# The Middle East

W. B. FISHER

# The Middle East

## A PHYSICAL, SOCIAL AND REGIONAL GEOGRAPHY

METHUEN & CO LTD

*First published* 1950
*by Methuen & Co. Ltd*
11 *New Fetter Lane London* EC4P 4EE
*Second edition* 1952
*Third edition* 1956
*Fourth edition* 1961
*Fifth edition* 1963
*Sixth edition, completely revised and reset,* 1971
*Seventh edition, completely revised and reset,* 1978
© 1961, 1963, 1971 *and* 1978 *W. B. Fisher*
*Printed in Great Britain*
*at the University Press, Cambridge*

ISBN 0 416 71510 9 *(hardback)*
ISBN 0 416 71520 6 *(paperback)*

# Contents

# Contents

# Maps and diagrams

# List of maps and diagrams

# List of maps and diagrams

# List of maps and diagrams

# List of maps and diagrams

# Preface

The aim of this book, retained in a new edition, is to offer a statement of the basic geographical facts relating to the region, together with discussion of the issues, theories and problems involved. There is at the same time an attempt to demonstrate the link between environmental conditions and the uniquely long historical tradition of the area. A large section of this volume is thus straightforward regional exposition: an approach which of recent years has been exposed generally to some criticism of professional geographers. But however one may employ the pitch-forks by specialist and systematic analysis, nature will return: there is now re-assertion of the validity of small territorial units, as human communities begin to stress local variation and the need for deeper understanding of the small-scale. Regionalism is a growing preoccupation among environmentalists, economists, politicians and field scientists; and geographers would do well to maintain the art for which they were – and still probably are – best known. Moreover there is growing appreciation that a region, far from being a commonplace and elementary system, is in fact a highly complex pattern, as yet intractable and beyond, rather than below, the capabilities of present-day modelling and analytical procedures.

In the third of a century that has elapsed since the ideas for this book were first sketched, changes have occurred within the Middle East on a scale unimaginable at the time. These changes have now brought certain parts of the Middle East to unparalleled wealth and influence; they have produced recurrent threats and actual outbreaks of war; they have

# Preface

fundamentally altered material ways of life, thought and culture for some groups; but they have not diminished the intense interest in Middle Eastern affairs by outside powers, and the determination of these latter to maintain or develop influence there. One difference, however, is that the process is now two-way, with more Middle Easterners involved in the economic and cultural life of the rest of the world – as participants in commercial activities, as temporary migrant workers (e.g. in Europe and the Americas), and as students. Moreover, the enormous expansion of air traffic and the limitation to flying over Communist territory, has meant that more than ever the Middle East with its expanses of open terrain, generally excellent flying weather has made the region a major centre of air routes, with increasing use of Great Circle trajectories: 'Concorde' flew first of all commercially to Bahrain. All this re-inforces the concept of 'Middle' in an expanding world.

Continued interest in this book from many parts of the world has allowed the appearance of a revised and improved, though slightly shortened, text, in which I have had the great benefits of assistance from numerous well-wishers. In particular, the Durham Centre of Middle Eastern and Islamic Studies with its Documentation Centre, second to none in Europe, has provided much valuable material. I wish also to acknowledge most gratefully support from British Petroleum Ltd, London, and Petroleum Development Oman, that has allowed field investigation in the Middle East.

I am greatly indebted to academic colleagues, diplomats, and other friends who have made available their specialist knowledge and expertise, particularly those in the Middle East. I wish especially to thank: Dr B. Booth of Imperial College London, and Dr D. P. McKenzie of Cambridge University and M.I.T., who have kindly allowed me to quote from their own research on plate tectonics, and to reproduce diagrams and material from their published work; Dr A. A. Ali of Cairo University who has made available from his own research on *khamsin* winds the material shown as fig. 3.8; Dr W. A. Abd el Aal for the information shown in fig. 17.11; and the secretarial and technical staff of my own Department for their considerable contributions.

Most of all, however, I wish to record with very grateful thanks the participation of Dr R. I. Lawless, acting-Director of the Durham Centre of Middle Eastern Studies, who has undertaken revision of certain chapters, and who has throughout provided overall comment and advice, as an indispensable collaborator.

W. B. FISHER

*Durham 1977*

xiv

# 1 Introductory

After many years of debate, acrid at times, and although the area itself
has risen to a position of major world significance, the term 'Middle
East' still cannot command universal acceptance in a single strict sense
– even counting in 'Mideast' as a mere abridgement. Perhaps the most
that a geographer can say, taking refuge in semantics, is that it can be
regarded as a 'conventional' regional term of general convenience, like
Central Europe or the American Middle West, with many definitions in
more detail feasible and logically possible.[1]

Use of 'Middle East' first arose in the early years of the present
century particularly with reference to the area around the Persian Gulf:
it was then a logical intermediate definition between the Mediterranean
'Near East', and a 'Far East' – although the position of the Indian
subcontinent remained anomalous – and after 1918 it was taken up by the
British Forces as a convenient label. During the Second World War, bases
and organizations previously located mainly around the Persian Gulf were
expanded greatly; and rather than erect an indeterminate, and divisive,
second unit, the term 'Middle East' was gradually extended westwards
with the tides of war. A military province stretching from Iran to
Tripolitania was created and named 'Middle East'. Establishment in this
region of large military supply bases brought the necessity to reorganize
both the political and economic life of the countries concerned, in order

---

[1] C. S. Coon's definition that includes Morocco and Pakistan, P. Loraine's restriction of
the term to Iran, Iraq, Arabia, Afghanistan; or the titles *The Nearer East* (D. G. Hogarth),
*The Hither East* (A. Kohn), and *Swasia* (G. B. Cressey).

I

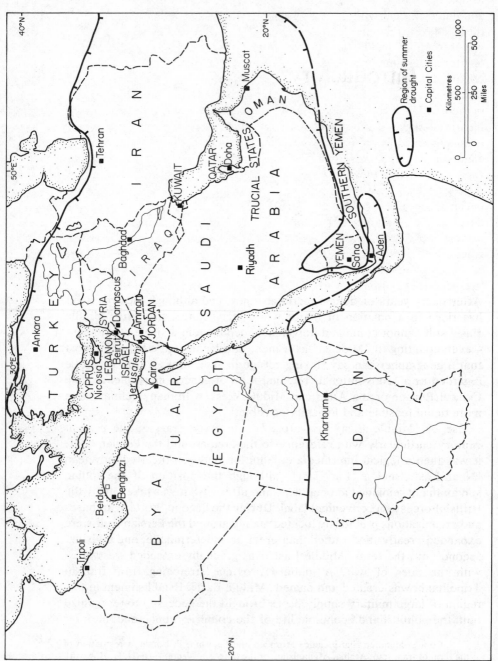

*Fig.* 1.1 The Middle East: countries and capital cities.

to meet the changed conditions of war. A resident Minister of State was appointed to deal with political matters, and an economic organization, the Middle East Supply Centre, originally British but later Anglo-American, was set up to handle economic questions. It was inevitable that the territorial designation already adopted by the military authorities should continue in the new sphere; hence 'Middle East' took on full official sanction and became the standard term of reference, exclusively used in the numerous governmental publications summarizing political events, territorial surveys and schemes of economic development. It has even been suggested as a possible explanation that France had strong military claims in an official 'Near East' theatre of war, but fewer in a 'Middle East', which was therefore much employed as a term and extended as a geographical concept when the situation of France vis-à-vis Britain became equivocal in 1940–41. Some colour is lent to this view in that, despite a deputation from the Royal Geographical Society in 1946 to protest, Mr Attlee's government continued the practice initiated by Mr Churchill's coalition, by which Egypt, Libya, Israel, Jordan and Syria are officially termed part of a Middle East.

Under these circumstances, it would seem difficult to challenge the validity of 'Middle East', particularly as the general public in Britain and America has become accustomed to the usage – in some cases as the result of first-hand acquaintance with the region during military service. It is true that there is little logicality in applying the term 'Middle East' to countries of the eastern Mediterranean littoral; yet, as shown above 'Near East' – the only possible replacement – has an equally vague connotation; and to some, moreover, taken on a historical flavour associated with nineteenth-century events in Balkan Europe. Thus, despite the considerable geographical illogicality of 'Middle East', there is one compensation: in its wider meaning this term can be held to denote a single geographical region definable by a few dominating elements that confer strong physical and social unity.

Within a territory delimitable as extending from Libya to Iran, and Turkey to the Sudan (including these four countries) it is possible to postulate on geographical grounds the existence of a natural region to which the name Middle East can be applied (fig. 1.1). The outstanding defining element is climatic: the Middle East has a highly unusual and characteristic regime which both sets it apart from its neighbours and also, since climate is a principal determinant in ways of life, the special climate induces highly distinctive and particular human responses and activities. It is true that this so-called unity is only partial, and therefore any definition of Middle East is open to criticism; but the common elements of natural environment and social organization are sufficiently recognizable and strong to justify treatment of the Middle East as one

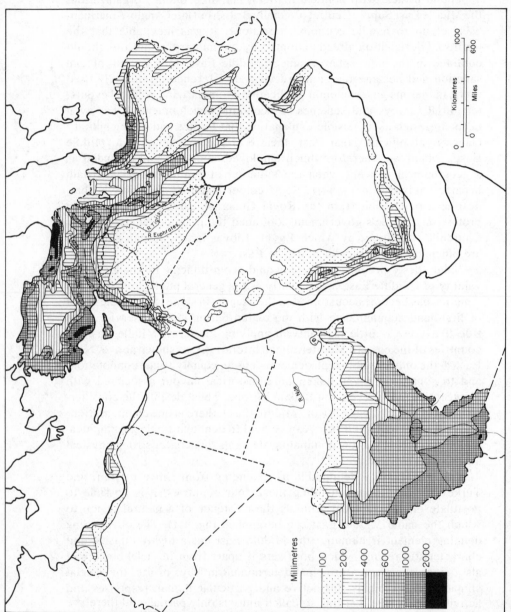

*Fig.* 1.2 Middle East: annual rainfall.

single unit. There are smaller intermediate areas on the margins: the southern Sudan in its physical and human geography is in certain respects closer to Central African conditions – though still part of the Nile Valley; extreme southern Arabia is brushed by monsoonal currents that give summer rain; whilst climatically and in much of its economic and social life Afghanistan has major affinities to a Middle East rather than to southern (monsoon) Asia. Thus, alternatives are possible: some modern geographers have written of a 'South-West Asia'; and 'Arab' or 'Moslem' World are sometimes used, the former explicit within linguistic boundaries, the latter logically capable of extension to include parts of south-east Asia and central and east Africa. All definitions have some objective in logic; none is wholly clear and unambiguous, and personal idiosyncracy may be introduced to reinforce validity. Therefore, as was once said in this very region over territorial pretension, *quod scripsi, scripsi*.

Within this region, definable principally by its climate and its culture, there are however remarkable local variations in way of life and living standards, widened still further during the last 20 years by exploitation of petroleum. Although almost all communities in the region have experienced some absolute increase in income, either directly or by 'spin off' from outside, for a fortunate few this change has been enormous, producing for these few the highest per capita income of anywhere in the world. Within one locality or minor geographical region can now be found merchants, politicians and financiers deeply involved in international markets, whose views receive closest world-wide attention, together with political, religious and intellectual leaders also highly conscious of their status as members of world organizations. Yet there also exist alongside them in the same areas significantly large communities of farmers and herdsmen some of whom are still living, despite recent improvement, at near minimum levels of subsistence with personal incomes still below the World Bank criterion of 'poverty'.

For long, complexity of geographical conditions – highly varied topography, prevalence of aridity with apparent absence of major economic resources, and consequent emptiness of many areas – retarded attempts at study. This was compounded by the reluctance of some indigenous communities, not unjustifiably, to admit outsiders; but above all by political rivalries and jealousies of outside powers, chiefly though not exclusively European, which were anxious to erect or preserve 'spheres of influence' particularly over routeways, and then as regards oil deposits. Now, however, with political independence, obstacles to investigation have greatly declined; and there is almost an opposite attitude – keen determination to understand the complexities and limits of the environmental endowment as a basis for technological and social development. There are now in a few areas situations approaching intensive investigation

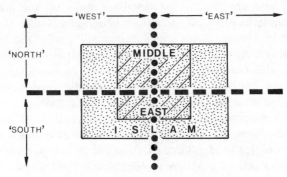

*Fig.* 1.3 The 'Interface' function of the Middle East.

with a risk even of over-survey, since all results and recommendations cannot be implemented, in many cases due to shortages of trained personnel rather than money.

Equally striking in recent times is the altered position of the Middle East in world affairs. Until the early twentieth century, and even later, south-west Asia and adjacent areas of Africa were largely isolated from the main currents of political and economic activity. Now, the region clearly ranks as one of the most significant parts of the world. Evidence of this could be adduced from the repeated personal visits by the Presidents of the USA and USSR, by the leaders of European opinion, and even by the Pope. Whilst some observers might dissent from the view of the Middle East as crucial in strategic matters, this is not true of the majority, and proof is to be seen in the fact that few major powers in the world can avoid having a 'Middle East' policy. Based primarily on reserves of petroleum, the largest in the world, and of natural gas, second largest after the USSR, certain Middle Eastern states have developed a level of industrialization and a financial strength that is now demonstrated by Middle East investment elsewhere in the industrial world: it is a long way in economic outlook, though certainly not in time, from the economic and political subservience of the 1930s and 40s to Arab and Iranian purchases of stocks and real property in Europe and North America: participation by Kuwait in London property, by Libya in Fiat and by Iran in Krupps and Daimler-Benz. The largest oil refinery plant, the largest petroleum export, gas refrigeration plant, the largest tankers, the most urbanized state and the best state medicine services in the world are now features in the Middle East, which also represents one of the best markets for sophisticated manufactures – most of all, armaments – outside Europe and North America.

Principally, however, the Middle East can now be regarded as a major interface area not only between East and West, which has long been its traditional role, but now between the newer alignment of 'north' and 'south' or in other terms, 'developed' and 'developing' nations. This latter role is increasing in significance with the Middle East more and more a consciously intermediate zone (fig. 1.3). Healthier in a few parts now than anywhere else in the world, with, for a minority, superb social services; a highly important market for some of the most sophisticated products of the industrial 'northern' world; and a respected mediator in world financial affairs, the Middle East has rapidly developed a new role. Yet at the same time, poverty of the majority, and geographical connection with Africa and Asia give the Middle Eastern peoples conscious affinity, economic, philosophical and political with the 'southern' world. Whilst the economic strength of OPEC since 1973 has been a major factor in world affairs, this has tended to reinforce intense interest by outside powers in Middle Eastern affairs, with sustained attempts to gain or retain political, economic and strategic advantages by possession of bases (now usually leased), trade links, and a patron–client relationship. Open dominance through Mandates has disappeared, but economic imperialism in the form of special trade relationships and 'tied aid' could be said to persist; and with the tense internal political situations recently described in 1977 by President Nimeiri of the Sudan as competing economic and armament imperialisms – Western and socialistic – the Middle East has significance much beyond its actual size or even numbers of population. Of recent years we have seen how the countries forming the Middle East have tended to be forced into the position of association with one or other of the major power blocs of the world. One or two Middle Eastern leaders, notably the rulers of Iran and Saudi Arabia, see their way to a vigorous national policy of independence, but for most others, support from outside, at least politically, is still necessary.

All this has produced a rapid change, amounting in some areas to crisis, in existing ways of life. Besides the pressures exerted on the natural environment by the spread of cities often on to the best agricultural land, the demand for water, increasingly polluted by human and industrial effluent, and the degradation of local ecosystems by various developments, there are urgent human problems. Forms of society that have endured over hundreds, even in some instances thousands of years are now in rapid decay, with urgent need for new groupings in replacement. Religious feeling, once the mainspring of most forms of cultural and political activity is now partly in eclipse, or subject (in an effort to restore it) to re-emphasis amounting in some instances to fanaticism or distortion: frequently materialist nationalism, sometimes dialectical, has taken its place, not always to advantage. Although new techniques of agriculture and industry have made considerable progress, ancient methods in husbandry, stock rearing and manufacturing still survive, so that for some communities the margin of existence is still extremely small, and living standards low. There has been enormous improvement since the 1940s, when it was possible to rank the Middle East as one of the worst nourished parts of the world; but changes have been highly uneven: in some regions very great; but in others slight. Population pressures are now a highly limiting factor, and for some countries, Egypt especially and possibly for Turkey, technological gains since 1940 have been largely nullified by extra human numbers to support. As well, given environmental limitations, one may be reaching the margin of effective utilisation of agricultural resources. Many Middle Eastern countries are experiencing the need for more and more food imports because increasing costs and decline of the rural labour force are placing limits on what can be produced from their own soil.

Change, amounting in some instances to disintegration, of internal society, and foreign pressures continuing from without, have increasingly forced Middle Eastern peoples to revise ideologies and adopt new ideas and techniques. In this connection one may note a situation special to the Middle East: close links between military elites and the 'common people' from whom many military leaders have come – there is a great deal of affinity between service officers and a new radical intelligentsia; with at the same time a strong nationalist feeling that can generate a negative attitude towards Communism. This means that the political and social paths open to Middle Eastern peoples may differ markedly from those so far shown by experience to be followed elsewhere: in short, the radical dialectic confidently predicted by some theorists as inevitably applicable to the West may not occur at all in the Middle East, or at least develop in a different form. Division and diversity, encouraged by factors of geography, may well continue for some time yet, as so often in the past, to dominate Middle Eastern affairs: and one essential step is to analyse how the geographical environment contributes to this situation. Only when we can be confidently aware of the real nature and influences of this environment will it be possible to formulate effective plans and policies.

Part I

# Physical geography of the Middle East

# 2 Structure and land forms

Though some doubts and uncertainties remain as to regional detail (and the commercial importance of oil-bearing strata has tended to retard complete public statements), knowledge of the geology and pattern of structural units is now much clearer. The situation of several decades ago, when one could note a near absence of published information for certain areas has now totally changed, as a result of the intensive surveys carried out for petroleum and other mineral exploitation.

Interest in the economic aspects of geological conditions tended to relegate the more theoretical questions of origins to a secondary role. This situation, however, has also improved in recent years, particularly following elaboration of the theory of plate tectonics, which has special applicability to the Middle East. We must therefore consider this theory in broad outline, with the reservation that much still remains to be worked out in detail for the Middle East, and ideas as so far stated are tentative and highly speculative.

It is apparent that whilst in some parts of the Middle East earth tremors and recent current volcanic activity are frequent, there is little or no trace in other parts of earth movement or volcanicity on any important scale. When the distribution of earthquakes, in particular, is plotted it becomes apparent that these occur within relatively narrow constricted bands surrounding much larger zones where disturbance is much less, or absent: i.e. large stable 'plate' areas with narrow boundary zones to which crustal disturbance is chiefly confined (fig. 2.1).

With this basis, elaborated by geo-magnetic observations and close

I I

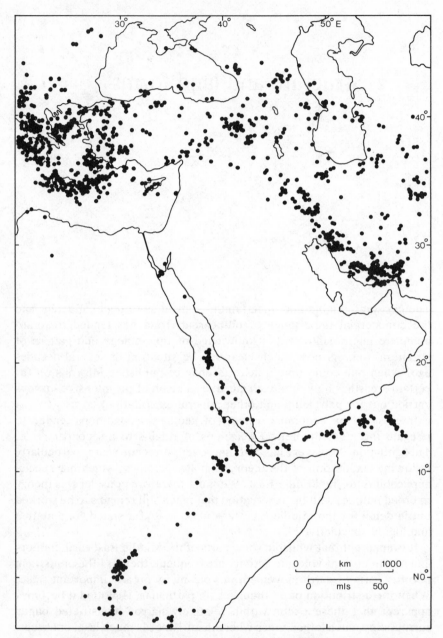

*Fig.* 2.1 Areas of tectonic activity (reproduced from *Nature* by permission of Dr D. P. McKenzie and Macmillan).

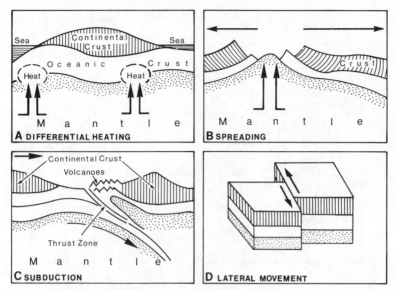

*Fig.* 2.2 Formation and evolution of tectonic plates.

observation of rock successions in relation to their origins, whether terrestrial, from oceanic deeps or otherwise, the theory of plate tectonics has been recently developed. Carrying further the earlier theories of Continental Drift, it postulates that the continental land areas are masses of less dense material floating as it were on a layer of denser material that tends to form oceanic deeps: there is a real difference, therefore, as regards rock character as between the deeper oceanic beds and the land surface. Differential heating, due it is believed to the presence of radioactive minerals, induces convection currents in the denser mass, which at great depths becomes plastic rather than rigid. Such convection currents in the earth's mantle first split up and then carry away the lighter plates that form the continental surfaces, rather like, to use an extremely crude analogy, ice-floes moved about by currents in denser sea water.

The plates may be forced apart or split off by upwelling from depths: this is spoken of as 'spreading'. Alternatively, two plates may be moved laterally against each other, producing tear or transform faults; whilst a third process, impinging and compression of one plate against another, leads to one plate being forced below the other, and its lower advancing edge then 'consumed' – a subduction zone. All these three processes are observable in parts of the Middle East (fig. 2.2).

In recent years, ideas of plate tectonics within the Middle East have been developed by various researchers very broadly as follows. In

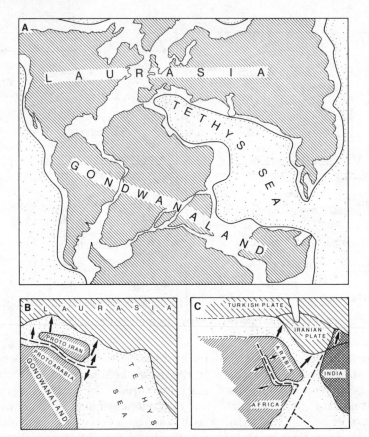

*Fig.* 2.3 Development of the Tethys embayment in Triassic–Jurassic times and later (reproduced from *The Geographical Magazine* by permission of Dr B. Booth and I.P.C.).

Triassic–Jurassic times (200 million years B.P.[1]) drifting continental plates had coalesced to form a very large land mass with two major lobes: one (in the north termed Laurasia) included much of what is now central and northern Asia, and the other (Gondwanaland) in the south, included much of Africa, India, Australasia and South America. Between these two major masses (which may have been joined in what is now the area of the western Mediterranean–east central Atlantic) occurred the extensive Tethys Sea, in which great sedimentary deposits, formed from erosion of the land plates to north and south accumulated, also as these sediments developed trapping the bodies of sea creatures that eventually gave rise to petroleum (fig. 2.3).

Spreading action in the north-eastern part of the Gondwana lobe during

---

[1]   B.P. = Before the present day.

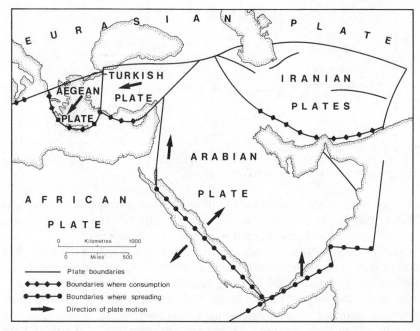

*Fig.* 2.4 Formation and movement of the tectonic plates comprising the Middle East area (after D. P. McKenzie and B. Booth).

the Cretaceous period produced a number of plate fragments to which the name proto-Iranian has been given. In addition, a second phase of spreading and fracturing impelled what is now the India plate north-eastwards. The effect of these movements was to reduce the width of the Tethys Sea, and to compress and then uplift its sediments. By the late Mesozoic the Indian plate had moved far away from the main mass of Gondwanaland (fig. 2.4), and one or more Iranian plates, of smaller size, were also separated. Around these smaller plates the Tethys sediments were later compressed to give the present-day local basins or micro-plates of Iran (e.g. the Tabas, Lut, and Helmand basins) and Asia Minor, with their surrounding fold garlands.

By the opening of the Cainozoic (Tertiary) era (65 million years B.P.) the Tethys had been reduced to a residual trough-line only partially occupied by sea; and further spreading had begun in what is now the Red Sea–Gulf of Aden area. The effect of this was to detach a major Arabian plate, that continued to move north-eastwards, impinging strongly against the Iranian plates, and in so doing elevating the main Zagros ridges of Iran. This movement, held to be active still at the present day, is regarded by some authorities (e.g. D. P. McKenzie and B. Booth) as responsible for the transform faulting that characterizes the Jordan valley,

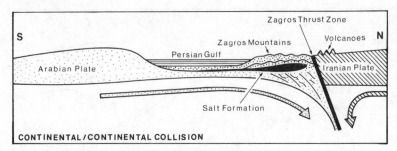

*Fig.* 2.5 Subduction of the Arabian plate against the Iranian plates, with formation of the Zagros–Makran ranges (after B. Booth).

and, perhaps more important, the movement of plates composing Asia Minor and the Aegean Sea, where considerable re-adjustment to stress is taking place, with consequent liability to earthquakes.

McKenzie and others recognize two plates in this area: a Turkish plate comprising most of central Asia Minor, and an Aegean plate immediately to its west. Because of the extreme pressures due to continued northerly motion of the large Arabian plate, the two smaller plates composing Anatolia and the Aegean are being thrust westwards, with transform faulting along their northern edges, and consumption of their southern edges against the African plate.

A recent view of conditions in the south-east of the Middle East (due to B. Booth) is that whilst the main Zagros folds represent the collision of continental plates, the Arabian being subducted and consumed below the Iranian plate-complex; further south, in the Makran, the collision has been between the Iranian plate and an oceanic plate, giving somewhat less spectacular subduction features (i.e. massive mountain ranges) as compared with the continental–continental collision which characterizes the main Zagros, where mountain chains are higher and wider.

It should finally be stressed that the ideas, as stated above in a very bald and elementary manner by the present author, are provisional and novel in many respects, with much more field research needed to establish the details of the processes by which the present continents and seas originated. But it is also right to say that the theories of plate tectonics go far to offer explanation of problems that earlier theories could not fully explain. The presence of wide variation in fold mountain structures in west and south Iran, as between the Zagros and Makran ranges; the confused structures of central Iran, about which so many differing theories have evolved; the timetabling of Red Sea faulting in relation to other geological events; and the peculiarities of the Suleiman Range to the east of Iran – all these become much more explicable when reference is made to the plate theory.

**Regional differences**

From the above, it will be apparent that one can regard the Middle East area as structurally forming two major zones: firstly the central and southern parts, which in the main are continental plate areas, interrupted only by the fault structures due either to spreading (as in the Red Sea zone) or to transform faulting (as in the Aqaba–Jordan–Orontes system). The second zone is where moving plates impinge strongly, due to the northward movement of the Arabian and African plates. Here there are phenomena of consumption and subduction on a large scale.

*The continental plate area*

This includes most of Libya, Egypt, the Sudan, and the Arabian peninsula. The fundamental feature is the basement of Archaean granites and other metamorphics, almost everywhere present, but usually underlying later rock series that are as a rule deposited in horizontal or only slightly tilted layers. Towards the north of the area, the basement is usually overlain by younger sedimentaries, of increasing thickness towards the north, offering varied resistance to erosion, and generally in horizontal layers. Further south, in the Saharan and central Arabian areas, rather more of the basement is exposed, and differences in rock type can give rise to varied land forms. In some districts of southern Arabia, isolated massifs of granite stand at a higher level than surrounding schists; steep conical hills of pegmatite occur in the Hadhramaut; and in the Sinai, Nubia and the central Sahara, especially resistant quartzites outcrop as imposing ridges. The accordance of relief forms with structure is, however, by no means total and the Archaean basement itself, where it is exposed, is far from being a massive featureless plain.

The younger rock series overlying this primitive nucleus consist mainly of sandstones and limestones of varying composition, thickness and extent. Jurassic, Cretaceous and Eocene limestones are well represented, and a formation of particular interest is Nubian sandstone, a concretion of sand-grains laid down by aeolian deposition at differing geological periods: e.g. in parts of Libya this series is ascribed to the Carboniferous, but in most other areas to the Permian–Cretaceous. Individual sand grains are aligned along well defined axes, and recent geophysical research has suggested that the trend of these axes, where pronounced, may have been produced by prevailing winds. Hence these series may give an indication of planetary winds and pressure zones, and of the position of geographical poles and equator at earlier geological periods, and hence also the movements of tectonic plates.

Despite the absence of major fold structures in this central-southern

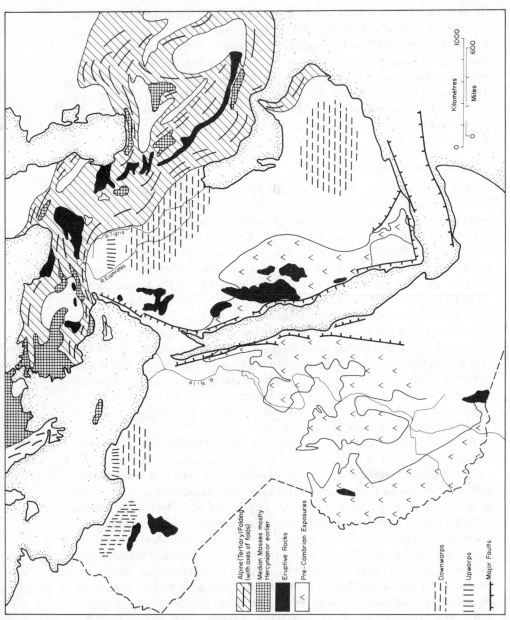

Fig. 2.6 Structural elements of the Middle East.

Alpine (Tertiary) Folding (with axes of folds)

Median Masses mostly Hercynian or earlier

Eruptive Rocks

Pre-Cambrian Exposures

Downwarps

Upwarps

Major Faults

R. Tigris

R. Euphrates

R. Nile

Kilometres

Miles

0    600    1000

region, variety in land forms does occur. The dominating element is often a plateau with a sharp delimiting scarp produced by erosive action. Under the particularly arid climatic regime of this zone, sandstones are much more readily eroded than limestones, hence valleys and depressions tend to develop on sandstone outcrops, with limestones as residual areas of more vigorous relief. Where erosion has been particularly active, there can be, typically, an extensive development of *hamad* – a level plain sometimes covered by exfoliated material (flint, rock fragments of various sizes) that are unsorted; or if there is episodic rainfall, these may be roughly graded by size. *Cuestas* resulting from differential erosion are also frequent: Egypt and Libya have these on a frequent and relatively small scale, whilst in central Arabia the same structural pattern gives rise to major relief features.

The general pattern of an impermeable, ancient base overlain by layers of often porous rock has great significance for water supply. Although the porous sedimentaries may not be continuous over very large areas, their general alignment means that water is held often in a series of gently sloping basins, that collect present-day rainfall by rapid percolation through highly permeable surface strata, but, probably more important, also by collection and retention of rainfall at earlier geological periods. There are thus important water tables or aquifers underlying both the Saharan and Arabian deserts – though the greater part of this water is, like petroleum, a fossil resource, not renewable if exploited. Libya, in particular, has considerable structures of this kind, at varying depths.

In certain areas, a combination of surface erosion together with hydrostatic pressure upwards from water-tables has resulted in the formation of depressions where groundwater appears at the surface. Largest of these are the oases of Kufra, and the Qattara depression of northern Egypt, and the interior of south-east Arabia but there are many more, now usually occupied by a salt-marsh – a fact which led some earlier investigators to suggest that they were relict marine formations.

The tectonic plate edges are defined by massive fault structures. Most impressive are the series of enormous fault-scarps delimiting the Red Sea trough, with extension northward into the Jordan valley. Besides these major features, however, there are relatively minor cross-faults aligned generally at right angles to the main north–south trend, and thus rock structures tend to be broken into rectilinear masses that exhibit what is sometimes called 'chess-board relief'. This is the case on a large scale in south-west Arabia, Asir, the Yemens, and part of the Hadhramaut, whilst the same features on a smaller scale are to be found on either side of the Jordan valley and adjacent Mediterranean coast, e.g. the 'steps' in the coastline at Tripoli (Lebanon), Beirut, and at Haifa are related to north–south and east–west running faults.

Some faults run back, as it were, into the centres of the continental plates. This is especially true of northern Arabia and north-east Africa, where a number of small rift valleys occur. These, partly enlarged by water action and aeolian erosion at earlier geological periods, are sometimes covered in places by loose sand, and serve (like the Wadi Sirhan) as routes to the interior. Whilst many fault lines appear sharply defined – in that they give rise to abrupt relief, with steep, unbroken slopes – it is also apparent that others have been extensively eroded back and now exist as primary or secondary fault-line scarps. These areas of complex faulting, with their sharp, varied land forms, stand in considerable contrast to the interior continental landscapes of the centre and south, and the topographic contrasts are often emphasized by extensive vulcanicity which has frequently occurred in association with the fault zones.

The most developed of these occur at the southern end of the Red Sea, and on either side of the Gulf of Aden. Here, basaltic 'trap' rocks have spread by fissure eruption over an area including much of the Yemen, Hadhramaut and Somali shores of the Red Sea and Gulf of Aden, as well as considerable areas further inland in Arabia, the Sudan and Ethiopia. The basalts, of Eocene age, occur in layers between 300–1000 m thick, giving rise to the imposing plateaus of the Yemen and Ethiopia. Vulcanicity of another type and later period (Miocene–Quaternary) is a feature in the same regions, producing well-defined cones and craters which often superimposed above the basaltic layer and uptilted plateau surfaces, produce striking effects of relief. The site of Aden town is formed of twin volcanic craters, and close by in the Strait of Bab el Mandeb are a number of volcanic islands still showing eruptive activity. Similar conditions, with slight eruptivity and the occurrence of solfataras and mofettes are characteristic of much of the southern Red Sea zone generally.

To the north, lava flows were of a quieter type, though equally extensive: many of the highlands of Asir and the Hijaz owe at least part of their height to superimposed basaltic sheets – the *harras*, which are barren lava fields showing various forms of eruption. Towards Sinai and the Gulf of Aqaba lava areas are less extensive, though again present.

On the east side of the upper Jordan depression volcanicity again becomes extremely widespread, with the Hauran, Jebel Druze and upper Jordan valley as the main zones. Here there have been many flows at successive geological periods resulting in an extremely complicated topography. The Jebel Druze region exhibits many types of cone: ash, acidic, and scoriae, together with convoluted sheet eruption. Maximum activity here would seem to have been during the Pliocene, but there has been much emission in Quaternary and even Recent times. Flows across the Jordan valley have impounded the Sea of Galilee and the former Lake

Huleh, and there are hot springs and solfataras around and beneath the Sea of Galilee, e.g. at Tiberias. Lava flows are also a feature, on a less developed scale, in western Syria near Homs and Aleppo.

Another major area of vulcanicity is the Libyan plateau south of Tripoli. Here there are also extensive *harra* areas like those of Arabia and Syria, with lines of volcanic peaks, e.g. the Jebel es Soda (Black Mountains), rising above plateau level. Another similar intrusive igneous feature is the Jebel Marra of the Sudan.

Finally, in discussing the 'continental' Middle East, reference must be made to the considerable sand areas. In some areas, the sands are very fine in texture, and are loose: thus very liable to shifting by the wind. These areas, at their most developed, form 'sand seas', the largest being those of Libya and western Egypt. Of highly variable, even chaotic surface features, such 'seas' have presented a formidable barrier to human settlement and even movement. Oases, even if established, can be quickly overblown by sand, and the shifting constantly varying landscape makes travel highly difficult. Elsewhere more regular and stable dune formation can be characteristic. Here dunes of up to several hundred metres in height and over 100 km in length can develop, with graduation to smaller size: the sand dunes show a classic cusp or crescent formation, even (as the Dasht-i-Lut of southern Iran) a conglomeration of cusps, whilst others tend to be straight ridges aligned in ranks. Where there is an extra fraction in desert sand such as silt, clay or salt efflorescence, dunes give way to flatter more stable formations that produce open plains, on which travel can be easy. Rock fragments, ranging from boulders to fine gravels, sometimes graded, sometimes intermixed, also occur. Thus 'the desert' may comprise many surface and local features, not only as regards topography, but, reflecting varied mineralogical origins, also as regards shape and colour.

## The northern and eastern plate margins

The generally northward and north-eastward movements of the African and Arabian plates would seem to have generated major effects on the structure and hence topography of the Middle East. Overall, there is the situation of two large-scale southern plates (the 'African' and the 'Arabian') impacting against an even larger 'Eurasian' plate, with a number of smaller plates or fragments occurring between: the various Iranian plates, the main Turkish plate, and the Aegean plate. Compression of the Tethys, with its considerable accumulation of sediments, led to the upthrusting of a succession of rock series many thousand metres thick.

It is therefore noticeable that the marine sedimentary layers which occur as relatively thin bands over the southern-central plate regions, become much more developed in variety and thickness towards the north and east. In addition, they become locally disturbed, though not at first strongly, so that a structure of anticline and syncline is traceable in a zone extending from Tripolitania and Cyrenaica through Israel, the Lebanon, Syria, Iraq, south west Iran and Qatar as far as Oman. Folding is on a very restricted scale, with very gentle arching of rock strata, often as single anticlines broken to a minor degree by local fractures; with overthrusting absent. The Jebel of Cyrenaica, the uplands of Judaea and the most developed of all, the Lebanon mountains, are all of this pattern. Further to the north and east, we may note the Jebel Ansarieh of Syria, and the somewhat more convoluted, but still open folds of Mount Hermon and the Anti-Lebanon which spread into smaller structures eastwards: the Jebel Qalamoun of Damascus, Jebel Bishri, near Palmyra, and others.

In Iraq there are two continuations of these wrinkles, as it were, in the sedimentary cover: the Jebel Sinjar and Jebel Makhal. In Iran, one can recognize the outer foothills of the central Zagros fronting the Mesapotamian lowlands as similar structures, whilst the very shallow upfolds of the Jebel Ahmadi (Kuwait) and the Jebel Dukhan (Qatar) are of the same type. Lastly, there is the single upfold of the Jebel Akhdar of Oman: and from Syria eastwards it is noteworthy that all these anticlinal–synclinal structures are associated with the occurrence of petroleum.

## The folded zone

Most recent interpretations suggest that the northern and eastern areas of the Middle East, topographically regions of high fold ranges, interior basins and tilted plateaus, could be regarded as a 'collision belt' where major movements of plate edges – in the form of over- and under-riding (subduction and consumption) or extensive lateral movements are the dominant mechanisms, although there may be some 'spreading' in the region of the northern Aegean sea. The presence of resistant blocks composed of older rocks is the other important feature: some are pre-Cambrian (or at least have lost any later covering), whilst others suggest origins at periods no earlier than the Hercynian – but all would seem to be subcontinental fragments welded into later plate formation.

In Asia Minor and the adjacent seas to west and south, movement of the plates is especially complicated; lateral torsion in the plate boundary that lies near the Black Sea coast, 'spreading' or lithospheric enlargement in the Marmara–North Aegean seas, and subduction (consumption) along two arcs: one through Crete and the other between Cyprus and the extreme south west of Asia Minor. As a result trends of folding are extremely varied, particularly in the western part of Asia Minor: narrow, high but in places abruptly ending at coasts – in short, confused, asymmetrical development, as might be expected from the involved tectonics of the region.

In Iran there is a contrast. Main feature is the thrust zone forming the main Zagros, and here, in response to a more unified and consistent (though none the less powerful) impinging of plates, there is great regularity of strike and continuity of folding over several hundred kilometres, that has produced closely packed, symmetrical parallel folds. To the north of this is a major area of dislocation, forming the high plateaus of Azerbaijan–Armenia, traversed by fault lines, with much differential uplift and downthrow, and once again the presence of volcanicity, which has covered parts of this plateau with sheet lavas, and in others given rise to volcanic cones such as Ararat (5000 m) and Suphan.

Conditions in northern Iran are less studied: some researchers, however, regard the southern Caspian area as a minor continental plate, with the Elburz range a zone of impaction. The narrowness of this range, with a great range of strata exposed (in some localities one can see almost an entire geological succession from Lower Palaeozoic to Recent) point to major disturbance though on a restricted scale. Basin structures of local or moderately large size, delimited by encircling high mountain ranges, are probably the most characteristic landform of this northern and eastern region. As well, there are a few large river valleys, sometimes defined even in their upper courses by fault lines, but more usually occurring as deep clefts, and often separate from the basins just described, many of which have no outward drainage.

**Land forms**

The vigour and freshness of relief forms in the Middle East, which, in the north especially, are outstanding features, are for the most part due to structural origin; but this is not the entire story. Evidence is present suggesting extensive cycles at different geological periods of erosion and peneplanation; whilst much deposition also occurs in the form of alluvial fans, outwash screes, sedimentation of lowland basins and, as already noted, the accumulation of aeolian deposits (sand, silt and loess).

Surveys by Awad and others have shown that an extensive erosion surface developed on the ancient Basement rocks in lower Palaeozoic times. Besides occurring in parts of the Sinai and eastern Egypt, this peneplain is best developed in Arabia, where it is revealed by later removal of younger sediments that were deposited on it. A second major period of erosion and peneplanation is also traceable in Arabia and parts of Iran. Erosion surfaces of various ages are observed round the upper Red Sea and lower Jordan rift, extending into Arabia: various levels are

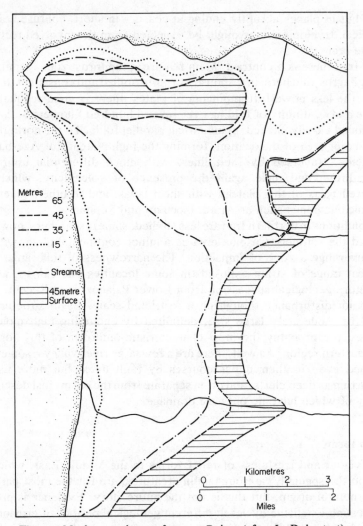

*Fig.* 2.7 Marine erosion surfaces at Beirut (after L. Dubertret).

ascribed to the Mesozoic (Red Sea area) and an extensive Oligocene
system at 900 m level, with two lesser developed surfaces at 1100 m and
1600 m.

In the Levant, oscillation of the surface was rather greater, and there
are numerous erosion surfaces: Eocene in the Lebanon, Anti-Lebanon,
Jebel Ansarieh and East Jordan; Miocene in the Negev, with numerous
surfaces and benches on a smaller scale round the middle Jordan rift.
The pattern in this area is so complex that it is not easy to reconcile the
various explanations: some surfaces may be due to climatic factors – high

and low levels of local water surfaces – besides the movement of land surface. Support for the idea of varied erosion periods and oscillation is to be found in the drainage pattern of the region: the curious courses of the Litani, Barada and Orontes rivers in relation to present day relief suggest partial superimposition and antecedent directions of flow controlled by pre-existing land-forms; the remarkable elbow of the Litani river which breaks through mountainous country to reach the Mediterranean instead of Lake Tiberias; the same feature repeated on the Orontes; and the way the Barada has cut through anticline and syncline to follow an obsequent trend inland.

In addition to major planifications there are many minor oscillations of coastline that are traceable in all the sea areas, but most of all in the Eastern Mediterranean. Eight coastal beach levels (ascribed to the Quaternary) are discernible on the Black Sea; whilst six to seven terrace levels can be traced in the eastern Mediterranean; and in the Red Sea. K. Butzer has attempted to correlate the various findings as follows: the lowest raised beach occurs at 1·5 to 5 m above present sea level, and is ascribed to the Flandrian period, with maximum development at +2·5 m. Other levels are: +5 to 10 m (Monastir), +10 to 20 m; +25 to 40 m (Tyrrhenian); +45 to 70 m (Millazzian); +70 to 110 m (Sicilian); +130 to 200 m (Calabrian). These levels (with the exception of the +2·5 m) can be traced in the Red Sea; whilst in the Persian/Arab Gulf there would seem to have been very many changes during the Quaternary, with the upper part completely dry for a time. Episodic downwarping (−2 to −4 m) is also observable in the eastern Mediterranean. Various investigators have attempted wider correlations: beginning with a high sea level in early Quaternary times, Fairbridge and Purser distinguish various terraces at up to +373 m in Oman and the southern Persian/Arab Gulf. Just before 100000 B.P. a period of markedly lower sea levels (with some oscillation) that at its maximum (20000 B.P.) brought sea level 100 m below its present level in the Gulf, initiated a period of landward erosion, and made the northern end of the Gulf dry land. This was one period of dune formation and migration in Arabia and lands adjacent to the Gulf, though not the main one (which antedates the Quaternary). Finally, since about 6000 B.P. sea level has been fairly close to present level with, however, minor fluctuations that have produced raised beaches and the development of coastal sabkha.

Reference was earlier made to the accumulation of sand in the desert interiors. It has been observed that the measured rate of accumulation of sand dunes implies a period of origin much earlier in many instances than the Quaternary, since dunes of several hundred metres in height and over a hundred kilometres in length could not have accumulated under present conditions of growth rate, within the last 100000 years. Dunes may move, and rates of displacement of up to 15 m/annum are known, but the most mobile dunes tend to be smaller ones: for the larger ones, stability is the main feature. One may observe the 'creep' of loose sand in many areas – some rocky hillsides in eastern Arabia can be seen to be 'plastered' by mobile sand, which has originated quite some distance away.

Of recent years, much investigation has centred upon the fluvial deposits that occur particularly on the piedmonts of the great mountain chains: the Elburz, Makran, Zagros, and in Turkey. These deposits, clearly of alluvial origin, are prominent features in quite a number of localities. Certain of these formations, amounting to infill or even the extension of highland forms, of several hundred metres in thickness, are thought to have been laid down in various erosional episodes that have been traced back to the middle Tertiary. Two important phases in northern Iran appear to have occurred, one between 40000 and 70000 B.P., and the other about 1000 years ago. Less investigated in detail, but still of significance, are wind-blown deposits, chiefly loessic, that have attained considerable thickness in parts of the Negev, and in certain of the basins of eastern and central Iran.

The effects of ice in modifying the landscape are restricted to the highlands. There are a few very small glaciers, and areas of near-permanent snow on the eastern Turkish hills above 3500 m close to the Black Sea: inland the snow-line rises to 4000 m and even 4200 m in Iran, with only such summits as Ararat, Demavand, Savalan and Taftan affected. But during glacial phases of the Quarternary the limit of snow and ice fell to about 1000 m above sea level in Asia Minor and 1200 m in the Iranian Zagros. Corries and numerous but small moraines are therefore to be seen in these areas.

More important at the present day are the formations known as *kavir* and *sabkha*. The former are water-bodies that maintain themselves in the sumps of interior basins, in regions of especial aridity. Sometimes open water surfaces, kavir may also include expanses of highly viscous mud, and be wholly or partially covered by hard plates of crystallized salt, that curl upwards at the edges to give sometimes a sharp edge reminiscent of a polar ice-floe. Known rates of stream flow and normal underground percolation seem in some cases inadequate to explain the persistence of water under conditions of great evaporation; thus it could be that the mineral content of the kavir and surrounding areas is sufficiently hygro-scopic to extract sufficient moisture from the atmosphere to maintain a water-balance.

Sabkha is coastal salt marsh, particularly developed on the southern shores of the Persian/Arab Gulf. As over quite considerable areas (and including the Mediterranean) sabkha has now developed out of range

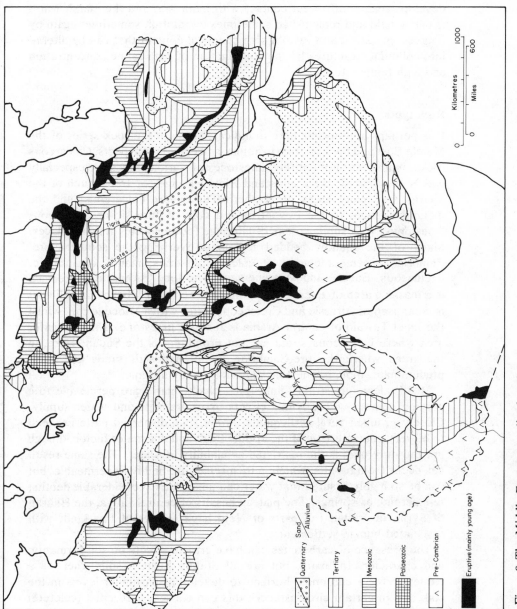

Quaternary
Sand Alluvium

Tertiary

Mesozoic

Palaeozoic

Pre-Cambrian

Eruptive (mainly young age)

Tigris

Euphrates

Nile

1000
600
Kilometres
Miles
0

*Fig.* 2.8 The Middle East: generalized geology.

of the tidal replenishment, it is not just a matter of sea water being temporarily retained. What seems to occur is that algal formations develop, sealing off direct contact with main sea, and the marsh water is partly held and replenished sometimes by rainfall, sometimes again by hygroscopic attraction, with a high chemical content that can be altered into colloidal structures by the combination of high saline concentration and high temperatures.

### Rock types

It is perhaps appropriate here to indicate some of the rock series of the Middle East and their relation to human and economic aspects. Calcareous rocks, mainly but not entirely limestones of various kinds are especially widely distributed: the Zagros and Elburz Ranges of Iran, much of the Taurus and many areas of northern Turkey are calcareous; and the mountain ranges of the Levant have a core of Jurassic or Cretaceous limestones, with similar rocks of later age forming a cap in many places. Many of the shallow bedded sediments overlying the southern pre-Cambrian basement consist of calcareous series, mainly of Jurassic, Cretaceous, Eocene and Miocene ages. The Jebel Akhdar of Cyrenaica is a massive arch of Eocene limestone, the northern Jebel of Tripolitania is composed of Jurassic and Cretaceous series with a Miocene cap, whilst the Jebel Tuwaiq of central Arabia is Jurassic limestone. The one major area where calcareous strata are not prominent is the Sudan. Here, in the areas where the pre-Cambrian is not exposed, sands and clays predominate, though limestones are not wholly absent.

Most calcareous strata – limestone, chalk, marl – are permeable to a varying degree, with obvious effects upon drainage and water supply. Closely grouped rural settlements, rather than dispersed patterns, tend to be very characteristic of the Middle East, and one major factor, though not the only one, is the restricted availability of water. The same result can occur from basalts, which in themselves are highly impermeable, but can be so highly fissured that water can penetrate to considerable depths, re-emerging as springs. The plateau basalts of central Libya, the Hauran of Syria, of Jordan and parts of Nejd have springs of this kind, with associated human settlements.

The presence of carbonates can have critical effects on soil formation and character. In many, but not all Middle Eastern soils, there is a tendency for a carbonate horizon to develop at particular levels in the soil, and in certain circumstances this can cause a hard crust (calcrete) to build up: a matter discussed in the section relating to soils. Most, though not all, of the petroleum deposits of the Middle East occur in porous limestone series: Jurassic in Saudi Arabia and Qatar, Cretaceous in Turkey and Syria, 'Main' (Eocene–Miocene) in Iraq. 'Asmari' (Oligocene–Miocene) in Iran.

Most other mineral wealth, other than iron, coal, lignite and phosphates, is associated with the igneous intrusion within the folded and overthrust areas of the north. A wide variety of minerals has been proved in Turkey, though wide irregularity in occurrence and quality of the ore bodies has restricted production, and Iran has also more metallic minerals than was at one time supposed. The goldfields in the Sardis district of western Turkey (once the domain of King Croesus) and copper of Cyprus were among the earliest to be worked; but modern attention is now focussed on copper, chromium, lead, manganese and zinc. Precious and semi-precious stones have a scattered but fairly wide distribition in the Middle East, but individual deposits are not rich (some indeed, having been worked for centuries, are now partially exhausted).

Other mineral wealth, associated with sedimentary measures, consist (besides petroleum) of iron, coal, lignite, phosphates, mineral salts, gypsum and pure limestone for cement making. Highly important deposits of iron have been discovered in north-east Africa within the last few years; phosphates are more extensive than was at one time thought, and the wide availability of limestone, with local natural gas and oil fuel, is the basis for one of the most widespread of Middle East industrial activities: cement production which is basic to the current boom in building construction.

### Hydrography

A fundamental demarcation can first be made between regions where rivers have a regular permanent (perennial) flow, and regions where river flow is only seasonal. The latter area is surprisingly extensive, including central Iran, the whole of Arabia and plateau of central Syria, the Sinai peninsula, and apart from the Nile valley and delta, the whole of north-east Africa. In this non-perennial flow zone, dry ravines or watercourses may fill rapidly after a fall of rain, but only for a limited period. A rushing torrent may rise 3 m or even 6 m carrying abundant fine sediment, pebbles and sometimes boulders. Erosion during this period can be very rapid, but lower down there can also be rapid deposition of eroded material by a stream that then quickly subsides. The lighter material, when dried out may also be re-deposited by wind action.

Such valleys, or *wadis*, tend to be irregular in section and in thalweg, with the floor often consisting of a series of rock basins, each with a layer of silt and pebbles. In spite of the relative fertility of water-borne deposits cultivation in these valleys may not be straightforward owing to the possibility of flooding, change of course of the stream, and above

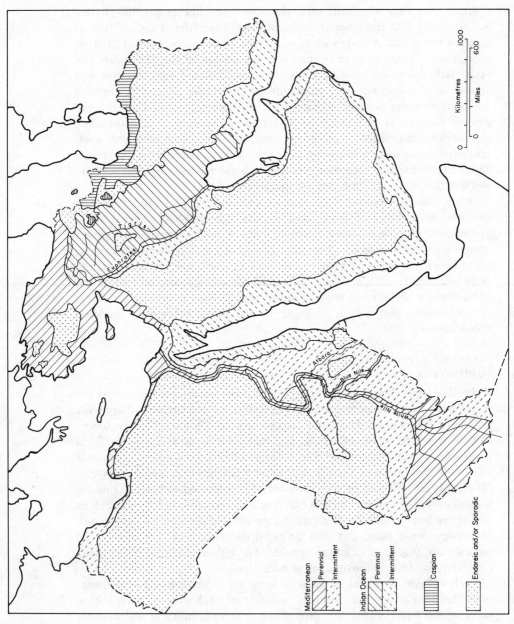

Fig. 2.2 The Middle East: drainage patterns

Mediterranean
Perennial
Intermittent

Indian Ocean
Perennial
Intermittent

Caspian

Endoreic and/or Sporadic

Tigris

Euphrates

Atbara

Blue Nile

White Nile

Kilometres

Miles

1000

600

0

0

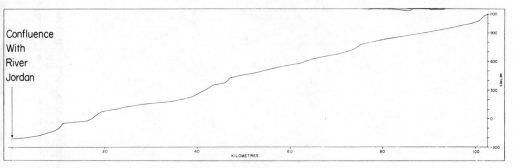

*Fig.* 2.10 Thalweg of the river Zerqa (Jordan).

all by the deposition of silt and other material. Dams and irrigation channels can thus become filled with sediment brought down by floods: many instances are known of Roman or mediaeval Arab dams being buried by alluvial deposits, and many present day irrigation works (though by no means all) can count only on a limited period of 30 years or so in use – a factor producing high irrigation costs. As many as ten to fifteen very short floods (*seil*) may occur in a particular valley, especially where this latter is deeply incised and formed of impermeable strata. Such is the case in Arabia, especially in the south and west, where rainfall can be moderately heavy for a short time, and where volcanic or pre-Cambrian rocks are exposed. Elsewhere, floods are less violent, but can be equally erratic, and even normally dry areas like the Sinai or Libya can have torrential flows for a few days in some years. Not long ago a major road in Saudi Arabia was largely washed out because it was built on an embankment with few drainage culverts. A large lake accumulated, which then burst through the embankment.

The area of perennial rivers corresponds in the main with regions where there is a water surplus of more than 100 mm/annum, which in turn corresponds broadly to annual precipitation of 600 mm/annum or more. Presence of permeable strata is important, in that winter rainfall is partially absorbed, re-emerging as springs later in the year to feed rivers during the dry season from June to September; and this, together with delayed melting of snow means that the effects of a limited annual rainfall, which in warmer and geologically impermeable areas might be dissipated rapidly as a flash-flood, are spread throughout the year. The contrast on the Euphrates, which after leaving Turkey has no right-bank tributaries but a number of major streams on its left bank fed from percolation and snow melt, is a good example.

There are only two rivers of really major size in the Middle East that are wholly fed from indigenous rainfall: a third river, the Nile, is maintained almost entirely by rainfall in Ethiopia and East Africa.

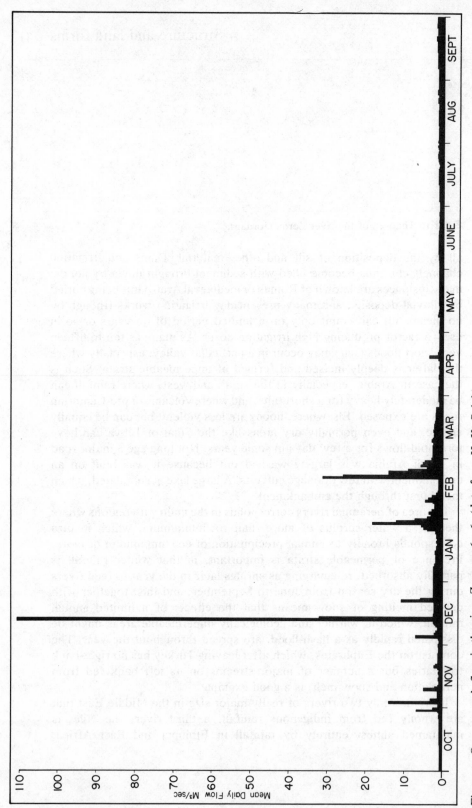

*Fig.* 2.11 One season's flow in the river Zerqa 1960–61 (data from H. K. Saleh).

Various estimates of river water available have been made, chiefly by
C. G. Smith, as given below.

Estimates of river water available

| | Mean annual flow (billion m³) | |
|---|---|---|
| Egypt, Sudan | 84 | Overall figure: the Sudan has rights to 18·5 billion m³ |
| *Turkey | 80 | (50% in the Euphrates and Tigris systems) |
| Iran | 42 | (22 billion m³ in the Dez and Karun systems) |
| *Syria | 28 | (24 billion m³ in the Euphrates) |
| *Iraq | 76 | (50 billion m³ originates outside Iraq) |
| †Israel | 0·75 | (includes half of the Jordan flow) |
| †Jordan | 0·75 | (including half of the Jordan flow) |
| Lebanon | 1·5 | |
| Libya | 0·05 | |
| Saudi Arabia | 0·1 | |

* These totals have been altered since 1974 by barrage construction, chiefly on
  the Euphrates.
† There is not necessarily, in fact, equal allocation of river Jordan waters *between*
  Jordan and Israel. In addition, surface water potential (derived from rainfall)
  has been estimated for certain areas by the United Nations:

| | million m³ |
|---|---|
| Iraq | 80 000 |
| Jordan | 850 |
| Lebanon | 3 800 |
| Syria | 32 000 |
| Saudi Arabia | 2 200 |
| U.A. Emirates | 220 |
| South Yemen | 1 500 |

The second major feature of Middle East hydrography is the extent
of endoreic (i.e. closed or inland) drainage. The main influencing factor
is of course low annual rainfall, but structure and physiography have
important roles. Interior basins shut off from the sea by encircling fold
ranges; recent lava flows across existing valleys; and development of
tectonic basins along fault-lines – all of these, in a region of episodic, often
scanty rainfall, with high evaporation and surface porosity have given
rise to extensive areas of inland drainage, usually as a complex of sumps
or basins.

Defined by an upland rim, often mountainous, these closed drainage basins often have an outwash area or 'alluvian fan' immediately below the mountain slopes, composed of rock debris gravels and silts. At lower levels still the topography becomes more level and plain-like with finer silts that may be re-deposited by aeolian action, though there can be benches or relict shore-lines that break up the level surface. Finally, at the lowest level, there is usually an expanse of water, marsh, salt desert or *kavir*, shallow and highly variable, often saline (sometimes very strongly), but not inevitably so. Iran has the greatest extent of inland drainage, since no major river has broken through the encircling fold ranges, and thus the interior is divided among *kavir* and endoreic basins: Lake Rezai'yeh (Urmia) and the Helmand (Hirwan) lake system being the largest of these latter, with open water. Only in the extreme north and west are streams sufficiently developed to have cut back deeply into the mountain chains. Arabia, with climate and a geology that favours considerable underground seepage and percolation, has little surface drainage, and *kavir* formation occurs mainly in the extreme south east, on the borders with Oman: the eastward tilt of rock strata is responsible.

Although heavier rainfall on the northern and western coastal margins has led to a greater development of rivers, many of which have cut back through the coastal ranges to reach the plateau basins of the interior, there remain a substantial number of closed drainage basins in Asia Minor, chief of which are Lakes Tuz near Konya, and Van.

A well-known, but relatively small basin of inland drainage is that of the river Jordan, with the Dead Sea at its lowest point. Further to the north, as we have noted, the rivers that occupy the tectonic trough – the Litani and the Orontes – have both broken through to the sea; but an area of endoreic drainage lies just to the east: Damascus and Aleppo both lie on the alluvial zones of small closed basins, in the upper reaches where the water is still sweet. In North Africa apart from the Nile Valley, there are also a number of drainage sumps, but none has a feeder stream: instead there is upwelling of water from porous rock strata.

Thus, apart from a very few large rivers, most Middle East rivers consist of relatively short streams making a rapid, though sometimes tortuous and intermittent way down steep mountain flanks. The Anatolian plateau is ringed by a number of such rivers that are broken by cascades and waterfalls and frequently hidden in the depths of huge gorges, with only a few more developed rivers such as the Büyk Menderes (Meander). Similar effects on a much smaller scale characterize the western Lebanon. Most of all, perhaps, the western Zagros shows an elaboration of short immature streams that have cut spectacular gorges even across anticlinal ridges, and because of their erosive power carry immense quantities of silt – the Karun in particular. Yet in its lowest reaches even the Karun becomes buried in its own alluvium, with only a seasonal flow reaching the sea.

These and other anomalies and unusual phenomena in Middle Eastern rivers have excited the curiosity and wonder of those who, over the centuries, have been able to observe them. The majestic Euphrates and Tigris, changing their relative level as they flow in a single valley, the underground Lethe of Cyrenaica and mysterious open artesian wells of the Sahara and eastern Arabia, the sacred Adonis river of Phoenicia, clear in summer but red in spring, the holy Jordan and the Abana, have all appeared as near miraculous to many living near them. But most of all was the riddle of the Nile, a river that regularly produces enormous floods just at the hottest and totally rainless season of the year. It is not surprising that Middle Eastern water has entered in as an intimate part of religious practice: in Christian baptism, and in the compulsory ritual ablutions for followers of Islam.

## Irrigation

This, for many parts of the Middle East, is an essential basis for cultivation: rain-fed agriculture is often precarious and variable in its results. Irrigation, on the other hand, if properly controlled, can be efficiently applied, and thus produces in normal years much heavier crops. Obviously, too, there are extensive areas of good soil that without irrigation, could produce little or nothing. Irrigation is, however, much more than the mere application of water. Type or quality, as well as quantity of water available, the crops grown, soil character, geomorphology (in respect of slope and porosity) and the level of technical competence, commitment and 'cohesion' of the human society involved are all relevant. Irrigation, for complete success, must be multivariate in its relations.

Simplest forms of irrigation are of the basin kind: where topography allows, dams on small or large scale divert river water or retain seasonal floods for long enough to ensure crop growth. This was the traditional method in ancient Egypt and elsewhere, and because it needs relatively little effort, is the cheapest form. It is now normally used for cereal growing, or, in lower Iraq, for watering date-palms.

The second type, channel irrigation, involves leading water in relatively small quantities from a river, well or other source by channels into prepared beds, often on a rota basis. This involves quite an amount of labour both in varying the intakes of the channels in rotation, and often in operating a mechanical water lift, or walking to control a draught animal that operates a hoist or wheel (this is what Old Testament writers meant when they spoke of watering the land by the foot). Such types of irrigation need regular maintenance and operation (often with a 'Water Committee' to ensure fairness and general participation). Such schemes

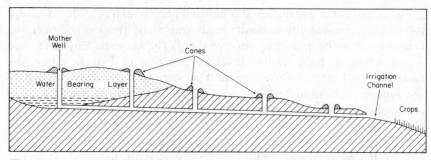

*Fig.* 2.12 A *qanat* or *foggara*.

are consequently more expensive in manpower and often in materials
– hence the higher value crops: fruit, vegetables and, of course, rice are
grown under this kind of irrigation, the *huerta* or *vega* as it was termed
in southern Spain, where it was introduced from the Middle East by
Moslems.

The most elaborate form of channel irrigation is probably that of a *qanat*.
This is essentially a very gently sloping tunnel driven from a water-bearing
layer to an emergence point at lower level, allowing collection of water
in its upper part, and gravity flow downwards to the surface or a
collection point. The first step is to sink a ' mother well' from the surface
to a water-bearing layer and thus prove the existence of underground
water. Then, when an emergence point has been decided upon, a
connecting tunnel is driven from it to the mother well.

As construction proceeds, numerous small shafts are cut from the
near-horizontal tunnel to the surface (at intervals of 5–20 m) in order to
give fresh air to the tunnellers, and allow disposal of soil: this is piled
round each shaft, giving the characteristic pattern of a line of small
volcanoes. A *qanat* may be of considerable length (some of 50 km and
a few even of 100 km are known) and may be to some extent independent
of local topography. They are mostly driven through relatively uncon-
solidated strata (alluvium, gravels, etc.) but may in some cases bore
through solid rock. The sides of the tunnel may be lined (usually with
a specially made fired clay ring or tiles) or supported by wood, and normal
tunnel sizes are 50–100 cm in width and 100–150 cm in height. Even a
tunnel of minimum dimensions for work, and with a minimum of vertical
shafts will involve shifting 3000–4000 tons of spoil/kilometre.

The main value of a *qanat* is the regularity of flow (provided the tunnel
is maintained at regular intervals); but this can be wasteful (e.g. at night)
or in the wet season: thus sometimes storage tanks or reservoirs are used
as adjuncts. Their other great merit is low maintenance when once the
tunnel is dug; though this calls for skill and effort, comparable with coal
mining by hand in the ' lowest' seams. Although the rock material is harder,

the coal miner has better facilities for disposing of his 'spoil' and he does not encounter the occasional snake or scorpion.

Iran has by far the largest number of *qanats* in operation, and was probably the originator (they were known 4000 years ago). Clusters of *qanats* of up to one hundred occur, the average rate of flow is around 50 m³/h (although figures of 300 m³/h are known); and there is considerable seasonal fluctuation. For long the city of Tehran was largely supplied by *qanats* some of which were over 20 km in length, and provided an aggregate flow estimated at 1·3 million m³/s. The natives of Yazd are especially renowned as skilled in *qanat*-building and maintenance, and even today their services are much in demand.

Elsewhere in the Middle East *qanats* are known as *foggaras* (Levant), *karez* (Iraq) and *fellej* (plural *aflaj*) in Oman and the south; and in the first area (as also in Tripolitania) quite a few of Roman date are still producing water. But with the rise in cost of human labour and availability of well-boring machinery and motor pumps, *qanats* are declining in importance: far fewer are dug and some go out of use, though many still continue. But over the last 2 or 3 years there have been crop failures in some parts of Iran because the motor pump broke down at a critical period and spares were lacking: this has led to a local return to the traditional *qanat* and their Yazdi constructors, and so debate has recently opened as to whether *qanat* systems can be improved and made useful by modern technologies.

In recent times modern methods of irrigation have come in. Sprinklers are used in Libya, Israel, parts of the Nile Delta, Lebanon, Syria and Saudi Arabia. The high initial cost restricts their use to high-quality and high-return crops; and one disadvantage is high water loss due to evaporation – in some areas and in seasons of low humidity this can be 45–50% of all water sprayed. The most modern system of all, used only in a very few areas for highest quality cultivation of luxury crops, is by underground drip percolation from plastic piping buried at root level, and controlled by a central computer programme to do the watering at night when evaporation and transpiration are minimal. Initial cost is very considerable, so such schemes are not widespread and thus used only for very high value crops, but once installed, they reduce needs for manpower. On the other hand, they are particularly prone to induce soil salinity.

Another major problem is the supply of water to the cities. Besides increased demand for water due simply to increased numbers, higher living standards also mean that the demand for water personally by each town dweller also increases, and there is also expanded demand owing to industrial development. It was recently stated at an international conference that the consumption of water by some rural populations may have increased by a factor of over 6 between 1952 and 1972. Some cities (mostly in oil-rich countries) now distil sea water; some (e.g. Kuwait) have a dual system (distillate for drinking and saline water separately for household purposes), but rising demand is now posing serious questions such as balance of available resources between agriculture and the cities; or the extent to which known supplies should be conserved – a few towns have drawn off all the local groundwater, and in some coastal areas (e.g. in Israel and some parts of the Persian/Arab Gulf) seawater has percolated into inland water-tables. Recycling of sewage for non-domestic use has begun in a few areas, but this treated water is saltier than normal supplies. The level of ground-water in some parts of Arabia has fallen by 5 to 20 m, and although there is some replenishment by percolation of rainfall, this amount is insufficient. Construction of water schemes on rivers that flow from one country to another are now seriously affecting downstream users, along the Tigris, Euphrates, Jordan, Nile and Helmand systems. In almost all major cities of the Middle East it is fair to say that problems of supplying water (and then treating contaminated effluent and sewage) are coming to be of critical importance. Most now experience a period of reduced or interrupted supply at certain times of the year, and ideas of long-term conservation are only just beginning to have an impact. One particularly unfortunate aspect is that in many cases, development of water supply projects are contracted to foreign developers, some of whom are interested only in short term plans, since their own commitment is limited. A most recent development is for the identification of rock structures favourable to water accumulation by the use of air satellite photography.

As a final element in this cursory survey of hydrology, we must note something of a discrepancy between the relatively feeble and sparse drainage system described above and the actual land forms of the Middle East, which show considerable effects of fluvial action: erosion and deposition. The physical map reveals a very considerable number of structures that in better-watered areas would be described as heavily dissected land forms: Arabia in particular, though devoid of permanent rivers, shows considerable peneplanation and deep erosion by valley formations.

The extent of water erosion and its effect on the landscape is even more apparent to the traveller by air. Broad *wadis* several hundred kilometres in length, and occupied by water only spasmodically or by a tiny trickle in summer; extensive outwash, and alluvial basins never wholly covered even by a flood; and cols, gorges or even wide valleys in high mountain ranges – these phenomena are found not merely in the hill country of the north, but in the drier south. Even in the region of perennial streams round the north-east Mediterranean, small rivers of moderate volume only lie in crevasses and canyons several thousand metres deep; and the greater part of the Syrian desert is diversified by well marked stream beds trending towards the Euphrates. Few of the present streams, it would seem, which trickle for a few days in each year could have carved out the rock basins marking their course, or deposited the masses of sediment that cover their beds. What we have at the present day would seem to be a shrunken and misfit hydrological system, a relic of earlier, wetter periods.

# 3 Climate

Of recent years, there have been two marked changes in approach to the study of climate and weather: first, appreciation that the atmosphere forms overall a continuum, in which, whilst local variables occur, the major features of weather arise from large-scale processes affecting the whole atmosphere; and second, that many of the conditions that give rise to weather changes occur in the middle atmosphere – that is, at heights generally between 5000 and 10000 m – and are hence by no means restricted to that part of the atmosphere near the ground.

The atmosphere receives heat not only directly from the sun in the form of short-wave radiation, but surface features and also clouds receive this radiation, which is then re-emitted to the atmosphere as long-wave radiation. Some of this latter radiation is directed upwards into space and so largely lost to the surface; but some (a small fraction) is absorbed by the atmosphere. When skies are clear, much heat is radiated upwards and lost, but a cloud cover inhibits this and consequently serves to retain the heat at or near the earth's surface. The net effect of this somewhat complicated situation is that two processes go on: heat is received from the sun, and heat is also re-radiated outwards into space. These two processes would seem to be in balance, since the earth's climates do not appear either to be heating up or cooling down in any steady way. Although there have been major fluctuations of climate, these have been either towards greater heat or towards greater cold; both sorts of change have occurred, and not just one.

It is observed that an excess of heat is received from the sun in low

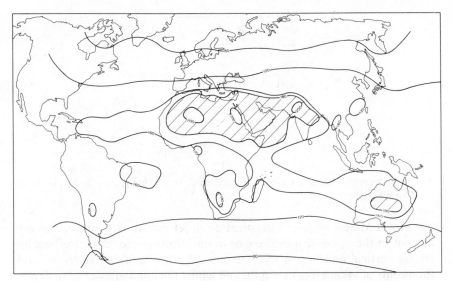

*Fig.* 3.1 Total insolation received at the surface (in g cal/cm²/annum); data from
I. Budyko.

latitudes, whilst north and south of latitudes 40°N and 40°S there is an
excess of outward radiation (i.e. heat loss). This means that there must
be a continuous exchange of heat from low to high latitudes, otherwise
the extreme north and south would get progressively colder, and the
equatorial zone steadily warmer, which obviously we know is not the
case. This process of heat exchange is carried out mainly by three
mechanisms: (1) currents of air moving directly from one zone to another
(major wind systems), (2) the movement of ocean currents, and (3)
movement of air masses (other than wind systems) from one region to
another. This is what is meant by regarding the atmosphere as a
continuum: there is a continuous process of heat exchange affecting the
whole earth, with different situations in different regions. Yet, although
the process may be continuous and world wide, we know that its effects
can also obviously be extremely different regionally. For instance, the
major area of heat increment is not, as was once loosely assumed, at
the Equator, but lies in a zone from the southern Sahara through central
Arabia to the Punjab (Budyko) (fig. 3.1).
    It has just been said that one important mechanism of heat transfer
is by air currents which move from areas at thermal highs to areas of
thermal 'lows', i.e. cooler zones; and of recent years much attention has
been given to these. During and after the Second World War many new
observations were possible by radio-sonde and satellite rocket, following
which there arose the concept of the 'jet stream'. As now defined by

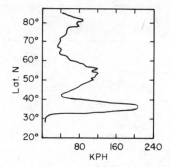

*Fig.* 3.2 Average wind maxima at 500 mbar level (velocities in km/h) after G. Essenwanger.

the World Meteorological Organization, a jet stream is a 'strong narrow current in the upper troposphere or in the stratosphere, characterized by strong vertical and lateral wind shears'. A jet stream is usually several thousands of kilometres in length, and whilst the minimum speed to define a 'jet' is arbitrarily set at 108 km/h (or 30 m/s), speeds of up to five or even ten times this amount have been observed.

Jet streams are most frequent in the upper troposphere but are also observed to occur nearer the surface of the earth, and in the stratosphere, where they are frequent over polar and equatorial zones. Rossby of Chicago, one of the earliest researchers into jet streams, speaks of a belt of great but varying wind speeds, at altitudes of approximately 10 km, 'which surrounds the entire two hemispheres in wavy meanders'. The causes of origin of the jet streams would seem to be (1) the great differences in observed temperatures between various regions – broadly, though not in total detail, the colder areas lie north and south of the Equator (giving a temperature gradient that falls away north and south of the Equator), and (2) the rotation of the earth, including the coriolis effect. The jet streams behave like the currents blowing round high and low pressure zones, i.e. they do not blow directly to or from areas of heat and cold, but as the geostrophic winds blow *at right angles* to the pressure gradients so the jet streams blow generally at right angles to the thermal gradient. With this gradient lying (as we have just noted) north–south, the jet systems consequently tend to have an east–west direction. Easterlies are observed to occur at highest levels in the stratosphere.

Another important characteristic of the jet stream is to display some limited seasonal variation in strength and also in its track. This has important effects in Asia, where contrasts between summer and winter temperatures are extreme, so it is observed that there is a tendency in winter for jets to occur as several linked or braided streams, north *and* south of the Himalaya, whilst in summer the system unites and moves further north, to exist as a single jet system entirely north of the Himalaya.

Many researchers now distinguish a Polar Front Jet Stream, which tends to occur in temperate latitudes and at 9 km altitude, and a Subtropical or Southern Jet Stream, which occurs at 12 km level. Much observation (including, recently, motion pictures taken from satellites) shows that frontal systems are not rigid boundaries, but rather continuously active zones that are forming and dissipating, and they cannot be traced as a single system round the globe. As regards the Middle East, it would seem that the Subtropical Jet lies over the north-east Mediterranean in summer, and displaces southwards, and also increases in velocity during winter, when its core lies as far south as the northern Red Sea.

With the existence of these jet streams as an upper zone of disturbed currents moving strongly in definite but narrow paths within the middle atmosphere, new appraisals must be made regarding the lowest layers of the atmosphere, in which the phenomena of weather occur. The Polar Frontal Theory of Bjerknes, with its associated ideas of air masses and clearly defined boundaries ('fronts'), must be modified, since the presence of strong currents of air aloft will introduce extra factors: convergence or divergence of air leading to pressure changes, and shear, or 'vorticity', which will 'steer' or modify the boundary zones beneath. Moreover, despite a now very developed network of ground reporting stations, giving in some parts of the world an extremely close 'gridding' of weather reporting, forecasts are still not wholly reliable, and therefore full understanding of weather would not seem to be possible from ground data alone. Interest therefore has shifted to the upper layers of the atmosphere as having important influences on weather, and supplying the extra information now regarded as essential to better analysis of meteorological conditions. The Polar Frontal Theory, though a useful and important step forward, has inadequacies: it does not fully explain observed changes of pressure at a frontal zone; it cannot offer explanations of why some systems move as they do, or why some perpetuate and others do not; and it cannot always explain observed precipitation. The obvious difficulties in obtaining data from the upper troposphere and stratosphere retard developments, especially for some regions of the world, but sufficient is now known to make clear the need for modified views on the origin of weather.

With this highly generalized and summary preamble, it is now necessary to consider the Middle East within the general context of the new approaches. Unfortunately, the limited technical level of many Middle Eastern countries, their late entry into scientific research, and the general lack of aerological experience, coupled with an intermediate location

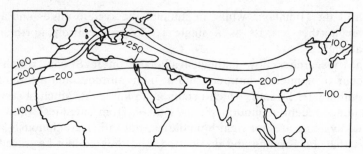

*Fig.* 3.3 Average wind speeds at 200 mbar level (km/h) during February 1956, showing jet development over the Mediterranean (after Krishnamurti).

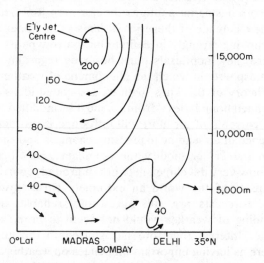

*Fig.* 3.4 Atmospheric circulation (easterlies and westerlies) over India (km/h) during July 1955 (after Koteswaram).

between Europe and southern Asia (both with more varied climatic conditions that have produced intensive study), means that still relatively little is known in detail.

The presence of major jet streams over the Mediterranean was established in the 1940s and after (partly from bitter experience in the loss of aircraft), local contributing factors probably being the presence of the unduly warm Sahara in juxtaposition to the cold mountain masses of south-central Europe (fig. 3.3 gives a typical example). Further east there are also major effects due to the monsoon of the north-west Indian Ocean, now increasingly recognized as a highly special, if not even unique, condition: the south-west monsoonal air current is now thought to build up rapidly as an extremely deep current (5 km – 16500 ft) which is twice that of the North-East Trades – but it thins out very rapidly to the northwest, towards the coasts of Arabia and the Makran. Above it, westerly jet streams prevail during November to March, at the other time of year (when the south-west monsoon develops fully) there is an *easterly* flow in the upper atmosphere (Koteswaram), that would seem to have significant effects for the southern Middle East, in that it induces vorticity and mixing at mid-atmospheric levels, drawing in moist air from the Indian Ocean that gives the summer rainfall of Ethiopia, the southern Sudan, and the Yemen uplands.

**Pressure**
*Summer*

Intense heating of the southern part of Asia gives rise to the well-known monsoonal low pressure area of the Indian subcontinent. This low pressure zone, shallow in that, as we have noted, it does not extend into the upper atmosphere, is however a permanent feature of the months June to September, and has a major centre over north-west India and west Pakistan, prolonged as far as south-east Iran and the Gulf of Oman. The strongly developed wind system to which it gives rise affects not only southern Asia but much of the Middle East, since the low pressure zone is prolonged over the Persian/Arab Gulf towards Iraq and Syria, with the development of a minor but extremely persistent low pressure centre over the island of Cyprus. This minor low lasts again throughout the summer months and markedly affects pressure and wind distribution in the Middle East. The other major factor is the seasonal extension of the Azores high which intensifies and pushes north-eastwards across north-west Africa as far as Libya and Egypt (fig. 3.5). The Cyprus low develops primarily as the result of differential heating of sea and land with a marked development of local convergent uplift. For a small island, Cyprus shows remarkably high summer temperatures, its basin-like topography probably contributing to this as a lens – it has been described as a *plaque chauffante* even in the warm Mediterranean.

The main result of these pressure conditions is to draw air from the north and east southwards over much of the Middle East. A further contributory element would seem to be the presence of the Subtropical Jet over Asia Minor and the Caspian: eddies (lateral and vertical) are generated with a clockwise (anticyclonic) circulation that both reinforce the northerly surface wind pattern, and also contribute to atmospheric stability, producing marked inversion. To the north of the jet, cyclonically circulating eddies tend to develop; this can be held to explain the tendency for summer rain on the eastern Black Sea coasts.

The well-developed northerlies, termed Etesian Winds or Meltemi,

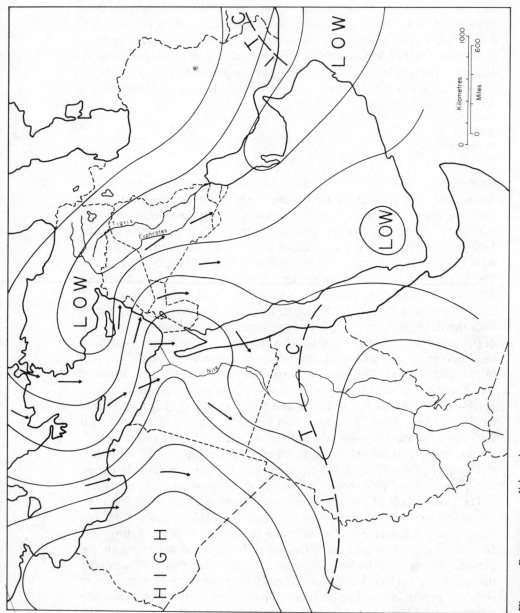

*Fig.* 3·5 Pressure conditions in summer.

develop consistently over the Aegean, and as far south as the coasts of Libya and Egypt, where they are strongly reinforced diurnally by the sea-breeze effect. Further east, however, over Israel, Lebanon and Syria, the prevailing winds are strongly south western, due to the 'pull' of the Cyprus low pressure, again reinforced by a sea-breeze effect which reaches as far inland as Damascus, Amman, and even Palmyra. This air, though northerly, is continental and from the interior of Eurasia (Asia especially) rather than from Europe, and so it is dry, being warmed at low levels as it moves south, and at highest levels by the inversion described in the previous paragraph. Thus there is entire absence of rainfall, except for two special instances – the north east Black Sea coastlands already mentioned, and the coastlands of southern Asia Minor between Antalya and Antakya (Alexandretta) where slight surface convergence towards the Cyprus low, a sea track and the presence of high mountains fronting the sea would appear to produce a very slight summer rainfall confined to the coast.

In the south of the Middle East, conditions are more complex. As we have noted, there is the upper jet system (the Tropical Jet stream) that develops in June to August and blows from the east strongly and at heights of 10–15 km. Below this at low levels, there is the transgression of southern Hemisphere Trade Winds across the Equator into the northern Hemisphere where they are deflected to become south-westerlies – in response to the northern migration of the Hyetal Equator and, correspondingly, the Subtropical (westerly) Jet that in winter lies over northern Egypt. Consequently, in summer there are convergent winds at low levels: dry northerlies and north-easterlies, and humid south-westerlies off the Indian Ocean, which between them produce what is termed the Intertropical Convergence Zone (I.T.C.). Above this is the seasonal high-level easterly, with considerable disturbance and eddying that is held to produce in a more developed form immediately further east, the monsoonal 'cell' of the northern Indian Ocean. Where topography produces mechanical uplift (as in the plateaus of Ethiopia, the Yemen and Asir), considerable summer rainfall occurs from the damp southerly maritime stream over-running the drier northerly currents. This may be held to explain why there is very little or no summer rainfall at sea level along the Red Sea and Gulf of Aden coasts, but considerable rainfall (up to 2 m) on the high mountains inland. This newer view offers a better explanation than that of a westerly upper air current from the Gulf of Guinea affecting east Africa and southern Arabia which was accepted 20 years or more ago. It is, however, as well to emphasize what was said earlier: this whole region remains as yet one of the least well provided with upper air reports and facilities for intensive study.

The composite pressure systems as outlined above tend to be permanent features from June until September. Relatively minor variations of surface pressure occur from time to time, with slight deepening or falling of the systems; but in general quasi-stability of the pressure situation remains; hence regularity in surface wind patterns and in weather conditions are the chief characteristics.

*Winter*

In the lower atmosphere, high pressure covers the interior of Asia, and extensions of this may reach as far as Iran. In Asia Minor, because of its elevation and consequent low temperatures, a second, much smaller and rather more intermittent anticyclone may form – unlike the larger Siberian 'high' it can disappear from time to time.

Over the entire Middle East, the westerly Subtropical Jet Stream becomes very well established and at higher velocity with its axis over the southern Mediterranean coast, and this is especially favourable for the elaboration of small low pressure zones ('depressions') to form in the lower atmosphere. Winter is therefore characterized by a succession of disturbed cyclonic conditions, broken from time to time by a temporary build-up of high pressures over Asia Minor and the mainland of south-west Asia. At the same time, the easterly Tropical Jet Stream characteristic of July in the extreme south is no longer present, hence the convergent air flow is much less marked, and there is very little rainfall in the southern Sudan and southern Arabia.

Depressions may pass, already formed, from the Atlantic, via north-west Europe, Spain or north-west Africa, into the Western Mediterranean basin. Rejuvenated by contact with the sea and maintained or even steered by the upper jet streams, the depressions continue via the Mediterranean as far as Armenia, Iran and the Persian/Arab Gulf to Pakistan. A few of these move southwards along the Red Sea to give slight winter rainfall to the coastlands.

As well, however, and on average distinctly more frequently, new low pressure systems develop or greatly intensify within the Mediterranean basin. It would appear that the impact of jet streams on major mountain masses is especially favourable for the development of 'lee depressions' – vortices or eddies in the lee of major hill massifs such as the Atlas or northern Apennines. As well, cyclogenesis can take place in the Gulf of Sirte and over Cyprus – with important effects on the weather of Libya, Egypt and the Levant.

This means that the Mediterranean in winter has its own pronounced system of weather. Sometimes fully formed depressions may continue on a track from Europe or the Atlantic, but often a change or new development takes place. Frontal systems of the Bjerknes type associated

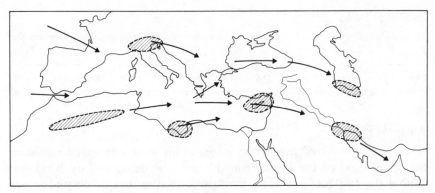

*Fig.* 3.6 Tracks of depressions and areas of cyclo- and frontogenesis over the Mediterranean.

with 'lows' are by no means necessarily the same in the Mediterranean – warm sectors in particular, which in higher latitudes are associated with extensive layer cloud, high humidities and much precipitation, may well in the Mediterranean be almost cloudless and quite dry.

A further point of difference arises in the relative shallowness and small extent of Mediterranean depressions. Whereas Atlantic depressions may cover half the entire ocean, with a minimum pressure approaching 960 mbar, disturbances in the Mediterranean are usually much smaller, and pressure rarely falls below 990 mbar. This does not mean that the depression is less intense; but the duration of bad weather is definitely shorter and greater variety in conditions is experienced.

It is not considered necessary to follow the tracks of Mediterranean depressions in much detail. Carefully defined routes tend to be somewhat misleading, since a feature of any depression is its irregularity of movement. Broadly speaking, however, depressions tend to follow a sea track. From northern Italy, they frequently pass down the Adriatic into the Ionian Sea. Here the track divides, under the influence of the land mass of Asia Minor. Many depressions continue eastwards into the Levant and Iraq, whilst others move northwards into the Aegean and Black Seas, ultimately reaching the Caspian. A second route lies in the south of the Mediterranean basin. In this case an uninterrupted sea track brings rain to the Levant coastlands, and depressions often reach the Persian/Arab Gulf, or even the interior of Iran (fig. 3.6).

In summer and very early autumn, cyclonic disturbances rarely affect the Middle East. A more northerly track takes them across central Europe and the northern Balkans to the Black Sea, where convergence with the northerly air streams, together with orographical effects intensifies the rainfall of the north-east coast of Asia Minor (see conditions at Batum).

Rainfall at Batum (mm)

| J | F | M | A | M | J | J | A | S | O | N | D | Total |
|---|---|---|---|---|---|---|---|---|---|---|---|---|
| 258 | 153 | 156 | 128 | 71 | 150 | 154 | 209 | 305 | 226 | 309 | 254 | 2473 |

**Air mass climatology**

In earlier editions of this book, reservations were expressed regarding the application of the Polar Frontal Theory as developed by Bjerknes. Within the last few years, as more investigation has taken place, it is increasingly accepted that modification of the Bjerknes model is necessary even in temperate latitudes, while the Polar Frontal Theory cannot account for many of the weather phenomena of low latitudes. Pedelaborde goes so far as to state that the fronts are rare in low latitudes, and Reiter, though aware of the value of the Bjerknes theories in explaining some weather sequences, has also drawn attention to several considerable difficulties of a technical nature. The Middle East as a mid-latitude zone is thus between the two very different systems of cool temperate zones, where the Bjerknes model of 'Fronts' still retains validity as a concept, and the areas of the Tropics, where it now does not. We therefore must be ready to accept the intermediate position that under some circumstances 'lows' will appear to have frontal systems of the 'classical' type, whereas on other occasions a different approach will be necessary in analysing weather conditions.

A most useful approach to understanding the weather of the Middle East is by considering the nature of the various air masses that move successively over the region, some on a quasi-seasonal periodicity, some much more sporadic and irregular. Here the special location of the area is of great importance. A link between Africa and Asia, the Middle East lies close to two of the hottest regions of the world, the Sahara and north-west India; yet at the same time it forms a part of the continent of Asia, which in winter develops the lowest temperatures occurring on the globe. Intermediate between these regions of extremes, the Middle East can easily fall for a short time under the influence of one or the other; and the relative closeness of such reservoirs of heat and cold means that little modification can take place as air currents make their way outwards from their regions of origin. Here is the first contrast with cool temperate latitudes: air arriving in north-west Europe, for example, whether polar or tropical in origin, is nearly always considerably modified during its long journey north or south, and best described as relatively cold (polar) or warm (tropical); but in the Middle East little doubt as to area of origin is possible. By reason of its scorching heat and dust-laden appearance, African air can be felt and seen to be a 'breath of the desert'; whilst at other times cold spells of near-Siberian intensity may freeze rivers in the north and east.

It is customary to divide air masses according to their area of origin, either polar or tropical. Further division is then made on the basis of humidity – continental air is generally drier than that originating over oceans. This gives four main types of air masses: polar maritime and polar continental, and tropical maritime and tropical continental. Division on these lines is, however, not entirely satisfactory for the Middle East, since maritime influences are less important, and continental origins cannot always be simply defined as tropical or polar.

For present purposes. it would seem useful to consider the Middle Eastern air masses as follows:

(1) Summer conditions.

(2) Maritime air from the Atlantic, reaching the Middle East via the Mediterranean. This can be either tropical or polar in origin.

(3) Tropical continental air.

(4) Polar continental air.

*Summer conditions*

As we noted above, air of somewhat varied origin is drawn over the Middle East during the summer months. Some of this air can be described as dried-out monsoonal air related to the lower-level monsoonal system of India; this air has had a long land track over the north of the subcontinent, and then crosses the Suleiman and Hindu Kush mountains, as the result of which it undergoes an adiabatic warming on descent over Iran. Such air is quite dry, but, from its previous history, so to speak, it is capable of absorbing moisture if it follows a sea track; this is especially apparent in the lower layers, where the air blows from sea to land, as in the eastern Mediterranean, Persian/Arab Gulf and the Red Sea. Humidities may thus become extremely high, though hardly any rain falls. In the north, much continental air is also drawn in from Russia – Asiatic and European. This is initially less stable, and also likely to be affected by the passage of low pressure systems or frontal conditions associated with Europe; and where the types of air meet over sea areas (as in the southern Black Sea and Caspian) mixing takes place. Given the further factor of high topography, there can develop a major convergent movement tending to uplift; and so, in the two angles fronting a major water surface, where mountain ranges meet, a zone of marked summer precipitation occurs. The two instances are the western Caspian shorelands between the Elburz and eastern Caucasus ranges, and north-eastern Turkey.

Otherwise, the air masses forming the major (almost sole) element are dry, giving almost no rainfall. Towards the west (Libya, Egypt and north-west Sudan) stability associated with subsidence tends to increase, under the influence of the subtropical high pressure zone which is a marked feature over most of northern Africa.

For the Middle East as a whole the general result in the extreme south is to produce several months of clear skies. Near the coasts there is a regular diurnal variation: totally clear skies at night and a small amount of fair-weather cumulus during the day, with sometimes slightly more over the sea. Inland, however, cloud amounts are very small and many days may pass without any cloud whatsoever, allowing uninterrupted insolation by day, with consistent high temperatures, but considerable night radiation, providing relatively cool nights.

Towards mid-September the first signs of change become apparent. Bursts of maritime air from the Mediterranean increasingly disturb the summer flow; pressure patterns in the lower atmosphere begin to change; and by late October other air masses are dominant.

### Maritime air

Somewhat higher general humidity is one characteristic, but a generally lower temperature is also found. This air usually originates over the Atlantic, passing into the Mediterranean either by way of Europe, Spain or north-west Africa. There may thus be considerable differences in the air mass itself, some parts being polar and others tropical in origin. Temperature characteristics are, however, modified during the long passage over land and sea. Humidity is, on the other hand, largely unaltered, as the track of the air has lain over sea areas. On uplift, or on intermixture with other masses, considerable condensation takes place, with consequent heavy rainfall. These maritime currents blowing generally from a westerly direction penetrate most of the Middle East, with the exception of the far south. Closely influenced by the Subtropical Jet Stream, which as we have noted intensifies at this season, vortices form from time to time, with an intermixture of air of differing types. Strings of small surface 'lows' can hence be a feature of the maritime régime (fig. 3.7A).

Maritime air currents blowing generally from a westerly direction penetrate the entire Middle East region between October and May.

Differences set up by slight changes within the air mass itself, or by interaction with other masses of more widely divergent type, give rise to disturbances which produce a kind of weather similar to that of the cyclonic belt of cool temperate latitudes. Strings of small depressions are the feature of the maritime régime, and the intensity of these latter

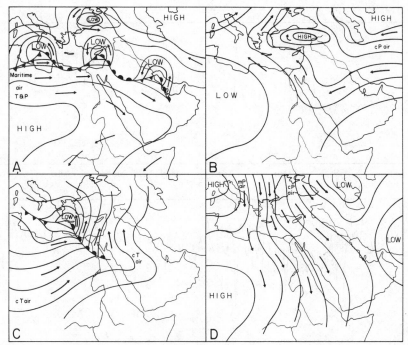

*Fig.* 3.7 Pressure conditions in winter.

depends upon the degree of contrast in temperature and humidity of the
varied air masses that form them (fig. 3.7A).

Maritime air exerts its greatest influence on the western margins of the
Middle East, but we have seen that depressions can penetrate as far east
as Iran. Like the monsoon current in India, the westerlies of the Middle
East become progressively drier as they advance into the continental
interior, and the weather disturbances to which they give rise become
increasingly feeble.

The inflow of maritime air, although predominant throughout much of
the year between October and May, is interrupted from time to time by
outbursts of air of two largely differing types, that are yet to be
considered.

## Tropical continental air

A feature of the Middle East is the proximity of wide expanses of desert,
from which intensely hot and dry air may be drawn by the passage of
depressions. If a southerly gradient of pressure develops, air from north
Africa and Arabia floods northwards on a large scale, producing highly
special weather conditions (fig. 3.7C).

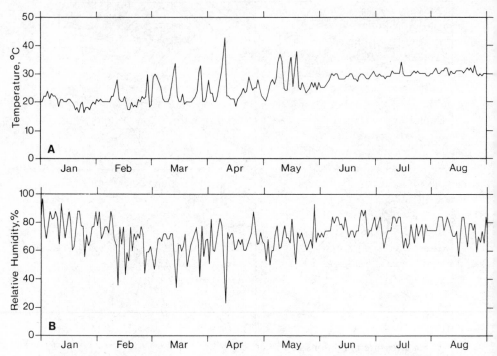

*Fig.* 3.8   Typical *khamsin* conditions at Alexandria, Egypt 1974 (data by A. A. Ali).

A portion of the great quantity of heat energy is transferred to the pressure field, giving rise to strong winds, which frequently reach gale force. Temperatures rise – sometimes by 16–20 °C in a few hours – and relative humidity falls to figures of less than 10%. Crops may be withered in a day and a rise in the death-rate is often noticed in large cities,[1] particularly among babies and young children. Nervous tension, even irritability, can affect many people, and static electricity can interrupt communications and become a danger to telephone operators. The most prominent effects are, however, driving sand and dust, which can cover roads and penetrate into houses. Best protection at home is to keep all doors and windows closed, despite the heat.

The effect is so marked that local names have been given to these southerly winds. In Egypt the word *khamsin*[2] is used, *ghibli* in Libya,

[1]   Such an effect, common today in the cities of Egypt, may explain in part the Tenth Plague of the Old Testament.

[2]   The word *khamsin* (Arabic *fifty*) has been variously understood to refer to the average duration of the hot wind (50 h), to its annual frequency (50 times) and to its season of maximum onset, the 50 days on each side of the spring solstice. The third explanation seems closest to the truth.

and *shlouq* in the Levant. In Iran, *simoom* (poison wind) is a good description. Similar winds on a somewhat smaller scale are termed 'Santa Annas' in California, and 'brickfielders' in Australia. A minimum definition for a *khamsin* is now taken as a rise of 6 °C (dry bulb) within 6 hours, but much higher figures are of course known.

Winds of *khamsin* type develop most often when tropical air is drawn in as the warm sector of a rapidly moving depression formed in maritime air. Such depressions give the most extreme weather conditions, but are usually of short duration. In desert areas, sandstorms are almost invariably produced by strong southerly winds, and these storms, often violent, may spread into settled areas. Cairo itself is not immune from visitations; and Herodotus records the fate of a Persian army which, setting out from Egypt against a rising south wind to subdue the oasis of Siwa, lost its way and was never heard of again. *Khamsin* depressions are a considerable hazard still, especially as regards aircraft flights.

Autumn and spring, particularly the latter, are the chief seasons at which hot winds occur. In spring, the southern deserts heat up rapidly whilst the rest of the Middle East is still cold, and favourable conditions are thus established for mixture of differing air streams. Owing to the extreme dryness of the desert air, rainfall, which normally results from mixing of two air masses, is very scanty or entirely absent. Quite often, however, as cold air comes in at the rear, there is a most spectacular build-up of cumulo-nimbus cloud, with extremely strong convection. Soil and dust carried upwards can give rise to coloured clouds and coloured or mud rains; and there are authentic instances of small living creatures, even fish and frogs, being carried into the air and then descending in rain. On one occasion, in 1968, dust from the Sahara was carried as far as southern England, where it eventually gave muddy rain, clearly to be seen on car roofs.

Apart from these major inconveniences and possible structural damage, by far the greatest ravages occur to crops. The frequency of hot spells (with or without sand winds) during the season when new crops are beginning to grow is particularly unfortunate (chiefly spring, but also autumn, as both winter and summer crops are grown). Much damage can be done to young plants.

*Polar continental air*

In winter and spring, waves of cold air flow southwards and westwards from the intensely cold interior of Eurasia. Two widely differing types of air can be distinguished. The first, originating in south-central Asia, overflows into Iran, and may for a short time reach the Mediterranean. The air is cold, but very stable, deriving from the Siberian anticyclone, and days are fine and clear. Over the Iranian and Anatolian plateaux very low temperatures occur, but sunshine during the day mitigates the worst effects, particularly as humidity is low (fig. 3.7B).

Further to the west, the air undergoes slight adiabatic heating as it descends the edges of the Zagros and the plateaux of Anatolia and Syria. Fine weather prevails, with low temperatures inland, but moderately warm conditions on the coastlands. Fog, the frequent accompaniment of winter high pressure in western Europe, is absent, as the air is very dry.[1] Anticyclonic waves are frequent in the Middle East during autumn and the early part of winter; but later in the year continental air of a very different type makes its way in from the north-west (fig. 3.7D).

Anticyclonic conditions frequently develop in central and eastern Europe during January, February and March. A reservoir of cold air builds up, and this, unlike the air outflowing from the dry heart of Asia, is damp, since it is merely chilled and modified maritime air originating from the Atlantic. From time to time currents of this European air are drawn into the rear of a cycle of depressions moving east along the Mediterranean; and on reaching the Middle East, the lower layers of this quasi-continental air have been subjected to contact heating during the southward passage over the warm sea. Considerable quantities of moisture have also been absorbed.

Unlike the adiabatic heating of the Asiatic continental air, which affects all layers, differential heating of only the lowest layers in the European current produces much instability; this, together with high humidity, gives rise to heavy rainfall of a showery type.[2] Practically all the snowfall and much of the rainfall of the Middle East develop in outbursts of cold damp air from central and eastern Europe. Late winter and early spring are unpleasant seasons, liable to prolonged periods of raw, cold conditions, with frequent and heavy precipitation. If these conditions persist for any length of time, they may become intensified as much colder Arctic air ultimately becomes drawn across central Europe from the north. This can give periods of thoroughly unsettled and unseasonable weather for a few days even as far south as the Sahara, central Egypt and the upper Persian/Arab Gulf, and cool spells in the Sudan.

[1] Fog occurs for the most part in the Middle East only during inflow of maritime air from the west.

[2] Heating applied equally to an entire air mass raises the temperature absolutely, but does not alter the temperature *difference* between highest and lowest layers and has therefore no effect on the stability of the air mass. Heating applied only to the lowest layer increases this difference, and hence tends to produce instability.

### Air masses and fronts

Thanks in part to the daily television bulletins, the ideas of Bjerknes on air masses and fronts are now a commonplace for many members of the public, at least in Europe and North America. We have noted, however, that there is need to modify the Polar Frontal Theory even for cool temperate latitudes – the details are beyond the scope of the present study – and that, as regards subtropical and warm temperate zones, significant limitations on a wider scale enter in. We have seen that, whilst the winter season in the Middle East is a season of fluctuating pressure systems, the summer has broadly a fixed pattern of high pressure to the west, and a complex series of 'lows' to the east and south-east. These 'lows' are, however, non-frontal and do not, except in the extreme south, exhibit marked discontinuities of temperature or of humidity. The weather therefore remains for the most part settled and fine. Non-frontal lows can also occur for a short period in winter.

Recent research has tended to show that the impinging of warm air against cold (the Bjerknes 'Warm Front') can, contrary to previous ideas, be an area of upper atmospheric instability. This may be particularly true of the Middle East; and there is the further factor that, as the warmest air tends to originate over continental areas, the air mass may be initially very dry, and so long as no long sea track is involved, cloud and precipitation do not develop. But a short sea track can produce instability, especially at higher levels; and so, while it is still reasonable to say that warm fronts of the true Bjerknes type are, generally speaking much less developed in the Middle East, warm fronts of a somewhat different character (i.e. without the extensive layer cloud characteristic of cool temperate zones, and with a much less humid warm sector) can occur, and they have some, but restricted, influence on rainfall.

Much, though not all, rainfall in the Middle East is from cold fronts, which show a very marked development. Usually regions of pronounced instability, this tendency is greatly increased by the presence of highly varied relief. Mechanical uplift thus occurs as cold air masses encounter mountain ranges; and the alignment of these ranges may produce an extra convergent effect which adds a further element of uplift. This can be seen off the coast of the Lebanon, where the presence of the Lebanon range (max. 3000 m) close to the coast gives rise to a slight convergent effect off shore, indicated visibly by a semi-permanent line of cumulus cloud when the wind is strongly on shore, as it is for much of the year. Cold fronts meeting mountain ranges or plateau edges are therefore much intensified; but rapid weakening also occurs on the leeward side of the high ground. In this way wide variation in climatic conditions may occur, since local topography assumes great importance in the development of

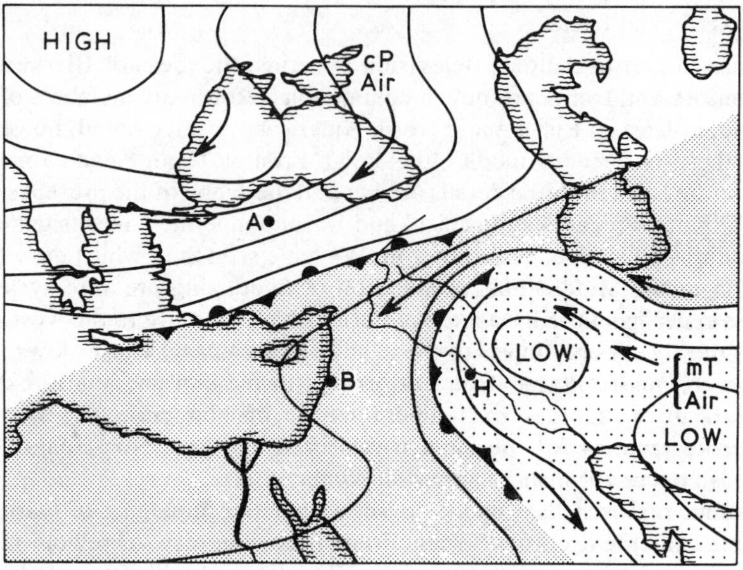

*Fig.* 3.9 Variation in air mass, with characteristic alignment of fronts and mass boundaries, during period 24–26 March 1945. A – Ankara, temp. +2 °C; B – Beirut, 16 °C; H – Habbaniya, 22 °C. Unmodified tropical air in south-east; modified polar air stippled; polar/Arctic air in north.

weather. Rainfall is heavy on the windward side of mountain ranges, but much reduced on the leeward side. This helps to explain why the edge of the Syrian desert approaches so closely to the shores of the Mediterranean, although prevailing winds are on shore throughout most of the year.

Another feature of the Middle East can be the alignments of fronts (or, better, air mass boundary phenomena) parallel to isobars, rather than across them, which is more usual further north. This occurs when air masses of different origins and qualities may come together and flow side by side without giving rise to the rapid formation of a lower atmospheric 'depression', as tends usually to happen in more northerly latitudes. Weather phenomena – cloud formation and precipitation – can frequently occur at these boundary fronts, but they are less identifiable as 'warm' or 'cold'; instead, if the colder air becomes more established and the front drifts over territory lately covered by the warm air, then there is a tendency in the weather to follow a cold front (instability) pattern; if the warm air becomes more established then warm weather front conditions tend to occur. In fig. 3.9 the front over Asia Minor could move northwards as a warm front, or southwards as a cold front – all that this means is, in the first case, that warmer air (with larger cloud) replaces cold, and in the second that colder air replaces warm (with resulting instability cloud). More research is, however, necessary for the Middle East region, especially as regards the movement of these shallow air masses near the ground in relation to the upper jets, especially the Subtropical Jet.

## Temperature and humidity
### Temperature

Chief features are the high temperatures of summer, and a wide range, both annual and diurnal. Clear skies are the main influencing factor here, since during the day intense solar heating of the land surface can give rise to very high temperatures. During the night, however, there is equally little check in heat radiation from the land surfaces, and so temperatures fall considerably away from the sea areas. It is first useful to note the general contrast with regions which, although close to the Equator, and therefore with even greater solar radiation, nevertheless have much rainfall and cloud restricting direct insolation. The warmest parts of the earth occur where summer skies are clear, rather than at the Equator, where cloud is more prevalent (fig. 3.1). 'Sun drenched' is for the Middle East both a description and a definition.

Average July temperatures

|  | °C |  | °C |
|---|---|---|---|
| Cairo | 28·3 | Colon | 26·6 |
| Beirut | 27·2 | Freetown | 25·5 |
| Basra | 36·1 | Mombasa | 25·3 |
| Tehran | 29·4 | Singapore | 27·2 |

Another important effect is that of altitude. In this connection it should be recorded that, whilst some parts of the Middle East are very low lying, there are very extensive areas – most of Asia Minor and Iran, for example – that lie at 1000 m or more above sea-level. This does not so much reduce the summer maxima (since the ground is warmed directly) as reduce winter temperatures, which can be very low indeed for the latitude. Further, though minor, influences are the mountainous coastline in many parts, which limits the tempering effect of the sea to a narrow strip, the basin-like character of many interiors, which concentrates insolation, and the absence of soil and vegetation, which allows both intense surface heating and nocturnal radiation.

In view of the wide daily and seasonal ranges of temperature, averages tend to be misleading, and it is better to refer to average maxima and minima temperatures in order to appreciate actual conditions. For instance, in the table above, it would seem that conditions in Beirut and Cairo are very similar; in fact, Cairo may have summer day temperatures of over 40 °C, but with a markedly cool night, whilst Beirut rarely rises above 35 °C, but with only 6 °C difference between day and night temperatures.

A marked simplicity of rhythm prevails throughout the Middle East. With a few exceptions July is the hottest month inland, but on the coast the maximum is delayed until August, because of the slower absorption of heat by the sea. Egypt shows a good example of this tendency, with a July maximum in the Nile valley and an August maximum on the Mediterranean and Red Sea coasts. Towards the extreme south the maximum is earlier, June in southern Arabia and Upper Egypt, and even May in much of the Sudan – due to more direct solar heating at the solstice.

January is everywhere the coldest month, but any considerable rise in temperature is often delayed until the end of February or early March. Once begun, however, this is rapid. Considerable differences are apparent in winter between the north-eastern part of the Middle East, and the centre and south. Proximity to the Eurasian interior means that continental influences are very marked in the north and east, and these are intensified by the effects of topography. Many of the higher parts, therefore, have really severe winters – very much colder than normal for the latitude. Motor oil may freeze, iron implements like axes become brittle, and humans migrate to the more sheltered valleys. Extremely low temperatures occur in Asia Minor, Armenia and much of Iran. Meteorological observations are scanty, but one small permanent glacier is known to exist in the Zagros, and conditions at Erzerum indicate the intensity of winter cold (January mean $-11$ °C, average day max. $+1$ °C, average night min. $-27$ °C, absolute min. $-40$ °C).

The Bosphorus and Black Sea sometimes become jammed by pack-ice; inland snowstorms isolate many districts, even as far south as Syria and Jordan. Small quantities of snow may fall in regions of lower elevations, and except for the lower lying parts of southern Arabia and all of the Sudan, no part of the Middle East can be said to be entirely free from snowfall. The lower Nile valley, the highlands of the Yemen and the hills of northern Libya experience slight falls when cold air makes its way south from Europe. Exceptionally, the Jebel of Tripolitania may have up to 1 or 1½ m of snow, and there can even be snowfalls in Southern Yemen and on the Jebel Akhdar of Oman.

Diurnal variation of temperature is important at all seasons, but most developed in summer. In coastal areas, maritime influences restrict the

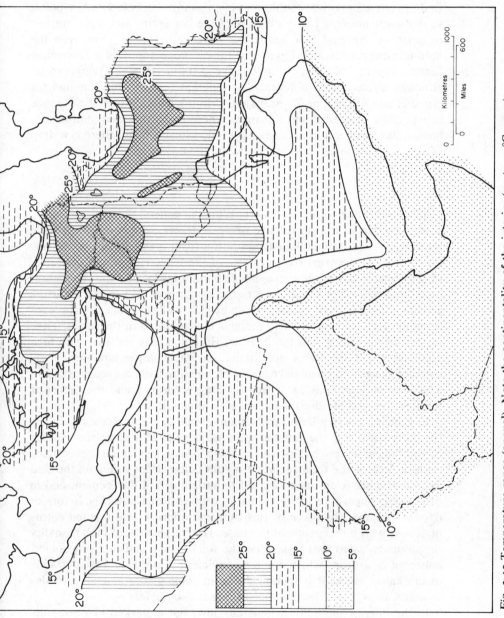

*Fig.* 3.10 Temperature range (annual). Note the continentality of the interior (up to 27°C range).

temperature range; but at a short distance inland, great heat during the day gives place at night to a most refreshing coolness. In Egypt and the Red Sea coastlands night cooling may even bring the air below its dew-point, so that early morning fog is a feature of the late spring and early summer in parts of the Red Sea coast, the lower Nile valley, and even the Mediterranean coasts of Egypt and Libya. Topography is a controlling factor – regions of high altitude have a reduced night temperature, although by day little difference is apparent (cf. the July minima for Istanbul and Ankara, or for Basra and Tehran). This altitudinal difference is especially marked in the Lebanon, where numerous mountain resorts have a day temperature of over 25–27 °C, whilst at night there is a drop of 10–15 °C, as compared with 5–6 °C on the coast.

### Humidity

Considerable local variation occurs. Whilst in general the average is low, due of course to the prevalence of open desert, some areas may have remarkably high humidities. Evaporation from major inland water surfaces, such as the great river systems of the Nile, Tigris and Euphrates, or the Dead Sea, may give rise to high humidities locally, but the highest humidities are often found in certain coastal zones. Wherever a narrow coastal plain is backed by a mountain barrier, well-developed sea breezes bring in much moisture, which remains concentrated in the coastal zone instead of spreading into the interior. High humidity together with high temperatures make living conditions extremely unpleasant during the summer season, when inland transfer of moisture from the sea is greatest. The Persian/Arab Gulf coast was for long notorious, and the shores of the Red Sea and Mediterranean are also affected.

In some places (e.g Beirut and Oman) humidity is actually at its highest for the year during the summer months, in spite of a complete absence of rainfall, and dew can occur on 200–250 days per annum, producing up to a fifth of the total recorded precipitation. Heavy dew on the Red Sea coastlands is an important aid to agriculture in the Yemen, and in this respect one will recall the similarity with western California. In former days advantage was taken of this by some nomads who erected cairns of stones with a receptacle at the base. During seasons of high humidity the stones radiated heat faster than the soil or sand, and so, being colder, collected dew drops which could be sufficient to produce a small trickle of drinkable water. It is reckoned that in some places dewfall provides as much as 25% of effective moisture usable by plants.

In the interior humidity is generally low, but a marked increase may occur in winter with a westerly or northerly air stream. Hence winter mist and even fog are by no means uncommon, particularly in riverine areas, and salt marshes may also experience dense mist.

Number of days with dew at Haifa (15-year mean)

| J | F | M | A | M | J | J | A | S | O | N | D | Total |
|---|---|---|---|---|---|---|---|---|---|---|---|-------|
| 0 | 3 | 2 | 11 | 18 | 25 | 19 | 19 | 23 | 18 | 0 | 0 | 138 |

*Tolerance*

High temperatures may be tolerated by humans so long as humidity remains low, and so the summer heat of the interior may often be more easily borne than the muggy conditions of the coastlands. Beirut, with summer average maxima of 30–32 °C and 70–75% relative humidity, may feel more exhausting than Damascus (37–40 °C, 30–40% relative humidity). There are some localities where the wet bulb temperature may rise for a time above blood heat (38 °C) and with these conditions sustained human activity becomes very difficult. It should, however, be added that, with the development of artificial air-conditioning, one of these traditional handicaps to life in the Middle East has been greatly diminished – at least for the better-off. In most cities, especially the oil towns of the Gulf, summer now experiences peak demand for electricity due to extensive air-conditioning.

One other, opposite effect is due to prolonged low humidity, as the result of which the nervous system is overstimulated, giving rise to strain and irritability. The French speak of this as 'cafard'; the British originally developed the term 'round the bend' during 1940–44 to refer to the same state of mind.

Having mentioned deleterious effects of certain features of Middle Eastern climate, a more important opposite aspect remains. Average conditions approach closely to the optimum for human and plant life, and with a 'continentality' that swings seasonally from cold to heat, drought to downpour, there could be the variability of conditions that Ellsworth Huntington regarded as the best basis for human advancement. This last apart, the extremes of growth-retarding cold and overwhelming heat are limited to certain regions only and for many areas, especially the coasts, conditions are almost always genial. Thus it is possible to suggest that the influence of climate on the Middle East has been a profound influence on the rise of civilization. Early man, unable greatly to change his material environment, found best help in the struggle to move from the primitive to the civilized afforded by a climate of 'summer's shine and winter's rain'.

## Rainfall

Except for the two small coastal regions of northern Iran and north-east Asia Minor, the Yemen uplands and adjacent areas in southern Arabia and the southern Sudan, which, as we have seen, are climatically special cases, the whole of the rest of the Middle East has a strongly marked 'Mediterranean' rhythm of summer drought and winter rain. During summer higher pressures over the western Mediterranean and north Africa act as a buffer between the low pressures of the north Atlantic, the Cyprus low and the monsoonal lows of the lower Persian Gulf and east-central Africa, thus shutting out seasonally oceanic influences from the west. For the western Mediterranean as far as and including western Libya the northward migration of subtropical high pressure can be regarded as directly responsible for the development of dry conditions. But, as has already been stated, pressures in the eastern Mediterranean and further east are actually lower in summer than in winter.

Atmospheric pressure (monthly average in millibars)

|      | Benghazi sea-level | Istanbul sea-level | Limassol sea-level | Basra sea-level | Muscat sea-level |
| ---- | ------------------ | ------------------ | ------------------ | --------------- | ---------------- |
| Jan. | 1010               | 1019               | 1017               | 1019            | 1019             |
| July | 1005               | 1012               | 1007               | 997             | 998              |

Rainfall occurs first in early autumn when the dry summer air masses are displaced by damper and more unstable currents from the west. A few short showers only occur during September, but towards the end of October heavier and more prolonged falls, often with spectacular thunderstorms, announce the end of summer. These usually clear up after a few days, and a relatively fine period ensues until December. The real rainy season does not begin until about Christmas, and may even be delayed until the New Year. Over the western half of the Middle East January is the rainiest month with a slight tendency to a December maximum noticeable in a few areas. Towards the east, the maximum is increasingly delayed. Syria shows a January maximum in the extreme west, and a February maximum in the remainder of the country. In eastern Iraq, in Iran and in parts of Asia Minor, March is often the wettest month; in these landward areas the influence of interior winter high pressure generated by intense cold may deflect the rain-bearing lows elsewhere, and it is not until these collapse in spring that maritime air can reach the interior.

Partly but not entirely for this reason the shores of the Caspian and southern Black Sea coasts have a double rhythm, with a minor maximum in spring, a major maximum in autumn, and no month without rain.

By the middle of June, rain has ceased over most of the Middle East (except for the extreme north and the south) and in many parts no rain normally falls for a period of 10 to 15 weeks.

The distribution of rainfall in the Middle East is largely controlled by two factors: topography and the disposition of land and sea in relation to rain-bearing winds. It must be remembered that the Middle East is predominantly a continental area, influenced only in certain regions by proximity of relatively small areas of sea. Hence air masses reaching the Middle East from the west, even though of oceanic origin, have lost some of their moisture; and it is only where a sea track has allowed partial rejuvenation that considerable rainfall can develop.

It might therefore be said that in most regions rainfall tends to occur in proportion to the length of coastline – or even in proportion to the length of westward-facing coastline. Regional contrasts are striking: the westward-facing shore of the Gulf of Sirte has a marked effect on the rainfall of Cyrenaica; and the absence of such configuration in Egypt condemns the country to a scanty rainfall. At Benghazi, at the western end of the Cyrenaican Jebel, annual rainfall amounts to over 270 mm as compared with 77 mm at Port Said. The narrowness of the Red Sea is reflected in the lower rainfall of Arabia: whilst, on the other hand, the influence of the broader Mediterranean is clearly shown in Asia Minor and the Levant. Proximity of the Persian/Arab Gulf and even the extensive water surfaces of lower Mesopotamia have a favourable effect on the rainfall in the Zagros.

With such a delicate balance between dampness and aridity, it is inevitable that topography should exercise a control equally as important, if not more so, than that of physical configuration. It has already been stated that the greater part of the Middle East rainfall develops under conditions of instability, to which the uplift of air currents as they are forced to rise over mountain ranges is a very powerful contributing factor. Warm frontal rainfall develops over a vertical distance of as much as 7500 m; and a few thousand metres of uplift in the lowest layers have no undue effect, as ascent of air has begun independently of conditions near the ground, and precipitation continues after high land is past. On the other hand, a cold front may not develop any precipitation whatever until the 'trigger action' of sudden uplift over high ground is first applied, with very considerable dynamical uplift following. Adiabatic heating on rapid descent from coastal mountain range to interior plains is another important influencing factor. Thus control by topography can be so great that isohyets tend to follow contour lines, with westward-facing mountain ranges or plateau edges experiencing heavier rainfall at the expense of eastward-facing slopes and lowlands. The swing of the isohyets in response to the south-eastward curve of the Turkish highlands towards the Zagros system gives rise to the beautifully developed 'Fertile Crescent' of steppeland linking the east and west of the Old World. Control by topography has resulted in the elaboration of striking regional contrasts – a short journey brought the Israelites from the rain-shadow areas of Sinai and eastern Moab (Jordan) into the milk and honey of the damper uplands of Judaea; and Palmyra, a caravan city of the Syrian desert, could pasture its beasts of burden on the grassy spurs of the Anti-Lebanon ranges a few kilometres away.

Occurrence of much Middle Eastern rainfall under conditions of instability means that much of it may be heavy, but short in duration, and extremely capricious both in period of onset and in distribution. The coastlands of the Levant with annual falls of over 700 mm receive more rain than parts of Britain, but this is crowded into little more than 6 months; and even so, the wettest months have only 14 to 18 rainy days.

A great deal of rain may thus fall in a short time – 25 mm/h is by no means unusual. In 1945 Damascus (annual average 240 mm) received 100 mm in a single morning; and in 1969 400 km of a newly constructed highway in central Arabia were washed away by one night of rainfall. 'Cloudbursts' or 'rain like stair-rods' are a feature on a few days in many years, but their effects are often extremely local, so that one side of a street may be quite dry, whilst the other is streaming with rain. Jarvis described a small valley of the Sinai region that had produced a record grain crop, yet 3 km away there had been insufficient rain to germinate the seed. It is such intense though short-lived rainfall that is by far the most dangerous as an agent in soil erosion, since very considerable transportation of material can take place, even of large boulders.

Averages for rainfall tend to be misleading, since few regions outside the highlands of the north can count on a really regular rainfall. Whole areas in Egypt, Arabia and the northern Sudan may go years without a fall of any kind, and in Libya it is reckoned that drought will prevail 2 years out of every 10. A heavy fall once in several years may thus appear in climatic statistics averaged out as an annual figure. Some, but not all, of the summer rain in Turkey and Iran is of this type; in successive years, Jerusalem once had 1060 mm of rainfall, then 307; and Baghdad 432 and 56 mm.

### Evapotranspiration

What is an arid zone, and how may it be defined accurately? The question is much more awkward than it at first seems. Major difficulty arises from the fluctuation in amount of rainfall received: should one merely define aridity as below a fixed criterion in total annual rainfall – for example, is a region arid when it receives less than 250 mm on average per 12-month period? In general, perhaps, yes – we know what we mean broadly by a dry climate and a wet one. But when fixed-scale definitions are needed, say, for study of the soil potential for agricultural development, of water supply for irrigation, or for storage in reservoirs, then there is need for more precise definitions.

A rough 'yardstick' was supplied by Penck, who suggested that a region was arid if it had no regular river flow – if it had, it was humid. More subtle and sensitive approaches were worked out by de Martonne and by Köppen, both systems being based on 'wet' and 'dry' months, with an arbitrary figure (calculated with reference also to temperature) being taken as defining 'wet'. This in practice was set at 60 mm/month for a 'continuously humid' month.

The idea of taking 'wet' and 'dry' months is, however, open to criticism, in that, within a highly seasonal régime, such as that of the Mediterranean and that of the Monsoon (both of which mainly affect the Middle East), a rainy season may shift: rain may be concentrated heavily in a short period, which may be confined entirely within 1 or 2 calendar months, or it may in a given year spread into 3, 4 or even 5 – with 60 mm as a criterion this could certainly happen. Moreover, annual averaging diminishes 'peaks' of rainfall data, and tends to give a figure which for a significant number of years does not correspond to actual conditions experienced. This may not matter to the reader of textbooks or the candidate for examinations in geography (here it is all to the good), but with regard to effective rainfall as an influence on agriculture or engineering projects, deviation from a theoretical mean is very important. For successful farming, is it the same to have heavy rain in one short period, or light rain over a much longer time? And one contributory cause to the 1969 'washout' of the Saudi Arabian highway at Al Kharj mentioned above was failure to provide enough culverts in an embanked road to let an exceptional flood stream away.

These considerations led to the Thornthwaite concept of 'evapotrans-piration' – that is, evaporation from the surface plus transpiration of water by plants. Two kinds are possible: *actual* evapotranspiration (the amount of water that actually evaporates and is transpired) and *potential* evapotranspiration (the maximum amount of moisture that would evaporate and transpire if it were freely available in and on the ground). If potential evapotranspiration exceeds or falls below actual evapotrans-piration then there is, respectively, a deficit or a surplus of soil water, and this 'water balance' can be used as an index of aridity. D. B. Carter has developed interesting maps of potential evapotranspiration for parts of south-west Asia using categories that correspond to standards of

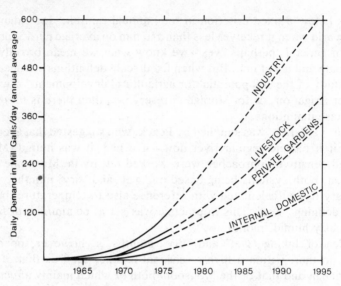

*Fig.* 3.11 Water demand (actual and potential), Kuwait.

aridity. A potential evapotranspiration of less than 285 mm annually is defined by Carter as a 'tundra' condition; 285–570 mm is a microthermal range, 570–1140 mm a mesothermal range, and 1140 mm and above is the megathermal condition, G. B. Cressey points out that the cultivated areas of Iran have an annual potential evapotranspiration of 900 mm, and in the Rub al Khali of south-east Arabia the figure exceeds 1900 mm.

The practical uses of evapotranspiration and water balance concepts could be important; but there are significant reservations also to be made:

(1) Actual figures for evaporation and transpiration are, in practice, very difficult to obtain. Evaporation is not constant, and an obvious difficulty arises when the surface is to be regarded as wet or dry, because latent heat of evaporation enters in here. How dry is average soil and to what depths?

(2) Air humidity, the extent of turbulent air mixing, and differing wind velocities at differing heights even over a small vertical range all enter in to affect evaporation, but are extremely difficult to measure accurately.

(3) Transpiration from plants is a very variable factor. The same species of plant alter their rates of transpiration according to climatic conditions, their degree of luxuriance and the density of their growth. Thornthwaite summarized this by saying that evapotranspiration cannot therefore be measured directly, but must be computed from a number of variables, including length of day (which, of course, greatly affects insolation); and also he came to accept an assumed value (of 100 mm) for the water storage capacity of the soil – an assumption that has been challenged by others.

All this is not to belittle the real contributions made by the researchers mentioned above, but it remains questionable how far, in practice, one can draw maps of climatic factors, including evapotranspiration, for the Middle East that do more than indicate an approximation based on a number of reasonable assumptions. Consequently, the present writer suggests that only the general ideas of climatic regions and conditions are necessary in the Middle East, with perhaps a limited need only for the elaborate subdivisions of Köppen and Thornthwaite. When detailed results are required it is better to observe local conditions as closely as possible and work from these, rather than apply ideas from generalized maps resting on concepts that inevitably must involve fairly general assumptions and 'rules of thumb' – even though, being expressed in suitably formidable algebraic equations, they appear to have full scientific validity. However, this problem has recently been tackled by FAO and UNESCO, in their major programmes of arid zone research. Classification of conditions, with a multivariate base including temperatures, rainfall totals and incidence, relative humidities, mist, dew, photo-synthesis of sunlight inhibitors and general patterns of climatic phases, have been arrived at, with the aim of deriving relationships that can be seen to relate to human and other living organisms.

Apart from slight tendency to mist and even fog in a few areas and the temporary *khamsin* conditions, the Middle East stands out as one of the areas of the world where the air is usually clear and unpolluted.[1] This situation is now rapidly changing for the larger towns, where atmospheric pollution is coming to be a serious problem. Near coasts, there are usually fairly strong breezes, especially in summer; but inland, particularly where cities occur in hollows or large basins, the air is stiller, particularly in winter, when as we have noted, stable atmospheric conditions due to high pressure can develop. Increased use of oil, both for heating, cooking and for air conditioning, the vast growth in motor and air transport (some of the former being incorrectly 'tuned' and therefore giving out unnecessary emission), and (in Turkey and part of Iran) the use of low grade coal and lignite have contributed to produce what is now regarded as a serious problem. Ankara, where low grade coal is extensively used (and the winter is cold) and Tehran, which has plenty of oil, are probably the most affected. In Ankara the problem is one of sulphur 'smog'; in Tehran high summer temperatures and sunlight induce photo-chemical reaction which produces nitrogen dioxide from exhaust emissions, and other effects which irritate the eyes and reduce general visibility – the problem particularly associated with certain Californian cities. As Middle Eastern cities grow, and petrol/kerosene remains relatively cheap, the incidence of atmospheric pollution is inevitably going

[1] One might even define the Middle East, in strictly scientific terms, as the largest continuous area of the world that receives maximum insolation (fig. 3.1).

to increase unless governmental action is taken to reduce emission of smoke and exhaust emission. Though two cities have been mentioned, there is the same problem on a smaller but varied scale in Alexandria, Amman, Baghdad, Beirut, Cairo, Istanbul, Jerusalem and Tel Aviv, and as a number of these are expected to have well over a million population by the end of the century (Cairo 10 million, greater Tehran 6 million, Ankara 5 million) atmospheric pollution may well become acute.

## Variation of climate

One cannot proceed very far in any study of environment in the Middle East without encountering the problem of possible variations in climate. It is clear that major climatic fluctuation is a feature of the differing geological periods; and in the single Hal Far cave of Malta there is a collection of animal remains buried in silt and clay that successively ranges from hippopotamus and rhinoceros to Arctic species such as the polar bear and arctic fox. Reference has already been made to the attenuated and misfit river systems of the present day, with a geomorphology that often suggests more humid conditions. Above all, there is the striking paradox in human occupancy. Looking today at the arid wastes that characterize many parts of the Middle East, it is difficult to reconcile present hostile environmental conditions to the brilliant historical past. How could man have achieved in these localities such significant and fundamental advances from Palaeolithic to Neolithic and then Classical cultures in advance of most, possibly all, other parts of the world?

In general, conditions would appear strongly to suggest marked climatic change at a relatively recent period, with progressive desiccation as the main feature. It is in fact indisputable that, in comparatively recent geological time, a wetter climate prevailed. Many of the rock series of late Tertiary and Quaternary age were deposited locally in the Middle East under conditions of greater precipitation; and other evidence suggests that in Quaternary times cycles of colder, wetter weather, comparable to those of Europe, produced ice-cap conditions in the plateaux of Turkey and Iran. Further evidence comes from archaeological sources, indicating that early human settlement was considerable north and south of the mountain zone, but sparse or entirely lacking in the highlands themselves.

Present-day land forms in the Sinai and central and eastern Lebanon are, in the view of some, at least in part the work of ice; though these views are not undisputed, it is obvious that much of the erosion and deposition could not occur under a semi-arid climatic régime.

It is more certain that the erosive power of the Nile was in certain regions much greater than now, and the existence of extremely deeply incised *wadis* on the land surfaces around the head of the Red Sea suggests a phase of much wetter climate. Other evidence comes from the existence of 'fossil soils' in regions now too dry to produce comparable developments; and a further important feature 'is the occurrence of surface depressions, or closed basins, especially in Libya, Egypt and the Arabian deserts, which show some signs of original erosion by water – though this is by no means the whole story. Finally, there is recent evidence (from pollen analysis) that as late as 3000 B.C. a fully 'Mediterranean' flora extended as far south as the Tibesti highlands – i.e. some 1500–3000 km further south than now.

Much within the historic period can be interpreted as evidence of desiccation. Many irrigation works now stand ruined or neglected in completely arid areas. Buried dams, empty channels and dry wells or cisterns, often located in places where there is no obvious water supply, would seem to show that surface water has become scarcer. In some instances, modern efforts have been made to repair ancient irrigation works, with varying results: some remained dry, others have a flow of water, sometimes exactly on the scale of former conditions.

Greater wealth and power in ancient times of countries of the Middle East is at least in part an indicator of a large population and higher level of economic development. For many regions of the Middle East, it is easy to point to at least one former period of outstanding prosperity; and for certain areas, if not the whole region, it would seem true that the population was more numerous in Roman and early Islamic times even than at the present day. Numerous ruins, particularly on the desert margins, indicate both a richness of culture and an intensity of economic exploitation that are often far in advance of modern conditions. In north-west Syria whole towns lie abandoned – Devlin and Gillingham counted over a hundred settlements of Byzantine age within 80 km of Aleppo – and in Iran many caravan routes are bordered by now deserted villages. Roman Palmyra was a commercial metropolis with continent-wide relations; the modern town is less in extent than the burial grounds of the ancient city.

To these physical and human considerations must be added certain biological factors. Ancient Egyptian and Mesopotamian art frequently depicted crocodiles or such animals as the lion and the gazelle – all of which are at home in a damper environment. Many areas now bare and without soil appear to have been wooded, in some instances quite densely.

At the same time, there is evidence of an opposite kind, which tends to suggest that conditions have not greatly altered. Many irrigation works appear to have been abandoned not because of a declining rainfall, but due to misrule, exaction and devastation produced by war and barbarian invasion. In a survey of the economic potentialities of Iraq in 1911, Sir

W. Willcocks stated that the problem was in large measure that of restoring the ancient irrigation system, rather than that of developing entirely new canals. Yet it is undoubtedly true that in some instances the water-table in the soil has fallen. This can, however, be ascribed either to a lowering of the base line of drainage, due to continued erosion of the bed of the river;[1] or to a loss of subsurface water because of soil erosion following destruction of the surface vegetation, including deforestation. The latter is a pronounced feature of many parts of the Middle East. Reckless cutting of trees for timber and fuel, unrestricted grazing by herds of animals, and unintelligent methods of agriculture in a land occupied continuously since the dawn of history have greatly contributed to extensive soil erosion, with consequent decrease in water resources.

Moreover, archaeological research has shown that many of the deserted settlements were not contemporaneous – that is, they were not all inhabited at one particular time. Many factors – security, economic resources, or even, as commonly in the Middle East, a growing problem of sanitation – may have caused the abandonment of one site in favour of another; so that a survey of settlement cannot, of itself, be taken as a reliable indication of population density. Even now, it is unwise to regard the size of a modern Oriental city as strictly indicative of the number of its inhabitants, because although some parts are heavily overcrowded, others may be partly derelict and abandoned.

The long continuity of life in the Middle East suggests that there can have been relatively little major environmental change since the original 'challenge' of desiccation postulated by Toynbee. Desert herders – 'plain men living in tents' – are as characteristic of modern times as of the age of Jacob; and agricultural technique, portrayed in ancient literature and art, still survives in many places with little alteration at the present day. Much of the literature dating from early times seems to indicate ways of life and natural conditions similar to those of today: the steppe life of Abraham, the Sinai and Moab Desert, from the Bible; the actual weather conditions mentioned seem often to have been like those of today; and many of the relics of Ancient Egypt would hardly have survived had the climate of the country been damper.

Another important point is the permanence of overland trade routes across arid regions. Caravans have followed tracks through certain oases for many centuries, and any deviations that occurred were largely due to unsettled political conditions – routes now drier than those at present in use do not seem ever to have been followed. It is difficult to see why such cities as Damascus and Aleppo should have maintained their function as points of departure for desert traffic over several thousand

---

[1] The river Nile is known to have lowered its bed by 7 m at one point since 1900 B.C., and though this is an extreme case, other instances could be cited.

years if we assume that the cities did not at one time lie on the border between steppe and desert. The existence of the series of ancient caravan centres – Medina, Petra, Jerash, Bosra, Damascus, Palmyra, Aleppo and Dura-Europus – can be related to present conditions of rainfall; if we move the desert boundary further inland, these towns lose their *raison d'être*. Similarly, many other ancient settlements of the Middle East show careful siting in relation to water supplies.

One sustained attempt to link and assess this mass of evidence has been made by K. Butzer, who comes to the conclusion that from about 8000 B.C. to the present day climatic conditions have remained broadly the same, with, however, (*a*) local and temporary oscillations affecting limited areas for short periods, and (*b*) more serious local and permanent effects due to the effects of natural erosion in lowering the water-table, and in removing soil and vegetation, often intensified here and there by the activities of man. On the other hand, Vita-Finzi has also drawn attention to sedimentation and terracing in river valleys, which point to a markedly different and rather wetter condition in early historic times. For earlier periods, Butzer suggests correlations with the great Ice Age of Europe, in the following way:

During the Mindel phase, indirect and scanty evidence suggests a pluvial period, followed by an interpluvial (Mindel-Riss) characterized by drier, warmer conditions. This was succeeded by the Riss pluvial period, during which distinctly colder and markedly wetter conditions prevailed. A Riss–Würm change towards drier but possibly not very much warmer weather may have resulted in extensive sub-aerial erosion.

A marked pluvial phase, well evidenced in much of the north of the Middle East, would appear to have characterized the early Würm period, oscillating to drier conditions temporarily, to be succeeded by the main Würm effect, datable to 25 000–18 000 B.P., during which temperatures fell markedly by an average of 4 °C. Greater precipitation occurred in the north of the Middle East, with extension of glacial and peri-glacial conditions in Iran and Anatolia, and some comparable effects traceable in the Lebanon and Anti-Lebanon ranges. South of latitude 22° the Würmian effects would appear to have been minimal, with little or no extra rainfall.

From 18 000 to 11 500 B.P. extremely dry conditions occurred, producing extensive wind erosion; to be succeeded in 11 500–10 500 B.P. by a shorter cold and moist phase, and then during 10 500–8800 B.P. a slightly warmer and markedly arid condition. From 8800 B.P. (= 6800 B.C.) to 5000 B.C. we enter the historic period, which was marked by a return to moister conditions, giving a climate very similar, in the view of Butzer, to that prevailing again in the nineteenth century A.D.

He further distinguishes:

(1) 5000–2400 B.C A 'Neolithic' moist interval of distinctly higher

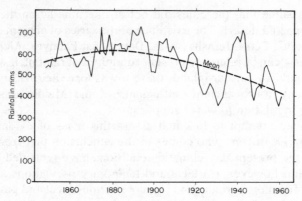

*Fig.* 3.12 A rainfall phase at Jerusalem, 1850–1960, showing a tendency to aridity.

rainfall and more varied temperature incidence – some localities with distinctly warmer conditions than now, others much the same.

(2) A period marked by temporary cycles of aridity, and lasting from *c.* 3600 to 2400 B.C.

(3) 2400–850 B.C. A phase of greater warmth, and a decrease in rainfall with one major wetter spell at *c.* 1200 B.C.

(4) 850 B.C.–A.D. 700. Becoming drier, with marked temporary drought cycles towards the end of the period; conditions broadly similar to those of today, perhaps with slightly warmer winters.

(5) After A.D. 700 to present. Many short-term fluctuations, with occasional bitter winters at first, e.g. ice-floes were reported in the Nile in A.D. 829 and A.D. 1011–12.

(6) Finally Butzer postulates for the present period a temporary oscillation towards drier, warmer conditions. As evidence he quotes the retreat of the snowfields in Europe and, to a very limited extent (since they are small), also in the Middle East; the lowering of the Caspian and Dead Sea levels, as shown by strand-lines; and instrumental records, which show an average rise of mean temperature of 0·4–0·5 °C at Alexandria and Beirut between 1890 and 1940, together with a 10–15% decrease in rainfall (see also fig. 3.12).

However, since 1940, there is some but not total evidence of a slight swing back to cooler, wetter conditions. There remains the fascinating question of attempting a linkage, if any is possible, between these suggested phases of climate and the major human responses – migratory, peaceable and warlike – and the rise and decline of economic conditions and hence of local cultures and civilizations. Besides this, and recalling the original statement that climate has not undergone really major changes, we must assess other effects which have undoubtedly had a major influence on the environment of the Middle East. These are (*a*) lowering of the bed of the streams as the result of normal erosion; this has also lowered the water-table in the soil itself, and left many irrigation canal intakes above the new water level; (b) soil erosion, due to wasteful agricultural methods, or to destruction of existing types of vegetation; and (c) probably greatest of all, misrule, wars and invasion. In this connection it is interesting to note that experiments in Algeria have shown that when the slope of land brought under cultivation exceeds 3–5%, continuous cultivation using normal methods of ploughing will lead to almost complete soil erosion within 10 years, to the point that the terrain is no longer usable.

By this means, and influenced by the minor fluctuations in historic time listed above, an originally deeper layer of soil and a thicker vegetation cover, both relics of earlier wetter periods, were gradually removed. This natural patrimony might have been preserved by careful utilization, but once soil and vegetation had disappeared, natural conditions were against a renewal. Thus it is man, and not natural causes, who is chiefly responsible for the gradual deterioration of conditions in the Middle East; and human occupation, not climatic variation, appears as the main factor in alteration of environment. This fact gives some hope for the future, because, whereas man can do little to influence the operation of natural forces leading to climatic change, he can do much to repair damage that he himself has caused. If soil and vegetation could be restored, the prosperity of ancient days might return; and accordingly, emphasis is now being placed on soil conservation, reafforestation and intelligent exploitation of the land as essential elements in the future development of economic life in the Middle East.

# 4 Soils and vegetation

## Soils of the Middle East

The study of soils in general could be said to be in transition. Under the influence of Russian workers in the subject, earlier approaches tended to be based upon the concept of zonality – that is, geographical location in the broad sense – and therefore the prime influencing factor in the development of soils was held to be climate. Soils can be zonal, where drainage is good; intrazonal on valley floors or benches or flats, where drainage is impeded; or azonal, where there is immaturity or considerable erosion. This approach was followed at first by most workers, including Reifenberg, one of the first to study Middle East soils, who held, for example, that Terra Rossa soils could develop wholly independently of parent rock, irrespective of whether this were limestone or basalt, because of the predominant effects of climate.

In recent years, however, the idea of zonation as a basis of classification for soils has been increasingly questioned. S. A. Harris shows that, for Europe, an accepted classification of soils on a zonal basis (that of Tavernier and Huckenhausen in 1960) shows little correlation with the Trewartha–Thornthwaite climate maps of the same area – which obviously it should if climate were the chief formative element.

In 1941 H. Jenny put forward a concept which, while derived from much previous thinking by others, emphasized that soils are the result of interaction between a complex of effects deriving from climate, parent rock, topography and biological activity (including action by man), all

76

operating over a varied period of time: the longer the period, the greater the possibility of interaction and therefore a differing end product. There is also the view of soil development as a catena: that is, within a given zone, there will be a gradual change from soil character at higher altitudes towards lower levels. In physical, and therefore also chemical and biological character, zonal ranking is still accepted by some, notably the Russians (I. P. Gerasimov, 1968), but many other workers (probably a considerable majority) now prefer to follow the ideas of Jenny in various ways. One of these is to classify soils by co-ordinates; that is, to take a number of properties as points of references or axes – texture, drainage, profile development, organic content, for example – and identify differing soils by position on a multi-dimensional axial model. This is the scheme adopted in British and Belgian national soil surveys. Reference to qualities and co-ordinates rather than zones also facilitates analysis by computer.

In the study of soils, a general division may be made concerning horizons. An *eluvial* horizon is one *from* which soluble compounds and finely divided insoluble material are removed by erosive agents, chiefly soil moisture derived from rainfall: and an *illuvial* horizon, one *into* which these materials are carried and redeposited. 'A' and 'B' horizons are summary ways of restating this variable process and a 'C' horizon is that close to the parent material.

In humid climates, the greater transfer of soil water is downwards and the top layers of soil therefore tend to form the eluvial horizon, with the illuvial layer below. In arid climates, scanty rainfall may penetrate the soil, but as the result of capillary attraction due to strong surface heating, it is soon drawn back to the surface, so that the final transfer of water may be upward, so that an accumulation of mineral salts may occur at or near the surface (fig. 4.1). When downward transfer of soil moisture is strongly predominant, then the upper layers of soil are said to be leached, or podsolized, and they often tend to be acidic, with a low pH (under 7). This is characteristic of regions of low evapotranspiration and a moderate or heavy rainfall, i.e. cold to cool and damp climates. In the Middle East such conditions occur only in restricted localities of considerable altitude, such as the mountains of the north; and where soil exists – in many parts it does not – it may be of the podsol type. Over much of the Middle East, however, a deficient rainfall and high average temperatures give rise to the opposite conditions: concentration of salts near the surface, with pronounced soil alkalinity (high pH, over 7). As well, there are the heavy alluvial soils of the riverine valleys, and in many areas skeletal soils – rock debris incompletely weathered into true soil – with, overall, wide variability as a distinguishing characteristic.

Regional soil studies in the Middle East have been very much on an *ad hoc* basis and there was little overall uniformity in classification until FAO/UNESCO commenced their project of compiling a soil map of the world (at scale 1:5000000, in 1968–70). Furthermore, pedological studies have reflected the training of the various research workers. The Dutch, in Iraq, have not concerned themselves in any great detail with classification problems of the soil but have mainly dealt with the agronomic problems resulting from the salinity characteristics of the Tigris/Euphrates alluvial soils. On the other hand, Reifenberg (Palestine), Oakes (Turkey) and Moorman (Jordan) have attempted soil classifications, based mainly on the 'Major Soil Group' approach similar to that proposed by Thorp and Smith, and did not attempt to make a detailed study of soil potential for agriculture.

Most national classificatory systems proposed for Middle East countries are now based on the Major Soil Group approach, but nomenclature may vary from country to country. As a result, there can be a certain amount of confusion in the literature, since soil surveys have been chiefly limited to cultivated areas. Comparatively little is known in detail about soils away from the irrigated areas. Three new approaches are important when discussing the classification of Middle East soils: the US Seventh Approximation and its supplement; the FAO/UNESCO classification; and the various land capability approaches.

The purpose of the Seventh Approximation is to group major soils in such a way that relations among them and between soils and their environment can be seen. Most of the characteristics used to classify the soils are grouped by the recognition of diagnostic horizons, but classification in the lower categories tends to be dependent upon environmental characteristics – for instance, Typic calciorthids, Ustollic calciorthids and Xerollic calciorthids are distinguished from each other by the number of days that the depth 18–50 cm in the profile is moist – and also soil temperature characteristics. The Seventh Approximation has many advantages, mainly due to its comprehensive character, but as we have just seen, for effective distinction as between soils in the lower categories a considerable amount of environmental data is required. This is as yet largely absent from most of the Middle East countries.

The Seventh Approximation has, however, proved to be extremely valuable when used in conjunction with land capability studies. Land capability studies for agricultural purposes are based on a much broader appreciation of the environment than are pure soil surveys. Because they are usually carried out for a specific purpose, they lack the comprehensive nature of a soil classificatory system, but the additional environmental information makes them eminently suitable for use in conjunction with the Seventh Approximation, thus allowing prediction to be made about soil behaviour at places where experience or experimentation is absent

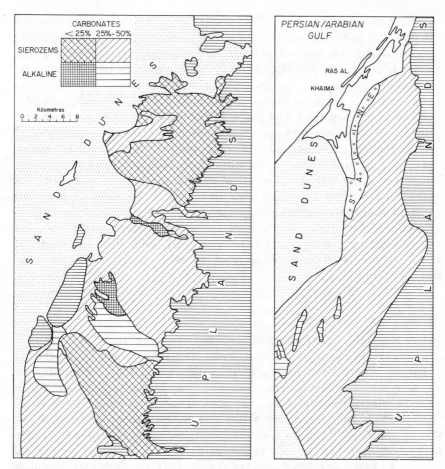

*Fig.* 4.1 Soil types in an area of the UAE (survey by J. H. Stevens).

from areas where there is knowledge about the behaviour of similar soils. This type of approach has been used successfully by Hunting Technical Services in the Sudan and Iraq.

The FAO/UNESCO classification attempts to clarify the confused situation resulting from the use of different systems whereby one soil has been known under a variety of names. It does mean, however, the introduction of a new language of soil nomenclature. In the initial stages, production of maps on a scale of 1:5 000 000 means that for any project a considerable amount of further research will be required, but it is hoped that such a map will enable a pattern of soils to emerge, making it then suitable for broad-scale planning.

Pending the appearance of the general soil map of the world, one can do no more than indicate broad categories for the Middle East. Approaches to classification have been made on a basis of environment, with climate the dominant element. G. Aubert distinguishes the soils of the true deserts, of the arid steppes, of the sub-arid areas, and of the sub-humid areas, being careful to make clear that, whilst one can speak of certain soils as highly characteristic of a particular zone, soils classified under one zone may well be found in another as well. It will be noted that here there is less emphasis on the absolute effect of climate (as was invoked by Reifenberg and Lang, by using 'rain factors') and more reference to general conditions involving the wider environment. For instance, Aubert defines a 'desert' as having less than 100 mm annual rainfall, and an 'arid area' 100–250 mm, whereas Lang developed a formula: total annual rainfall divided by the mean temperature of the rainy season, which gives a 'rain factor' from which exact categories were erected: 'arid' as corresponding to a 'rain factor' of 0–15; 'semi-arid' from 15–30, etc.

We may now set out a summary of the varied types of soil that occur in the Middle East.

*Desert zone (lithosols)*

Here the soil-forming processes are at a very early stage, and the main feature is physical breakdown under the influences of temperature changes, strong winds and transport by the rare but powerful flash-floods. Coarse sand (the fine material is carried away by wind action) and gravel can be interspersed with masses of stone of various sizes. Here and there, at lower horizons there may be patches of sandy loam, and deposits of salts, gypsum, etc. Many areas of loose sand occur – ranging from pale grey, white, brown to red, yellow or black – including *nebkhas* (small dune-like forms developed round plants or small obstacles), *regs, barchans* (moving crescent-shaped dunes) or *ergs*, which are a larger development of *barchans*, sometimes several hundred metres high and many kilometres in length.

Salt efflorescences are common in desert soils. The surface may harden temporarily into a light crust that will allow passage of a car over otherwise loose sand. Another feature of the desert is the presence on rock masses of a hard coating resembling enamel. This 'desert lac' may be formed by the interaction, within extremes of heat and cold, of compounds of iron. In other cases, a patina due solely to mechanical abrasion of the rock surface may be more characteristic. Two terms have been introduced by UNESCO: the first, Ergosol, refers to sand dune formations – 'dynamic' if the dunes are shifting, 'semistatic' or 'static' if they are partially or fully stabilized. The second term, Ermolithosol, describes the hard pavement often to be found in deserts, with subdivisions of lithic (stony), gravelly or argillic.

Other deposits associated with deserts are the accumulation of salt deposits in naturally formed basins (*kavir, sabkha*). In some desert areas, there may be development of loessic type soils as the result of wind transportation. This deposit is formed by the accumulation of fine sand, silt and clay (the last two being derived in the first instance from wash and erosion), together with a slight organic content which is due to the growth of plants on an original friable rock-exposure. Such loess deposits can form fairly rapidly, and in parts of western Libya, and also in the Negev and Sinai, the margins of the desert are becoming covered by loess deposits. Archaeological evidence suggests that near Gaza approximately 3 m of loess have accumulated within the last 4000 years. Given a suitable water supply – non-saline, which is not always realizable – such loessic soils and even the sandy loams may be capable of cultivation, and in some regions, good crops are now being raised on them.

*Arid steppes*

Here, several general types of soil occur. Where aridity is particularly pronounced, the alteration of mineral compounds and the organic processes that give rise to humus have restricted effect only, so that soils are immature. Of this kind are the steppe soils, basically sandy in texture, and of grey, grey-brown or grey-red colour, sometimes loamy, sometimes with clay, and often with carbonate or gypsum concentrations. Some authorities attribute the reddish colour (where it occurs) to damper climatic phases. Cementation due to lime or gypsum may also be present.

Where aridity is somewhat less pronounced, the process of soil formation may develop further, and produce *sierozem* soils. These are rather more mature than the soils just described, with a somewhat more extensive (though still small) organic content, and a higher lime fraction, both being fairly evenly distributed throughout the profile. Salinity and the development of gypsum layers can be a prominent and serious feature, but maximum concentration in a *sierozem* tends to be at a shallow depth, rather than at or near the surface.

*Semi-arid to humid areas*

As aridity becomes less and less pronounced, soils of markedly different qualities are found. Some of these are given below.

(*a*) *Brown or yellow-brown soils* These may be associated with a wide range of parent rocks, and siliceous and cherty facies can in some areas produce a particular kind of stony, brown soil type. The soils may range from silty clays to clay loams, and another obvious feature is frequent stoniness, both at the surface and at depth. Colour may range from a dull brown to browny-red or brown-yellow; silt content is from 25% to 45%, and on the Jordan plateau, where these soils occur frequently as large tracts, pH values are observed from 6·9 to 7·4, with little colour change at depth.

Terra Rossa soils are distinguishable first by their distinctive bright red colour, and also by their heavier texture, due to a relatively high clay content (50–70%), with a correspondingly lower sand content. Enriched in sesquioxides of iron and in silica, there is also evidence of decalcification, with little or no free lime, despite frequent association with a limestone parent rock; pH values vary from 7·0 to 8·0.

Another important feature of Terra Rossa is its high moisture-holding capacity, which allows it to store considerable amounts of rainfall. This, together with its relatively high fertility, makes it an extremely useful soil for agriculture – though it is liable to erosion; and when this happens, besides the heavy 'slumping' and removal of the soil itself, an earlier stage under very heavy episodic rainfall may be the formation of a thin slurry-like material which seals the surface pores of the soil, thus promoting rapid run-off of rainfall rather than absorption – a further factor making for soil erosion.

A highly important effect in certain soils of the Middle East is the occurrence of a 'hard pan' or crust (calcrete). Much debate has occurred concerning these formations, which may appear as a layer of hard, concrete-like material sometimes a few centimetres thick only, but instances of several metres are known (one of 4 m occurs near Saida in the Lebanon). It would now appear that these crusts are formed by a complex and prolonged process involving three major factors: (a) leaching of steppe soils (which are rich in calcium, gypsum, carbonates and sulphates); (b) capillarity from the lower soil layers, by which moisture is drawn towards the surface – this soil moisture is thought to originate from lateral infiltration, or the accumulation of temporary water supplies following heavy but highly episodic rainfall; (c) the effect of algae.

Some crusts are of ancient origin, and held to be related to earlier pluvial phases of climate; but others have been demonstrated to be of much more recent age; and whatever their origin, the presence of a hard pan can have considerable economic and social effects. Only relatively shallow-rooted plants such as cereals can grow unless a hole is first driven by man through the hard layer. Orchards and groves of trees may thus represent much effort on the part of the cultivator, each tree having required an individual break-through to the subsoil. Once established, fruit trees are not easily replanted elsewhere – a factor in the extreme traditionalism of agricultural methods.

Areas of extensive crustal development have, as a result, a very characteristic appearance – wide, open landscapes, often highly cultivated

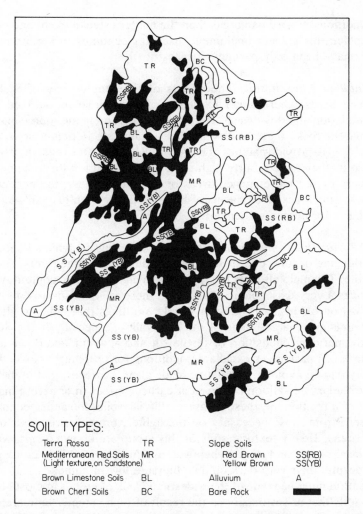

*Fig.* 4.2 Soil types in an area of Jordan near Irbid (survey by author and colleagues).

with cereals but entirely devoid of natural bush and woodland, and planted with a few fruit trees only in the vicinity of settlements. The absence of any kind of timber prevents the use of beams and rafters in building construction, and the normal flat-roofed houses of the peasants are not found. Instead, a domed roof of hardened mud is characteristic, giving the impression of a cluster of beehives; around Aleppo and in Sistan many villages of this sort occur. Moreover, the presence of hard pan at a shallow depth demands a special technique of ploughing. The light wooden *araire* which can follow varying depths of soil is better adapted to conditions in hard pan areas than the modern steel plough; and efforts to replace this ancient implement, used for centuries in Mediterranean lands, have been only partially successful.

(*b*) *Infill and bench soils* The effects of topography may often be to produce areas where small expanses of soils develop, derived from accumulation and downwash. Depending in part upon the source material and parent rock, these infill soils that accumulate in depressions or on 'flats' tend to provide patches of better arable land. Often reddish or brown in colour, they have a fairly high silt or clay content, with some humus. In many of the more rugged areas of the Middle East, the occurrence of these small, scattered basins of better soil – or even just soil – are the sole basis for human settlement.

(*c*) *Alluvial* (*hydromorphic*) *soils* These are soils in which temporary waterlogging occurs, due to seasonal flooding from large rivers, such as the Nile. The main effect is to give rise to a higher organic content, which produces a very dark colour. Sometimes there are reddish-brown streaks due to iron oxides, with grey or purple mottlings that indicate gleying. Such soils are characteristic of the Nile valley, especially in the Sudan, and the periodic deposition of fertile silt and alluvium laid down above the dark soil base gives excellent conditions for cropping, provided that salinity can be avoided. It must be made clear, however, that in the case of the Sudan, deposition occurred at earlier periods in or before historic times. Cultivation of these heavier alluvial soils demands techniques different from those necessary on the lighter, brown or red soils of the drier areas. Heavy-textural soils of this group are known as *grumosols*. These are plastic and sticky when wet, and hard and liable to crack when dry; despite their very dark colour, they are low in humus.

Mention must be made of the widespread lack of humus in most Middle East soils that arises mainly as the result of high summer temperatures, which, in effect, burn out much organic material. There is also basically less organic material available; many trees are evergreen and do not shed their leaves annually, hence there is less natural surface litter.

Because of the generally higher temperatures and high capillary movement of soil water, fertilizing by organic or by artificial compounds is less effective or, rather, inherently different in some respects from that practised in cooler, temperate latitudes.

## Irrigation

From what has just been said, it will be apparent that because of the nature of the soils of the Middle East and the climate, special attention is necessary when crops are irrigated. The high surface temperatures attained – those on the actual surface of the ground (as distinct from inside a shaded meteorological screen above ground) can reach 70–75 °C – give rise to strong capillarity and evaporation, thus changing in some instances the structure of the soil and bringing to or near the surface extensive salt and gypsum deposits. The Euphrates and Tigris double their salt content during their passage through Iraq, and the Nile contains appreciable quantities of soluble salts. Hence uncontrolled irrigation can produce deleterious effects: waterlogging, loss of structure and, above all, increased soil salinity. It is estimated that nowadays 1 % of the total area under cultivation in Iraq becomes saline and unusable each year, and 80 % of the total crop area is to some extent saline. The Nile delta lands are definitely becoming saline to the extent of inhibition of certain crops; and in many other smaller areas there is the same story of development for a very few years after inauguration of an irrigation scheme, soon followed by salinity and decline. The Dujaila scheme of Iraq in 1958, the pilot Khuzistan development project of the 1940s, and others (the latest being the Dez scheme of the 1970s) show how irrigation can induce salinity problems unless extreme care is taken. Besides sodium ions, which are not only toxic to many plants but also induce a breakdown of soil structure leading to impermeability, calcium, magnesium, chlorides and sulphates are present. Even when the soil itself is not basically saline, use of saline irrigation water can turn the soil saline after a short time. This has happened in many places, one of the latest being in the United Arab Emirates, where use of saline water has raised salinity levels to 8000 parts per million – the maximum for possible plant growth is 3000 ppm.

The remedy is not to let water remain in or on the soil for long, or where salinity is established, to 'wash out' salts by rapid water leaching. Once a crop has absorbed what it needs, and no more, water should be led away off the fields by means of an underground drainage system. This in low-lying territory may mean much attention to outfall, or even, in some cases, pumping the water artificially back to the surface; but it is necessary if soil deterioration is not to take place. The extra cost of this double system of channelling water at the surface and leading it away again at shallow depths may be considerable, but there is only one alternative – sterility after a few years – if this is not done. Hence the great importance of preliminary soil surveys in any major irrigation scheme, parallel with studies of the quality of water available. Much water obtained from wells and artesian borings can be brackish and therefore of restricted use, and even originally sweet water may become contaminated by contact with mineral salts. Irrigation canals, wells and *qanats* must therefore be made with great care, to avoid contact with saline layers.

Saline water can, however, in certain instances be used for irrigation, provided that its use is carefully controlled in relation to soil type, and to kind of crops grown. In Israel saline and non-saline water supplies are artificially mixed to give an acceptable level of salinity.

Besides the question of salinity, irrigation may disturb a delicate ecological balance involving human disease. At the Middle East Agricultural Conference of 1944, it was stated that in one area of Egypt the effects of increasing supplies of irrigation water had raised the incidence of bilharziasis and malaria from 5% to 45% or even 75% of the total population of the region. Malaria is nowadays fairly easily controllable, but the incidence of bilharziasis, transmitted from a virus that lives in the body of a water snail, still spreads at a disquieting rate with the extension of irrigation. Provided these kinds of problem are borne in mind at the outset, it is certainly possible to minimize or even avoid totally these harmful 'side effects' of irrigation; but sufficient has perhaps been said here for it to be apparent that irrigation involves much more than just problems of structural engineering. The land reforms undertaken during the 1960s can be criticized because of the lack of attention they paid to water problems. In Iraq careless and hasty action directly increased soil salinity and put large areas out of cultivation; in Iran, though salinity problems were fewer, the effects of reform were reduced because relatively little attention was given to problems of water supply – it is insufficient to make over land to peasants if control of the irrigation of water necessary for exploitation remains in landlord hands.

**Natural vegetation**

Control by climate is very clearly apparent in both the character and the distribution of vegetation within the Middle East. Most outstanding are, of course, the effects of widespread aridity and high summer temperatures; and we must first discuss the influence of these upon the plant life of the region. There are two ways in which vegetation can survive a prolonged period of heat and drought: the first is by completing the cycle of growth during the cooler, rainy season; and the second is by special structural adaptation to resist deleterious conditions.

Plants of the first group usually germinate in late autumn, with the first onset of heavy rains, and grow rapidly throughout the winter, reaching maturity in late spring or early summer. As summer draws on, the plant itself is shrivelled and dies; but the seeds survive, to repeat the annual cycle during the next season. To this group belong grasses and cereals – wheat, barley and millet, some of which are indigenous to the Middle East and have later spread into other lands.

Structural adaptation to counter lack of rainfall may take the form of

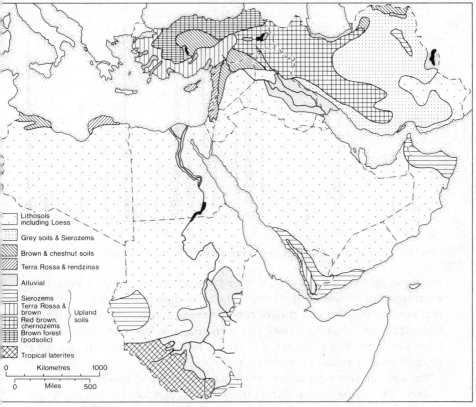

*Fig.* 4.3 Sketch of soil type distributions.

very deep or extensive roots – as for example in the vine. In some instances roots spread out just below the surface, and are hence able to absorb quantities of night dew which, as we have seen, is a feature of summer in coastal regions. Other plants lie dormant during the dry season, losing much or all of their portion above ground, and maintaining a stock of nutriment in bulbs, tubers or rhizomes. To this group belong the anemone, asphodel, iris and lily, tulip and narcissus – plants characteristic of the Mediterranean – which flower in spring and die down with the onset of summer.

Another group of plants remains in more or less active growth during the hot season, but shows special structural adaptation with the object of reducing water-loss. Certain species develop a thick outer layer: on the stem or trunk, as in the case of the cork oak; or on the leaves, as in the case of evergreens (laurel, evergreen oak and box). In other instances, leaf surface and size are reduced – the olive being of this type – and the process may be carried further by the shrinkage of leaves to

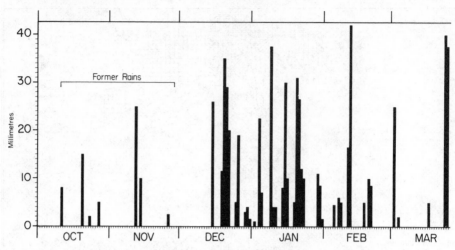

*Fig.* 4.4 Former and Latter Rains (average year in the Levant).

scales or spines, e.g. in tamarisk and thorn bushes. Leaves may even be dropped at the onset of summer, the stem then performing the normal function of leaves; and this occurs amongst certain species of broom and asparagus. Finally, a thick hairy coating may develop, by which the inner fleshy parts are protected from the heat. An example of this latter development is found in the hyssop.

Because of this adaptation to climatic conditions, involving in many instances a resting season during the summer, agricultural practice in the Middle East differs considerably in certain respects from that of cooler regions. Sowing can take place in early autumn; and although outside a narrow coastal zone frost may retard growth for some weeks, the rapid change to warmer conditions in March allows harvesting during April, May or June. Some plants, notably the orange and lemon, bear during the winter, and cropping begins in November, lasting until February or March.

The rainfall régime has a special significance. Heavy showers in the latter part of October mark the end of summer, and the beginning of the annual cycle of growth. These showers are the 'Former Rains' of the Bible – the reviving influence that quickens new plant life. Then in the mid spring there is usually a final onset of rain: a week or 10 days of intermittent showers following on an increasing dry spell. This is the real end of the rainy season; and the 'Latter Rains', as the Bible terms them, though not of necessity particularly heavy, are of great importance in the agricultural life of the Middle East (fig. 4.4). A prolongation of the rainy season for even a short period can have very considerable difference as regards crop yields and also in the 'flushes' of natural grassland which support the nomads' animals.

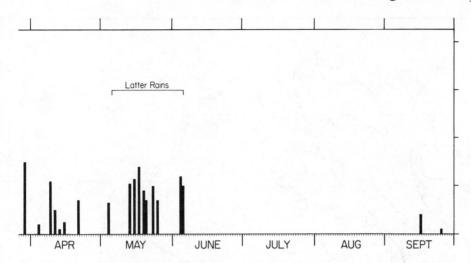

Where abundant water supplies are available, as in the great river valleys, or especially favoured irrigable zones, the short cycle of growth for some plants may allow several crops in one year. By careful husbandry, involving the maintenance of soil fertility, as many as three or even four crops per year are sometimes obtained in the Nile valley; and with judicious use of cereals, vines, fruit trees and vegetables, together with such cash crops as cotton, a type of mixed farming with an almost continuous yield is possible. Certain districts of the Middle East are capable of considerable further development, providing the two limiting factors of low soil fertility and deficient water supply can be overcome.

Aridity is, however, by no means characteristic of all parts of the Middle East; towards the north, more abundant rainfall gives rise to extensive forests. It has been shown how closely rainfall in the Middle East is related to topography, and the generally higher rainfall of mountainous areas, together with lower temperatures, favours the growth of a vegetation type very different from that of the warm, dry lowlands. In certain parts of the high plateaux of Asia Minor and north-west Iran, conditions even approximate to those of the fold mountains of central Europe, with a characteristic alpine vegetation of pasture and dwarf plants. Special conditions obtain in the Sudan, where, despite a fairly uniform relief in most parts, rainfall varies from almost nil in the north to a maximum of 2000 mm in a few mountainous localities of the extreme south, with consequent variation also in vegetation type, from desert to savanna and forest. The presence of the braided streams of the Nile system also leads to development of the well-known Sudd vegetation.

Reference must be made to a second controlling factor in the vegetation

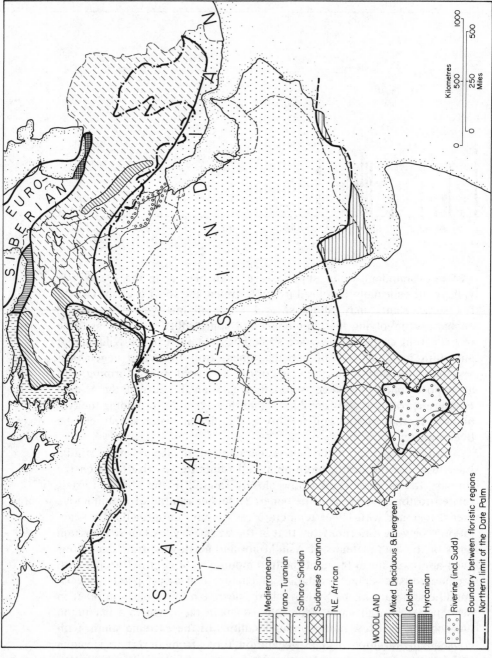

Fig. 4.5 The Middle East: natural vegetation

Mediterranean

Irano-Turanian

Saharo-Sindian

Sudanese Savanna

N.E. African

WOODLAND

Mixed Deciduous & Evergreen

Colchian

Hyrcanian

Riverine (incl. Sudd)

Boundary between floristic regions

Northern limit of the Date Palm

Kilometres

0    250    500    1000

0    500    Miles

types of the Middle East – that of adaptation by man, which in some important areas is so extensive as to justify the view that there is now no really natural vegetation left. Long occupation by man has meant that much of the original plant cover has been removed: the most striking change is the replacement in many parts of forest and woodland by scrub and heath. The practice of annual burning of the grassland and scrub carried out in many parts of the central and southern Sudan is important here. Deforestation has been especially widespread, especially in the Levant where the accessibility of the wooded areas, their relative absence in Egypt close by, and reckless use without conservation in the present century – even as railway fuel during the First World War – has denuded whole areas. Similarly, the Elburz uplands have lost much of their former dense tree cover, particularly since the growth of motor transport allowed the trees to be reduced to charcoal for sale in the towns – Tehran most of all. Once destroyed, woodland may not easily be renewed, since in some areas it is really a marginal growth, with natural conditions only barely suitable for its continued existence. In one sense, some (though not all) forests of the Middle East can be considered as expendable legacies from an earlier, wetter past. Once removed, the balance turns against renewed growth: soil is quickly eroded, the water-table may fall, and tree seedlings are not sufficiently vigorous to thrive on competition with scrub vegetation that springs up on deforested sites.Recent experimentation has, however, shown that for some areas it does in fact remain possible to re-afforest, though much effort is necessary, including careful physical and legal protection of the seedlings.

Most harmful to natural or artificial regeneration is, however, the practice of unrestrained grazing, chiefly by goats, which destroys the seedlings as they develop. In the opinion of many, such unrestricted grazing, particularly by 'sharp poisoned tooth of the goat', is one of the fundamental causes of agricultural backwardness in the Middle East. Gradual loss of forest cover leads to uncontrolled water run-off, with resultant soil erosion; and this in turn lowers the water-table in the subsoil, making difficult the supply of water for cultivation. For many areas this problem is acute, and differing solutions are arrived at. Sometimes, as in Jordan and Libya, the practice continues, in other areas nomads are excluded. The difficulties of holding a just balance between the claims of herders and the rights of agriculturalists are hence fundamental matters in certain parts of the Middle East.

A word must be said regarding the extreme richness of plant life in the Middle East. In the desert and on its margins alone, over 2000 species of plants occur, and many of these are indigenous to the Middle East, whilst 10000 species have been recorded in Iran alone. The corridor aspect of the Middle East is again important, for in addition to a type of flora associated specifically with the Mediterranean, there are plants belonging to two other botanogeographic provinces, one predominantly Asiatic, and the other African. Moreover, the southern Sudan, the Black Sea coastlands of Asia Minor and the southern Caspian lowlands each possess a special and distinctive flora quite different from that of the rest of the Middle East. In some localities, these last especially, the present-day flora has subsisted without major change since Pliocene or even late Miocene times; in northern Asia Minor this would frequently seem to be the case and, despite changes in climate in the Quaternary, the resulting drop in snow-line would have been insufficient to produce major alteration at moderately low altitudes.

## Vegetation types
### Mediterranean vegetation

This has a relatively restricted distribution, being mainly confined to the wetter parts of the Mediterranean coastal area – that is to say, to the narrow coastal plains of Cyprus, Israel, the Lebanon, Syria and Turkey, together with the lower flanks of the mountain ranges immediately inland, including the northern slopes of the Jebel Akhdar of Cyrenaica and parts of the Jefara and Jebel of Tripolitania. In addition to the 'classic' plants of the Mediterranean régime – vines, wheat, olive and fruit trees – a large number of shrubs and herbs, many evergreen, flourish in regions of thinner soil. During the spring numerous bulbs make a brilliant show. Walnut and poplar trees flourish in the damper places. Cactus, introduced from the Americas and used as hedges round fields or houses, has extended widely in the Levant, where it has 'escaped' from its earlier, limited use to become 'wild'.

Besides the plants mentioned above, the Mediterranean flora includes several highly characteristic plant complexes or groupings. Best known is the *maquis* or *macchia*, which, most fully developed in Corsica, is fairly widespread throughout the Mediterranean basin, in association with siliceous soils. Densely set evergreen oaks, myrtles and broom, with a thick undergrowth of thorn bushes and shrubs, form a vegetative covering that is sometimes sufficiently extensive to afford shelter to refugees and outlaws. Because of this connection, the term *maquis*, once of botanical significance only, has taken on a wider meaning involving human and even political relationships. *Maquis* is not especially widespread in the Middle East; instead, two degenerate types of *maquis* vegetation, garrigue and phrygana, are more characteristic.

Garrigue is associated with the thinner soils of calcareous outcrops. Evergreen oaks, which are tolerant of greater aridity, persist – although at wider intervals than in true *maquis* – but tall shrubs are much less common, and a low scrub of dwarf bushes and thorns takes their place. Because of the more open nature of this vegetation, which rarely exceeds 2 m in height, perennial plants can develop, and for some weeks after the spring rains, a carpet of flowers and herbs makes a striking display, Garrigue is often discontinuous, with bare patches of soil or rock interspersed with plants; and if *maquis* is cleared, it is frequently found that garrigue takes its place, especially if animal grazing prevents the regrowth of taller trees and shrubs. For this reason, garrigue is more characteristic of the Mediterranean zone of the Middle East than is true *maquis*, and much of the vegetation of Cyprus, north-west Cyrenaica and the western Levant is of the former type.

Phrygana, a term employed by the ancient Greeks, denotes a special type of thorn scrub, which is restricted to western Asia Minor and the Aegean region. Unlike garrigue, which includes many differing types of plant, phrygana consists principally of thorn bushes, of only moderate growth, but very spiny and closely set. Bands of thorn scrub, occupying the deeper valley bottoms, can be a considerable obstacle to movement in districts where they occur.

## Steppe vegetation

A special type of vegetation has evolved under the influence of steppe climate, of which the chief features are wide seasonal variation of temperature and generally lower rainfall. A botanical province has been recognized, corresponding to the geographical distribution of steppe conditions; and to this province the name Irano-Turanian is given. As the name implies, Irano-Turanian vegetation is best developed in central Asia, but a westward extension has occurred through Asia Minor and Iraq into central Syria.

On the lower slopes of the mountains flanking the steppe, a park-like vegetation is found, with scattered carob, juniper and terebinth trees, and bushes of Christ thorn, wild plum or thorn and wormwood, separated by expanses of smaller shrubs (sage, thyme and thorn cushions) or creepers. In regions of true steppe trees are absent, and various species of grass appear, although these have sharply restricted seasonal growth. Many grasses show adaptation to semi-arid conditions: one species has a hygroscopic seed casing with a stiff pointed top, by means of which the seed, after being driven into the hard ground, is supplied with water; and another has developed a system of propagation by means of small swellings on parts of the leaves that remain underground.

More than half of the plants of the steppe region disappear in summer. There is hence a considerable difference in aspect between late winter and early spring, when numerous species of flowers and grass are in rapid growth, and the rest of the year, when most plants are shrivelled up or have not yet germinated. For a few weeks each year the steppe presents an amazing picture of luxuriant, almost lush vegetation; but with the approach of summer, only hardier bushes and thorns remain above the ground, and vast expanses of bare earth appear, upon which are strewn the withered remains of earlier plant growth.

The steppes are the home of pastoral nomadism, and it will easily be seen how narrow is the margin of existence in these regions – an extra week of rain (i.e. prolonged Latter Rains) will mean a more than corresponding lengthening of the spring pasture season, with great increase of flocks and herds during the ensuing year; early cessation of rainfall means a long summer with much hardship until the next spring. Under such conditions even a small climatic fluctuation can have a disproportionately large effect upon human activity, and a few seasons of deficient rainfall may lead to widespread movements within the steppes, culminating in the invasion of adjoining lands, with vast consequences for human societies as a whole. Such great events as the Indo-Aryan invasions of Europe and the Middle East during the second millennium B.C., the Israelitish occupation of Palestine and the rise of Islam in the seventh century A.D. can all be traced to slight changes in environmental conditions within the steppelands of Eurasia.

## Desert vegetation

To a third major botanical grouping, characteristic of arid conditions, the name Saharo-Sindian has been given. Many plants of this grouping show an extreme degree of adaptation to dry or saline conditions; of these, thorns (chiefly tamarisk) are the most important.

Camel thorn, a shrub of the pea family, and also certain kinds of tamarisk, exude a brown, sweetish sap, which, when hardened on contact with the atmosphere, forms the Biblical manna. Other desert plants complete their growing cycle within a few weeks after the end of the winter rains, and throughout late spring one sees an extraordinary variety and abundance of flowering grasses. Such vegetation may, however, last only for a matter of days.

## Mountain vegetation

Four distinctive types of vegetation occur on the higher mountains of the Middle East. Of these, three are forest growths, and the fourth is Alpine pasture or heath.

The first type of woodland is of mixed evergreen, coniferous and deciduous trees. Evergreen oaks generally grow on the lower hill slopes, up to about 1000 m, and associated with these are the carob and a species of pine that is native to the Mediterranean basin. At higher levels are found cedars, maple, juniper, firs and two other species of oak and pine – the valonia oak, which yields an extract valuable for tanning leather, and the Aleppo pine, which, like the Mediterranean variety, is smaller and more bushy in appearance than the conifers of northern latitudes. The famous cedars of Lebanon, large but extremely slow-growing trees, now exist, as we have noted (fig. 4.6), only in scattered clumps as the result of centuries of exploitation. The largest of these clumps, numbering 400 trees, occurs at a height of over 200 m between Tripoli and Baalbek; and, like many isolated groves in the Middle East, has acquired a semi-sacred character that may help towards its future preservation. By far the greatest extent of forestland exists in Asia Minor (with limited extensions southwards along the crests of the Zagros) and in western Syria and the Lebanon. About one-eighth of the state of Turkey is classified as forestland.

Above 1500–2000 m, or exceptionally, 2200–2500 m in the Elburz mountains of Iran, forests die out and are replaced by scrub or dwarf specimens of true forest trees. In eastern Anatolia and Azerbaijan, temperatures are lower than elsewhere in the Middle East, and a kind of Alpine vegetation appears. In the wetter parts, small areas of grassland reminiscent of Swiss pastures may occur, but, more often, conditions are too dry and vegetation is limited to bushes, creepers and 'cushion' plants.

The second type of forest is found on the northern slopes of the Elburz mountains, towards the Caspian Sea. Oak, hazel, alder, maple, hornbeam, hawthorn, wild plum and wild pear are the characteristic trees, and these are festooned by a dense growth of brambles, ivy and other creepers. Here and there are openings occupied by box, thorn bushes, pomegranate and medlar trees. To this luxuriant growth, peculiar to the region, and developing under conditions of abundant rainfall throughout the year with high or moderate temperatures, the name Hyrcanian forest is sometimes given. One interesting feature is the absence of conifers.

A third type of woodland – the Colchian or Pontic forest – has developed in response to the warm humid climate of the southern Caucasus and eastern Black Sea.[1] An indigenous species of beech, with oak, hazel, walnut, maple and hornbeam, form the chief trees, and a dense undergrowth of climbing plants is again found, with widespread occurrence of the rhododendron. Best developed near the southern Caucasus, the Colchian forest extends westwards in an increasingly attenuated form

[1] One element in the unusually high winter temperatures of the south-eastern Black Sea coastal margins is the frequent occurrence of Föhn winds which descend from the high inland plateaux of eastern Anatolia.

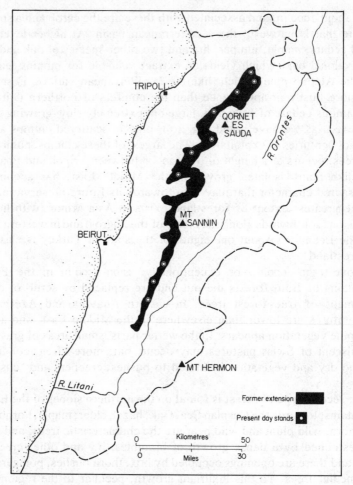

TRIPOLI

QORNET
ES
SAUDA ▲

R. Orontes

MT
▲ SANNIN

BEIRUT

▲ MT HERMON

R. Litani

Former extension ■

Present day stands ⊙

Kilometres
0 ———————————— 50
0 ———————————— 30
Miles

*Fig.* 4.6 Cedars in the Lebanon (in part after W. M. Mikesell).

along the north-eastern edge of the Anatolian plateau as far west as Sinop. It has been suggested that, like the Hyrcanian forest further to the east, the Colchian forest is the remnant of a flora that was characteristic of much larger areas of the Middle East during Tertiary and early Quaternary times.

### Savanna

In the Sudan broadly south of latitude 15° N savanna-type vegetation becomes dominant, in response to the markedly different climatic régime and soil types of the southern Sudan. Grassland develops, which then becomes interspersed with tall trees: various acacias only in the drier areas (under 450 mm annual rainfall) and then an intermixture with broader-leaved deciduous species. As rainfall becomes more abundant, the height and luxuriance of the trees tends to increase. Grasses also occur, even when (as is common) the branches of individual trees may meet; these grasses can be sharply seasonal in growth, or more continuous. Bulbs and herbs are also found. The intermingling of grasses and tall trees in some parts of the Sudan and the absence of trees in others (leaving a grass savanna only) has been explained in different ways. One view is that grassland without trees is a climax controlled by soil type – deep clays or sands; others believe that the habit of regularly burning the savanna grass results in the extinction of trees and the perpetuation of the more rapidly growing grasses, which can regenerate rapidly, whereas trees take longer to re-establish themselves, and are in any case (as saplings) highly sensitive to burning of the grass.

In the extreme south of the Sudan the heavily wooded savanna passes here and there into full tropical rain forest, with a closed canopy and gallery-type forest.

### Riverine vegetation

The extensive alluvial lowlands of the great rivers have a special type of vegetation. Aquatic grasses, papyrus, lotus and reeds that sometimes attain a height of 8 m make up a thick undergrowth in deltaic regions in the Sudanese reaches of the Upper Nile system and in the lower courses of the Tigris and Euphrates. The vegetation is so dense in the southern Sudan as to form a real barrier to movement of the water, hence the name Sudd (blockage). Elsewhere, scattered willow, poplar and alder trees may occur, but the commonest tree is the date palm, which is extremely tolerant of excessive water, provided that the temperature remains high. Cultivated palms are therefore a feature of riverine lowlands in Egypt and lower Mesopotamia. Another wild plant of economic importance is the liquorice, a bush that is fairly widely distributed along the banks of the middle and upper Euphrates and Tigris. Juice is extracted from the underground stem, and this forms an important item of trade in the districts of Aleppo and Mosul.

### Changes in vegetation

There remains the interesting question of how far the present vegetation distributions in the Middle East can be ascribed to climatic changes since the later Quaternary, and how far the changes are due to human action. The fact that many relatively small or isolated areas now show extreme richness in plant species – this is the case especially in Iran and Asia Minor – suggests that plant migration was once able to take place over broader zones, which later have been reduced or obliterated owing to changes in climatic conditions. The corridors or linkage-areas would seem in certain instances to have been much more extensive and developed than is now the case. But, as has been mentioned above, there would also seem to be the fact that many species have appeared to have survived *in situ* and largely unaltered, from mid-Tertiary times onwards. The Quaternary period most probably had the effect of depressing snow-lines in many upland areas of the northern Middle East, but this does not appear to have caused major changes in vegetation, at least at medium or lower levels.

We thus have human agencies as a principal factor in the erosion and degradation of woodland in the Middle East. This has undoubtedly been a major matter. Various literary sources indicate the extent of exploitation: the Bible (use of cedars for roofing as one of the few trees capable of yielding a large baulk of timber that could span a wide expanse such as a large room); and some classical writers, who describe the careless and in some cases organized exploitation of timber either for metal-smelting, for building or even for clearing that would convey a title or ownership. During the First World War local timber was certainly cut for fuel on the northern parts of the Hijaz Railway; and the cold winters of many interior parts of the Middle East provide a ready market for wood that is usually made into charcoal, which offers a more manageable small-scale fuel.

Hence it is necessary even now to take positive steps towards protection of the remaining woodlands even, in some parts, to the extent of maintaining fences and an armed guard. Uncontrolled grazing by goats is still a great handicap to regeneration, the saplings likely to be cropped off regularly, whilst summer heat and aridity allow devastating fires. We have noted the situation in the southern Sudan, where deliberate burning by humans is a major ecological control. Many Middle Eastern governments are becoming aware of the importance of tree cover, and are taking steps to achieve this, or even one positive step further, the elaboration of re-afforestation schemes. But the gap between good intentions of a ministry located in a capital city, and actual conditions on a remote hillside with only tenuous local governmental authority, is apt to be very wide.

Because of long continued human occupation and intensive use, it is now the case that much, if not most of the former 'natural' vegetation of the Middle East has either been profoundly modified or even replaced by other forms. The distinction between natural climax and controlled forms has greatly altered, with the variations of climate over the last millennia acting as a major determinant. Introduction of cactus from the Americas after the sixteenth century – now ubiquitous and much-used form of 'hedging' for houses or cultivation – is another variable in the extremely complex pattern of vegetation adaptation and development.

# Part II

# Social geography of the Middle East

# 5 Peoples

Few regions in the world can surpass the Middle East in heterogeneity of population. From earliest times, the region has attracted waves of immigrants from various parts of the Old World, and fusion of diverse elements has sometimes tended to be slow, or even incomplete. Frequent references in the literatures of various peoples of the Middle East indicate an acute awareness of racial and cultural distinction; and insistence by these groups on their separate identity can be taken as an indication of the close juxtaposition of many types of racial stock, cultural patterns and social organization.

The pictorial art of ancient Egypt was always concerned to depict the Egyptians themselves, by means of a special coloration, as a separate and distinctive group; and there is little need to comment on the theme of fierce tribal exclusiveness that permeates much of the Old Testament. The Greeks, too, had a marked appreciation of racial differences, not merely as between themselves and their neighbours, but also in a wider sense, as for example, when Herodotus notes that Egyptian skulls could be distinguished from Persian, owing to the greater fragility of the latter. Distinctions between Jew and Christian, Believer and Infidel, Turk or Arab, Semite and Hamite, or between mountaineer and plainsman, and Badawin (herders) and Hadhar (cultivators), have long coloured the geography of the Middle East, and are still at the present day factors of prime importance in the human relations of the region. Despite improved communications and the spread of education, it is currently an unfortunate tendency of societies the world over, and not just in the Middle East, to have become latterly more rather than less conscious of nationality and cultural divisions. Race, colour, culture and nationality (whatever any of those terms really mean) are increasingly with us.

It has proved difficult to established criteria by which the peoples of the world may be subdivided. Appearance and physique, blood serum character (in a strictly biological sense), language, religion and nationality have all been invoked as a basis of definition, but no single one of these can provide a wholly satisfying and acceptable point of reference. For the Middle East, this insufficiency is easy to demonstrate. We may speak of an 'Arab' people, but how is this to be defined? What, in short, is an Arab? Physical type among Arabs can range from the slight, spare Badawin of the Arabian and African deserts to the heavily built, large-framed, muscular Lebanese or Egyptians. Colour of skin is a limited guide only: must all Arabs be brown? And, if so, dark, very dark or light? What does 'dark' mean?: some Arabs are no darker than Spaniards or Greeks. Language might be a better basis of classification, with Arabs defined as Arabic-speakers; but then there would be included a number of inhabitants of Iran living in the central Zagros area; whilst Armenian-, Circassian- and Greek-speaking minorities living in Egypt, Lebanon, Syria and Jordan would be excluded, together with the Aramaic-speakers of Ma'aloula (Syria) and the Berbers of certain Libyan settlements. With religious beliefs as criteria, we find firstly that a number of undoubted 'Arabs' are Christians; secondly, that Islam itself is much divided, with sectarian divisions almost as extensive as those of Christendom; and thirdly, that religious life within the Middle East shows an infinite gradation from almost complete paganism to the fullest development of Christianity, Islam and Judaism.

Nationalism is an increasingly potent element, political consciousness having greatly developed over the last 20–30 years. But smallness of numbers, intermingling with other, equally conscious groups, or external political obstacles, have tended to inhibit effective realization, so that existing national frontiers can hardly be said to allow complete political expression to all nationally conscious groups. The Kurds are the most obvious example here; but there are also the southern tribespeople of the Sudan, and the Turks of Cyprus until the dramatic events of 1974, to name only a few. Finally, there is a wide range of political structure, from the socialistically inclined republican units typified in Egypt, Syria and Iraq, to the monarchical oligarchic and even semi-theocratic forms of government that prevail in some other countries. Pan-Arab, pan-Iranian, pan-Turkish, pan-Kurdish movements and *enosis* (union of Greek-speaking peoples) are at present political issues of varying intensity, but they all encounter practical difficulties which have so far prevented their full realization. In an attempt to throw further light on the complicated question of cultural, political and social organization, the populations of the Middle East will be considered in turn from the standpoint of the five criteria of race, language, religion, social organization, and national consciousness. This examination will, however, of necessity be limited in detail, since in some instances, our knowledge of the factual and even intellectual basis of these attempted categorizations is far from complete.

As a preliminary to this examination, it is first useful to note the influence on the peoples of the Middle East of certain geographical factors. The region has a dual aspect – that of a broad corridor linking several major parts of the world, either overland, or by short sea journeys often almost totally within sight of land. Here and there, however, local environment – desert, mountain or inauspicious location – has favoured the preservation of distinctive physical human types and cultures, some- times emphasizing these through interbreeding, or else merely fostering the continued existence of individual culture patterns and ethnic groups that in more accessible areas have been submerged by later arrivals.

A somewhat discontinuous belt of fertile steppe and oasis runs along the southern slopes of the Elburz mountains of Iran, and is followed by an ancient route that in the opinion of some anthropologists was one avenue by which certain types of early man spread into western Eurasia. Further to the west the route divides, one branch turning south west into south-west Iran and Iraq, and the other continuing through Azerbaijan to Asia Minor. A zone of steppeland in inner Anatolia completes the link between central Asia and Europe.

More strongly marked is the steppe area of the Fertile Crescent which links western Iran, Iraq, south-east Anatolia and the Levant. By this route numerous invaders from the east and north have gained the shores of the Mediterranean and the Nile valley; and as a return movement Egyptian culture has also spread into Asia. The Mediterranean itself has facilitated rather than impeded intercourse between the peoples near its shores. The island-studded Aegean was a nursery for man's first sea adventures; and it is not surprising that some of the earliest cultural developments occurred in Cyprus, which is visible both from Asia Minor and the mainland of the Levant. In the south, close physical connection between Arabia and north Africa is paralleled by similar cultural contact. The Sinai has formed a major route for movement of peoples, and some authorities stress the importance of the Bab el Mandeb region as the gateway between Arabia and the Sudan.

Alongside this *durchgangsland* of the Middle East, there occur regions in which difficulty of access or hostile natural conditions have restricted penetration. Largest of these is the desert of Arabia, the Jezirat al Arab (Island of the Arabs), where, in the words of Hitti, 'ethnic purity is a reward . . . of ungrateful and isolated environment'. Other such regions

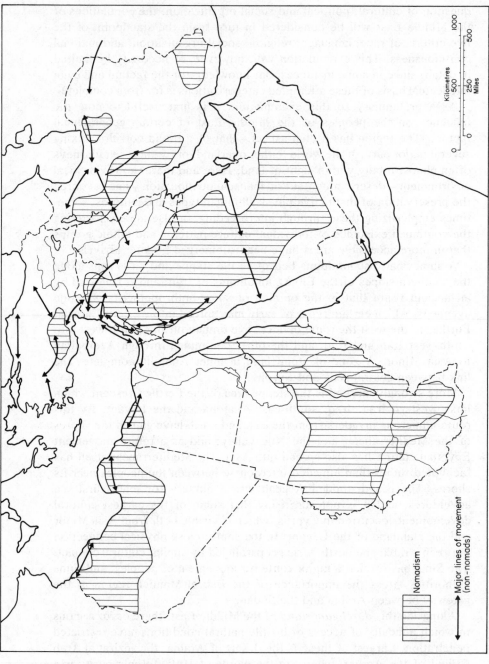

Fig. 5.1 Nomadism and lines of movement in the Middle East

Nomadism

Major lines of movement
(non-nomads)

Kilometres
0        500        1000

0    250    500
Miles

may be seen in the highland plateaux of the Mediterranean seaboard, and here Samaritans, Druzes, Maronites, Metwalis, Alawites and various sects of Asia Minor, such as the Bakhtahis and Takhtajis, have preserved a certain cultural autonomy, if not always a pure racial type. Further east, the Kurds of the Anatolian and Zagros mountain belts have maintained a separate identity; and smaller units can be traced in the Yazidis of the Jebel Sinjar of north Iraq, the Circassians (Cherkasski) and the Turcomans. Variation on a large scale is also characteristic of the Zagros. But it is also necessary to note that nowadays several influences are working to erode the separation and distinctiveness of these long-standing minority communities. One is the increased efficiency of communications media, which allow formerly isolated groups to reach and be reached by motor bus and radio; another is the enhanced 'pull' from new occupations and better living conditions in the cities, due in large part to the prosperity based on oil-exploitation – this has, for instance, drastically reduced the number of nomads in Kuwait state over the last few years. A third influence is the medical care usually available only in major urban centres but now much sought after by all; and finally, there is the stronger incidence of central government which, also using modern methods of communication, is able to reach out far more effectively and consistently to impose centralized rule upon once isolated and ignored communities.

## Race

In the past, anthropologists attempted to erect a system of racial division based on skin and hair colouring, on stature, and on shape of the cranium, and this system of 'Mediterranean', 'Alpine' and 'Nordic' classification was applied to the Middle East. This approach, however, proved unsatisfactory, and it has now been abandoned. Other more objective systems of analysing racial diversity have therefore been developed, based particularly on blood grouping but also on other genetically controlled factors.

Quite distinctive elements, often directly relatable to genetic factors (and hence easily traceable), can be isolated in human blood, and many individual systems of classification are therefore possible. The best known of these is the ABO system, which is based on the presence (or absence: O) of two substances on the red cells of the blood, with complementary antibodies in the blood serum. An individual person may have A quality only, or B quality only, or both (AB), or none (O); and occurrence would seem to reflect the effect of geographical location, since the proportions of A, B or O are not random, but vary by recognizable amounts, sometimes (as in north-east England along the line of the lower Tees river) by relatively sharp breaks. Fig. 5.2 shows the distribution of the B factor

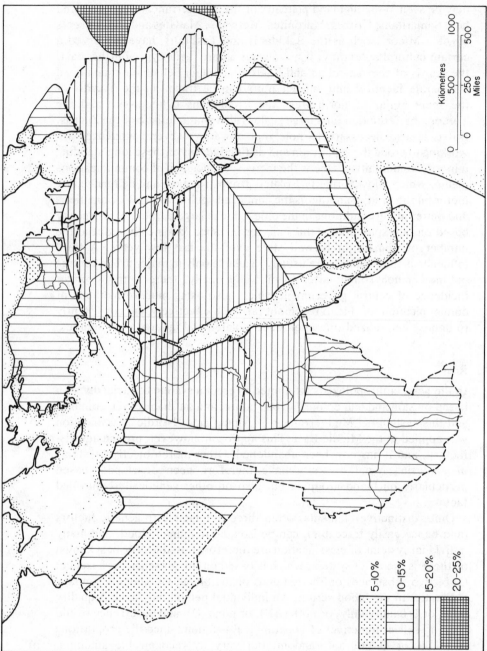

5-10%

10-15%

15-20%

20-25%

*Fig.* 5.2 The Middle East: distribution of the B blood group gene (after F. Sunderland and others)

Kilometres

0    250    500    1000

0    250    500

Miles

for parts of the Middle East, although it must also be stated that data for this region are still relatively few. It will be seen that the distributions shown in fig. 5.2 appear to have no relation whatever to other racial or cultural distributions.

Recognition of quite other blood-group substances allow further, separate systems: the Diego, Duffy, Lewis and Kidd, Kell, Lutheran, MNSs, P, Rhesus and Sutter systems, some of these being named after a particular gene or groups of genes, the others after their human discoverer. Besides being easily measurable and objectively determined – they are demonstrably present or not – racial grouping on this kind of genetical basis has the merits of showing linkages, geographical and historical. That is, two communities, even though separated in habitat but of similar blood grouping, could be shown to be derived from a single, common group. Such connection has been demonstrated, for example, for the gipsy communities of Europe and the Middle East (hence the sound basis of Gipsy = Egyptian?). As well, close relationship to genetic factors allows the tracing of outside influences such as geographical intermixture or isolation, social barriers or inbreeding.

Of especial interest here is the position of the Jews. For long, anthropologists have disputed whether or not it was possible to define or recognize a distinctly Jewish physical type, or whether this type, where it existed, was really only a part of a 'Semitic' race that also included Arabs and Armenoids. Some Jews could be demonstrated to be distinctive in appearance from surrounding communities; whilst others maintained equally positively that there was no difference, and the term Jewish was therefore purely a cultural or social (religious) distinction. Blood grouping has, however, shown that many (though not all) Jews show certain similarities among their own group (i.e. with other Jews) and fewer similarities with the surrounding communities: that is, they do have a biological basis which is to some extent distinctive. This and associated problems, now that the country receives immigrants from many parts of the Middle East, is of importance for the present-day Israeli state, and in 1970 led to an impassioned debate in the Jewish Knesset (Parliament) on 'What is a Jew?' This debate still goes on, with undiminished intensity.

Other blood factors, enzyme deficiencies and biological traits, such as the ability to taste or smell various chemical substances, would seem to have a patterned distribution among human groups, suggesting some form of differential response to environment. The importance of this would seem to lie in that there appear to be recognizable regional variations between communities of human being, with, however, variability rather than uniformity the principal factor.

In summary, we are left with a distinctly complex and even confused picture. There are indubitable differences between human groups as groups, but these tend, in the main, to occur spatially as gradations rather than as sharp divides. Moreover, the elements that vary are not confined to matters of skin colour or physical appearance: these are part, but only a limited part, of the whole, highly involved complex that make up biological distinction between man and man. No single 'nation' or 'race' is entirely homogeneous in its physical attributes, yet at the same time, persistence of genetical differences – whether of skin colour, hair types, blood group or response to tasting phenylthiocarbamide[1] – suggests that these qualities confer some sort of genetical advantage, in that those humans who possess them are better adapted for life in the particular environment that they inhabit. Otherwise, these qualities would have tended to die out, or at least, regress to an average.

### Language distribution

As regards language, the position in the Middle East is much clearer. Although it is possible that at one time each racial group had its own language, intercourse soon breaks down linguistic differences, and one language may quickly establish a dominance, to the exclusion of others. Whereas physical characters can persist through many generations as a result of biological inheritance, a cultural feature such as language often becomes modified within a short time, and may even die out, particularly if the language itself possesses no literature.

Our present purpose is merely to note the distribution of existing languages within the Middle East, with incidental references to earlier periods only as they affect modern conditions. In the north, Turkish, as the language of Osmanli conquerors, became dominant in Asia Minor. Spoken only by Asiatic nomads, Turkish at first possessed no alphabet, and Arabic characters were borrowed; but as these letters are not particularly well adapted to expressing the sounds of Turkish, Roman letters replaced Arabic script in 1923, by decree of the Turkish Republic.

At the present time Turkish is by no means universally spoken in Asia Minor. Towards the east, Armenian, a more ancient language with its own characters and literature, still persists; and further to the south, Kurdish has a wide extension. In the difficult and inaccessible hill districts near the Russian frontier many remnants of Caucasian languages occur – Circassian, Lazi and Mingrelian being among the chief. Some of these represent ancient cultural or racial groups submerged by later arrivals, but others are Finno-Ugrian dialects brought in at comparatively recent dates by invaders from the east.

At one time Greek was spoken by a considerable minority in western

[1] The large majority of Amerindians can taste this substance, but some 30% of the populations of Eurasia cannot.

Anatolia; and until the forcible deportations in 1922, Izmir (Smyrna) was at least as much Greek as Turkish. At the present time, Greek is still spoken in the islands of the Aegean and is the native tongue of at least three-quarters of the inhabitants of Cyprus – the remainder speaking Turkish. Until the Turkish invasion in 1974 and the *de facto* partition of the island into Turkish and Greek zones, Greek cultural influence predominated in the life of the island. The question of the union of Greek-speaking peoples remains a political issue of some importance.

From the interior of Arabia have come two great groups of languages, North Semitic and South Semitic. To the first group belong the Aramean and the Canaanitish dialects – Aramaic proper, Hebrew, Phoenician and Palmyrene (the now extinct language of the inhabitants of Palmyra); to the second group, Arabic. In the first and second millennia B.C., extensive folk migrations spread North Semitic languages into Mesopotamia, Syria and the Levant. Aramaic, the language of a people living in the western edge of the Syrian desert, became current over a wide area in the Middle East, most probably because of the extensive commercial relations developed by the Aramean states. Aramaic dialect was the vernacular of Palestine during the time of Christ; and at least one of the Gospels can be considered as pure Aramaic literature, with several words even surviving unaltered in the English translation of the Bible.[1] Aramaic also had a considerable effect on certain languages spoken in Iran, and traces are still apparent in the north-west of the country today. The language is not completely dead; it lingers still in a few villages near Damascus and Mosul, and is the sacred language of a number of Christian sects in both countries. A revived and simplified Hebrew has been adopted as the official language of the State of Israel.

Arabic, originally spoken by a small group of traders, townsfolk and desert nomads in the district of Medina and Mecca, was the language of Muhammad and his early followers, and with the rise of Islam in the seventh century A.D. quickly replaced existing languages in Libya, Egypt, the Levant and Iraq. As the language of the Koran, Arabic is one of the great unifying influences of the Islamic world, since although local deviation in vocabulary and pronunciation occur, a standard form of classical Arabic is understood by most literate Moslems.[2]

It should be noted that the dominance of Arabic in the Middle East is by no means complete; penetration of the mountain zone of the east and north did not occur, and over much of the Sudan languages other than Arabic are current, from Nubian in the extreme north and Beja in

[1]  E.g. The Last Words of Christ (Mark 15: 34).
[2]  North African, Egyptian, Palestinian, Syrian, Iraqi and southern Arabian 'dialects' of Arabic occur. Some of these differ only in pronunciation (e.g. as between spoken English in London, Lancashire or Scotland), but in other instances the colloquial forms may be as wide apart as, say, French, Spanish or Italian.

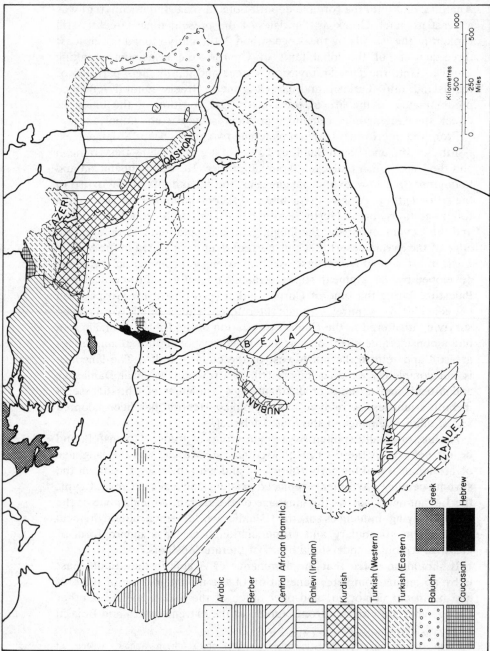

**Legend:**

- Arabic
- Berber
- Central African (Hamitic)
- Pahlevi (Iranian)
- Kurdish
- Turkish (Western)
- Turkish (Eastern)
- Baluchi
- Caucasian
- Greek
- Hebrew

QASHQAY

AZER

BEJA

NUBIAN

DINKA

ZANDE

Kilometres
1000
500 500
250
Miles

0

*Fig. 5.2* The Middle East: language distribution

---

1 *Read from right to left:*

Arabic,  في البدي كان الكلمة

Aramaic (Syriac),  ܕܘܒܪܐ ܐܘܡܘܡܣ‌ܘ ܗܘܐ ܡܠܬܐ

Hebrew,  בראשית היה הדבר

2 *Read from left to right:*

Armenian,  Սկզբանէ էր Բանն

Greek,  Ἐν ἀρχῇ ἦν λόγος.

Cyrillic (Russian),[1]  Въ началѣ было Слово.

The examples given are all translations of John 1: 1, 'In the beginning was the word'.

---

*Fig.* 5.4 Specimens of scripts in current use in the Middle East.

the Red Sea hills to the many central African languages of the south. Arabic has, however, intermingled in many areas of the country. In Asia Minor, as we have seen, Arabic script only was adopted, and the numerous non-Semitic languages of the region remained in current use. Similarly, Iran retained its own distinctive speech, which can best be described as an ancient indigenous language (termed Pahlevi) much modified by extraneous influences, but using Arabic script. Extensive interchange of vocabulary and ideas between Iranian and Arabic shows that the cultural influences of Arabic have been strong, yet not sufficient to drive out the native form of speech. Again reminiscent of Asia Minor, Iran has a number of minority languages, chiefly spoken by tribes living in the Zagros regions: Turkic, Arabic, Baluchi, and Kurdish. There are also other minority languages in south Arabia – the Hadhramaut particularly.

Broadly speaking, the Middle East can thus be divided into (*a*) an Arabic area, in which a single language predominates to the virtual exclusion of all others; and (*b*) composite regions, in which many languages, recent and ancient, remain current. It may be significant that the boundary between these two areas coincides for the greater part with the southern edge of the geological folded zone; and the effect of topography in restricting the spread of language would seem to be marked.

[1] Used by a very few Slav-speaking groups formerly living in the Balkans and Russia, e.g. the Circassians of Jordan.

### Religious differences

The most highly developed of all religious systems in the world – Zoroastrianism, Judaism, Christianity and Islam – have arisen within the Middle East region.

## Zoroastrianism and Judaism

These were the first of the monotheistic religions. Zoroaster, or Zarathustra, a native of Iran, lived during the period 700–50 B.C. and his teaching that human life is a battleground for opposing forces, good and evil, was adopted as the official creed of the Persian Empire under Cyrus and his successors (p. 157). The religion of Zoroaster, by its insistence on moral and ethical standards, represented a great advance on the older pagan and polytheistic creeds, which had frequently appealed to the baser human instincts of self-interest and sensuality. The older gods were, however, not entirely abandoned, but retained as subsidiary in influence to a single Lord of Goodness and Light, or sometimes as demons. Association of the Lord of Goodness[1] with light led in time to the use of fire as an important element in Zoroastrian worship; and with the spread of religion amongst peoples who found difficulty in appreciating the abstract conceptions of Zoroaster, some earlier ideas were abandoned in favour of a simpler form of belief that was greatly influenced by pre-existing pagan creeds. Fire also came to be used as the principal element of ritual. Thus Zoroastrianism became associated with fire-worship, and remained the distinctive religion of Iran until the rise of Islam. One of the largest fire temples was at Masjid i Suleman, in the Iranian Zagros, where a natural oil seepage occurred. Moslem persecution over a long period has reduced the fire-worshippers to a small remnant, who now exist as a minority in the Kerman and Yazd districts of Iran. Large numbers emigrated to India, where they form the Parsee community.

The Jewish people entered Palestine during the second millennium B.C. and successfully established a small state in the highlands of Judaea. It was subsequent to this entry into Palestine that the religion of the Jewish people, at first worship of a purely tribal deity and strongly influenced by a pastoral way of life,[2] developed the lofty conceptions which now characterize it. Following conquest by the Assyrian king in 722 B.C. the first dispersal of the Jewish people took place, when numbers of Jews were forcibly settled in Mesopotamia. Later, however, these immigrants

---

[1] Ahura-Mazda, or Ormuzd. Cf. a modern commercial use of the name.
[2] Of all the books in the Old Testament, only one, that of Ruth, shows the predominating influence of an agricultural tradition.

were allowed to return, and the Jewish state revived. In A.D. 71, as the result of a revolt against Roman overlords, a second and more permanent Dispersal (Diaspora) took place. Jews became established in many parts of Europe and Asia, where they absorbed much of the culture and even some of the racial traits of the peoples amongst whom they settled. Yemenite, Persian, Turcoman, Georgian and even Abyssinian Jews are distinguishable at the present day; and by reason of their Oriental culture and outlook, these groups are in sharp contrast to the Jews of Europe. Numbers of Oriental Jews settled in Palestine during the Ottoman period, and for a time in the twentieth century showed some disinclination to identify themselves with Zionism. However, since the creation of Israel in 1948 a mass exodus of Jews from Arab countries has taken place, although sizeable Jewish communities survive in Turkey and Iran.

Of the European Jews, a minority settled in the Iberian peninsula and adopted much of the Spanish-Arab culture of the region. These Jews, spoken of as Sephardim, have been considered by some to be the élite of the Jewish people. The remainder, settled chiefly in Poland and adjacent countries, are known as Ashkenazim; and it is from this latter group that the majority of modern European immigrants to Israel have come.

*Christianity*

In A.D. 313 Christianity was adopted as the official religion of the Roman Empire.[1] This adoption led to many changes in Christianity itself, which, from being the fiercely held creed of an active, but disliked and mistrusted minority, became an accepted and integral part of the Roman state. In undergoing this development, Christianity was subjected to two influences. The first, an attempt at defining a single body of dogma and ritual in order to preserve unity within the Church itself, is of little concern to the geographer; but the second, the creation of administrative provinces on a territorial basis, has much geographical interest.

Within the Roman world, four cities could claim a certain material and intellectual pre-eminence. Rome itself, for long the centre of the empire, began to decline in influence with the increasing economic and political importance of the lands of the eastern Mediterranean during the later Roman period; and a symptom of this shift of balance was the corres-

---

[1] There were many reasons for this change, some of which were mainly political in character. The Roman Emperor Constantine saw in Christianity a strong, positive social bond, by which the increasing disunity of a declining empire might be counteracted. The older Roman state, vigorous and secure, could afford to ignore the cohesive power of religion, and therefore tolerated many religious beliefs within its frontiers. At a later date, in face of disintegration within and barbarian pressure without the empire, tolerance was abandoned in favour of a single religious system from which the state could derive support, and which in turn could benefit from official recognition.

ponding rise of Constantinople, which supplanted Rome as the capital of the Roman Empire in A.D. 330.

Further to the east, Alexandria and Antioch, both extremely wealthy commercial centres, had each developed a distinctive tradition based on special regional interests. Accordingly, the early Christian Church was organized into four provinces, based on the four cities, with each province headed by a patriarch. Within a relatively short time, however, instead of the unity that had been hoped for, strong regional particularism came to be manifest.

The province of Constantinople was in closest touch with the seat of government, and therefore came to be identified with imperial authority. Moreover, by reason of its location, the Church in Constantinople was greatly influenced by Classical Greek rationalist thought, and, like the older pagan religions of the country, tended to employ much painting, sculpture and music in its ritual.

In the west, the patriarch of Rome inherited much of the ancient authoritarian tradition of the former capital city, and in spite of the newer supremacy of Constantinople, was able to exert a dominating influence on the Christians of the west. Far less affected by Greek thought, the Church in Rome developed a separate tradition of its own, more particularly as a western European church.

Christianity in Alexandria and Antioch was influenced to a varying extent by Oriental mysticism and speculation. Traces of the religion of ancient Egypt were manifest in the dogma and ritual adopted by the province of Alexandria; and other differences became apparent in Antioch. How far we can ascribe these variations in observance to historical accident, and how far to the slow operation of geographical factors, is a matter beyond our present scope; the main result is, however, of immediate importance, since within a relatively short space of time increasing divergence in doctrine and ritual led to a complete separation of the four provinces. From Constantinople arose the Greek Orthodox Church; from Rome the Roman Catholic or Latin Church; from Alexandria the Coptic Church; and from Antioch the Syrian or Jacobite Church (from St James); all of which soon came to possess complete independence in organization.

Further division, reflecting other regional diversity, rapidly occurred. By the fourth century, an independent Armenian (Gregorian) Church had come into existence; and the teachings of Nestorius, denounced as heresy in the west, were adopted by many in Iraq, Iran and countries further east. At a somewhat later period the sect of Maronites, followers of a Syriac monk named Maroun, came into existence in north-west Syria, and established themselves in northern Lebanon during the seventh to eleventh centuries A.D.

Later political developments in Europe and western Asia had great influence on the various religious communities of the Middle Eastern region. The supremacy of Constantinople passed away, and effective leadership amongst Christian peoples was taken over by the Church of Rome. The impact of Moslem conquest fell chiefly on the Christians of the east, so that groups like the Copts, Jacobites, Maronites and Nestorians (or Chaldeans) dwindled to tiny communities, whilst the Churches of Rome and Constantinople continued to flourish. At a later date, further expansion of Moslem power reduced the importance of the Greek Orthodox community, but later still this decline was partly offset by the rise of Russia, which adopted the Greek faith in preference to that of Rome.

During periods of Moslem persecution, the autonomous Christian sects of the east obtained support from the Church of Rome, but often at the price of obedience to Rome. Agreements were made whereby in return for recognition of the Pope as head of the community, local usages in doctrine and ritual were permitted to continue. Hence a number of eastern Christians broke away from sects such as the Jacobites or Nestorians and formed what are known as the Uniate Churches, i.e. communities with practices that differ widely from those of the main Roman Church[1] but which nevertheless accept the supremacy of the Pope. There have thus come into existence the Armenian Catholic, the Greek Catholic, the Syrian Catholic, the Coptic Catholic and the Chaldean (Nestorian) Catholic Churches. The entire Maronite Church entered into communion with Rome in the twelfth century. Formation of the Uniate Churches did not extinguish the older sects, some of which preferred a precarious independence; hence at the present time representatives of both groups, Uniate and non-Uniate, are to be found in the Middle East.

The Lebanon and western Syria, where a mountainous topography has afforded shelter to refugees, yet has also offered some reward to exploitation, now hold the greatest number of religious sects; and it is noteworthy that even as late as 1939, when the region of Alexandretta (Iskanderun) was ceded to Turkey, a number of Armenian Christians preferred to emigrate to Syria rather than remain to become Turkish citizens.

## Political effects

The origin and character of certain religious communities has been described at some length, because many features of social and political life in the modern Middle East derive from religious matters. Following conquest of much of the region by the Osmanli Turks during the fifteenth

---

[1] Chief of these are the use of Aramaic or Arabic instead of Latin in the liturgy, and a dispensation allowing lower orders of priests to marry.

Christian sects of the Middle East

| Ecclesiastical provinces of the later Roman Empire | Churches which derive from Roman provinces (independent) | Uniate Churches (in communion with Church of Rome) |
| --- | --- | --- |
| Constantinople ⟶ | Orthodox (Greek) | Greek Catholic |
| Rome ⟶ | Latin (Roman Catholic) | |
| Alexandria ⟶ | Coptic (Egyptian) | Coptic Catholic |
| Antioch ⟶ | Jacobite (Syrian) | Syrian |
| | Later Churches (also independent) | |
| | Armenian Orthodox | Armenian Catholic |
| | Nestorian (Chaldean or Assyrian) | Chaldean Catholic |
| | Maronite (until twelfth century) | Maronite (after twelfth century) |
| | Protestants (small in number; due to missionary activity in nineteenth century from Europe and America) | |

and sixteenth centuries, the *millet* system was adopted as the basis of civil administration in the Turkish Empire. This system merely institutionalized and refined an arrangement which had existed since the rise of Islam.

A *millet* was a separate religious community, with a leader who was recognized by the Ottoman Sultan as having important religious and civil functions.[1] This arose from the fact that, owing to the view that Islam was both a religious creed and a form of civil government, the status of non-Moslems was dubious, and had to be regulated in a special manner. Each head of a *millet* was a member of the local provincial administrative body, with right of direct access to the Sultan; and was in addition permitted to maintain a kind of law court of his own, which supervised such matters as marriage and dowries and even the inheritance of property among his co-religionists. A most important feature was the fact that non-Moslem communities were in some cases allowed to operate their own code of law, even when this differed from the official law of the Ottoman Empire.

Hence, in addition to his ecclesiastical function, the head of a *millet* had a considerable legal and civil power; and he could also call upon

[1] Many, but not all, of the Christian sects enumerated above were recognized as *millets*. Most important was the Greek Orthodox *millet*. The Jewish community also obtained *millet* status.

Turkish civil officials to give effect to his decisions. Moreover, consider-able economic power sometimes lay in the hands of the head of a *millet* by reason of the Moslem system of land tenure, which, particularly where there was a group ownership, gave him considerable responsibility for the allocation of holdings among tenant occupants.

The result of such organization was ultimately to create a number of 'states within a state'; and as time elapsed the heads of certain *millets* grew sufficiently powerful to obtain substantial privileges from the Sultan.

Another feature of the *millet* system was the opening given to interference by outside powers. France, as 'eldest daughter of the Church', assumed the role of champion of the Roman Catholic and Uniate communities; and, after the eighteenth century, Russia, a Greek Orthodox state, increasingly intervened in favour of the Greek Christians. One of the many issues of the Crimean War concerned the rivalry of Uniate and Orthodox communities in Jerusalem, and their relation to the Ottoman government.

In the nineteenth century, American, British and German Protestant missionary activity gained a small number of converts[1] and gave rise to a number of educational and cultural establishments in various parts of the Middle East – American, British, French, Prussian (German), and Italian. These enterprises were unofficial, and, generally speaking, the various national governments concerned made little attempt to use them as grounds for intervention in the politics of the Middle East. Although now declining, the intellectual influence of these institutions has, however, been considerable, especially as regards American schools and the American University of Beirut, which dates from 1866 and draws students from many parts of the Middle East.[2] A number of present-day leaders of the Palestine Liberation Movement are A.U.B. alumni.

A further feature deriving from the *millet* system has been the emphasis given to religion as a basis of political grouping. Although *millets* ended with the fall of the Ottoman Empire in 1918, the habit of associating politics with religion still persists in the Middle East. Insistence on sectarian differences as a basis of political grouping has tended to produce an atmosphere of strife and conflict, and the restlessness, faction and extreme individualism that characterize many present-day political affairs hinder co-operation, and hence retard the development of a stable form of government.

The influence of religion on political organization still persists. The Lebanon is an extreme example. Until 1975 the structure of government

---

[1]  The Protestant Armenians were given *millet* status in 1847.
[2]  It is probable that during the French occupation of Syria and the Lebanon the Mandatory power did not always view the American educational establishments of Beirut, Tripoli and Aleppo with wholehearted approval, because of the non-French outlook of these institutions.

itself was organized on a religious basis. There was an understanding that the president should be a Maronite and the prime minister usually a Sunni Moslem, with the other government portfolios and parliamentary seats allocated on a *pro-rata* basis per religious group so that the religion mattered more than the individual cabinet minister himself. Other instances are known, especially in Israel where the relationship between religion and the state is particularly complex. An important factor is the existence of religious political parties of which the largest, the National Religious Party, has been a member of most governing coalitions since the state was founded in 1948. The question of just how much Judaism there should be in a modern Jewish state remains a critical and as yet unresolved issue. In Turkey, extremist religious political parties also hold the balance of power between Right and Left; and in 1977, Egypt, in an effort to appease Muslim zealots, proposed that apostacy from the Islamic faith could be punishable by death.

*Islam*

Shortly after A.D. 600 Muhammad,[1] a fairly poor member of the important family of Qureish, began to preach a doctine that had come to him by divine revelation. His message was first received with amusement and indifference, later with hostility; so that in A.D. 622 he decided to leave his native city of Mecca and established himself at Medina. This flight, or *Hegira*, from Mecca to Medina is taken as the beginning of the Islamic era, though it was not until some time after that Muhammad's teachings were accepted by the Meccans. Much of Muhammad's teaching was his own; part was derived from Christian and Jewish beliefs, with which he had a slight acquaintance. Born into a merchant community in the trading city of Mecca, he was a citizen not a nomad, and Islam as he conceived it was, by virtue of its social constraints and its spiritual demands, very much a city religion. The rhythm of Islamic religious practices is made for city dwellers.

Muhammad preached submission (*Islam*) to the will of one god, Allah, of whom Muhammad was the chosen prophet. Besides the profession of faith, the chief ritual duties enjoined on Moslems include (*a*) prayer, five times daily, (*b*) fasting during the month of Ramadan, (*c*) the giving of alms, and (*d*) pilgrimage, if possible, to Mecca. In addition, mention should also be made of the Moslem prohibition of alcohol and pork.[2]

---

[1] This form of the name is somewhat closer to the Arabic sound than the more usual Mohammed.

[2] The geographer may note with some interest the possible operation of a climatic factor. Pigs in the Middle East are much less healthy than in cooler latitudes, being often infested with parasites that can be transferred to humans. It would also seem that in a warmer climate the intoxicating effect of alcohol is heightened.

Although there are other elements of belief and practice that set Islam apart from other religions, the five 'Pillars of the Faith' remain the most distinctive. Islam has no consecrated priesthood, and the *imam* (leader) who conducts the faithful in prayer and the *sheikh* (elder) who delivers the sermon are laymen not necessarily occupying positions of prominence but generally respected for their moral and intellectual qualities. In fact the act of prayer can be carried out anywhere, although Moslems are supposed to meet together at the chief mosque for the prayer at midday on Friday. The mass of the people, however, found that observance of the basic duties of Islam was not enough, and the worship of saints spread rapidly, often integrating local religious traditions. This innovation, which quickly became an important part of popular religious life, was eventually accepted as orthodox practice.

The five 'Pillars of the Faith' are central supports of the *Sharia*, the Islamic law. Divinely inspired, the Sharia has been revealed to man through the Koran and through the recorded actions and statements of Muhammad known as the *hadiths* (traditions). The task of interpreting the legacy of the Prophet and building the Sharia was achieved during the first three centuries of Islam, mainly through the achievements of the *ulema*, Moslem theologians and legal experts. Nevertheless, although agreed on many essentials, there emerged among the *ulema* many different schools of interpretation, varying 'pathways to the truth' as they were known. They ranged from mildly liberal in their outlook to strictly fundamentalist. Four legal schools still exist today, named after their founders – the Maliki, the oldest, found in North Africa and the Sudan; the Hanafi, the most flexible and the official school in most countries of the Arab east (except for the Arabian peninsula); the Shafii, which prevails in northern Egypt; and the Hanbali, found in Saudi Arabia. The first two schools are somewhat modernistic and progressive; the last two conservative in outlook. However, in spite of these differences, each school has long accepted the others as orthodox, and in many countries a person may choose to be judged according to a school different from that officially recognized by the state.

One important feature of Islam has been the close connection between religion and civil government. To Moslems Islam provides a full way of life, with complete interpenetration of civil, religious and even economic activities, and codes of law, derived from religious bases. Islam and the State, for the devout, are one, recognized by the fact that formerly the political head of state held religious functions, under the title Defender or Leader of the Faith (Caliph). This makes for great cohesiveness in society, but is also a difficulty for modernists – can one really divorce a modern secular state properly from Islam?

Within a very few years, from being an obscure doctrine held by a small group of townsfolk and nomads in the arid interior of Arabia, Islam had spread into Palestine, Syria, Egypt, Iraq and Iran. The surprising political success of the new religion in establishing itself alongside the Byzantine and Iranian Empires, which at that time divided the Middle East, is startling when one considers how poor were the followers of Muhammad in numbers and material resources. In order to explain how a group of shepherds, merchants and camel drivers came to wrest the greater part of the Middle East, within a few decades, from the successors of Imperial Rome and Sassanid Persia, a number of factors must be considered.

Politically and militarily, both the Byzantine Empire to the west and the Sassanid Empire of Iran were exhausted. Long-continued warfare between the two powers, with Armenia, Syria, Iraq and Palestine as a battleground, had achieved no definite results, since both belligerents were too large and too remote to be entirely overrun by the other. Border raids and skirmishes had, however, devastated much of the central part of the Middle East, and the high taxation and misery that resulted had made local populations very ready to acquiesce in a change of masters. Rigid social divisions and indifference to the lot of the peasant did not serve to popularize either Byzantine or Sassanid rule.

Spiritually too, the common people of the Middle East had become weary. Unending theological debates in the Christian world, with intricate discussions of forms of belief and doctrine, were frequently beyond understanding by the average Anatolian or Syrian peasant; but the charges of schism and heresy that resulted led to much general persecution and oppression, first by one sect, then by another. This, in contrast, had obvious effect on the native population. In Iran, the finer ideas of Zoroaster had become overlain by a number of gross practices borrowed from earlier religions, or else were too abstract in conception for the mass of the people. In either instance, the appeal of a new religion, direct and simple to understand, with a clear relationship to matters of everyday life, and which offered a brotherhood of man in place of the formalities of Zoroastrianism or the strict class distinctions of Byzantine society, had an immediate appeal. Buttressing all this were the material gains to be made from conquest. Sectarian differences among Christians were in fact so acute that on some occasions persecuted minorities opened the gates of Byzantine cities to Moslem attackers. The rapidity with which Islam developed and spread, with enormous impact on life and culture in an area extending from China to France, is one of the most remarkable features of history. One has to wait for the spread of Communist doctrines during the present century for any real parallel.

*Sectarian divisions within Islam*

Over the centuries, although there have been numerous sectarian divisions in the House of Islam, these sects account for only some 10% of the Moslem World, and the orthodox or Sunni branch (*Sunni* means majority or orthodox) has prevailed as a powerful majority. All four legal schools, for example, are Sunni. The appearance of divisions within the Moslem community was a direct consequence of the nature of Islam itself. An important feature, already noted, was the close connection between religion and the state. In the early centuries because Islam and the state were one, a revolt against the central power was often accompanied by a religious crisis. Indeed, as politics and religion were inextricably interwoven, religion provided the only possible expression of sustained opposition. Sectarian divisions were therefore nearly always political in origin, but later differences of doctrine and outlook developed.

Muhammad left no male heirs nor did he nominate a successor so that his death in A.D. 632 precipitated a political crisis. In the course of the 7th century a struggle developed for the succession to the caliphate between Ali, Muhammad's cousin and also son-in-law, and the younger Omeyyad branch of the Prophet's family. During these events, two main heretical groups developed, expressing in religious terms the opposition of certain parties to the existing social and political order. The earliest of the dissident sects, the *Kharijites* (or 'seceders') believed that the caliphate should be open to all Moslems and not merely men of Muhammad's own family. They have been described as the anarchist wing of revolutionary opposition in Islam. Their egalitarian fervor played an important role in the Islamization of the Berbers of North Africa, but today only small scattered communities survive in the Middle East – in the Jebel Nefusa in Libya and in Oman.

The second and by far the most important opposition group was the party of Ali, commonly known as the *Shi'a* (partisans). After Ali was eventually defeated by the Omeyyads, his loyal followers refused to accept his abdication. When he was assassinated in A.D. 661 by the Kharijites, his supporters started a movement to restore the caliphate to the family of Ali, and this political group rapidly developed into a remarkable and distinctive religious sect. The Shi'a were convinced that the Omeyyad and Abbasid caliphs set out systematically to eliminate the descendants of Ali, and they transformed these victims of political manoeuvering into semi-divine martyrs, known as *imams*. A decisive element of separateness became the importance attributed by the Shi'a to the imams and the virtual exclusion of Muhammad. Many other factors separated Shi'a from Sunni Moslems but particularly important are their intense emotionalism (expressed especially during the focal point of their religious year, the first 10 days of the month of Muharram), their ingrained suspiciousness over religious matters and their intolerance born of periodic repression and persecution over the centuries. The Shi'a also have their own holy places, notably the tombs of their imams at Karbala and Nejf (Najaf) in Iraq, which are more important to the Shi'a as places of pilgrimage than Mecca or Medina.

Today the strongholds of the Shi'a are in Iran and Iraq. In the past some authorities have seen in the differences between Sunni and Shi'a a reflection of the separate cultural evolution of the Iranian world. Shi'ism has been portrayed as a liberal revival of the Persian national genius and as a resurgence of the Aryanism of Iran against the alien Semitism of Arabian Islam. But persistent identification of Shi'ism with Iran and the expression of racial conflict must now be abandoned. Research has revealed that the main centres of the early Shi'a movement were among the predominantly Semitic-speaking peoples of southern Iraq and that Shi'a Islam was first introduced into Persia by the Arabs themselves, and for many years found its main supporters among the Arab soldiers and settlers. The Shi'a gained their earliest political successes in north-west Africa, Egypt and Arabia, and it was not until the sixteenth century that these doctrines were imposed on a predominantly Sunni population in Iran by the Safavid rulers who were of Turkish origin. Their success can thus be explained only in terms of the moral and political condition of Iran during the sixteenth century and not by reference to the schisms and conflicts of earlier times.

The majority of the Shi'a recognize the existence of twelve imams beginning with Ali, and are known as *Twelvers*. The twelfth imam is believed to have disappeared and will one day re-emerge as the Mahdi or new Messiah. This group is dominant in Iran – the only state where Shi'ism is the state religion; they represent over half the population of Iraq; they form a compact community in southern and eastern Lebanon under the local name of Metwali; and considerable numbers are also found in Bahrain.

Not all Shi'a are Twelvers. The *Zaidis* only recognize the first four imams, and there is little in their beliefs and practices to distinguish them from orthodox Moslems. At the end of the ninth century the Zaidis established their control over North Yemen, and although the majority of the population remained Sunni, Zaidi imams continued to rule there until the 1962 revolution, which led to the creation of a republic. Another group, the *Ismailis* or *Seveners*, originated in the belief by some Shi'a that Ismail, the son of the sixth imam, was unjustly accused of unworthy conduct by the Twelvers. They set out to vindicate him, and during the ninth century launched a vigorous campaign to overthrow the orthodox Abbasid caliphate. They did not succeed, but a group of Ismailis seized power in North Africa in the tenth century and established the Fatimid caliphate which ruled in Cairo until the twelfth century. With the decline of the Fatimids, the Ismailis did not disappear. In the eleventh century a Persian leader of the sect founded an extremist political group, the Assassins, some of whom were drug takers (hashishin = assassins). Their executions of key political figures were acts of ritual murder. From their strongholds in the Elburz and Syrian mountains they terrorized much of the Middle East until they were suppressed in the mid thirteenth century. A remnant of the sect still survives in north-west Syria with other communities scattered through Iran, Oman, Zanzibar and India, and in the nineteenth and twentieth centuries they emerged from obscurity under a leader known as the Aga Khan. They now depend on business success to advance their cause rather than assassinations.

Ismaili missionary activity also resulted in the creation of some sects incorporating so many non-Islamic practices that they are sometimes regarded as separate faiths. The most notable are the Alawi and the Druzes. The *Alawi* (worshippers of Ali) carry to the extreme the Shi'a deification of Ali. They retain certain features of pagan cults and follow a ritual adopted largely from Christianity, including the celebration of Christmas and Easter. Today their main centre is in the Jebel Ansarieh in north-west Syria, and the present President of Syria is an Alawi.

The *Druzes* trace their origins to an eleventh century Ismaili missionary, Darazi, whose supporters recognized the Fatimid Caliph Hakim as the hidden Imam. Druze doctrine and practice differ widely from Moslem orthodoxy. Belief in the transmigration of souls is widespread; they do not observe Ramadan or make the pilgrimage to Mecca; and polygamy is forbidden. To escape Sunni persecution the Druzes found refuge in the mountains of southern Lebanon and in the Jebel Druze in southern Syria.

A modern heretical movement in which Ismaili doctrine played a prominent role is the *Bahai* faith. The movement began in the mid nineteenth century in Iran where a young religious teacher declared himself to be the hidden Imam. As a reaction against materialism, corruption and self-seeking the movement won many converts in Persia but was repressed with great severity by the government. The survivors became known as Bahis, after Bahaullah a disciple of the founder, and are noted for their tolerance, and their strong commitment to social improvement and international peace. Although subjected to intermittent persecution in Iran, the Bahai faith has spread beyond the Middle East, and there are now scattered communities all over the world.

Unlike the Christians and Jews, these heretical Moslem sects were not allowed the status of millet, and instead it was persecution – especially by the Ottoman Turks – which strengthened the bonds uniting their members. While the 'peoples of the book' (i.e. Jews and Christians, whom Muhammad knew) became concentrated mainly in the urban centres where they enjoyed the protection of the ruler, the Shi'a and other heretical Moslem sects installed themselves at a distance from centres of urban power and orthodoxy in remote regions, mountain refuges and desert oases. Geographical segregation, isolation in regions difficult of access, poor communications, and distance from an often weak central authority were important factors which helped these communities to remain coherent units and retain their identity. In recent years, however, increased security, improved communications and new economic opportunities have resulted in the gradual abandonment of many of these refuges. Migration from the mountains to the plains – of the Druzes from the Lebanese mountains and the Alawi and Ismaili from the Jebel Ansarieh in Syria – and from remote rural areas to the towns and cities, are breaking down the old pattern of religious segregation. Even the residual elements are being subjected to more and more vigorous processes of assimilation.

### Sufism

Sufism is the spirituality or mysticism of the religion of Islam. Its main tenet is belief in a mystical union of the human soul and the Deity, with omnipresence of God's purpose and guidance: in many ways man acts as inspired directly by God, and is not a wholly free agent: there could be an element of predestination. Meditation, spiritual possession, prayer and asceticism are components of the Sufi way of life, which aims at human behaviour determined by God's will. The term *Sufi* is derived from the Arabic word for wool (*suf*) and refers to the coarse woollen garments worn by the early Sufi ascetics. Nearly two hundred major Sufi *tariqas* (orders) are recorded during the history of Islam. Each tariqa consisted of a leader (sheikh) and his disciples (dervishes) who were supported by lay members. Two distinct types of brotherhood emerged – the urban orders such as the Qadiriya and Naqshbandiya, characterized by moderation and with close links with Sunni orthodoxy; and the rural orders, the Rifaiya and Bektashi, with wider popular support and often following practices (walking through fire, eating glass, self-wounding without pain) borrowed from paganism, Shiism or Christianity, and denounced by orthodox Moslems.

A revival of the orders occurred in the nineteenth century with the appearance of a number of new movements including the Sanussi. The Sanussi movement affected Algeria, Egypt and Arabia but took deepest root in Libya where it played a leading part in the Arab struggle against Italian penetration after the withdrawal of Ottoman Turkish rulers in 1912–18. Following the Second World War, the (by then) exiled Sanussi leader, the Emir Idris, was recognized as head of the Libyan people; and, with the attainment of Libyan independence in 1951, ruled as king of Libya until the Revolution of 1969.

At the beginning of the twentieth century, the hold the Sufi orders exercised over the people was still strong, but as the century progressed their popularity declined with government action against them, and the spread of secularist ideas. This process of change has greatly undermined the orders, and many have declined or virtually disappeared, though the Green Dervishes of Konya (Turkey) still have some political influence, and there is a Dervish mosque at Damascus.

### Wahhabism

Wahhabism began during the eighteenth century in the Arabian peninsula as a reaction to the popular practice of Sufism and its preoccupation with saints and sheikhs. The founder, Muhammad ibn Abd al-Wahab, and his followers called for the purification of Islam and a return to the primitive nature of the faith as preached by Muhammad. It was felt that there had been much backsliding; many of the precepts of Islam, especially those relating to self-indulgence,[1] were ignored; and, in addition, much superstition and unnecessary elaboration had crept into religious observance. The Wahhabi preached a return to austerity and simplicity, and may thus be called the Puritans of Islam.

At an early date, the Wahhabi formed a political alliance with the Saudi family who had their capital at Riyadh in the centre of the Arabian peninsula. The Wahhabis came into great prominence a the beginning of the twentieth century when the Saudis under the leadership of Abdul Aziz ibn Saud succeeded in conquering the Holy cities of Medina and Mecca compelling the rest of the Moslem world to give attention if not acceptance to Wahhabi doctrines. The present state of Saudi Arabia, the creation of ibn Saud, remains a stronghold of Wahhabism and of Moslem conservatism.

### Paganism

Older beliefs and practices have not entirely died out in the Middle East, and their influence remains to colour the observances of the newer religions – often to a surprising degree. The Greek Orthodox Church has recognized as saints and martyrs a number of which would seem to be local deities of an older pagan pantheon; whilst in the Lebanon a group of trees near the mouth of the Nahr Ibrahim, once hung with votive offerings by the worshippers of Adonis, is still decked with strips of cloth at Eastertime by a Christian population, and until fairly recently barren

---

[1] I.e. the prohibition of smoking and drinking alcohol.

women made pilgrimages to the area in the hope of having children. Perhaps more striking still, the Ka'aba or Black Stone at Mecca, now a holy relic of Islam, had originally no connection in any way with Muhammad, but was worshipped long before his time as a tribal fetish. Also, other influences deriving from more primitive forms of religion, such a fertility rites and cults, tend to occur in some rural areas alongside more orthodox religious observances. Two distinct communities practise religious observances in which both Christian and Zoroastrian borrowings can be discerned – curiously enough, little seems to have come from Moslem sources.

The Yazidi of the Jebel Sinjar region in north-west Iraq are sometimes spoken of as worshippers of Satan. But, in fact, far from being devil worshippers their prime tenet is antidualist, denying the existence of evil, sin and the devil, and it is for this reason and not out of reverence, that they abhor the name of Satan. The Yazidi owe their survival as a separate religious community to centuries of persecution by both Kurds and Arabs, Sunni and Shi'a and to the difficult nature and isolation of the terrain they inhabit. But what persecution failed to achieve is being rapidly realized by the modernization of Iraq. At the beginning of the twentieth century there were 150000 Yazidi: today there are probably no more than 30000.

The Mandeans or Sabians live in the marshes of lower Mesopotamia in close proximity to the rivers. About one fifth of the community lives in the Iranian districts of Ahwaz and Khurramshahr, the rest in Iraq. Their beliefs are derived from the gnostic sects which sprang from the dying struggles of paganism with advancing Christianity, blended with some Zoroastrian elements. Their notoriety in the West has been for their discipleship of St John the Baptist, and for their strict practice of baptism in flowing water. Unlike the Yazidi, the Mandeans were not persecuted by their Moslem neighbours, and like the Christians and Jews they are mentioned in the Koran as 'people of the book'. They are famous as boat-builders in their native marshes, and in the suqs of Amara, Baghdad and Basra as Iraq's finest silversmiths. Today, Mandeans number no more than 20000.

*Religion and modern life*

In the past religious groupings were the main focus of political and social loyalties in the Middle East, of a sense of belonging. The present age is of sharp religious transition and reappraisal, and one in which influence of Western imperialism and rising nationalism has been profound. Different views regarding the role of religion and the state have emerged. In some states, notably Turkey, Egypt and to some extent Iran, nationalism is tending to replace religion as the principal socially cohesive force.

Westernizing reforms have been imposed, often ruthlessly, including the nationalizing of *waqf* revenues and the introduction of modern Western-style, legal and educational systems. Increasingly identity is defined and loyalty claimed on national rather than communal lines, while criticisms and aspirations are expressed not in religious but in secular terms. In contrast, in certain other countries religious feeling is still the mainspring of rule. In Saudi Arabia the political authority of the ruler traditionally derives from his alliance with the Wahhabi movement, and in Libya the regime of Colonel Gaddafi sees politics as true religion controlled by the religious state. Sectarian relations remain a fundamental issue in Lebanon, and in Israel too, differences between traditionalist and modernist inter-pretations of Judaism are highly important matters. Religious groupings retain some of their former importance as a social framework, although rapid urbanization and economic change are leading to the formation of new allegiances based not on religion but on occupation, wealth and social class.

The drive for reform and for change in the Middle East is widespread. Some believe that this can only be achieved through a rejection of the West and a return to the fundamentals of Islam – the Moslem Brotherhood is an example of such a movement; for some a secularization of society through, for example a socialist or Marxist approach represents the only way forward; while others attempt a middle way. Recently a view has been put forward which rejects the ideologies of both capitalist and socialist systems in favour of a more 'authentic' Islamic socialism. Yet whatever the future, Islam remains a force in the Middle East. It can still be a powerful rallying cry, and an attack on God and religion can arouse the anger and resistance of the Moslem masses. The wholesale repudiation of Islamic traditions in Turkey during the 1920s and 30s contributed to the eventual defeat of the Republican party in the 1950 elections, and the victorious Democratic party quietly restored religious education in state schools and made other concessions to Islam. It is also interesting to note that in recent years the self-styled 'revolutionary' states, notably Syria and Iraq, have become more, not less, self-consciously Islamic, and a number of Middle Eastern states have been influenced by the political assertion of Islam by certain oil-rich Arab states. Even those Moslems who have rejected Islam often retain Islamic habits and attitudes; and new values and ideologies are sometimes merely an artificial and superficial veneer. Moreover, with the manifest limitations of present-day secular forms of government, there would seem to be nowadays a very marked and large-scale turning towards and revival of religion, especially Islam as a political force. An appreciation of Islam is still very necessary in order to understand the contemporary Middle East and its peoples.

# 6 Human society
# in the Middle East

For centuries human society in the Middle East has been divided into
three different types of communities – nomads (*Badawin*), settled cultivators (*Hadhar*) and townspeople. Through history, many writers have
been impressed by the contrasts in ways of life and social organization
shown by these three groups; and until recently there was a tendency
to stress the isolation of the cultivators and the Badawin from the
'civilizing' influences of urban life. P. W. English, however, has put
forward a modified approach – the concept of the Middle East ecological
trilogy. He emphasizes that although Middle East society was divisible
into three distinct types of communities, these were mutually dependent
'each with a distinctive lifemode, each operating in a different setting,
each contributing to the support of the other two sectors and thus to the
maintenance of total society'. Commerce was one activity which played
an important role in the development of close mutual relations within this
ecological system. Besides the merchant body directly engaged in
exchange of products, the organization of long-distance transport involved
a supply of foodstuffs and other agricultural products, and hence the
Hadhar of the rural areas were involved. Badawin were also employed
as guides and drivers; and safe conduct money was sometimes paid to
nomads. Woodmen, tent and harness makers also had a marginal part
to play. Nevertheless, the benefits of this interdependence were unequally
divided, and urban dominance is central to the concept of the ecological
trilogy. Recent changes, however, have disturbed the equilibrium between
these three communities, and the forces of modernization are producing
new patterns and new relationships.

## The Badawin

The main feature of this group is, of course, regular movement in search of pasture for animals. For the greater part this movement is from one district to another, i.e. true nomadism; but in mountain regions different levels in the same district are occupied successively and this is termed transhumance. The nomadism is, in effect, horizontal movement; transhumance is more a change in altitude. The Badawin of Arabia may be cited as true nomads whilst certain of the Kurds of Anatolia and the western Zagros tend rather to practise transhumance.

With rainfall, and therefore pasture, both scanty in amount and liable to much variation from one year to another, the nomads have found that experience provides the best means of survival. Thus to the oldest members of the group is given the task of making decisions which guide the activities of the entire community – accent is, so to speak, on age, not youth. Frequently too, in the face of sudden crisis (failure of wells or attack by outsiders) rapid decision is called for, and one man alone rather than a group is looked to as supreme leader – in warfare particularly more confidence is felt in a single man than in a committee. This type of social organization, termed patriarchal, places the life of a community under the control of a chosen man, and is highly characteristic of nomadic pastoralists. The chief (sheikh) of the community has considerable personal power, which is tempered only by precedent (the collective experience of the group as a whole) and by the opinion of older members of the tribe. There is little place for individuality or for innovation, and patriarchal communities have kept their way of life largely unaltered through many centuries.

A sharp limit to the size of social groupings amongst nomads is set by natural resources, which in a given district can support only a relatively small number of people. Thus the unit amongst Badawin is the tribe – a group large enough to profit by advantage of numbers, yet small enough to exist under desert conditions. Family relationship is strong, and perpetuated by emphasis on intermarriage within the group. Yet although tribal solidarity and discipline are conspicuous features, it has been the weakness of Badawin society throughout the ages that political combinations larger than the tribe have been achieved merely for a very short time. An outstanding leader has brought together a number of tribes into one larger unit, but union has proved temporary: more often than not, on the death of the leader his organization has dissolved again into smaller groups. Large-scale political organization is not, therefore, a feature of Badawin society, and resulting intertribal feuds, inveterate warfare, political instability, and inconstancy, have had an effect not merely on desert and steppe life, but also on that of the settled lands of the arid borders. To each tribe belong certain rights of pasture and occupation.

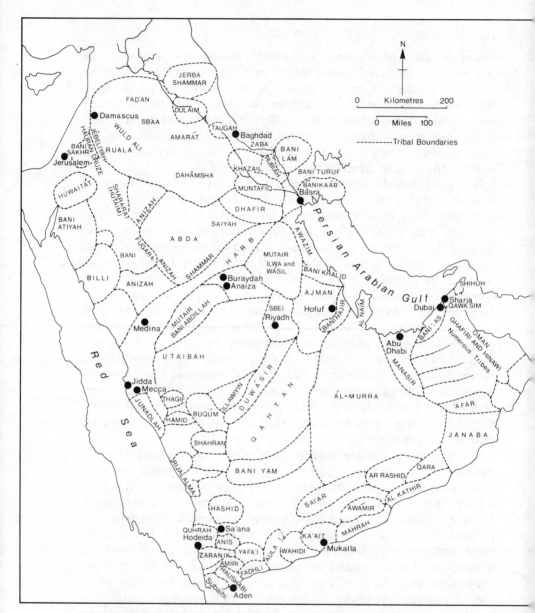

*Fig.* 6.1 Tribal map of Arabia (not all tribal groups shown); data in part from H. P. Dickson.

The limits of each tribal territory are carefully defined, and generally comprise a summer and a winter camping ground. Exact size of territory usually has a certain relation to the physical force and prestige commanded by each tribe, and limits, therefore, vary from one period to another. Weaker tribes seek 'protection' from a larger.

Environmental conditions within desert areas vary considerably, with resulting variation in influence on the precise way of life of the inhabitants. For example, the northern part of the Arabian desert is a vast open tableland, dissected into occasional shallow valleys or closed basins; whilst further south, topography varies from a succession of jagged uplands, *poljes*, lava-fields and highly eroded basins and valleys, passing eastward into distinctly more subdued relief. Climate, especially rainfall, also shows significant variation: in western Arabia there can be sufficient for sporadic cultivation, with or without irrigation. Human response to these conditions is extremely varied in character. Near the Euphrates, relatively short-distance movement with sheep- and goat-rearing is the rule, with an approach to transhumance rather than full nomadism in the extreme north on the edge of the mountain rim of Turkey–Kurdistan. Further south, in the open zones between Damascus, Baghdad and Jordan, more extensive migration based on the use of the camel is characteristic; whilst in Arabia proper there are all stages from extensive movement, involving camels as the basis of the economy, to partial nomadism only, with an approach to cultivation and semi-settlement. A similar state of affairs exists in the deserts of Libya, whilst Sven Hedin described certain nomads of Iran who sometimes covered 2000 km in an annual movement between the interior deserts and the Elburz uplands. On the Jebel Akhdar of Cyrenaica, nomads have a complicated annual routine involving a double seasonal movement to and from the uplands with an approach to cultivation. Further south, movement is around wells within the more arid zones, whilst the presence of oases allows the existence of completely settled agricultural communities. Camels can go several days without watering, sheep four, cattle one or two.

It is thus possible to draw a summary distinction between camel-nomads, who usually cover great distances; shepherds, whose territory may be more confined; and semi-nomadic or transhumant groups, often with cattle, who practise some degree of cultivation. This pattern is in constant fluctuation, partly as the result of climatic vagaries, and also with slower changes in numbers and influence. Where tribal territories cross international frontiers, special problems arise, and whilst agreements give to nomads temporary nationality of the country in which they find themselves, this arrangement is not wholly agreeable to the governments involved.

Because of the necessity for constant movement, the material culture of the Badawin is poor. Chief possession of the tribesman, after his animals, is a tent, usually black or brown and woven of camel or goat hair. When in good repair, these tents are quite waterproof – sufficient to withstand the infrequent but severe downpours which occur – and the size of the tent, shown by the number of tent poles used, is an indication of the affluence and social standing of the owner.

Clothing of the Badawin is simple. A long robe of thick material is the principal garment, with in winter, a waterproof cloak of woven camel hair. A voluminous headcloth, held in place by a rope or band, is wound round the head so as to given protection to the face and neck, and rawhide, heel-less sandals are worn on the feet.

Water is usually too precious for much washing – indeed, the Koran permits the ceremonial use of sand in the daily ablutions which are enjoined on all Moslems – and animal urine is frequently used as a substitute. Badawin food is monotonous and scanty. Most important are milk products: curds, buttermilk, various kinds of cheese – of which *labne*, a kind of cream cheese, is the most widespread – and *samne*, or butter. In addition, wheat and barley and occasionally a little rice are obtained from agriculturalists, or else grown very sporadically by the nomads themselves.[1] Small amounts of dried fruit, usually dates, are also eaten. Meat is provided only as a great luxury, since animals themselves are in effect a kind of fixed capital – owners must live from the yield, not upon the animal itself. Apart, then, from occasions of high festival, when special slaughtering takes place, only those animals that die naturally are eaten. In general, the standard of nutrition of the Badawin is low – in the opinon of some, below the level necessary in other regions to sustain life. As a result, the Badawin are small, even stunted and lightly built, though their physical powers and endurance are great. Life is, however, very hard; and by forty, particularly in the case of women, old age has begun. Fifty years is a long life for a nomad.

One means of supplementing the deficiencies in arid areas is by raiding. Amongst the Badawin the *ghazu* is a recognized activity amounting almost to sport, but it also fulfils a definite economic function. The effects of a bad season are mitigated, as when rains have failed in the desert, the Badawi has a choice of taking what he requires by force from other people, or of starving. The word 'sport' has been used because, although fundamentally a serious matter, Badawin raids are conducted under certain conventions – almost, one might say, rules.[2] Rapid, unlooked-for coups, using cunning and guile, are most favoured: bloodshed is as far

[1] Patches of ground are roughly sown with grain, and later in the year tribesmen return to harvest the crop.

[2] There are only three sources of amusement or distraction in Badawin life: conversation round a coffee hearth, family life, and raiding.

as possible avoided, although goods, women-folk and children become the property of the victors under a kind of slavery. Successful leadership in tribal raids is the means by which personal reputation and power are built up: King Ibn Saud, originally a dispossessed nomad, gained absolute power in Arabia through successful tribal encounters on an increasingly large scale. Badawin raids may be directed against other tribes, but frequently toll is levied on agricultural settlements on the fringe of the desert. Less able to resist, and with more at stake than the nomad, settled cultivators sometimes remain under permanent tribute to Badawin tribes and supply a quantity of needed foodstuffs to their overlords. The name *khaoua* (tribute of friendship) is applied to such transactions. Raiding is now greatly declining, because of increasing control by local governments, but in addition to the political problem presented in controlling outbreaks, there is the economic factor of providing alternative occupation to ensure a livelihood. Though declining, the practice is still not totally extinct. Even in 1946, J. C. Crowfoot could write: 'Arabs are now raiding each other in Fords and Chevrolets'.

Strict discipline, necessary both in everyday routine and because of liability to attack, has left its mark on Badawin ways of thought. In religion, there is little room for compromise or doubt – a strong, vivid and intolerant faith is held. Similarly, there is a strict code of behaviour. Hospitality, in an environment without fixed routes or settlements, is a highly regarded virtue, and ordinary social intercourse has been developed into an elaborate code of manners and conduct. In view of the vagaries of human existence amongst the Badawin, it is hardly surprising that superstition and fatalism are also strongly marked. The operation of the 'evil eye' and malevolent spirits is seen in everyday life – nothing is praised directly without attributing its excellence as due to God – and men, animals and even motor vehicles carry charms. Possibly as a result of reduced physical strength, and their enforced preoccupation with household tasks, the status of women is low, although they are not veiled, like many of the women of the settled areas.

Nomadism is a special response to environment, by which the frontier of human occupation is pushed further within a region of increasing difficulty. In the past, nomadism has often been regarded as an unsatisfactory alternative to agriculture; it was believed that primitive man passed from a life of hunting and collecting first into a stage of pastoralism, and later, in places where conditions were favourable, to the fullest development of a life based on cultivation. It is clear that pastoralism may in certain instances represent a development from cultivation – a dynamic response to environmental and social conditions, and not necessarily a regression or half-stage between hunting and gathering and settled cultivation.

At a particular historic period, or in a special locality, it is possible to observe the shift towards nomadic pastoralism in response to various pressures. At the present day, however, it is right to say that the tendencies are strongly in the opposite direction, i.e. towards sedentarization of nomads. This is apparent in almost all areas, due to the 'pull' of increased opportunities of employment in towns and higher urban standards, and the 'push' by reduction of natural grazing grounds as these are taken over for other purposes, and the pressure by governments which often find nomads unsatisfactory and unreliable citizens. In the recent past, forcible measures have been taken to settle nomadic tribesmen (e.g. in Iran and Turkey), but it was often found that poverty and disease increased to such an extent as to bring about virtual extinction of some communities.

Despite these considerable changes, it can be argued that pastoral nomadism has a continuing part to play, though of greatly reduced significance. This is because, in certain localities, pastoralism is still the only possible means of land evaluation. Cultivation may not be possible or other resources non-existent, hence semi-arid lands can produce the wool, milk and meat now increasingly required in the towns. To achieve this, an enlightened policy will be necessary: provision of rural credit, grading and marketing schemes for animals, co-operatives, provision of health, education and veterinary services; and above all, an acceptance by the central government that nomads are not to be regarded as second-class or dangerous citizens.

Reliable figures of numbers do not, for fairly obvious reasons, exist, but a figure of 5–7% of the total population would seem to be a reasonable approximation for all countries other than the Sudan. Most nomads live in the Sudan, Turkey, Iran and Arabia, with 750000 to 1·5 million possibly in each of the last three countries. Syria has about 150000, Iraq about 60000, Egypt under 50000, Israel and Jordan about 25000–30000, and there are perhaps 200000 in Libya. The Sudan is a special case. An official census (1973) gives 11% of the total population of the country as nomadic, but some writers put the figure at 30–40%, i.e. 4–6 million.

### Villages and cultivators

The decline in nomadism, especially since the late nineteenth century, contributed to an increase in the settled rural population in the Middle East, and today, despite recent rural to urban migration, between one half and two-thirds of the region's population live in village communities, the vast majority as cultivators. To take Iraq as an example, the settled rural population increased absolutely from just over half a million in the mid nineteenth century to nearly 2·25 million in 1930, and relatively from 41–68% of the total population; since 1930 the total rural population has continued to rise but there has been a relative decline from 61% in 1947 to 56% at the last census in 1965.

From time immemorial the village has been the typical form of rural settlement in the Middle East, and there are few isolated farms and farmhouses. Dispersed settlement is impractical in many parts of the region because of the scarcity of water – the primary determinant in the distribution of population and the location of villages. Lack of security and protection from attack, and the common practice of collective ownership of land, where lands were held in the name of the whole village, were also factors favouring nucleation. Other influences contributed to the survival of this pattern of settlement. The big landowners and their agents could supervise and control the tenants and sharecroppers more easily and effectively in nucleated villages than in scattered farmsteads. A communal pattern of agriculture and co-operative forms of production prevailed in some parts of the region, especially in Iran, with open fields for grazing and frequent redistribution of holdings by the landlords. Government taxes were levied on the village as a unit, and not on individuals. In some areas, notably in Egypt, where cultivable land is in short supply, construction beyond the limits of the village was actually forbidden. Over the centuries, social customs developed in such an environment have become obstacles to any change to a more dispersed pattern.

Most Middle Eastern villages are small, the average size being about 400–500 people. However, where population densities are unusually high, the villages become larger, pressure within them increases, and they occur in greater frequency. Villages in Egypt, for example, are generally larger than those in other Middle Eastern countries, and village population size ranges from 300–20000 people; on the other hand, the majority of Iranian villages have an average population of only 160 inhabitants.

In the plains and along the major river valleys, settlements are compact clusters of low dwellings normally built of mudbrick and separated from one another by narrow, winding, alleys and unpaved streets. They are situated on the least productive plots of ground, on rocky outcroppings, or along the edge of the desert and the sown, in order to avoid wasting valuable agricultural land. The traditional type of dwelling usually consists of a number of dark rooms built around an open courtyard which the family sometimes shares with their animals. Most homes are meagrely furnished one-storey structures. Many have no furniture except mats made of straw or blankets which, together with a few cooking and eating utensils, comprise most of the villagers' possessions. Water may have to be carried considerable distances, and is thus too precious for much washing; and though the kerosene stove has appeared widely in the last 10 years, dried animal dung may still be used as fuel for cooking, and the family may keep warm in winter from a pan of hot charcoal. In the mountains villages are usually less compact, and often comprise a number of loose clusters of dwellings with stone replacing mudbrick as the main building material. Courtyards are much less a feature, because of the shortage of land suitable for building, and houses sometimes have a second storey.

Few amenities are found in the villages beyond the mosque, a bathhouse and a few shops, usually located around a central square which functions as a meeting place for all the inhabitants and is sometimes the site of the weekly market. Some villages also have one or more guesthouses which act as a convenient meeting place for the men. The monotonous appearance of the villages is only broken by the variety of building materials and external decoration employed, and particularly by the different rooftypes found. Where a single building material is used, however, one village looks very much like another.

Until recent years the tone and pattern of village life in the Middle East had changed little for centuries. Poor health, high infant mortality rates, illiteracy, oppressive forms of tenancy, crippling debts through high interest rates, poverty and extremely low standards of living were widespread. The majority of villagers lived in ignorance and isolation, hunger and servility beneath the sway of the big landowners.

Rents and taxes often absorbed as much as five-sixths of the total produce of a holding so that the tenants were forced to turn to the moneylenders who might demand rates of between 50% and 200%, if not more. The cultivator rarely escaped from the moneylender once he had made their acquaintance. Traditionally, right to profit from agriculture rested on provision of five elements: land, water, seed, implements (including animals) and labour, each rating sometimes 20%. Thus a landless tenant cultivator might be regarded as entitled to as little as 20% if he supplied only his own labour. Because of poor communications all the produce of one district tended to find its way to a single market where in times of plenty the price fell because of a glut, and high prices occurred only when crops failed. Under such conditions 'cornering' by middle men could easily take place.

A survey of Iranian villages as late as the early 1950s found severe to appalling conditions among the poorest peasants. The majority were seriously diseased, annual interest rates of 240–800% were common, and in some areas the cultivators existed on locusts and clover as their main food supply. There were villages where peasants made as little as US $8 a year. Equally depressing descriptions exist from other parts of the region.

Today, although many villagers still live near the margins of subsistence, rapid, irreversible and fundamental changes are occurring in the countryside; changes which are usually for the better, but not always. Major road building programmes have improved communications between many villages and the main towns and smaller administrative and market centres. Journeys which once took many hours, even a whole day, along poor tracks often impassable for part of the year, can now be undertaken in a fraction of the time by car, taxi or bus along decent metalled roads. A growing number of villages now have piped drinking water, and some at least also have electricity. Medical centres of various kinds have been established in rural areas, but all too often they are inadequately manned, and their staff undertrained and underpaid, while more centres are urgently needed. Nevertheless, the health of the villagers is improving, if only slowly. Since the Second World War, many new state elementary schools have been opened in rural areas. Much progress has been achieved, and the attitude of the villagers to public education is changing with growing awareness of the importance of formal education in occupational success. The new government buildings bringing the village some of the services of urban life have interrupted the monotonous appearance of many settlements; new building materials – cement and redbrick – are now being used, and a few entirely new, regularly planned villages have been established, particularly in areas of land reclamation schemes.

Thanks to the influence of the mass media, especially the transistor radio, the villagers' horizons are beginning to expand beyond their own small community after centuries of isolation. The transistor radio can be seen everywhere in the villages. In Lebanon there are radios in 91% of all rural households; in Egypt agricultural workers even wear them in their belts as they work in the fields and most shops and vendors' stalls have them playing to entertain the customers. The radio is particularly effective because it overcomes the barrier of illiteracy; and it can be considered a fundamental in the process of change. It brings the villagers information about life in the towns, and about events in other countries, and it has been used by the governments of the region not only for political and ideological communication but also for promoting various social and welfare programmes such as family planning. The radio has brought new ideas and an increased political awareness among the villagers who have become familiar with words such as imperialism, nationalism and socialism. Television is also beginning to reach some villages, and, although it is still far less important than radio as a popular means of communication, in the future its influence on attitudes and behaviour will increase.

New crops, improved agricultural technology, and new techniques of cultivation are modifying the agricultural bases of village life. In most countries, land reclamation and irrigation schemes both large and small are increasing the cultivated area and permitting more intensive cropping. In many areas cultivation is no longer merely for subsistence. Foodstuffs, particularly wheat and barley, still remain the most important crops for the majority of villagers, but the cultivation of cash crops for export (e.g. cotton, vegetables and fruits) has greatly expanded. With the introduction of fertilizers, insecticides and improved equipment, the villagers are now able to achieve much higher yields for their crops. Following major land reform programmes and the breakup of multi-village estates, some cultivators have become landowners for the first time, although their holdings are often very small. New co-operatives have been set up to provide credit and technical advice; to arrange for the marketing of agricultural produce; and in some cases to supervise farm production.

Unfortunately not all cultivators have received land. In some cases agrarian reform has merely aggravated existing social divisions resulting from the introduction of money and market principles and produced new tensions in rural society. Various studies have revealed the importance and complexity of the pattern of class division or stratification which is based not merely on ownership of land, for there are different strata even among the landless. A modest improvement in the income of the small landowners, especially the beneficiaries of land reform, has occurred as a result of government sponsored agrarian policies, and in many cases it is these richer peasants and their families who have secured control of the new co-operative and have acquired the political and economic influence to dominate the rural areas where the power of the great landlords has been broken. Tenant farmers also appear to have made some gains from the reforms, whether they operate under cash rents or as sharecroppers. The most unfortunate group remains the landless labourers who have often suffered a loss of income and employment as a result of the reforms. Among the landless the position of casual labourers, hired for short periods often under extremely oppressive contracting arrangements, is particularly acute. One example is the *tarahil* casual labourers of Egypt, recruited for the maintenance of canals and other rural public works, and probably the poorest of the rural poor. Landless peasants already constitute a sizeable proportion of the rural population, and their numbers are increasing from year to year as a result of the high rate of population growth.

Amidst these changes, kinship ties and religious observances remain important among the cultivators. The family – husband and wife, their married and unmarried sons and unmarried daughters – functioning within the clan structure, is still the basic social and economic unit. Obedience and respect to father and elder brother as well as to clan elders led by the clan head and loyalty to close relations and clansmen are basic rules of social life. In villages of Moslems and most Christian sects marriage within the clan is generally preferred, and in many places there is a traditional hostility between different clans of a single village. Disputes over land, water, women or appointment of the village headman can occur with sometimes violent consequences. Indeed it is generally recognized that loyalty to clan and religous sect has served to undermine the unity of the Middle Eastern village community.

Today some changes are certainly taking place. New information, objectives, ideas and resources from outside are altering existing social relationships within the village. Common residence among kinsmen, though still widespread, is no longer the dominant pattern everywhere, and the number of nuclear family residences is increasing. Fathers now have decreasing control over their sons, the young are generally less deferential and less obedient to the older members of the village, and women are already less submissive to their menfolk. The appearance of political parties has also begun to undermine the system of kinship solidarity and rivalry. But in a number of important areas – marriage, childbearing and religion – there is considerable evidence that change is resisted. A recent national survey of all Turkey, for example, revealed that 90% of village respondents reported that a son ought to begin married life in his father's household – an interesting comment on the survival of traditional values about sex and marriage in rural areas.

In spite of a number of very real material improvements in the lives of the cultivators the villages remain unhealthy and depressing places, and the gulf between countryside and town is still very wide. At the same time, growing contact with the world outside the village has given rise to aspirations and expectations among the cultivators that the limited opportunities available within the village cannot fulfil. Indeed in most villages the falling deathrate is causing an increase in the number of mouths to be fed, in people to share land resources, and in hands available for work. One result has been the acceleration of labour migration to nearby towns, to neighbouring countries, and even to Western Europe – a process which in itself has become one of the most important factors in change in the Middle Eastern village. The remittances which the migrants send back to their villages often support those who remain at home. Some migrants eventually return to the village but many others settle permanently in the towns where they are joined by their wives and children. Links with their native village are nevertheless maintained and regular visits are customary, reinforcing and increasing the villagers' knowledge and experience of urban life and in this way contributing enormously to further permanent migration.

In a whole variety of ways the Middle Eastern village is becoming increasingly integrated into a national system of government, and into a national society. State intervention in the countryside has increased steadily in recent years, and the growing importance of the central government and its changing relations with the countryside is one of the major developments of the last two decades. There are now regular visits from the police, party officials, agricultural officers, bank and co-operative officials and health workers. Local branches of national political and economic organizations have been set up in the villages. The teachers in the state elementary schools in the villages follow a national curriculum and bring national values to the children. In many countries all men must serve in the armed forces. Thus the major forces that have set in motion the processes of change have come from outside the village, and consequently more progress is made *for* the villagers than is made *with* their participation. Government intervention, moreover, although aimed at reducing inequalities in the countryside and narrowing the gap between town and countryside has, in fact, produced new tensions within the rural community.

*Strata of adult male agriculturalists widely found in Iranian villages* (after N. R. Keddie)

*Non-cultivators*
1  Absentee landlord, including the state, crown, and *waqf* trustees.
2  Large-scale renter from above, often absentee.
3  Village officials: headman, landlord's agent, water official, field watcher, etc.
4  Non-cultivating small owner.
5  Non-cultivating small renters from strata 1 or 2 (one village or less).
6  Non-cultivating leaser of productive instruments, usually cattle, sometimes water.
7  Non-cultivating head of work team, providing at least one instrument of production.

*Cultivators*
8  Cultivating small owners.
9  Cultivator paying a fixed cash rental.
10  Cultivating head of work team.
11  Sharecropper with some productive instruments, usually oxen, not head of a work team.
12  Sharecropper with only his labour to sell, but with a regular position on work team or on land.
13  Labourer with regular wage, in cash or kind.
14  Casual labourer, without a place on work team or land, often hired by the day only at peak seasons.

Almost every village in Iran has several of these strata with some peasants in more than one of them. During the recent land reforms only

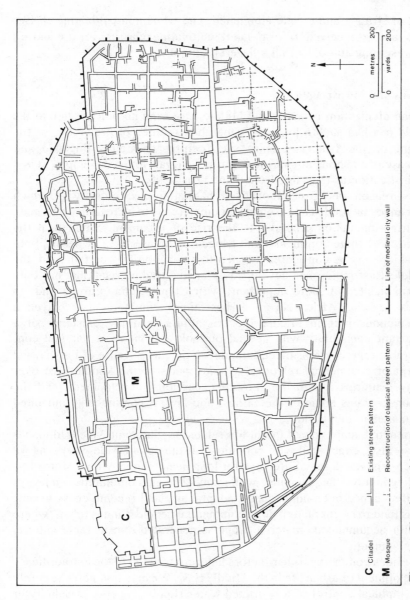

C Citadel    ⊣├ Existing street pattern

M Mosque    ⊣¦├ Reconstruction of classical street pattern

⊣├ Line of medieval city wall

*Fig.* 6.2 Classical grid remnants in ground plan of old Damascus (after P. Sauvaget).

part of strata 1 and 2 were eliminated, and while non-cultivating classes 5, 6 and 7 received reform land, cultivating classes 12, 13 and 14 (representing 40–50% of all villagers) did not.

## Towns and townspeople

Urban civilization began in the Middle East, and no other region in the world has had such a long and venerable tradition of urban life. At the height of the Islamic Empire such centres as Cairo, Baghdad and Damascus outshone any of their European rivals in the development and sophistication of their intellectual and artistic life.

By reason of its need of fixed habitation and security in which exchanges of goods can take place, commerce is to be regarded as a main contributing factor generally to the rise of urbanism. Situated at the junction of three continents, and fringed by areas of sea or desert, both of which may be considered as open to navigation of a certain kind, the Middle East region has developed extensive trading relations, not only within itself, but more important, with China, India, Europe and, to a less extent, Africa. From earliest times commerce has played a conspicuous part in Middle Eastern affairs, and the existence of a merchant community with special outlook and interests has had considerable repercussions on cultural development. Because of the unusual extent of commercial relations in many parts of the Middle East over many centuries, urban life showed exceptional development, and the region contains some of the earliest and largest continuously inhabited town sites in the world.

An active and evolved urban life related to continent-wide trading has often, also, contrasted with conditions in the countryside where, as we have seen, standards of life have for long been relatively low. Moreover, trading involves acquaintance with many different communities and ways of life – hence open-mindedness, adaptability and receptiveness to new ideas tend to be characteristic of commercial peoples, and in towns, where wealth accumulated, material progress generated considerable cultural development.

Besides commerce, other factors have contributed to the extraordinary development of urban life in the Middle East. We may first note the purely geographical control of a restricted water supply; because of salinity or deficiency of water, people have been forced to congregate in a few favoured spots where supplies were available. Secondly, the course of Middle Eastern history reveals that time and time again, a vigorous yet small community has asserted political domination over a large area, but because of numerical inferiority, has been unable to undertake extensive colonization; instead, a hold has been maintained on towns, from which

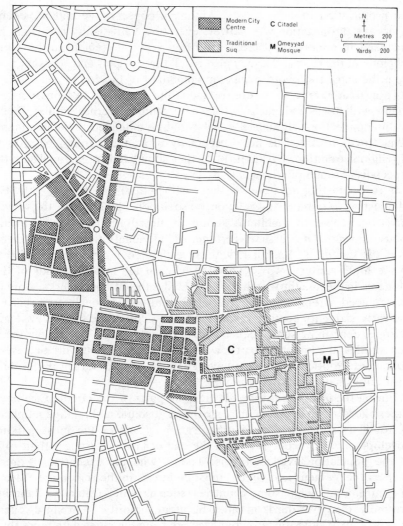

*Fig.* 6.3 Central Damascus, showing juxtaposition of traditional and modern city (after J. Dettmann).

an alien countryside has been ruled. The ancient Persians, Greeks and Romans, the early Arabs and the Turks all followed this plan, so that a tradition of rule and dominance has come to be characteristic of the towns.

Thirdly, there is the religious aspect. As we have now seen, the great religions of the Middle East spread from small beginnings, and this spread has been easiest and most marked among urban populations, who by their receptiveness to outside ideas formed a favourable ground for the propagation of new creeds. Among a conservative and backward peasantry, propagation was slower: even now Christianity and Islam as practised in remote rural areas are often very different from the same religions in the towns. We may also recall that 'pagan' and 'peasant' are from the same root word *pagus* (an inhabitant of the countryside).

To a great extent, therefore, religious life has come to be associated chiefly with towns and cities – we need only think of Jerusalem and Mecca in this connection, although the list could be extended to include many other towns regarded as holy, especially in Iran and Iraq. The growth of religious traditions has, in turn, further stimulated commercial activity especially through pilgrimage.

It is interesting to observe that, with a basis of trading activity, administrative control and religious association, the cities of the region have been able to maintain an uninterrupted tradition over several thousand years. Of course the fortunes of individual cities have fluctuated over the centuries. Baghdad, with an estimated 1·5 million inhabitants in the ninth century, was devastated when it fell into the hands of the Mongols in the mid thirteenth century. Under the Ottoman Turks Istanbul experienced a remarkable revival after centuries of decline so that by the early sixteenth century it was the largest city in the Middle East and Europe, containing some 400000 people. Nevertheless, throughout these vicissitudes, the importance of towns and the deeply rooted urban pattern continued. Political groupings have come to an end but, in the Middle East, cities have outlasted empires.

During the last two or three decades all parts of the Middle East have experienced a considerable increase in the absolute and relative numbers of town dwellers, and rapid urbanization is one of the most striking developments of recent years. At the end of last century less than 10% of the population lived in towns. Today, with the exception of areas such as the Yemens and Oman, most countries in the region are at least one-third urban, while some countries (such as Israel, Qatar and Bahrain) are more than two-thirds urban. The great majority of urban dwellers in nearly all Middle Eastern countries are found in cities with more than 100000 inhabitants. Istanbul, Ankara, Cairo, Alexandria, Tehran and Baghdad each contain over 1 million inhabitants, and the Greater Cairo region (8·4 million inhabitants) is one of the world's major conurbations.

The growth of many of these cities owes much to migration from villages in the surrounding regions, as in the case of Ankara, Baghdad, and Cairo; or to in-migration from other parts of the Middle East, as in the main towns of the Gulf states. Nevertheless, natural increase is also an important, and in many cases the predominant, component of urban growth. In the past, cities were centres of disease and high mortality. Today mortality, especially infant mortality, is much lower than in rural areas as a result of better working and housing conditions, enormous improvements in sanitation and hygiene, and a marked concentration of medical facilities in urban centres. At the same time fertility remains high, in some cases higher than in rural areas.

The gulf which has always separated rural from urban has been greatly accentuated in recent years, because it is the towns and cities which have been the main beneficiaries of modern social and economic development. By contrast to China, where towns are of relatively minor importance and social life derives most strongly from the countryside, urban life in the Middle East stands out sharply against a background of rural poverty and backwardness. The town dweller has by far the larger share of available amenities in buildings, communications, public health, education and entertainment. An important feature is that relatively few professional men practise outside the towns; and lack of amenity means that few senior civil servants or administrators will live outside the large towns if they can avoid it. The better off, with only a few exceptions, do not regard the Middle Eastern countryside as attractive – it is rather archaic, underprivileged and uncomfortable, sometimes hostile. Consequently, in the words of Dubertret and Weulersse, 'there is an extraordinary inequality between town and country. The former gathers to itself power and wealth, whilst rural communities remain significantly disinherited'. The process has tended to develop even faster with the exploitation of oil. It should also be mentioned, however, that many Middle Eastern towns, especially those without major international trading links, function mainly as the focus and outlet of their region – acting as collecting and distributing points for the surrounding countryside, the centre of local manufacturing and seat of government. P. W. English draws attention to certain Iranian towns where there is clearly no outside contact of great magnitude – the city functions principally for its region as a 'central place'. Indeed the notion of a sharp separation between urban and non-urban life in the Middle East is now being challenged by some researchers who argue that the idea of a rural–urban continuum is a more accurate view of the complex reality of Middle Eastern society.

The morphology of Middle Eastern towns has undergone striking changes in recent decades, and in many cases one finds a juxtaposition of two distinct urban styles – the traditional form and architecture of the pre-industrial city or *medina* often existing side by side but in sharp contrast with the Western-style layout and buildings of the modern suburbs or extensions.

The physical form of the traditional city is best understood by reference to the relationship between social organization and spatial patterns. In most cities there were districts which were primarily commercial and the centre of public life, and others that were primarily

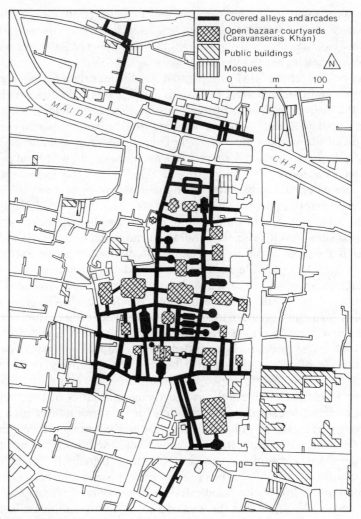

*Fig.* 6.4 Tabriz: bazaar (after G. Schweizer).

residential. The commercial areas – the bazaars or *suqs*, consisted of a complex network of narrow streets and alleyways, sometimes open, sometimes covered, lined with the workshops of the artisans, storerooms, and shops, stalls and alcoves where goods were displayed for sale. Within the busy and noisy bazaars, shopkeepers and artisans were grouped by trades so that one could find whole streets where the same commodity was produced or sold – grain, copperware, cloth and jewellery. The religious and political life of the community was also concentrated here. The suqs had mosques and *madrasas* (religious schools); and in some cities the main markets were situated close to the citadel or fortress.

Public and private space were clearly differentiated, and in the residential quarters the emphasis was on privacy and security. Here was a maze of narrow alleys, twisting lanes and cul-de-sacs surrounded by the high compound walls of the houses. Life centred on the interior courtyard or garden completely shut off from the street. Houses tended to present few openings to the outside, with solid bare walls devoid of ornament, heavy doors, and window shutters. Within these quarters the citizens were grouped by religious sect or community rather than by wealth, resulting in the close juxtaposition of large and humble dwellings. It was common for Jews, Armenians, Greeks and Europeans and the various Moslem sects to occupy a distinct quarter of the city, in some cases walled off from the others; in Antioch, perhaps the classic example, forty-five such quarters have been identified. This pattern derives in part from the *millet* system, or from forcible colonization by an autocratic ruler, and partly from the general need for solidarity and protection. Most streets were too narrow for wheeled vehicles and offered access only to pedestrians. Until recently drinking water could be scarce, and water-borne sanitation non-existent. Civic feeling often had difficulty in finding adequate expression, and it is only within the last few decades that there have arisen municipal councils with elected representatives and general powers over urban development. Nevertheless, the pre-modern Middle Eastern city was far from being a formless jumble of houses and streets; there was a definite and logical organization of space. L. Carl Brown draws attention to the fact that the walls and gates dividing the city's different quarters represented 'a security arrangement that relied less on personnel than on a spatial organization controlling mobility', while the narrow winding streets were 'a sort of built-in system of traffic control producing an informal but effective zoning plan'.

Beginning in the late nineteenth century and gathering momentum since the Second World War, the traditional urban setting in many, particularly the large cities, has been reshaped and often radically transformed by physical expansion and the introduction of Western-style town-planning, Westernized architecture and building techniques, and new urban attitudes. Wide avenues have been laid out for motor vehicles, and the number of cars, taxis and trucks has increased enormously. Modern buildings have sprung up along these new thoroughfares – multi-storey office blocks for government and private business, high-rise apartment blocks, department stores, hotels, smart restaurants and cafes, cinemas and theatres. Street lighting has been introduced together with piped water supplies and public sewage systems.

Where the earlier urban centres have survived intact, the contrast between the old medina and the new modern city can be visually sharp, as for example in Jerusalem and Aleppo and among many provincial towns throughout the region. In Beirut, however, the walled medieval town has been almost engulfed by the rapid expansion of the modern agglomeration, and in Kuwait the original city has been virtually erased to make way for a new capital better suited to modern transport and commerce. In some areas the scarcity or absence of indigenous urban centres resulted in the establishment of entirely new towns such as Dhahran in Saudi Arabia and Abadan in Iran, built by foreign oil companies.

Under the impact of Westernization, the centre of gravity of urban life has moved from the market areas of the medina to the central business district of the modern city which has absorbed most of the evolving modern functions. Everywhere there has been a movement of the urban elite out of the traditional quarters into the new suburbs where houses and villas are less crowded together and street patterns more regular. In turn, the older quarters have been occupied by rural migrants often too poor to maintain the houses, which rapidly fall into disrepair. Increasingly proletarianized and overcrowded, and congested with traffic that it was never designed to accommodate, in varying degrees the medina has become peripheral or marginal to modern economic activity.

As a result of rapid urban growth the supply of housing has not kept pace with demand. Average occupancy densities have increased steadily and shanty towns, sometimes referred to as spontaneous or overnight settlements, have proliferated on the outskirts of many Middle Eastern cities, sometimes with, more often without the permission of the authorities. Almost two-thirds of the inhabitants of Ankara do not have full permission, and thus have imperfect legal status for their houses. Recent research has revealed that these squatter settlements, built of traditional materials (reeds, sun-dried mudbricks or stone, and sometimes new materials such as tin) may be areas of second settlement for migrants who have moved out of the overcrowded slums of the inner city. Generally regarded as undesirable by urban planners, they represent, nevertheless, an attempt by the new urbanites to solve their housing problems by their own efforts and provide minimal shelter. Unfortunately, the location of these settlement is rarely in line with the overall pattern of planned urban expansion, whilst high densities and absence of basic services present severe health risks and serious social problems.

Amidst rapid urban growth and the changing functions and technology of modern urbanism, the long tradition of the quarter as a corporate entity, based on ethnicity, religion or occupation, and of co-operation *within* the separate quarters of the city, appears to have survived to a remarkable degree in the Middle East. In new urbanizing districts there is evidence that the inhabitants of squatter settlements try to organize themselves according to social affinities – kinship, religious sect, ethnic identity or village of origin. Janet Abu Lughod, in her important work on the nature of adjustment of rural migrants to urban life in Egypt, has described the

constant 'ruralization' of the cities, particularly Cairo, and the incorpora-
tion into the metropolitan region of pre-existing village communities
and their occupants. She found that migrants tend to reproduce for
themselves a semblance of the way of life they left behind, and have
developed a variety of informal institutions such as the village benevolent
society to make their transition to urban life more gradual and thus reduce
cultural shock. Other case studies highlighting the importance of social
networks and family ties are avilable from such varied urban centres as
Tripoli, Baghdad and Beirut. The extent to which these urban cultural
patterns and social behaviour can continue to withstand the impact of
changes in the form, scale and organization of the modern Middle Eastern
city remains debatable. Some writers deplore the survival of these
'traditional' social patterns and maintain that they effectively block the
'modernization' process. Others suggest, on the contrary, that physical
planning should encourage the survival of these smaller sub-systems rather
than destroy them, because they have a vital role to play in preventing
the social disorganization of Middle Eastern urban society. Such thinking
has coloured the attitude of planners in Abu Dhabi who have deliberately
constructed 'intermediate' semi-tribal housing layouts.

Very different views have also been expressed about the concentration
of urban population in the largest cities. Cairo, for example, contains
almost one half of all urban population in Egypt; in Iraq two-thirds of
the urban population live in Baghdad; and Amman has over half of
Jordan's urban population. The growth of Tehran is also causing extremely
severe problems. Some observers are increasingly alarmed by the degree
of imbalance in the urban hierarchies of the Middle East; by the growing
concentration of industry, services and government in a few major
centres at the expense of the small and medium-sized towns, and by the
striking intra-urban contrasts emerging within the region. Many point to
the need for decentralization to encourage the growth of small towns and
for vigorous regional development programmes in order to reverse this
trend. In Tehran, for example, even in 1972 the *per capita* income was
2·4 times the national average; 76% of *all* vehicles were operating in the
one city, and more than half of all manufacturing industry was located
there. Others see the tendency for urban populations and functions to
gravitate to the largest metropolitan centres as a normal and healthy
development, reflecting the increased scale of contemporary society and
appropriate to the new technological situation. They admit that the
emergence of primate cities has given rise to serious problems. However,
because of the need for greater integration and mutual exchange within
the modern economy, they maintain that the answer lies in the creation
of linear conurbations with close linkages between the major city or cities
and the secondary subcentres; small towns located outside these dominant

axes are destined to decline. Indeed they suggest that the outlines of these new metropolitan regions are already visible, e.g. between Cairo and Alexandria, and Baghdad and Basra.

Finally, evidence suggests that in recent decades urbanization in the Middle East has outstripped both general economic growth and industrial development so that a significant part of the urban population is unemployed, underemployed or forced into that expanding group of activities sometimes labelled 'the urban informal sector'. Bartsch, for example, maintains that official figures on urban unemployment in the Middle East are often misleading, and by applying a revised methodology to a poor district of Tehran he identified much higher rates of worklessness than those reported by the Iranian census. It is held by some that most countries in the region are now over-urbanized, and, instead of stimulating modernization, further urban growth may hinder economic development. If this proves to be the case the cities of the Middle East face a bleak future, physically, economically and socially. The question is an important one for by the end of the century over half the region's population will live in towns and cities.

**Human disease**

The extent to which human activity, and therefore economic life, is affected by the incidence of disease, is so considerable that an outline of the main problems involved can justifiably be discussed as an aspect of the social geography of the region. The wide variation of climatic conditions within the Middle East, with generally high temperatures; its position between large centres of population to east, west and south; and the flow of pilgrims of various races towards the shrines of Arabia and Palestine; all are in part responsible for a relatively high rate of disease. Further factors must be sought in the mode of life of the people. Overcrowded, insanitary conditions in many areas are responsible for much ill health; and these, in turn, are related to certain geographical factors: a general deficiency of water, lack of material resources in food and building materials, and social and political conditions such as methods of land tenure, or frequent foreign invasion.

Some of the more widespread diseases originate directly from environmental conditions. Malaria, yellow fever, kala-azar and various other fevers are all spread by insects, the distribution of which is controlled in large part by climate. Other diseases, such as bilharzia, dysentery, trachoma, typhus and infestation by parasitic worms, are caused mainly by insanitary conditions, and are therefore a more specific human problem. A third group of diseases, chief of which is pellagra, is due entirely to malnutrition, and is thus related to economic productivity.

It should also be stated that in some sectors at least, especially as regards malaria, the situation has improved – dramatically in certain instances – over the last 20 years. Up to and shortly after the Second World War, it could be said that as many as 75% of the total population of Egypt was affected by one if not two diseases; surveys revealed villages in Asia Minor, Palestine and Iran where 50–90% of the people examined had chronic malaria; and dysentery was a minor but disabling affliction in most parts. Now, thanks to much improved public health, based on better water supply, improved sanitation and medical care and the use of new insecticides, the situation has been transformed; and the former mosquito nets, once to be found in every hotel bedroom of any pretension, are almost entirely absent.

The Middle East was once a stronghold of malaria, which affected most well-watered lowlands and hills up to about 1500 m. The riverine areas of Iraq and Egypt, the Yemens, the Caspian coast of Iran, parts of western Asia Minor, Cyprus and the valleys of western Syria, and the Lebanon, were particularly affected. Dusting by D.D.T., attention to water-flow to eradicate small stagnant pools in which the mosquito larvae could develop, stocking of standing water by predatory small fish, and public education, have resulted in virtual eradication of the disease from many areas: Cyprus was, for instance, declared entirely free in 1950.

In consequence, a great deal of low health and disablement due to chronic malaria has begun to disappear, with resulting beneficial effects on human energy and productivity. In 1943 three villages round the now drained Lake Huleh at the head of the Jordan valley had respectively 85, 92 and 97% of the total inhabitants suffering from chronic malaria. The rate is now almost nil: and here is one index of what can be achieved.

Yellow fever is a dangerous disease because of its high mortality rate, which is over 25%. Not widespread in the Middle East, it is nevertheless more endemic in central Africa, into which it spread from the original source of South and Central America. Yellow-fever-carrying mosquitoes can be introduced by aircraft, and there are now stringent measures to prevent the spread into such areas as the Sudan.

Now that malaria has decined, the most widespread disease of the Middle East at the present time is probably bilharzia. Even more than malaria, this disease is a disease of irrigated lands. Spread of the disease is related to the occurrence of a species of water snail which acts as first host to a bilharzia parasite passed out from an affected human body by defecation. After developing in the body of the snail, the fully grown parasite then enters a second human body through the soles of the feet and makes its way to the intestine, producing bleeding and severe debility which can continue as a chronic condition for many years. Bilharzia thus has considerable effects upon the energy and initiative of rural populations, and is increasing, not declining. Napoleon in his blunt way spoke of Egypt as 'the land where men menstruate'.

Egypt and the Sudan are probably the most seriously affected region of the Middle East, with the lower Tigris and Euphrates, but the disease may spread to any newly irrigated area where there is not effective sanitation. Control of bilharzia can be achieved by destroying the water snail by means of copper-sulphate solution, by eradicating insanitary habits among the human population, and by wearing footgear within the fields. All these cost money, not always available.

Another widespread parasitic disease is hookworm or ankylostomiasis, which is more directly related to insanitary conditions concerning disposal of faeces. Egypt, where some years ago 40% of the rural population were known to be affected, is the chief centre of the disease, but it is well known also in Iraq, Iran, Jordan, the Sudan and Turkey.

Typhus (Plague), carried by lice and rat-fleas, is another disease of insanitary conditions and one more likely to affect urban populations. Severe epidemics can occur from time to time, although with better conditions in the towns and the greater number of medical men as compared with the country, urban epidemics are becoming far less frequent. The stronghold of typhus was Iran, but other parts of the Middle East are affected, particularly in the neighbourhood of ports. Dysentery is also caused by lack of cleanliness, and in a mild form is almost ubiquitous, so that the native inhabitants seem to have developed a very limited degree of 'conditioning' to the disease – the worst sufferers can often be new arrivals.

Trachoma, a severe affection of the eye that often leads to blindness, is specially characteristic of the Middle East. Lack of cleanliness is an important contributing factor, and the infection may be spread from one baby to another by flies settling on the eyes and thus transferring the disease from an infected infant. Once again, Egypt would seem to be an endemic area, but the disease occurs all over the Middle East, especially among nomads, who have limited access to water. Cholera epidemics occur from time to time, the latest occurring in 1975.

In colder areas, for instance Asia Minor and northern Iran, tuberculosis remains a problem. Confined, shut-in conditions for part of the year mean that risk of infection remains high. Smallpox also affects a number still, though vaccination has spread widely of recent years, and eradication is in sight. Contagious hepatitis continues as a minor danger.

The south of the Sudan remains as one area where levels of public health still continue low. Although yellow fever, smallpox and typhus have decined, malaria, bilharzia, kala-azar, tuberculosis, ankylostomiasis, draconiasis and meningitis have not, and may possibly be increasing. In addition, in forested areas, sleeping sickness, leprosy and simolia (Sudan blindness) are endemic.

Veneral disease is held by some observers to be widespread in certain parts of the Middle East, often in a chronic rather than acute form – for example, one writer, A. T. Sharaf, stated that in 1963, 4–7% of the total population of Khartoum province was infected. But in other regions both the incidence and strength of the disease have been much reduced of recent years, and for these areas rates are no higher than those of swinging London or happy Los Angeles.

Rabies is a present danger in all parts, due to the presence of many scavenging dogs – this is why dogs are not encouraged as household pets in the Middle East – and anthrax and foot-and-mouth disease are also prevalent in pastoral areas.

Despite the considerable improvements of the past 20 years, there are still some grounds for concern. Since 1970 a more virulent strain of malaria has appeared in the south – notably Arabia and Oman: and malaria has never disappeared from the piedmont areas of Yemen.

Lassa (Marburg or Green Monkey) fever, with no known cure and a very high mortality, has spread into the southern Sudan from tropical Africa: there was an epidemic in Juba during 1976; but perhaps most disturbing of all is the faster spread of bilharzia in Egypt. The relatively rapid current of the Nile prevented upstream movement of certain species of water snail that are vectors for a particularly virulent bilharzia strain; but since the current has become slow and intermittent in consequence of the building of the High Aswan Dam, these snails, hitherto confined to the lowest reaches of the Nile, are able to move upstream. Once again, here is an example of change in one element of an ecosystem having totally unexpected repercussions on another.

# 7 Aspects of the historical geography of the Middle East

**Early political units in their geographical setting**

The change generally from nomadic wandering as hunters or gatherers to settled occupation of the soil with the development of plant cultivation as the first real stage in growth of civilization, is generally thought to have taken place first in some part of the Middle East, though opinions as to more precise locality differ, and the date at which such changeover on a significant scale would seem to have occurred is being pushed steadily further backwards as more results of archaeological investigation become available. This is not the place to enter into detailed discussion, but the present view is that the Natufian peoples of western Palestine were among the first known to have developed a way of life based on cultivation, (with some herding of animals) as a secured and fixed, rather than nomadic, base. The time of this development is put very close after the last glacial period, 12000–10500 B.P., with other developments *c.* 8000 B.P. at Çatal Hüyük (Asia Minor) and Jericho (Palestine). Rapidly improving ecological conditions, from previously near peri-glacial in many parts of the central zone of the Middle East, gave first, a warm, temperate, lightly wooded environment (Mediterranean oak, olive and carob, with swamp reeds in the riverine areas) that later became drier and still warmer. One theory first advanced to explain the origins of agriculture by V. Gordon Childe was that this desiccation led to crowding of plant species, animals and humans into certain small but favoured areas: oases of a kind; where domestication by humans then occurred. Other researchers have since put forward views that cultivation arose from growth in population numbers in certain areas which were increasingly affected by climatic deterioration towards aridity: one argument is that marginal hunters and gatherers, faced with more numerous competitive communities, were driven to adopt domestication of animals and plants; another interpretation is that, with such ecological pressures, it was the 'core' communities living in the better spots in greater numbers which experienced demographic pressure and therefore evolved a more complex social structure that then led to cultivation and closer dependence on the local area.

We are so far considering small numbers, in small-scale conditions. The development of communities other than on a purely local basis involves extra factors, since cultivation must then be necessary on a scale large enough to produce the surplus of wealth necessary to support specialist crafts and the services of professionals as administrators, priests and intellectuals. Here the presence of the two major river systems of the Middle East – Tigris–Euphrates and Nile – is of major significance, since it was in these two valleys that the organization of political units on a wider-than-local scale first took place. In both instances one can observe the operation of a number of separate factors. First, and most important, was the existence of a large alluvial tract, watered annually by river flooding that also renewed fertility by deposition of silt. Next, spatial location – connection with the contacts with other groups – from which a synthesis of experience could be made, and in addition, a wider human gene-pool could evolve. In this connection it is useful to note that at this early period there would seem to have been three major ethnic groups within our area: Semitic related to the Arabian peninsula; Hamitic in north-east Africa; and various groups of Indo-European cultures in the northern mountain zone: Aryans who spread into Iran by 4000 B.C., Hittites who entered Asia Minor by 2000 B.C., and various Caucasian groups.

Another element, ability first to absorb and develop, and then show capacity for social and political co-operation at wider levels, is also involved in the process of civilization, and with the development of the city which offers a better environment for all these, the process gained even greater momentum.

There has been controversy as to where this 'urban' level, which we can term 'civilization', of recognizably Neolithic character, and involving integration of a spread of rural territory and a number of organized urban communities, first actually occurred. Mesopotamia and Egypt are generally recognized as the earliest in the world where this developed, and present archaeological opinion is that the oldest major culture is that of Sumer, c. 3500 B.C., with a parallel but slightly later development in Egypt c.

3100 B.C. Both had a high technical level of cultivation (grain yield in Sumer *c.* 2300 B.C. is held to have been as good as that in the best areas of present-day Canada) which supported a highly evolved social life, with organized civil and religious bodies. Copper and bronze were used, though on a limited scale, and trading contacts had begun, especially with Syria, which, located between the two prime areas and endowed with natural resources not present in the other two (e.g. timber), participated in the general material and cultural advances initiated from Egypt and Sumer.

It is interesting to note that, though the first development of all can be related to the Tigris–Euphrates valley, conditions here might appear to be less favourable than along the Nile. The Nile is a single stream without tributaries in its lower course, and with regular seasonal floods that are confined within the incised trench of the valley, only on average about 10 km wide. The Tigris and Euphrates are on the other hand braided streams in a very open shallow valley, and the former receives important affluents throughout the length of its course which bring down much silt that impedes the lower stretches of both rivers, giving rise to swamps, lagoons, and embanked river beds that are hence liable to change course. Moreover, Mesopotamian floods are somewhat more erratic since they derive directly from Middle Eastern rainfall (which as we have seen can be very variable) whereas Nile floods are produced by more regular Tropical zoned rains. Flooding in the Tigris (which can be especially sudden and variable) and in the Euphrates occurs hard upon the end of the rainy season, giving a long dry period throughout much of the year: in Egypt the floods come later, splitting the year into four shorter and rather more 'manageable' seasons: one of very slight rainfall followed by drought, then summer flood again followed by drought.

Geographers might be tempted to suggest that the initial 'challenge' in Mesopotamia was therefore greater, and hence produced precocious response and development of civilization. In Egypt, however, because of intrinsic regularity and manageability, with richer alluvium derived from the volcanics of Ethiopia, early development passed directly from pre-civilization direct to large scale organization without an intervening period of city-states; maintaining at the same time unrivalled ability to organize collective effort from its peoples basically in agriculture and then in public works, with a stable, centralized and highly traditional form of government. The same factors may also explain why Syria, though geographically closer to Mesopotamia, should have tended to lie under the influence of Egypt rather than Mesopotamia.

The second millennium B.C. saw much invasion and disturbance with a relative decline in the influence of Mesopotamia and Egypt. From the more arid areas of Arabia the Hyksos (Shepherd Kings) entered Egypt, and Aramaean peoples, among them Canaanites, Israelites, Philistines and Phoenicians, established themselves in the better-watered regions of the

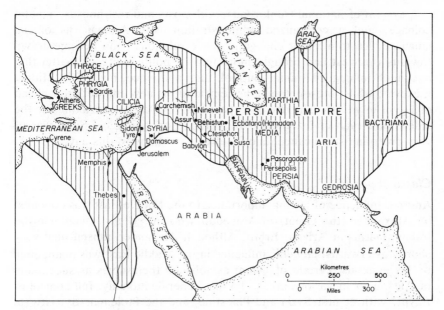

*Fig.* 7.1 The Persian Empire *c.* 500 B.C.

Levant, whilst the Kassites entered lower Mesopotamia. In the north, originally pastoral peoples, the Mitanni and the Hittites, invaded and introduced the horse and the chariot: the Hittites would also have appeared to have invented iron smelting round about 1300 B.C. At the same time, because of extensive commercial relations developed by the Phoenicians, whose chief cities were Tyre, Sidon and Arad (Ruad), Aramaic languages began to spread over much of the Middle East, as far as Europe and Iran, and with the Phoenician alphabet were a considerable advance on the cumbersome hieroglyphics of Egypt and the cuneiform of Mesopotamia, which was adapted best for incision on clay tablets.

After a relatively short period that saw the rise of an Assyrian empire (1200–1000 B.C) based on an area of rain-fed cultivation on the plains of the upper Tigris – a feature that illustrates the progress of agricultural techniques – there came the rise of Persia. Settlement had developed in parts of the inner plateau of Iran as early as 5000 B.C., and in *c.* 1000 B.C. there occurred irruptions of Indo-Aryan peoples, among whom were the Medes who settled in the north-west, and the Persians (Farsi) who settled further south, around Fars. Unification by conquest was achieved by the Achaemenid dynasty, most outstanding monarch of which was Cyrus. His conquests, beginning in 539 B.C. with Mesopotamia, brought together under a single unified administration, and for the first time, a territory that ultimately extended from the Hindu Kush to the Aegean and North Africa including Egypt.

A system of national trunk roads, with posts and rest houses, a metal coinage, and a centralized administration with Aramaic as official language, led to a major change in space relations. Iran became drawn towards the west and brought more into its political life – a matter that has much influenced Iranian outlook then and since, making it 'Middle Eastern'; whilst Mesopotamia, as central to the new empire, drew ahead of Egypt in wealth. The rise of a specifically Aryan culture alongside the older non-Aryan civilizations of Egypt, Mesopotamia and Syria was of very profound significance; and its effects continue to this day.

*Classical period*

Another influence of lasting importance to the Middle East was conquest by Alexander (the Great) of Macedon who in 331 B.C. overcame the Iranian Darius at Arbela (Erbil). Although Alexander himself died very shortly afterwards, Hellenic influence in the Middle East was maintained by his generals, certain of whom established themselves as successors of Alexander in various areas. To one general, Ptolemy, fell control of Egypt, with at first Syria and Palestine, and the Ptolemaic dynasty (to which belonged Cleopatra) ruled Egypt until the Roman conquest of that country in 30 B.C. Another general, Seleucus, established a dynasty in Iran, Mesopotamia, and at a later date in Syria. Themselves of partly Indo-Aryan origin, the Macedonians who shared with the Iranians a strong military tradition with extensive use of the horse, intermarried to form a Perso-Macedonian ruling class. Both groups, as often since in the Middle East, found that as a minority their influence could best be exercised amongst urban populations, rather than rural cultivators and herdsmen. Accordingly, emphasis was placed on town and city development: old centres were expanded and new sites carefully chosen – Haleb (Aleppo) and Carchemish were re-named Beroea and Doura, whilst new towns were created, for example Alexandria, Alexandretta, Laodicea (Latakia – from the name of a sister of Seleucus), Antiochia and Heliopolis (Baalbek), to name only a few. Thus within the towns, Hellenism was often dominant; in the countryside, older Semitic traditions persisted. This was the situation at the time of Christ in Judaea, as shown by Pontius Pilate's inscription on the Cross – in Latin, the language of the conquerors, in Greek, the language of townspeople and officials, and in Aramaic, the Semitic language of the peasantry.

In time Seleucid rule declined, to be replaced by a new, native Parthian state in Iran, and the growing Roman Empire in the west. For several centuries this division between Parthian and Roman spheres was the basic geopolitical fact within the Middle East. Despite the power of Rome, the centres of the Parthian Empire, doubly screened by the Syrian desert

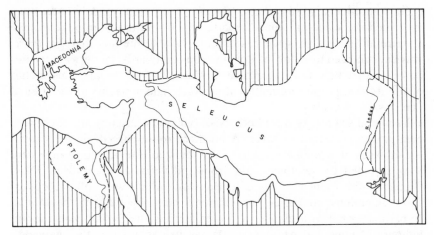

*Fig.* 7.2 The Empire of Alexander the Great, and its division between Ptolemy and Seleucus.

and by the rampart of the Zagros mountains, were too remote to be attacked in strength; conversely, the Parthians could never conquer the western provinces of Syria, which were ultimately sustained by a powerful Roman fleet.

Under Roman rule, western Anatolia, Syria, Palestine, North Africa, and Egypt entered upon a period of prosperity which has probably never since been equalled, unless at the present day. Tranquillity of conditions led to a great expansion in agriculture and trade. Irrigation was practised on a scale greater in places than any until the present day; and, in addition to supplying a numerous local population, the rich cornlands of Egypt and Syria had a constantly increasing market in Italy itself. As Italian agriculture declined in the later Roman period, the greater became the demand for Middle Eastern wheat. Increase in material prosperity stimulated a demand for manufactured goods. A textile industry, first woollen and linen, then silk, had the advantage of abundant raw materials and natural dyes – saffron, umber, and purple from the murex shells of Tyre. Glass-blowing and metal-working also reached a high level; and at a number of centres on the coast easily accessible woodlands provided material for shipbuilding.

The Middle East as a whole derived much profit from the expansion in world relations which took place under the Romans. Besides the two empires of Rome and Parthia, there were now equally highly developed civilizations in India and China; and trade contacts between Rome and the east began to assume importance. Silk was for long a Chinese monopoly, but an extensive demand by wealthy Romans led to a considerable transit traffic through Parthia and the Middle East. Other eastern products were jewels, spices, drugs and sandalwood. Pliny estimated the value of annual importations from the east into the Roman Empire at 100 million sesterces; and, in view of the fact that this traffic was not balanced by a flow of Roman goods eastwards, modern authorities consider that between one-quarter and one-half of the precious metals of the Roman Empire ultimately drained to Asia in payment for Oriental luxuries.

Land and sea routes were both used, but land transport, although more costly, was preferred as safer. A northern route passed via the central Asian oases of Khokand, Bokhara and Merv to Hamadan in Iran, where it was joined by another route from India via southern Iran. From Hamadan the route continued to Babylon, which was still a focus of communications, and then turned northwards by way of the Middle Euphrates, whence a choice of routes skirting the Syrian desert led to Palmyra, Aleppo and Antioch, or Damascus. Access was then gained to the numerous Syrian ports. A more southerly route utilized the Indian Ocean and Red Sea as far as the Gulfs of Suez and Aqaba. From the latter point shipment then took place by way of Petra, Jerash and Philadelphia (Amman) to the south Syrian ports; from Suez, a route also led overland through Egypt to Alexandria, which rivalled Tyre and Sidon as an entrepôt. The amazing prosperity of the Roman Middle East, with its dense population and high level of culture, is attested by the numerous remains which are still to be seen. Of these, the temple of Heliopolis (Baalbek) is one of the most impressive. Situated at an altitude of 1000 m, on the low watershed between the Orontes and Leontes (Litani) rivers, the temple was erected in A.D. 200–400, partly from stone quarried in Egypt, and rests on a foundation course that consists of hewn stone blocks each weighing 450 tons. Antioch, the metropolis of Roman Syria, is estimated to have had a population of three-quarters of a million, a number in excess of the combined populations of early twentieth century Aleppo, Beirut and Damascus; even so, the greater number of Syrians lived in the country rather than in the towns.

Further to the east, the Parthians also derived much advantage from trade routes. It is customary in the west to regard the Roman empire as surrounded by barbarians; as concerns Parthia, this was by no means the case, since both states dealt politically on equal terms, and both appreciated the value of commercial activities. The Parthians maintained active trading relations with China, India, Arabia and Siberia, in addition to those with Rome; but they were particularly anxious to keep a monopoly of trade in their own region – foreign merchants were not welcomed in Parthia itself, and all dealings were strictly supervised. The Romans have left an extensive literature, but the Parthians have left almost no written records, and much of our impression of them is thus derived

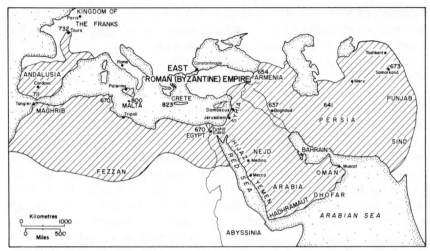

*Fig.* 7.3 The expansion of Islam.

from extraneous and not always impartial contemporary sources. Nevertheless, it is clear that the Parthians had a relatively high level of cultural development in which, however, the Hellenic influence of Seleucid times gradually gave way to an increasingly local and Oriental outlook.

In A.D. 224 the Sassanids gained power in Parthia, and though most of the existing Parthian way of life continued, the later Iranian Empire showed itself increasingly Oriental in its internal life, and in external affairs more aggressive in the west, against the slowly weakening power of Rome. A long period of intermittent fighting between Rome and Parthia, with border skirmishes and occasional major expeditions, continued until the downfall of both Empires in the seventh century A.D. The Roman Empire had at some time previously fallen into an eastern and a western portion, and of these, the former, now spoken of from A.D. 373 as the Byzantine Empire, took up the Iranian challenge. The Middle East from the Black Sea to the deserts of Arabia became a battleground, and the inconclusive results of this warfare, prolonged over many years, led to the ultimate exhaustion of both sides. The resulting material devastation, ideological intolerance and crippling taxation of the native populations were, as we have already noted, important contributing factors in the rise of Islam during the seventh century A.D.

## Arab period

The Arab conquest of the Middle East between A.D. 630 and 640 brought an active, virile, but rough and uncultured desert community into contact with the rich and highly evolved civilizations of Rome and Iran. The early followers of Muhammad were largely desert Badawin – 'plain men living in tents' – and without any tradition except that of a hard, patriarchal society existing as pastoralists or caravan traders.

The rapidity with which these semi-nomads were absorbed into existing life in the Middle East, and the extraordinary cultural development that resulted from the fusion of the two groups, must be considered one of the outstanding events in the development of human society, unparalleled in its speed until the spread of Communism in our own time. The explosion of Islam can probably be related, at least in large part, to the decline of hitherto prosperous communities in south-west Arabia ('Arabia Felix'). This decline may, in turn, be related to climatic catastrophe, as shown by the breakdown of the irrigation systems, e.g. at Marib, in what is now the North Yemen Republic, during the fifth and sixth centuries A.D. Politically the Islamic state at first enjoyed unbroken success. With the capture of Mecca in A.D. 630 as a beginning, there followed in 636 the seizure of Syria, of Egypt in 641, and of Libya in 642. Within a century, the whole of north Africa and most of Spain had become Moslem, and France and Italy were threatened. In the east, Islam had reached the oases of Turkestan, and was stretching towards India and China. Only in the north was expansion arrested, and that only temporarily, by a reduced but revivified Byzantine Empire.

Materially, the impressive level of achievement of the Roman era was maintained. Egypt and Syria retained a high agricultural productivity; taxation was lighter than in Byzantine times; and a degree of religious toleration allowed collaboration between various sects, with a fruitful interchange of ideas.[1] In Mesopotamia, the development of irrigation reached its highest point with the construction of numerous canals, many of them navigable, linking the Euphrates and Tigris. We may recall the statement in an earlier chapter, that many of the modern irrigation problems of Iraq would be largely solved by the reconstruction of the early Arab system of canals; this is in fact now occurring.

An important number of manufactures – metal-work, leather and textiles[2] – gave additional prosperity, and ancient trade routes between Europe and the Far East continued in full use. Intellectually, at a period when learning was practically extinguished in Europe, the Arabs took over and expanded classical philosophy, particularly in the fields of medicine and science, adding a considerable body of new thought, partly developed by themselves, and partly derived from Iran and even Hindu sources.[3] It may therefore be said that, almost until the Renaissance, the

[1] A number of high officials of the early Arab state were Christians.

[2] The names *damask*, *muslin* (Mosul) and *tabby* (Arabic *attabi*, originally cloth with stripes in various colours) indicate the extent of Arab textile production.

[3] Our debt to the Arabs is indicated by the words alchemy (from which chemistry), algebra, alcohol, alkali, admiral, julep and soda. A number of chemical substances, such as borax,

main stream of traditional classical culture deriving from the Ancient World was to be found in Arab lands rather than in Europe; and Arab commentaries and expositions on ancient authors were used as textbooks in European universities until the seventeenth and eighteenth centuries. It was in studying these in part at Salamanca University that Christopher Columbus decided that the world was round.

The Caliphate, or political leadership of Islam, was on the death of Muhammad first established in the family of the Omeyyads, who reigned from Damascus. After a century, a rival family, the Abbasids, supplanted the Omeyyads; and the political centre of Islam shifted to Baghdad. To this period, during which material prosperity in Mesopotamia probably reached its greatest peak, belongs the Caliph Haroun al Rashid (A.D. 786–809).

Later, towards the end of the ninth century, the political unity of Islam broke down, partly due to the great cleavage between Sunni and Shi'a. Ever since the original rise of Islam the Byzantines had succeeded in holding Asia Minor; and the existence of this advanced base of Christianity greatly favoured the operations of the first European Crusaders, who in A.D. 1079 landed in Asia Minor, and proceeded to an invasion of Syria.

### Crusader period

Within a short time, the coastal area of the Levant, from Cilicia to central Palestine, had fallen under Crusader domination. Feudal principalities were established on the European model, and Jerusalem was held from 1099 until its recapture by Saladin in 1187. The Crusaders did not, however, penetrate far inland. Except for somewhat more extensive, but short-lived kingdoms in Cilicia (kingdom of Armenia) and Judaea (kingdom of Jerusalem), their influence ceased at the crest of the mountain ranges backing the coast, and the important cities of Aleppo, Hama and Damascus remained in Moslem hands.

The Crusaders were not wholly inspired by religious motives. Trading activities had attraction, especially to the Genoese and Venetians, who supplied sea transport for crusading armies in return for substantial commercial concessions. Throughout most of the hundred years of occupation by the Crusaders, a considerable volume of trade in precious stones, spices, silks and other luxuries was carried on with the Moslem

sal ammoniac, nitre and sulphuric acid, were brought into use by the Arabs, who also introduced paper from China, where it was first invented (Arabic *rizma*, a bundle, hence *ream*). Two other contributions were the present system of numerals, a great advance on the cumbrous Roman figures, and the use of the zero sign.

In view of the extent of Arab dominions, and the necessity for pilgrimage, great attention centred on geographical studies, and to the Arabs must be ascribed the regional concept in geography.

*Fig.* 7.4 Crusader states in the Levant.

states, part being a transit traffic from China and India. It is also
interesting to note that, on balance, the East had more to offer than the
West in the way of material and cultural amenities. The Crusaders learned
much from Islam – an indication of the advances made in the Middle East
during the period of the Dark Ages in Europe.

During the thirteenth century Arab power revived, and the Crusaders
were gradually driven from Syria. By 1299 Acre, the last Christian
stronghold, had been taken. A remnant of Crusader refugees fled from
the mainland of the Levant, and established themselves in the island of
Cyprus, where European control, first under a Crusader dynasty named
Lusignan, and later under the rule of the Republic of Venice, lasted until
1571. The Lusignan period was one of great brillance in the history of
Cyprus, for the island became an entrepôt between Europe and the East.
Trading posts on the mainland of Asia, first developed under the

Crusaders, continued to function after the Moslem re-conquest; and European traders, chiefly Italian and French, had depots at Latakia, Tripoli, Beirut and Alexandria. Much commerce passed through Cyprus, which, secure from attack because of the lack of a seafaring tradition amongst the earlier Moslems – a situation that altered at a later date – took its place as a natural centre of the eastern Mediterranean. The wealth of individual merchants of Famagusta, Limassol and Nicosia is said to have exceeded that of many European monarchs; and the extensive Gothic buildings still existing in Cyprus somewhat incongrously among classical Greek and later Islamic architecture testify to the prosperous condition of the island under the Lusignans. It was not until the sixteenth century when a new power, the Ottoman Turks, had been sufficiently long in contact with the sea to have developed a maritime tradition, that invasion was attempted, and the island passed to Moslem control.

From the Crusader period onwards, repeated incursions of Mongols from the steppes of central Asia caused much destruction and devastation from which certain regions of the Middle East have never really recovered. The brunt of Mongol attacks fell on Iran, where between 1220 and 1227 the 'hordes' of Genghis Khan sacked and almost completely destroyed many cities, massacring the inhibitants. Many of the irrigation works maintained for centuries now fell into disrepair, and vast stretches returned to steppe or desert. By 1258 the terror had reached Mesopotamia, Baghdad was destroyed and the Abbasid Caliphate extinguished.

A century later, fresh Mongol invasions occurred. The armies of Timurlane reached Syria, where Aleppo, Homs and Damascus were burned and looted; whilst in Iran the Nestorian Christian community, which had played a great part in the intellectual life of the country, was reduced to a tiny minority. Mongol invasions were, however, arrested in Asia Minor, where a new power, the Ottoman Turks, had risen to importance.

*Ottoman period 1517–1923*

In the thirteenth century A.D., a small group of Mongols known as the Ottoman or Osmanli Turks invaded Asia Minor, and received a grant of territory in north-west Anatolia from a somewhat uneasy Sultan.[1] By 1400, the Ottomans had extended their domains to include central and many parts of western Anatolia, together with a considerable area of Balkan Europe. In 1453, after a number of previous attempts, the great city of Constantinople was taken, and the Byzantine Empire, of which it had been the capital, finally destroyed. Thence onwards, the expansion of

[1] One may recall grants of land, under somewhat similar circumstances, to the followers of the Saxons Hengist and Horsa, and also to Rollo, first Duke of Normandy.

the Ottoman state was rapid. By 1566 the entire north coast of Africa as far as Algiers had been occupied, together with Egypt, Syria, Palestine, Anatolia and Iraq. In addition, the whole of south-east Europe between Croatia and the lower Don fell into Ottoman hands, and Austria found herself menaced. A number of campaigns had led to a stalemate in the east, where a 'debatable ground' in the region of eastern Armenia, the Caucasus and Zagros mountains separated the Ottoman state from Iran, which retained its independence.

The early expansion of Ottoman power was accompanied by a process of administrative reorganization, as the result of which there came into existence a form of government that lasted without serious change from the fifteenth to the twentieth centuries. Certain features of Turkish rule are extremely interesting as showing to a marked degree the influence of the social background of the early Ottoman tribesmen, who became the ruling class of the new Empire.

The Ottomans had entered Anatolia as pastoral nomads from the steppes of Asia; and it has been said of them that they brought to the task of administering their Empire much of the technique that had served them in the handling of animals. In the first place, as a herdsman keeps separate his sheep and goats, the Ottomans made no attempt to develop a single, unified state, but were rather content to allow existing differences of race, religion and outlook to continue. At first, this tolerance of division amongst peoples of the Ottoman Empire was probably mere indifference; but at a later period, it became an important basis of policy: 'divide and rule' was the principle by which the weaker Ottoman Sultans were able to maintain their rule over a restive but heterogeneous population. Moslem was turned against Christian, Shi'a against Sunni, Kurd against Armenian, and Orthodox Greek against Roman Catholic. Sectarian feeling was provoked and increased by the creation of the *millet* system, and after the seventeenth century the grant of Capitulations to various non-Turkish nationals was a further recognition of the separate status of certain communities within the Empire. Provided that the subjects of the Sultan showed themselves amenable to rule, and willing to pay the taxes demanded and in some instances support military conscription, many communities could exist largely in their own way.

The Ottomans created a special corps of picked subjects to police the Empire. These men, known as Janissaries, were brought up from earliest youth in military barracks, under the strictest discipline. Bought as slaves from neighbouring states, or obtained as tribute – usually from Christian families – within the Empire, the Janissaries were separated from their parents, whom they never knew, and hence grew up without family ties or local sympathies. Obedient and ruthless, and fanatically Moslem by reason of their early training, the Janissaries were the instrument by which

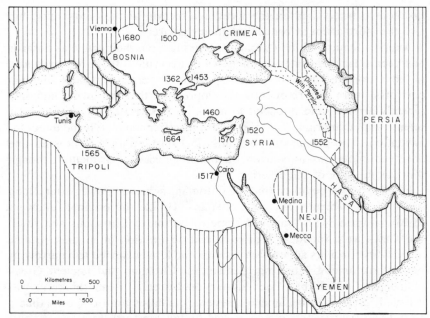

*Fig.* 7.5 The Ottoman Empire.

the Turkish government maintained a hold upon its mixed population. Those among the young Janissaries who displayed bookish rather than military abilities were trained as administrators, and often provided the Ottoman state with excellent civil officials.

As a purely pastoral tribe, the Ottomans had had no tradition of industry and commerce, and in their Empire both tended to be despised or ignored, and left to Armenians, Greeks, Jews or foreigners. Trade activities were tolerated, but little positive encouragement was afforded by the government; and from time to time, rapacious and arbitrary exactions were levied on commercial communities. Much business was therefore carried on half secretly, as far as possible without attracting attention, in the face of indifference or worse, from official quarters. Even the houses of many merchants were miniature fortresses, capable of withstanding attack. This long tradition of secrecy and dissimulation in business has had a most harmful effect. Even in some modern Middle Eastern states, methods inherited from the not-too-remote past still persist amongst small-scale traders. Accounting systems are rare, banks are often mistrusted, 'presents' are frequent accompaniments to commercial transactions, and fixed prices, even in retail shops, are by no means universal.[1] A problem of many modern governments has been to apply

[1] The process of haggling over prices has during the last twenty years greatly declined in most areas, but is still by no means extinct.

taxation to traders, often the wealthier section of the community, but also the more adept at concealing their resources.

Another feature of the Ottomans deriving from their origin as nomads has been a lack of material amenities in everyday life. It has been said of an Ottoman household that, as regards furnishings and material comforts, there was frequently the impression that the owner had only recently arrived, and intended to move off the next day – furniture was scanty and utilitarian, and the house itself incompletely adapted for habitation. The palace of the Sultan in Constantinople impressed one observer merely as a 'warren of undistinguished apartments', though this was not true of the exterior.

Finally, it may be noted that the Ottomans achieved power after a long series of wars mainly against Christians. Unlike the original followers of Muhammad, who practised some toleration of Christians and Jews, the Turks were fanatical Moslems, and destruction of infidels became a highly meritorious action. Intolerance and fanaticism led to a narrowing of outlook among Moslems themselves: Christian and ancient Greek philosophy, which had been drawn on by early Arab thinkers, was rejected, and Islam became for several centuries until our own time a closed and rigid system which ceased to develop further.

The discovery in 1498 by the Portuguese of the Cape route to India had a profound effect on the Middle East. A transit traffic between Europe and Asia, which from time immemorial had enriched the countries of the Middle East, was now diverted to the sea; and despite efforts by the Ottoman Sultan to intervene against Portuguese traders in the Indian Ocean, the flow of goods through Iran, Syria and Egypt ceased. Establishment in 1514 of a Portuguese fort at Ormuz at the head of the Persian Gulf excluded the Ottomans from any possibility of interference with Portuguese communications with India; as a result, the Middle East entered upon a period of decline. It was not until the cutting of the Suez Canal in 1869, and the development of motor and air transport later still, that the region recovered some of its ancient importance. Between the sixteenth and late nineteenth centuries the Middle East was increasingly remote from the main commercial currents of the world.

In the political sphere, the Ottoman Empire reached its maximum of power during the seventeenth century, when Austria was threatened and Vienna besieged. From this high-water mark, with a turning-point at the repulse of the Ottomans outside Vienna in 1683, the Empire entered on a period of slow decline. One reason for the decline was pressure by newly developing states such as Russia and Austro-Hungary, but the principal factor was unrest amongst non-Turkish subjects of the Empire, especially amongst Christian communities. A symptom of the growing weakness of the Ottomans was the rise of autonomy in outlying provinces, where the governors, at one time mere officials appointed by the Sultan from Constantinople, tended to follow an increasingly independent policy, and ultimately became hereditary rulers. The Sultan could do no more than issue a formal confirmation on the succession of a new provincial ruler. Such a development occurred in Algiers, Tunis, Egypt and the centre and south of Arabia, all of which by the nineteenth century had evolved into more or less independent states.[1]

Commercial decline in the Asiatic and African provinces of the Empire, together with the rise of political autonomy in certain regions, caused the Ottoman rulers to devote greatest attention and interest to the European part of their dominions. By the later nineteenth century, however, the rise of national feeling amongst Balkan peoples and the aggressive action of outside powers were rapidly reducing Ottoman territory in Europe, and the Sultan felt it necessary to revise the system that had been followed in non-European districts. Accordingly, a 'forward' policy, designed to reassert Turkish supremacy, was undertaken in the Middle Eastern provinces. Its exponent, Sultan Abdul Hamid II, was aided by the recent construction of the Suez Canal, which allowed the easier movements of troops from Turkey southwards. Garrisons of Ottoman soldiers were established in the Hijaz (1869), the Yemen (1872) and Hasa (1871).

Further steps in the strengthening of Turkish control in the Middle East were taken by the construction of railway routes that were designed to bring outlying provinces into closer contact with Constantinople. Lines were built with the aid of foreign capital (chiefly German) from Anatolia south-eastwards to Baghdad via Aleppo, and southwards from Aleppo through Damascus and Ma'an as far as Medina. The latter railway, said to have been built well away from the coast in order to be out of range of the British fleet, was rendered unusable during 1914–18, but is now in process of reconstruction.

The efforts of Abdul Hamid delayed but did not prevent the break-up of Ottoman power. Nationalist feeling continued to develop, and although at first restricted to the Christian peoples of the Balkans, this later became a disruptive factor amongst the Islamic populations of the Ottoman state. Arab as distinct from Turkish national feeling was fostered by the rise of semi-independent tribal leaders in Arabia, and by the organization of secret political societies of anti-Turkish complexion, chiefly in Syria. By the twentieth century, nationalism had begun to affect the Turkish people themselves. In 1908 a revolution occurred, as the result of which Abdul Hamid was deposed, and a more strongly nationalist impulse given to the policy of the Empire. Six years later Turkey entered the First World

[1] Egypt, although in effect completely independent during most of the nineteenth century, remained technically a part of the Ottoman Empire until 1914, as did Cyprus.

War on the side of Germany; and following her defeat in 1918, the complete extinction of Turkish power seemed at hand. An unlooked-for revival under Mustapha Kemal and his Nationalist party altered the situation, however; and a new, purely Turkish state came into being. For a short time the Ottoman Sultanate continued, although without effective power; but in 1923 Turkey was declared a Republic. A year later the religious title of Caliph, which had been borne by the Sultan, was also extinguished, and since that date Turkey has functioned as a nationalist, secular state.

## The political background A.D. 1800 to the present day

### Western imperialism

One element in the long-continued decline of Ottoman power was the control gained by foreigners over much of the economic life of the Turkish state. As the result of Ottoman indifference to commercial development, the way had been largely left clear for activities by outsiders. Even in the sixteenth century, when Turkish power was at its height, commercial treaties was negotiated with France, by which French merchants enjoyed special privileges within Turkish dominions. During subsequent years, other European nations followed the French lead, with the result that by the end of the nineteenth century a considerable body of rights, concessions and privileges, known collectively as Capitulations, had been granted to foreign traders. Capitulations gave to nationals of Austro-Hungary, France, Germany, Great Britain, Italy and Russia virtual exemption from most of the internal taxation of the Turkish state, together with immunity from police search of foreign-owned premises. Foreigners were also immune from trial in a Turkish court of law, special tribunals being appointed for each nationality.

Concessionaires gained control of resources which were then exploited without regard to the general interests of the country; and by lending money at usurious rates foreigners gained a stranglehold on much of the economic life of the whole Ottoman Empire – e.g. most gas, electricity and water companies, where these existed, together with the greater part of the railway system, were foreign-owned; and the fact that all mineral resources of the Empire were regarded as the personal property of the Sultan, to be disposed of as he wished, led to a form of exploitation that benefited only a few foreign commercial interests.[1] Profits from economic

[1] Sultan Abdul Hamid raised money for immediate needs by the sale of mineral concessions. Once sold, however, the concessions brought no further profit to the Turkish state; and by the opening of the twentieth century the availability of new concessions was running short, and Turkey had in effect almost ceased to derive advantage from the existence of mineral wealth within her boundaries. As well, the Turkish Sultan sold plots of land in Palestine to the first Zionists – with immeasurable consequenses for the region.

activity were drained away from the country, and, at the same time, the Turkish state was confronted with numerous non-Turkish communities over which it had no legal jurisdiction. In effect, further 'states within a state' had been created, and thus Capitulations were a kind of economic *millet*.

Further emphasizing the economic dominance of foreign powers, the Ottoman government had been forced to agree that its national debt, amounting to some £150 million ($750 million) should be administered by an international committee, the 'Council of Administration of the Ottoman Public Debt', which, presided over alternately by a Frenchman and an Englishman, was composed of nationals from Austro-Hungary, Germany, Holland, Italy and Turkey, together with a representative of the Imperial Ottoman Bank which was itself largely foreign-owned. The Council repaid interest and capital from the ordinary revenues of the Turkish state and hence had a certain control of taxation with Ottoman dominions.[1]

Economic penetration of the Ottoman Empire was accompanied by equally active political pressure. The remark of the Tsar in 1844, 'We have a sick man on our hands. It would be a grave misfortune if we were not to provide beforehand for the contingency of his death', could be taken as a summary of the attitude of most of the powers of Europe; but actual break-up of Turkish domains was delayed because of mutual jealousies among these interested powers: at times various European states were prepared to acquiesce in a continuance of Turkish power and postpone their own designs, rather than see a rival gain advantages. So in 1854 Britain and France went to war to thwart Russian schemes of expansion at Turkey's expense in the Black Sea and eastern Anatolia, and the former again threatened war in 1878 – a policy that was reversed in 1914; whilst the role of protector of Turkish interest, undertaken first by the British and later by Germany, could not be called an entirely disinterested one.[2]

In Ottoman affairs, the nineteenth century was a period of accelerated decline as the result both of internal weakness and of outside pressure. The more outlying provinces of the Empire, those of north-west Africa, achieved virtual independence, only to fall later under French, Spanish and Italian dominance; and by the opening of the nineteenth century even the position of Egypt as an Ottoman province had become increasingly doubtful.

[1] Chief creditors were: France (60% of the total debt), Germany (20%), Britain (15%). Staff of the Council of Administration numbered in 1912 approximately 9000 persons.
[2] Witness the cession of Cyprus to Britain in 1878 'as a base for the defence of the Ottoman Empire', and the grant of concessions for the 'Berlin–Baghdad' railway to Germany.

## Egypt and the Sudan

During this period an Albanian adventurer named Mohammed Ali rose to power in Egypt. At one time it seemed as though Mohammed Ali might successfully overturn the Ottomans in Syria and Crete, and establish an Egyptian Empire; but European intervention, with Austria and Britain supporting the Turks, and France supporting Mohammed Ali, led to the defeat of Mohammed Ali's wider aspirations, although he remained as ruler of Egypt, where his dynasty reigned until 1953.

French influence and support remained in Egypt: the campaigns of Napoleon in 1798 had stimulated European, and particularly French, interest in the country. It is not always remembered that Napoleon included a number of archaeologists and scientists in his invading army, or that the deciphering of ancient Egyptian hieroglyphics may be said to date from the discovery of the Rosetta Stone during French occupation. Mohammed Ali, an exact contemporary of Napoleon (both were born in 1769), had great admiration for the conqueror of Europe, and imitated his methods, often with success. Traces of French influence came therefore to be a feature in the state of Mohammed Ali and his successors; and it is significant that at the present day French language and culture still persist among the educated classes of Egypt. Publication of several daily newspapers in the French language is an indication of the strong Francophile tendencies of certain groups of the population.

A further link between Egypt and France was the construction by de Lesseps in 1869 of the Suez Canal, a project that had been actively opposed by Britain. It seemed as though Egypt was slowly moving within the French orbit, but in the words of H. A. L. Fisher, 'it was England that stumbled into the inheritance which France had marked for her own'. In 1874 a successor of Mohammed Ali, the Khedive Ismail, who had been allotted a large number of foundation shares in the Suez Canal Company, found himself in difficult financial straits, and decided to sell his holding in the Canal Company. At the instigation of Disraeli, then Prime Minister, the British government quickly came forward as a buyer, and, by the purchase of the Khedive's shares for £4 million, found itself the principal shareholder in the Suez Canal Company, and the possessor of an important stake in Egyptian affairs. This sale by the Khedive did little to ameliorate his financial position, and within a very few years, as the result of continued extravagance, Ismail was once more heavily in debt, chiefly to British and French bond-holders.

The British government ultimately determined to take action in order to secure repayment of its nationals who had lent money in Egypt, and France, encouraged by Bismarck who was anxious that France should find colonial commitments,[1] joined with Britain in securing the deposition

[1] As a distraction from a possible war of revenge over Alsace–Lorraine.

of Ismail, and the reorganization of Egyptian finances. The latter proved
to be a longer and more difficult task than had been anticipated, and France
subsequently withdrew. As a result, control of Egyptian affairs fell
entirely to Great Britain.

Before 1800, the Sudan had stood in relation to Egypt somewhat in
the same position as Arabia in relation to Turkey – i.e. a vague suzerainty
existed, although in fact various local rulers were more or less completely
independent. The position had, however, been altered by Mohammed Ali,
who undertook a reconquest of the Sudan, and was later able to use
Sudanese troops in his campaigns against the Ottomans. Garrisons of
Egyptian troops were maintained in the Sudan both by Mohammed Ali
and his descendant Ismail, so that when British intervention in Egyptian
affairs began, these garrisons, precariously maintained by a now weakened
government among a hostile population, had become a special
preoccupation.

In 1881 an outbreak of religious fanaticism occurred in the Sudan, where
an obscure Moslem from Dongola proclaimed himself the Mahdi and
announced as his object the conquest of the world. After initial successes
against both Egyptian and British forces (during which General Gordon
was killed at Khartoum), the military power of the Sudanese dervishes
was finally broken at Omdurman (1898), by combined British and
Egyptian forces under Kitchener, and joint rule by Britain and Egypt (a
Condominium) established.[1]

Rule by Condominium in effect gave by far the larger share of influence
in the Sudan to Britain, but it is necessary to note that Egypt's special
position as legal co-ruler was recognized until the final attainment of Sudan
independence in 1956. This gave rise to much difficulty, since to most
Egyptians the Sudan was and perhaps should still be an integral part of
national territory. Besides the political supremacy established before
British occupation of Egypt, there is the highly important economic factor
of Nile river control: with the present situation of, in effect, complete
utilization of Nile water within Egypt, the key to future expansion of
irrigation development lies within the Sudan – everything that could be
done within Egypt was achieved by the Nasser High Dam project. Many
Egyptians hoped that the Sudan would opt to join with Egypt; and
although the Sudanese have so far preferred complete independence, there
is no doubt that union with the Sudan remains one of the highly desired
aims of Egyptian policy, and the declaration in 1970 of 'association' is
welcomed in Egypt.

In 1914, on the declaration of war by Turkey, Egypt, which had
remained nominally under Ottoman suzerainty, was declared independent,

[1] Although, in fact, the reconquest had been carried out by British troops, it will be
remembered that the Sudan was technically an Egyptian province, and that Britain was
merely acting legally on behalf of Egypt in intervening in Sudanese affairs.

though in fact internal control remained largely in British hands, and British forces were stationed in the country.[1] At the end of the war, Egyptian agitation developed, with the aim of securing effective independence, and in 1924 a treaty was signed by which Britain handed over control of the bulk of her affairs to Egypt herself, retaining the right to maintain garrisons of British troops in Egypt for the defence of the Suez Canal. Later changes in the political situation – the eclipse of Italy, the enhanced wealth of Egypt following the war of 1939, together with a decline in British influence following the Second World War – led to more and more insistent demands for complete independence. By slow stages British garrisons were withdrawn and bases evacuated; until, following the 1956 Suez episode, the last remaining groups – civilian technicians in Canal Zone bases – were withdrawn. Egypt then found herself entirely in control of all her territories, and the triumphant acknowledged leader of Arab nationalism in the Middle East.

We must go back a little to the situation in the Sudan. So long as Britain remained in effective control of Egypt, relations with the Sudan under Condominium meant, as we have noted, parallel rule of the Sudan by the British, who found it extremely convenient from many points of view to regard themselves as in theory part-agents and in fact total rulers. From time to time Sudanese insurrection occurred, and it was not until 1916 that the last dissident province, that of Darfur, was fully brought under rule from Khartoum.

However, with Egyptian independence after 1924, the Sudan passed first from direct rule in effect by the British into a period of Indirect Rule or Native Administration, with a parallel 'Southern Policy' applied to the non-Islamic peoples of the south, who were regarded as possible adherents to a federation that might in the future be based on East Africa. Moslems were impelled to move out of the southern areas, which were declared 'Closed Districts', with the aim of discouraging migration out of them by their non-Islamic inhabitants, and migration outwards by Moslems. It was during the period of Native Administration (1924–43) that the Gezira Cotton Growing Scheme was expanded from its early, private beginnings.

Nationalist feeling developed in strength, but was faced with a dilemma: total independence, or connection of some kind with Egypt? When in 1953 the monarchy in Egypt came to an end, a way seemed clearer towards solving this problem. Egypt under Nasser believed that the Sudan Union political party would opt in favour of permanent union with Egypt, and supported it, so that its leader was able to assume power in 1955 as head of an independent state of the Sudan. On doing so, however, he declared for total independence rather than any form of union with

[1] Cyprus, also technically Ottoman territory, passed at the same time under direct British rule as a Crown Colony.

Egypt. During the 1960s there was much insurrection and separatism in the non-Islamic areas of the south, due partly to heavy-handed, uncomprehending rule from Khartoum, but mostly reflecting the ferment for national freedom and aspiration that swept much of central Africa at this time: if an independent Kenya or Uganda, why not a separate southern Sudan? After a period of unsuccessful military action by the north against the south, which led to a mass flight of southerners as refugees in adjacent territories, an amnesty was declared in 1965, and since that time conditions have improved, very slowly at first, but much faster after the declaration by President Nimeiri (who came to power in 1969) establishing regional autonomy for the south, which, at first organized in three provinces, was re-organized into six during 1976 in order to facilitate development and planning.

## Asia Minor and the Levant

Throughout the nineteenth century Asia Minor and the Levant – 'heartland' of the Ottoman Empire – remained outside foreign political control. As we have seen, attempts at political domination were largely thwarted by international rivalries. Penetration of these regions was limited to the economic and cultural spheres, and in the latter instance sectarian differences provided the main opening for intervention: Russia remained in close contact with Orthodox Christian minorities, France championed the Uniates and Britain supported Muhammadanism, sometimes orthodox, sometimes heretical, as in the case of the Druzes during the 1840s. In 1860 massacre of Maronites by the Druzes led to intervention, chiefly by France, and the creation of limited autonomy for Lebanese Christians in the form of an 'Organic State of Mount Lebanon', which, limited to the higher parts of the northern Lebanon range, was cut off from the sea and contained no important towns. Baabda, a village on the outskirts of Beirut, served as a winter capital, and Beit-ed-Din, a mountain settlement, seat of the former Emirs of the Lebanon, fulfilled a similar function in summer.

Reference has previously been made to the growth of Arab as distinct from Turkish nationalism during the last century; and by 1914 a number of secret societies designed to advance Arab nationalist aims were in existence, chiefly in Damascus and Beirut. When war broke out between Turkey and the western powers, these societies attracted the attention of Britain, and encouragement of Arab nationalism both in Syria (i.e. Syria in 1914, which included Palestine and Transjordan) and Arabia proper came to be appreciated as a useful political weapon in the struggle against Turkey. A small group within the Allied armies in the Middle East was allotted the task of fostering Arab revolt against Ottoman overlords by

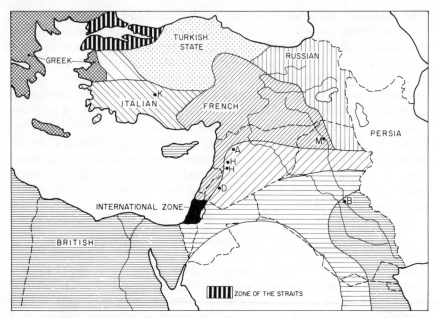

*Fig.* 7.6 The Sykes–Picot Treaty of 1916. Wide shading: sphere of influence; narrow shading, control.

means of monetary subsidies and small-scale military assistance, and best known of this group was T. E. Lawrence.

Besides Arab nationalism, the Allies had other war aims of far greater interest. With Britain, France and Russia now committed after decades of hesitation and suspicion to a break-up of Ottoman power, new arrangements could be considered. An important complicating factor was the position of Italy who, having seized the Dodecanese Islands and the northern coastlands of Tripolitania and Cyrenaica during Turkish preoccupations in the Balkan wars of 1910–12, was party to the Triple Alliance that ranged her on the side of Germany and Austria. It became an object of Franco-British policy to detach Italy from the Central Powers by offers of territory: and in 1916 the Sykes–Picot Treaty delimited precise future allocations within the Middle East of territories, either in full possession or as spheres of influence in a reduced Turkish state. The Sykes–Picot agreement never came into effect, however, since Tsarist Russia collapsed in the following year, before Turkey was defeated, but the treaty is interesting not only as reflecting the balance of power as it existed in 1914–16 between the three countries, but as showing intention to partition the Middle East.

With the defeat of the Ottomans in 1918, it seemed as though the end of Turkey as a state was at hand. Despite Russian preoccupations, which prevented her claiming her allotted share in the division of the country, British, French, Italian and Greek influence was paramount, and the Treaty of Sèvres, proposed as a political resettlement of Asia Minor in 1920, would have resulted in a virtual extinction of Turkish power. In effect, the position of Britain, France, Italy and Greece as previously defined in 1914–16 was to continue unaltered; new elements were that the zone of the Straits, formerly allocated to Russia, was to pass under international control, and American interests led to proposals for an Armenian state to be created in the former Russian zone of eastern Anatolia. The Treaty of Sèvres can be regarded as the high-water mark of European intervention in the Middle East – had it been implemented, practically the whole of the Middle East region, except for Iran and inner Arabia, would have fallen under foreign domination or influence.

Faced with the possibility of near extinction as a political unit, the Turks rallied, and, owing partly to division between the Allies (especially as affecting Britain and France), partly to general war-weariness, and partly to their own courage, sustained by desperation, an unlooked-for revival of Turkish power occurred under the leadership of Mustapha Kemal Pasha. After some months of fighting, the French withdrew claims to the part of Anatolia allotted to them under the Treaty of Sèvres. A year later the Greek-held city of Smyrna (Izmir) was taken by storm, and a large Greek population, numbering over half a million, fled to Greece or was forcibly expelled – many being literally driven into the sea or massacred. The total of Greek deaths is estimated at one million. In this manner a great measure of ethnic and political unity was achieved in western Asia Minor, though at a heavy price both in human suffering and in economic disruption. The former Greek population was highly skilled, and formed the greater part of the artisan and trading classes in Turkey – communities that the new state, deeply involved in reconstruction problems, could ill afford to lose.

In the east, the Armenian question had been to some extent resolved by the massacre of large numbers of Armenians by the Kurds; and outside military support from one of the great nations would have been necessary in order to erect a separate Armenian state. This support was not forthcoming, and to date the nearest solution of Armenian problems – though hardly one which is satisfactory to all Armenians – has been the creation of an Armenian Soviet Republic within the Soviet Union. Hence, untouched on the east and victorious in the west, the new Turkish state was able to negotiate a more advantageous peace settlement, the Treaty of Lausanne (1923), by which control of Asia Minor and the adjacent area of European Turkey remained firmly in Turkish hands. Since that time Turkey has developed further in internal strength, as the result of fundamental social and economic reforms undertaken by Kemal Pasha (Ataturk). Now, in terms of area, population and economic potential, Turkey regards herself as certainly one of, if not the leading Middle Eastern state. The growth of Russian power, always dreaded in Turkey, has driven the country, unlike most others of the Middle East, actively to seek alliances in the West; and at her own pressing request, Turkey joined NATO in 1952. America has provided considerable amounts of military, financial and technical assistance, and an economic link of longer standing with Western Germany has also greatly revived since 1945. The relations of Turkey with the USA have latterly been cooler following American disapproval of Turkey's part in the partition of Cyprus, despite the presence of what was described in 1977 as 'a six billion dollar military infrastructure' in Turkey.

*The Levant*   In enlisting Arab help (as an 'irregular right wing' on the flank of the Turkish army) against the Ottomans during 1914–18, the promise was made by the British that Arabs should achieve independence and sovereignty in Arab lands captured from the Turks. A reservation was, however, made in the case of Palestine, concerning which promises had also been made to the Jews. Following the entry of the Arabs into Damascus in 1918, the Arab leader Feisul took over, with British acquiescence, control of government in Syria. France had long entertained the ambition to rule in Damascus and Aleppo, and, not being a party to the negotiations between Britain and the Arab leaders, considered herself free to follow another policy in Syria.

In 1920, after some months of uneasy joint occupation of the Levant by British and French troops, during which time France became increasingly mistrustful of the presence of Feisul's government in Damascus, the French determined to bring Syria more effectively under French control. Following the proclamation by Arab nationalists of Feisul as king of an independent Syria, the French undertook a military campaign to expel him, and with the defeat of his army outside Damascus, Feisul was forced to leave the country. Thence onwards, Syria was administered under mandate, as a federation of territorial units. This scheme, by which six theoretically autonomous political units were created, proved unworkable after a few years, and was later modified.

The ruling of Syria proved an onerous task, and relations between France and the local population were rarely harmonious. One major rebellion took place in 1925, when French hold over Syria was severely shaken for some months. During the next 15 years Syrian exasperation mounted as first Egypt and then Iraq shook off British tutelage, the former by the treaty of 1924, the latter by the ending of the British mandate in 1932. A treaty reducing French influence in Syrian affairs had, however, been negotiated during 1938; but this was rejected by the French Chamber of Deputies in Paris, and the war of 1939 began with Syria firmly held as a part of French overseas possessions. In 1941, with the occupation of metropolitan France, Syria came to be used as a German base for operations in the Middle East. When this trend became apparent, British and Free French forces invaded Syria, and after some months of fighting occupied the country. It was stated at the time of entry of British and Free French troops that Syrian and Lebanese independence would be recognized,[1] but for some time, partly because of the exigencies of war, no action was taken to make this independence effective. In 1944, when the tide of war had receded from the Middle East, differences between Free French and Syrians once more became acute, and in the following year open military clashes occurred. The French undertook a bombardment of Damascus, in order to reduce the main centre of Syrian nationalism; at the same time French garrisons in some other towns of Syria were made prisoner by the Arabs. A large-scale rising, involving the whole of Syria and the Lebanon, seemed imminent; and in view of the importance of Syria as a part of the corridor linking Europe to the war areas of the Far East, the British government decided to intervene.

British forces in Syria were increased, and energetic steps taken to end the military clashes in Damascus and elsewhere. Within a year, both French and British forces had been withdrawn from Syria, and complete independence was at last attained, with a formal ending of the mandate and the creation of sovereign republics of Syria and the Lebanon. For some years the two countries maintained an economic union; but in 1950 this was dissolved, and eight years later Syria joined with Egypt to form the United Arab Republic, a situation that ended with the withdrawal of Syria from the UAR in 1961. It is to be questioned how far British action against France in 1944 produced or exacerbated the attitudes of General de Gaulle over Israel and later over British application for entry to the EEC.

Since her resumption of full independence in 1961, Syria has increasingly aligned her policy towards understanding with the Soviet Union and the Comecon powers.

*Palestine*  At the same time that France received a mandate for Syria, Britain was also allotted a similar mandate for Palestine and the region lying east of the Jordan river. In the former area Britain was committed to what has since proved the impossible task of creating a 'National Home for the Jews' without prejudicing the rights of Arabs living there; in the

---

[1] Declaration by General Catroux, commander of the Free French forces at Damascus, September 1941. It should be noted that on occupying Syria, the Free French authorities assumed full control of the country, as the legal rulers recognized by Britain.

latter, a purely Arab area, the Emir Abdullah, an elder brother of the Emir Feisul, was proclaimed ruler of a state of Transjordan, under British Mandate. Though small and poor, the country of Transjordan proved for several decades to be a stable political unit, and after some twenty-five years as mandated territory, during which a slow but consistent development took place, the full independence of Transjordan was recognized in 1946, and since 1949 the country has been known as the Hashemite Kingdom of Jordan.

In Palestine, unrest and disturbance have continued since the end of the First World War down to our own times. Increasingly large-scale immigration of Jews after 1918 aroused apprehension among the then Arab majority – later to be justified – that Palestine would eventually become predominantly Jewish; and in fact the earlier Jewish call for 'refuge' and 'a home' within Palestine gradually turned into more insistent demands for a sovereign Jewish state.

Jewish observers see Jewish colonization of Palestine/Israel as occurring in a series of 'waves'. In the later 1880s, alongside an Arab population of about 440000, there grew up some 25000 Jews – chiefly refugees from Tsarist Russian pogroms. A 'second immigration' took place in the first years of the twentieth century, again composed of Russians, this time of more pronounced socialistic and communistic leanings. It was these immigrants who started the *kibbutz* idea. A third wave of immigrants after 1918 was made up of dispossessed refugees from the devastated areas of central Europe. Another considerable increase in immigration, this time of Jews affected by anti-semitism in Poland, took place between 1924 and 1928. Persecution in Hitlerite Germany then led to the fifth 'wave' of immigration, on this occasion by German Jews.

Such mounting entry of Jewish immigrants led to serious riots and civil disobedience by the Arabs in 1929 and again in 1936–39. This disorder and rioting achieved a certain success in that a limit (75000 persons within five years) was placed on Jewish immigration, but the lesson that the mandatory power was amenable to influence by rebellion and armed revolt was not lost on the minority group in Palestine.[1] During the war of 1939 arms and ammunition were accumulated by both Arabs and Jews, and with the end of warfare in 1945 the extremist section of the Zionists opened a campaign of terrorism and intimidation to effect a return to unrestricted Jewish immigration, as the first step to the final objective of a Jewish Palestine.[2]

[1] 'The Jews in Palestine are convinced that Arab violence paid.' Report of the Anglo-American Committee of Inquiry, 1946.
[2] This movement in favour of unrestricted immigration from Europe into Palestine had a certain amount of support from France, Russia and USA. In all three countries motives were mixed – there was a humanitarian desire to help the distressed Jews of central Europe, freed from persecution in Hitlerite Germany; but there was also some tinge of

In 1947 the question of settlement in Palestine was referred to the United Nations Organization, and a Commission – the nineteenth in twenty-five years – once more surveyed conditions in the country. The report of the Commission was in favour of partitioning the country between Arabs and Jews, with Jerusalem under international control. But mounting terrorist action, chiefly by Zionists, prevented implementation of the report, and in May 1948 British Mandatory rule was officially declared at an end. Three months later the last British forces were withdrawn, and fighting immediately broke out between Zionists and the states of the Arab League. Some 700 000 to 1 million Arabs fled from Palestine into nearby Arab countries, where most still remain as destitute refugees. Eventually an armistice was declared, with existing battle-positions stabilized to form a frontier. A small strip near Gaza occupied by the Egyptian army was incorporated into Egypt, and portions of the Judaean highlands and Jordan valley held by the forces of King Abdullah formed an enlarged state of Transjordan, then renamed Jordan. The remainder of Palestine (including the New City of Jerusalem but not the Old City) became the Jewish state of Israel. Between 1949 and 1951 the population of Israel doubled, mainly due to massive immigration, this time mainly from Arab countries, where Jewish groups, often of long standing, were no longer desired. Late in 1956, following a secret agreement with France and Britain (details of which did not appear until ten years later) Israel occupied the Gaza strip (a region where Arab refugees were concentrated), the entire Sinai as far as Suez, and islands in the Gulf of Aqaba. United Nations action led to later Israeli evacuation of these territories; but in 1967 a demand by Egypt for the withdrawal of the UN peace-keeping force led to the 'Six-Day War' during which Israel, after a brilliant campaign, was able to re-occupy the entire Sinai region as far as the Suez Canal, over-run all the Jordanian West Bank (including the Old City of Jerusalem) and push the frontier with Syria over the Golan summits to threaten the lowland leading to Damascus. This brought a further 1·1 million Arabs under Israeli rule in the so-called Occupied Territories (450 000 in the Gaza strip, and 650 000 in the West Bank). At first, with the exception of the Old City of Jerusalem which was fully absorbed into a single Jewish municipality, Jewish settlement in the Occupied area was not permitted, but gradually a cluster of Jewish settlements of various kinds has developed mainly but not solely in the Jordan valley zone. The 'legality' or otherwise of some of these settlements is now a major issue both as regards external politics and also within Israel. Jerusalem has been rapidly colonized by

political animus against Great Britain, as the result of which none of the three countries was wholly averse to witnessing an increase in Britain's difficulties. France, in particular, had reason to recall the events of 1944–45 in Syria, and the part Britain had played in bringing about the end of the French Mandate; whilst the Jewish 'vote' in the USA is of considerable importance.

Jews: in 1977 it was stated that 34000 new dwellings (chiefly high rise flats) had been built in the last three years or are planned for the future.

## Iraq

The present political unit came into existence after the Versailles settlement of 1919, when it was to a great extent inevitable that control of the lower valleys of the Tigris and Euphrates should fall to Britain. River navigation and rail communications had for long been in British hands; the development of oil in Iran had enhanced the value of the river ports of the Shatt el Arab; and British influence was paramount in the Persian Gulf.

Britain was first allotted a Class A mandate for Iraq south of latitude 35°N,[1] and shortly afterwards the Emir Feisul was elected king by almost unanimous plebiscite. Thus Britain could claim that promises made to Arab nationalists were to a great extent fulfilled – states ruled by the leaders of the revolt, Feisul and Abdullah, had come into existence, though subordinate for a limited term of years to a mandatory power.

Difficulty was experienced over frontiers. On the north, the Mosul Vilayet, with its future oil possibilities was until 1926 in contention between Britain, Turkey and France, with some interest expressed from the USA: in that year the Vilayet was finally awarded to Iraq. In the south-west, most of the population was for long nomadic, with pastoralists moving between Saudi Arabia, Iraq and Kuwait. Eventually, two lozenge-shaped 'neutral territories' were created to facilitate movement; but these were partitioned in the 1970s, in view of their enhanced value as oilfields. The frontier between Iraq and Kuwait is still a matter of controversy, with independent Iraq claiming from time to time that Kuwait is geographically part of the Mesopotamian valley, and thus alienated Iraqi territory. In 1961 and again in 1973 and 1976 frontier 'incidents' occurred, with an international peacekeeping force from other Arab countries interposed for some months in 1961.

Although British Mandate ended in 1932, and a treaty was negotiated by which Iraq took over full powers of government,[2] the political evolution of the country can hardly be said to have been of the happiest. The death in 1933 of King Feisul, a sagacious and far-seeing ruler, was a great loss to his country, since his attempts to develop a broad unity of sects and parties with a high standard of probity and disinterest were not continued to the same degree after his death. A massacre of Assyrian Christians

---

[1] A Class A mandate – under which Syria and the Lebanon, Palestine, Transjordan and Iraq were all held – envisaged a limited term of rule by the mandatory, following which independence would be granted.
[2] Britain retained the right to maintain certain airfields in Iraq.

by Kurds was allowed to pass unpunished by a Moslem cabinet; and rifts between the then governing groups, largely Sunni, and the mass of Shi'a peasantry, grew in extent. In 1958 a revolution overthrew the Hashemite dynasty, and since that time Iraq has pursued political aims aligned, like those of Syria, towards socialism and greater friendship with Russia. A long-continued source of internal strife has been the demands of Iraqi Kurds for autonomy in the area of the Zagros that they inhabit; as this includes the Kirkuk oilfield zone, the demand was resisted by Baghdad. The result has been a long period of intermittent insurrection, with periodic civil war. Iraq, like Syria, has increasingly oriented domestic and foreign policy towards social and political links with the Communist states, but relations with Syria, despite this, have not always been good.

## Iran

Events in Iran have been influenced by the internal decline of the country from the position of great strength in the eighteenth century, when northern India was held as an Iranian dependency; and by the accompanying rise of Russia as an imperial power. By the end of the eighteenth century a Russian advance south-eastwards had absorbed the Tartar tribes of the lower Volga region, and had begun to extend along the western shores of the Caspian Sea, directly threatening Iran. In the first years of the nineteenth century Iranian-owned territory was reached with the occupation of Georgia.

French interest in Iranian affairs provoked counter-measures from Britain, and when in 1807, after the Treaty of Tilsit, French policy veered round to friendship with Russia, French influence in Iran declined. In 1814 a defensive alliance was concluded between Britain and Iran, by which Iran was to assist at need in the defence of Afghanistan, in return for a money subsidy.[1]

Despite this alliance, Iran lost much territory between 1804 and 1828. As we have seen, the ruler of Georgia, formerly a client of the Shah, was forced to accept Russian suzerainty in 1800, and Iranian attempts by war to recover Georgia led to the loss of further territory. By the Treaty of Turcomanchai, which closed the war in 1828, Iran was forced to agree to the loss not only of Georgia, but also of the districts of Erivan and Lenkoran; to the payment of an indemnity to Russia; and to the grant of capitulatory rights within Iran to Russian citizens.[2] It was this treaty that brought into existence the present Russo-Iranian frontier

[1] It should be noted that this treaty was directed against France, who had recently threatened India. Nothing was stipulated regarding Russia, with which Britain was at the time an ally, in the war against Napoleon.

[2] Capitulations had previously been granted to British nationals during the seventeenth century.

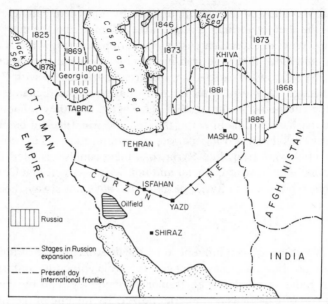

*Fig.* 7.7 Russian expansion in Iran, and the Curzon Line.

between the Black Sea and the Caspian; and thence onwards until the present Iran was rarely able to face Russia on politically equal terms.

Thus reduced in influence, and unable to resist either Russian or British inroads on her sovereignty, Iranian diplomacy aimed at playing off one country against the other: the most that Iranians hoped to achieve was a stalemate between the two. This situation was the fundamental feature in Iranian affairs down to the present, and although one side has at times gained a temporary advantage, the balance has in the main been preserved, and still continues its uneasy existence, with, however, the USA replacing Britain as principal opponent of Russia. Iran is currently of prime importance as a political unit in the struggle between East and West, and having gained markedly over the past few years in economic strength, is now able to derive much political advantage from this 'uncommitted' position.

With the western shores of the Caspian occupied, the Russians were free to turn their attention to the east, and, after 1840, a series of aggressive expeditions brought Turcoman and Uzbeg tribesmen living in the Aral region under Russian rule. In 1864 Tashkent was taken, in 1886 Samarkhand, in 1873 Khiva, and in 1876 Khokhand. The final state was reached between 1880 and 1893, when the northern slopes of the Kopet Dagh ranges were occupied, and Merv, loosely held by Iran, passed to Russian control. A series of boundary commissions fixed the final

Russo-Iranian frontier east of the Caspian Sea, as the result of which the fertile lower slopes of the Kopet Dagh were allotted as part of the Russian Empire, to the disadvantage of Iran.

During the same period, the Iranian frontier with Afghanistan was demarcated by a number of British officials: but Iran remained dissatisfied, and the question was finally settled by a Turkish arbitrator during 1934–5. On the west, the ancient indefinite frontier zone between the Ottoman and Iranian states was precisely delimited by an Anglo-Russian commission, following which a small area now developed as the Naft Khaneh oilfield passed under Turkish (later Iraqi) ownership. A feature reflecting the relative weakness of Iran was the allocation of the entire Shatt el Arab to Turkey (Iraq) with the frontier at the eastern bank to the detriment of Iran, and not down the *thalweg* (centre of the waterway). Thus Iran controlled only the immediate approaches to Abadan, Khorramshahr and Khorzabad, and had no possibility of developing other ports on the Shatt el Arab. This situation ended in 1975 when the frontier was rectified to lie along the river *thalweg*.

With Iran closely enveloped on the north, attention subsequently shifted to the Persian Gulf, where at first Iran found herself strong enough to maintain or even extend her hold over a number of islands (Qishm, Hormuz, Larak and Henjam). Here in the south, though, the influence of sea-power based on India gave to Britain a specially advantageous position; and on the southern shores of the Gulf a number of Arab sheikhdoms (Bahrain, Kuwait, Muscat) were induced to accept British protection. One reason for British interest in the Gulf was the prevalence of slave-trading, with victims seized from east Africa and Baluchistan. Other prominent activities were gun-running and piracy; and it was largely owing to British efforts that all three practices were more or less suppressed. Iran had, however, regarded herself as involved to the extent of ruling in parts of the southern Gulf coast – especially Bahrain: this claim was based on the undoubted presence of many Persian and Baluchi inhabitants in the sheikdoms, and the undoubted fact that Bahrain was ruled by Iran on several occasions, the last being 1602–1782. When the British withdrew in 1971 Iran forthwith occupied two small islands, Abu Musa and Tumbs; these islands lie offshore of Sharjah, and Iran has been successful in gaining participation in the offshore oil field that surrounds the islands.

In the last few years of the nineteenth century, Russian eyes were turned towards the Persian Gulf as a possible site for a warm-water port. This provoked strong reaction from Britain, and Russia was directly warned that attempts to establish her influence in the Gulf would be forcibly resisted (Curzon Declaration of 1902).

Within Iran itself, however, the situation was very different, being by far the more favourable for Russia which directly enveloped Iran on three sides. It therefore seemed credible to assume at the beginning of the twentieth century that the whole country would ultimately fall under Russian influence – Russian traders were most numerous in the region, the rich Caspian provinces, with valuable sturgeon fisheries, were tending to become economic dependencies of Russia, and, as a symptom of the control exercised by Russia, we may note the fact that Russian opposition successfully prevented Baron de Reuter from obtaining a mining concession with Iran during 1872. The long-continued expansion of Russian power was, however, checked by the Russo-Japanese war of 1904, which revealed unsuspected Russian weakness; and in 1907 a compromise was arrived at over Iran by which the country was partitioned into three zones, one Russian, one British and one neutral[1] (fig. 7.7). Russia held exclusive rights concerning economic matters within her own zone, as did the British in the south, and both nations were free to seek concessions and influence in the neutral zone.

As at first drawn up, the treaty of 1907 seemed to give by far the greater advantage to Russia, since the Russian zone included most of the towns and the fertile land of Iran. But the subsequent discovery of oilfields in the neutral zone, and their development by British capital with the British government as a large shareholder, made the entire neutral area in effect a British preserve, thus restoring the balance. Once again, Britain and Russia were able to confront each other in Iran on equal terms.

With the outbreak of war in 1914, Iran, though ostensibly neutral, found herself immediately involved, as both warring sides fought across her territory. A Russian attack on north-eastern Turkey, partly over Iranian soil, provoked a counter-attack by the Turks in the district of Lake Urmia; whilst further south, Turkish armies attempted to penetrate from Mesopotamia through the Zagros mountains by way of Kermanshah. From the start British forces had occupied the head of the Persian Gulf in order to protect the oilfields of south-west Iran; and Turkish and German agents attempted to embarrass the British by fomenting guerrilla warfare and attacks on the oilfields by nomadic tribes living in the Zagros. These attempts were on a considerable scale and gave anxiety on many occasions.

British intervention in Iran increased after the Russian collapse in 1917, and a British force was sent to north-west Iran to resist German and Turkish pressure in the Caucasus district. This force was supported at first by scattered White Russian units, so that the British became increasingly at odds with the newly formed Bolshevik armies, and events finally reached the stage of active warfare for a time between Britain and Soviet Russia.

[1] Another reason for the conclusion of the 1907 treaty was the rise of an aggressive Germany – a potential enemy both of Russia and of Great Britain.

This friction gave favourable conditions for a revival of Iranian strength, and from 1919 onwards a marked improvement began. The revival, like that in Turkey, was fostered by an ex-army officer, Reza Khan, who by means of a *coup d'état* in 1921 marched on Tehran and seized power from the hands of a feeble and bankrupt Shah. A treaty, remarkably favourable to Iran, was negotiated with the Russians, who relinquished all their commercial and economic rights in Iran, with the exception of control of the Caspian fisheries. Strengthened in this way, Reza Khan was able first to undertake a reduction of British influence, and later, a pacification of the tribal areas, which had for long been almost independent of Tehran. Kurds, Lurs, Qashqai, Bakhtiari, Baluch and Khuzistan tribesmen were in turn subdued by military force; and thus, master of Iran, Reza Khan was able to secure the deposition of the reigning Shah, and to assume the title himself (1925).[1] One will note the close similarity between events in Iran and the policy of Kemal Pasha, whose activities in Turkey were an example and stimulus to his fellow autocrat in Iran.

After 1925, Reza Shah embarked on a policy of extensive modernization. Besides enforcing the wearing of European dress, and the emancipation of women, attention was paid to expanding economic life by the development of modern industry. Perhaps most important of all, since the greatest number of people were involved, numerous nomadic tribesmen were forcibly settled and compelled to adopt cultivation as a livelihood. There was in this an underlying political motive – as a sedentary population, the tribesmen would be less independent and troublesome.

During his reign, Reza Shah achieved many beneficial results: stagnant life in Iran revived, and a certain amount of prosperity began to return. It seemed that the country might successfully follow the example of Turkey in surviving the upheavals of the early twentieth century, and in adapting herself to modern conditions. But when in 1941 the Shah refused to expel German agents at the request of Britain and Russia, he over-estimated the strength of his own position. Under stress of events in Europe, Anglo-Russian differences were temporarily forgotten, and for Iran it was no longer possible to follow the traditional plan of playing off the two rivals one against the other. A joint Anglo-Russian invasion followed, and the Shah was deposed, to be succeeded by his son, who now rules.

During the war years, 1941–45, Iran became an important supply base for the Middle East, particularly as regards the transference of materials to Russia. Roads and railways were built to link the Persian Gulf and Russia; but this and also the increased volume of demand for Iranian products were offset by very considerable inflation. After the end of the

---

[1] Reza Khan took the title of Reza Shah Pahlevi – an emphasis on the purely native origin of the new ruler (Pahlevi means Persian).

war, Iran found herself again subjected to political pressures. There were some local demands in the north-west for regional autonomy, and Russia remained in occupation of the Tabriz area for several years after the end of the war. For some years the Tudeh (left wing) party engaged in opposition to the Shah's government, with tacit support at least from the USSR; and internal unrest from tribal elements – chiefly the Bakhtiari and Qashqai – produced a situation of near civil war in some of the more distant areas of the mountains.

For a number of years, therefore, the Iranian government was subjected to tensions within and pressures from without the country. However, the economic situation began to improve in the late 1950s, and the Shah found himself able to undertake the 'white revolution' of forcing land reform on reluctant landowners. This was successful, and so the political strength demonstrated reacted on the economic prospects, which over the past 20 years have been totally transformed by the rapidly rising level of oil revenues. A series of Five Year Plans, amended as necessary as revenues rose, has greatly expanded infrastructures and allowed a wider range of economic activity, particularly in the industrial sector: in some recent years annual growth rate has been of the order of 20–25%. As a result Iran is now certainly one of the leading political units not merely in the Middle East, but also now in a world context, as a highly influential member of OPEC.

## Arabia

The peninsula of Arabia long remained, as the result of isolation and poverty in natural resources, for the greater part outside the main sphere of imperialist influence. It was only on the coast that European occupation occurred – Britain, anxious to secure bases for her sea routes to India, obtained control of the Aden district in 1839. Further British expansion in Arabia followed, with the double aim of ending slave-raiding and acting as a counterpoise to Russian designs in Iran. With the southern shores of the Persian/Arab Gulf in British hands, Russian influence in the north could be checked; the route to India safeguarded. Hence a number of treaties were negotiated with the sheikhs of coastal territories in Arabia, by which British protection was accepted, but internal affairs were left to the jurisdiction of native rulers. This was a policy *par excellence* of 'marginal control', and the precise degree to which British influence extended inland was never fully defined.

In the interior, Turkish hold on the tribes was shadowy and precarious even after the Ottoman revival under Abdul Hamid II. Away from the garrison towns of Mecca, Medina and Sana'a tribal government and intertribal rivalry and warfare persisted. Most important of the non-

Turkish rulers in Arabia at the beginning of the twentieth century was King Hussein, Sherif of Mecca, Hereditary Guardian of the Holy Places of Islam, and direct descendant of the Prophet Muhammad. In 1914, Hussein was persuaded to take up the cause of Arab nationalism and though Hussein himself had no active share in the fighting, his son Feisul assumed command of the Arab army that conducted irregular operations against the Turks in Arabia and Syria; and it was to this army that T. E. Lawrence was attached during the campaigns of 1914–18.

The early years of the twentieth century also saw the rise of a second Arab leader in Arabia. This was Abdul-Aziz Ibn Saud, formerly an indigent and dispossessed chieftain of the uninfluential Wahhabi sect, who were regarded with suspicion and some derision as ultra-reactionary upholders of a primitive form of Islam. The energy and skill of Ibn Saud brought him and his followers, as time went on, to a commanding position in Arabian affairs; and, after the war of 1914, the Wahhabi were able to dispute with the Sherif Hussein the leadership of Arabia. In 1925, Ibn Saud defeated the Sherif, who retired to Cyprus; and for the first time in many centuries the interior of Arabia was united under a single ruler. It is noteworthy that the association of King Ibn Saud with the British was less close than in the case of the Sherif Hussein. Although Ibn Saud accepted British subsidies during 1914–18 to fight against the Ottomans, he at times forcibly opposed British policy in Arabia; and in the Sherifian-Wahhabi war of 1925 he overthrew a ruler who had strong claims on British support. Generally speaking, King Ibn Saud pursued a more strictly Arab policy, increasingly aligned after 1945 to collaboration with the USA, rather than British interests. For a time in the 1950s and 1960s Saudi Arabia, like other oil-rich and monarchical states, was criticized and opposed by radical Middle Eastern states, led principally by Egypt under President Nasser. But the rising wealth of Saudi Arabia, backed by cautious but sagacious and quietly determined policies, has now brought Saudi Arabia to the position of leader, arbiter and patron of Arab opinion and policies. The radical states have become clients rather than opponents; and Saudi Arabia has developed a foreign policy of its own that is increasingly impinging not merely on the Middle East, but in adjacent areas of Africa.

The sheikdoms of the Gulf (nowadays called by the inhabitants of its southern shores 'The Arab Gulf')[1] have had a varied political evolution. Kuwait, which in 1869 had become a British protectorate – its ruler feared

[1] The present writer, aware of this, and equally aware that to Iranians it is rightly the Persian Gulf (a fact validated by almost all literary and historical references of pre-1960s age) is perforce in equity driven to refer to the Persian/Arab Gulf – a variant that, hardly surprisingly, pleases no one, other than those who agree that nearest inhabitants have some and equal right to determine the name of geographical territories adjacent to their homeland.

Turkish occupation – gained independence in 1961 and as it were became a model and leader for the political evolution of the other Protectorates of the Gulf. Bahrain, as we have seen, was claimed in the 1960s as sovereign territory by Iran; but local feeling led to a report by United Nations which proposed independence, and this came into effect, with Iran dropping the idea of union, during 1971. The seven remaining of the Gulf states (other than Muscat), some with oil and rich, others lacking oil and poorer, but all very small in population and territory – the principal revenue for a time of one state came from the sale to collectors of rapidly changing sets of postage stamps – led, after some initial hesitation, to the creation of the United Arab Emirates. There had been quite a number of boundary difficulties, since these had remained undefined in detail, representing as they did tribally held territories sometimes detached from the capital area. Within a short time, however, agreement had been reached not only with other emirates, but, as in the case of the Buraimi oasis, with Saudi Arabia. Gradually, centralization of functions is taking shape, with Abu Dhabi, the wealthiest of the seven, being most active in this.

The other political units of the Arabian peninsula are the Yemen Arab Republic (North Yemen), the Yemen People's Democratic Republic (South Yemen – formerly Aden and the Protectorate) and Muscat (formerly Muscat and Oman). As regards North Yemen, difficulty of access – much of the country is over 1500 m in altitude – and scantiness of resources aided the country in maintaining aloofness from the currents of foreign penetration that affected the rest of the Middle East. There was some Italian attempt to develop influence during the 1930s, but the Yemen remained independent first under the despotic rule of the Shi'a (Zaidi) Imam, then after 1962 divided between Royalists and Republicans, with seven years of civil war. The king of Saudi Arabia (whose father Ibn Saud had invaded the Yemen in 1934 in order to impose a frontier settlement between the Yemen and the Saudi province of Asir) gave support to the royalist cause, whilst Egyptian troops were sent in by President Nasser on the republican side. Periods of rapproachment between Egypt and Saudi Arabia meant de-escalation of the war in the Yemen, with the converse also true. Events moved generally towards a Republic, with the USSR giving material support, and Britain (influenced by Yemeni support for dissidents in Aden) refusing recognition until Egyptian troops were withdrawn. Earlier attempts had been made to bring about federal union between Yemen and the United Arab Republic had come to nothing, and with Egyptian difficulties after the 1967 war with Israel leading to evaculation of Yemen, it was possible to negotiate a 'moderate' settlement in 1970. Two years later, after a period of fighting this time against South Yemen (formerly Aden). it was agreed that both

Yemens should form a single unitary state, with a capital at Sana'a. Despite intermittent lip-service to this programme, it still remains an ideal rather than a reality. Since 1975 the North Yemen state has greatly increased its links with Saudi Arabia, which in 1976 announced considerable military and financial aid: at the same time the Yemen has markedly drawn away from the USSR.

The southern coastlands of Arabia were ruled by Britain under treaties with various local rulers. Aden city was occupied in 1839 by troops of the British East India Company, and down to 1944 was administered from India. Extending some 800–1000 km further along the coast were some 23 Arab states whose rulers had accepted British suzerainty in foreign affairs. This was the Protectorate, organized as a loose association of units that varied in size and influence; and in 1967, after a series of varied experiments in administration, none of which proved viable or successful, the British withdrew, and the Peoples Republic of South Yemen succeeded to all the mainland territories of the former Colony and Protectorate. The Kuria Muria Islands, formerly part of Muscat prior to British occupation, reverted to Muscat. Closure of the Suez Canal and withdrawal of British assistance had severe economic consequences for the South Yemen, so that for a time, limited assistance had to be sought first with the Eastern bloc countries with China, and then with the oil-rich Arab states. Re-opening of the Suez Canal has been valuable in restoring the activities of Aden as an *entrepôt*, but so far the overall level of activity is far less than anticipated.

Until the exploitation of its oil in 1967 the Sultanate of Muscat and Oman (now Oman) remained away from the main economic and political currents, isolated from the land by deserts, and either agriculturally self-sufficient or looking towards the sea, with the British responsible for foreign affairs. Movement and contact were strongly discouraged by a despotic Sultan of mediaeval outlook (down to 1970 the city gates of Muscat were firmly locked at 9 p.m. daily) who ruled from Salalah; and the lack of education and possibility of advancement had driven many Omanis abroad. Tribal dissidence at times fostered by an Imam based on Nizwa and supported after 1967 by South Yemeni troops and arms (of Chinese/Russian origin) was a highly complicating factor. Intermittent guerilla fighting on the borders of South Yemen–Dhofar was only put down in 1976, after the Omani troops had been supported for three years by Iranian and other royalist Arab contingents. Previously the Sultan had been deposed by his son, under whom, with a very different outlook and rising oil revenues, Oman is following the pattern of breathless material development as an oil-state.

*Libya*

At the opening of the present century, Libya was under Ottoman rule, with Turkish officials and military garrisons. Economically, the region was extremely retarded: two mainstays had been piracy[1] and a small but regular slave trade across the Sahara. The former had ended in the early nineteenth century; the latter ceased in the 1930s (the last slave was publicly sold in 1934), and the trans-Saharan caravan trade dwindled to tiny proportions. In 1911–12 during Turkish preoccupations in a Balkan war, Italy occupied Tripoli, and at the start of the First World War was in process of extending its hold on the country. Main opposition to Italian penetration came from the Sanussi under their leader, the Grand Sanussi, who was seconded at first by a number of notable Turkish officers, among them Kemal and Enver Pasha. The presence of a Sanussi-Turkish army was for some time a threat to the British position in Egypt; but after 1918 Italian forces gradually subdued the coast, and later the interior. Pacification was, however, not complete until about 1934. Under Mussolini Libya was divided into four provinces: Tripolitania, Misurata, Benghazi and Derna; and about 250 000 settlers from Italy were established as artisans, shopkeepers, farmers and officials.

During the Second World War, the British entered into an agreement with the Grand Sanussi of the time (who was living in exile in Egypt) and recognized him first as the ruler of Cyrenaica, where Sanussi adherents are most numerous, and later as king of a united Libya. Full independence was gained in 1951 (after Russia had put forward a request for a mandate); and for a time Libya was governed as a federation of three territories: Tripolitania, Cyrenaica and the Fezzan, with the capital of each acting in turn annually as Federal capital. This proved unworkable, and was dropped in 1963. In 1969 a bloodless coup under Colonel Gaddafi overthrew the Sanussi monarchy in favour of a republic; and since that time Libya has followed a highly idiosyncratic policy aligned strongly to the extreme left, with increasing links with the USSR, and its oil revenues used to support dissidence and revolution in various parts of the Middle East and the world in general. A 'love-hate' relationship with Egypt, oscillating between imperious demands for unity and warlike acts on a limited scale, with expulsion of Egyptian workers in Libya (who, an essential element, number about ¼ million) has been a feature of the Gaddafi regime; which is able to derive especial benefit generally from the location of Libya close to European oil markets, and on the 'right' side of the Suez Canal.

[1] One of the earliest exploits of the American Corps of Marines (commemorated in the National Anthem) was a punitive expedition against Libyan corsairs.

*Present political grouping*

It has largely been inevitable that the present national frontiers drawn in lands where sectarian and social divisions are strong, and where political consciousness is a rapidly developing phenomenon, should in some instances give incomplete realization to the political needs and aspirations of all Middle Eastern peoples. We have the example of change in Africa generally following the break-up of colonial rule, and the emergence of sovereign states. Yet even though it is probably impossible to devise frontiers that would enclose viable states on a pattern that would be satisfactory to all, present boundaries (despite the growth of native government in place of colonial or imperialist rule from outside) offer a number of special difficulties. Besides the Israeli–Arab issue, with its associated problems of refugees, there are also the Kurds, Armenians, and Cypriots, Turkish and Greek.

*The Kurds* These are a mountain people, partly semi-nomadic, but now mainly settled agriculturalists, who themselves claim to be the descendents of the ancient Medes. Their language is clearly Indo-European, related to Farsi (Persian), and not Semitic; and, whilst about three-quarters are Sunni Moslems, the remainder (especially those within Iran) are chiefly Shi'a Moslems, Sunni Dervish, or even Yazidi, who could be said to be an offshoot from Zoroastrianism. In the past, many Kurds practised semi-nomadic pastoralism, with transhumance between summer quarters on the higher mountain slopes, and winter quarters in the valleys and lowlands. There are few towns: the largest could be said to be Diyarbekir in eastern Turkey, with about 200000 inhabitants – another is Suleimaniya in Iraq.

The Kurds have rarely been independent and their homeland is now divided between Turkey, Iraq and Iran, with enclaves of Kurds also in Syria and in the USSR. It has been said of this people that they have claims to racial purity and to continuity of culture that are stronger than those of any European nation, since the Kurds have been settled in their present home since about 2400 B.C.; but the term 'culture' must be taken in a limited sense: their organization is still chiefly tribal, with large numbers of landless peasant cultivators, and they live in remote mountain villages still with very few communications and other infrastructures. As a result, three-quarters are still said to be illiterate, and there is a high death-rate, general and infantile, as compared with the totality generally for the three countries they inhabit. They have been renowned as a warlike people, from the days of Xenophon onwards, and down to our own time they have remained as partially free: at best, neglected and victims of central government indolence, at worst, actively oppressed.

Estimates of Kurdish numbers *c.* 1974

|  | Maximum ('000s) | Minimum ('000s) |
|---|---|---|
| Turkey* | 8000 | 3200 |
| Iran | 5000 | 1800 |
| Iraq | 2500 | 1550 |
| Syria | 600 | 320 |
| Lebanon | 70 | 40 |
| USSR (Armenia, Georgia, Azerbaijan) | 300 | 80 |
| *Total* | 16470 | 6990 |

* In modern Turkish statistics, the Kurds are described as 'Mountain Turks'.

Few reliable figures exist as to the numbers of the Kurdish people: isolation plus difficulties of language and organization are compounded by the strong desire of the 'host' countries to minimize numbers. Recent studies have assembled varying figures (estimates only); and there are further difficulties as to whether to include such groups as the Bakhtiari and Luri tribes of Iran, and the Yazidi of Syria.

The Treaty of Sèvres (1920) actually made provision for the creation of an independent Kurdish state, alongside an Armenian one, but the rise of Kemal Ataturk prevented any implementation. In 1946 Iranian Kurds attempted to set up a 'Mahabad Republic' which only lasted a few months. Fig. 7.8 shows in an extreme form the territory claimed as Kurdish, a territory covering ½ million km². It will be seen that these claims include the oilfields of Kirkuk (principal wealth of the present Iraqi state), and it is thought that the territory may contain other oil, coal, copper and possibly uranium.

In the past, there have been policies of 'divide and rule' followed by larger national governments, and these led to Kurdish action against others, e.g. the Armenians during the early twentieth century. Authoritarian rule in Turkey and Iran has given little scope for Kurdish separatist aims, but in Iraq where the internal regime is weaker, and the prize (of a major oilfield) greater, sustained attempts have been made since 1958 to assert some form of independence. The Kurdish–Iraqi war of 1970 led to an agreement to allow limited autonomy, but this was modified and not fully implemented, so warfare broke out again in 1974. This time the Shah of Iran, hitherto opposed to the Iraq government and a tacit supporter of the Iraqi Kurds, made an accommodation over the Shatt el Arab frontier-line, and withdrew support from the Kurds, who were then over-run by Iraqi military forces. Since that time there have been reports

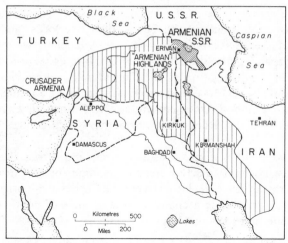

*Fig.* 7.8 Kurdish and Armenian territorial claims.

of forcible deportation of Iraqi Kurds from the mountains into the plains, with extensive attempts at 'arabicization'.

The Kurdish problem exemplifies many current dilemmas. Even at minimum estimates, there are enough Kurds to form a 'state' that would certainly be larger than others now existing in the Middle East; but if separatism and autonomy were granted, this could result in break-up of present larger states – Iran particularly, with its Azerbaijani and Baluchi dissidents, and Turkey, with its other non-Turkish minorities in the east.

*The Armenians* The Armenians once formed a majority in certain parts of eastern Asia Minor, where, in contrast to the Kurds, they lived as settled peasant cultivators, exploiting the occasional patches of richer land on valley floors. A markedly high birth-rate, coupled with lack of opportunity in their homeland, led to much emigration, so that Armenians are also found in other parts of the Middle East, and to some extent in Europe and America. Again, unlike the Kurds, the Armenians outside Armenia have settled as townspeople, and their frequently high level of intelligence has made it possible for them to enter commerce and the skilled professions. A relatively large proportion of the trade of the Middle East is carried on by Armenians, and many Armenian musicians, teachers, lawyers, doctors and dentists are to be found.[1] In some respects, therefore, and particularly by reason of their interest in commerce, and their mental and artistic ability, the Armenians can be compared with the Jewish people.

[1] Most Armenians can be readily distinguished by the fact that the majority of their surnames end in 'ian', e.g. Khatchaturian, Mikoyan.

During the war of 1914–18 the Armenians, as Christians, gave support to the Tsarist armies against the Turks, their overlords; and, following the retreat of the Russians in 1915–16, the Armenians were exposed to Turkish vengeance. About ½ million of the former were massacred by the Kurds, at the instigation of the Turks, and a larger number saved themselves only by flight – either into Russia, or into Iraq and Syria. There are now about 3 million Armenians in the USSR, including over 2 million in the Soviet Socialist Republic of Armenia, which centres on the city of Erivan.

In other adjacent regions, especially Iraq and Syria, the Armenian refugees were not particularly welcome, as imposing an extra burden on scanty local resources, and also as swelling a Christian minority in Moslem states, thereby provoking a change in the balance of political power. A recent estimate gives the numbers of Armenian refugees as follows:

| | |
|---|---|
| Syria | 120000 |
| European Turkey and Greece | 50000 |
| Bulgaria | 45000 |
| Egypt | 25000 |
| France | 55000 |

The Soviet authorities have made strong efforts to secure Armenian loyalty by furthering economic development in the Soviet Republic of Armenia. Outside observers have also agreed that a high degree of autonomy is allowed, and that no anti-religious policy is imposed. As a result, some 16000 refugees entered Soviet Armenia from the Middle East between 1926 and 1936, and others after 1945. The claims of Russia to have secured the continued survival of the Armenian people are therefore strong.

Like the Kurds, the Armenians have a desire for a politically independent national state, but here the comparison ends, because the latter people are scattered over the world, and as traders and intellectuals have means of forwarding their cause that are denied to the mountaineers of Kurdistan.[1] American interest in the Armenian problem was shown by the action of President Wilson in 1919, when he went so far as to draw up boundaries for a projected Armenian state – a proposal that, as we have seen, never reached realization; and latterly the question of Armenian aspirations has become directly related to Russian affairs. The problem is in one sense simple: Armenians have now the possibility of settling in an Armenian state, but at the price of accepting Russian tutelage – a condition that some Armenians, strongly religious or living by commerce under capitalist conditions, do not care to accept. Once again there is the further question of Russian influence in the Middle East. With a

[1] The parallel will be noted in this respect between Armenian nationalism and political Zionism.

majority of Armenians now resident in the Soviet Union, and as protector of the Armenian Republic, Russia has grounds for interesting herself in the districts of Turkish Cilicia and Lake Van, until 50 years ago the ancient homelands of the Armenian people, and now possibly a future component, with the Soviet Armenia as a nucleus, of a wider Armenian state.

*Refugees* Not counting the Kurds, there are now about 2 million refugees in the Middle East: a number that approaches the total population of a country like Libya or the Lebanon, and exceeds that of Kuwait, Cyprus, Oman, the UAE or South Yemen. Most are Arabs who fled from Palestine in 1948; a substantial number left the Judaean highlands and East Ghor of Jordan in 1967, as did 90–95000 Syrians from the Golan–Kuneitra region further north. Since that time there have been Kurdish refugees, mainly in Iran, some Cypriots, and since 1975 numbers of Lebanese, who fled to Syria, Cyprus and the Gulf States. Most of the Palestinian Arab refugees are destitute, still living in camps; but others who were more fortunate in having friends or an education have been able to move to various Arab countries where their abilities are used in professional and artisanal occupations, e.g. one-quarter of the population of Kuwait and 30% of that of the UAE are Palestinians. Most of the poorly-off are cared for by the United Nations Refugee and Works Agency (UNRWA), in camps or suburbs, and they left their homes, according to Arab views, under threat of imminent massacre by Israeli soldiers. The Israeli view is that they fled either of their own accord, or were deliberately moved away by Arab leaders in order to embarrass the Israelis. The Israeli government will not have them back, since they would be a dissident minority that would also be a serious long-term demographic threat, because their birth-rate is higher than that of the Israelis. Work is not provided for the refugees lest local economies and living standards become adversely affected.

The various Arab states are vehemently unwilling to absorb more than a very few of the refugees, on the grounds (*a*) that to do so would be tantamount to acquiescing in the permanent loss of Arab Palestine, and (*b*) that there would be enormous social and economic difficulties in trying to absorb them – for example, the population of Jordan would be more than doubled; and so long as the refugees remain as obvious victims, there is still hope even after twenty years that they might one day return or receive some reparation (as did ultimately and perhaps ironically Israeli refugees from Nazi Europe).

It is from the desperate, embittered, and forcibly idle menfolk in these camps, who have little to do except conspire and procreate, that the Arab guerilla leaders draw their recruits – the camps in Jordan and Lebanon

Palestinian Arab refugees 1975 ('000s)

| Location | In camps | Outside | Total |
|----------|----------|---------|-------|
| (a) registered with UNWRA | | | |
| Jordan | 231 | 679 | 920 |
| Gaza Strip | 198 | 133 | 331 |
| Lebanon | 140 | 100 | 240 |
| Syria | 51 | 131 | 183 |
| (b) national statistics | | | |
| Kuwait | — | 140 | 140 |
| Egypt | — | 33 | 33 |

are bases for guerilla organizations, as was demonstrated in the Lebanon in 1974–76. It is, however, important that both President Carter and the EEC political leaders have indicated during 1977 their awareness of the need for 'a homeland' for these dispossessed Palestinians.

*Summary*

This survey, though rapidly and incompletely given, will indicate the seriousness, wide range and complexity of Middle Eastern problems. Existing national states, having achieved a hard-won independence, are little disposed to tolerate any shift of internal power to minorities, even when this means denying to smaller groups the same rights that they claim for themselves. Any infraction of present unity – any 'boat-rocking' by dissident sects or parties – may lead to a break-up of existing political organization, and extreme methods, even direct repression and persecution, appear justified, so long as outward unity in political grouping is maintained. The position is complicated, too, by the existence of nomadic or minority groups, partly inside and partly outside various national states. Iran and Turkey went to war during the nineteenth century because both countries claimed the Kurds as their own nationals – a somewhat barren quarrel since the Kurds were little disposed to admit the effective suzerainty of either state.

Then there is a wider problem involving outside powers. French support of Uniate Christians, British interest in Druzes and Assyrians, and American activities on behalf of Armenians and Zionists, served to transform questions that were at first purely local into international issues involving major states and even 'blocks' of states. Turkish claims to possession of the Mosul region in 1926 immediately brought into discussion the position of the Kurds, Armenians and Assyrians; and Britain, as a Christian power, found herself in opposition not only to Turkey, but also to France, who was against any further extension of British influence in the Middle East. Turkish claims also received support from American organizations interested in the exploitation of oilfields. Similarly, and more recently, we have seen how Palestine/Israel, Syria and Egypt have embittered relations between Britain, France and the United States, and how the Jewish question is a hotly debated issue in America and Britain.

There is, over all, the question of the USSR. As the one major power that directly adjoins the Middle Eastern territory, Russia has a special interest and special advantages. No other country can influence Middle Eastern affairs so easily and quickly, either by direct action, or by using the aspirations and mutual jealousies of minorities within various national states. During the last 40 years, Russia has made use of Kurdish separatism once to thwart British influence in Iran (1918), and three times to exert pressure on the native government of Iran (1921, 1942, 1946), and, by creating an Armenian Republic within Soviet territory, she has obtained a weapon for use against Turkey. One reason for the reluctance in some quarters to support Kurdish and Armenian nationalist aims has been the thought that these would weaken both Iran and Turkey *vis-à-vis* Russia. It will, however, be apparent that besides the weapon of attack the USSR may now gain more by appearing as the supporter, political and economic, of 'leftish' Middle Eastern states (Egypt, Libya, Iraq, Syria, and Southern Yemen) against 'western' capitalist support of Israel, and against 'reactionary' monarchical governments.

It is thus easily possible to see in the present political situation of the Middle East a recapitulation on a vaster and more complex scale of the Balkan position of 1914. Local sectarian and communal feeling is painfully transforming itself into political organization, but the process is often crude and incomplete, with manifest deficiencies. These defects give possibility of interference for their own purposes by non-Middle Eastern powers; and as Austria and Russia opposed each other before 1914 over Serbia, so American, British, French and Russian interests now clash in the Middle East. Moreover, there are richer prizes at stake; unlike the Balkans, the Middle East is no isolated peininsula, but, as has been emphasized, a corridor of unique strategic importance between an awakened Asia and the West; and far more valuable than anything in the Balkans are the oilfields of the Middle East, the most important in the world. With national governments now in control of their own oil resources, it is not so much a question of direct exploitation by outsiders, as of ensuring continuity of supply to a petroleum-dependent West.

A further problem arises from the archaic social structure of many Middle Eastern countries. In general, contact by western nations has been with an élite – a ruling class based on hereditary position or wealth – since social grouping in the Middle East, often tribal or communal, has tended to concentrate effective power in the hands of a few leaders of great influence. Today, the basis of that order is being questioned, often successfully, as we have seen since 1952, in Egypt, Syria, Libya, Iraq and South Yemen. With the recent success of radical policies in south-east Asia, there is now a strenuous effort to bring over this remaining 'uncommitted' corner of southern Asia and northern Africa to one form of ideology or another. Described a few years ago as a 'political shatterbelt' between two more powerful world-wide systems, the Middle East could find itself merely in the position of being able to choose between these major blocs. But of late years the changed financial situation of some Middle Eastern states has given their rulers the possibility of a third alternative – that of balancing, as powerful but independent entities, between competing forces, and alternately looking for support from one side or another. This the present rulers of Iran, Saudi Arabia (as conservatives) and Syria, Libya (as more socialistic) see their way to achieving.

### Regional organizations

Since 1945 there have come into existence a number of organizations with varied political, economic and cultural aims. One of the first of these was the Arab League, founded in 1945, when for the second time in 25 years opposing armies from Europe had been fighting across Arab soil. Founder members were the six states of Egypt (which took the lead in formation), Iraq, the Lebanon, Saudi Arabia, Syria and (then) Trans-jordan, with representatives of the Palestinian Arabs. Now there are 21 members, and all Arab states from Mauritania and Morocco to Somalia, the Yemens and the Gulf States are now members. Located in Cairo, the League began explicitly with the objectives of resistance to Zionism and to foreign tutelage, but has extended activities into economic and intellectual issues. One major activity is the world boycott of Israel, operated through a 'black list' that has assumed more and more importance as the Arabs have become major traders and importers since the petroleum 'boom'. It operates a number of specialized agencies ranging from research groups into e.g. public health, forestry and arid zones to postal aviation and telecommunications unions: most important of these agencies are the Council of Arab Unity, which organizes an Arab Common Market and an Arab Monetary Fund, and the Arab Cultural Organization. So long as Egypt was the leading Arab power in the Middle East, as in the days of President Nasser, the Arab League appeared as the sole agent of Arab unity; but with the changed geopolitical and financial relationships of the last 10 years, the League is partly overshadowed by newer agencies, though its boycott is increasingly effective. Its financial agencies such as The Arab Fund for Technical Assistance, Council of Arab Economic Unity, and Fund for Economic and Social Development indicate one aspect of the League's activities.

Islamic solidarity on a wider geographical basis together with a sharpening of the opposition to Israel was advanced by creation in 1971 of the Islamic Conference, based in Jidda. This organization, of 38 members, includes (besides members of the Arab League) Iran, Turkey and African and Asian Islamic states such as Senegal, Guinea, Malaysia and Indonesia.

*The European Economic Community* In 1972 the EEC developed what is termed a 'global policy for Mediterranean states', reflecting a desire for consistency over what had been 'piecemeal' policies. As early as 1964–65, agreements had been reached separately with Turkey, Egypt, the Lebanon and Israel over tariff and customs preferences, and technical aid. These agreements, negotiated country by country, were of limited scope, but in some instances, e.g. as regards Turkey and Israel, they were regarded as definite preliminaries to closer union, with the ultimate possibility of eventual admission to the EEC. By late 1977 Israel will have free access for her industrial exports to the EEC, with reciprocal concessions to EEC imports in the 1980s.

In 1973, the EEC Foreign Ministers made a declaration in favour of Palestinian refugees, and the desirability of a return to the political frontiers of 1967. This led to an initiative by the Arab League that resulted in a general negotiation between Arab states of the Mediterranean area and the EEC – part of the 'global approach' announced a year earlier. Besides the limited agreements with Egypt, Turkey and the Lebanon, and the wider one with Israel (as mentioned above) negotiations began with Cyprus, Syria and Jordan. Suggestions that Iran and Saudi Arabia might also be interested were received at first coolly by the USA which was not anxious to see the enlargement of a preferential tariff area of which it was not a member – but this attitude is now changing.

From EEC-Arab contacts there developed a 'Euro-Arab Dialogue' that since 1974 has considered not only economic co-operation with Arab states, but political issues – notably Greek-Turkish relations over Cyprus as well as the question of Palestinian refugees.

*Oil Exporting Organizations* Finally, though this does not exhaust the list of regional political associations, there are the OPEC and OAPEC. The former, the 'Organisation of Petroleum Exporting Countries', has (1977) as members: Algeria, Ecuador, Gabon, Indonesia, Iran, Iraq, Kuwait, Libya, Nigeria, Qatar, Saudi Arabia, the United Arab Emirates and Venezuela – the world major producers, the USA and USSR excepted. Formed in 1960, with a secretariat in Vienna, OPEC has been the co-ordinating body behind the successful attempts to raise the world selling price of crude petroleum from $2 per barrel to $12 between 1973 and 1977; and in using embargo and joint collective action to bring about first increased taxation and then expropriation of western ownership and operation. It also operates a Fund for Aid to Developing Countries. The Organisation of Arab Petroleum Exporting Countries includes most (though not all) of Middle Eastern Arab oil producers, large and small, together with Algeria: Iran is not a member. Headquarters are in Kuwait; and besides co-ordinating a specific Arab and Middle Eastern oil 'policy', OAPEC is beginning to be involved in transport, shipping, sales of petrol retail, and financing petrochemical plants. It also has regular contacts with the EEC.

In conclusion, brief reference may be made to an underlying major difficulty in the Middle East – one that is closely linked to the future of the Arab League – the spiritual and ideological crisis referred to in chapter 1, which is bringing into question the entire basis of Arab society. Recent experience of domination by outsiders has exposed the weakness of the Islamic world alongside the West; and this had led to much self-questioning and self-criticism by Moslems themselves. The first problem in the minds of many is whether the Islamic way of life has failed. Does the future lie in complete abandonment of the former way of life, with rapid and unquestioning acceptance of all the beliefs, spiritual values and methods of Europe and America? It is possible to pursue a middle course between both Western and Islamic traditions? Or is it a failure fully to live up to the true Islamic code that lies at the root of present difficulties, and should there hence be a return to a more simple and primitive Islamic life? Can a fourth way be found – in a specifically Middle Eastern/Islamic socialist pattern, such as that exemplified in the Baathist movement? What then are the spiritual and social values of the outside world; a mixed economy like that of western Europe; or types of Marxist-Communist-Maoist-Baathist socialism? From time to time, one hears that, because of the non-class structure of early Islamic society, Islam itself remains a 'buffer' against the spread of communism; but, equally, this could logically be regarded as an ideology predisposing towards communism. What is clear is that Arabs tend often to appreciate direct and somewhat ruthless political methods: as a result Russia is admired, whilst the West has often had the worst of both worlds by its show of moderate force soon followed by a 'cave-in'. On the other hand, there is also acceptance by some Arabs of nationalism and materialism as potent and desirable objectives – these may bring a desire for linkage to Western objectives and policies. Yet overall there remains the matter

Armaments purchases

|  | 1961–71 | 1975 |
|---|---|---|
| *Declared expenditures ($ US million)* | | |
| Egypt | 2197 | 123 |
| Iran | 1100 | 1045 |
| Israel | 936 | 640 |
| Jordan | 290 | 95 |
| Kuwait | 46 | 1500 |
| Libya | 210 | 225 |
| Qatar | — | 20 |
| Saudi Arabia | 322 | 4100 |
| *Country of supply 1950–73 (%)* | | |
| South west Asian States | | |
| USA | 29 | |
| USSR | 48 | |
| UK | 11 | |
| France | 7 | |
| North African States | | |
| USA | 13 | |
| USSR | 33 | |
| UK | 9 | |
| France | 39 | |

Source: Institute for Strategic Studies.

of Zionism, for which Britain and the USA have a fundamental responsibility – France's part in 1956 as an ally of Israel seems forgotten. This
fact, in Arab eyes, of having introduced the deadly injection of an Israeli
state, underlies much political approach in the Middle East.

As another new factor, we also have the change in ideological and
historical pattern. Whilst older Arabs once tended to talk of pan-Arabism
and Holy War against the Infidel, younger activists speak of class
struggle and multi-nationalism in a federal context, supported by oil
revenues made available to all Arabs.

A reflection of the highly unsettled intellectual and political situation
is the enormous purchases of armaments in the last few years: in terms
of expenditure per head now the highest in the world.

# 8 General economic life

In this chapter it is proposed to describe in general terms a number of features of economic life that are common to many regions of the Middle East. This discussion should be viewed as a background to the detailed survey of economic activities given under the appropriate regional heading.

## Economic growth and structural change

Since the Second World War, the Middle East has enjoyed rapid economic growth (averaging some 6·5% per annum during 1960s) accompanied by substantial social advance. In almost every country private consumption has risen appreciably. The amount of social services extended by the governments in the form of education, health, cheap housing, drinking water and rural electrification has greatly increased, and as a consequence the level of living of the majority of the people is distinctly higher than it was 20 to 30 years ago. But in most parts of the region, incomes and wealth of the rich have risen still more rapidly and the distribution of both is probably more unequal than it was before the Second World War.

The rapid advance of recent decades may be attributed to three main factors; the large capital inflows resulting from the phenomenal growth of the oil industry since the Second World War, from the huge amounts of foreign aid received (more per head of population than any other area in the world except possibly Great Britain) – the provision of infrastructures (the construction of thousands of kilometres of roads, new ports and the improvement of older ports); and the development of human resources through the provision of greatly expanded and improved educational facilities.

Important structural changes have accompanied these high rates of growth. But while the transformation of the economic structure of the region is proceeding vigorously, the rate and pattern of progress varies from one country to another, and the economic paths chosen by different countries have differed because of internal political development as well as the influence of economic and social factors. Regional economic co-operation has so far been on a very small scale.

Looking at the region as a whole the two dominant natural resources are agricultural land and petroleum. Other mineral deposits are available but their regional significance as an economic resource is very limited. Agriculture accounts for a substantial portion of national income and is a major source of foreign exchange in several Middle Eastern countries, e.g. Egypt and Turkey. It is also the main source of employment in most countries of the region. In contrast, in Saudi Arabia, Libya, Kuwait and the Gulf states, oil production is the principal source of income and foreign exchange, and in Iran and Iraq, where oil production is a major activity, it contributes substantially on both counts. The trend in almost every country is towards a decline in the share of agriculture in the composition of G.N.P., a rise in that of services, and a marked increase in the industrial sector. The service sector is swollen by income accruing because of location (Suez Canal and airlines); by pilgrimage and tourism; by the large size of the government sector, including army and civil service; and by the receipt of massive foreign aid. One consequence of the growth of the public sector has been a great extension of government control over economic activity. Only in Lebanon does the government still play a minor part in economic activity. The growth in industrial output has gone primarily to the domestic market, although in a few countries (Egypt, Israel and Lebanon) exports of manufactured goods have increased appreciably.

Possibilities of maintaining a high rate of growth appear to be excellent given the enormous oil revenues that will accrue to Libya and the countries bordering the Persian/Arab Gulf during the next decade. Growing incomes should continue to be accompanied by rising rates of saving and investment, higher levels of living (for some at least), increasing industrialization and intensified agriculture. Unfortunately, growth may be seriously affected unless there is a permanent settlement of the Arab-Israeli dispute and a sharp reduction in the levels of military expenditure: the Middle East now has the highest expenditure per head on armaments of anywhere in the world. In some countries, notably

The Middle East – some agricultural statistical indicators

| Country | Economically active population (%) in agriculture | | Index of agricultural production (1961–65 = 100) | Index nos. of per caput agricultural production (1961–65 = 100) | No. of agricultural tractors | Cereal cultivation (% of area actually cultivated) |
|---|---|---|---|---|---|---|
| | 1970 | 1960 | 1975 | 1975 | 1974 | 1974 |
| Cyprus | 38·5 | 41·8 | 145 | 126 | 9 500 | 37·5 |
| Egypt | 54·4 | 58·4 | 139 | 103 | 21 000 | 69·9 |
| Iran | 46·0 | 53·9 | 165 | 117 | 25 000 | 42·3 |
| Iraq | 46·1 | 53·1 | 140 | 95 | 9 100 | 41·7 |
| Israel | 9·7 | 14·3 | 177 | 124 | 19 535 | 34·8 |
| Jordan | 33·7 | 44·0 | 55 | 37 | 3 300 | 20·6 |
| Lebanon | 19·6 | 38·2 | 157 | 112 | 3 100 | 19·8 |
| Libya | 32·1 | 53·2 | 215 | 144 | 4 100 | 16·4 |
| Sudan | 82·0 | 85·7 | 181 | 127 | 8 600 | 53·2 |
| Syria | 51·1 | 54·2 | 137 | 95 | 12 864 | 37·7 |
| Turkey | 67·7 | 78·5 | 155 | 115 | 199 812 | 47·2 |
| Yemen (Aden) | 64·5 | 70·5 | 138 | 105 | 1 180 | 2·7 |
| Yemen (Sana'a) | 79·2 | 83·2 | 147 | 99 | 650 | 95·1 |

Source: *FAO Production Yearbook 29* (1975).

Egypt, there is also a need to promote birth control and to provide incentives for the limitation of family size in order to reduce the high rate of population increase. Finally, some form of effective regional co-operation to channel surplus investment funds from the major oil-producing states to those without large oil revenues is essential if growth in the region as a whole is not to be accompanied by growing disparities between the oil-rich and non-oil producing countries.

## Agriculture

Agriculture is by far the most important economic activity in the Middle East, since about 50% of the total working population is directly engaged in cultivation (Table, p. 206), and a further proportion is dependent upon the products of agriculture either as a supplement to the main livelihood of pastoral nomadism, or as a source of raw materials for industrial occupations. Even in Iran, Iraq and to a lesser extent Libya, which have large incomes from oil, agriculture still plays an important role as the biggest employer and as a producer of foodstuffs. With the exception of the main oil-producing states and Israel, earnings from agriculture constitute the major source of foreign exchange; in Egypt, Sudan, Syria and Turkey about three-quarters of export earnings come from agriculture. Nevertheless, the contribution of agriculture to G.D.P. has been declining, and in most countries the proportion of the total population in agricultural employment (if not the absolute number), is also falling as a result of migration to the towns. In most countries agriculture accounts for less than 30% of G.D.P. and is very much less in countries whose income is derived mainly from oil. Despite this relative decline, agriculture remains the largest single sector in Egypt, Sudan, Turkey and Syria, while in Iran and Iraq it is second after petroleum.

The last two decades have witnessed rapid changes in agriculture in most countries of the Middle East, although the gains have been seriously diminished by the increase in population. Agricultural production has notably increased in all countries during this period, but the increase in *per capita* agricultural output has been much less. Egypt, Iraq, Jordan, Syria and the two Yemens, for example, have only just maintained their *per capita* output levels, or have actually suffered a decline. In the past agriculture has received less than its proportional share of public funds and attention, while agricultural pricing policies were in the interests of urban consumers rather than of rural producers. Yet Middle East agriculture still has great potential for change, and since the early 1970s most countries in the region have begun to place a new emphasis on the development of this important sector. Massive investment plans are either being carried out or are scheduled in almost every country in the region,

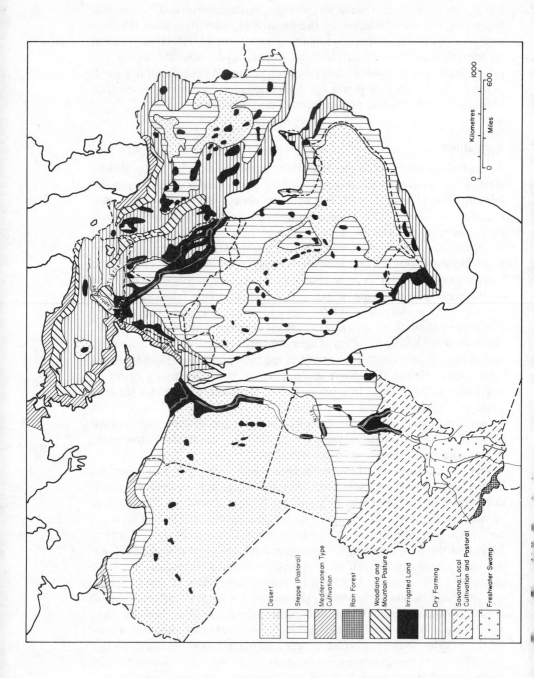

Desert

Steppe (Pastoral)

Mediterranean Type
Cultivation

Rain Forest

Woodland and
Mountain Pasture

Irrigated Land

Dry Farming

Savanna: Local
Cultivation and Pastoral

Freshwater Swamp

particularly Sudan, where an ambitious 25-year programme sponsored by the Arab oil exporters aims to transform the country into the granary of the Arab world. In many cases these developments include the introduction of advanced Western agri-business techniques. Food requirements in the Middle East are increasing rapidly as a result of population growth, the massive rise in the region's income, and considerable changes in consumption patterns. Thus unless food output is expanded quickly and substantially, imports will continue to rise; they have already increased six-fold (in value) between 1970–77. Many countries hope to achieve near self-sufficiency in food production in the future in order to reduce the threat of internal unrest over scarcity or high prices, and the insecurity arising from dependence on imported foodstuffs; but this target remains in many cases aspiration rather than reality.

### Cultivated and irrigated areas

Although agriculture plays such a large part in the life of the region, by no means all the Middle East is cultivated or even cultivable. The total arable area has increased during the last 20 years as grazing lands have been brought under the plough and irrigation systems extended. But over the region as a whole only 7·9 of the total area is actually cultivated. As the following table indicates there are also marked regional variations in land utilization. The ratio of cultivated land to total area ranges from below 1% in Saudi Arabia, about 3% in Egypt, to over 30% in Syria and Turkey. Some further reduction must be made to the figures because on average one-quarter to one-half of the land stated as under cultivation actually lies fallow each year. In irrigated areas, the proportion of fallow is much less, because annual flooding partially renews soil fertility; but in regions dependent on rainfall, fields are sometimes cultivated only once in 2, 3 or even 5 years.

The bulk of the region's arable land is devoted to dry farming or rain-fed cultivation which is confined almost entirely to areas with an annual rainfall of over 250 mm. It is therefore most widespread in Turkey, western Iran, the Levant coastlands and in the southern Sudan. Smaller areas occur in the southwest corner of the Arabian peninsula. Where rainfall is less than 250 mm, cultivation depends on irrigation, which is essential for human life in many parts of the Middle East. Were it not for their elaborate irrigation schemes many countries would hardly exist as they do now, certainly not at anything like their present level of population. The Middle East is fortunate in that it is partially crossed by three major rivers – the Nile, Tigris and Euphrates – that rise in the better watered south and north, and make their way across desert land. Some of the irregular and capricious rainfall also percolates underground

Agricultural land – Middle East countries (1974)

| Country | Total area ('ooo ha) | Actual cultivated area ('ooo ha) | % of total area | Irrigated area ('ooo ha) | % of cultivated area |
|---|---|---|---|---|---|
| Egypt | 100 145 | 2 855 | 2·8 | 2 855 | 100 |
| Cyprus | 925 | 432 | 46·7 | 94 | 21·7 |
| Iran | 164 800 | 16 280 | 9·8 | 5 350 | 32·8 |
| Iraq | 43 492 | 5 280 | 12 | 4 100 | 77·6 |
| Israel | 2 070 | 430 | 20·7 | 177 | 41·1 |
| Jordan | 9 774 | 1 360 | 14 | 60 | 4·4 |
| Lebanon | 1 040 | 348 | 33·4 | 85 | 24·4 |
| Saudi Arabia | 214 969 | 775 | 0·36 | 185 | 23·8 |
| Sudan | 250 581 | 7 195 | 2·8 | 870 | 12 |
| Syria | 18 518 | 6 027 | 32·5 | 578 | 9·5 |
| Turkey | 78 058 | 27 895 | 35·7 | 1 970 | 7 |
| Total | 884 372 | 68 877 | 7·9 | 16 324 | 23·7 (1·8% of all land) |

Source: *FAO Production Yearbook* 29 (1975).

into porous rock layers to produce water tables at varying depths. Certain of these cover many thousands of square kilometres under the deserts of Libya, Egypt and the Arabian peninsula. Irrigation has varied forms: by dams and barrages across surface rivers, by wells and pumps, and by qanat (see p. 36). Some techniques – the qanat and lifting devices such as the *Archimedean screw* and *shaduf* – have been in use for many centuries, but almost everywhere they are gradually being replaced by motor pumps. Since the Second World War a large number of huge multi-purpose dams have been constructed across the major rivers to provide irrigation water, flood control and hydro-electric power. Examples include the Aswan High Dam on the Nile, the Tabqa Dam on the Euphrates in Syria, the Dukan and Darbandikhan Dams on tributaries of the Tigris in Iraq, and the Dez Dam of Iran. Throughout the region irrigation is being extended, and a large number of new projects are planned or under construction. Yet a number of serious problems have appeared. Extensive use of motor pumps has lowered water tables drastically in many parts of the Middle East – the coastal plain of Israel, in northern Libya, central Saudi Arabia, and in Iran. As we have noted earlier, if too much water is applied certain Middle East soils can turn impossibly saline, owing to solution of soil minerals and then capillary attraction to the surface. Salinity is in fact now a serious problem, particularly in Egypt and Iraq. Drainage of surplus water is thus as necessary as irrigation but the laying of underground drains greatly increases the already high cost of reclaiming desert lands – estimated as US $2000 per feddan in Egypt.

## Land holding, tenacy and agrarian reform

The land tenure system in many parts of the Middle East, and particularly the areas which are now Turkey, Iraq, Syria, Lebanon, Jordan and Israel, as well as Cyprus, was based, until the introduction of land reforms in the 1950s, on principles which were influenced by Ottoman land law. It is useful to describe the main features of this system, although it is important to realize that the actual situation varied considerably, according to custom and to type of land, both within and between Ottoman provinces. It is also important to stress that the Ottoman Land Code of 1858, which summarizes the various forms of tenure and defines methods of registration of title, had little relevance to local conditions in many areas, although later generations of administrators were to treat the provisions of the Code as if they did reflect the actual situation.

There were four main categories of landholding, *mulk*, *matrūka*, *waqf* and *mīrī*, of which *mīrī* was by far the most important. Briefly *mulk* is equivalent to freehold, and was largely restricted to buildings and gardens; *matrūka* (lit., set aside) is land reserved for public purposes, such as roads and government buildings; *waqf* is land left for religious or charitable purposes, generally administered through a department of state or ministry; and *mīrī* covers the rest. The basic premise of Ottoman land law was that the State was sole landlord, and that it alone possessed *raqāba*, possessory rights. All grants to individuals were thus theoretically simply of *tasarruf*, usufruct, rather than of actual property rights, although the practical implications of ultimate state control were rarely felt. The state would grant out this usufruct to lessees, *multāzimīn* or *muhāṣṣilīn*, who could acquire the leases by making bids at periodic auctions. This was known as true *mīrī* or *mīrī sirf*, and such arrangements were, apart from customs and excise, the Ottoman government's main source of revenue, amounting for instance, to 42% of all income from the three provinces which are now Iraq in 1911. The arrangement was a cash commutation of the former *tīmār* system under which leases had been given to individuals in return for the provision of soldiers for the Ottoman army.

In most of the Ottoman Empire, however, the code did not fit around the kind of corporate communal ownership which prevailed. Both the *mushā'* system in Syria and the *lazma* system in Iraq were forms of joint customary ownership which were alien both to Islamic and to Ottoman law, neither of which recognized the existence of legal entities, or corporations. This meant that, in the future, leases could be given to individuals, and not to a particular village or tribe. Furthermore, it must also be remembered that in the second half of the nineteenth century much of the Middle East was gradually moving from an internationalized economy, based on subsistence farming or subsistence stock-rearing to cultivation for a cash market, either at home or abroad. Realization of the fact that there were profits to be derived from agriculture contributed to encouraging the sedentarization of nomads, and questions of boundaries, leases, and conditions of tenure began to assume a greater importance than in the past. This was especially true of areas which came under cultivation for the first time, whose potential was vastly increased by the extension of mechanized irrigation after the First World War.

These changes, which were in response to external economic pressures, were to cause, in the late nineteenth century and in the first half of the twentieth, immense changes in the structure of landholding throughout the Middle East. Over the period an original society of generally free tribesmen was transformed into groups of serfs, bound to the soil by debt and inertia, where traditional leaders and 'new' landowners gained unprecedented legal and economic powers over their peasantry. Communal landownership disappeared, and tribal sheikhs and absentee landlords in the towns became the unchallenged owners of vast estates.

Thus until the land reforms of the 1950s the land tenure system in the Middle East was characterized by extreme inequality in landownership. In Egypt before 1952, 2000 large landowners, representing about 0.08% of all proprietors, owned about 20% of the cultivated land. In contrast nearly 2 million peasants, 84% of all proprietors, owned only 21% of the cultivated area, in small plots of less than 2 feddans. The distribution of landownership was even more skewed in Iraq and Syria. In Iraq 2% of all landholders owned 68% of the land under cultivation, and in Syria 1% of all proprietors owned 50% of the cultivated area. A similar pattern of landholding was found in Iran (where 400–450 individual landlords owned 57% of all Iranian villages), and in Turkey. In spite of the dominance of large ownership units, operational units were usually quite small, and there were few economies of scale in farming operations. Landlords were often absentees who preferred to live in the cities rather than professional farmers and they played little or no part in the running of their estates. There were few 'improving landlords'; land was regarded merely as a secure form of investment – as a fixed real asset that could not be stolen or depreciate in value. As a result the countryside remained an area that provided a surplus for the cities but received almost nothing in return.

It was common practice for large estates to be leased to intermediaries who then divided them up into small holdings allocated to tenants or sharecroppers. In some cases there arose a whole chain of intermediaries between the small cultivator and the actual owner. In Egypt, for example, middlemen rented large areas and then sublet them to local farmers at rents 50–70% higher than they paid to the original landlords. A common form of tenancy was sharecropping. Under this scheme the landlord or his agent provided land and sometimes seed, implements and draught animals in return for a share of the harvest which varied according to the relative provision of the main factors of production. The proportions of the crop taken by the landowner also varied with the type of cultivation. In addition labour services were sometimes required of the tenants. At best sharecropping protected both landlord and tenant against the vagaries of Nature in a frequently difficult environment – the loss was equally borne if a crop failed – in practice the system was open to abuse, it discouraged innovation, and led to short term, exhaustive methods of cultivation. In pre-revolutionary Iraq, Doreen Warriner found that the main cause of rural poverty was not shortage of land but the fact that the sharecroppers paid two-thirds of the produce as rent. After the Second World War the practice of cash rents increased, especially in market-oriented areas and in some cases with the introduction of mechanization. In Egypt a widespread conversion from sharecropping to money rents occurred between 1939 and 1952 (from 17–75% of land under cash rents) which tied the peasants to the market economy but did little to improve their material condition. The monopoly power of big landlords over land and water resources kept rents so high that they absorbed about 75% of the net income per feddan. With virtually no access to the modern credit market, tenants and small farmers were compelled to resort to village moneylenders, merchants and brokers who extorted interest rates often in excess of 100% per annum. But if tenants and small farmers were caught in a vicious circle of debt they were better off than the landless labourers who neither owned nor rented land. As the least credit worthy members of the rural community these last could only sell their labour for subsistence, becoming either permanent labourers employed on an annual or longer basis, or casual labourers employed on a temporary, often a seasonal, basis. Payment varied from region to region but in many cases was partly in kind and partly in cash. These landless peasants, the poorest of the rural poor, constituted a sizeable proportion of the rural population – 48% in Iran and 44% in Egypt.

Paradoxically, another serious problem, particularly among the smaller landowners, was the uneconomic size of many farm holdings. This was the result of the Koranic injunction that inherited property must be divided among the surviving members of the family, at least among the male heirs, a practice that was merely aggravated in the late nineteenth

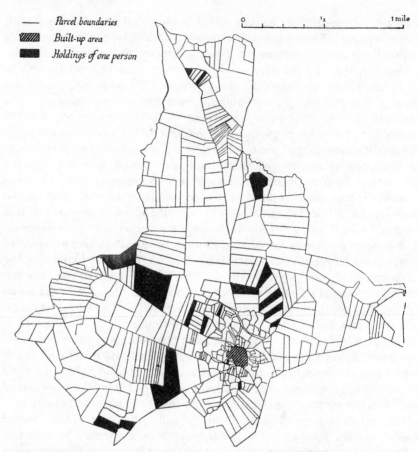

*Fig.* 8.2 Subdivision of land holding in an Arab village of Palestine 1945. (Reproduced by kind permission of Dr E. C. Willatts and the Royal Geographical Society.)

and early twentieth centuries by population increase and in some areas by the limited resources of cultivable land. Individual holdings were composed of irregular plots scattered through the village lands to take account of variations in soil and water, and this led to inefficient farming practices. Weulersse quotes the instance of Bar Elias, a Lebanese village where 2135 ha came to be divided into 32643 plots, and fig. 8.2 gives a similar example from Palestine. The uneconomical fragmentation of holdings meant that many properties were too small to support the owner and his family.

Since the early 1950s the Middle East has experienced a number of major land reform programmes. Their primary aim was political rather than economic, but the social and economic consequences have been far from negligible. In Egypt, Syria and Iraq land reforms were introduced following political revolutions with the immediate objective of breaking the power of the old ruling oligarchies dominated by large landed interests. Their long term aim was to bring about a restructuring of social and economic relationships in the rural areas. In South Yemen the first land reform measures were implemented immediately after independence in order to destroy the power and influence of those landowners who had worked for the British. In contrast, land reform in Iran (the so-called 'White Revolution') was carried out to strengthen the existing regime and give it a broader popular appeal by securing the support of the peasantry. Elsewhere, little progress has been made with land reform in Turkey or in Jordan. As yet no attempt has been made to introduce land reform measures in Saudi Arabia, Oman or North Yemen.

The land reform laws imposed limits on the size of holdings. The official ceiling varied from country to country and between irrigated and rainfed land. In Egypt, where all the cultivated land is irrigated, the maximum holding was set at 84 ha in 1952 but reduced to 42 ha in 1961 and then 21 ha in 1969. In Iraq the Agrarian Reform Law of 1958 fixed the limit at 250 ha on irrigated land and 500 ha on rainfed land, but the maximum size of holding has been progressively reduced since that date. In Syria after the 1958 Reform Law the permitted maximum was 80 ha in irrigated areas and 300 ha in dry farming areas. All land held above the official ceiling was expropriated by the state and redistributed in small plots to landless tenants. The amount of land received by beneficiaries of the reforms varied from an average of 1 ha in Egypt, where population pressure is greatest, to 7·5–15 ha on irrigated land and 15–30 ha on rainfed land in Iraq where land and water resources are more abundant. Land redistribution proceeded fairly rapidly in Egypt, and in South Yemen the peasants were mobilized to seize land from the landlords by force. There were long delays in Iraq and Syria because of the complex systems of land tenure, insufficient trained staff to implement the reforms, and lack of reliable records of land ownership. Thus, 10 years after the introduction of the first Land Reform Law in Syria less than one-third of the land expropriated had been distributed to cultivators. In Iran the problem of land registration was avoided by using the village as the basis for redistribution. Instead of a precise land area, landlords were allowed to retain no more than one village or selected fractions totalling one village. Landlords were normally compensated for the land expropriated, and the peasants made to pay for the land they received. However, in Iraq after 1970 and in South Yemen from the beginning of reform, no compensation was paid and land was redistributed free of charge.

The impact of land reform has been far reaching, but its consequences must be viewed in perspective. The proportion of the cultivated area affected by the reforms varies considerably – from 42% in Iraq to only 12·5% in Egypt. Not all the large estates have disappeared. In the case of Iran some landowners avoided confiscation by transferring ownerships to wives, children and relatives before the actual implementation of the reform, while orchards, plantations of tea and certain other crops, and lands under mechanized farming were exempt from expropriation. There was nothing to prevent landlords retaining the best lands, or in irrigated areas those lands which dominated the water supply for the rest of the village. Even where landlords lost much of their lands their social prestige often persists, and many have retained a measure of political influence over the peasantry. In general the beneficiaries of land distribution now enjoy higher incomes and an improved standard of living. Many tenant cultivators are also better off thanks to a number of measures regulating landlord–tenant relations. However, without adequate enforcement, traditional forms of tenancy can still survive under the guise of new leasing arrangements. Only a limited number of peasants have received land under the reforms – perhaps 14–15% of the total peasant population in Iran, 10% of Syria's peasants, and 9% of the Egyptian rural population. In many cases landless tenants were favoured over agricultural labourers, but by no means all the tenants on expropriated estates became beneficiaries of 'reform' land. Some have been forced to join the growing ranks of the landless unemployed. The demand for casual labour has declined with the break up of large estates, as only family labour is usually employed on redistributed plots. In this situation the position of the landless labourers has often deteriorated. In Iran the large labouring class has been given no protection, no minimum wage, no unemployment relief, and no land; while in Egypt it has proved impossible to enforce the statutory minimum wage because of the large surplus of unemployed. The largest section of the rural population, the landless labourers and the poor peasants living on minute plots of land, have generally not benefited from the land reform programmes. The effect of land redistribution on employment opportunities overall has thus been negative. In the future and in spite of continued rural–urban migration, increasing population pressure in the countryside will probably accentuate the problems of disguised unemployment and open unemployment among the rural population. These problems will only be avoided by the creation of additional employment opportunities in agriculture.

*Co-operatives* were set up following land reform to perform the functions previously undertaken by the landlords or their agents, and integrate the peasants into a new social and economic infrastructure. Membership is normally obligatory for recipients of reform land. In Egypt the co-operatives are responsible for the provision of most inputs, including seeds and fertilizers, credit facilities and the marketing of agricultural produce in the land reform areas. The land remains in private hands but operational units have been enlarged through consolidation of fragmented holdings. Farming operations on the enlarged holdings are directed and controlled by the co-operatives. Because of the success of crop consolidation, the co-operative system was extended throughout the country, and by 1962 membership was compulsory for all farmers. This type of co-operative was introduced in Iraq after 1958, but with less satisfactory results. The landowners retained considerable local influence which they used against the co-operative movement, and it proved difficult to maintain irrigation and drainage works and to market agricultural produce because of the serious shortage of qualified staff. Production co-operatives have also been established in South Yemen, but in Syria the government has stopped trying to coerce farmers into co-operating in crop production and is encouraging service co-operatives in which farmers own and work their own land but combine to buy inputs, rent machinery and in some cases market output. Government policy towards co-operatives has also fluctuated in Iran and was the main reason for the slow growth of the movement during the first phase of the land reform. At first co-operatives were mainly confined to providing credit and in some cases consumer items. A few villages, however, were converted into farm corporations, professionally managed, collectively owned farming units, and the peasants received shares in the corporation in proportion to the amounts of land and property each had contributed to the enterprise. Recently, producers' co-operatives have been emphasized, in which land is held individually, but a government official directs farming operations and arranges the marketing of crops. In spite of the growth of the co-operative movement in the Middle East traditional money lenders continue to play an important role. Although they charge higher interest rates than the co-operatives, application procedures are less complicated and borrowing is more flexible. Even in Egypt, where the co-operatives are the main source of rural credit, many poor farmers still resort to private money lenders, and in Iran a recent survey of prosperous peasant families revealed that money lenders provided about half their credit needs.

## Crops

Improved world prices for some crops, and better communications that allow access to wider markets, have brought quite a number of areas in the Middle East out of the stage of self-subsistence, and allowed the expansion of commercial agriculture. Overall, an older pattern of regular reliance on cereals and a very few extras, which had prevailed for several thousand years (and still remains characteristic of wide areas), has given way in many regions to a more mixed agricultural pattern in which cash

Cereal yields (kg/ha)

| Country | 1961–65 | 1975 |
|---|---|---|
| Egypt | 3310 | 3646 |
| Libya | 251 | 653 |
| Sudan | 815 | 834 |
| Cyprus | 1069 | 1458 |
| Iran | 930 | 1108 |
| Iraq | 831 | 776 |
| Israel | 1471 | 2371 |
| Jordan | 726 | 565 |
| Lebanon | 1027 | 1167 |
| Syria | 816 | 803 |
| Turkey | 1146 | 1629 |
| Yemen (Aden) | 1277 | 1560 |
| Yemen (Sana'a) | 739 | 884 |
| World | 1460 | 1840 |
| USA | 2736 | 3440 |
| West Europe | 2337 | 3205 |

Source: *FAO Production Yearbook*, 29 (1975).

crops, vegetables and fruit especially, with some fodder, play an important role. Commercial crops such as cotton, tobacco, sugar cane and oil seeds, have greatly expanded since 1950 and produce higher cash returns. The net value added per hectare for cotton is almost three times that for any grain crop. Nevertheless foodstuffs still remain the most important crops though some countries which are predominantly agricultural now import growing quantities of food. Foodstuffs account for about 30% of Egypt's total import bill, and for a quarter of all Iraqi imports.

In many areas agriculture has greatly improved with markedly higher crop yields. Output per hectare is highest in Israel and Egypt where cereal yields, for example, exceed the world average and compare favourably with those of the USA and northwest Europe. Elsewhere yields are still well below the world average and are particularly poor in Libya, Iraq and Yemen (Sana'a).

Tractors and steel ploughs are used frequently, and the mechanization of agriculture is increasing, but traditional implements still survive in many regions. After Israel, Lebanon has the most tractors per hectare of agricultural land, and their introduction has been encouraged chiefly by increasing labour costs. Increased mechanization can lead to an improvement in productivity but also to serious problems. In Turkey, for example, a tractorization programme after the Second World War encouraged overcultivation, serious soil erosion, and massive migration

Consumption of chemical fertilizers in the Middle East 1964–75

| Country | Total consumption (tonnes) | | Consumption per ha of agricultural land ('oo g) | |
|---|---|---|---|---|
| | 1964–65 | 1974–75 | 1964 | 1974 |
| Cyprus | 11411 | 12217 | 217 | 233 |
| Egypt | 304670 | 430300 | 1216 | 1507 |
| Iran | 31221 | 426690 | 13 | 156 |
| Iraq | 2963 | 34442 | 3 | 37 |
| Israel | 37100 | 64539 | 301 | 517 |
| Jordan | 4383 | 3220 | 34 | 22 |
| Lebanon | 25054 | 49520 | 873 | 1383 |
| Libya | 3792 | 15700 | 4 | 17 |
| Sudan | 23636 | 60316 | 8 | 19 |
| Syria | 16676 | 42037 | 13 | 34 |
| Turkey | 96349 | 617100 | 18 | 111 |
| Yemen (Aden) | — | 460 | — | 2 |
| Yemen (Sana'a) | — | 2500 | — | 3 |

from the countryside to the towns. In Egypt there are limits to increased mechanization because of the dangers of further reducing employment opportunities in agriculture.

The application of chemical fertilizers has also increased steadily in recent years. In the early 1960s the region's total annual consumption of fertilizers amounted to 624836 tonnes, but during 1974–75 it reached well over 2 million tonnes. For many years Egypt has used more chemical fertilizer per hectare of agricultural land than any other Middle Eastern country: the higher crop yields obtained in the Nile valley can be attributed in part to the widespread use of chemical fertilizers. In contrast, virtually no fertilizers were used in the Tigris–Euphrates region before 1960, and although consumption has increased during the last decade, Iraq's poor agricultural performance reflects the limited application of chemical fertilizers. Iran and Turkey have also emerged as major consumers of fertilizers in recent years, but consumption per hectare of agricultural land remains low – under one-tenth of Egyptian levels.

(a) *Cereals* Despite the changes mentioned above, cereal cultivation still plays the major part in Middle Eastern agriculture. For this, the direct need for local food, the relatively slow development of fruit trees, and until recently the conditions of land tenure (which encourage crops that are short term), can be held to be responsible. Wheat and barley grown as winter crops (i.e. sown in autumn and harvested in late spring or early summer) are most important, with wheat predominating, except in Egypt, Libya, Sudan and Yemen (Sana'a). The chief summer crops are maize (which, dependent upon irrigation, has become the principal cereal crop in Egypt and is likely to spread further with expansion of irrigation), millets of various kinds, and rice. Summer crops are usually sown in spring and harvested in late summer or early autumn. The millets are particularly important in the Yemens and the Sudan, whilst rice cultivation is of growing significance in the alluvial lowlands of the larger rivers, again expanding as more irrigation water is available. Oats and rye are grown in the cooler mountainous regions of the north.

Wheat and barley are natives of the Middle East. As a wild plant barley has a wide distribution, ranging from Tunisia through Tripolitania, Cyrenaica and the Sinai to the Levant and Asia Minor, with extensions to the north-east as far as Transcaucasia, Turkestan and Afghanistan. The fact that in Mesopotamia measures of barley were taken as standards of value at least as early as 2000 B.C. indicates the importance and antiquity of the plant which was, until recently, grown practically equally with wheat in Iraq.

The origin and distribution of wheat are a more complicated matter. In the first place, the bead wheat now in common use as a food would appear to be a hybrid, developed by cultivation from other strains, and not a domesticated wild species, as is the case with the remaining cereals. Ruggles Gates suggested that bread wheat has arisen from the crossing of two inferior wheat strains: (a) einkorn (alternative names dinkel and spelt), which is a small plant that grows wild in Greece and the northern part of the Middle East, and (b) emmer, a much more productive species, which is still widely cultivated in regions of warm dry summers. Most of the hard wheats used in the making of food pastes – macaroni, etc. – are of the emmer group. Wild emmer has a more restricted distribution; the only area where its occurrence seems definite is a narrow strip immediately to the east of the Jordan depression, between Syria and the Nejd. Another possible area is the northern Caucasus. A theory has been put forward to the effect that bread wheat formed by the crossing of einkorn and emmer must therefore, have been first grown in the region where both species grow wild – that is to say, in south-west Syria or Transcaucasia.[1] A second theory due to Vavilov places the origin of bread wheat in eastern Afghanistan, Iran or Transcaucasia. This theory is less generally accepted, since it conflicts in some measure with archaeological

---

[1] Further light on the origin of bread comes from certain features of cell structure. The cells of einkorn (Triticum monococcum) show a chromosome grouping of seven; those of emmer (typical varieties T. dioccum and T. durum) a grouping of fourteen; and those of bread wheat (T. vulgare) a grouping of twenty-one, strong evidence in favour of crossing the first two species.

evidence. Later views still suggest either spontaneous mutation, or hybridization between various wild and cultivated strains.

Except in Asia Minor, where some is still produced, *einkorn* is now little grown; but *emmer*, because of its tolerance of high altitudes and a cooler climate, is widely grown, particularly in mountainous or semi-mountainous regions. With bread wheat, *emmer* is the staple food grain of most agricultural areas of the Middle East, barley now being used increasingly for animal fodder, and for exporting as malting barley. Recently, new high-yielding dwarf varieties of wheat and hybrid maize have been introduced into the Middle East, and two long seed varieties of rice have been developed by Egyptian experts. The availability of effective advice and instruction for the cultivators is, however, critical to the success of these improved seed strains.

(b) *Fruit and vegetables* Because of lack of pasture, and hence of milk and meat, fruit and vegetables form an essential part of the diet of most peoples of the Middle East. Many workers make a usual midday meal of bread, olives and onions, with additions such as dates or figs. Orchards and gardens are hence an important complement to ploughed land, and, whenever possible, the cultivator tries to have a proportion of both. As we shall see later, it is sometimes possible to sow orchards with cereals; more usually, orchards and gardens are planted round houses, since shifting cultivation prevents the establishment of fruit trees on ploughed land.

Thanks to a climate which combines certain of the features of both tropical and temperate regimes, the already abundant natural vegetation of the Middle East has been enriched by the successful introduction of numerous other species from north to south. To the indigenous olive, vine, apricot, fig, pomegranate, cherry, peach and carob have been added the banana, orange and sugar cane, natives of the tropical south; and from the north, the apple, strawberry and potato.

Though rather less widespread than formerly, owing to greater cultivation of groundnuts, the olive still occupies 25–40% of the total area planted in fruit trees throughout the Middle East – an indication of the importance of the olive as a source of food. The better fraction of the oil is used in cooking, giving a characteristic style of food preparation; and the olive itself, easily stored and carried, is often eaten raw. A general lack of animal fat in Middle Eastern diet is largely made up from olive (and now groundnut) oil; and variations on the basic recipe of chopped vegetables mixed with oil are a typical food of the Middle East – one particular kind (*kubbeh*) is the national dish of the Lebanon. In addition, the poorer oil is used as an illuminant, and as the basis of an important soap industry, whilst the crushed stones are fed to cattle.

Closely adapted to the Mediterranean climate regime, the olive flourishes best in regions of abundant winter rain; yet a long, dry summer is essential to a full development, and it is remarkable how even a smaller summer rainfall will reduce the oil content of the fruit. Moderate winter warmth is also necessary, although the olive can stand up to 10° C of frost for a short time. In spite of its predilection for regions of moderate rainfall, the olive is tolerant of aridity, and can grow, with irrigation, on the borders of the desert. This explains its wide distribution outside the purely Mediterranean areas of the Middle East: as an oasis plant it extends as far east as Iran. Irrigation becomes necessary in regions of less than 200 mm rainfall, but care must be taken not to apply an excessive amount of water, in order to avoid reducing oil content of the fruit. Main growing areas of the Middle East are (1) the valleys of south-west Anatolia, centring on the Büyük Menderes (Meander), and (2) the lower Orontes, centring on Antakya (Antioch) and extending as far inland as Idlib. Other districts are the Seyhan plain of Turkey, and the environs of Latakia, Tartus, Tripoli (Libya), Damascus, Beirut and Tripoli (Lebanon).

The vine is second in importance to the olive. Production has varied at different periods, the Islamic ban on alcoholic beverages having had a restrictive effect. At the present time, some wine is made, chiefly, but not exclusively, by Christians and Jews – Cyprus, the Lebanon, Israel, Turkey, Iran and the Alexandria region of Egypt being the chief wine-producing areas. A large proportion of grapes are eaten as dessert, and a sweetish confection (*dibs*) resembling molasses is also prepared. In western Asia Minor, most of the grapes are dried and exported as sultanas.

The vine is much less tolerant of great heat, and is also liable to contract disease in the damp summer atmosphere of the coastal lowlands. Hilly country, therefore, suits the plant best; and the foothills of Cyprus, the Lebanon and Israel, almost the whole of the lower hill slopes of Asia Minor, and many parts of northern and western Iran, are the home of vine cultivation. In all parts of this zone, extending from the well-watered hills of Cyprus, western Anatolia and the Levant, to the high valleys of Armenia and Azerbaijan, and to the oases of central Iran, vines form an important adjunct to cereal cultivation. Phylloxera, said to have been introduced into Turkey by the construction of the Orient Express route in the 1880s, has now necessitated the introduction of American vine stocks (which are more resistant to the disease) in districts of intensive production.

Another plant showing considerable adaptation to Mediterranean conditions is the fig, which has been cultivated in the Middle East from earliest times. Like the olive, the fig needs a long hot summer, but is otherwise able to stand either aridity or abundant moisture, and is therefore of frequent occurrence on the Mediterranean coast and as far inland as the desert border. Associated with the olive, vine and fig, but of lesser importance, are the other fruit trees: apricot, peach, orange and pomegranate. Mention must also be made of the many nut trees – chiefly almond, pistachio and walnut – which are characteristic of the 'continental' inner zone of the Middle East from south-west Anatolia to Iran; and of the hazels that are more characteristic of northern Asia Minor. A cold winter is essential to the growth of many of these crops.

Another fruit crop of increased importance is the apple – difficult to grow except on the higher hill slopes. Apples are much in demand among the oilfield workers – they keep well, and are often less easily contaminated than the soft fruits. In the Lebanon, 'apple land' – above 500 m altitude – now commands higher rentals than warmer terrain nearer sea-level.

So far, little has been said of the southern portion of the Middle East. In this zone generally higher temperatures, with only a few short cold spells in winter, together with lower rainfall, give rise to a vegetation complex essentially different from that of the cooler and more humid north. Most typical of the south is the date palm, and the northern limit of its occurrence may be taken as a frontier separating the Middle East into two contrasting provinces. The significance of this division is greater than that of mere vegetation zones. To the north of the boundary lies the more specifically 'Mediterranean' area, with a characteristic social development related to the cultivation of wheat, olives and vines, and tending to look in some aspects of its political and cultural orientation towards the west and north. South of the boundary is a region showing some affinities to the tropics and to the monsoon lands. Here the date is a staple, and millet, sorghum, rice, maize and sugar cane tend to replace wheat and olives as principal crops. With this alteration go changes in agricultural practices and ways of life: irrigation becomes the basis of cultivation; and contacts with the south and east assume importance.

Date palms require prolonged hot and dry summers for successful growth of fruit. If temperatures fall below 18°C for any considerable period during the year, fruit will not ripen, although the tree itself may develop normally; and summer rain prevents fertilization of the flowers. Pre-eminently a tree of the hot deserts, date palms can exist on a minimum of water, and produce fruit even when partially buried in drifting sand. The palms can also stand considerable amounts of water, and heaviest yields of dates are obtained when irrigation is applied to roots so that date palms are also characteristic of most riverine areas in the south of the Middle East. In order to obtain a large crop, the female flower must be fertilized by hand with pollen obtained from a male flower, since natural pollination is somewhat slow and unreliable. A date grove will therefore include two or three male palms per hundred of females, and some trade in pollen dust is carried on from southern Iraq, where date palms are most numerous. The banks of the Shatt el Arab are the region of greatest cultivation, and a large surplus is available for export after local needs have been met. The date is also a principal item of diet in southern Iran, the Arabian peninsula, parts of the Nile valley and in Libya. Its high sugar content, relative resistance to contamination by the bacteria of human disease, and long keeping qualities make it suitable as a food for nomadic and semi-nomadic peoples.

Vegetables are becoming increasingly important. Hitherto, the summer drought has been an unfavourable factor; but with recent development of irrigation schemes this difficulty is being overcome: and a further stimulus has been provided by the growth of cheap motor transport. Market-gardening is therefore becoming a feature, especially in the neighbourhood of large towns, with a small but growing export trade, especially from Israel and also Egypt. Chief native plants are onions, cucumbers, pumpkins, beans, squashes, aubergines, artichokes, peppers and avocado pears; to these have been added tomatoes and potatoes. Tomatoes are fairly widespread (and increasing), being grown as a field crop, but potatoes tend to be restricted to the cooler and damper north, where again they form an increasingly important commodity.

(c) *Commercial crops* Chief of these are cotton, fruit (especially citrus), tobacco, sugar cane, sugar beet and oil seeds.

Cotton is a summer crop. The absence of late spring frosts, and a long dry summer followed by a distinctly cooler autumn, are markedly favourable factors: and where abundant water supplies are available (usually only in irrigated areas) the plant does well. Unfavourable factors are soil salinity, which has a marked deleterious effect, and liability to insect pests. Lower Egypt is the principal area of production and the famous long-stapled cotton of the region has a worldwide market.

Cotton also forms the principal export of the Sudan where it has been a traditional crop for over 50 years; and since about 1950 great expansion of cotton-growing has occurred in Turkey, Iran, Iraq, Syria, Israel and Cyprus.

Citrus fruit flourishes close to the Mediterranean coasts, and has become an important export commodity, not only for Israel, but the Lebanon, Cyprus and Turkey as well. The fruit begins to ripen in November, and is picked during the winter.

Tobacco, like cotton, is a summer crop, and is best grown on hill slopes in regions of moderate rainfall. Despite official Moslem disapproval of smoking, tobacco is widely grown throughout the Middle East for local consumption only, but in most areas quality is poor. In western Asia

Minor, and in the Latakia district of Syria, more careful methods of cultivation result in a better product, and an important export trade has grown up. Of recent years, the 'Turkish' tobaccos of Anatolia have lost much ground to the Virginian variety,[1] but Latakia tobacco, which is used mainly as a blending ingredient in pipe tobaccos, has maintained its position.

Sugar cane is a crop that needs considerable summer heat, and also copious water: its cultivation tends to be restricted, therefore, to the irrigated areas of the south (Egypt especially), whilst sugar beet, on the contrary, flourishes in cooler conditions, and in the Middle East tends to be grown in the hillier parts of the north (Iran, Turkey, Israel).

Groundnuts have been introduced in many parts, especially western Libya (the Tripolitanian Jefara), Cyprus and Egypt. Other oil-producing plants and seeds are grown on a fairly small scale.

Mulberry plantations for the rearing of silkworms have been a feature of certain parts of the Middle East ever since the cocoons were first smuggled from China in early Byzantine times. Within the last century, the extent of mulberry plantations has undergone considerable fluctuation: under the Ottomans, a heavy tax restricted development, and outbreaks of disease were frequent, necessitating the import of new plant stocks from America. More recently, the competition of foreign silk from Italy, France and Japan, and the use of artificial silk, brought about a crisis in the Middle Eastern industry, and many mulberry plantations were re-sown with cereals. During the war of 1939, however, the Middle East became one of the few sources of raw silk in Allied hands, and a rapid expansion of production took place, especially in the Lebanon. Now, a renewed phase of competition and decline has taken place, and whilst Bursa and a few other western Anatolian towns still maintain some activity, as does part of Mazanderan (Iran), the mulberry has practically disappeared in north Lebanon, where once it was widespread, and in Iraq.

The opium poppy and a form of hemp (hashish) are grown in the Middle East for medical purposes, as a source of morphine and its derivatives. Although production is very small, the high value of the drugs renders the plants extremely useful as cash crops, and there is considerable temptation in the way of the peasant cultivator to produce small quantities above the legal amount allowed. These ultimately find their way to the illicit drug markets of the world. In Turkey, where slightly less than half of the world's controlled supply of morphine is produced, strict governmental supervision is maintained; but elsewhere in the Middle East, although governmental prohibition exists, ineffective supervision led in

[1]  It is interesting to note the change in smoking habits in Britain since 1900. At that time Turkish cigarettes were fashionable, and it was felt necessary to apologize when offering a stronger Virginian 'gasper'.

the past to an illegal market. Now, drug pedlars in Iran are executed. Opium poppies need a dry and moderately warm spring, with absence of frost. Towards the end of the summer, incisions are made in the capsule of the flowers, and a juice containing opium flows for some 24–60 h, later coagulating into a sticky mass. Rainfall during this period and just before will result in loss of the opium both by washing away the exudation, and also by reducing the alkaloid content. Once grown in Iran round Yazd, but now prohibited, opium-growing is officially confined to Turkey. Hashish is sometimes produced in the Lebanon, and at one time it may have been a principal export commodity of the Lebanon.

## Pests and diseases affecting plants

Agricultural production is greatly reduced by losses due to pests and diseases. The locust is probably the greatest single menace to crops, since one-half to three-quarters of the entire yield of a holding may be eaten during one visitation. Locusts originate in the deserts of Arabia and the Sahara, later moving outwards in immense swarms towards the cultivated areas.[1] As the locust is relatively large, measuring some 4–12 cm in length of a body, a considerable quantity of greenstuff is eaten, and whole districts can be stripped bare within a few hours. The Sahara locust which feeds for preference on grain and fruit, is regarded as more destructive than the Arabian variety, which prefers the leaves of trees. Because of their rapid migration by flight, locusts are an international problem; and a joint committee[2] has been established by a number of Middle Eastern states to develop methods of control. These include crushing the female locusts by heavy rollers, ploughing the eggs into the ground before they can hatch, the use of flame-throwers, and also insecticides such as sodium arsenite, against the adult locust.[3] Another method is to sweep the young locusts into specially dug trenches before their wings are properly developed.

[1] An interesting relation between climate and the occurrence of locust swarms has been described by Dr Uvarov. Between periods of invasions by locust swarms, small numbers of locusts have been found to exist as individuals, quite dissociated from any swarm, and harmless to crops. Such 'solitary' locusts approximate closely in appearance and behaviour to ordinary grasshoppers. If, however, the progeny of solitary locusts are reared under crowded conditions (e.g. in a cage) physical changes occur, so that the solitary grasshopper type of locust becomes transformed into a true swarming locust. These changes, demonstrated under laboratory conditions, have also been observed to take place in grassland areas, when, following a season of drought, locusts are forced to congregate in a few relatively low-lying and damper spots. Hence locusts of the swarming type would seem to develop during cycles of slightly increased aridity, and it would thus appear that the factors producing an invasion by locusts are largely climatic.

[2] The Office International des Renseignements sur les Sauterelles de Damas.

[3] Spraying from aircraft has proved markedly successful. Another advance has been the discovery of gammexane, an insecticide that, unlike arsenical preparations, is harmless to vertebrate animals, and may therefore be used in grazing areas.

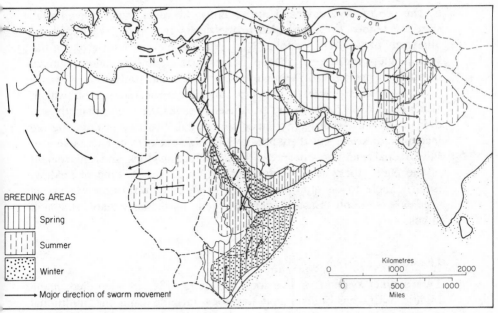

*Fig.* 8.3 Locusts in the Middle East.

Another pest is the *sunn* or *sunna* insect, which attacks the ears of
cereals, just as they are ripening. The *sunna* seems to be most widespread
in the damper, cooler parts of the Middle East and, like the locust, the
insect passes the first part of its life cycle outside cultivated areas,
migrating into these regions only when fully developed. This habit offers
the possibility of control by man, since if crops can be harvested before
the arrival of the insect, much loss is averted. Hence quick-growing
cereals are favoured in regions infested by the *sunna*; and barley, which
ripens earlier than wheat, is less likely to be attacked.[1] Another form
of control is to root out and burn the affected plant, thus destroying the
insect, which, being very small, remains inside the ear. Losses from *sunna*
infection are only slightly less great than those from the locust; up to
60% of the crops may be affected. The *sunna* does not migrate in large
numbers over long distances, so that control measures on an international
scale are not attempted.

The production of dates suffers from the activities of certain species
of spiders, which cover the ripening fruit with thick, close webs. In the
dusty atmosphere of date-growing regions, the webs collect sand particles,
with the result that sunlight no longer reaches the fruit, and development
is arrested. Other insect pests attack both citrus and soft fruit trees. Aphis
and the saw fly do much damage each year, though losses can be reduced

---

[1] This is one reason why in some Middle Eastern countries barley is more important than
wheat.

by the use of insecticides. Until recently, however, such preventative spraying tended to be confined to the citrus groves of Israel, and the vineyards of western Anatolia. Now that commercial fruit-growing has become more widespread, there is increasing tendency to employ chemical methods of pest control, though this is by no means universal.

Citrus fruit is liable to develop small black or red scales, which, although of little harm to the fruit itself, render the crop unsightly and difficult to sell. Hydrogen cyanide spraying is effective in reducing the incidence of scale, but there are obvious drawbacks to its extensive use. Phylloxera is another widespread disease affecting vines, and replacement of the plant stocks is the only effective cure. Rust, a kind of mildew, is also liable to develop on ripening grain and, unfortunately, native species of Middle Eastern cereals seem particularly liable to such attacks.

### Livestock production

Two distinct systems of livestock production may be identified in the Middle East – pastoralism and livestock farming – and the traditional separation of these systems from each other has accentuated the inherent differences between them. Pastoralism is practised by nomadic herdsmen making use mainly of natural rangelands beyond the cropped area for animal feeding. Animals and animal products form the basis of the nomads' economy. In contrast, livestock farming is practised by sedentary communities and provides only a part of their total income. Animals are raised within or on the edges of the cultivated area as a secondary activity to that of crop production. Within these communities agriculture and animal husbandry are often separate occupations and many villages still maintain one or more shepherds to look after all animals in common, whilst the great majority of farmers devote themselves entirely to cultivation. Even in Saudi Arabia, despite the traditional dominance of pastoralism, 38% of the total livestock population in 1970–71 was raised among settled communities. However, a mixed farming system, characterized by the close integration of livestock rearing and cultivation, as developed in Western Europe, is relatively rare in the Middle East and is found mainly in Israel, in parts of the Nile Valley and in Lebanon.

At present livestock accounts for about 40% of agricultural output in Iraq and Israel, about 33% in Egypt, Lebanon and Jordan and less than 25% in Syria. The quality of animals tends to be low, and yields of food and other products restricted. The size of such animals is less than in some other parts of the world, and yields of milk and meat are small, with hides quite often of indifferent quality, partly due to parasites. Middle Eastern wool tends to be 'hairy' and tough, so that it cannot be used

Livestock numbers 1961–65 to 1975 ('000s)

| Country | Cattle | | Buffaloes | | Camels | | Sheep | |
|---|---|---|---|---|---|---|---|---|
| | 1961–65 | 1975 | 1961–65 | 1975 | 1961–65 | 1975 | 1961–65 | 1975 |
| Egypt | 1 565 | 2 271 | 1 559 | 2 280 | 174 | 105 | 1 657 | 1 982 |
| Iran | 5 060 | 6 500 | 247 | 130 | 234 | 60 | 30 410 | 35 000 |
| Iraq | 1 531 | 2 116 | 238 | 332 | 200 | 338 | 10 138 | 15 829 |
| Israel | 228 | 300 | — | — | 10 | 10 | 190 | 197 |
| Jordan | 61 | 49 | — | — | 17 | 16 | 752 | 792 |
| Lebanon | 100 | 84 | — | — | 1 | 1 | 200 | 232 |
| Libya | 106 | 121 | — | — | 266 | 120 | 1 378 | 3 329 |
| Saudi Arabia | 230 | 311 | — | — | 460 | 606 | 2 288 | 3 102 |
| Sudan | 8 111 | 14 665 | — | — | 2 000 | 2 600 | 8 255 | 14 000 |
| Syria | 454 | 504 | 2 | 1 | 11 | 8 | 4 035 | 5 310 |
| Turkey | 12 621 | 13 387 | 1 162 | 1 022 | 54 | 19 | 32 863 | 40 539 |
| Yemen (Aden) | 71 | 101 | — | — | — | — | 201 | 232 |
| Yemen (Sana'a) | 1 260 | 1 100 | — | — | 54 | 120 | 3 289 | 3 200 |

| Country | Goats | | Horses | | Mules | | Donkeys | |
|---|---|---|---|---|---|---|---|---|
| | 1961–65 | 1975 | 1961–65 | 1975 | 1961–65 | 1975 | 1961–65 | 1975 |
| Egypt | 780 | 1 410 | 50 | 25 | 10 | 4 | 1 236 | 1 554 |
| Iran | 13 006 | 14 000 | 449 | 350 | 130 | 120 | 2 041 | 1 800 |
| Iraq | 2 209 | 2 675 | 159 | 130 | 95 | 37 | 560 | 607 |
| Israel | 156 | 138 | 12 | 4 | 5 | 2 | 15 | 5 |
| Jordan | 592 | 400 | 6 | 2 | 15 | 8 | 78 | 44 |
| Lebanon | 456 | 330 | 3 | 4 | 5 | 4 | 31 | 26 |
| Libya | 1 281 | 1 109 | 31 | 15 | 1 | — | — | — |
| Saudi Arabia | 1 468 | 1 722 | — | — | — | — | 105 | 148 |
| Sudan | 6 579 | 9 300 | 21 | 20 | 1 | 1 | 583 | 672 |
| Syria | 668 | 684 | 67 | 60 | 68 | 50 | 195 | 251 |
| Turkey | 22 665 | 18 746 | 1 247 | 878 | 197 | 299 | 1 899 | 1 522 |
| Yemen (Aden) | 809 | 923 | — | — | — | — | 17 | 31 |
| Yemen (Sana'a) | 7 993 | 7 400 | 3 | 4 | — | — | 472 | 640 |

Source: *FAO Production Yearbook*, 29 (1975).

in weaving fine modern-type textiles, but instead finds best use in the making of carpets. One compensation for the small size of Middle Eastern sheep is the prevalence of the fat-tailed variety, which provides an extra delicacy when eaten.

The preponderance of sheep will be noted: this holds in almost all areas. Sheep are important in both systems of livestock production. Besides providing a small convenient carcass of excellent meat which can be eaten by a single family in a short time – a factor of importance in view of the hot climate – the sheep provides milk and wool, and because of its ability to travel considerable distances between pastures it is better adapted than are cattle to existence under semi-arid climatic conditions. Goats are also kept in large numbers and are found under both systems of livestock production, and also in urban areas. These animals are more agile than sheep, and can find sustenance on less abundant vegetation, though, as we have seen, their voracious cropping of all green plant-life makes them a menace in certain parts of the Middle East. Goats are kept for their meat and milk, and for their hair, which can be woven into a thick, smooth cloth that will resist soaking by rain, and is hence favoured for the making of tents and Bedawin cloaks. The finer hair from Angora goats (mohair) produced in small quantities – chiefly from Turkey – is almost all exported.

Outside the Sudan cattle are far less numerous than sheep or goats, and tend to be kept in cultivated areas rather than on the arid and semi-arid rangelands where water sources are far apart and the vegetation too poor to support them. Except in Egypt, Israel and the other relatively few (though expanding) areas where fodder crops are specially grown, animals often have to find a limited subsistence on stubble pasture after cereals have been harvested, on scrub or steppe, or in the uncultivated borders of arable land. However, with the recognition of the benefits of legumes as an element in crop rotation, fodder growing for such animals is now becoming more widespread. Mutton and lamb are still much preferred to beef by most people, so cattle tend to be lean, and kept mainly for milk and for use as draught animals. Dairying has developed around many of the larger towns, with animals sometimes stall-fed. In recent years there has been some importation of dairy breeds – Brown Swiss, Holstein and Jersey.

Because of Jewish and Islamic religious prohibition, pigs are relatively unimportant in the Middle East. They are found in Israel, Iran, Lebanon and Turkey, but numbers are not large. Water-buffalo are important in the marshes of lower Iraq and Egypt, the Caspian provinces of Iran and the alluvial coastlands of Turkey, where in addition to providing milk they are used for ploughing rice-paddy fields.

Donkeys are the principal draught animals of the Middle East, and numbers have increased almost everywhere. Hardy, surefooted on broken ground and tolerant of indifferent pasture or poor fodder, these animals are used both for ploughing and for transport of people and goods. Mules, much less important, are decreasing in number.

Camels have also declined in importance, though some still occur in all countries of the Middle East, and in Saudi Arabia and Sudan numbers have actually increased in recent years. Besides the Arabian (one-humped) animal which is adapted to the warmer deserts of the south, the two-humped Bactrian species (which can tolerate winter cold better) is found in Iran and Turkey, with cross-breeds between the two. Today camels are rarely used as transport animals, and among the surviving nomadic pastoralists they are raised mainly for meat production.

Horses are the least important of the draught animals in the Middle East, since their natural habitat is the cooler steppe of central Asia, and they have been introduced only with difficulty into the Middle East. Pasture is usually too rank or poor for much grazing, and keeping a horse is a matter of considerable expense. Hence they are little used as beasts of burden, but for riding and racing, as in the West.

As a result of the traditional nature of livestock production system in the Middle East and the lack of any major efforts at modernization and development, livestock rearing is one of the most underdeveloped sectors of the Middle Eastern economies. In agricultural development priority has been given to crops, often cash crops, and little investment has been diverted to the livestock sector. Mutton and lamb production increased during the last decade in Turkey, Iran, Syria and Iraq, but only slowly; while beef production has done little better. The growing demand for meat and milk resulting from rising living standards has been met by a massive increase in imports of livestock and frozen livestock products. Until 1930 Saudi Arabia was self-sufficient in livestock products with a surplus for export; by the early 1970s about two-thirds of meat consumption was provided by imports.

Today pastoralism is in decline, owing to loss of vital manpower, the expansion of cultivation, and the serious deterioration in many of the region's rangelands. Official government policy has favoured the settlement of nomads in new farming communities, and few attempts have been made to help them become better pastoralists by understanding their problems and needs. Yet there are vast submarginal areas in the Middle East, entirely unsuitable for producing crops, that can be utilized efficiently by pastoral animals. Measures to conserve and improve the rangelands using imported range management practices and techniques are only beginning to be introduced. Greater efforts are being devoted to investment in intensive commercial livestock farming projects using Western management techniques, e.g. the Kufra project in Libya, and the Hofuf and Diab schemes in Saudi Arabia. The most ambitious projects are in Sudan, financed largely by the Arab oil exporters and managed by American and West European agri-business companies. One such project, set up by the Saudi controlled Triad Holding Corporation and the Arizona–Colorado Land and Cattle Company, involves the creation of a 400 000 ha ranch near the Blue Nile to turn 100 000 head of cattle into 17 000 tons of beef annually for export. These schemes are capital intensive and use little local expertise. High quality breeding stock is imported and animals are fed on irrigated fodder and often imported concentrates. Iran, Iraq, Egypt and Oman are also turning to agri-business techniques for a solution to the development of their livestock sectors, but success is by no means assured.

## Mining

Apart from oil resources, which will be discussed separately, the mineral deposits of the Middle East tend to be of rather limited importance, although significant discoveries have been made in the past few years and the general situation is better than seemed possible a few years ago. Even so, chrome ore, mined chiefly in Turkey and Iran, is the only non-petroleum mineral of which the region is a producer on a world scale. Many mineral deposits occur in relatively small amounts, though with exceptions (e.g. the iron ores of Turkey, Egypt, Libya and the phosphates of Jordan) and thus large-scale extraction plant is not always justified. A number of deposits are in remote, inaccessible areas: because of association with the folded zone of the Middle East, metallic minerals especially tend to occur at high altitudes in regions that are thus difficult topographically and climatically.

In consequence, there may be involved a long expensive haul to centres where ores can be treated or shipped abroad. Even in Israel high cost of transport over the 120 km to the coast has had some adverse effect on exploitation of Dead Sea minerals; and the long distance that separates Turkish coal from iron ore is a factor in the high cost of production of Turkish iron and steel.

Another disadvantage has been lack of coal, which, apart from the general effect on economic life, has a directly restrictive influence on the production of other minerals, since some ores cannot be treated or concentrated near the mines, but must be moved elsewhere (often out of the Middle East) for refining. Coal of good quality is found only in the Eregli-Zonguldak basin of north-west Turkey, and even here supplies are limited. Latterly, however, electric power generated from oil, or from the Aswan Dam water potential, is changing the situation in certain areas.

A fourth obstacle to mineral production is lack of labour. Most mining centres are well away from centres of dense population, and there is little inducement, in the scale of development of mining industries, to attract a large mining population to the hilly zones where minerals could be exploited. The severe winter of the north makes it impossible to continue mining throughout the year in many parts of Anatolia; and most peasants prefer, if at all possible, to combine with mining some part-time cultivation or herding. Even workers in the Turkish coal mines return to the fields for a short time during the harvest season.

A further but minor adverse factor is that exploitation of metals in the Middle East has been in progress, at least in a sporadic way, since the dawn of history. The gold of Lydia (Turkey), where coins were first issued, the copper of Cyprus, and the iron of Anatolia and Phoenicia, have all been partly exhausted of their richest ores; and although these considerations obviously do not apply to minerals like asbestos or chromium, certain areas formerly renowned as centres of mineral production have no modern activity. On the other hand, new discoveries have been made on old sites, and improved technique in extraction allows exploitation of ores that were rejected in ancient times as being of too low grade.

It is not proposed at this stage to outline the detailed distribution of the mineral resources of the Middle East: for the present it is sufficient to note a general picture. This is of rather sporadic and limited development of a surprisingly wide range of minerals, with (following more intensive prospection over the last decade or two, and the greater availability of capital for development) the growth of certain new activities. There is now a wide range of types of activity, from near haphazard collection of surface outcrops, with little attempt at actual mining, by workers whose major interest may be in agriculture or forestry, to intensive integrated exploitation involving the most modern large-scale plant. Collection of umber in Cyprus, or chrome in a few parts of Turkey and Iran, might exemplify the first, whilst the Aswan iron, Jordonian phosphates, Iranian copper, or Israeli Dead Sea potash, bromides and magnesium exploitation typify the second situation. Mining plays a significant role in the economy of Turkey and Iran which both possess a wide range of minerals, and phosphate mining in Jordan provides the country's biggest single export commodity.

**Industry**

Craft industries were once very widespread in the Middle East. Small-scale working of metals has characterized the region since earliest times. Highly tempered steel for weapons and harness were chief products: during the Middle Ages, Damascene steel and inlay work had a world-wide reputation, and something of the ancient tradition still lingers in the modern workshops of the district. Silverwork from Amara (Iraq) and from Iran has today more than a local renown.

Textiles have also been a traditional product. Raw materials are abundant: cotton, flax, silk and wool are all produced within the area, and camel- and goat-hair also are available in steppe regions. Some Middle Easterners use cotton, silk and now rayon and other artificial fibres, and cloaks of finely woven camel-hair serve as an impermeable outer garment for many Badawin. 'Traditional Arab' styles of dress are retreating before 'European' styles (less than a century ago almost all Syrians wore Arab dress), but a mixed style prevails still in many areas, and better-off men like to vary or mix the two types of garments. Saudi Arabian leaders still prefer traditional styles.

In addition to the production of textiles of everyday articles of clothing, the Middle East, particularly Syria and Iran, specializes in luxury brocades, which consist of metallic threads of gold or silver interwoven with a base of silk, or silk and cotton. Mohair, woven from the fine hair of angora goats, is produced on a very small scale, chiefly in Turkey; and there is some production of linen, mainly from Cyprus.

Wool produced in the Middle East, as we have seen, is often too coarse and too hairy for use in high-quality textiles. Instead, it is used in the manufacture of carpets and rugs, for which parts of Iran and Turkey are world famous. This activity is *par excellence* a small-scale craft: the finest Persian carpets in wool may have as many as 60–80 tufts/cm$^2$, whilst silk pile carpets in a cotton warp can have more: in each case months or years are needed for completion of a single carpet. The wool may be tinted (as in the finer carpets) by hand-made dyes, using processes that are sometimes family secrets, but cheaper aniline dyes (which give sharper, cruder colours) have come in. At the same time, falling values of money in Europe and the USA have made good Persian carpets an object of investment that does not easily lose value; and so there is a demand for carpets of high quality, especially in West Germany, France and the USA. In addition, the Middle East absorbs quite a number of carpets, not only among the remaining nomads, whose principal possession may be a few rugs, but in houses where they sometimes serve as coverings for divans.

Although some traditional crafts still survive, often maintained and sometimes revived by the influence of international tourism, the majority have declined to low levels as a result of competition from cheaper machine-made manufactures, and the changes in fashion which they brought about. Various attempts were made during the nineteenth century to resist the decline by establishing new industries along Western lines, but with little success. Modern industrial development only began in earnest during the Second World War and is thus a relatively new phenomenon in the Middle East.

Being largely cut off from outside supplies during the Second World War, with at the same time a very greatly increased demand for consumer goods from the temporarily stationed troops, the Middle East saw a considerable development of industrial production which has continued and expanded owing to population increase, greater wealth from oil, and the determination of many governments to foster industries where the strict economic return may not altogether have justified this. War, blockade and political and economic pressures from outside have also fostered a considerable desire to move closer to self-sufficiency in manufactures.

Modern industrialization began with the extraction of minerals and the processing of agricultural products, mainly for export. There followed the appearance of a range of light industries based on local raw materials

Manufacturing industry's contribution to G.D.P. and employment in manufacturing industry

|  | Contribution of manufacturing industry to G.D.P. (%) (1974) | Economically active population employed in manufacturing industry (%) (1970) |
| --- | --- | --- |
| Major oil producers |  |  |
| Iran | 20 | 9·7 |
| Iraq | 9 | 3·7 |
| Kuwait | 3 | 4·2 |
| Libya | 2 | 1·4 |
| Saudi Arabia | 7 | — |
| Non-oil economies |  |  |
| Cyprus | 13 | 11·3 |
| Egypt | 20 | 6·5 |
| Israel | 20 | 20·1 |
| Jordan | 9 | — |
| Lebanon | 16 | — |
| Sudan | 10 | — |
| Syria | 16 | 6·0 |
| Turkey | 23 | 3·6 |

Source: *UN Statistical Yearbook* (1974).

and producing for the domestic market – activities such as flourmilling, bottling, textiles (particularly cotton), cement manufacturing and some light engineering. In some countries higher value consumer durables – radios, television sets, refrigerators, motor vehicles – are now assembled locally using imported components, while the foundation has been laid for basic heavy industry with the establishment of several iron and steel smelting plants. Although most of the region's oil continues to be exported as crude, a growing number of refineries and associated petrochemical plants have come on stream in recent years, and many more are planned. The lack of fuel for industry, especially coal, is no longer a major handicap because of the increasing use of oil (either directly or as a basis for electricity generation), natural gas, and the greater development of hydro-electric schemes. Advances in technology have also played an important role; for example, high grade coking coal is no longer essential in steelmaking following the development of the direct reduction process used in conjunction with the electric arc furnace.

Industrial output has risen substantially during the last 15 years, achieving an annual rate of growth of over 10% during the 1960s. Israel, Egypt, Iran and Turkey have the most diversified industrial structure and dominate the industrial pattern of the region, while the UAE, Oman and the two Yemens are among the least industrialized countries. Nevertheless, manufacturing industry still makes a modest contribution to G.D.P. and to the employment structure of even the most highly industrialized states within the region. Some manufactured goods are exported, but industrial products make a major contribution to the export trade of only one Middle Eastern country – Israel. During the next decade, however, this picture could change dramatically. Following the completion of major industrialization programmes now underway in a number of countries, the Middle East could command at least 20% of the world's petrochemical market by 1985 and become a major exporter of refined petroleum products, and sponge-iron and semi-finished products.

Most countries in the region are committed to rapid industrialization, but the structure of industry and the planning strategies adopted in each country varies in response to political and economic aims and to resource endowment. For the major oil producers, petroleum represents a source of fuel, feedstocks and funds for industrialization which is regarded as central to the successful diversification of their economies ready for the day when the oil runs out. Iran, with important non-oil resources and one of the largest domestic markets in the region, already possesses a wide range of industries including food processing, vehicle assembly, tobacco products, home appliances, steel production, aluminium smelting and oil-related production in petrochemicals, with ideas of nuclear energy development. Priority in development planning is being given to rapid industrial expansion with emphasis on iron and steel and petrochemicals; manufacturing industry has become the fastest growing sector of the economy. With few financial constraints on development planning, Saudi Arabia is also investing heavily in petrochemicals and other capital intensive heavy industries such as steel and aluminium, and there are also plans to reduce dependence on imports. The aim of the current 5-year plan is to transform the country into a modern industrial state. In contrast, Kuwait, Qatar and the UAE have small territories, tiny populations and few resources other than oil. They have all embarked on major industrialization programmes, but because of the narrow domestic market and limited labour supply priority is being given to capital-intensive, export-oriented industries – gas liquefaction, refining, fertilizers and petrochemicals – and there are few plans for light industry geared to import substitution. Bahrain, however, with much smaller oil reserves and production than its neighbours, is following a different industrial strategy. Development and diversification began early, and this small island state already possesses a large oil refinery and an aluminium smelter, and a major drydock is under construction. There are no plans for further heavy industries, and priority is being given to light ancillary industry, mainly concentrated around the smelter and dry dock.

For the non-oil economies, the major constraint on industrial expansion has been lack of capital. Industrialization began early in Turkey, which, unlike most Middle Eastern countries, possesses a wide range of domestic raw materials for both heavy and light industry. It has the largest iron and steel industry in the region, a growing petrochemical sector, numerous assembly plants and important light industries – including textiles, paper, and food processing. Further expansion is planned in order to prepare Turkey for eventual full membership of the EEC, while the structure of Turkish industry is changing away from consumer goods to the manufacture of secondary and even capital goods. In Egypt agriculturally-based industries are dominant. The industrial structure is heavily dependent on textiles, but local mineral resources provide a base for heavy industry, and cheap H.E.P. is available from the Aswan High Dam. Priority is currently being given to petrochemicals, cement, tractors and agri-business, and a special effort is also being made to attract foreign-financed, export-oriented industries which will utilize Egypt's abundant skilled and semi-skilled labour. Israeli industrialization is in many ways a special case. Industrial development has not been restricted by shortages of either capital or skilled labour because of the large inflow of foreign aid and private remittances, and the existence of an already trained industrial labour force among the immigrant population. Industry was originally based on local raw materials to supply the home market and thus save foreign exchange. Later, tax and investment incentives were given by the government to encourage industrial exports which now contribute 80% of all Israeli's export trade. Food processing, textiles and clothing industries still produce mainly for the domestic market, and polished diamonds are the most important industrial export; production and exports of electrical and electronic equipment, particularly for military and communication purposes, have expanded rapidly in recent years.

Lebanon, like Israel, possesses a relatively skilled population, few natural resources and a small domestic market. Industry has developed around light manufacturing, while food processing, textiles and building materials account for nearly half industrial production and provide the most important exports. Lebanon holds a unique place in the regional economy, and industrial products are exported principally to other Arab states. Until the outbreak of civil war in 1975, the country's industrial prospects looked extremely bright.

In Egypt and Iraq, the two centrally planned economies in the Middle East, the state controls all key sectors of industry. The role of private enterprise is strictly limited in Iraq, but in Egypt private sector participation has been encouraged since 1973 and is seen as the key to further industrial expansion. In contrast, private firms dominate the entire structure of Lebanese industry. Elsewhere a mixed economy is more characteristic. In Turkey only about 40% of manufacturing industry remains under direct state ownership, and in Iran both local and foreign capital investment is encouraged in all sectors except the state-owned basic industries, mainly steel and petrochemicals.

Many Middle Eastern industries rely on a tariff wall to maintain an internal market. Costs of production tend to be high and quality mediocre, so export possibilities are not great and markets therefore small – an extra factor in keeping up costs. Acute manpower shortages are a serious problem, particularly in the major oil-producing states which have become heavily dependent on foreign workers in every sphere of industrial development, from high technology to unskilled labour. Although modern, large-scale plants are increasing in number, small workshops maintained by a single owner with five or six workers are still very characteristic. As in most developing countries, many industries operate at well below full capacity, in some cases at less than 50%. A common feature throughout the region is the strong concentration of manufacturing industry in relatively few centres, chiefly the major cities where it is now possible to see modern industrial quarters; there is an urgent need for greater decentralization of industrial activity. The rising demand for water for industrial use has already become a serious problem in some parts of the Middle East, and the only solution in the future may be investment in expensive desalination plants.

The future success of Middle East industrialization also depends on closer economic co-operation between the countries of the region. Regional co-operation is essential in order to overcome the limited size of domestic markets, to avoid excessive duplication and competition, particularly in the development of oil-based industries – and to encourage the capital surplus economies to invest in industrial projects within the region. Co-operation in industrial development would allow economies of scale, lower production costs, and higher quality products which should eventually make the Middle East's industrial products more competitive in international markets. Various plans and programmes for industrial co-operation have been drawn up, but few have actually been implemented.

Conditions of labour in industry remain varied. In some regions, or branches of industry, there are strong trade unions, with correspondingly high standards and some social security benefits; in other parts, the opposite is the case. Labour legislation, restricting hours of work and the employment of women and children, has been enacted in many states of the Middle East, but is sometimes allowed to become a dead letter because of lack of inspection and governmental control. Children of ten or less are to be found at work, sometimes under hard or dangerous conditions; and the large surplus of unskilled labour, due to high birth-rates and to the gradual extinction of handicraft industries, has meant that the collective bargaining power of the artisan has tended to remain low, although improvements have occurred in the past few years. Moreover, the lack of a sophisticated tax system means that much government revenue must be raised not by direct taxation, but by imposts on necessities – which bears most heavily upon the poorer sections of the community.

## Fishing

In view of the low standard of agricultural productivity, it might be expected that the Middle East, with its long coastline, would have developed an important fishing industry. This is not so; comparatively little sea fishing takes place, and of the meagre quantities of fish produced, slightly less than one-half is obtained from inland waters. There are several reasons for the lack of attention to fishing, and most of these have a geographical basis; but one is mainly psychological – the prejudice of the Moslem peoples, and of Shi'a Moslems in particular, against eating certain species of fish.

A second factor is the straight, harbourless and often sheer coastline, which offers little inducement to seafaring on a small scale. Even in regions where harbours are more numerous, local populations have in a few cases turned their back on the sea, and settled at some distance from the coast, because of the liability to piratical raids in the not too remote past. This is especially true of Cyprus, where one might expect fishing to be an important occupation. Other natural factors influencing sea fishing depend on local conditions; and these will now be examined in turn.

### Black Sea

Below about 80 m, the waters of the Black Sea are heavily charged with sulphuretted hydrogen. Fish are therefore restricted to the upper levels; and in winter, storms and ice produce a large-scale migration towards the calmer Aegean and Mediterranean, with a return movement in spring. Much fishing is, therefore, possible in the Bosphorus, the Sea of Marmara and the Dardanelles – one factor, incidentally, in the importance of Istanbul – and large quantities are caught in spring and autumn, at the times of migration, about three-quarters of the total being marketed at Istanbul. Pollution, however, is becoming a problem, and the considerable increase in turbidity in the Sea of Marmara may explain the decline in the Turkish mackerel catch in recent years. In the Black Sea itself fishing is also a seasonal occupation, and a surprising variety of fish is caught:

anchovy, mackerel, sardine, turbot and tunny being the chief. A proportion of the catch is canned at various ports along the Black Sea and at Istanbul. Turkish production of fish is higher than in most other Middle Eastern countries; but even so, further development could easily take place, especially in centres at some distance from Istanbul.

### Mediterranean

The Mediterranean is far less rich in fish than is the Black Sea, owing to a lack of nutriment for the fish themselves. This lack arises from a deficiency of calcium salts, which in other sea areas are produced by the entry of fresh water from rivers and by interchange of deep and shallow water under the influence of tides, currents and atmospheric turbulence. In the eastern Mediterranean, all these factors are of small effect; the Nile is the only large river, and where it enters the sea there occurs the one important fishing ground of the eastern Mediterranean. In the late summer and autumn, when the river is in flood, large shoals of sardine normally move towards the Nile delta to feed upon the nutriment in the fresh water; and heavy catches were obtained during the short season of Nile flood. These, however, have been very adversely affected by construction of the Aswan High Dam, which has almost ended the Nile flow into the Mediterranean.

Along the coast of the Levant, sardine, mackerel and mullet are caught, but the number of boats engaged is small. Some development has occurred in Israel, but a limiting factor is the scarcity of fish away from sea areas influenced by Nile water, and some Israeli boats even operate in the Atlantic. The eastern Mediterranean is, however, an important area for sponges, and a high-quality product is obtained in most areas, the best coming from the Egyptian coast immediately to the west of the Nile delta. The sponge industry is closely controlled by various governments concerned, since over-fishing can easily occur. Chief areas of production are the Dodecanese Islands, Cyprus, the island of Ruad (off the coast of Syria), Egypt and Cyrenaica (Libya).

### Red Sea

Fishing is not on a large scale (annual yield approx. 70 000 tons), since littoral populations are scanty and the waters of the Red Sea not outstandingly productive in themselves. Evidence suggests an increase in productivity from north to south, with the most productive waters those of the Yemen Arab Republic. Most of the fishing trade of the Red Sea has been developed from the African shore, chiefly from Port Sudan and Massawa. The total fish landings from the Red Sea by Saudi Arabia are estimated at only 6–8000 tons per annum. Catches include snapper, rock cod, emperor fish, mackerel, jack and tuna, almost entirely for local consumption. Some attempts are being made to expand activities from the Red Sea ports of Saudi Arabia, and there appears to be scope for commercial exploitation by modern fishing units to supply local markets and for export.

## Indian Ocean

In contrast to conditions in the Red Sea, fishing on the coasts of southern Arabia is one of the principal activities of the people. In the words of Worthington, the sea is equally as, or more productive than the land. During summer, shark are caught; and in winter immense shoals of sardine approach the shore, followed by numerous tunny, which prey on the sardines. The local population live for the most part on fish, fresh and dried, which in inland regions is also fed to transport camels, and even forms the chief fodder for cattle in the eastern areas of South Yemen and in Oman. There was once a large export of dried and salted fish from the southern coasts of Arabia to India and East Africa but the trade has declined substantially. It is not surprising to note the inhabitants of south-east Arabia were known to the ancient Greeks and Romans as the Ichthyophagi (fish eaters). Most of the fish caught still supplies the local market, but efforts are now being made in both South Yemen and Oman to build up a modern fishing industry capable of exporting large quantities of fish and fish products.

## Persian/Arab Gulf

Although diving for pearls has greatly declined, there has always been small scale in-shore fishing, since, like the Indian Ocean, the Gulf has a considerable fish fauna. Of late years, the Iranian government has made efforts to develop fishing, and the state-owned South Fishing Company operates from five Gulf ports where cold storage units have been established, including Bandar Abbas and Bushire. The Gulf's shrimp resources are already well-exploited, and as local consumption is small, the bulk of the catch (totalling 10000 tons in recent years) is exported to Europe and North America. The yield of other fish is only 40–45000 tons annually by commercial methods and a further 10000 tons by traditional means, and there is considerable scope for further expansion. In 1975 a project was launched to survey and develop the region's fisheries involving all littoral states.

*Caspian Sea*

Fishing in the Caspian has only limited possibilities, since although present production is relatively high, the sea is rapidly shrinking in size, and restriction will be necessary in the future in order to conserve supplies of fish. Conservation of Caspian Sea resources is being promoted through Iranian–Soviet co-operation. The production of caviare from the roes of the sturgeon is particularly important and in 1975–76 reached 200 tons of which 170 tons were exported. Production, however, has fallen in recent years because of heavy pollution in the Caspian Sea, and the government is giving considerable attention to breeding sturgeon in artificial lakes. Other types of fish are caught (total catch reached an estimated 4000 tons in 1975–76) and the demand within Iran for white fish from the Caspian has been increasing.

*Inland fishing*

This is, relatively speaking, of considerable importance. One reason is the concentration of population in many riverine areas as the result of which markets for the catch and a supply of labour are both easily available. Many Marsh Arabs of lower Iraq are fishermen, and in Egypt areas of inland water are considerable. The catch from inland fishing is thus several times greater than from the sea; and areas are now stocked with fry to replenish supplies. Several thousand inland fishermen are active.

In Israel great attention has been given to breeding fish in ponds and tanks, and this provides a very useful supplement to diet. Besides this, there is some fishing on the Sea of Galilee, but the lower Jordan and Dead Sea are too saline. Israel has also purchased a number of British trawlers, and trained Jewish crews in the North Sea. Some North Sea and Atlantic catches are even transported to Israel.

**Foreign aid**

In closing this general discussion of Middle Eastern economy, some reference may be made to the assistance proffered by outside agencies, governments and individuals to various Middle Eastern countries. Aid may be direct, in the form of outright payments; as loans on commercial terms; in the form of purchases of Middle Eastern products on advantageous conditions, as technical subsidies, either in cash or by the provision of materials and personnel; in the form of scholarships, training grants or other educational subsidies to Middle Eastern nationals; by payments for the use of Middle Eastern facilities, e.g. military bases; or finally as 'military aid'. The stage has been reached of direct competition between the Western bloc and the USSR to offer aid to Middle Eastern countries; for example, when America withdrew offers regarding the financing of the Aswan High Dam, the Soviet Union almost immediately made more acceptable proposals. Soviet aid was also provided for the Helwan steel plant in Egypt and the Euphrates Dam in Syria, and during the last two decades the USSR has supplied some 48% of all arms imported by Middle East countries. Of total US overseas aid allocations in 1976–77, about half were destined for the Middle East, with Israel and Egypt the two major recipients. Israel is heavily dependent on US aid for its survival; revenue from grants and loans, mainly from the US and the major Arab oil producers, accounted for half the state expenditure of Jordan in 1975; and Egypt would be in serious default on its foreign debts (estimated at $9–10 billion – much of it owed to the USSR), but for gifts and grants from Saudi Arabia, Kuwait and the UAE. Indeed, in recent years, and particularly since 1973, the major Middle East oil producers have undertaken to provide substantial credits and grants to poorer states in the region, and also to other Third World states in Africa and Asia. Aid is distributed mainly through national and multinational funds such as the Kuwait Fund for Arab Economic Development, the Saudi Development Fund, the Arab Fund for Economic and Social Development and the OPEC aid fund. In addition assistance is offered through contributions to the World Bank, IMF and the UN Emergency Fund. In 1974–75 the Middle East oil producers provided 30% of total borrowings from the World Bank compared with only 8·5% of the total in 1972–73.

# 9 Oil resources of the Middle East

## Theories of origin of oil

Petroleum would seem to have been formed by the decomposition of various types of marine life – chiefly plankton, but also algae and lowly animal organisms. As the remains of these organisms collected on the floors of seas and estuaries, they were gradually covered by deposits of thick, fine sediment that excluded air and light. Under such conditions, the normal process of decay did not operate; instead, partial decomposition, produced by certain bacteria that exist in anerobic conditions[1] seems to have transformed the original organic material into globules of petroleum. It is also possible that chemical reactions involving mineral salts contained in the surrounding water and silt played some further part in the process of decomposition.[2]

As sedimentation continued, compressions of the mass of silt led to its consolidation into rock measures of various kinds. The recently formed oil globules, at first widely dispersed throughout the entire mass of silt and intermingled with water-drops, were hence squeezed out of their original parent rock, and forced to migrate, together with water and natural gas (also a product of organic decomposition), to any near-by rock measures such as limestone or sandstone. There, a slow process of

[1] I.e. without air.
[2] It is interesting to note that the same process of sedimentation and organic decomposition appears to be in process at the present time on the bed of the Black Sea. Similar conditions would also seem to be present in the Gulf of Oman. Black, strongly smelling mud with a high organic content is being deposited, and the waters of the Black Sea below 80 m are heavily charged with sulphuretted hydrogen.

separation began, by which oil, as a lighter fluid, floated on top of the denser water, and gradually collected, under the influence of gravity, into large pools. Above the oil, and sometimes partly dissolved in it, occurred a quantity of natural gas; below was always to be found an accumulation of saline water.

In order for concentration of scattered oil globules to take place, some slight disturbance or irregularity of the rock measures would seem to have been necessary. Without the presence of some kind of trap or basin in which liquid could accumulate, the globules of oil would remain dispersed throughout a considerable thickness of rock, in a way that would preclude all possibility of commercial exploitation. Much of the oil might seep gradually away, and be lost. The occurrence of oilfields is therefore closely linked with geological structure; a limited amount of folding and dislocation is essential to allow the accumulation of petroleum in reservoirs, but excessive disturbance may break up the basin-like retaining structures and allow escape of the oil. Petroleum deposits are therefore associated with the outer margins of fold structures, where disturbance of the rock measures, although present, is greatly restricted in extent. It is perhaps not necessary to remark that the oil does not occur as a vast underground 'lake' – rather, it is held in the interstices within porous rock measures.

A further condition for concentration of petroleum in large quantities is the existence of an impermeable rock layer, which acts as a seal immediately above the porous oil-bearing rock. Without this seal, or cap-rock, oil would not be retained in amounts sufficient to allow commercial extractions. Oil accumulation hence depends upon a conjunction of factors: (a) original richness of oil-forming material, (b) the occurrence of porous strata, (c) tilting or other changes in the rock succession to allow separation of oil from water, and its concentration in workable quantities, and (d) impermeable cap-rocks to prevent leakage of oil to the surface. The main types of geological structure favourable to oil concentration are shown in fig. 9.1, and of these, the first, or anticlinal/synclinal type, is by far the most widespread.

Conditions in the Middle East are favourable to a remarkable degree for the occurrence of oil. Reasons for this are: (a) long-continued sedimentation in the geosyncline of the Tethys, as the result of which oil was formed in rocks of many different ages and character, (b) the fact that the Tethys was a warm-water sea, and consequently rich in animal life, (c) the further fact that, although extensive fold movements took place, these were reduced in intensity over wide areas by the presence of an underlying crystalline platform,[1] (d) the frequent occurrence of strata

[1] In Iran folds are steeper than in other oil-bearing areas of the Middle East. This is probably because the later series became detached from the crystalline basement as the result of shearing along the underlying Cambrian salt-beds.

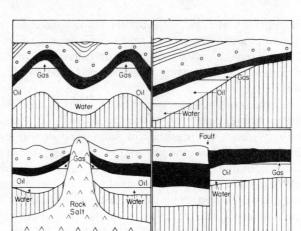

*Fig.* 9.1 Types of oil-bearing structures, cap-rock in black.

that are porous either because of their structure, or because of later fissuring, and (*e*) a similar abundance of impervious, and sometimes highly plastic rock series near or at the surface: e.g. the occurrence of impermeable beds of sandstone, shale, gypsum, anhydrite and rock-salt. As a result, even though geological exploration is by no means complete, the petroleum deposits of the Middle East are on a vast scale – so far, the greatest known in the world. On a basis of proved reserves (though the world situation changes) the Middle East is the principal potential source of petroleum, with about 60% of the world total – over six times the reserves of the United States. Three countries, Kuwait, Saudi Arabia and Iran, now each have more petroleum in reserve than that in the entire USA. In 1976, taking only the largest fields (i.e. with reserves of over 1000 million barrels) the situation was as shown in the table on p. 247.

A special technique of geological surveying, known as the Seismic Refraction Arc Method, has been developed as a means of locating the oil deposits of Iran, which are for the greater part associated with limestone series. It has been discovered that vibrations from an explosion travel much more quickly through limestones of a certain type than through other, non-limestone formations. Hence a charge of explosive (usually 1–2 tons) is detonated underground, and the results recorded at a number of seismometers spaced along the arc of a circle, the centre of which is at the source of the explosion, or shot-point. The seismometers are 15–25 km away from the shot-point, so as to give time for differences in speed of travel of the vibrations to become clearly apparent; and after allowance has been made for variations in altitude, the readings of each seismometer are compared. Because vibrations travel most rapidly through limestone, the seismometer placed at a point where an under-

Major world oilfields (excluding the USSR)

| | Year of discovery | Cumulative production to 1975/6 ('ooo million barrels) | Reserves ('ooo million barrels) | Years of production at 1975 levels |
|---|---|---|---|---|
| *Saudi Arabia* | | | 149 | 58 |
| Ghawar | 1948 | 12 | | |
| Safaniya | 1951 | 3 | | |
| Abqaiq | 1940 | 5 | | |
| *Iran* | | | 65 | 33 |
| Agha Jari | 1938 | 6 | | |
| Gach Saran | 1928 | 4 | | |
| Marun | 1964 | 2 | | |
| Bibi Hakimeh | 1961 | 1 | | |
| Ahwaz | 1958 | 2 | | |
| *Kuwait* | | | 68 | 100 |
| Burgan | 1931 | 10 | | |
| *Iraq* | | | 34 | 42 |
| Kirkuk | 1929 | 7 | | |
| Rumaila | 1953 | 2 | | |
| *Libya* | | | 26 | 48 |
| Sarir | 1961 | 1 | | |

lying bed of limestone approaches nearest to the surface will be among the first to record the explosion. In this way, by taking a number of arcs, buried anticlines and synclines in limestone formations can be mapped, even though these may lie uncomfortably with the surface strata. When the general trend of folding has been established, more precise observation of the exact crest of an anticline is made by grouping the seismometers in a straight line passing over the shot-point. By this means, using the same theoretical principle, not merely the position of the crest but also its exact depth can be ascertained. Elsewhere in the Middle East, the more usual method of prospecting by reflection is followed.

### Oil-producing areas

In a broad regional sense, the main productive oilfields of the Middle East are located (1) under and around the Persian/Arab Gulf, with its geosynclinal extension into Iraq as far as north-east Syria and south-east Turkey, (2) along the Red Sea–Aqaba rift zone, as far north as Israel, and (3) the northern rim of the shield or basement of north-east Africa, with deposits in the interior deserts of Libya and western Egypt.

*Persian/Arab Gulf area*

*Khuzistan fields* These lie on the western flanks of the Zagros mountains
in the region between Bushire and a mountain range known as the
Pusht-i-Kuh. The western Zagros is composed of a series of large
anticlinal ridges, all aligned in a north-west–south-east direction, but of
unequal longitudinal extent. One such ridge, the Pusht-i-Kuh, forms part
of the extreme western edge of the Zagros in the latitude of Baghdad.
The range is only some 300 km long, and where it dies out, both to the
north-west and the south-east owing to downward plunging of the fold
structures, it is not immediately succeeded by other ranges. Hence the
western edge of the Zagros mountains approaches nearer to the river
Tigris, and descent to the plain of Mesopotamia is abrupt; but further
to the north-west and to the south-east there are wide lowland embayments
within the highland region, where the plain rises more gradually, by a
series of foothills, to the main ridges of the Zagros. It is in these two
areas of foothills that the major oilfields of Iran and Iraq lie. The southern
embayment, drained by the Karun river, contains the Khuzistan fields;
in the northern embayment occur the second group of fields – those of
north Iraq and north-west Iran – with the Pusht-i-Kuh range as a zone
of separation between. Only in the two enclaves, where the transition
from plain to mountain is less sudden, and where, as a result, folding
is less intense, are oil domes found. In the region of the Pusht-i-Kuh rock
series plunge steeply below the sediments of the Mesopotamian plain,
and so far have not yielded oil in any quantity.

The valley floors of the foothill region lie at an altitude of 150–250 m
above sea-level. Between them run anticlinal ridges, often dissected and
terraced, and giving the impression of small plateaux. Towards the west,
ridges and plateaux reach a height of about 300 m above the valleys, but
further east, topographical features are more strongly marked, with ridges
attaining 1000 m. On one such ridge, the Kuh-i-Seh Qaleitun, is situated
the main production unit of the Gach Saran field, from which oil flows
by gravity to tide water on the Persian/Arab Gulf.

The oilfields of Khuzistan are related to the occurrence of a bed of
limestone, some 300 m in thickness, which acts as a reservoir for
petroleum. This rock known as Asmari limestone and of Oligocene-
Miocene age, is not, however, in itself especially porous, and were it not
for numerous fissures which have been developed in it as the result of
folding movements, oil would not flow in quantities large enough for
exploitation. Wells must therefore reach a fissure in the Asmari series
before they become productive, but when this is achieved, flow of oil in
a single well has sometimes attained 1 million gallons per day. Because
of the presence in the lowest levels of the Asmari beds of a quantity of

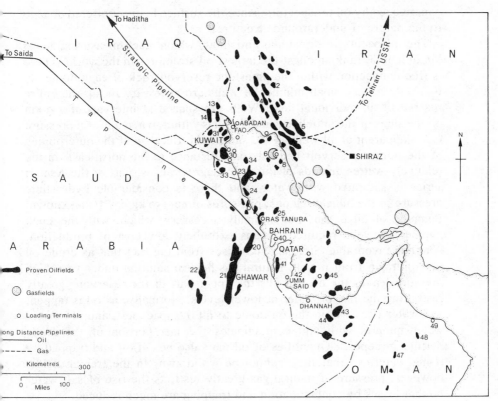

*Fig.* 9.2 Oilfields of the Gulf area.

water, which can be traced downwards without break through several thousand metres, it is inferred that oil has migrated into the limestone from a considerable number of other rocks of differing character.

In the foothill region, the Asmari beds are folded in a number of simple anticlines. Further to the south-west, however, they dip sharply under the sediments of the Mesopotamian plain, sometimes at an angle of 70°, while towards the north-east they outcrop at the surface among the main Zagros folds well to the east of the foothill region. Above the Asmari series is a complex of shale, salt and anhydrite beds of Miocene age, known collectively as the lower Fars series. These beds act as an impermeable cap-rock, except where a number of faults allow some seepage of oil and gas to the surface. Because of the plastic nature of the salt-beds, folding in the lower (Asmari) series did not conform exactly with that in the upper (Fars) series, so that in the oilfield regions a number of synclines in the lower Fars strata are underlain directly by anticlines in the Asmari measures. Until this disharmony was discovered, much difficulty was experienced by oil prospectors, since the surface features offered no clue to the nature of underground structures.

The oil occurs in dome-like anticlines, which, each measuring 20–30 km in length, rank amongst the largest oil structures in the world. There is free connection within the limestone reservoir rock of each dome, so that only a very small number of wells are necessary to tap the entire reserve of an individual field. Wells are spaced at intervals of 2–3 km on the sides of the anticlines; and, as oil is withdrawn, a uniform pressure fall is apparent at all wells in the same field. Because of the outcropping of the porous reservoir beds at some distance to the north-east, in the relatively wetter uplands of the main Zagros ranges, part of the Asmari series is saturated with water, and there is considerable hydrostatic pressure in the oilfield regions, pressures of 60–150 kg/cm² being known. Pumping of oil is thus not normally necessary, which, with the small number of wells required, means extremely low cost of production. Another favourable circumstance arises from the fact that as crude oil is withdrawn from a well, natural gas held in solution under very high pressure leaves the oil and fills the upper part of the reservoir, greatly restricting the rise of water at lower levels. Normally, as oil is tapped, salt water rises within the oil dome to fill the space left, and ultimately water mingles with and contaminates the last portion of the crude petroleum deposit. Quantities of oil may also be cut off and trapped by rising water, so that they cannot be withdrawn. In the Iranian fields, however, pressure of natural gas greatly restricts the rise of salt water so that losses by contamination and trapping are much reduced.

Oil was first produced in 1908, from the Masjid-i-Suleiman field (1). After 1918, output steadily increased; and in 1928, the Haft Kel field was developed (2). The remaining fields came into production during or after the Second World War down to the present day. The fields of Iran are now grouped in three major complexes: the so-called Central Area fields (actually north of the other two), which are linked by pipeline to Abadan; the 'light-crude' export fields, which include Agha Jari (3) (currently the largest single producer-field in Iran) and Marun (4); and the 'heavy-crude' export fields, Gach Saran (5) being the chief. The second two areas export mainly through the more recently developed terminal of Kharg Island (6), though some fields (e.g. Pazanun (7)) are also linked by pipeline to Abadan.

In addition there are off-shore producing fields, located under the waters of the Persian/Arab Gulf. These, in distinction from the three complexes mentioned above, are exploited jointly by the National Iranian Oil Company and various foreign partners: American, Italian, Indian and Japanese. Most important of these producing areas are the Darius, Cyrus, Esfandiar and Feridun fields (8) which have pipelines to Kharg Island, the Bahregansar and Nowruz fields which have pipeline connection to a terminal at Emam Hassan, the Sassan field, and the Rostam field.

In 1910–13 the first major pipeline, 240 km long, was constructed from Masjid-i-Suleiman to Abadan, then a small port on the Shatt el Arab. Here a refinery was erected to treat the oil which flows from the producing fields largely by gravity. Port and refinery have been extended, so that Abadan, with a refining capacity of over 400000 barrels per day was for long the largest installation in the world. It is now equalled by Ras Tanura (Saudi Arabia). Expansion has also occurred at Khosrowabad a short distance downstream from Abadan; but with the considerable developments also at Kharg Island and other terminals Iranian oil is no longer almost entirely routed through Abadan.

*Fields of Iraq*  These fields lie in the more northerly of the two embayments previously described. Many of the structural features of Khuzistan are repeated in the north: there is the same foothill topography some 80–150 km broad, flanking the main Zagros ranges that lie further to the east; and folding follows a similar pattern of broad anticlines in the foothill zone, with sharper dips to the south-west. The reservoir rock, of Eocene-Miocene limestone (termed Main Limestone), is closely comparable with the Asmari series of Khuzistan, but of rather greater thickness. Four oilfields have been developed, at Kirkuk, Naft Khaneh and Ain Zaleh in Iraq, and at Naft-i-Shah in Iran, the latter lying very close to Naft Khaneh of which it is really a part, but on the opposite side of the Irano-Iraqi frontier.

At Kirkuk (10) there is a single narrow anticline between 80 and 90 km long – an immense size for an oil dome – and, as in the Khuzistan fields, open connection within the reservoir rock allows free flow of crude oil, so that under fifty wells are sufficient to tap the whole length of the anticline.[1] First developed in 1927, the Kirkuk field now produces from three centres; and this oil moved originally by pipeline across the Syrian Desert to terminals on the Mediterranean. Political difficulties have resulted in progressive shut down: the Haifa branch closed in 1947, and the others in 1976. In 1976–7 two replacement pipelines, one to Basra ('the strategic pipeline') and another via Turkey to Dortyol near Iskanderun came into operation. Prior to interruption of supply via Syria, the terminal at Banyas (Syria) was handling over 500000 barrels per day and Tripoli (Lebanon) about 350000 barrels, which produced $100 million net revenue to Syria and $10 million to Lebanon.

In 1939 oil was discovered at Ain Zaleh (11), north of Mosul, but invasion threats in 1941 led to a suspension of activities, and production

[1]  A gas and oil seepage from the crest of this anticline, at Baba Gurgur, is traditionally associated with the 'fiery furnace' of Nebuchadnezzar (G. M. Lees).

did not start until 1952. The oil is held in a layer of Cretaceous limestone (i.e. distinctly older than the 'Main Limestone' of Kirkuk). With a daily production of under 30 000 barrels from only eight wells, Ain Zaleh and a smaller site, Butmah (12), rank as the third most important field in Iraq, and this region is connected by pipeline to Kirkuk. Another later but larger field (second to Kirkuk) has very recently been developed at Zubair (13) and Rumaila (14) near Basra. Here the reservoir rock is of Cretaceous sandstone, and geological conditions are closely similar to those described below for Kuwait and Saudi Arabia. Two pipelines with a total capacity of 8·5 million tons per annum connect Zubair with a loading terminal at Fao on the Persian Gulf.

Other regions of Iraq have been surveyed for petroleum resources, but disappointment has resulted. Large quantities of oil were found at Qaiyara on the Tigris, and in the region between Hit and Ramadi on the Euphrates, but in both cases the crude oil was of very high gravity, so that it was impossible to pump the oil from the ground; and there was in addition a sulphur content of 5–10% (cf. sulphur content of crude oil at Kirkuk, 2%; at Masjid-i-Suleiman, 1–2%). Oil of a similar heavy type has been found in other districts of the Iraq lowlands, but again little can be done, at the present stage of technological development, to exploit these resources. Possibly in the future some method will be discovered by which these heavy low-grade oils can profitably be used.

*Saudi Arabian fields* Conditions in Arabia and on the southern shores of the Persian/Arab Gulf are in marked contrast to those of Iran and Iraq. Folding of the sedimentary measures has been greatly restricted because of the presence of the ancient continental platform of Gondwanaland; hence oil structures are very broad, open anticlines. In some localities, anticlinal structures are visible at the surface; in others, surface topography offers no guide to the presence of oil domes. The oil reservoir rocks of Arabia range from Jurassic to Cretaceous in age, and are thus considerably older than those of Iran and Iraq. Another point of difference is that in parts of Arabia petroleum is often held in porous sandstones, not limestone.

At Abqaiq (20) there is a very shallow dome, 6 km long, with the reservoir rock (of Jurassic limestone) at a depth of 2000 m below the surface, and a layer of anhydride as cap-rock. In some other areas, the oil-bearing limestone lies at 3000 m depth.

In 1954 it was realized that four producing centres hitherto regarded as separate structures formed one single oil-pool of enormous dimensions. The first 'strike' of oil was in 1948 at Ain Dar, and 6 months later a second at Haradh. Following discoveries in 1951 and after at Uthmaniya and Shedgum it became clear that this pool, or field, now known as 'Ghawar'

(21) extended for 200 km from north to south, and 25–30 km from east to west. The one Ghawar structure, with oil reserves equal to the entire total of those in the USA, is the greatest single producer in the world, and has various sections: from north to south, Fazran, Ain Dar, Shedgum, Uthmaniya, Hawiyah and Haradh. Further to the north are Abqaiq and Dammam, while a new area developed in 1968 is Khurais (22).

Further north is a complex of producing areas, some located inland, some off shore. The largest, Safaniya (23), occurring just south of the Neutral Zone 5 km off shore, is the world's largest off-shore 'field' and was discovered in 1951, with the oil held in a sandstone reservoir. Other off-shore fields are Manifa (1966) (24) and Abu Safa (1967) (25), with four others proved but not yet developed. An off-shore field is Hursaniya, whilst the Berri field lies partly off shore and partly on shore. Production from the Abu Safa field is shared with Bahrain, and there is a complex of pipelines linking these various areas and the refinery at Ras Tanura. A feature of the Saudi Arabian oilfields is the occurrence of extensive artesian water supplies (see chapter 16) in porous rock strata above the oil-bearing layers. Special precautions are taken to conserve this water in order to make it available for use both in the oil settlements and for irrigation.

Oil from the Saudi Arabian fields is passed by pipeline to export terminals and refineries at two centres on the Gulf: Ras Tanura and Bahrain, and to Saida (Sidon) on the Mediterranean. Construction of the well-known 'Tapline' (Trans-Arabian Pipeline) of 30–32 in. diameter over a distance of 1800 km was achieved in 1950 after many delays (some of which were political, and some due to world shortages of materials). Ras Tanura can now handle 11 million tons of crude oil per annum, Bahrain a slightly smaller amount, and the capacity of Saida is 25 million tons per annum.

*Kuwait fields* Here there are two reservoir layers of Cretaceous sandstone, about 300 m thick (as compared with 70 m in some of the Saudi Arabian fields), at a depth of about 1200 m. Production began in 1946, at Burgan (30) and later at Magwa/Ahmadi, whilst other fields were brought in after 1950 north and west of Burgan: Raudhatain, Bahra and Sabriya (31), and Minagish and Umm Gudair (32), respectively. Oil is piped to loading terminals at Mina al Ahmadi, where there is a refinery; a large off-shore loading base to accommodate supertankers was opened in 1969. This is located 16 km east of Mina al Ahmadi in the open sea, with a dredged approach channel to the south-east, and is linked to the shore by submarine pipelines.

It is worth remarking that the Kuwait field offers exceptionally low costs of operation. The crude oil is under water pressure (not gas pressure as in Saudi Arabia) and can be led to the crest of a low ridge (128 m above sea-level) overlooking Mina al Ahmadi, from where it flows by gravity to tide water – a total distance from oil well to the coast of only 25 km. The large size of deposits at relatively shallow depth, and the open nature of the country, mean that considerable economies of scale and organization can be effected. Nevertheless, concern over size of reserves has led the Kuwait government to reduce its operations drastically from a maximum of 1·2 billion barrels in 1972.

*Partitioned zone* This territory, shared equally between Kuwait and Saudi Arabia, has both on-shore and off-shore oilfields. The on-shore fields are at Wafra, South Fuwaris and Umm Gudair (33), and are exploited jointly by the American Independent Oil Co. (Aminoil), which holds its concession from Kuwait, and the Getty Oil Co. (US) which has its concessions from Saudi Arabia. Pressure is low, so that pumping is necessary, and there is a high sulphur content of up to 4%, besides which reserves are not thought to be very large. The Aminoil share of production is exported via a refinery and terminal at Mina Abdulla in Kuwait, and the Getty share moves to refinery and export terminal at Mina Saud.

Off-shore exploitation is carried on by the Japanese-owned Arabian Oil Co. (AOC). Five fields have been located since 1960; at Khafiji, Al Hout (34), Lulu, Ratawi and Dorra – so far only the first of these is actually producing. Submarine pipelines bring the crude oil to a refinery and loading terminal at Ras al Khafiji, which exports almost entirely to Japan.

*Bahrain and the Emirates* A small, but long-standing production area is located at Awali (40) on the island of Bahrain. Reserves are now within sight of exhaustion, and as no new discoveries have been made, exploitation is at a moderately low level in order to conserve output. Crude oil from the Saudi Arabian mainland is now brought to the Awali refinery to make effective use of excess capacity.

Oil was discovered at Jebel Dukhan in the Qatar peninsula (41) during 1939, but for various reasons war conditions brought about a complete cessation of activity, which was not resumed until 1947. The petroleum occurs at a depth of nearly 2000 m in Jurassic limestone, and pipelines carry the crude 80 km to an export terminal at Umm Said on the opposite (eastern) coast, where there is also a very small refinery now in process of extension.

Off-shore fields have been developed from Qatar: at Idd al Aharghi (1964) (42) some 50 km from land, and Maydam Mahzam 20 km further to the north-east from Sharghi, with pipeline connection to a loading terminal at Halul Island.

After a number of earlier disappointments, oil in substantial quantities was discovered in Abu Dhabi, and production began in 1962. The first field to be discovered was at Murban (43), with a later extension to Bu Hasa (44), and exports of crude are through a sea terminal at Dhanna. Production is now considerable.

Off-shore deposits were also discovered around Das Island; at Umm Shaif (45), 30 km east of Das and 130 km from the mainland; Zakum, about 100 km east of Das (46); and Al Bunduq, 30 km south of Das Island. All these are linked to extensive storage facilities (some actually undersea) and a loading terminal on Das Island. During 1969 production also started from off-shore fields located near Dubai. In 1971 Iran occupied the island of Abu Musa, off-shore from Sharjah, and an off-shore field, Mubarak, came into production in 1974. Revenues are shared between Iran, Sharjah and Umm al Qawain. Exploration in the other Emirates has so far been unrewarding.

Initial expensive disappointment followed by substantial discoveries has occurred in Muscat and Oman, where highly variable and disturbed rock series – ranging from serpentine to porous sandstones and limestones – were paralleled by an uncertain human and political situation. The earliest concessionaries largely withdrew, but the first commercial field was discovered in 1962, at Yibil (47), with two further fields at Fahud and Natih (48). These fields are some 300 km from the Batina coast, and a pipeline now links them to a terminal at Mina al Fahal (49), from which exports began in 1967.

### Suez–Sinai fields

On both sides of the Red Sea and Gulfs of Suez and Aqaba, geological structure is exceedingly complex, with a wide variation of rock types that range from pre-Cambrian to Recent. Strong faulting movements at the time of formation of the Red Sea rift have produced severe dislocation, hence structures favourable to the large scale accumulation of oil are less frequent; and of smaller size than those of the Persian/Arab Gulf zone previously described.

Discoveries have been made since 1913 in various localities on either side of the Gulf of Suez, in a zone extending as far as southern Israel. Some wells were short lived, others had crude oil of a high sulphur content, but despite these drawbacks the overall position is markedly better than a few years ago. Israel developed two very small fields near Gaza, at Heletz and Kohar, and until the western Sinai was occupied (between 1967–75) these were, with accompanying gas, a mainstay.

Since 1974 there has been a marked change in Egypt, with important discoveries on-shore and off-shore in various places around the Gulf of Suez. Most important so far is the El Morgan field (1965), but greater potential is thought to exist in the Ramadan area (1974). The July field (north of El Morgan) also seems important: these three zones, all off-shore, and with a reservoir rock of Nubian sandstone at 2000–3500 m. Older fields of longer production are at Abu Rudeis, Ekma, Feiran and Sidri, and these were operated by Israel, who, Egypt claims, extracted 400 m barrels. Smaller production also comes from the Amir, Bakr, and Shuqair fields on the west of the Gulf of Suez where wells of long standing are now declining in output. On the other hand, significant discoveries have been made in the Western Desert of Egypt, at Alamein (site of the Second World War battle), Al Gharadiq, and Al Razzaq. These, and possibilities along the Suez Canal (at Kantara) encourage the Egyptian government, already self sufficient in oil, to hope for a total of about 1 m barrels per day by the 1980s.

The numerous open fold structures of north Syria and the adjacent foothill zone of Turkish massifs are structurally the northern terminal of the great oil geosynclinal that stretches away through Iraq and Iran to the Gulf. In 1940 a discovery of oil was made at Ramandagh, 100 km east of Diyarbekir, where a reservoir of Cretaceous limestone lies at a depth of 1200–1600 m, from which oil with a high sulphur content was produced. Better-quality oil was later found nearby at Garzun, Germik and two other centres, but the total production from this entire field is only 15000 barrels a day. Another smaller field occurs at Bulgar Dagh-Selmo, also in the Siirt region, which gives 10000 barrels per day. A third field, with wells at Kayakoy, Kurkan and Baykan, produces 35000 barrels daily.

In 1958 a strike of oil was made at Karachok in north-east Syria, and this field would seem to be linked structurally with the Ain Zaleh field of northern Iraq. Production is from three centres, Karachok, Rumelan and Suweida, and these fields are linked by pipeline via Homs to Tartus and Banias on the Mediterranean coast.

### Libyan fields

In contrast to the relatively modest, though extremely useful scale of exploitation in Turkey, Syria, Israel and Egypt, Libya ranks among the most important producers in the world, comparable wholly with Iran and the Gulf zones. The first strike of oil was made in the extreme south-west of the country – at Atshan in the Fezzan – during 1957, but by far the largest discoveries have been in the hinterland of the Sirte Gulf, where a broad lowland embayment extends southwards and eastwards, bounded to east, west and south by 'sand-seas'.

Largest current producing fields are those of the Oasis Company, which has a minority American participation. The Libyan Government is a major

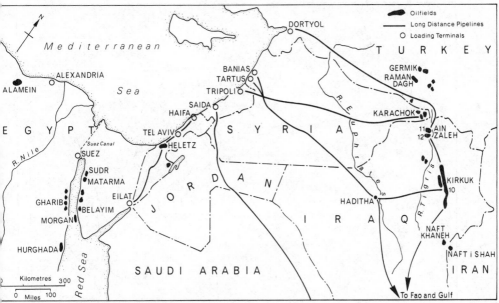

*Fig.* 9.3 Oilfields of the north and centre.

participant in all Libyan oil companies. The fields include the Dahra, Defa, Bahi, Waha, Gamah and, Zaggot fields, which are linked by pipeline to an exporting terminal at Es Sidr. Next in importance is the Occidental group (American minority) which operates the Zuetina terminal west of Agedabia. Main fields are the Intisar group (formerly known as Idris). The Zelten field was the earliest to be developed (1954) and is connected to the Marsa Brega terminal. Besides being a major producer of oil, there is a considerable export of gas with one of the world's largest plants. Minority participation is by Exxon (US).

Largest reserves in Libya appear to occur in the Sarir field of south-east Libya, but the oil has a high wax content, which makes exploitation difficult. There is a terminal at Marsa Harija near Tobruk, and the field was totally expropriated by the Libyan government from US and B.P. interests. A similar situation obtains for the Beda and Nafoora fields, which, though scattered, are linked to a sea terminal at Ras Lanuf. Production from the Amal and Hofra fields (minority West German holding) is also handled at Ras Lanuf. The remaining major Libyan field is in eastern Cyrenaica, with pipeline connexion to Zuetina. Italian interests participate in this company.

There have also been discoveries in western Libya, and exploration is active both on land and in off-shore areas. Various cut-backs ordered by the Libyan government for conservation of stocks and political

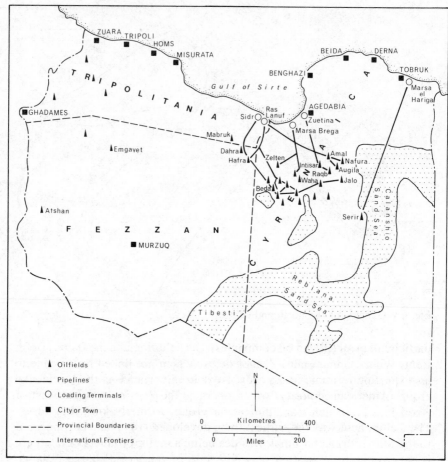

*Fig.* 9.4 Oilfields in Libya.

reasons have so far inhibited pipeline development in this western zone, though there are plans for a new terminal at Zuara. There is a small production by a Libyan–French company in the Sorit area.

### Quality of oil

There are considerable variations in crude oil: some is clear, light golden in colour and free flowing, whilst other types may be black, viscous or near-solid, and strong smelling ('sour'). Besides physical impurities such as sand, salt and water, there are other constituents, chiefly sulphur, but also gases such as methane and nitrogen and metals, especially nickel and vanadium. A broad grouping by characteristics is now used to define

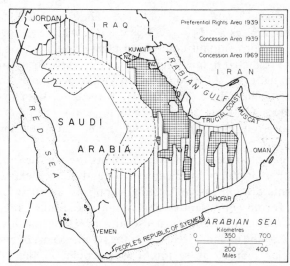

*Fig.* 9.5 Aramco concession changes: 1939–69.

crude oil: heavy, medium and light. Sulphur content and 'pour point' are also important determinants, e.g. Arabian heavy oil can have 2·9% sulphur content, and Abu Dhabi (light) o·75%; while some east Libyan crude solidifies at 10°C. All these affect the cost of refining, and the different types of fields that can be produced – hence also the selling price. A high concentration of vanadium is harmful to boilers, whilst other constituent chemicals affect the catalysts used in refining.

Grades are assessed by specific gravity: degrees API, ranging from very light (42° API = specific gravity of o·816) to heavy (25° API; o·904 sp. gr.) At 25° API there are 6·98 barrels per metric ton of crude; at 42°, 7·73 – hence the difficulty of converting a simple statistic of production in barrels per day to tons per annum.

A most important matter is the range of refined products that can be obtained from a particular crude, with four main categories: petrol (gasoline) including feedstocks for petrochemical industries; paraffin (kerosine); gas oil (for domestic heating); and heavy fuel oil for steam raising, chiefly in electric power stations and industrial plant. The heaviest fraction is bitumen (for road surfacing). Each has a related specific gravity – o·70–o·78 for aviation petrol, o·71–o·79 for motor petrol, o·78–o·84 for paraffin, o·82–o·91 for diesel oils, o·92–o·99 for heavy fuels. In broad terms, there are therefore 8½ barrels of aviation petrol to 1 metric ton, and 6 barrels of heavy fuel oil.

In the Middle East, there are significant differences as between various oilfields. Arabian 'heavy' yields 18% petrol, 11·5% paraffin, 18% diesel oil, and 52·5% heavy fuel oil, whilst for Iranian 'heavy' the corresponding proportions are 21%, 13%, 20% and 46%. The same vital statistics for Arabian 'light' are: 21%, 15%, 21% and 43%. All these, together with other factors such as sulphur content, viscosity, and location in relation to markets are reflected in finely tuned prices. In early 1977, for example, Libyan Brega light (40° API) commanded $13.81 per barrel, Iranian light (34°) $12.81, Arabian light (34°) $12.09; Kuwait medium (31°) $12.37; Arabian medium (31°) $11.69, and Arabian heavy (27°) $11.37. These variations may seem in themselves fairly small, but when multiplied by millions, they are obviously not.

It is possible to convert the lower fractions (heavy fuel oil, etc.) into petrol and other products by means of a catalytic 'cracker', but such 'cracker' plants are expensive, costing at present about twice as much to construct, for an equivalent throughput, as the primary refining plant. Nevertheless, 'cracking' is a most useful process in that it can absorb crude oils of varying equality to produce the required sort of end products for a particular market or region. For example, in the USA petrol (gasoline) accounts for nearly half of all 'oil' consumption, but only 18% in Japan and 20% in Europe. Thus in the United States a 'cracker' plant (secondary plant) is normally included with primary refining plant in the ratio of 1:3; whilst in Japan and Europe 'crackers' are fewer, in the ratio of 1:20, since the greatest demand is for the 'heavier' refined oil products (for industry, domestic heating, power generation, etc.). However, this also means less flexibility, and Europe and Japan must therefore exercise more care in buying crude oil, because they have less possibility of meeting a changed pattern of demand: the USA can, if necessary, treat a wide variety of crudes to produce gasoline: Japan and Europe are more dependent on buying crudes with a higher proportion of the lightest fraction if they wish to increase their 'petrol' production.[1] (The alternative is of course to build more 'cracker' plants.) All this has political repercussions in that possession of a wider range of refining possibilities allows consumer countries to be more selective in their purchases of crude – to 'shop around' more. If Middle Eastern producer countries extend their own refining activities, as they now wish to do, refinery policy in consumer countries could be seriously affected: and in more than one way.

**Natural gas**

Considerable quantities of gas (over 60%) are still flared off, as unusable and unwanted (in that gas among other things causes corrosion in pipes).

[1] The unlooked-for cut in petrol prices during July 1977 in Britain arose from heavy demands for fuel oil during the previous unusually cold winter, which left an unwanted surplus of petrol.

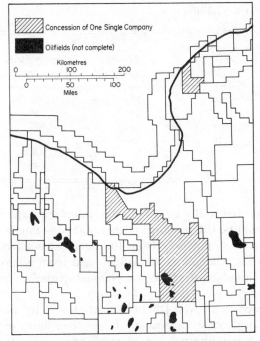

*Fig.* 9.6 Concession pattern in Libya, 1969.

Nevertheless, determined efforts are being made to achieve better usage of what is too often considered in the Middle East as a marginal product. One difficulty has been the discovery of natural gas in large quantities nearer areas of consumption in Europe (e.g. the North Sea deposits, which now supply the whole of the UK) and the possibilities of other major discoveries; competition from Algeria in Western Europe; and the greatest technical difficulties (and therefore costs) of exporting gas, either in natural or liquid form. The costliest ship afloat is a liquid gas carrier.

Nevertheless, natural gas is increasingly used within the Middle East first for re-injection into oilwells in order to maintain pressure, thus allowing more oil to be extracted, and then for local industries: metal smelting (iron and aluminium especially), and for domestic use.

Iran has substantial gas-fields unassociated with oil, and reserves are thought to be the second largest in the world (16% of world total, 35% USSR, 10% USA). Two major fields are (1) off-shore in the Persian/Arab Gulf near Bushire, and (2) Sarrakhs in Khorassan. In addition, much gas is collected from the southern oilfields, where on average one barrel of crude contains 700 ft³ of gas, and piped northwards along the Iranian Gas Trunk line running from Ahwaz via Isfahan to Astara on the Soviet frontier. Some of the gas is used *en route* for Iranian industries, but most

Gas flared off 1976 ('000 million m³)

| | Total gas produced from oil | Total flared off | Total of estimated gas reserves |
|---|---|---|---|
| Iran | 50 | 28 | 10 592 |
| Saudi Arabia | 47 | 37 | 2 448 |
| Kuwait | 11 | 4 | 1 800 |
| Iraq | 10 | 8 | 779 |
| Abu Dhabi | 15 | 14 | 708 |
| Libya | 18 | 4 | 630 |

is at present exported to the USSR. By the 1980s it is expected that gas, rather than oil, will be the principal energy source within Iran; with also a considerable export, not only from the oilfields, but from Sarrakhs, where a pipeline is planned to the USSR, and from Kharg Island and Bushire, where liquefaction plants are planned to allow export to Japan and the west.

Proved gas reserves in Abu Dhabi have tripled in the past few years and may be as large, or even possibly larger than those of Iran. Apart from a relatively small internal use, most is exported.

Although the total for the entire Middle East (including Libya) is thought to be only about 26% of total world reserves, as compared with 55–60% of petroleum, nevertheless, only the Communist World with 36% has a greater regional share.

### The economies and politics of oil concessions

The first concession in the Middle East was given in Iran (1872) to Baron de Reuter; but the first productive concession was that granted to an Englishman, W. K. D'Arcy, as the result of which the Masjid-i-Suleiman field began operation in 1908 (the original well-head and drill are preserved on site). During the 1920s further concessions were granted in other parts of the Middle East – principally in Iraq. After allotting 5% of the holding to Mr C. S. Gulbenkian, the Armenian intermediary responsible for negotiating the terms, four groups participated equally: British Petroleum, holders of the Iranian concession, Standard Oil (later to be known as Esso/Exxon), Royal Dutch-Shell, and Compagnie Française des Pétroles (later Total). Slightly later, a consortium of solely American interests – (Exxon, Texaco, Standard of California (Socal), and Mobil) – known as the Arabian American Oil Co., gained exclusive concessions in Saudi Arabia.

The original concessions were very extensive, covering half or more of an entire country; and terms were either a fixed royalty per ton of oil (usually 20–25 cents), or a percentage royalty on net sales. Iran, where the latter scheme operated, felt increasingly vulnerable, since in bad years (e.g. the Depression of 1931) royalties sank to very low levels. By the end of the 1940s the four Middle Eastern governments where oil was exploited (only Iran, Iraq, Egypt and Kuwait) had become very critical of the concession arrangements, on the following grounds: (a) the financial terms were too low; (b) the national state had no control over rate of prospecting or of exploitation – some wells had been shut down during the war years, and known oil deposits were 'left' for future use; (c) the concession areas were too large and on too long a lease, and (d) the operating countries employed a majority of expatriate personnel, who operated the concessions as 'states within a state', exporting through Company terminals, and importing goods that sometimes paid no customs duties – in short, a kind of wealthy colony parallel to the national state.

In 1948 two independent American companies (Aminoil and Getty) 'undercut' the prevailing pattern by accepting a concession for the (then) Neutral Zone between Kuwait and Saudi Arabia on terms much more favourable to the two Arab governments; and in the same year the Venezuelan Government legislated to acquire 50% of oil company profits, and approached the Middle Eastern oil states to follow suit and demonstrate solidarity. Accordingly, being sensitive to events, the Aramco and 'majors' in Iraq and Kuwait then offered a 'fifty–fifty' basis, which had the effect of broadly quadrupling the royalties paid to Arab governments from 20–25 cents per barrel to 75–85 cents.

Iran was not within this agreement, and felt especially deprived. A wave of nationalist feeling, basically anti-oil company (there was only one, B.P./Anglo-Iranian) and anti-British, in that the major shareholder in the AIOC had been the British Government itself ever since 1910, swept Iran led by Dr Moussadeq. Even the Shah's government, which had appeared willing to accept a 'fifty–fifty' revision, was severely shaken. This was also the era of extensive nationalization for the first time in Britain, and so in 1951 with Dr Moussadeq as Prime Minister the Iranian Majlis took the highly important opportunist step of declaring the AIOC concession nationalized. Despite its attachment at home to the principle of nationalization, the British government (through the AIOC) and other oil 'majors' in effect declared a joint embargo on Iranian oil, and after 3 years of trying to break the boycott and internal difficulty, an accommodation was reached in 1954. The principle of nationalization remained, with a 'fifty–fifty' sharing between the Iranian state and a new Consortium, no longer exclusively British, with major American participation equal to a now reduced British share at 40% – a reminder of the part now played by American interests in Iran. The remaining shares were allocated to Shell (14%) and French CFP (6%).

Thence onwards, there were gradual moves towards (a) reduction of concessions both in area covered and in duration, (b) increased shares to the national state, by for example, concessionary priced crude oil, or local arrangements regarding pricing, accounting procedures, and taxation; and (c) participation by newer, smaller oil companies ('independents' or 'minors') which were willing, in order to gain a foothold in what was now clearly a growing area, to accept less favourable financial terms, such as smaller concession areas for shorter periods. The first concessions in Iran, Iraq and Kuwait were for 40–100 years and covering thousands of km$^2$; by 1970 the average concession period had been reduced to about 10 years and hundreds only of km$^2$: the emergence of Libya as a major oilfield was the 'tryout' of the new system.

Dissatisfaction by the producer states over reductions in price made by major companies in 1959–60 led to the formation of OPEC (Organisation of Petroleum Exporting Countries). Because of the dominance of American producers at that time in the world's markets oil prices generally were fixed by reference to conditions in the US/Mexican Gulf, with a charge ('freight absorption') to take into account theoretical cost of transport into and out of this Gulf area from other parts of the world, whether or not the transfer was actually made. This led to the situation that in 1960 a barrel of oil cost much the same to buy in any part of the world, but the price of a barrel of Texas oil, being the 'marker' on which prices were calculated, represented only local costs of production (which were high), whereas selling prices of Arabian crude (the same as for Texas) comprised costs of production (which were lower than Texan costs) plus a differential of $1.20 which had been introduced in order to allow, theoretically, for transport costs from the Persian/Arab Gulf. By 1971 it was clear that OPEC, with Libya a leader in applying pressures to the oil companies, was in a dominating position to exact increasingly favourable royalty payments. Declining production within the USA led to more and more imports from the Middle East (these tripled between 1971 and 1973) and in 1973, the year of war involving Egypt and Syria against Israel, the Middle East OPEC members (OAPEC) decided to use this new supremacy as producer as a direct political weapon: in September 1973 they determined on a price-rise larger than anything ever before achieved, and also a cumulative embargo: exports to states directly supporting Israel (in practice this was held to be the USA and Holland) were reduced by 5% every month, together with a 25–30% overall cutback.

This reduced (temporarily) production from some states by about one-third; and so Western buyers began to look for oil from elsewhere in the world, and showed themselves willing to pay what seemed at the time crisis prices – up to $12–$16 per barrel. This demonstration of what consumers really could and would pay for oil was not lost on OPEC which declared a price increase of 130%: Iran wanting more, and Saudi Arabia less. This had the dramatic consequence of, in effect, quadrupling or quintupling prices to consumers over 1972 levels. Since 1974 the power of the oil companies has been further reduced by takeover and nationalization, amounting to complete state ownership, that has been a feature of 1975–76. Thus by 1977 it could be said that, with only a few exceptions, the production of petroleum in the Middle East was now mostly in the control of individual national governments with foreign companies agents or minor associates. It was also apparent that the divergence of view over price-rises could no longer be overcome: in 1977 Iran raised prices by 10% and Saudi Arabia by only 5%, giving some point to the view that oil pricing is more the result of political and strategic considerations than merely supply and demand.

Middle Easterners, however, argue that these price rises only reflect higher costs of manufactured imports to them, brought about by devaluation and 'floating' of world currencies (especially the American dollar) since 1971 – the increases are merely a form of 'price indexing'. Thus to Middle Easterners the enhanced prices are basically a prudent and equitable response to a world situation in which Middle Eastern oil has come to have a dominant position. The level of royalty income accruing to Middle Eastern governments is of interest:

Oil revenues to Middle Eastern governments (US $ million)

|              | 1960 | 1965 | 1970  | 1973  | 1975/6 |
|--------------|------|------|-------|-------|--------|
| Saudi Arabia | 310  | 655  | 1 200 | 7 200 | 27 000 |
| Iran         | 247  | 534  | 1 093 | 5 600 | 20 500 |
| Kuwait       | 425  | 671  | 895   | 2 800 | 7 500  |
| Iraq         | 210  | 375  | 521   | 1 900 | 8 000  |
| Abu Dhabi    | —    | 33   | 233   | 1 200 | 5 500  |
| Qatar        | 60   | 69   | 122   | 600   | 1 700  |
| Libya        | —    | 371  | 1 295 | 3 000 | 6 000  |

Before the quintrupling of prices, taxation by Western governments raised the selling price of a gallon of petrol in a motor service station by a factor of 2½ to 3½, i.e. the principal gainer from the sale of a gallon of petrol in a service station was the local national government. This inequity, by which, say, the British government got 40% or more of selling price from the sale of petrol, compared with 10–20% by the Iranian government, has now, in Middle Eastern eyes, been altered by the new

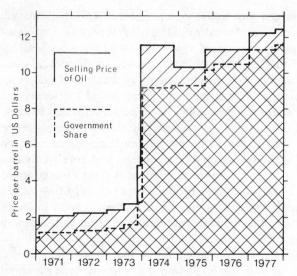

*Fig.* 9.7 The increase in average selling price of oil, and the proportion received by Middle Eastern governments.

higher prices for crude oil only to give 50–50 returns as between the Middle Eastern producer state and the foreign national state where refined petrol is sold.

### Pipelines and refineries

With the Middle East now supplying most of Europe's needs in petroleum, and the USA since 1953 an oil-importing country, the bulk of Middle Eastern oil moves westwards – though, however, the markets of eastern Asia, Australasia and east Africa are increasingly important. Because of the geographical location of the oilfields and the configuration of south-west Asia, sea transport of oil to Europe is a relatively expensive matter, owing to the distance from the Persian/Arab Gulf to the eastern Mediterranean (some 6500 km). Suez Canal dues have been a further important factor. Because a pipeline can be in continuous use, not empty for half its life as is a tanker, despite high constructional costs, the necessity of paying way-leave royalties to the states lying *en route*, and political vulnerabilities, savings of the order of $5–6 per ton were achieved by by-passing the Suez Canal.

Now the situation has greatly altered because of the advent of super-tankers, which give very considerable economies of scale – for example, unit costs have fallen by over 30% in financial terms, and whilst it takes five and a half hours to load 20 000 tons of crude oil, four times this amount can be loaded in ten hours into a larger ship. Thus Middle Eastern oil can be transported profitably via the Cape of Good Hope; and as regards the growing market of Japan, costs have fallen even further with the advent of supertankers. A saving of $1 per ton can be made by using a 300 000 ton tanker. Even by 1967 the Suez Canal was nearing saturation point, and its closure from 1967–74 led to the establishment of permanent tanker routes elsewhere – reopening of the Canal has diverted back only smaller tankers, since these alone can be handled. There is also the growing export of gas, either liquefied or not. Dependence of Middle East governments on foreign owned tankers (even though some states are now beginning to operate tankers of their own), plus the operational savings from pipelines, have led to construction of new oil and gas lines. These are (some have been mentioned earlier); the gas line from southern Iran to Astara and the USSR (with another planned in north-east Iran to the USSR); the SUMED oil pipeline from Suez to Alexandria, which is part of the industrial 'build-up' now in progress in the north Delta area of Egypt; the Eilat-Askelon line from the Gulf of Aqaba, which allows Iran to reach western markets more directly; and the north-south 'strategic' and Kirkuk–Dortyol lines from the Iraq fields – this last, completed 1977, is 981 km in length, with a capacity of 35 million tons.

There are now ten major refineries in the Middle East each with a capacity of over 100 000 barrels per day, and a further 24 smaller ones: those of Abadan, Ras Tanura, Ahmedi (Kuwait), and Sitra (Bahrain) are by far the largest. It is proposed to build another major refinery (of 400 000 tons capacity, approximating to the two largest present refineries at Abadan and Ras Tanura) at the Alexandria terminal of the SUMED pipeline.

The price increases and production cuts of 1973–4 have produced great changes. A world (especially the 'developed world' that had hitherto complacently looked forward to steadily increasing energy consumption) has experienced cut-backs and decline, with the future prospect of accommodating to reduced energy use. At the same time, extreme concern by environmentalists (including President Carter) together with technical difficulties have greatly retarded the development of nuclear sources of energy. Consequently, unless there is a dramatic break-through in the discovery of new energy sources (solar, wave-power etc.) which is at present not likely, oil will remain as it is now, the prime world fuel with some revival possible in the use of coal.

Various estimates and projections for the late 1970s and early 80s have been made, based on these and other assumptions, and none suggest that there will be an absolute decline in the demand for oil, rather that the rate of annual *increase* will decline from 7 to 8% in the early 1970s to something nearer 4%. But this is still an increase overall; and whilst new

Oil production 12 months to June 1978 (million tonnes)

| Saudi Arabia | Iran | Iraq | Kuwait | Libya | Qatar | |
|---|---|---|---|---|---|---|
| 418 | 282 | 105 | 100 | 93 | 21 | |

| Abu Dhabi | Egypt | Dubai | Oman | Syria | Turkey | Bahrain |
|---|---|---|---|---|---|---|
| 74 | 22 | 17 | 16 | 10 | 3 | 2 |

| USSR | USA | Britain |
|---|---|---|
| 557 | 475 | 44 |

Totals: *World*     *Middle East*
            30120*       11750§

\* 103% of 1973 total.
§ 92% of 1973 total.

oil discoveries (e.g. the North Sea) can be expected to contribute a greater proportion, the Middle East will in absolute terms still remain a major area of production, and the principal supplier to Europe and Japan: one other estimate (1977) is that over 70% of oil requirements in these areas will be met from Middle East sources. With the tendency, now increasingly established, that oil prices ought to keep pace with world inflation, there would seem, for the relatively short period, a continuance of the oil revenues at least at their level of the last 2 years (in real terms). In short, the Middle East will remain for some time a principal world supplier, with all that is implied for national revenues. The 1977 estimate is that oil, now providing 54% of total energy in the non-Communist world, will still provide 48% in 1990, involving an annual demand of 28 billion barrels per annum. Further, annual consumption is currently 17 billion barrels per year, and rate of discovery of new sources 15 billion barrels, with no obvious likelihood of this discovery rate being greatly expanded.

There remain three basic problems for Middle Eastern states: first, to ensure that the benefits of the new incomes (for Saudi Arabia, the Gulf States and Kuwait the highest per head of population in the world) reach as widely as possible among their own people. Second, to make provision by development of other activities, for the time when oil wealth will become exhausted, and third, to devise a means whereby the enhanced economic power of the oil-states is used on a world scale, in a positive, constructive way. All this can only be achieved by political stability within the Middle East – hence the over-riding need for peace based on equitable solutions to problems.

# 10 Demographic trends

Nothing in geography has been more remarkable than the extent to which population questions, once little regarded, are now accepted as central and crucial to any discussion of social geography. In the Middle East the population situation is of critical importance, partly because of the very unequal distribution between densely occupied areas where pressure is acute and areas still undeveloped through scanty population, and partly because of high rates of growth, amounting in some regions to over 3% per annum.

Moreover, because of differing ethnic or cultural groups, the situation of population numbers can have the most important political implications, as in Israel, Iraq, Cyprus and the Sudan. In Kuwait and certain of the Gulf States, recent immigrants now outnumber the indigenous populations.

Unfortunately, details of population are not always as detailed or even available as would be desirable. No census figures exist for the Lebanon, Muscat and Oman, the Yemen and Southern Yemen; and a figure of 3297000 obtained by a census during 1962–3 in Saudi Arabia has been set aside as unrepresentative, with a figure of 6870000 for 1967 accepted instead as official. A census of Libya in 1964 suffered from the fact that large territorial units only were employed as a base, thus making detailed breakdown by local area impossible: the 1973 census was better. In addition, registration procedures are regarded as inadequate or deficient in some degree, hence an Arab demographer (El Badry) considers that census data published for Iraq, Syria and Jordan are only partially

269

reliable. In other countries, e.g. Kuwait, Cyprus and Israel, the situation is much better.

### Population distribution

This is extremely uneven. There are considerable areas, e.g. the central Kavirs of Iran, the Rub al Khali of Arabia, the Saharan deserts of Egypt, Libya and the Sudan, and the south-centre of the Sudan, where populations are either non-existent or at most tiny in numbers. On the other hand, in certain of the larger and well-watered alluvial river valleys, population densities are high, with the Nile valley of Egypt far and away the most heavily peopled; here in 1978 an estimated 1200–1400 persons live on every square kilometre of cultivable land. Moreover, even in the desert areas, there are oasis settlements that are densely populated, sometimes by an agricultural population, sometimes by mixed groups of cultivators and oil-exploiting workers. Regional imbalances are thus the principal distinguishing feature, with, for example, still over 99% of Egyptians living in the 4·5% area comprising the Nile valley and delta, over half of the population on about 14–16% of the area in Jordan and in Iraq, and almost 60% of the people of Israel on 10% of the area. Adequate rainfall is a principal though not total influencing factor: this is well seen in Asia Minor and along the Caspian coast of Iran, but something of the contrary is demonstrated by the relative emptiness of the well-watered southern zone of the Sudan. It is obvious also that irrigation potential as distinct from natural local rainfall plays a considerable part in conditioning population distribution; and some writers regard density of population per square kilometer of cultivated land a better index of the real situation.

The figures given above must obviously be accepted only with much caution; and the further reservation to be made is that they take no account of migration, outward or inward. Migration has very considerable effects in the Gulf States, where a majority of the inhabitants of Kuwait and the United Emirates are incomers, and even in Saudi Arabia a comparatively large proportion may be from the Yemens and Oman. Clearly too, there are very large migrations affecting Israel, the Lebanon and Jordan, Palestinian refugees being the major, but not the only element here. The position of Cyprus, with supposed influx of mainland Turks into the north, Lebanese refugees in the south, and displaced Greek Cypriots is also unclear.

It is immediately apparent that there are considerable differences both in absolute size of populations, and in densities. The annual incremental growth in numbers in the three largest states (Iran, Turkey, Egypt) is in each case larger than the total populations of seven states listed above

Population (1976) (estimated, usually from latest census, taking into account annual growth)

|  | Last census | Population (millions) | Birth rate | Death rate | Annual growth (%) | Infant mortality (per 1000 births) |
|---|---|---|---|---|---|---|
| Bahrain | 1971 | 0·2 | 44 | 15 | 2·9 | 78 |
| Cyprus | 1960 | 0·7 | 18 | 10 | 0·8 | 28 |
| Iran | 1976 | 34·6 | 45 | 16 | 3·0 | 139 |
| Iraq | 1965 | 11·4 | 48 | 15 | 3·3 | 99 |
| Israel | 1972 | 3·5 | 28 | 7 | 2·9 | 23 |
| Jordan | 1961 | 2·8 | 48 | 15 | 3·3 | 97 |
| Kuwait | 1970 | 1·1 | 45 | 7 | 5·9 | 44 |
| Lebanon | — | 2·7 | 40 | 10 | 3·0 | 59 |
| Libya | 1973 | 2·5 | 45 | 15 | 3·7 | 130 |
| Muscat and Oman | — | 0·8 | 50 | 19 | 3·1 | 138 |
| Qatar | 1970 | 0·1 | 50 | 19 | 3·1 | 135 |
| Saudi Arabia | 1963 | 6·4 | 49 | 20 | 2·9 | 150 |
| Sudan | 1973 | 18·2 | 48 | 18 | 2·5 | 141 |
| Syria | 1970 | 7·6 | 45 | 15 | 3·0 | 93 |
| Turkey | 1975 | 40·2 | 39 | 12 | 2·6 | 119 |
| UAR (Egypt) | 1971 | 38·1 | 38 | 15 | 2·3 | 98 |
| UA Emirates | 1968 | 0·2 | 50 | 19 | 3·1 | 130 |
| Yemen (North) | — | 6·9 | 50 | 21 | 2·9 | 152 |
| Yemen (South) | — | 1·7 | 50 | 21 | 2·9 | 152 |

The figures of annual growth do not include the effects of migration.

even though these three 'blocks' of population are in themselves not particularly large: Turkey in 1977 ranked as the seventeenth largest state in the world.

Principal causes of the remarkable variation in densities occuring both between political units, and, as we have noted, even within one country itself are clearly geographical – in particular the availability of water: riverine, from direct rainfall or in relation to underground flow. But water resources alone, or even other factors of physical geography such as terrain, do not provide a complete explanation of population distribution. Certain areas, e.g. the Lower Nile valley, the hill country of the northern Levant, north-west Jordan, the uplands of Syria lying east of the Orontes river with their continuations into south-central Asia Minor, and finally the uplands of Asir and the Yemen – all these have a distinctly greater population density than those of neighbouring areas, in which occur approximately similar water resources, climatic conditions and even topography. Hence to explain these anomalies it is often necessary to invoke economic, historical and social factors – an illustration both of the complexity of conditions and also of the interplay of widely differing influences, some of which are political – e.g. the desire or need to live in ethnic communities; whilst others are social – what has been termed 'gregariousness': the desire to have close neighbours and co-operation in work, or its opposite: mistrust and separation.

### Population fertility

Birth-rates now appear to range in general between 39 and 50 per 1000 of population. This is high, but parallels occur elsewhere in the Third World. There are, however, communities where birth-rates are lower than this range: in Africa, for instance towards the equatorial regions (i.e. in the Sudan), some birth control is practised, and there are significant numbers of sterile females. Also, absence of men who are working overseas, as for instance in the Yemen and Hadhramaut, may delay age of marriage and so reduce family size. There are also clear differences often between Moslems who have uniformly high birth-rates, and other groups e.g. in Cyprus and Israel. The implications of this situation are important, and will be discussed later.

In general, however, the pattern of reproduction is one of high fertility. Causes of this are: almost universal marriage, with polygamy and easy divorce amongst Moslems, which means that relative sex-ratios are less important than in areas where monogamy is the rule; second, early marriage, with emphasis on quickly having a family, and infertility ample grounds for a divorce; social conditions, which allow child labour and emphasize the value of numerous adult offspring to care for one in old age – this is still significant in countries that do not have state retirement pensions; and lastly, unwillingness to accept contraception on any wide scale. Although there is no specific religious ban, as in some other communities, birth control is not extensively practised, at least in Moslem communities.

Until recently, death-rates were also high, but, as elsewhere in the world, have been greatly susceptible to improvements in public health and social amelioration. Improved nutrition through better living standards, more widely available medical care – now in some countries highly subsidized by the state – and perhaps above all there are the attacks on disease through much improved public health measures such as chlorination of drinking water, eradication of disease vectors by modern insecticides and the use of antibiotics; with parallel improvements in personal medical care, hygiene and education. These effects can only be described as dramatic, and in many areas have compressed into two or

Population: composition and projections 1977

| | Rural population (%) | Popula-tion under 16 years (%) | Life ex-pectancy from birth (years) | Number of years to double popula-tion | Population in A.D. 2000 (millions) |
|---|---|---|---|---|---|
| Bahrain | 22 | 44 | 61 | 24 | 0·5 |
| Cyprus | 57 | 32 | 71 | 87 | 0·8 |
| Iran | 49 | 47 | 51 | 23 | 67 |
| Iraq | 39 | 48 | 53 | 21 | 24 |
| Israel | 14 | 33 | 71 | 24 | 5 |
| Jordan | 57 | 48 | 53 | 21 | 6 |
| Kuwait | 22 | 43 | 69 | 12 | 3 |
| Lebanon | 39 | 43 | 63 | 23 | 6 |
| Libya | 71 | 44 | 53 | 19 | 5 |
| Oman | 65 | 47 | 44 | 22 | 2 |
| Qatar | 24 | 35 | 60 | 22 | 0·2 |
| Saudi Arabia | 82 | 45 | 45 | 24 | 13 |
| Sudan | 87 | 45 | 49 | 28 | 38 |
| Syria | 56 | 49 | 54 | 23 | 16 |
| Turkey | 61 | 42 | 57 | 27 | 71 |
| UAR (Egypt) | 57 | 41 | 52 | 30 | 64 |
| UA Emirates | 35 | 34 | 60 | 22 | 0·5 |
| Yemen (North) | 93 | 45 | 45 | 24 | 14 |
| Yemen (South) | 74 | 45 | 45 | 24 | 3 |
| | | | | Total | 339 |

three decades the improvements that took a century to achieve in Europe. Whole regions that were very highly malarial only twenty years ago are now very different, and piped water is replacing insanitary surface channels and polluted wells. All this means that death-rates in most parts are now under 20 per 1000, with some areas where the figure is under 15 per 1000 balancing as it were those few other parts where mortality still remains high.

The effects of this situation are now seen in the rates of increase which for most countries of the Middle East now run at about 2·9% per annum. Implications of this situation are considerable. First, it means that populations are likely to double in less than thirty years – more precise indications are given below.

A second matter should be noted: some countries (e.g. the United Arab Emirates, Kuwait, possibly Saudi Arabia) owe a substantial part of their overall population increase to immigration, and so in assessing the implications of the table above, one must distinguish between natural growth and that due to in-migration. Thirdly, the high proportion of young people is a major phenomenon, and one that is tending to increase: 10 or so years ago there would have seemed to be only five countries of the Middle East where those aged under 16 numbered more than 45% of the population: now, a majority of countries are in this situation.

The implications of age structure with over 40% of total population aged under 16, and about 5% only older than 65, are considerable. With large numbers still illiterate, the need for schools is great, yet the funds and trained staff are not always available. The Middle East must avoid having an untrained mass of young people for whom no employment is available, yet mechanization and nationalization are reducing the demand for labour in the principal employment sector, which is agriculture. Industrialization is one obvious answer, but we have seen some of the difficulties involved. There is also, for some countries, the effect of over-production of college and university graduates in non-technological subjects – undue raising of expectation in a society that cannot absorb too many service workers and officials. The social and political consequences of high population growth beginning with the probability that in some areas (e.g. Egypt and Iraq) the gains from technological improvements in agriculture have been nullified by extra population numbers, will be likely to bulk larger in the future. Movement of rural populations to the towns result in the concentration of under-employed rootless city immigrants, housed at low levels. Experience in Europe and North America has shown that reproductive rates in industrialized and urban communities tend to decline, but the recent trend of events in southern Asia does not altogether substantiate this view. Because cities have a disproportionate share of physical amenities and, above all, far easier access to medical care, their death-rate may fall to very low levels, even below 10 per 1000, so that, although births may also decline somewhat, net reproduction still remains high. Industrialization may thus be desirable on economic grounds, but it may not be an automatic process leading to reduction in population growth. This situation is exemplified in Kuwait, which with an overwhelmingly urban population has the lowest death-rate of any Moslem country, but, with a high (though not outstandingly high) birth-rate, it has at present a net reproduction rate of 44–46 per 1000, i.e. 4·4% natural increase. The mere fact of a very 'young' population can, of course, also give rise to a low mortality rate: this is especially true of Israel and Kuwait which have crude death-rates of about 7 per 1000, produced by the combined effects of a 'young' population and good medical care.

**Growth of towns**

The fact of high natural increase in towns, together with the phenomenon of rural emigration, explains one feature which is especially characteristic of the Middle East: the rapid growth of towns, which prior to 1914 probably contained under 10% of the total population of the Middle East, but now urban dwellers form a near-majority in most countries, and their proportion overall is likely to reach 50% during the 1980s. J. I. Clarke considers that natural increase plays the major part in producing this situation, and that immigration from rural areas is the chief element only in a few cases: Kuwait, certainly, with other towns like Abu Dhabi, Doha and possibly Benghazi. The larger the city, the more likely is it that growth is due to its own natural increase. Thus amenity and opportunity operating as factors mainly to reduce mortality, and to a minor extent to attract an immigrant population from the countryside, are the chief causes of town growth, along with the habit of high natality that keeps up even among urbanized populations.

As we have noted in another chapter, urbanization is a very important feature of the Middle East not only because of numbers. Although actual definitions of an 'urban population' vary, it is possible to say that townspeople amount to one third of the total population in all states, and in some countries – the states of the Arab Gulf, Israel, Libya and the Lebanon – the proportion rises to over two-thirds. Turkey and Saudi Arabia stand out as amongst the least urbanized. Another tendency is for the largest cities in each country to grow even proportionately faster than the rest. This is especially true of Iraq, Iran, Egypt, the Lebanon and the Sudan; but not so in Turkey and Libya, where the 'second' town is growing faster than the 'first'. The considerable pre-eminence and primacy of some chief cities is now recognized (particularly in Iran) as likely to inhibit development in the rather smaller towns and, in Iran at least, special policies have been devised to attempt to correct such hierarchical imbalance. At the other end of the scale, town development is less prominent in the Yemen, Muscat and Oman, and Cyprus, which may be regarded as under-urbanized, not merely in relation to the generally high level prevailing in most of the Middle East, but even in comparison with non-Middle Eastern areas.

**Migration**

Besides internal movement which is chiefly from country to town, from poorer areas to oil-rich territories, and from war-torn areas (i.e. as refugees), there is a fairly considerable outward migration.

Arabia (especially the Yemen, Southern Yemen and Hadhramaut where about one million may be temporarily absent) has a considerable outward human migration not only to nearby regions of the Middle East such as lower Iraq, Jordan and Syria, together with Eritrea and Somalia, but also further afield to the East Indies (where there are 70000 in Java alone), east Africa, Pakistan and India. Mostly, the emigrants work as labourers, traders and seamen, with a minority of soldiers and officials. Another region important as a source of emigrants is the Lebanon and Syria. Most migrants are small peasant-proprietors who can sell up their lands to find passage-money; and the chief areas of origin are the hinterland of Beirut as far inland as the Beqa, the hill country behind Tripoli, the Alawi area, and the uplands north-west and south-west of Damascus. Warfare and disturbance have acted since 1975 as a major 'push' factor. More Lebanese migrate than Syrians; and the chief receiving countries are: once Egypt, now West Africa, Brazil and the Argentine, and to a limited extent the USA, chiefly the motor-producing areas near Detroit. At least 750000 to 1 million Lebanese have emigrated; and there are nearly 1 million inhabitants of Brazil and the Argentine that are either new immigrants or of first generation maintaining contacts (such as citizenship and by sending remittances) with the Middle East.[1] The fact that the Lebanon continues to count some such emigrants as its citizens has political implications.

Many Cypriots have migrated, chiefly to Britain, where there are about 60000, and to a lesser extent to Australia. Another feature of the last few years has been the movement of educated Arabs to other Arab countries, where they fill professional and technical posts. Many Egyptian teachers staff schools in Libya, Saudi Arabia and in the Persian/Arab Gulf states; oil companies recruit all over the Middle East, and Syrian businessmen are widely scattered especially in Egypt, where there are also a number of Sudanese, especially Nubians. Palestinians of good education also find similar employment in many Arab countries, professional occupations and administration, and as skilled workmen. It should also be noted that two major displacements of Arabs occurred, the first in 1948 involving ¾ million Palestinian Arabs (about 50% of the total population of Palestine), and again in 1967 when the West Bank was over-run by Israel. Altogether, Palestinian Arabs now number 3·2 million, 16% of whom have remained in Israel proper (though they may in some instances have been 're-settled' to make way for Jewish colonists), 36% in Israel-dominated areas, 10% in Syria and Lebanon, and the remainder in Jordan (30%). Some 1·6 m Palestinian Arabs are still of refugee status, with minimum standards of living, and fertile ground for extremist propaganda, as well as posing severe problems for host countries.

[1] Annual average totals of emigration by Lebanese and Syrians are estimated as follows: 1860–1900, 3000; 1900–29, 8000; 1929–38, 1700; 1945–75, 2700.

Establishment of the Israeli state also led to considerable in-migration of Jews from other parts of the Middle East: from Iraq and the Yemens especially, but over-all involving 90% of Middle Eastern Jews – about 300 000 (North Africa not included). Total annual immigration into Israel has varied considerably: the largest single number in one year being 239 000 (1949). In 1976 the figure was 15 000.

The Israelis of Oriental origin now pose serious questions for the other Israelis, whom they will soon out-number because of higher birth-rates. Whereas an Israeli-born woman has on a statistical average, 2·95 children, Afro-Asian Jewish immigrant women have 4·22 children, and European-American immigrants 2·78 children (1972 figures). Some 25–28% of Oriental immigrant families are housed with three or more persons to a room; 90% of all families with 4 or more children are of 'Oriental' origin; and conviction of Jewish juvenile offenders (1957–69) were five times as great for children of 'Oriental' origin as for 'non-Oriental'. This is a recital of deprivation: it partially explains the intense desire of the Israeli government to achieve social equality and integration.

**Differential fertility**

A highly important matter is the differential fertility as between various communities of the Middle East. Moslem reproduction rates are, as we have seen, high, whilst those of other communities tend to be markedly lower. For example, Jewish birth-rates, despite the 'young' age structure of the Jewish population in Israel, have oscillated in the 1970s between 20 and 26 per 1000 of population, as compared with a rate of over 45 per 1000 for Moslems living either in Israel or in the West Bank areas of Jordan occupied since 1967. Whereas the Jewish birth-rate has shown a marked tendency to fall from levels of 30 or more per 1000 in the late 1940s, the Moslem rate has risen considerably, hence whilst reproduction rates for Jews have changed from about 25 per 1000 in the 1950s to only 15–20 per 1000 in the 1970s, comparable rates for Arabs over the same period are respectively 32–37 and 40–47 per 1000. Despite considerable Jewish immigration, the *absolute* number of Jewish babies born has not greatly risen over the last 20 years, whereas more Arabs are born and more now survive.

Similar though less striking differences occur as between Moslems and Christians. This is apparent in the Lebanon, where a slight Christian preponderance in the 1930s and 40s has altered to a Moslem majority. Something of a similar situation exists in Cyprus between the Greek Christian and Turkish Moslem communities, as regards the Copts of Egypt, and also for the non-Moslems of Iran – chiefly a very few Christians and Parsees (Zoroastrians). In these latter instances, non-

Population densities: 1976

| | Total popula-tion (millions) | Area ('ooo km²) | Density/ km² | Rural popula-tion (millions) | Area of per-manent crops (km²) | Popula-tion density on farm land |
|---|---|---|---|---|---|---|
| Bahrain | 0·2 | 6 | 334 | 0·04 | — | — |
| Cyprus | 0·6 | 9 | 69 | 0·34 | — | — |
| Iran | 34·1 | 1 648 | 20 | 16·7 | 170 000 | 98 |
| Iraq | 11·4 | 438 | 26 | 4·4 | 75 360 | 58 |
| Israel | 3·5 | 21 | 169 | 0·5 | 4 850 | 103 |
| Jordan | 2·8 | 95 | 29 | 1·6 | 10 700 | 149 |
| Lebanon | 2·7 | 10 | 260 | 1·1 | 3 000 | 366 |
| Libya | 2·5 | 1 760 | 1·5 | 1·8 | 25 100 | 72 |
| Oman | 0·75 | 272 | 3 | 0·5 | — | — |
| Saudi Arabia | 6·4 | 2 150 | 3 | 5·2 | 9 000 | 578 |
| Sudan | 18·2 | 2 506 | 7 | 15·8 | 70 920 | 223 |
| Syria | 7·6 | 185 | 41 | 4·3 | 68 450 | 63 |
| Turkey | 40·2 | 779 | 52 | 24·5 | 246 270 | 99 |
| UAR (Egypt) | 38·1 | 998 | 38 | 21·7 | 28 430 | 763 |
| UA Emirates | 0·2 | 84 | 2 | 0·07 | — | — |
| Yemen (North) | 6·9 | 200 | 34 | 6·4 | — | — |
| Yemen (South) | 1·7 | 34 | 5 | 1·3 | 2 500 | 500 |

Moslems are a small minority, hence the social and political effects of differential reproduction rates are less acute than in Israel and the Lebanon. Even 'Oriental' Jews formerly living in Arab countries, and who formerly had a 'Moslem' pattern of birth-rates, have tended to take on patterns of lower natality after only a few years as immigrants into Israel, so that Israel must rely on immigration rather than natural increase to expand her Jewish population. Since 1965, at least half of the Moslems living in Israel are under 14 years old; but only about 30% of the Jews are of this age group – or, in other words, the average age of a Jew is between 25 and 30 and rising upwards, of an Arab it is 14 and falling.

The considerable anomalies in distribution, density and living standards that now clearly exist between various human groups in the Middle East invite the question of how far more positive action to spread population and amenity would be desirable and feasible. There are certain obvious areas where population pressure is great – as in the Nile valley, and in parts of Asia Minor; but equally, there are areas, such as the Mesopo-tamian lowlands of Iraq, and less certainly, parts of Iran and the coastal uplands of Libya, that are under-cultivated. We have the phenomena of already highly urbanized areas drawing even larger numbers most of all

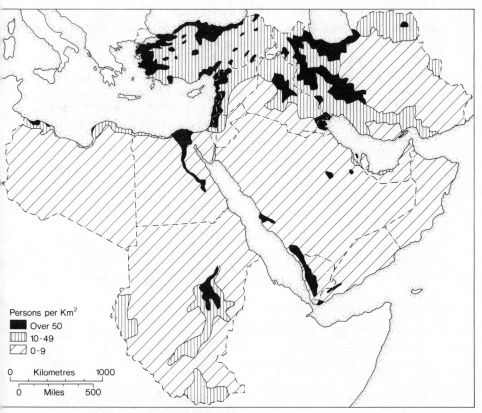

*Fig.* 10.1 Sketch of population density, 1976.

into the primate cities, and then into rather smaller urban centres, with all the strains on infrastructure and provision of social benefits that this rapid urban growth entails. There are also 2 million refugees, which in a territory where several states of far less than 1 million exist, represents a problem that would be extremely acute for any state, but is desperate in the context of the small-scale political pattern of the Middle East.

There is wealth, most of it from oil; but how far could effective redistribution, even if this could be achieved, solve any of the Middle East's demographic problems? Will urban life and industrialization really be able to produce a change in the prevailing demographic pattern of high, and increasing, net reproduction? How far are other means – contraception and possibly sterilization on a massive scale, and drastic social and fiscal measures – to reduce natality likely to have to enter in before too long, with resulting fundamental changes in outlook and family life?

Islam has shown itself extremely resilient as a way of life –
'indestructible' is one description by an American writer. Will it be able
to adjust to bring about a reduction in high reproduction rates, or must
any major change wait until Islam as a way of life is ineffective or
destroyed? All these questions deepen the surface of political issues within
the Middle East, and whilst the situation is not yet wholly desperate, in
that there are some lightly peopled zones and also much wealth, matters
which distinguish the region from, say, India, nevertheless time is short
for effective action.

Part III

# Regional geography of the Middle East

# 11 Iran

As a high plateau ringed on all sides by higher mountain ranges, Iran displays a markedly physical unity based on separation from its adjoining regions. To the south and west, the contrast between the massive ranges of the Zagros and the lowlands of Mesopotamia is particularly striking; and on the north, there is an equally abrupt descent from the Elburz ranges to the plains of Russian Turkestan and the basin of the Caspian. Elsewhere, however, the mountain ring of Iran continues with much less interruption into the highlands of eastern Anatolia, and into the more broken massifs of Baluchistan and Afghanistan.

In determining the extent of natural regions various solutions are possible. In other work, the present writer has followed a somewhat different plan: the variation arises from the difficulties of subdividing a mountain ring that is continuous but different in its various sub-regions. For a discussion of these points the reader is referred to the Cambridge *History of Iran*, I; here, an alternative view will be followed – that of regarding the Zagros and Elburz ranges as extending far to the east, even though in both instances these eastern portions become attenuated to a marked degree.

## Structure

Conditions have long been recognized as extremely complex, and again various interpretations are possible. One of these, based on a system by J. V. Harrison, and solely geological, would recognize seven or eight distinctive units (fig. 11.1).

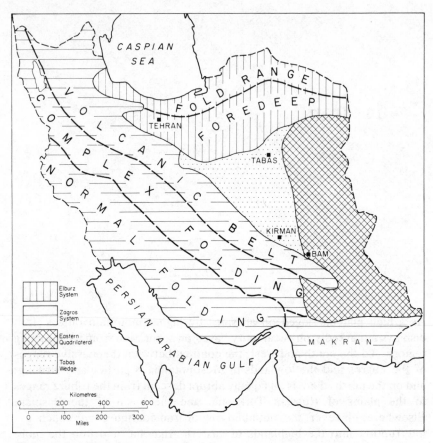

*Fig.* 11.1 Iran: structure.

The first unit would include the Elburz mountain system, and associated with it the region immediately south of it, termed by Harrison the Elburz Foredeep. The Elburz range is moderately folded, with some areas of fairly intense dislocation and thrusting, which is probably most developed just to the north of Tehran. Rocks of many ages are involved, from pre-Cambrian onwards. Associated with this to the south is a foredeep in which has occurred extensive fracturing and foundering: in the south-west, it is estimated that there has been a later infilling by upper Tertiary sediments up to 7500 m in thickness. Topographically the area is, as would be expected, lower lying than the Elburz, and forms part of the inner basin system of Iran.

In the west and south, there is a massive disturbed and uplifted zone mainly associated with the Zagros range. Harrison recognizes three broadly parallel zones, from south-west to north-east: (*a*) a zone of normal folding, then (b) one of complex folding, and finally (c) a volcanic belt. In (a) the main rock series is massive limestone overlying first sandstones and clays, with, as a basal element, a complex of dolomite, calcium sulphate and pre-Cambrian rock-salt. Lateral pressure has folded the mass of rocks into a series of long hog's back ridges. The pre-Cambrian salt-beds, being more plastic, have in response to folding also forced a way through the overlying sediments to produce swarms of salt domes at or near the surface in a number of localities.

The complex zone differs from the zone (a) in that extreme dislocation has occurred, with overthrusting and nappes the main features. Movement has been so intense that often one nappe is entirely unrelated to its nearest neighbour, with totally different rock series involved, or fragments of one nappe may have been caught into another. Extremely intense distortion of rigid rock series produces *schuppen*, which are lens-shaped masses that result from shearing under high pressure, and these are especially characteristic in the south-west parts of the complex zone. Nappe 'fronts' may provide important elements in the landscape: this is especially true near Niriz, where such a front runs for over 150 km.

The volcanic zone comprises a series of Tertiary and Mesozoic rocks through which extrusive and irruptive rocks have forced a way. Vulcanicity began in late Cretaceous times and reached a climax in the late Eocene, though it still continues to the present day. Granites, lavas, and ash are characteristic in this zone, and folding and faulting of both the intrusive igneous rocks and the surrounding sedimentaries are a feature. Generally speaking, vulcanicity is in a decadent phase, with activity linked to mud flows from craters and fumaroles (emission of gas). But the impressive ash cones and extensive basalt cover in some areas is a reminder of the recent nature of much of the activity in this zone.

Along the eastern border of Iran there extends an area of much structural irregularity. The whole zone, very roughly a quadrilateral in shape, may have been formed as a resistant horst compressed against the Tabas wedge to the west and another block formation located to the east in Afghanistan. Part of the quadrilateral is low lying, with extensive basin formation, but much also is elevated, with differential movement along fault-lines, and the occurrence of major domes, or anticlines. Rise of magma along fissure-lines is also a feature.

The final structural element recognized by Harrison is the Tabas wedge. This is a mass of Jurassic strata underlain by older series reaching as far back as the Cambrian. There is a region of downwarping in the extreme south-east, but in the main the wedge suggests a mass or block of relatively stable strata involved partially but not overwhelmed by the enormous tectonic movements around it – a sort of fundamental nuclear unit. One can also interpret these structural units as being the rigid edge of a major tectonic plate, with the plate of Arabia being driven down below it and consumed. The occurrence of major folded belts, succeeded further towards the centre of the Iranian plate by a volcanic zone, strongly support this hypothesis.

### Geographical units

References made above on structural features do not necessarily imply a similar pattern of geographical units, since altitude, climate and accessibility (to name only a few) are other factors which fortify recognition of an environmental unit. Hence in the discussion that follows, we may distinguish natural regions as follows:

(I) The Zagros area, extending in a series of arcs or cusps from Armenia to Baluchistan and subdivisible into north-west, central and south-east portions. Associated with this is also the portion of the piedmont and plain of the Tigris that lies politically within Iran.

(II) The northern highlands – a narrower but well-defined series of folds that run between the Caucasus mountains of southern Russia, and the Hindu Kush of Afghanistan. Again there is an associated lowland: in this instance the Caspian coastal zone.

(III) The eastern uplands – a more varied, broken, region.

(IV) The central plateau.

### The Zagros

This can be subdivided into three contrasting zones, the north-west, which could be held summarily to lie between the 35th and 39th parallels of latitude; the centre, which extends from latitude $35°$ N to about $27°$ N; and the south-east portion, termed in its eastern part, the Makran, which lies between the Strait of Hormuz and Baluchistan.

(a) The north-west Zagros Adjacent to Anatolia, land forms have been developed primarily as the result of differential tectonic movements along well-marked faults. Horst blocks and downthrow basins are therefore prominent, though in places the outlines of these have been modified by intense erosion. One of these downthrow basins is that of Lake Urmia (or Rezaiyeh), which covers over 50000 km²; and others occur (i) at Khoi, north of Urmia (with the narrow ridge of the Mashu Dagh acting as a separation between the Urmia and Khoi lowlands); (ii) in the Moghan district of the lower Aras (Araxes) river; and (iii) in the upper reaches of the Qara Su (Ardebil region).

The uplifted horsts form a series of blocks that increase generally in elevation towards the north-west, giving the appearance of an extensive

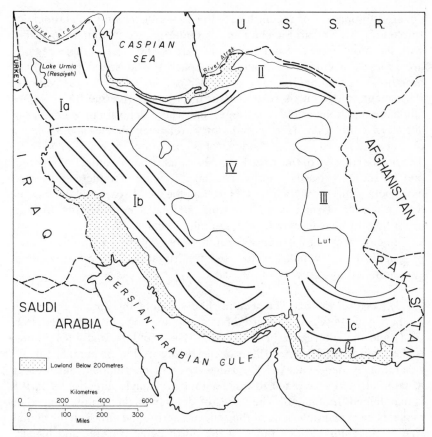

*Fig.* 11.2 Iran: geographical units.

but irregular plateau that is tilted towards the south-east. Numerous deeply incised valleys separate the individual blocks, so that, despite the general impression of a plateau, relief is extremely varied. Some of the river valleys are no more than gorges or defiles; but others (owing to tectonic action) are much wider, e.g. the Aras valley, which forms a corridor some 15–60 km wide, and serves as a frontier between Iran and Russia; and the Safid Rud (named in its lower course the Qizil Uzan), where there is a lowland basin 25 km in width, in which stands the town of Mianeh.

A third important topographical feature in the north-west Zagros is the presence of numerous volcanic zones, formed by the rise of magma along fracture-lines: this zone is the most developed portion of the structural 'volcanic zone'. Besides much basalt pavement, there are imposing peaks such as those of Savalan (4300 m), Sahand (3650 m) and Kharazana (3520 m). Generally speaking, the plateau uplands, stony and undulating, or covered by masses of recent lava, offer few inducements to settlement. Intolerably hot and arid in summer, and bitterly cold in winter – possibly with the most extreme climate of any part of the world – these regions are sparsely occupied by nomadic shepherds who spend the summer months in searching for pasture, and pass the winter in the valleys. Permanent settlement is restricted to the broader riverine tracts where climatic conditions are less extreme, and where deposits of water-borne silt allow cultivation. Here population is relatively dense, and a variety of crops are raised – wheat, barley, tobacco, cotton, vegetables and fruit. The most extensive of these settled areas is that situated round Lake Urmia and extending towards Tabriz. The lake is without outlet, and hence extremely saline – only a little less so than the Dead Sea. Unlike the Dead Sea, however, Urmia is shallow and fluctuates considerably in area according to season and recent rainfall. Because of the two factors, settlements occur at a distance from the shores of the lake, on the banks of small streams which can be used for irrigation before the water is contaminated by contact with the lake.

(b) *The central Zagros* The second subdivision of the Zagros comprises the part lying between Bandar Abbas at the opening of the Persian/Arab Gulf, and the sub-region just described. Here folding, and not faulting, is the main feature, hence there occurs a succession of parallel ridges, separated by deep valleys. The ridges are not continuous, but die out at intervals and give place to others, though a single direction of strike is maintained throughout. The series of densely packed folds, aligned in ranks, is most characteristic of the central Zagros, and although the actual size of the folds varies – those in the north being broader and higher, those in the south smaller and finer – they form the principal, almost the only, topographical feature in the region.

On the south-west, towards the Mesopotamian lowlands, the folds are relatively open, consisting of simple anticlines (ridges) and synclines (valleys). This is where the zone of 'normal folding' is at its best developed, and it indicates the relative geological youth of the entire range. Towards the interior, one passes into the zone of complex folding, which as we have noted is characterized by shearing and nappe formation. Extensive dissection by rivers has led once again to the development of narrow, steep-sided valleys, some of which are mere slits or defiles, too narrow or too recent in formation even for the smallest alluvium-covered terraces to occur. In certain places the rivers appear to follow a direct path to the Tigris lowlands, and plunge directly through the most massive ridges by a series of enormous clefts or gorges. These gorges, named *tangs*, often cut across the highest parts of the ridges, and it therefore at first seemed unlikely that they could have been formed by river action – to the earliest observers, the *tangs* appeared to be great cross-faults developed at right angles to the main axis of folding. Recently, however, T. M. Oberlander has demonstrated that the elaboration of the drainage in the central Zagros would seem to be due mainly to straightforward and highly active differential erosion of a series of anticlines formed of a succession of strata that are in some cases resistant and in others much less so. Extensive capture is also a further complicating feature, but the main effect due to normal erosion acting upon the particular structures and lithological succession of the region. Capture could, however, be held to explain the fact of some *tangs* not now being occupied by a stream.

All this has led to the development of an extremely intricate drainage pattern. In some areas rivers flow in longitudinal valleys, weaving a tortuous transverse course from one syncline or trough to the next. In others there is a much more direct but narrow and even precipitous riverine reach that makes a rapid descent toward the Mesopotamian plain.

Because of the uniformity of the mountain ridges, one finds fewer outstanding single peaks than in north-west Iran; but there is a greater extent of highland, and a considerable number of domes attain an altitude of 4000–5000 m. Parts of the Zagros are vegetation-covered, particularly in the north, where rainfall is heavier, but much of the central region consists of bare expanses of rock often startlingly coloured in red, yellow, white, grey, green or black. Between some ridges lie deep open valleys, the floors of which are 1200–2500 m above sea-level; and, in contrast, most of these floors are vegetation-covered, with parts wooded. Here water is available, cultivation is possible on small fields or terraces cut in the sides of hills; but to a far greater extent the region supports a pastoral population. The grassy valley bottoms are used at various seasons of the year, and a well-organized transhumance, reminiscent of that in the Alps, is a prominent feature. Conditions in Iran are, however, somewhat sterner than in Switzerland – one does not often hear of a Swiss shepherd kicking footholds in the snow for his animals by means of his bare feet, a not uncommon occurrence during spring in the Zagros.

Minor but striking topographical features of the southern portion of the central Zagros are numerous salt hills or plugs, some of which rise to heights of 1500 m. It is thought that these plugs have been formed as the result of isostatic pressure on a deep-seated and plastic layer of rock-salt that is Cambrian in age. As later sediments accumulated above the salt, this relatively plastic layer was pressed upwards through younger series in the form of giant eruptions. Some of these plugs are in active upward motion at the present time, forcing their way through overlying strata, and raising impressive glistening sugar-loaf cones above the surrounding country; others have been eroded after eruption to the surface, and the covering rocks have collapsed into the resulting crater as a bewildering jumble of strata.

Another minor feature of the central Zagros is the occurrence of small lowland basins where the north-easternmost of the Zagros folds have impinged upon the buckled edge of the central plateau. Some of these basins, e.g. those of Shiraz and Niriz, are enclosed, with aretic drainage, and hence have salt marshes or lakes in the lowest part; in others a stream has broken through the surrounding highland rim, and there is a normal drainage outwards towards the south-west. Certain of these basins, intensively cultivated in the non-saline stretches away from the lowest parts, have been the centres of important cultural movements. Niriz was the homeland of the early Persians, who established a continent-wide empire: Shiraz was later renowned as the cradle of Persian poetry, the home of Hafiz, Saadi and Omar Khayyam.

(c) *The south-east Zagros (Makran)* Immediately east of Bandar Abbas, the trend of the Zagros ridges alters abruptly. For a distance of 250 km between Bandar Abbas and Jask, the direction of folding is north–south; then, eastwards of Jask, there is a second change, with, first of all, a trend from west-north-west to east-south-east, and later, from west to east.

In striking contrast to the massive, elongated and regularly aligned ridges of the central Zagros, topography in the south-east is much more irregular and broken, and on a far less imposing scale. A narrow coastal plain bordering the Gulf of Oman and the Indian Ocean is succeeded inland by a zone of plateau country of an average elevation of 600–900 m and this plateau is crossed in places by lines of hills that occasionally reach 1800–2100 m. Between these hills lie numerous river basins, noteworthy in that they run directly to the sea, with a more directly consequent alignment than the valleys of the central Zagros, which, as we have seen, tend more to have a trellis or rectangular plan.

Northwards, the plateau zone gives way to an extensive trough, the Jaz Murian basin, which consists of a depression with its lowest point at an altitude of about 300 m. This basin is partly filled by a thick layer of silt and wind-blown material deposited in dunes. There is no drainage from the basin, and the centre is occupied by a salt lake fed by two streams, the Rud Halil and the Rud Bampur. Other streams from the surrounding high ground fail to reach the lake, and soon disappear beneath the drift cover. The Jaz Murian basin is defined on the north by a single narrow line of highland, which acts as a divide between the Jaz Murian depression and the interior plateau of central Iran. The average height of the ridge is about 1200 m, but in the east the eroded volcanic cone of the Kuh-i-Baznan exceeds 3300 m.

Most of the south-eastern Zagros region presents a vista of rugged desolate landscapes, either bare rock or sand dunes, with occasional patches of cultivation of cereals and cash crops in a few favoured spots where water is available. Dates are a staple, supplemented by small amounts of cereals, by dried fish brought from the coast, and by meat and milk from the few animals that find pasture on the scanty grasses of the lower mountain slopes. The Jaz Murian plain thus has few inhabitants, some nomadic; but development is now taking place at places, such as Iranshahr, which have better water supplies, and on the coast at centres such as Chah-behar and Bushire.

### The northern highlands

The northern highlands of Iran consist of two distinct groups: the Elburz range in the west with its outlier, the Talish hills, and the more extensive chains of the north-east – chief among which are the Kopet Dagh and the Ala Dagh. Between the two masses lies a trough, part of which is occupied by the Atrek river.

The Elburz consists of a relatively narrow series of folds disposed in a shallow crescent along the southern border of the Caspian Sea. Although narrow, the fold ridges are extremely steep, and a number of summits exceed 3000 m, within a distance of under 50 km from the Caspian shore, which is now almost 30 m below sea-level. Erosion has been very active on the northern slopes of the Elburz – annual rainfall exceeds 2500 m – and this region is hence broken by deep gorges, at the bottom of which great torrents flow directly northwards towards the Caspian. Further to the south, when the northernmost crests are passed, there is a development of longitudinal or strike valleys, recalling on a smaller scale those of the central Zagros, in which flow a number of longer and better-developed rivers, e.g. the Shah Rud and the Nur. Although only 100 km wide in its broadest part, the Elburz region exhibits marked climatic variation, and its southern flanks, where rainfall is moderate or even scanty, are much less dissected by streams, so that here the east–west trend of the folds is more apparent than on the north. As in the north-west Zagros, volcanic cones are a feature, the best known of which, Mount Damavand, an ash cone of Quaternary age, located north of Tehran, attains 5500 m, and carries a permanent snow-cap and a very small glacier.

The northern slopes of the Elburz are well wooded up to a height of 2100–2450 m, but further south a sharp change occurs, and vegetation soon becomes less luxuriant, passing ultimately, in the extreme south, into scattered patches of scrub, with most of the hillsides entirely bare. When water is available, many parts of the southern Elburz are extremely fertile, especially the alluvial cones and river terraces, where there is a thick deposit of rich soil. In some places, however, the river bed is too deeply incised to allow the deposition of silt, and such valleys are uninhabited.

Bordering the northern edge of the Elburz range, and its western

continuation, the Talish hills, lies the coastal plain of the southern
Caspian. This varies between 15 and 110 km in width. Close to the
Caspian shoreline is a zone of sand dunes, behind which lie salt marshes
and lagoons. These are succeeded by slightly higher and firmer ground,
most of which was densely covered by the Hyrcanian vegetation to which
reference was made in chapter 4. Of recent years many parts of the
Hyrcanian forest have been cleared for cultivation, leaving only vestigial
patches of the original vegetation. The coastal plain of the Caspian is
now one of the most closely settled of any part of Iran, containing 15–20%
of the total population of the country.

The Caspian plain has been uncovered by a gradual retreat of the
Caspian Sea, which once extended as far south as the foothills of the
Elburz range. Over the last 70–80 years the level of the Caspian has fallen
by over 2 m, the precise annual rate depending upon inflow from various
rivers, chiefly the Volga. Despite its irregular shrinking, the Caspian is
much less salt than most sea water, and is only one-quarter as salt as the
Mediterranean. The retreat of the Caspian Sea is having a most unfortunate
effect on the economic life of the Iranian ports on its shores, which can
now only be approached by specially dredged channels resembling canals.
A project of long standing, sponsored by the Russians, aims at cutting
a canal to link the Caspian and Black Seas, by which the deficiency of
water may be made up.

In the extreme east, at about longitude 56° E, the Elburz range dies
down and is succeeded by a trough or plateau, the lower parts of which
are grass-covered and support a population of pastoral nomads. It is hardly
correct to speak of this trough as a lowland, since the average altitude
is about 1500 m, but it serves to divide off the higher Elburz to the west
from the more massive and widely spaced ranges to the east. These
eastern ranges have a predominantly north-west–south-east trend, in
contrast to the due east–west alignment of the Elburz. The most northerly
of the ranges, the Kopet Dagh, lies partly in Iran and partly in Russian
Turkestan, the frontier following the eastern foothills of this range. The
Kopet Dagh (termed Kuh-i-Hajar Masjid in its south-east portion) reaches
3000 m in maximum elevation, and is then succeeded by a second chain,
named the Kuh-i-Aleh (northern part) and the Kuh-i-Binalud (southern
portion). In between the Kopet Dagh and Kuh-i-Aleh lies a well-defined
valley, occupied by two rivers; the Atrek flowing north-west to the
Caspian, and the Kashuf flowing south-east towards Afghanistan.

Main interest centres in the lowlands of the Atrek and Kashuf, which
provide a natural corridor between the Caspian region and the Turcoman
steppes of the district of Merv. Most of the highland is barren and empty,
serving only as grazing ground for occasional nomadic tribes; but the
riverine lowlands are relatively densely peopled, with numerous cultivated

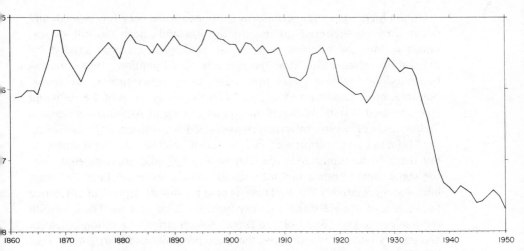

*Fig.* 11.3 Variation in level of the Caspian Sea.

areas. The richest part is the upper Kashuf valley round Mashad and Nishapur, from which comes a substantial proportion of the wheat and barley of Iran. From the abundance of ruins of many ages scattered in this district, it would seem that there was once a very dense population. Tribal wars, invasion and liability to earthquakes were for long retarding factors; situated at the principal natural gateway into eastern Iran, the Mashad region bore the brunt of many Mongol raids, but with stronger rule since the 1920s there has been a considerable revival of economic activity in the region.

## The eastern uplands

This term can be applied to the broken and irregular highland region lying between the region just described, and the south-east portion of the Zagros. There is little geographical unity: the highland massifs are irregular in trend and disposition, and give place in many localities to wide lowland basins. Generally speaking, the entire eastern region is markedly barren and unproductive, for besides the difficulties of irregular topography, with much loose scree, jagged peaks and drifting sand, there are considerable climatic drawbacks – extremes of heat and cold, great aridity, and a special feature, a persistent and violent wind which blows with great regularity throughout the summer season, and sometimes reaches a velocity of over 120 km/h. (In winter, blizzards of 200 km/h are not unknown.) As a result great quantities of sand are lifted, giving rise to a kind of natural sand-blast. In time, the lower courses of buildings can be etched away by the wind and fall in ruins.

On the higher ground, permanent settlements are very few indeed, and occur only in sheltered gullies. In the lowlands near the hill slopes, outwash fans of pebbles, and scree of jagged material eroded by exfoliation, alike offer little inducement to cultivation. In the neighbourhood of the few rivers that exist, some agriculture is, however, possible. Most important of such areas is the lower basin of the Helmand river, termed Sistan. Water from streams rising in Afghanistan reaches Sistan, and cultivation by irrigation is carried on. Unfortuately, however, the Helmand river terminates in a series of shallow lakes and marshes, but there is the remarkable phenomenon of episodic drainage each year for some weeks into a natural swamp, which serves to keep the main lake waters relatively fresh. There is also an annual deposit of silt, since the waters of the Helmand are very turbid in flood season. Thus, despite the liability to the 'Wind of 120 Days', which strips vegetation of leaves and causes intense evaporation, there are possibilities for irrigation. Iran is unfortunate, however, in that most of the Helmand basin lies politically in Afghanistan; and an American–Afghan irrigation scheme started in the 1960s has hardly been a major success. Nevertheless, the situation remains that Sistan, like the Mashad region, once supported a larger population, and could again, give right development.

### The central plateau

The inner part of Iran, amounting to about one half of the total area of the country, is occupied by a series of closed basins from which there is no outward drainage of any sort. In the main, the lowest parts of these basins lie at an elevation of 600–1000 m, although they are sometimes 300 m lower than this in the south-east; and the mountain ring, which almost completely encircles the inner plateau, falls little below a general level of 2500 m.

At an earlier period – probably late Tertiary and Quaternary – the basins were occupied by lakes, which have left thick deposits of alluvial material. The central plateau is now almost rainless, and so for the most part the region is one of unrelieved desert. There are, however, certain unusual features. The lowest parts of the basins have a deep deposit of black mud, and evaporation at the surface has resulted in the formation of a salt crust. The salt is precipitated in the form of angular blocks or plates, about 2–3 cm thick, and several square metres in area. As evaporation proceeds, the crusts increase in size and are forced one against the other, so that in time they become arched upwards, and their rough, sharp edges protrude above the surface, giving an appearance rather similar to that of a glacier or ice-floe. Beneath the salt crust lies a sticky mass of salt marsh or mud, with drainage channels at intervals

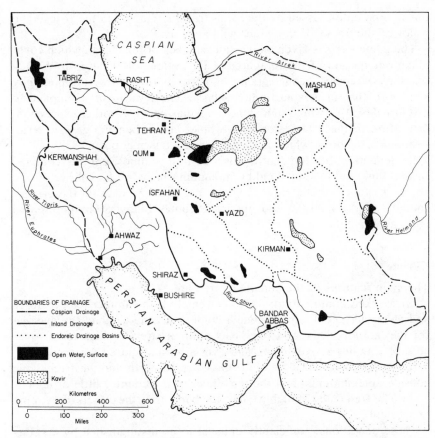

*Fig.* 11.4 Iran: drainage pattern.

that are filled with watery ooze or slime. It is something of a mystery
how such an arid area still retains extensive swamps; but possibly the
water is a remnant of the old lakes, supplemented at the present by
soakage from the mountain crests. The presence in the swamps of
magnesium chloride, a strongly hygroscopic substance, may also attract
a certain amount of moisture from the subsoil and from the atmosphere.

The salt marshes are extremely dangerous to travellers, since the sharp
edges of the salt crust can cause serious injury to men and animals.
Moreover, the layer of salt is often insufficient to bear the weight of a
man, and the scattered drainage channels, which occur underneath and
of which there is no indication on the surface, are deep enough to
overwhelm anyone caught in their sluggish waters. Movement in the region
is rendered even more hazardous by frequent winter fogs. As a result,
widespread areas of the marshes are uninhabited and were for long

unexplored until crossed by the Swiss traveller Gabriel in the 1930s, who followed the tracks of the larger wild animals.

The name *kavir* is given to the salt marshes of inner Iran which cover about one-quarter of the total area of the region. Elsewhere, firm sandy or stony stretches occur, giving a more 'normal' desert topography similar to that of Arabia or the Sahara. The term *dasht* is applied to this firm desert, in which sand dunes (*rig*) may occur. Another expression, *lut*, refers to the arid region as a whole, and is hence a generic term, denoting a region in which both *dasht* and *kavir* may occur.

Settlement within the central basin of Iran is almost entirely confined to the flanks of the surrounding mountain chains – e.g. Tehran on the southern slopes of the Elburz; Qum, Yazd and Kirman on the eastern foothills of the Zagros – and important routes follow a circumferential path, avoiding the centre of the *lut*.

### Climate

The main features of the climate of Iran are:

(*a*) Marked continentality, with extremely high summer temperatures and an usually cold winter – much colder, in general, than the average for the latitude. This is in large part a direct effect of high relief: over 90% of Iran lies above 300 m, and over a third at more than 1500 m.

(*b*) Great contrasts in rainfall, the extreme north and west receiving considerable amounts, and the remainder of the country little or none.

(*c*) The frequency of high winds, which intensify the effects of extreme temperature.

These conditions, sufficiently unusual to be distinguished by de Martonne as a separate climatic regime,[1] arise chiefly as the result of the mountainous nature of the region, and its situation as part of the heartland of Asia. In summer, dry continental air associated with the peripheral circulation of the low pressure areas centred over north-west India and the Persian/Arab Gulf cover most of Iran, and give temperatures comparable with those of the Thar Desert, whilst in winter the country can easily fall under the influence of the Siberian anticyclone, with few topographical barriers to prevent the south-westward spread of intensely dry, cold air. On the other hand, maritime influences are excluded by the high mountain wall, most fully developed on the west and south, so that milder, damper air from the Mediterranean and Caspian Seas, and Persian/Arab Gulf, affects only the outer regions of Iran.

Altitude is partly responsible for the unusually cold winters (Tehran and Isfahan mean January temperature 4 °C – cf. Aleppo and Beirut in the same latitude, 6° and 13 °C; or Seville, 11 °C) and, although altitude

[1] The 'Iranian' type.

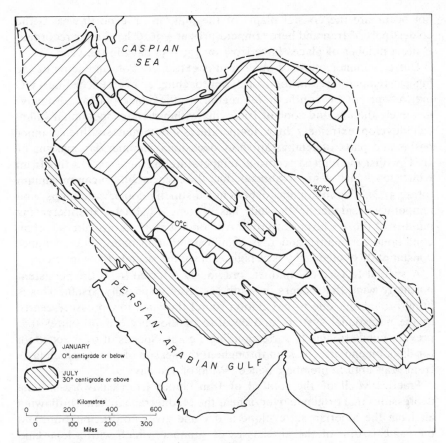

CASPIAN SEA

30°c

0°c

PERSIAN-ARABIAN GULF

JANUARY
0° centigrade or below

JULY
30° centigrade or above

Kilometres
0     200     400     600

0     100     200     300
Miles

*Fig.* 11.5 Iran: summer and winter temperatures.

does not much mitigate the intense heat of the day in summer, it does produce a rapid fall of temperature at night (Tehran, altitude 1191 m, mean day max. July 35·8 °C, mean night min. July 22 °C; Mashad, altitude 986 m, mean day max. 33·7 °C, mean night min. 17·9 °C; Qum, altitude 928 m, mean day max. 38·2 °C, mean night min. 22·2 °C). Annual range of temperature on the central plateau varies from 20° to nearly 50 °C, with an average January temperature of zero in the northern and western districts and 8 °C in the south and east. Frost is, therefore, normal in most parts of the central plateau during late autumn, winter and early spring; and in the higher parts of the surrounding mountains temperatures are lower still, so that snow may lie for many months (mean January temperature at Tabriz, −1 °C). Temperatures well below freezing have even been recorded on the Shatt el Arab, at sea-level, where occasionally ice formation has been seen. The only regions of Iran where frost does not occur are the coastal plains of the Makran. The north-west is the coldest part of Iran and here temperatures at −36 °C have been recorded. Quite a number of places have frost on 130–150 days in the year.

During summer, most of inner Iran is extremely hot, and some of the highest temperatures in the world, approaching or even exceeding 55 °C may occur in the southern *lut* region of the inner plateau. Equally, however, the lowland zone of Iran lying within the Mesopotamian valley can develop extremely high temperatures – both the south-east inner basins and parts of Khuzistan show occasional summer day maxima of 50 °C whilst the highest recorded temperature in Iran is 53 °C – this from Khuzistan which also, at Shustar, has the highest July mean maximum (of 47·3 °C). The mountains experience distinctly cooler conditions, and temporary residence in the hills has become a habit for the increasing number of those who can afford it. Air conditioning has also altered urban conditions for many, and it is significant that in many cities summer consumption of electricity is as high as in winter, despite the winter cold.

A special feature of summer, previously referred to, is the persistent northerly wind that occurs in south-east Iran, especially Sistan. This is in all probability due to circulation round the main low pressure centre of the monsoonal system, and because of the very low pressures that prevail, wind strength is correspondingly great. Speeds of over 100 km/h for days on end are common throughout the season of onset, which lasts from May until September, hence 'Wind of 120 days'.

Practically all of the rainfall of Iran comes from eastward-moving depressions that originate over or near the Mediterranean Sea. Outflowing air from the Siberian anticyclone is dry and gives no precipitation, and the same is true of the air masses of summer, which with a long land track round the summer monsoonal low, have little moisture on passing over Iran. Hence the summer is completely arid (except in the extreme north along the shores of the Caspian), and rainfall at other seasons depends on the arrival of maritime air masses from the west. Depressions in this maritime air stream are, however, greatly weakened, as most of their moisture is deposited on the highlands of Asia Minor and the Levant; and the remaining moisture is precipitated during the crossing of the Zagros ranges, so that little or none falls in the central plateau.

When the track of a Mediterranean depression has lain over land, the quantity of rainfall occurring in Iran is very small, but when a sea track has been followed, the amount of moisture is greater, i.e. depressions moving towards Iran via the Aegean and Black Seas give the heaviest rainfall, whilst those moving due east across Syria and Iraq are almost dried out.[1]

[1] It has been suggested that a partial regeneration of these exhausted depressions may occur over the swamps of lower Iraq and the Persian Gulf.

Percentage relative humidity

|                                  | J  | F  | M  | A  | M  | J  | J  | A  | S  | O  | N  | D  |
|----------------------------------|----|----|----|----|----|----|----|----|----|----|----|----|
| Tehran                           | 76 | 64 | 44 | 46 | 51 | 50 | 47 | 49 | 50 | 54 | 66 | 77 |
| Mashad                           | 83 | 83 | 77 | 68 | 59 | 48 | 45 | 46 | 49 | 62 | 76 | 79 |
| Abadan                           | 77 | 75 | 59 | 45 | 33 | 25 | 25 | 29 | 33 | 39 | 60 | 75 |
| Jask                             | 63 | 71 | 65 | 65 | 64 | 67 | 68 | 72 | 64 | 64 | 62 | 62 |
| Lenkoran (Russian Caspian provinces) | 86 | 87 | 87 | 84 | 81 | 75 | 73 | 76 | 82 | 88 | 89 | 89 |

Thus, as might be expected, north-west Iran experiences by far the heaviest rainfall, and the distribution of rainfall in general is closely related to topography. Isohyets tend to follow contour lines, and the north-west Zagros and Elburz regions, lying close to sea areas, receive by far the heaviest rainfall that can amount to as much as 200 mm. The amount decreases towards the south-east, markedly so in the lower central plateau, more slowly in the mountain zones. Hence the Kopet Dagh and Ala Dagh of the east, and the south-east Zagros, have annual totals of under 250 mm, whilst on the central plateau a rain-shadow area occurs in which rainfall is under 100 mm (Yazd has only 40 mm).

The season of greatest rainfall varies somewhat over the country. In the north (Caspian provinces excepted) the maximum occurs in spring with March as the wettest month; but in the south, the maximum falls earlier (December at Ahwaz and Khorramshahr, January at Jask). Again, as is usual under Middle Eastern conditions, rainfall is capricious, varying greatly in amount from year to year, and in onset – even in regions where annual rainfall is below 250 mm, falls of 50 mm in 24 h are known, and years may pass without any precipitation.

Great contrasts exist in humidity. Over most of Iran the air is dry – as would be expected, in view of a deficient rainfall – and figures for Tehran and Mashad, showing a winter maximum, may be considered as typical. On the Caspian coast, however, humidity is high throughout the year, though still with a winter maximum; but in the Persian Gulf humidity is highest in summer, giving rise, in combination with the very high air temperature, to extremely oppressive conditions. Where sea-breezes carry in moisture from sea to land, as at Jask, summer humidity is high. At Abadan, the opposite occurs, and with the prevailing wind from the north-west (i.e. from the land) humidity is low. This difference in humidity is all the more striking in view of the complete absence of summer rainfall at both places.

Cloudiness in general is extremely low. The Caspian region, with an average cloud cover of seven-tenths, stands out; but the general lack of

Cloudiness (in tenths of sky covered)

|          | J | F | M | A | M | J | J | A | S | O | N | D | Mean |
|----------|---|---|---|---|---|---|---|---|---|---|---|---|------|
| Tehran   | 4 | 5 | 4 | 4 | 4 | 1 | 1 | 1 | 1 | 2 | 4 | 4 | 3 |
| Mashad   | 5 | 4 | 5 | 5 | 3 | 1 | 1 | 0 | 1 | 2 | 4 | 5 | 3 |
| Sistan   | 3 | 3 | 2 | 1 | 1 | 0 | 0 | 0 | 0 | 0 | 0 | 2 | 1 |
| Lenkoran | 7 | 7 | 8 | 7 | 7 | 5 | 5 | 4 | 6 | 6 | 8 | 8 | 6 |
| Bushire  | 4 | 4 | 4 | 3 | 2 | 0 | 1 | 1 | 1 | 1 | 3 | 5 | 2 |

cloudiness is an important factor in the wide range of temperature, both seasonal and diurnal. During the days of summer, the sun blazes down on an uncovered land surface: at night, and in winter, much terrestrial heat is given out unchecked to the atmosphere.

It remains to discuss the special climatic regime of the Caspian region. Here, as the result of the presence of the Elburz range, and proximity to two expanses of sea which form a 'storm track' for depressions, rainfall is very much higher. Moreover, the low altitude of the coastal plain gives winter temperatures more in keeping with the latitude. In summer rainfall occurs, though on a reduced scale, and the resulting cloud cover helps to reduce insolation, so that the high temperatures characteristic of the rest of Iran are not found – it is very unusual for the thermometer to reach 37 °C, and the July mean is only 24–27 °C. A hot but not torrid summer, and a winter milder than in the adjacent areas of Iran, together with abundant rainfall, well distributed throughout the year (maximum in early autumn), indicate that climatically the Caspian provinces stand apart from the rest of the country, with conditions that are closer to those of the humid tropics.

### Agriculture

Although the rural population amounts to about one-half of the total (it was some 60% in 1968 but is declining), the contribution of agriculture to gross national product is calculated (1977) at 11–13%, with the average annual income of each peasant about $US 250, compared with $1400 for townspeople. More than half of Iran is regarded as uncultivable, non-agricultural land, and only 11–12% is actually cultivated. Of this, about a half at any one time is under fallow; and 25–28% of cultivable land is irrigated, with rainfed agriculture dominant in the Caspian provinces, Kurdistan, Azerbaijan and the north-west Zagros. Cultivated lands occur generally as relatively small patches surrounded by vast tracts of grazing gound, by unexploited desert or mountain or by what is termed land capable of reclamation and development, but hardly used except for grazing.

Climatic data: representative stations in Iran
*Temperature (°C) and rainfall (mm)*

| | J | F | M | A | M | J | J | A | S | O | N | D | Total |
|---|---|---|---|---|---|---|---|---|---|---|---|---|---|
| **Tehran** | | | | | | | | | | | | | |
| Temperature | | | | | | | | | | | | | |
| maximum | +9 | 11 | 15 | 22 | 28 | 33 | 36 | 35 | 31 | 24 | 15 | 10 | |
| minimum | −1 | 0 | 4 | 10 | 15 | 19 | 22 | 22 | 18 | 12 | 5 | 0 | |
| Rainfall | 31 | 29 | 35 | 35 | 14 | 3 | 0 | 2 | 2 | 8 | 38 | 24 | 224 |
| Rainy days | 4 | 4 | 5 | 3 | 2 | 1 | 0 | 1 | 1 | 1 | 3 | 4 | 29 |
| **Mashad** | | | | | | | | | | | | | |
| Temperature | | | | | | | | | | | | | |
| maximum | 7 | 9 | 12 | 19 | 26 | 31 | 34 | 33 | 29 | 22 | 13 | 9 | |
| minimum | −3 | −2 | +2 | 8 | 11 | 15 | 18 | 16 | 11 | 5 | 0 | −2 | |
| Rainfall | 32 | 31 | 61 | 51 | 25 | 4 | 0 | 0 | 1 | 6 | 17 | 20 | 249 |
| Rainy days | 3 | 3 | 5 | 5 | 2 | 1 | 0 | 0 | 0 | 1 | 1 | 2 | 23 |
| **Abadan** | | | | | | | | | | | | | |
| Temperature | | | | | | | | | | | | | |
| maximum | 19 | 21 | 26 | 32 | 38 | 43 | 45 | 45 | 42 | 36 | 27 | 19 | |
| minimum | 7 | 9 | 12 | 17 | 22 | 26 | 28 | 27 | 23 | 18 | 13 | 8 | |
| Rainfall | 20 | 15 | 19 | 15 | 4 | 0 | 0 | 0 | 0 | 1 | 26 | 41 | 146 |
| Rainy days | 6 | 5 | 3 | 3 | 1 | 0 | 0 | 0 | 0 | 0 | 3 | 4 | 25 |
| **Yazd** | | | | | | | | | | | | | |
| Temperature | | | | | | | | | | | | | |
| maximum | 13 | 16 | 20 | 26 | 32 | 37 | 39 | 38 | 34 | 27 | 18 | 12 | |
| minimum | +1 | 3 | 7 | 13 | 17 | 22 | 24 | 22 | 18 | 11 | 5 | 2 | |
| Rainfall | 15 | 3 | 8 | 9 | 4 | 1 | 1 | 0 | 0 | 1 | 16 | 8 | 68 |
| Rainy days | 3 | 1 | 3 | 2 | 1 | 1 | 0 | 0 | 0 | 0 | 3 | 2 | 15 |
| **Rasht** | | | | | | | | | | | | | |
| Temperature | | | | | | | | | | | | | |
| maximum | 12 | 12 | 12 | 19 | 25 | 27 | 30 | 30 | 26 | 22 | 16 | 13 | |
| minimum | 3 | 2 | 4 | 8 | 13 | 16 | 18 | 19 | 16 | 12 | 6 | 3 | |
| Rainfall | 81 | 105 | 159 | 51 | 50 | 59 | 40 | 67 | 198 | 246 | 195 | 107 | 1355 |
| Rainy days | 8 | 10 | 12 | 5 | 5 | 6 | 4 | 7 | 16 | 23 | 15 | 10 | 131 |
| **Bushire** | | | | | | | | | | | | | |
| Temperature | | | | | | | | | | | | | |
| maximum | 19 | 20 | 24 | 31 | 35 | 37 | 39 | 40 | 37 | 33 | 27 | 21 | |
| minimum | 10 | 10 | 14 | 18 | 22 | 25 | 28 | 27 | 24 | 19 | 15 | 12 | |
| Rainfall | 61 | 22 | 19 | 9 | 5 | 0 | 0 | 0 | 0 | 1 | 48 | 93 | 259 |
| Rainy days | 5 | 3 | 2 | 1 | 1 | 0 | 0 | 0 | 0 | 0 | 3 | 4 | 19 |

In comparison with the tremendous growth in other sectors of the Iranian economy, agriculture remains the least developed. Reasons for this are to be found in the intrinsic environmental handicaps of a difficult topography, aridity, extremes of temperature, tendency to soil salinity in some areas (including one of the richest farming areas – in Khuzistan), and prevalence of pests and plant diseases. Further factors are limited

Land utilization in Iran 1968 (million ha)

|  |  | % total area |
|---|---|---|
| Cultivated land | 19·0 | 11·5 |
| (a) Annual and permanent cultivation | 7·1 | |
| Of which: irrigated | 3·1 | |
| non-irrigated | 4·0 | |
| (b) Fallow | 11·9 | |
| Pasture and range land | 10·0 | 6·1 |
| Forest and woodland | 19·0 | 11·5 |
| Uncultivated but capable of reclamation | 31·0 | 18·8 |
| Uncultivated (mountain, desert, cities, etc.) | 86·0 | 52·1 |
| Total | 165·0 | 100 |

communications, restricting access to markets; poor infrastructures and technologies – implements, seeds, and handling; whilst methods of exploitation tended to be primitive. As a result, yields are low, and the peasants, 90% of whom are subsistence farmers, are severely undercapitalized. Perhaps the greatest single factor in this generally low level of agriculture was, however, the system of land tenure, with, in the words of A. K. S. Lambton, one single person coming to exercise the functions of local civil and military governor, tax collector and ground landlord, with the consequent emergence of a powerful landed group ('the thousand families') and a landless peasant class.

This last has, however, been greatly changed by the Shah's 'White Revolution' or scheme of land reform. The Fifth Development Plan (1973–8) aims at an annual growth rate of 7%, as compared with an actual 2–3% in the previous Plan; and, because of growing shortages of foodstuffs (which necessitate imports on an increasing scale), more finance was applied in the Fifth Plan to agriculture than ever before (in all, $8 billion is allocated). Land reform, farm mechanization, improvements in seeds, and more widespread use of fertilizers have produced larger crops in the 1970s, but a significant part of the improvement has come from taking in new land, often with expensive irrigation, rather than better cultivation of existing fields.

*Crops*

Wheat is the chief crop, and is grown over most of Iran. The regions of greatest production are: (a) the Mashad region of Khorassan province, (*b*) the valleys of the north-west and central Zagros, particularly the disticts of Lake Urmia, Hamadan, Kermanshah, Isfahan, Shiraz and Niriz, and (*c*) the better-watered parts of Khuzistan. In most instances, wheat is grown as a winter crop, but in the high valleys of the Zagros and Elburz, sowing is in the spring, so that the harvest takes place in July and August, Iran is not self-sufficient in wheat owing to rising standards of living, and over 2 million tons are now imported annually. Barley has declined to being Iran's third most important cereal, and is grown in the same districts as wheat. Barley has the advantage of ripening 3 to 4 weeks earlier than wheat, and thus escapes the ravages of the *sunna* insect, which, appearing in late summer, is particularly prevalent in Iran.

Rice is now the second most important cereal, and is grown in the Caspian provinces of Gilan and Mazanderan, with the Rasht district the region of most intensive production. Quantities are also grown in the newly-irrigated areas, for example of the Dez system; and this has made rice a much more significant crop. Khuzistan, Kermanshah, Isfahan and the Shiraz basin are of growing importance as areas of production. Rice cultivation demands much labour, as several ploughings are necessary – the first to break up the land, and again when the paddy fields have been covered in water, and the surface must be broken down to the consistency of mud. For this purpose mountaineers from the Elburz (and to a lesser extent the Zagros) are employed as seasonal workers. The fields are broken up in late winter, then the fields are flooded to a depth of 30–50 cm in April, and sowing takes place in May. Later, the crop is thinned out, either by transplantation or by trampling down unwanted shoots by foot. Harvesting takes place in August or September. Until the introduction of rice in the tenth century A.D., the Caspian provinces were much less productive, because the climate, with cloudy summers and a very rainy early autumn (i.e. closer to monsoon conditions), does not altogether favour the cultivation of wheat and barley.

Two minor cereal crops are maize and millet. Maize cultivation is expanding in areas of summer rainfall (i.e. the extreme north) and with irrigation, as in Khuzistan. Millet is more a crop of warmer, drier areas.

Fruit-growing is of considerable importance, since fruit forms an important part of the everyday diet of most Iranians. The main regions are situated in the north-west of the country, but small orchards occur in most districts. Iran is famous for its apricots, said to be the finest in the world, and the wide extent of hilly country favours the cultivation of the vine. Many varieties of the latter occur: some are dried as sultanas and raisins, others are used in wine-making,[1] whilst large quantities are eaten fresh. Grapes from the Shiraz district, reputed to be the finest in

[1] Despite Moslem disapproval, wine-making has long been carried on in Iran, as the poetry of Omar Khayyam shows.

the Middle East, are exported as far as Iraq and India. The vine is found at altitudes up to 1500 m in most parts of the country, and many of the lower hillsides are terraced as vineyards. Other fruit crops are figs, peaches, lemons, melons and oranges. Some oranges grow to a size of 20 cm in diameter, and melons are also of enormous size. In the north-east, towards Russian Turkestan, the latter attain a weight of 50 kg.

Citrus fruit growing is generally confined to the Caspian coastlands, and to the outer foothills of the central Zagros. The wide extent of upland massifs allows a well-marked gradation of cultivation of fruit crops: at the lowest levels oranges, peaches, pomegranates and melons are found, succeeded at heights of 30–600 m by apricots, nectarines and the vine. In the cooler zones about 1200 m there is a variety of temperate fruits – plums, cherries, pears, apples and strawberries. Olives are less important, and cultivation is mainly limited to the Elburz range, with the Manzil region of the middle Safid Rud as the chief centre. Scattered olive groves are, however, also found on the eastern side of the Zagros range, towards the inner pleateau of Iran. Oil seeds (sesame, sunflower), groundnuts and soya beans are cultivated on an increasing scale for food.

In the south of Iran date-growing assumes very high importance, and in the south-east Zagros and Makran districts, dates form a staple of diet. About one half of the productive date palms of Iran, which in total number about 10 million, are found round Minab on the Strait of Hormuz, and most of the remainder in Khuzistan, near the Shatt el Arab, or in the extreme east of Iran.

*Commercial crops* Cotton is by far the most important crop, since besides supplying home demand there is a significant export both of raw cotton and processed yarn. Irrigation is essential, and growing is, therefore, restricted to the north and west of the country. A moderately long-stapled variety of cotton known as *Filestani* is grown in Azerbaijan, Kermanshah, Fars and Khuzistan provinces, and accounts for about 50% of the total of cotton grown. A shorter-stapled American variety is found mainly in the Caspian district, whilst a third kind, a native short staple of inferior quality, though hardy in growth, is restricted to marginal (i.e. dry or hilly) areas. The cotton plant is also grown extensively for its seed, which yields an edible oil that replaces olive oil as food in many areas. Well over 100000 tons are produced annually.

Silk is a traditional product of Iran, but there have been many vicissitudes, the latest being competition from synthetic fibres. Mulberry-growing tends to be a feature of the eastern Caspian lowlands, in Mazanderan. Opium, too, was once more widespread, but in 1955, following severe international criticism, cultivation was prohibited by law.

Production of major crops (1974–75 estimate) (million metric tons)

| Wheat | 5·2 | Cotton | 0·66 |
|---|---|---|---|
| Rice | 1·4 | Potatoes | 0·49 |
| Barley | 1·0 | Oil seeds | 0·58 |
| Sugar beet | 4·6 | Tea | 0·11 |
| Sugar cane | 0·09 | | |

*Other crops* Sugar beet was introduced by Reza Shah, and its production has latterly been greatly fostered by the Iranian government as a means of reducing the country's dependence on imports. Because of an environment that is in the main too warm and dry for really intensive cultivation – the beet is more at home in cool temperate latitudes – there is only a low sugar content. The beet crop is totally dependent upon irrigation, which, however, must be very carefully applied, in order to avoid damage to the plants. Cultivation is confined to the regions of Tehran, Tabriz, Kermanshah, Shiraz and Mashad. Cane sugar, widely grown in Iran during the early Muhammadan era, is now restricted to the Caspian provinces (Gilan and Mazanderan) and to Khuzistan. Planting takes place in March or April, and the cane is cut in November.

Tea is another crop that owes its extension to the efforts of Reza Shah. Chinese experts were introduced to develop cultivation on the northern foothills of the Elburz and Talish hills, overlooking the Caspian plain, where climatic conditions somewhat resemble those of the lower Himalaya. Abundant moisture is necessary, so the crop tends to be restricted to the western portion of the Elburz, where rainfall exceeds 900 mm per annum. The eastern province of Mazanderan is used for jute-growing, but production of this latter crop is very small.

Tobacco is grown in most districts for local use, but the more important areas are the north-west and south-east Zagros, and the Caspian provinces. Quality is not high, so that there is little or no export. A number of dye-plants are important in the carpet-making industry. Production is mainly from the central Zagros region, and the adjoining province of Kirman in the central plateau: the chief crops being indigo, henna, madder, saffron and oak-gall. Output has greatly declined since the introduction of aniline dyes during the last 50 years.

Recently, fodder crops, oil seeds and market gardening have greatly increased in response to expanding demand for dairy produce and vegetables. Potatoes especially are more and more grown as a winter crop. Production of all these is being stimulated as general living standards increase, and it is government policy to encourage this in order to reduce imports.

### Irrigation and land reform
*Irrigation*

Some 13% of Iran receives less than 100 mm of rainfall annually, and a further 61% less than 250 mm. Only 9% of the country receives more than 500 mm (this is a fairly generous figure for secure cultivation, but not too high, in view of the considerable evaporation due to high summer temperatures). As a result, Iran has severe water problems, some deriving from the nature of the physical environment – steep gradients, encased drainage and the loss of stream water, either outwards into other countries or into closed saline drainage basins. Evapotranspiration is considerable – at Tehran annual rainfall is 224 mm, but potential evaporation is 2700 mm – whilst archaic laws and customs and social restrictions further inhibit effective utilization of what water there is. At first new crops (sugar beet and cotton) were introduced without much irrigation, but their spread was dependent on better water supply, and so governmental finance has increasingly been applied to irrigation works, some large, others small, with which are often associated electricity generation and flood control. Of the total rainfall received in Iran, it is estimated that 60–65% evaporates or is lost below ground, 15% fills underground aquifers, and the remainder, 20–25%, remains at or near the surface. Besides many small local barrages and 50000 *qanats*, there are twelve major irrigation works now completed, with a further seven in construction.

It is believed that the area of cultivated land could be doubled, with greatest potential occurring in the Khuzistan area. So far, a number of important projects have been completed or begun, and many smaller-scale improvements undertaken to existing dams, *qanats* and canal schemes. Caution is necessary, as some areas, e.g. along the Karun river, are susceptible to soil salinity if over-watered; and in earlier years, enthusiasm sometimes outstripped finance and sound planning, so some schemes had to be modified or delayed. The largest projects are in the north-west (Dez, Karun, Karkeh) and the north (Safid Rud), but, as fig. 11.6 shows, developments are spread over much of the country where rainfall and topography offer possibilities of reservoir construction.

*Land reform*

Up to 1960 between a quarter and a fifth of Iran's 48000 villages were owned by proprietors who possessed at least five villages and were thus frequent absentees. Many were members of the Majilis (Parliament), and the power of this landlord group ('the thousand families') had for long been an obstacle to those who wished to attempt to achieve a fair distribution of crops and profits as between cultivating share-croppers

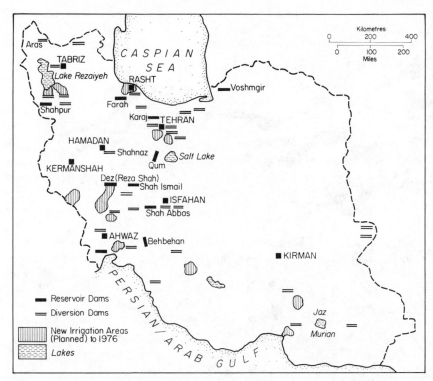

*Fig.* 11.6 Crops and irrigation development (1976).

('metayers'), who might receive only 20–30% of what they produced, and landlords, who receive the rest. However, from 1951 onwards the Shah began redistributing Crown land (which was considerable) to peasant-occupiers, and a wider land reform programme developed on a modest scale in 1961, to be expanded in 1964 over the entire country. Under provisions of various new enactments, land had to be redistributed if a holding exceeded a given maximum, which was large in an area of low fertility, and proportionately reduced in a highly fertile region. Landlords were compelled to divest themselves of excess holdings in one of four ways: selling direct to peasants, leasing for a 30-year period, or dividing the land with the peasants in the ratio that formerly prevailed in the division of crops (e.g. in a village where the landlord received 40% of the crop annually, he would retain 40% and the peasants would receive 60%). The fourth method of redistribution is by joint exploitation through a local organization. Orchards and woodlands and also land worked by mechanical methods could be retained by the landlord. Compensation was paid by the central government, at low values in some areas, but at higher values in some others – one factor sometimes being the declared value

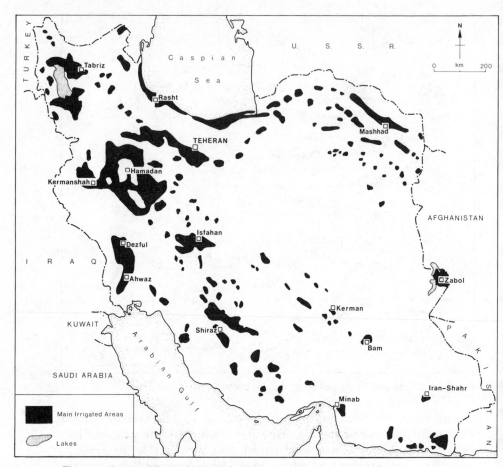

*Fig.* 11.7 Iran: major existing irrigation.

as previously stated by the landlord for income tax purposes. Later phases of the reform encouraged consolidation of fragmented holdings and mechanization, whilst in the 1970s co-operatives (now nearly 3000 in all) have been set up, first small in size but now larger in scale, with nearly 3 million participants. Some 60–70 farm corporations (i.e. farming enterprises with peasant stock-holders) have been formed, to undertake more intensive methods. 'Agri-industrial complexes', eventually to cover 8% of irrigated land, are developing: these include integrated fodder/dairy, almond, fodder/meat-packing activities.

Critics of the reforms suggested that the new peasant owners would lack capital and expertise, and that their lands would thus be less efficiently farmed. Governmental bureaucracy would be incapable of handling the practical and technical problems involved; and a large mass of labourers would still remain unaffected and therefore without land.

Transfer to peasants was made in the event relatively smoothly and efficiently; levels of production did not fall off, and the governmental officials proved generally equal to the demands made on them. But, owing to population growth and higher living expectations, Iran still needs to import quantities of basic foodstuffs, and efforts are now being made to extend co-operatives and agri-industrial units as the best means of closing the gap. There is now a critical shortage of trained, skilled workers in agriculture.

*Pastoralism*

Nomadism, once extremely significant in Iranian life, is now in accelerating decline: many nomadic pastoralists have taken up sedentary life either as the result of pressure by government, or because of the 'pull' exerted by the growing towns, where unskilled workers are now much in demand. Yet pastoralism remains the best form of resource-evaluation in many hilly or semi-arid areas; and provided facilities such as education, co-operative marketing, medical and veterinary services, and equality of political treatment, can be made available, the nomads can still contribute to the economic life of Iran in a substantial way. Apart from the value of milk and meat, wool for carpets is in considerable demand.

Sheep are most numerous, with a probable total of (1977) about 24 million, and these animals are kept either in semi-arid or mountainous areas, where they form the main wealth of nomadic tribes, or else close to partly settled agricultural regions. In the latter areas a village herdsman usually takes care of a single large flock, and is repaid in kind by the owners. Shearing takes place in May and September, and the wool is used locally for clothing and blankets, or else sent to market centres to be sold.

Goats are next in importance, numbering about 12 million. Besides providing milk and meat, their hair is woven into cloaks and tent-cloth. Cattle are less numerous – about 5 to 6 million. Whilst many are employed in agricultural districts as draught animals for ploughing and irrigation, an increasing number are now kept in and near large towns for dairying. Buffaloes are of importance in the rice areas of the Caspian lowland. Latest estimates suggest about a quarter of a million. Poultry-keeping is also increasing.

Camels, once numerous in the south and east as pack animals, and also for meat, are less in evidence owing to the spread of motor transport. An Iranian breed – the Khorassan – has been developed by crossing the Arabian (single hump) with the Bactrian camel (two-humped). The Khorassan camel can carry twice the load of the Arabian species, and is better adapted to the winter cold.

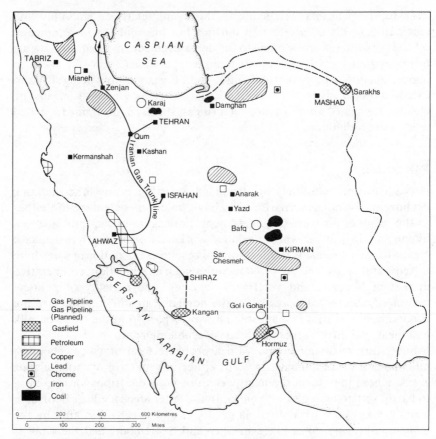

*Fig.* 11.8 Mineral distribution in Iran.

## Minerals

Intense exploration over the past few years has established that Iran has a number of very useful mineral deposits, wide in range, though relatively small in size of actual deposits. For long this situation, together with difficulties of access, restricted exploitation, but within the last 10 years the government in its national Plans has laid increasing emphasis on the development of Iran's mineral resources.

Coal of Jurassic age occurs in the Elburz, mainly north-east of Tehran and north of Damghan. For many years there has been small-scale production from such centres as Shimshak and Lasherak. More important deposits have now been proved in the Kirman area, where reserves may exceed 150 million tons. Mining occurs in two centres near Kirman (Pabedana and Bab Naizu) and is used in the new steel complex at Isfahan. Important new fields were discovered during 1974–75 at Tazreh near Shahrud; and east of Bujnurd. The former may eventually produce half a million tons of coal annually – possibly more; but development in both fields is not yet complete. These new discoveries provide a most useful basis for growing Iranian industries, and as some coal is of coking variety, integration with metallurgical activities is now possible, with new fully mechanized plant.

Iron is worked in a number of localities: near Karaj (where there is a blast furnace), round Isfahan and round Kirman. Most interest now centres on the newly discovered Gogohar field near Baqf, between Kirman and Bandar Abbas. Reserves of magnetite and haematite here are now put at 200 million tons, and of high grade (up to 60%). But the ores are difficult to work and chemically complex, hence major investment is now being made by Plan Organization; and the ores will be treated at Isfahan where a Soviet-financed plant that opened in 1973 is now in process of expansion to reach a target output of 2 million tons per year in 1978 – one-third of Iran's projected total production of steel. Iron oxide occurs in quantity on the island of Hormuz, in association with a rock-salt dome, and has long been worked as 'red ochre'.

Copper will assume major importance, with the exploitation of two newly discovered deposits. The first is at Sar Chesmeh, south of Kirman. Estimated reserves of 750 million tons (half of high grade) make this deposit one of the largest in the world, and the government plans a new town with a rail link to Bandar Abbas, 400 km distant, in what is now an arid, remote area of the Zagros. The second discovery, north of Zahidan in the extreme south-east of Iran, suggests a reserve of over 100 million tons, giving Iran a total of 1000 million tons. By 1978–80, Iran could well rank among major world producers of copper. Other significant producing areas are Anarak, Abbassabad, Zenjam-Tarom, and the Azerbaijan area north-east of Tabriz.

A similar pattern of major new discoveries holds for chrome, which has long been produced on a small scale in the Elburz. Important new discoveries have been made at Bafq, Minab, and Shahrud, in the hill areas behind Bandar Abbas; and around Kirman. Although overall reserves are smaller, Iran could become an important world producer.

Lead and zinc (often in association) are known in many areas, chiefly Anarak, Mianeh, and between Kashan and Isfahan. Plans are in hand to raise production to 150–200000 tons annually. Bauxite is being developed in the region of Kirman – a small smelter is located at Arak, but again plans are in hand for a new and far larger smelter to be located in the southern region.

Turquoise, once regarded as the finest in the world, has for centuries been exploited in Iran, particularly at Nishapur, but competition from American and synthetic stones restricted output. Now, with the world boom in jewelry, prices have risen, and a new major discovery has been made at Damghan. Sulphur, produced mainly from the Zagros west of Bandar Abbas, is also a minor, but useful export.

## Industry

Apart from the Anglo Iranian Oil Company's installation, no really modern industry of any kind could be said to exist in Iran before 1934; though Iran produced some manufactured goods, these were either made by hand, or by simple machinery. Major efforts were made by Reza Shah during 1930–41 to introduce modern plant, and this process has continued, with considerable development in the 1960s of light and moderately heavy industry. Over the past 10 years, major efforts on a massive scale have been made by the government to foster industrial growth in order eventually to be independent of oil revenues. Large 'package' deals involving participation of countries such as the USA, USSR, France, Great Britain, Japan, Italy and West Germany in joint development schemes have been a feature, whilst the Iranian government itself has been a major, sometimes sole participant (for example, as in the Sar Chesmeh copper development). Already, industry contributes over 25% to G.N.P. (more than double that of agriculture) and employs over 2 million workers.

It has long been a basic principle to spread industrial activities as reasonably widely as possible throughout the populated parts of the country, and at the same time to place particular industries close to sources of raw materials, where labour was available and communications good. This meant that whilst most provincial capitals and major route centres obtained some new industrial activities, geographical advantages in location and presence of resources inhibited an even spread. In particular Tehran developed a considerable industrial complex which has made it far and away the largest city in Iran.

About a half of Iranian raw cotton comes from the Isfahan district, and so this town has developed as the principal cotton textile centre of the country, with minor centres at Kasvin, Kirman, Mashad and Yazd, and in the Caspian area (Shahi and Behshahr). Woollen goods are again chiefly produced in Isfahan, being placed conveniently in relation to the great pastoral areas of the central Zagros, but Tabriz, the regional capital of the northern Zagros, and Kasvin are also significant. Jute is woven on a small scale of Rasht and Shahi, whilst silk from local sources is woven at Chalus (Mazanderan).

The carpet industry, for which Iran has long been famous, remains a craft industry carried on by hand, though not now always in small units. There are a growing number of larger factories, but many carpets are still made in the bazaars, or even by tribesmen and women at home. Wool is the chief material used, but cotton is often employed as a foundation or 'warp', because it allows finer work. Silk is sometimes used also. The finest (i.e. closest) work can be done on a cotton or silk warp, and up to 50 knots/cm$^2$ can be achieved with woollen tufts, and 400/cm$^2$ with pure silk tufts. When woollen warp is used, the carpet is heavier, and of a deeper pile, though less fine. Compared with Turkish and Caucasian products, the better Persian carpets have a more vigorous, flowing or curvilinear design, freedom in pattern and brightness, and more varied colours. Turkish and Turki carpets in particular show a stronger influence of patterns based on straight lines or simple motifs, with simpler, cruder colours.

Traditionally, each district of Iran developed its own distinctive designs and colour combinations, e.g. Tabriz specimens employ pastel tints, whilst Sultanabad carpets are more vivid; and the lighter, finer rugs, made on cotton or silk warps, come from Kirman, Tabriz and Tehran. Heavier carpets in wool are associated with the uplands of the Zagros – Shiraz, Hamadan and Khurrumabad. But of late years successful or popular designs have been reproduced outside the region of origin, so the association of a pattern with a locality or style of weaving is now less strict or frequent than it used to be: there is no 'appellation controlée', as with French wines. Kirman is probably the leading carpet-making centre, with other producing towns (besides those already mentioned) Arak, Mashad, Bijar, Kashan and Senna (Sanandaj). Young children, having small fingers, are often employed, and the finished products have a world-wide sale, chiefly in America, to wealthier Middle Easterners, and in Germany and France. Demand has latterly much increased, as a good Persian carpet is a 'hedge' against inflation, hence carpets now rank as 'number one' manufactured export, and second only to petroleum in the general export list. This demand has, however, led in the last few years to poorer workmanship and increasing use of low-grade materials, so the Iranian government is now anxiously seeking remedies to conserve what is, after all, a major national activity, earning $200–400 million annually.

Food-processing still occupies the largest single group of industrial workers. Sugar-refining (beet and cane) is now carried on in a number of centres (chiefly Tehran, but also in the Zagros areas), and flour-milling, fruit- and fish-canning, and oil-pressing are widely distributed. Cement-making has also developed greatly.

Over the last 10–15 years, engineering (mainly light, but increasingly of the 'heavy', basic kind) has developed very rapidly. Besides producing consumer goods on an increasing scale, there is now an electrical and machine industry, with assembly plants for tractors, cars and heavier vehicles, with most major world manufacturers participating. An increasing number of the parts and now whole vehicles are Iranian made. Larger electrical and electronic industries are being set up, and petrochemicals (both heavy and high-grade) are also being developed. Seven more steel mills are planned for the late 1970s: at Isfahan, Ahwaz, Mashad, Bandar Abbas and Bushire. Most of the new industries have developed in or around Tehran, which now has, as an accolade of modern development, a 'smog' problem (as noted earlier), with Isfahan next in importance.

*Five Year Plans*

Iran began her Fifth Five Year Plan in 1973, but the rapid rise in oil revenues at the start of 1974 allowed a major upward revision of all targets, which originally envisaged an average annual growth rate of 14% (the Fourth Plan had achieved one of 10%). The revised Plan expects over 25% annual growth up to 1978 (7% for agriculture, 18% for industry and mining, and 52% for oil and gas). Oil revenues (1974 levels) were assessed at $100 billion for the remaining period of the Plan. Besides petroleum, Iranian officials now believe that Iran has the second, or possibly the largest reserves of natural gas in the world: most of these fields are located offshore and onshore near Bushire and Kangan (Persian/Arab Gulf) and at Sarrakhs in the extreme north-east beyond Mashad. Considerable quantities of gas are now exported by pipeline to the USSR via Asterabad; and there is now a plan to construct a new major pipeline via Orenburg that will bring Soviet and Iranian gas to industrial areas of the Comecon countries, and export a considerable quantity to West Germany.

Another relatively important source of income is tourism. Although Tehran itself is modern and without any really antique building, many Iranian towns, Isfahan, Mashad and Shiraz especially, have mediaeval and older antiquities of great beauty, and the scenery in parts of the Zagros and Elburz is very attractive: foreign tourists now number ½ million, providing growth for a hotel industry; whilst 3 million 'internal' pilgrims visit Mashad. The Fifth Plan, therefore, includes a large item for hotel development.

Overall, the Plans are aiming at bringing Iran to world rank as an industrial 'developed' power. Already, Iran ranks twelfth in the world in terms of terms of foreign reserve holdings, and aspires to rank with EEC countries as regards G.N.P. per head of population. The progress achieved is impressive: in 1960 there were perhaps 72 000 motor vehicles registered in Tehran, and now there are 1 million, and per capita income rose by 600% in 10 years, even prior to the major oil revenue increases of 1974. On the other hand, there are certain serious obstacles to realization of Plan aims. These are (1) the lack of skilled manpower and technical ability, particularly in the 'middle range', where ¾ million skilled workers are needed – Iran is moving towards recruitment of Turkish workers repatriated from Europe, (2) difficulties over imbalance of resources and settlement, (3) insufficient infrastructures – communications, schools, etc., and (4) since 1975 a shortage of new capital. In this year Iran was forced to realize that development was proceeding too rapidly, at least for the time being, and had to borrow abroad to maintain cash flows for projects and commitments already entered into. Given further rises in the price of oil, this may be no more than a temporary 'hiccup', but as in many other parts of the world during 1975–76, spending plans had to be cut back to some extent.

## People

The first census of Iran in 1956 showed 18945000 people exclusive of nomads who may have numbered 1½ to 2 million: it is now regarded as an under-enumeration. A second census 10 years later gave 25800000 inhabitants: this is thought to have been over-generous with urban populations; whilst the latest census (1976) reported 33,591,875 people. As will be seen from fig. 11.9, densities vary considerably, with most Iranians living in the north and west of the country, and fewest in the south and east, with several regions almost uninhabited. Water, soil and topography are clearly the dominant influencing factors, with the increasing dominance of Tehran as a metropolitan area, not only itself as a very rapidly growing city, but also in that former small towns in its vicinity are also sharing in its expansion: Karaj, for example, a small road junction until quite recently, now ranks as 16th largest town in Iran, after being merely 70th in 1956.

Over the past 10 years, the population of Iran has increased by 2·7% annually – some 34000000 persons. The natural rate of increase of the rural population would, however, appear to be approximately 3% per annum; but there is migration on a massive scale to urban areas, and so by the later 1970s there is expected to be an even balance between urban and rural groups, moving rapidly towards greater urbanization, with, by the early 1990s, approximately 30% only rural and 70% urban. With a present annual growth rate of 3·1% but a lower, and declining, birthrate in towns, projection of future population numbers is hazardous, but Iran's present 35 million is expected to become somewhere near 50 million, or possibly over 60 million, before the end of the century. Family planning, now energetically fostered by government, will, it is hoped, bring down the annual rate of growth to under 2% per annum.

One most obvious feature in Iran is, therefore, the rapid growth of

Iranian towns, with heavy demands on infrastructure: communications, schools, water, electricity and housing. These are not always met at once, and so the development of 'shanty' suburbs can be a feature in some towns, though distinctly less than elsewhere in the Middle East. It is, however, also right to state that in Iran there has been energetic reconstruction in many towns (e.g. Shiraz and Tabriz) with broad new streets laid out through former slums. Although there is a risk of only temporary and precarious employment, boom conditions of the last few years, with growing shortage of skilled manpower, have exerted enormous 'pull', by which the arduous daily agricultural routine, with few free days and the cramping social and financial restrictions of village life, can be exchanged for a more 'industrial' type of existence with more restricted hours of work, freedom to change one's occupation, the glitter (such as this may be to a poor immigrant) of urban shopping centres, and, above all, the chance of sudden opportunity, which is much more likely in a growing town than in a stagnant village. It is this last element which brings so many Iranians into the town. Now that public order and security are stronger, fewer are willing to live frugal harsh lives in remote spots under the feudal control of a landlord. The motor bus to Tehran or Isfahan has altered this – hence formerly moderately densely populated hill areas in the Elburz and northern Zagros especially are losing their inhabitants.

The same process has greatly affected the nomads, who were once particularly numerous and powerful, usually with a tribal organization. The broken nature of the Zagros especially has fostered the emergence of various sharply differing cultural groups. The Kurds speak an Aryan language and are fairly strict Sunni Moslems, the Qashqai are of Mongoloid ancestry and use a Turki language; there are others who use Arabic and Baluchi, whilst the largest tribal grouping of all, the Bakhtiari who speak an Aryan language related to Kurdish, are only nominal Moslems. With the severe decline in numbers, from over 2 million a few decades ago, to about ⅓ million or less, tribal life now plays a far smaller part in Iranian life.

A fourth element in the Iranian population is the heavy predominance of young people. Some 55% of the population is aged 20 or less, and the 'working' element in the population has fallen from 32% to 28% over the past few years, even putting the start of 'working life' at twelve years of age, as do official statistics. Again, this is no new feature, since Iran shares the problem with most other Middle Eastern countries, but it highlights the need for school building, and the extent to which juvenile labour remains a feature of the country, the more so as very few women, still, work outside the home. A final feature, now giving much concern, is a 'brain drain' of some of the best educated and active elements of the population. This mainly affects doctors and scientists, who settle in America and Europe (West Germany especially). For a country which

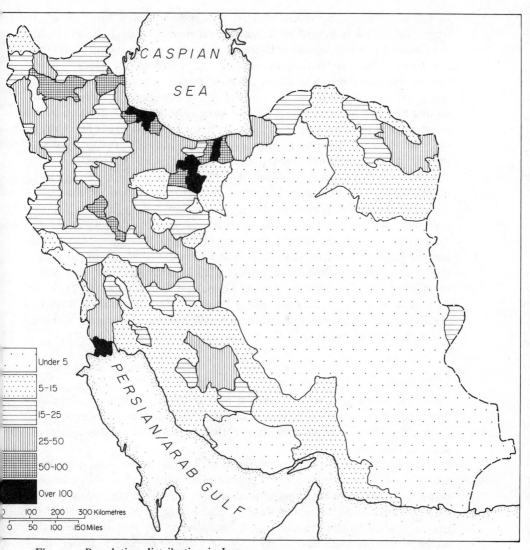

*Fig.* 11.9 Population distribution in Iran.

is crucially in need of trained manpower, this annual loss is highly important. Apart from those practising in Tehran, there are no more than 1200 Iranian trained doctors in the rest of the country.

## Communications and towns

Iran has long been a centre of routeways linking east and west, but as a result of invasion and misrule in the later Middle Ages, and the change in space-relationships which diverted commerce from China and India to the sea, the road system of Iran decayed, and was for a time an important factor in retarding economic advance. In a large country – it is 1300 km from the Caspian to the head of the Persian/Arab Gulf, and 2500 km from Tabriz in the north-west to the extreme south-east – road construction and maintenance is difficult, but of late years much effort has gone into constructing all-weather roads between the larger cities, so that by the late 1970s Iran will have 50000 km of roads, of which over a quarter will have an asphalt surface. A major new highway is in building from Mashad via Kirman to Bandar Abbas. This will greatly open up the east and south, particularly the new mineral areas of Kirman.

Railway building has been slow: it is said that Iran is one of the most difficult areas in the world for construction. Before 1927 two non-standard extensions entered Iran, one from the Indian rail system as far as Zahidan, and the other from the Russian system through Julfa as far as Tabriz. In 1927 Reza Shah planned the first trans-Iranian railway from Bandar Shah on the Caspian via Tehran to Bandar Shahpur on the Gulf, and 11 years later the line was complete. Later extensions have been made to Mashad and Tabriz and towards Qum; and a link with the Turkish system is now complete. Plans are in hand to join Isfahan with Bushire via Shiraz, and extend from Kirman both to Zahidan and to Bandar Abbas. Electrification has started in the Tehran area.

*Towns*

These have long held a predominant part in the life of Iran, and recent immigration has swollen their size considerably. A few years ago, only four cities had a population larger than 200000; now the figure is approaching fifteen.

The exceptional size and importance of Tehran (pop. 1975, 4000000) arises from its position on the Veramin plain – the largest of a number of tongues of fertile land that extend southwards from the flanks of the Elburz range into the central desert – and partly from its command of routes. Owing to the presence of a 'dead heart' in Iran the choice of a capital has not been easy – any town was bound to have an ex-central position, and relations with the rest of the country would be of necessity rather difficult. Tehran is, however, situated astride the important east–west route that follows the southern slopes of the Elburz, at a point where the route divides, one branch continuing west-north-west towards Azerbaijan and Asia Minor, the other turning south-westwards to the central Zagros, Baghdad and the Persian/Arab Gulf. From Tehran northwards, three separate passes, from east to west the Gudar Guduk (2150 m), the Imamzadeh (2750 m) and the upper Chalus (3500 m), give access to the densely populated Caspian lowlands.

The supremacy of Tehran dates only from 1788, when it was chosen

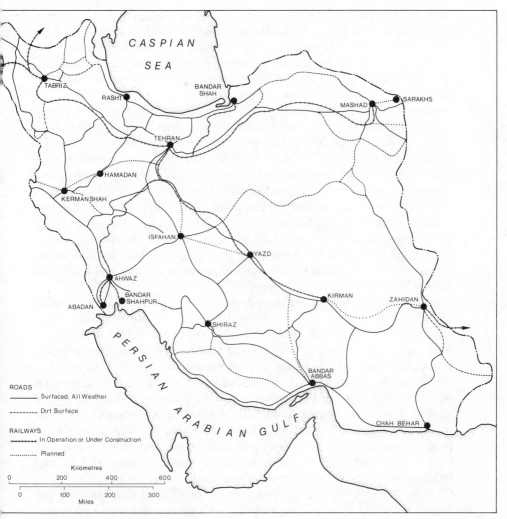

CASPIAN
SEA

TABRIZ
RASHT
BANDAR SHAH
MASHAD
SARAKHS
TEHRAN
HAMADAN
KERMANSHAH
ISFAHAN
YAZD
AHWAZ
BANDAR SHAHPUR
ABADAN
KIRMAN
ZAHIDAN
SHIRAZ
BANDAR ABBAS
CHAH BEHAR

PERSIAN

ARABIAN GULF

ROADS

———— Surfaced, All Weather

--------- Dirt Surface

RAILWAYS

++++++ In Operation or Under Construction

............ Planned

Kilometres

0    200    400    600

0    100    200    300
Miles

*Fig.* 11.10 Communications in Iran.

as capital by the Qajars who had hitherto used it as a wintering centre for their animals. Other cities throughout Iranian history, mainly in the south-west, had functioned as national capital, and one can see in this shift of influence the operation of several factors: firstly, the difficulty of finding an adequate central site for a capital; secondly, the enhanced economic importance of the northern provinces within the last two centuries; and thirdly, the change in political influence as reflected in the northward movement of the capital.

As the result of extensive building first by Reza Shah, and then during the unprecedented 'boom' of the 1950s and later, Tehran has a very modern air, with none of the medieval or later monuments that characterize Isfahan or Shiraz. Towards the foothills which the suburbs of the city now reach, there is an expensive residential quarter; towards the south lies a rapidly expanding industrial zone. Besides the occupations related to function as capital city – administration, services, catering, printing, etc. – the city is now the principal industrial centre of Iran, with engineering, consumer goods, chemical, textile, electronic, building (bricks and cement) and food-processing industries, amounting to about one-third or more of the modern plant in Iran.

Important factors in the rise of Tehran have been the growth of road and rail communications during the last 30 years, and the development of nearby coal resources, with other minerals within moderately easy reach (copper from Anarak and Abbassabad; lead, antimony, nickel and sulphur from Samnan). But most of all, Tehran is now the indisputable metropolis of Iran with 15% of the total population of the country, nearly 25% of all industrial workers, over 35% of gross national production, two-thirds of all students, and three-quarters of all cars and lorries. It is growing at about 5% per annum.

Isfahan is now the second largest urban centre of Iran and, in contrast to Tehran, its history as a continuously inhabited site goes back to c. 1000 B.C. It is located in the centre of a basin watered by the Zaindeh Rud. Abundance of water supplies and a rich soil make Isfahan a highly productive agricultural region, but its location on the piedmont at the transition from mountain to desert, and above all its strategic command of routes (Isfahan means 'troop assembly point'), particularly those leading through the Zagros to the Gulf and the Tigris lowlands have given the city continuing importance. With supplies of raw cotton and wool produced in the neighbourhood, and now supplemented by imports of wool from Australia, Isfahan is the largest textile centre of Iran, the industry being carried on in modern mills and as a bazaar and home craft. Clothing, carpets and luxury cloths are the chief products, but there are large food-processing plants, milling and paper- and cement-manufacturing. The new steel mill is an important adjunct. Isfahan is one of the ancient capitals of Iran, and its most splendid monument is perhaps the Maidan, an enormous open square in which the game of polo is said to have originated – an indication of the links with horse-breeding and pastoralism, as well as with military activities. This and other monuments attract a growing number of tourists.

Tabriz is situated in the upper part of the Maidan Chai, one of the largest valleys that drain into the Urmia basin, in a district where there are numerous small alluvial fans formed by erosion of soft lava. The soil is hence extremely fertile, and this, together with the presence of non-saline water, makes Tabriz a rich agricultural area. Moreover, the site of the city, close to the Turkish and Russian frontiers, gives it an importance as a centre of communications. There is considerable exchange of products between the farmers of the lowlands round Tabriz and the pastoralists of the more distant uplands; and a large market is one of the features of the city. Industries based on the agricultural and pastoral products of the two regions (tanning, fruit-drying, soap-boiling, distilling and textile manufacturing) are carried on, partly by means of modern plants introduced by Reza Shah. Carpet-making is on an extensive scale, and there is a growing amount of trade with Turkey and the USSR. The largest town of the north-west and a former capital of Iran, Tabriz is the chief city of Azerbaijan, and has played a notable part in political affairs, often as the centre of Kurdish and Azerbaijani dissident movements – Turkish is as important a language here as Pahlevi. For this reason it has received rather fewer of the state-sponsored industries than, for instance, Isfahan, which has overtaken it in point of size. Tabriz, however, is now starting to benefit by the improved communications, especially by road with Europe. One handicap is, however, location on a major tectonic fracture line, making the city liable to earth tremors, hence buildings are not generally built high.

Mashad has profited latterly from better, quieter political conditions and is also developing rapidly as the regional capital of the extreme north-east. It grew after the destruction of a nearby settlement, Tus, in 1220. Mashad was deliberately created in the nineteenth century a major centre of Shi'a pilgrimage, but in addition it exercises the functions of regional market and administrative centre, with a variety of smaller-scale transformation industries and light engineering.

The other Iranian towns have the functions of route-centre, local market and, often, manufacturing site. Centralizing the economic activities of their region, they facilitate exchange of agricultural, pastoral and manufactured products, and have developed manufacturing trades based on local raw materials. They also function as staging-posts for bus transport, and as administrative bases – in a relatively empty land, a regional centre still has important, undisputed functions. Specialization may exist: Rasht has jute, tea, and flour mills, and handles most of the trade (in caviare, tea, isinglass and salt fish) with Caspian Iran and the USSR. Carpet-making is prominent in Kirman and Kashan, sugar- and oil-refining at Kermanshah, and oil-pressing at Yazd. Textiles (chiefly cotton) are important at Shiraz, and wine-making is a minor industry in many places, especially at Shiraz and Kazvin. Qum is another major centre of pilgrimage.

*Ports*

Iran now has a major port problem. The enormously increased volume of imports during the last few years has meant that the ports, small both in number and in scale, that sufficed for Iranian trading are now quite inadequate. Abadan, built by the former Anglo Iranian Oil Co. after 1910 purely as an oil terminal, is by far the largest installation, but its function is still chiefly to handle oil, and its landward communications (partly because of the braided nature of the river channels) are restricted. Most Iranian traffic (well over half, excluding oil exports) is handled at Khorramshahr (Mohammerah), which lies 18 km above Abadan, at the confluence of the Shatt el Arab and the Karun river. Until recently the fact that the entire Shatt was in Iraqi territory (with the frontier at the east bank and not along the thalweg) was a further handicap. Now, ships must wait to unload, and in 1977 the delay was several weeks. Even when goods are unloaded, they may not be moved off the port because lorries and lorry drivers are in short supply – there is a 'black market' in the former. Currently, up to 1 m tons of imports may be warehoused or stood in the open awaiting clearance inland.

Hence major efforts have been made to improve port facilities: chiefly at Bandar Abbas, which is now equipped to handle 2 million tons per year. About two-thirds of this capacity is for general cargo, and the remainder for mineral ores other than petroleum. This development is related to the increased attention now given to expansion in the south, undertaken partly to diversify and reduce the pressure of the Shatt el Arab, and partly for political reasons – to avoid dependence on the Shatt el Arab and upper Gulf, and also to bring a hitherto isolated and little developed region of Iran more fully into national life. Another important development is at Bandar Shahpur, the regional terminus of the Trans-Iranian railway, which now ranks second after Khorramshahr as a port: between them, these two so far handle over 70% of Iran's trade by sea (oil always excluded). Bandar Abbas has also undergone development, both for commerce and also as a base for the expanding Iranian navy, which is now a significant element in the geopolitics of the Gulf. Bandar Pahlevi (formerly Enzeli) is the chief Iranian port on the Caspian, the planned railport terminus at Bandar Shah having been badly sited and now silted up. Ahwaz is a transhipment point on the Karun, Iran's only navigable river. A stretch of rapids above the town makes further ascent impossible, and the importance of Ahwaz has much increased since the opening up of south-west Iran by oil interests.

A development of some interest, deriving from the new affluence in some strata of Iranian society, is the growth of seaside resorts for holidays and weekends, as for example, at Chah-behar, formerly a tiny and remote fishing centre, and at a number of centres on the Caspian shore, once described by an English poet as 'lone', but no longer so, with tourist hotels that range from the modest to opulently luxurious.

# 12 Asia Minor

## Physical

Like Iran, Asia Minor consists essentially of an inner plateau ringed by mountain ranges that for the great part fall away steeply on their outer margins, either to the sea or to lowland areas. Only in the extreme east of Asia Minor are the mountain ranges continued without break; and there the confused highland topography of eastern Anatolia merges on the north-east into the Caucasus, and on the south-east into the Zagros. Structurally, Asia Minor consists of fold systems grouped round two nuclear areas: the Menderes block in the south-west, and the Kirsehir block in the centre (fig. 12.1). Geographical sub-regions may be distinguished as follows:

(1) The Black Sea coastlands extending from the Caucasus of Russia as far west as the region of the Bosphorus.

(2) The Aegean-Marmara coastlands, designated respectively (a) and (b) in fig. 12.2.

(3) The Mediterranean coastlands.

(4) The central plateau.

(5) The eastern highlands, subdivisible into the main highland area (a), and the piedmont (b) that overlooks and drops eventually to the Tigris–Euphrates lowlands.

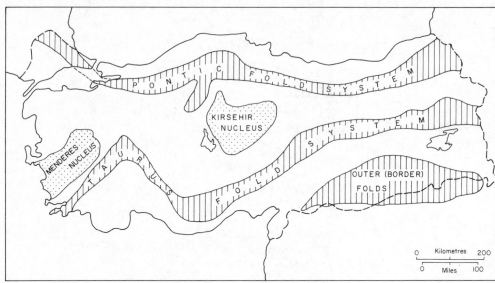

*Fig.* 12.1 Asia Minor: structure.

## The Black Sea

Present features have come into existence as the result of the foundering of the Black Sea region in Pliocene times. An extensive series of east–west trending fracture-lines was developed on the northern side of the main plateau of Asia Minor; and differential movement along these fracture-lines, with downthrow mainly towards the north, has produced the present abrupt and harbourless coastline. Fracturing did not, however, take place in a simple pattern; faults are arranged in arcs rather than in a single straight line, so that between Eregli (Heraclea) and Sinop there is a northward bulge of the coastline which is sharply defined by a small number of bold fracture-lines; whilst further east, between Sinop and Samsun, smaller interlocking faults have given rise to an embayment with a somewhat more irregular and indented coast. In the extreme east, beyond Samsun, there is a return to a simpler pattern of a few large faults comparable with those in the west; but extensive lava flows along the fault-lines have obscured the fault-planes, and again produced a broken, irregular coastline that contrasts markedly in appearance with conditions in the extreme west, although fundamentally there is a similarity in structural origin. A modern interpretation of this structural pattern is that it represents part of zone of lateral displacement between major tectonic plates.

The steep and rocky coast of the western Black Sea region, which is only occasionally broken down into bays and estuaries by the erosive action of rivers, is succeeded inland by an irregular line of highlands that

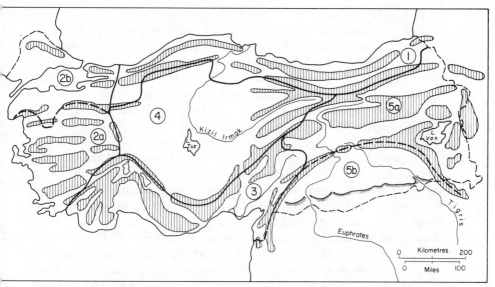

*Fig.* 12.2 Turkey: geographical units.

rise to 2000 m within 25–35 km from the sea, with only a restricted area of coastal plain, sometimes entirely absent. Eastwards of Sinop, mountains front the coast on an even more imposing scale. Behind Trabzon (Trebizond) and Rize the maximum heights attained are 3000–4000 m, and the ranges are distinguished by special names. At Trabzon the coastal ranges are known as the Cakirgol Dagh, and further east, near the Caucasus, as the Tatus Dagh. The entire coastal uplands are really a series of horst blocks, some relatively undisturbed, others tilted; and the higher elevation of summits in the east is due to the outpouring of lava, giving a series of volcanic cones and vents superimposed upon the general plateau level.

Further inland still, towards the south, the coastal ranges give way to a series of lowland troughs that are defined once again by east–west running tectonic lines, most probably part of the lateral tearing between plates. Cross-faulting and minor displacement have occurred so that this inland lowland region is not a single simple rift, but rather a series of irregular downwarped basins, sometimes opening one from another, sometimes separated by low divides. Later erosion by rivers has reduced the height of these divides, so that an interior lowland valley system, broad and open in the west, but increasingly narrow in the east, is now a feature of the total Black Sea coastal region, and can be traced from the Gulf of Izmit in the north-east of the Sea of Marmara as far as the Russian frontier.

The rivers of the Black Sea coastlands consist chiefly of short torrents cascading from the coastal ranges towards the sea. Here and there, however, valleys have been cut back far enough to reach the inner lowland trough, where an east–west (longitudinal or subsequent) drainage pattern has developed. The larger rivers, therefore, consist of two distinct portions: a long upper reach, with a generally east–west trend, and a shorter lower stretch aligned from south to north, in which the river breaks through intervening ridges – often by a gorge or rapids to reach the Black Sea. Examples of such rivers are the Çoruh, Çelkit, Kizil Irmak, and Yenice.

The steep and rocky nature of the coast, absence of harbours, and difficulties in the way of penetrating inland, have all restricted human activities in this region, so that whilst population densities are higher in the western coastal zones than in the immediate interior, they are distinctly lower than those in the Trabzon-Rize area further east. On the west, the absence of harbours is particularly noticeable; further east, where the coastline is more indented, the mountain barrier is higher. Another disadvantage is that, because of the cascades and gorges on the lower courses of the rivers, very few river valleys provide easy routes inland – it is significant that none of the rivers mentioned in the previous paragraph have any major settlement at their mouth, and all important towns stand away from the larger streams. Instead, the inner lowland region has come to serve as a line of communications, which, therefore, tend to run from west to east from the Aegean region, rather than southwards from the Black Sea coast itself. In the western half of the trough access from one lowland basin to another is relatively easy, and rail and road construction are facilitated. A considerable handicap throughout the whole region is, however, a liability to frequent and devastating earthquakes related to active plate movements. Thus population densities are somewhat lower than might be expected in comparison with the Aegean coastlands. Whilst a narrow coastal strip in the extreme east carries what is for Asia Minor a dense population, inhabitants are more scattered along the western coastlands and concentrated in a relatively small number of districts where there is a special advantage, e.g. the presence of coal, easy access to the interior, or a patch of level fertile terrain.

## The Aegean coastlands

There is no distinctive break between the Black Sea coastlands just described and the Aegean region. The great fault-lines that define the coast of the eastern Black Sea continue without interruption as far as southern Bulgaria, and the foundered trough zone of the interior can be traced from the lake-studded lowlands at the head of the Gulf of Izmit into the

Gulf itself, and finally into the northern basin of the Sea of Marmara. Thus east–west trending tectonic lines are again outstanding in the Aegean area, not merely in the extreme north near the Black Sea, but also as far south as the island of Rhodes. The broad valleys of the Gediz and Büyük Menderes are east–west running rifts enlarged by later erosion.

Besides the existence of east–west fracture-lines, two other major influences must be noted. These are (*a*) extensive cross-faulting with a north–south trend, and (*b*) foundering of the central portion of the Aegean, with consequent invasion by the sea. Occurrence of cross-faulting and foundering in the Dardanelles and Bosphorus justifies the inclusion of the Straits district with the Aegean region, rather than as a continuation of the Black Sea coastal region; and differences in geomorphology and human occupance justify further separation as a Marmara sub-region (*a*) and an Aegean sub-region proper (*b*). Cross-faulting and later drowning have led to the development of a highly intricate, broken coastline, with many irregularly shaped islands and long, twisting estuaries. The islands are small horsts standing above the sea floor; and on the mainland of Asia Minor the same conditions are repeated, with irregular upland horsts serving to separate broad and shallow rift-valleys. Broad similarities in tectonic pattern to the Suez–Sinai region of the northern Red Sea suggest small, but important oil possibilities, a matter now in dispute between Greece and Turkey; and there have in fact been oil 'shows' known for many years in the Marmara region.

Involved cross-faulting with later erosion and drowning have been responsible for the formation of the Bosphorus and Dardanelles. In the extreme north along the Black Sea, an extensive mass of resistant granite and gneiss has been fractured by the east–west trending faults, leaving a narrow neck of upland joining Europe and Asia, with the Black Sea to the north, and the Sea of Marmara to the south.[1] This neck, or long narrow horst, broadens out westwards to form the Istranca highlands of European Turkey, and is tilted towards the south, so that there is a scarp-face towards the north, down which a number of small torrents fall steeply to the Black Sea. On the southern (Marmara) side there is a much gentler dip slope, and a more extensive drainage system has developed. In many instances lines of weakness due to small north-north-east–south-south-west trending faults have been eroded into narrow valleys, and a number of small synclines have also been occupied. Thus erosion along one such north-north-east running fault gradually pushed back the head of a small stream flowing to the Sea of Marmara, until the highland ridge was cut through, and a channel opened between the

[1] The scale of this fault system can be gauged from the extent of downthrow in the Sea of Marmara, which reaches over 1000 m in depth, with parts of the nearby coastlands 500 m above sea-level.

Black Sea and the Sea of Marmara. A tributary of this stream that flowed partly in a synclinal valley also entered the Bosphorus on the western side: and subsequent drowning of this tributary has given rise to the Golden Horn (see fig. 12.1). The Bosphorus is 25 km in length, and on average 1·5 km wide, but it narrows in places to less than 200 m. Both banks, Asiatic and European, rise steeply from the water, and form a succession of cliffs, coves and landlocked bays, which provides a highly scenic, increasingly attractive effect. Most of the shores are densely wooded, and are occupied by numerous towns and villages.

The Dardanelles Strait has been formed in a similar manner – by erosion along fracture-lines, and later drowning; but the rock series of this latter region are much softer, being composed of limestones and sandstones, hence erosion has been much more extensive, and land forms are gentler. The Dardanelles is 40 km long, and increases in width towards the south, from 4 km at the northern extremity to 7·5 km in the south. Another contrast is in vegetation – the shores of the Dardanelles are only sparsely covered by trees, the chief vegetation type being a low garrigue. Again unlike the Bosphorus, the Dardanelles has few settlements of any kind along its shores; the whole region being generally empty and desolate and given over to rough grazing. Because of intense evaporation in the eastern Mediterranean, together with considerable supplies of river water in the Black Sea, there is a continuous flow of markedly cold water southwards from the Black Sea, producing a strong current in the Bosphorus and Dardanelles. This current averages 5 km/h at Istanbul, and 2·5–3 km/h in the Dardanelles. There is also a deep counter-current that flows close to the bed, in a northerly direction. The feat of Leander, who apparently swam across and back regularly to meet his girlfriend, is thus more than would first appear from just looking at the map.

Further south, the immediate hinterland of the Aegean Sea is made up of a complex of east–west trending fault-valleys, broken at frequent intervals by rather less strongly developed north–south running fractures. This development has imposed a markedly rectangular pattern of detached horsts and somewhat fjord-like valleys. An excellent example is the valley of the Büyük Menderes, with its numerous sharp elbows and tributary valleys set at right angles to the main stream.

Other similar, but less extensive valleys are (from north to south): the Sakariya, which runs mainly in a north–south trending rift, and hence reaches the Black Sea, though passing within a short distance of the Gulf of Izmit; the Simav, which enters the Sea of Marmara; and the Gediz and Dalaman, both of which reach the Aegean. Generally speaking, all valleys are broad and flat-bottomed and have relatively steep sides. The floors are covered by rich alluvium deposited in great quantities in the lower reaches, and as a result, an extensive floodplain has been built up,

*Fig.* 12.3 Western Asia Minor.

upon which the river develops a classic 'meander' pattern. To find well-developed meanders in a region of broken plateaux and highland massifs may seem unusual, until it is remembered that the lower valleys of most rivers have been formed entirely by tectonic action, and not by fluvial erosion. Large quantities of silt are carried down towards the coast, and the lower ends of the valleys are being steadily filled up, so that the mouths of the rivers are advancing westwards towards the Aegean Sea. The Büyük Menderes mouth is now, for example, some 45 km further west than it was in Roman times.

The Marmara sub-region is characterized by generally smoother topography, though not without imposing contrasts, by the greater extent of lowland (some of which, as we have seen, is lake-studded), and above all by intensity of human exploitation and occupation. About one half of Turkey's urban population is concentrated in this region, mainly, of course, in Istanbul and satellites, but also in a number of moderately sized towns such as Bursa and Izmit. On the Asiatic side, in contrast to conditions in European Turkey, rural population is relatively dense.

The Aegean area proper – sub-region (b) – has more craggy and arresting topography, with higher peaks and restricted areas of lowland. When drained and cultivated the valleys are extremely productive, and, with the Marmara sub-region, the Aegean still remains the most prosperous and advanced part of Turkey. Malaria was for long a major disadvantage, but this has declined. Certain of the larger valleys are important as routeways to the interior of Asia Minor, since they rise relatively gradually to the inner plateau region. In some instances, however, as with the Simav and Dalaman valleys, the lowland ends at a cross-fault, with the valley shut in by mountain massifs, and hence useless for major communications. This partly explains the dominance of one city, Izmir, in this southern region.

### The Mediterranean coastlands

Here there is a sharp contrast with the last region described, since fold ranges, not rift-valleys and horst blocks, are the chief structural feature. Along the southern edge of the Anatolian plateau, a series of folded arcs has been developed; but because of the complexity of the inner plateau region, around which the arcs have been folded, the fold structures themselves are highly irregular, with sudden changes in trend. Structural features consist in some parts of parallel ranks of folds, in others of single anticlines, and again in others of overthrusts and nappes.

The westernmost arc can be traced from the district of Fethiye north-eastwards towards Afyonkarahissar, then south-eastwards towards Silifke. This series of folds, known as the Western Taurus, is not disposed entirely symmetrically, since the western limb of the arc is shorter and more irregular than the eastern limb. In the north, the Western Taurus folds are closely packed against the plateau of Anatolia; and, because of recent formation, rivers occupying synclinal valleys have not always been sufficiently long in existence to have cut valleys leading outwards to the sea. Numerous lakes – most of which are saline – are therefore characteristic of the northern part of the Western Taurus; a second feature is the completeness of the mountain wall, which acts as a barrier to movement. Roads are few; no rail communications exist with the rest of Turkey, and the whole of the region is in marked isolation from its neighbours.

To the south, fronting the Mediterranean, small streams reach the sea, and have built up a lowland plain, that is spoken of as the Plain of Antalya. Here the soil is fertile, although marshy in some places; but the prevalence of malaria and difficulties of communication with the remainder of Turkey for long hindered development. The coast is straight and shelving because of the rapidity of deposition of sediment from the rivers; and harbours are thus poor and infrequent. As a result, the Antalya plain for long remained sparsely populated, but with eradication of malaria, improved communications and attraction to tourism, there is now considerable development in this area of very fertile soil and favourable climate.

East of Silifke, the Western Taurus gives way to a second arc, with an abrupt change of trend. This second fold range, the main Taurus, runs north-eastwards from Silifke as a single narrow fold, and though distinctly narrower than the Western Taurus, the main Taurus is much higher, reaching 3700 m in the Ala Dagh region. Owing, however, to its restricted width, erosion has been more active, and, as we have seen, a number of narrow and precipitous river valleys have been cut right through the entire chain at certain points. These gorges offer practicable routes through the mountain barrier, and one such defile, that of the Yeziloluk, a tributary of the Tarsus river, forms the well-known Cilician Gates – a relatively easy, but rather indirect route between central Anatolia and the Mediterranean coast: another valley, that of the Çakit river, offers a more direct but steeper passage, and is now used by the railway from Ankara to Aleppo.

To the east and south-east, a further series of fold ranges runs parallel to the main Taurus system. These are known in a general way as the Anti-Taurus range, but the name is loosely applied, and two smaller ranges, structurally an undoubted part of the Anti-Taurus and of a similar trend, are separately distinguished as the Amanus range and the Kurd Dagh. The latter can be termed the last member of the Anatolian mountain system: further to the east and south-east the land drops to form the low plateau and plain of northern Syria; whilst to the south-west the Amanus and Kurd Dagh can be traced respectively into the Karpass and Troödos ranges of Cyprus.

The Anti-Taurus region is topographically difficult and geologically complex. Its northern portion is largely buried under lava sheets, some of ancient, some of recent origin. Between the upfolds lie valleys, sometimes mere slits and gorges, sometimes, especially towards the east, broader alluvium-covered lowlands that support a relatively dense population. Chief of these lowland areas are the Elbistan plain and the upper Ceyhan valley centring on the town of Maras. Five parallel ranges can be discerned within the Anti-Taurus system, four of which die away about 65 km to the north-east of Adana and give rise to a lowland basin, the Seyhan-Ceyhan plain. The fifth range continues further to the south-west as the Misis Dagh, and forms the western side of the Gulf of Iskanderun. The Gulf lies between two fold ranges, the Amanus and the Misis Dagh, and owes its continued existence as a deep-water gulf to the absence of any large river entering it from the north-east. A short distance to the west, what would appear to have been a similar gulf between fold ridges has been filled up by silt brought down by the Seyhan river, and now forms a plain, with a low-lying, lagoon type of coastline.

The Seyhan plain is in many respects similar to the Antalya plain of the western Mediterranean coastlands: there are the same features of low relief, a rich alluvial soil, a straight shelving coastline and, formerly, considerable prevalence of malaria. The Seyhan plain is, however, much less isolated by its surrounding mountain chains, as a number of cols give access to central Anatolia, eastern Asia Minor and north-western Syria. Hence the Seyhan region carries a markedly denser population than its western counterpart, particularly in the slightly higher parts where drainage is easier; and certain districts have greatly developed recently as important crop-growing areas (cotton especially).

### The central plateau

This region consists essentially of an extensive and irregular plateau ringed on all sides by higher mountain ranges. In the north, east and south the mountain ring is well defined, being 600–1200 m higher than the plateau it surrounds; but on the west, towards the Aegean coastlands, the hills are fewer and less imposing. The plateau itself consists of a rolling upland diversified by numerous sunken basins, or *ova*, that are occupied by marshes and mud flats; and also by small highland massifs that consist either of volcanic cones or horst blocks. The floors of the *ovas* stand at about 1000 m above sea-level, that of the largest *ova* (Lake Tuz) being 980 m in altitude. The general level of the plateau surface may be taken as between 1000 m and 1500 m, whilst the upland masses reach 1800–2500 m above sea-level. Because of its *ova* morphology, Lake Tuz is shallow, and varies enormously in area according to recent rainfall – from little more than a salt marsh to many hundreds of square kilometres in extent.

Towards the east, the plateau is about 300 m higher and, in contrast to the confused structures of the western plateau, uplands tend to occur more often in the form of definite ridges with a well-marked trend. Volcanic cones on a large scale are also a feature, some reaching 3000–3700 m in height.

At one time the entire plateau region of Anatolia probably consisted of a series of small basins of inland drainage, with no outlet to the sea, i.e. conditions closely approximate to those of present-day Iran. Differential earth movements related to warping of tectonic plates – downthrow on the northern (Black Sea) side, and uplift on the southern (Taurus) side – seem, however, to have increased the erosive power of streams on the northern flanks of the plateau, so that these have cut back through the mountain range and now drain wide areas of the plateau itself. The basins of the Sakariya, Kizil Irmak and Yesil Irmak cover more than half the plateau, leaving only the south-west as a region of aretic drainage. The rivers themselves are often deeply entrenched below the level of the plateau; and their valleys, consisting in places of a series of captured *ovas* linked by gorges, are irregular and discontinuous. The whole surface of the northern plateau is deeply eroded, with, in many districts, precipitous valley walls, and sheer, rugged hillsides.

The enclosed basins of the south-west are disposed in a rough crescent between Afyonkarahissar (west), Konya (south) and Kayseri (east). In the absence of drainage, there are no deep valleys, and the whole region is open and undulating, a feature which has favoured the growth of road and rail communications. It will be recalled that Konya was the starting point of the old Baghdad Railway.

Because of its enclosed nature, much of the central plateau of Asia Minor is arid and supports little plant or animal life. Wooded areas are confined to the extreme north-west and north-east; and cultivation is restricted to the neighbourhood of rivers, in parts where the valleys are sufficiently wide to allow terracing, or where an *ova* structure provides a stretch of level ground. For the greater part, the central plateau is bare and monotonous country given over to grazing.

## The eastern highlands

There is little physical unity in eastern Turkey. The sub-region distinguished as 5 *a* in fig. 12.2 consists in the main of a series of very considerable mountain ranges eroded here and there into narrow valleys, whilst region 5 *b* could be distinguished as a foreland, first (in the north) of hill ranges that are, however, distinctly lower in altitude and more broken, and then (in the extreme south) the northernmost limits of the undulating plain that continues on through Syria and Iraq. Further diversifying elements are the presence of several large river basins – those of the Aras, Tigris and Euphrates – and the occurrence of a number of *ovas*, some with outward, some with closed drainage. Vast outpourings of recent lava have buried whole valleys, giving a high-level plateau surface – fairly level but climatically inhospitable – and one such eruption from the cone of Nemrut has blocked a river valley and impounded the water to form Lake Van.

The mountain ranges have a confused trend. On the north, the folds bordering the Black Sea coast run at first in an east–west direction, but later, as in the Gavur Dagh near Erzerum, the trend alters to south-west–north-east, turning once again to the original direction on approach to the Caucasus system. Further south, in the region of Erzincan–El Aziz, the line of the Anti-Taurus is continued by a series of folds that later swing round in a great arc towards the south-east, where they form first the Kurdish Taurus (south-west of Lake Van), and finally merge with the Zagros range. In the hollow part of the arc lies an expanse of plateau country (region of Diyarbekir, Mardin and Urfa) which topographically can be regarded as the northernmost extension of the Syrian steppe.

The northern and eastern parts of eastern Turkey form the ancient country of Armenia. Here, because of the extremely recent volcanic outpourings, soil cover is often very thin or entirely absent. The rivers have cut immense gorges in the soft lava, and often lie several hundred, or even over a thousand metres below the level of the surrounding plateau. Their upper reaches are too narrow for settlement, but lower down expanses of alluvium have been deposited, and these, when cultivated, are extremely fertile. The region of Lake Van once supported a moderately dense population, though because of the brackish nature of the lake water, cultivation was limited to the middle levels of the lake basin, as is the case round Lake Urmia.[1]

Because of their altitude (over 2000 m) and barren surface, the lava uplands are for the most part uninhabited. Here and there immense volcanic cones rise several thousand metres higher (the largest, Ararat, reaches 5165 m above sea-level), and the heavier rainfall near such peaks allows a scanty Alpine flora that provides seasonal grazing for Kurdish shepherds. The population was greatly depleted by the massacres of 1916–18, and for some years since 1945 the Turkish government has been following a policy of settling immigrants from the west and from Bulgaria in the empty Armenian valleys.

Further south, in region (*b*), which contains as two major towns Diyarbekir and Urfa, topography is much less rugged, and general elevation lower. Rivers tend, however, to be deeply slotted into the plateau surface, and the extent of cultivable land is greatly restricted. Certain districts where water can be more easily raised to the fields,

---

[1] The waters of Lake Van are less saline than those of Lake Urmia, but contain a high proportion of sodium carbonate.

support a number of agricultural communities, but in large measure pastoralism is the predominant way of life. Lower elevation, though facilitating movement, condemns the southern part of eastern Turkey to semi-aridity.

## Climate
### General

The climate of Turkey, like that of Iran, is one of extremes. Parts of the western coastlands never experience frost, yet in Armenia snow lies even in the valleys for a third of the year; and in respect of rainfall much of the entire country has a deficient water supply, whilst the north-east has an excess. Season of onset of rainfall also varies, from winter in the south and west, spring in the central plateau, summer in the northern coastlands, and autumn in the extreme north-east. The reasons for such contrasts are to be found in (a) relief, (b) the position of Asia Minor on the margin of the 'Mediterranean' and interior Asiatic climatic zones, and (c) the extent of sea, which has a modifying influence on the western part of the country. It should be noted that the Anatolian plateau is considerably higher on average than the interior of Iran, although the surrounding mountain chains are less developed. This gives rise to lower winter temperatures, and hence to the frequent occurrence of a separate and distinctive high pressure system over Asia Minor during the months between November and April. The effect is to divert rain-bearing depressions as they move along the eastern Mediterranean either to the north or the south of Asia Minor, so that relatively few can penetrate into the interior of the plateau. This is why a winter maximum of rainfall is by no means universal in Turkey.

During the summer and autumn, on the other hand, the north of Asia Minor lies on the outer margins of the air mass system that brings air that is dry but capable of absorbing moisture rapidly on its circuitous passage round the Cyprus low pressure zone. Intermixture over a colder sea (fed by cold Russian rivers) with air from eastern Europe moving southwards, and also a damper, often cooler stream associated with the 'westerlies' of western Europe can thus give rise to the development of cyclonic rain in the Black Sea regions; and the effects of such mixing are enhanced by the contrasts of relief along the northern coast of Turkey.

As in Iran, the high encircling ranges receive a disproportionate share of precipitation, and the interior lies in a rain shadow area. Aridity is, however, much less complete than in Iran, since the eastern portion of the plateau stands at an elevation of 1500–2100 m, and so receives more rain than the lower-lying interior basins of western Anatolia.

### The Black Sea coastlands

It is convenient to discuss the climate of Asia Minor on a basis of the natural regions already distinguished. In the Black Sea coastlands winters are mild, summers moderately hot, and little difference is apparent between east and west. Rize, on the extreme east, shows an average January temperature of 6 °C, Samsun one of 6·6 °C and Trabzon one of 7·2 °C. Highest temperatures occur in August and corresponding means are Rize 21·6 °C, Samsun 20 °C and Trabzon 23·3 °C. Inland, the moderating influence of the sea is much less felt – Merzifon, a short distance south of Samsun, in the interior lowland trough, has a January mean of −1 °C, and a July mean of 20 °C. A special feature of the eastern Black Sea coastlands is the prevalence of Föhn winds in winter. These occur when heavy stagnant air from the interior plateau streams towards the coastlands. As much as 16–22 °C of warming may take place during the 2000–3000 m of descent from the interior; hence, although the air may be initially below freezing point, temperatures of 15° or even 30 °C may be attained at sea-level. Thus, instead of a beneficent wind that tempers the rigours of winter, an unduly warm blast may occur and actually wither growing vegetation, and is responsible for the barren condition of many of the foothills of the region, which would normally be thickly forested. It is significant that at Rize and Samsun temperatures of 21 °C have been recorded in January and February, and over 27 °C in March.

Rainfall is almost everywhere abundant in the Black Sea coastlands, and ranges from 600 mm in the west to 2500 mm in the east. At Izmit (extreme west) February is the wettest and August the driest month, although no month is without rainfall. Rize (annual rainfall 2450 mm), with a maximum in November and a minimum in late spring, has a rainfall that is well distributed throughout the year.

### The Aegean coastlands

Temperature conditions in this region have some similarity to those of the Black Sea region, though local variation is somewhat more prominent and there is a marked rise in temperature towards the south. In winter there is a January minimum of 5–8 °C on the coast and 2–4·5 °C inland, whilst in summer July and August show little difference in temperature, each having figures that range from 23 °C at Istanbul to 27 °C at Izmir. Despite the presence of the sea, diurnal variation of temperature is very pronounced during the summer months, and much more prominent than in the Black Sea region; day temperatures frequently exceed 32 °C during July (and also in the south during August), with correspondingly cooler nights – indications that the Aegean comes more definitely within the Mediterranean régime. Even Istanbul has a mean July maximum of 32·7 °C.

Rainfall is fairly evenly distributed over the entire Aegean coastlands, with amounts ranging from 500 to 750 mm per annum near the coast and 400 to 500 mm in the extreme east on the borders of western Anatolia. December is everywhere the wettest month, and it may be noted that, although many areas have a fall of under 25 mm during each of the 3 months, June, July and August, there are few instances of an entire absence of rain during the summer. One feature of the west is the steady northerly winds (termed Etesians, or Meltemi) which blow throughout the summer, and, except in the sheltered lowlands, temper the heat of the day. In the deeper valleys, which are often shut in the hilly massifs, moisture can be brought in by sea breezes, and humidity is high – too high, often, for comfort and sustained human activity.

### The Mediterranean coastlands

These have slightly hotter summers than in the Aegean region (mean 28 °C, mean daily max. 33–35 °C), with August always the warmest month on the coast, and July further inland. This clearer difference between July and August temperatures as compared with conditions in the Aegean may arise as the result of the straighter coastline – maritime influences are restricted to a narrower coastal belt, and are not carried inland by long estuaries or broken fretted shorelines. Winters are considerably warmer, at least, on the coastal lowlands, January temperatures ranging from 9 °C at Adana to 11 °C at Iskanderun. Rainfall is moderate in amount, but considerable local variation occurs, depending on aspect and altitude. In general, the south-facing ranges of the Taurus systems receive more than 750 mm per annum, whilst the seaward-facing plains at the foot of the mountains receive between 500–750 mm, though in a few districts that are especially open to the sea (e.g. Antalya and Fethiye) rainfall is slightly above 750 mm.

December or January are the wettest months, July and August the driest. In summer a very slight rainfall is recorded, usually less than 10 mm in the 2 months together. Towards the east, in the regions of the Seyhan plain and the Hatay, the total fall is higher.[1] Summers are therefore not entirely arid, like those of the Syrian, Lebanese and Israeli coasts.

Humidity is again high during summer, and maxima for the year tend to occur during June, July or August – a feature common to the eastern Mediterranean and Red Seas. Iskanderun, with a relative humidity of 59% in January and of 74% in August, is a typical example, though it should be remembered that the Hatay and adjacent Seyhan lowlands, ringed by mountain chains and open to the prevailing south-west winds, are a little damper than the Antalya region further west.

[1] Cf. the extent of cloudiness, during July and August. Antalya 0·9 and 0·6 tenths of sky covered; Adana 1·0 and 1·8, Iskanderun 1·8 and 1·1.

## The central plateau

This region is characterized by a wider range of temperature and by greater aridity. Winters are cold, with January temperatures averaging − 1 °C over most of the plateau; and all districts have more than 100 days of frost during each year (cf. Izmir 13, Adana 16). Summers are warm, with high day temperatures and cool nights, though the mean for July (the hottest month), as the result of distinctly cooler nights, lies between 20 and 23 °C. At Ankara and Konya day temperatures during July rise to 30 °C but fall at night to 12 °C. Diurnal variation is also pronounced in winter, day maxima in January averaging 3 °C and night minima − 8 °C to − 5·5 °C.

Between 250 and 525 mm of rainfall are received annually, the precise amount depending largely upon altitude. Konya and Ankara, at approximately similar elevation, have 350 and 250 mm respectively, whilst Sivas, situated 300 m higher, has 525 mm. It is somewhat remarkable that May is in general the wettest month, and July and August, only a few weeks later, are the driest. This curious régime is most probably due to the occurrence of a high pressure system in winter − on its collapse in late spring, rain-bearing winds can more easily penetrate into the interior. As is common in regions of deficient rainfall, irregularity of onset is a prominent feature, and most areas record whole months without any precipitation: at Ankara, for example absolute drought can occur on seven out of the twelve months of the year.

## Eastern highlands

Like adjacent parts of Iran, eastern Turkey is a region of great extremes, with a climate that is one of the most varied and severe in the world. Summers are hot and arid, particularly towards the south and east, where, as the steppes of Syria are approached, maximum temperatures exceed 38 °C, and in the deep calm valleys figures of 43–49 °C are attained. Summer temperatures are a little lower in the north-east; but 32 °C during the day is common, although marked diurnal variation, with a cold night, brings the daily average to 18–21 °C.[1]

Winters are cold, even in the extreme south, where Diyarbekir has a mean January temperature of − 0·5 °C. Further north, cold becomes intense; and Kars, in the extreme north-east of the region, has a *mean* January temperature of − 13 °C, with a night minimum of − 21 °C. Absolute minima of − 35 °C have been recorded; and on the higher plateaux − 40 °C is not unknown. Thus it is not surprising that snow lies for over 120 days

[1] A diurnal variation of the order of 27–30.°C can bring the night minimum below freezing-point even in summer.

Climatic data: representative stations in Asia Minor
*Temperature (°C) and rainfall (mm)*

|  | J | F | M | A | M | J | J | A | S | O | N | D | Total |
|---|---|---|---|---|---|---|---|---|---|---|---|---|---|
| **1 Black Sea** | | | | | | | | | | | | | |
| *Trabzon* | | | | | | | | | | | | | |
| Temperature | 7·2 | 6·6 | 8·3 | 10·5 | 16·1 | 20·0 | 22·7 | 23·3 | 20·5 | 17·7 | 12·7 | 9·4 | |
| Rainfall | 64 | 66 | 64 | 61 | 40 | 56 | 40 | 56 | 97 | 87 | 115 | 105 | 850 |
| **2 Aegean** | | | | | | | | | | | | | |
| *Izmir* | | | | | | | | | | | | | |
| Temperature | 7·7 | 8·3 | 11·6 | 15·0 | 20·0 | 24·4 | 27·2 | 26·6 | 22·7 | 19·0 | 13·8 | 10·0 | |
| Rainfall | 110 | 120 | 76 | 41 | 36 | 11 | 3 | 3 | 21 | 54 | 84 | 123 | 682 |
| **3 Mediterranean** | | | | | | | | | | | | | |
| *Adana* | | | | | | | | | | | | | |
| Temperature | 9·0 | 10·0 | 13·3 | 17·2 | 21·6 | 25·5 | 27·7 | 28·3 | 25·5 | 21·6 | 15·5 | 10·5 | |
| Rainfall | 108 | 102 | 64 | 41 | 51 | 18 | 5 | 5 | 19 | 49 | 61 | 97 | 620 |
| **4 Central Plateau** | | | | | | | | | | | | | |
| *Konya* | | | | | | | | | | | | | |
| Temperature | −1·0 | +1·0 | 5·5 | 11·1 | 15·5 | 20·0 | 23·3 | 23·3 | 18·3 | 13·3 | 7·2 | 1·6 | |
| Rainfall | 46 | 33 | 28 | 33 | 36 | 21 | 8 | 0 | 13 | 33 | 36 | 42 | 329 |
| **5 Eastern Turkey** | | | | | | | | | | | | | |
| *(a) Kars* | | | | | | | | | | | | | |
| Temperature | −13·0 | −10·0 | −5·0 | 3·8 | 10·3 | 13·6 | 17·2 | 17·9 | 13·1 | 7·5 | 0·7 | −7·0 | |
| Rainfall | 28 | 29 | 28 | 44 | 87 | 74 | 54 | 53 | 31 | 41 | 31 | 25 | 525 |
| *(b) Urfa* | | | | | | | | | | | | | |
| Temperature | 5·0 | 6·1 | 11·3 | 15·2 | 21·8 | 27·1 | 31·0 | 29·9 | 26·3 | 21·2 | 14·3 | 7·4 | |
| Rainfall | 119 | 64 | 56 | 41 | 13 | 0 | 0 | 0 | 3 | 23 | 46 | 77 | 442 |

each year in the north-east but only for 7 to 10 days at Diyarbekir and Urfa.

Because of greater altitude, eastern Turkey is better watered than the central plateau, this despite an inland position; and the total rainfall varies between 450 and 600 mm. The months of heaviest rain tend to be January to March, but towards the north-east there is some approach to conditions of the Black Sea region (i.e. a maximum in summer or autumn), so that at Erzerum November is the wettest month, and at Kars, May or June.

The climate of eastern Turkey stands out as one of the most difficult and inhospitable in the world. Summers are hot, arid and markedly dusty; winters are bitterly cold, and spring and autumn are both subject to sudden hot or cold spells – the former due to Föhn winds and to southerly (*khamsin*) winds from the Arabian desert, the latter to outbursts of cold air from inner Asia, which may give snowfalls as late as the month of May. As a summary of weather on the entire Anatolian plateau, there is the widespread view that one cannot easily travel and undertake field visits until mid-April.

## Agriculture

In many respects Turkey has a successful and relatively highly developed agricultural economy. Nearly two-thirds of the population derive their living from the land, agricultural products accounted for 55–60% of exports in 1975, quality of many products is high, and self-sufficiency in most foodstuffs other than wheat has been a feature of the last 25 years. Under the Ottomans, little attention was paid to agriculture, though it occupied the overwhelming majority of the people, and massive imports of food became necessary. But after 1923 serious attempts were made to improve conditions through technical education of peasants in better methods and provision of infrastructures such as communications and marketing facilities. Production rose markedly, amounting in the 1950s to what some termed a 'green revolution', but in the 1960s there was a fall-off, with little more than half of achievement asked for in the national plans (2·5% annual growth: planned, 4·2%). In the 1970s, however, more national resources were allocated, with the result that irrigation became more widespread, and the use of fertilizers and machinery increased dramatically. A national Land Reform started in 1974 will ultimately redistribute about 4 m ha to half a million peasants – 10% of Turkish farmers are landless.

The effect of technical improvements plus good weather combined in 1975–7 to give excellent, even record harvests in many areas.

*Cereals*

About 50–55% of the cultivated area is given over to cereal growing (as compared with 80–90% 20 years or so earlier) with wheat occupying three-fifths of this. This underlines the increasing importance of cash crops and the decline of a subsistence economy. At the same time it should be noted that only about 30% of the country is cultivated, with about one-third of this in fallow at any one time, so actual cultivation covers no more than 10–15% in good years, and in poor years 8–10%. Wheat is grown over most parts of Turkey, but particularly important is the west-central plateau interior, where larger-scale methods are more possible. Here there is a wide extent of fairly flat territory, and rainfall is a little heavier than in the centre of the plateau. Another important wheat-growing region is the northern Aegean region, inclusive of European Turkey.

Since 1967 an important development has been the use of imported Mexican strains of wheat seed. This, planted on the fertile coastal areas of the west and south, gave dramatic results – two to three times the yield as compared with indigenous seed. In 1968, however, extension of Mexican wheat to the Anatolian plateau took place with distinctly less favourable results. It would seem that it is as yet too early to assess the longer-term significance of what could ultimately be an extremely important break-through.

Barley is the second cereal crop, occupying about 30% of the acreage of wheat; though, because of its tolerance of heat and aridity, yields per

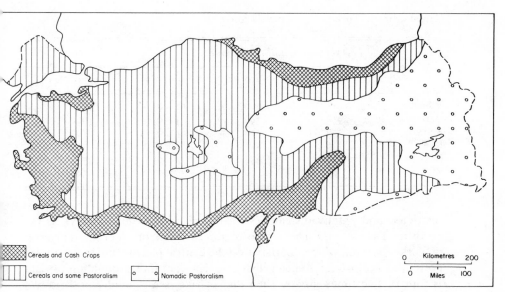

Cereals and Cash Crops
Cereals and some Pastoralism
Nomadic Pastoralism

Kilometres 200
Miles 100

*Fig.* 12.4 Land use in Turkey.

unit cultivated are often higher. Its main use is as a fodder crop, and it has a wide distribution, notably on the steppe zones flanking the inner plateau of Anatolia (districts of Ankara, Konya and Corum especially), and also on the inner coastlands of the Aegean, with Konya by far the most important region. In all of these regions it is often grown on the drier parts, where annual rainfall is from 350 to 450 mm. Over most of Asia Minor all the three cereals, wheat, barley and spelt, are sown as winter crops (i.e. in autumn); but in the extreme east, winters are too cold, and sowing takes place in spring with the harvest delayed until late summer.

Next in importance after wheat and barley is maize, which flourishes most in the warm and humid Black Sea coastlands, especially round Samsun, and, with irrigation, in the Aegean coastlands. Rye is also important as a cereal of marginal lands, where conditions are too dry or too cold for wheat or barley. Eastern Turkey and the inner parts of the central plateau, away from the salt steppe region, are the main districts of production. In places where the soil is poor but climatic conditions a little more favourable, a mixture of wheat and rye termed *maslin* is often grown.

On the low, humid plains of the Mediterranean coast, rice is an increasingly important crop, with the Mediterranean lowlands towards Adana one important area. Rice-growing has also expanded markedly in the upper Euphrates area, around Maras and Diyarbekir, with more

Cereal crops in Turkey ('ooos metric tons)

| | Average annual production | | | |
|---|---|---|---|---|
| | *1934–38* | *1950–52* | *1968–69* | *1974–75* |
| Wheat | 3412 | 4700 | 12800 | 13000 |
| Barley | 1954 | 2340 | 3750 | 3900 |
| Maize | 557 | 738 | 1100 | 1300 |
| Rye | 336 | 521 | 900 | 700 |
| Oats | 223 | 334 | 480 | 380 |
| Rice | 64 | 70 | 120 | 165 |

restricted and patchy distribution in the marshy Aegean valleys as far north as Thrace, and also in the region of Trabzon. Yet another crop of Turkey is oats, which flourishes on the central plateau and in the cooler north and north-west Aegean districts. The fact that production of oats is four or five times greater than that of rice is a reminder of Turkey's position as the most northerly of Middle Eastern countries; outside Asia Minor oats grow only with some difficulty on the higher uplands regions, and have small importance as a crop.

Potatoes are now of considerable importance, production having increased greatly since the 1930s. Here again a colder climate is an advantage, since only the sweet potato (yam) will grow in many parts of the southern Middle East. Iran, Cyprus and the Lebanon are the only other countries which rival Turkey in the growing of potatoes, and at present production in Asia Minor is in excess of the individual output from all the other countries. Potato-growing tends naturally to be restricted to the north, and to the higher parts of the central plateau; and the plant is now of increasing value in the extreme east.

*Fruit crops*

These are extremely important in most districts of Asia Minor, and the wide extent of fruit-growing arises from (*a*) a generally favourable climate with, in the west and south, mild winters and long sunny summers, (*b*) a rich volcanic soil in many areas, which is particularly advantageous for vine-growing, and (*c*) varied topography that allows a wide range of species, from subtropical to temperate fruits, on the same hill slopes.

Vines rank as the most important commercial crop of Turkey in area, with a large proportion exported, mainly as sultanas. Improvements in quality have been marked, following the import of French and American vines which were then distributed by the government, and, despite competition from Australia and California, Turkey is in some years the principal world exporter of raisins. Vines are grown over most of the country except in the north and east, with especial concentration in (*a*) the Aegean area round Izmir, and (*b*) Turkish Cilicia, close to the Syrian border. Large-scale production for export is confined to the Aegean region (vilayets of Izmir and Manisa, with the best fruit coming from the small zone between the Büyük Menderes and Gediz valleys). North of the Gediz valley, slightly cooler and damper climatic conditions lower the yield very markedly. The grapes are dried in the sun on sheets of paper spread on the ground, then cleaned, bleached and packed for export as sultanas. At present 70000 to 110000 metric tons are exported. Other species of grapes are used for making wines and spirits, the production of which is now between 12 and 15 million litres annually.

Olives are also an important crop, but most are consumed locally and are hence never marketed, in contrast to sultana grapes. The olive flourishes best on sloping ground, and highest quality oil tends to come from dry stony ridges, since a rich soil and abundant water produce large luxuriant trees but a watery crop. Hence the foothills of mountain ranges close to the sea are usually given over to olive-growing (away from the sea, at about 100–150 km inland, yields fall off), with the western and southern coasts the areas of intensive cultivation. Izmir is a centre for processing and export of olive oil, and production is at about 800000 metric tons annually.

Figs are also grown on a considerable scale for export, and once again the Büyük Menderes–Gediz region is the chief centre of production. Turkish figs have a special flavour that is said to be due to the presence in the fruit of numerous seeds, which are fertilized by certain species of insects that occur only under the special climatic conditions of the Aegean coastlands. The figs ripen in August, when the hot dry Meltemi winds are fully developed. For some weeks previously, during the late spring, westerlies have prevailed, and the succession first of mild damp maritime air swells the fruit, and then later the hot modified continental air of the Meltemi completes the ripening stage. After drying in the sun, packing of the figs takes place at Izmir. Considerable quantities – even as much as 40–50% of the total crop – may be lost during the drying period, when a single slight shower can spoil large numbers; and as few figs are actually picked (most are allowed to drop off the trees), many are over-ripe. The rejected fruit is used in the manufacture of industrial alcohol. About 200000 metric tons are produced.

In the valleys of the Aegean coastlands, there is a well-marked sequence of cultivated plants according to altitude. On the lowest parts of all, which are liable to flooding, small fields of rice are found, and elsewhere on the valley bottoms, vines and cereals grow. On the lowest slopes of the valley sides, figs are planted; then, at slightly higher levels, olives replace figs. Sometimes cereals are also grown among olive plantations. Above this, at slightly varying heights (450 m in the north, 600 m in the south), scrub forest and nut trees occur.

Besides olives, vines and figs, large quantities of other Mediterranean fruit are grown chiefly for home consumption. Apricots and peaches take the place of figs in the eastern and central provinces; cherries are abundant on the Black Sea coastlands – Giresun (Cerasus) is the original home of the cherry – and plums are grown in the northern Aegean (both in European and Asiatic Turkey) and on the damper parts of the central plateau. Some of these plums are dried – prunes from the Edirne (Adrianople) district of European Turkey having a high reputation – and quantities are exported. The cultivation of citrus fruit has greatly increased – up 10 to 15 times as compared with 1950 – with tangerines on the Black Sea coast, and the largest crop ('jaffas') on the southern coasts, giving a total annual average production of 600000 tons. Bananas are grown in the hot steamy valleys of the Mediterranean coastlands, whilst temperate fruits, especially apples, are a feature in Anatolia, particularly in the east, where they outnumber other species of fruit.

Another important export is that of hazel nuts, which accounts for about half the world's marketed supply. The oil is used as a lubricant in aircraft, and as a varnish, whilst the nut is eaten as dessert or in confectionery. Some 250000 tons are gathered annually, two-thirds being exported.

Chief areas of production are the 'Pontic' forests that clothe the ridges of the Black Sea coastlands; and the nuts are shipped from Giresun, Trabzon and Samsun. The Aegean region also produces important quantities of both hazel nuts and walnuts. Almonds and pistachios are grown in the south-east, round Maras and Diyarbekir, and also in the central plateau.

*Commercial crops*

Besides cereals and fruit, Turkey produces a number of commercial crops, chief of which are: cotton, tobacco, sugar beet, oil seeds (sunflower and sesame) and opium. Cotton is grown in two main areas: the Seyhan plain between Adana and Mersin (with a centre at Cukurova), and round Izmir, with smaller-scale production in the south-east, round Diyarbekir. Great efforts have been made by the government to stimulate production by provision of irrigation and sponsored co-operatives for selling and provision of equipment and fertilizer. Production now runs at over 2 million bales, with about 1 million from each of the two major producing areas, and about half is exported, chiefly to the West, but also in smaller quantity to eastern Europe. After a decade of 'boom' in which much expansion took place, there was recession in 1968, with parts of the Adana cotton area replanted in Mexican wheat. However, marked improvement occurred in the mid-1970s, with over 500000 tons produced annually. Raw cotton accounts for 20–25% of Turkish exports, values having more than doubled since 1960.

Sugar beet is an introduction since the 1930s, and, as in Iran, its development was fostered in order to reduce dependence upon imported cane sugar. About 800000 tons are produced and chief regions are: on the western fringes of the central plateau, in the districts of Eskesehir, Afyonkarahissar and Birejik; in European Turkey; and in the Pontic region behind Samsun. All these have good rail communication for transport to refineries. Cane sugar is also grown on a small scale in the plain of Adana, but accounts for only a tiny proportion of Turkish output of sugar.

Tobacco is a traditional Turkish crop, and because of its high value ranks as a principal export commodity. At one time tobacco was widely grown all over Turkey, but in an effort to improve quality, the government has restricted cultivation during the last 30 or so years to two main regions: the Aegean coastlands (chief centres Izmir and Bursa, near the Sea of Marmara) and the Black Sea coast with centres at Samsun and Trabzon (the latter producing a stronger, darker variety). Tobacco is an exhausting crop, hence rich soils with a varied mineral content and an adequate water supply are necessary. Heaviest yields are obtained in the Izmir region, but highest quality occurs round Samsun and Bursa. The crop is controlled as a governmental monopoly, and normally about one half of the total production is retained for home use, and the rest exported. There has been much fluctuation in demand, but generally speaking dollar shortages and difficulties in Rhodesia had tended to act as a stimulus, so that production has risen to about 170000 tons with, however, much annual fluctuation.

The valonia oak grows only in the borderlands between the Aegean and western Anatolia, and is for the most part restricted to altitudes exceeding 100 m. From the cup which holds the acorn an extract useful in tanning, and known as valonea, is obtained. The main regions of growth of the valonia oak are the uplands at the head of the Büyük Menderes, Gediz and Simav rivers; and the inner slopes of the Western Taurus and main Taurus. Acorns and cups are picked during the period August to October, then dried in the sun for several weeks, following which some acorns are exported, and some treated at Izmir to obtain the extract. About 50000 tons of acorns are produced, and of these about two-thirds are exported, the principal buyers being France, Great Britain and the USA. Liquorice grows wild over much of Asia Minor, but occurs mostly in the drier parts of the south and east, towards the Syrian steppe. No actual cultivation takes place, but some 30000 tons are gathered annually, and

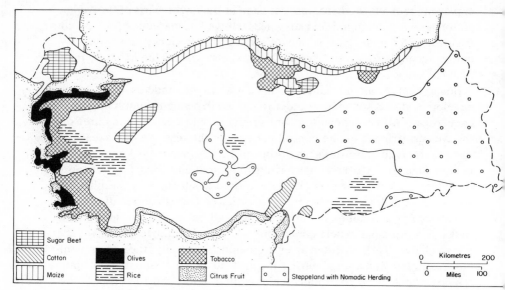

Sugar Beet

Cotton        Olives        Tobacco

Maize        Rice        Citrus Fruit        Steppeland with Nomadic Herding

0        Kilometres        200

0        Miles        100

*Fig.* 12.5 Crop distribution in Turkey.

most of this is sent either as dried root, or in a concentrated extract, to the United States, where it is used chiefly for flavouring tobacco, and also as a sweetmeat.

Sesame and sunflowers are grown for oil seed in many parts, especially the coastal areas of Marmara, Antalya and Adana, but production is now inadequate for home needs. Opium is a crop of volcanic soils of the western plateau, especially round Afyonkarahissar (*afyon* = opium) and Konya. Like tobacco, opium production is a state monopoly, and Turkey produces 250 tons. Although only 30000 ha are legally planted with the opium poppy, the value of the crop is very high, and occasionally, if other crops have failed, farmers may obtain permission to grow a small amount as recompense for other losses. Between 1972 and 1974, as the result of American pressure, the Turkish Government placed a total ban on opium growing, but this was ended as a gesture, at the time of the invasion of Cyprus.

Another crop of enhanced importance is tea, developed since 1933 in the Rize area, where conditions are in certain respects comparable with those of Assam and the Caspian coast. Because of lower temperatures, however, yields of tea are smaller in quantity, though quality is moderate or good; with a production of 40000–45000 tons, Turkey is self-sufficient in this commodity and exports about one-third of the crop. Other, less important agricultural products of Turkey are gum tragacanth, aniseed, hemp, attar of roses and madder (for dyeing of rugs and carpets). Mention must also be made of the greatly increasing cultivation of vegetables of all kinds in response to the rapid growth of town populations.

## Irrigation

The irrigation problems of Turkey differ in certain respects from those of most other Middle Eastern countries. In the first place, with slightly higher rainfall, river water is actually more abundant, but in the interior, the extremely deeply entrenched and slotted river courses make it difficult to raise water to the surrounding agricultural land; whilst, closer to the coast, broad alluvium-filled tectonic troughs are most often subjected to floods, and become filled with marsh and swamp. Irrigation in Asia Minor is thus often combined with river control and draining of marshes – particularly in the north and west of the country – and existing works are on a relatively modest scale, hardly comparable with those of the Nile, Euphrates or Tigris. Only about 7% of the cultivated area of Turkey is irrigated.

One large barrage is that on the Seyhan river just north of Adana, from which over 10000 ha of land is at present irrigated. This scheme, which also produces electric power, is in process of extension; and already the output of cotton from the Seyhan lowlands has more than doubled owing to irrigation, with wheat- and rice-growing also expanding. Further west, reclamation of swamp has taken place near Tarsus, and, as a result, this lower valley of the Seyhan has developed into one of the most significant agricultural regions of Turkey.

Irrigation and flood-control works on a smaller individual scale have developed in many parts of the Aegean coastlands, notably the valleys of the Great and Little Menderes, Gediz and Simav rivers; and the aggregate acreage of land involved is expected ultimately to exceed that of the Adana irrigation scheme. Improvements are also taking place along the course of the Yesil Irmak, where marsh reclamation allows increased cultivation of tobacco, cereals and fruit. Other important dams are on the Sakariya river, and at Hirfanli on the Kizil Irmak – the latter being one of the largest barrages in the country.

Mention must also be made of developments in the central plateau. A large barrage has been built near Ankara (the third largest in Turkey), partly to secure a good domestic water supply for the city, and also to allow increased cultivation of cereals and vegetables. Round Eskeşehir, 4000–8000 ha are developed for sugar-beet production.

The Euphrates in the region of Malatya has seen much extension of irrigation. Here, in the main, the river is rather less deeply slotted into the plateau, and a system of small-scale barrages and canals has come into existence from which fruit trees are irrigated. At Keban, where two major branches of the Euphrates river join, a dam 200 m high, the largest in Turkey, was completed in 1973 that will ultimately produce a lake 115 km long, from which extensive irrigation will be possible, together with a doubling of Turkey's hydro-electricity output.

After several decades of experience, it is now recognized that irrigation has not proved wholly successful, or even popular. Some reasons for this situation are: (a) lack of knowledge by farmers of suitable techniques – necessary changes in crop rotation, choice of seeds, etc., and the use of fertilizers and insecticides, (b) the relationships of drainage to soil salinity, and (c) soil erosion and reservoir silting. Because of the special geographical nature of Turkish rivers an unusually high proportion of silt is carried – on the Kizil Irmak (Red River) floodwaters may carry as much as 80 g of sediment per litre. Thus, rapid silting of irrigation works can often be expected, and the useful 'life' of the barrage is thus in some cases no more than 50 (or even 20) years – an extremely important factor in the cost of operation of irrigation schemes. Moreover, soil erosion in certain of the catchments of the dams has become a serious problem, and there are now attempts to reduce this by controlling the land utilization, and by afforestation.

## Pastoralism

The large extent of mountain and semi-arid steppe, too dry or too cold for agriculture, has led to the development of stock-rearing on a considerable scale. In many areas considerable seasonal movement from winter to summer pastures takes place, amounting in certain districts of the east and south to semi- or full nomadism, whilst in agricultural regions a kind of mixed farming prevails, with stock-keeping as an important supplement to cultivation. The importance of animal-rearing in Turkish economy is shown by the fact that Turkey comes second only to Great Britain as a European producer of wool, and surpasses all other Mediterranean countries.

Sheep are most numerous, and, though widespread over practically the whole country, greatest concentration occurs in the western districts of the central plateau (centres: Eskeşehir, Afyonkarahissar and Kayseri), in the provinces bordering Syria and Iraq, and in European Turkey. Milk, wool and meat are obtained, and there is a considerable trade in live animals with neighbouring countries. Normally some 250000 sheep are exported, mainly to adjacent countries. Turkish wool is, unfortunately, rather coarse, and cannot be used in making of good-quality cloth; but within recent years, the government has had success in improving the yield of wool by introducing merino sheep, which now number 200000.

Goats are often kept with sheep, since both animals thrive on the

Livestock in Turkey 1973–76 ('000s)

| Sheep | 41000 | Horses | 800 |
|---|---|---|---|
| Goats (black) | 13000 | Water-buffaloes | 1100 |
| Goats (Angora) | 6000 | Mules | 300 |
| Cattle | 13000 | Camels | 20 |
| Donkeys | 1400 | | |

limited vegetation of the central plateau. Angora goats are especially valuable as yielding mohair, a soft, fine fibre about 15 cm in length, which is woven into a durable, silky cloth. As the name suggests, the Ankara region is the main home of these goats; and elsewhere, the ordinary black goat is most common.

Cattle are less important than either sheep or goats, since these animals are much less tolerant of semi-arid conditions, and cannot travel long distances in search of fresh pasture. The main regions of cattle-rearing tend, therefore, to occur in the damper coastlands of the north and west; and relatively few are kept in the centre and south-east of Asia Minor. Breeds are poor, and the yield of meat and milk low, but, as in the case of sheep, the government has made efforts to improve methods and stock by the establishment of model farms, research and breeding institutes, and by the introduction of foreign breeds. Along the Black Sea coast, water-buffaloes are still important both as a source of milk and even for transport and ploughing. Elsewhere, donkeys, horses, mules and even camels are still used for transport, but, as roads and motor transport spread, animal transport is declining.

Figures of land use, though highly approximate in some instances due to changes of category, show very important changes. The expansion of cultivation and market gardening are clearly indicated, together with a decline in grazing lands. There have been significant afforestation projects, but part of the recent increase is also due to inclusion of lightly wooded areas in the category of 'forest' due to adoption of FAO categories on density.

Agriculture in Turkey has, as we noted above, experienced vicissitudes. After the conspicuous improvements of the 1950s and early 1960s, there was a period covering the later 1960s when improvements fell away, and even the modest target of 4·2% growth was only 55% attained. Reasons for this were the diminishing returns from marginal lands taken in from pasture during the 1950s, with accompanying soil erosion, which, according to a statement by the Ministry of Rural Affairs had come by 1970 to affect 70% of all cultivated land. Mechanization by those farmers who could afford it made them better off, but the average peasant, who could

Land utilization in Turkey (official estimates)

| | Area ('ooos ha) | | | Percentage of total | | |
|---|---|---|---|---|---|---|
| | 1935 | 1966 | 1976 | 1935 | 1966 | 1976 |
| Land under cultivation | 10600 | 24000 | 25100 | 14 | 31 | 33 |
| Grazing land | 44300 | 28000 | 23500 | 57 | 36 | 31 |
| Market gardens and orchards | 1100 | 2400 | 3300 | 1 | 3 | 4 |
| Forest | 9200 | 10600 | 21000 | 12 | 14 | 28 |
| Unproductive | 12100 | 13100 | 5100 | 16 | 17 | 7 |

not, saw his status fall to that of partial or seasonal day labourer. However, by the early 1970s the effect of government planning, plus its Land Reform Act of 1973 which aims at redistribution of 3 m ha of land by the late 1980s, and greater provision of infrastructures (roads, irrigation and drains, education etc.) together with rural credit facilities, has had markedly beneficial effects. Irrigation has expanded – in some years up to 100000 ha have been brought in – the use of fertilizer has increased ten-fold since the 1950s, and there have been annual increases in production since 1970 of 5–10%, with the occasional poor year due to adverse weather. Still greater emphasis in National Plans on agricultural development is needed: even the amounts allocated (18% of total in the First Plan, 15% under the Second) were not fully spent. Turkey still remains marginally self sufficient: in good years enough foodstuffs are produced, except for wheat, and imports of this can be paid for by exports of other agricultural produce, which account for over 50% of the export total.

**Minerals**

Asia Minor has long been renowned as a centre of mineral production. The first coins ever to be issued were those of Croesus, king of Lydia, and these were fixed quantities of gold, the purity of which was guaranteed by the personal seal of the monarch. Gold was also an ancient product of the north-east; and here, the home of the legendary Golden Fleece, alluvial gold is still obtained from rivers by washing silt against an oily sheepskin, to which particles of gold adhere. Iron was first developed by the Hittites of Anatolia c. 1250 B.C., and copper was exploited at a much earlier date.

Turkey has a moderately wide range of minerals, greater in variety and amount (petroleum excepted) than in most other Middle Eastern countries.

Mineral production in 1976 ('000 metric tons)

| | | | |
|---|---|---|---|
| Bituminous coal | 4800 | Borax | 220 |
| Lignite | 5600 | Copper (blister) | 28 |
| Crude oil | 3400 | Chrome | 712 |
| Iron ore | 2600 | Sulphur | 18 |
| | | Manganese | 8 |

But development has been slow and partial, with, in some instances, full survey not yet completed. Irregular world demand, with widely fluctuating prices, has been one adverse factor; another is distance and indifferent communications; and a third is lack of capital for development. Turkey has not been able to find sufficient of this from internal sources, and experiences during the Ottoman period have made modern Turkish governments very chary of inviting in much foreign influence. As a result, nearly two-thirds of Turkish mineral output is produced by state-run or -financed organizations.

Coal is produced from the Eregli-Zonguldak region of the Black Sea coast. The coal, of good quality, and much of it of coking type, is inter-bedded with Carboniferous sandstones, and occurs in irregular, fractured, folded and tilted seams. Mining is difficult, and much coal is lost in handling. Output is subsidized, and of late years there have been various schemes of modernization, some of which have been successful. Nevertheless, the entire field may now have a life of under 10 years, and Turkey will become entirely dependent on lignite. Because of the broken, forested nature of the coastal interior, land transport of the coal is hindered, and much therefore moves by sea, even though there are on average 150 days of bad weather annually that affect loading of coal.

Lignite is fairly widespread in western and central Anatolia. One of the largest deposits is around Kutahya west of Ankara, where reserves of nearly 1500 million tons exist. Main centres of production are at Degirmisaz, Soma and Tunçdilek. Major developments are planned in order to increase output since most lignite is used in electricity generation.

Iron was until recently produced almost entirely from Divrigi, located nearly 500 km east of Ankara. This ore is of good quality (60–65% iron content) and reserves amount to over 20 million tons. Other deposits are known in the Izmir area and at Torbali, Hasancelebi and Elbistan in the eastern plateau region. The first blast furnaces were built at Karabuk, close to the Zonguldak coal basin, before the Divrigi deposits were known, and ore is carried nearly 1000 km by rail to this plant, which, despite reorganization not long ago, produces iron and stell at a price higher than that of steel from outside delivered in Turkey. In 1965 a sheet steel and rolling mill was set up at Eregli, and construction began in 1970 of a third steel plant at Iskanderun. This will use crude petroleum and oxygen as prime fuels, and is financed and designed by Russians.

Chrome has been produced in Turkey since 1848, and for long the country was chief world producer; but now Russia holds first place, with Turkey second. The mineral occurs as lodes or lenses in association with serpentine, and is usually quarried, mined by adit, or even collected from the surface. At Guleman (west of Lake Van) workings developed in 1925 produce 20–30% of total Turkish output, the remainder coming from a number of smaller mines in the districts of Bursa and Eskeşehir (north-west Anatolia), Fethiye and Antalya – the last two zones being worked by private companies. Production from Guleman is partly from surface outcrops, and the ore moves by lorry to railhead, then 650 km to Mersin and Iskanderun. Production is interrupted by cold weather for about 10 weeks each winter. A ferro-chrome concentrator was recently built, the first in Turkey, and almost all the chromium produced is exported.

Copper is mined at two places, Ergani Madeni (about 100 km north-west of Diyarbekir) and Borchka, on the Black Sea close to the Russian frontier. At Ergani, a high-grade deposit estimated to amount to 3 million tons is worked by open-cast methods, and fair progress has been made since the opening of the railway to Mersin, though the haul is 550 km. The Murgul mine at Borchka began production in 1950 and has larger reserves than at Ergani Madeni. A sulphuric acid plant is associated with the refinery at Murgul. Some copper is retained within Turkey, but the greater proportion is now exported.

Other minerals exploited on a smaller scale, yet collectively important, are alum (Black Sea region), antimony (Black Sea), asbestos (Kars), borax (Bandirma), lead-zinc (various regions), manganese (various), mercury (Izmir), molybdenum (Ankara) and sulphur (Kecibolu-Isparta). During 1954 deposits of tungsten containing also wolfram were found in the Uludagh hill region of Bursa. These are now thought to be among the richest wolfram deposits in the world. An aluminium plant planned with Soviet assistance has been in construction since 1968 at Seydisehir near Konya, where there is a reserve of over 30 million tons of bauxite.

Mining in Turkey was for long almost entirely controlled by the state, with immediate supervision in the hands of a government department, the Institute of Mining (M.T.A.), and finance supplied by the state E.T.I. Bank. Under the Ottomans, exploitation had come to be entirely in the hands of foreign concessionaires, who were nearly all bought out by the Republic – exceptions being certain of the chromium mines at Fethiye (French), boracite (American) and wolfram (German). Since 1950 a policy of denationalization has taken place, and private ownership is a feature

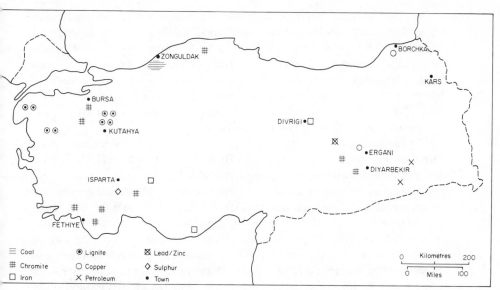

*Fig.* 12.6 Turkey: minerals.

in a few sectors of mining and industry – about one-quarter of the lignite, two-thirds of the chrome, half of the iron ore, and all the manganese are now privately produced.

## Industry

Like Iran, modern Turkey has attempted to stimulate major industrial growth mainly by direct state intervention. Five-year plans at intervals since 1934 (the latest covering the period 1973–77) have led to the situation of large-scale basic industry (amounting to about 30%) being undertaken by the state, and production of smaller consumer goods (70%) being in the hands of private enterprise. State direction of industry (étatism) derives from Kemalist ideas that national assets in resources such as mineral deposits and major basic manufacturing activities must be kept under closest governmental control, from the interlocking nature of much exploitation (e.g. coal, iron, communications) and because most of the funds available from outside have been channelled at governmental level (e.g. as 'aid' or for political motives). Earliest plans attempted to foster economic self-sufficiency in order to escape dependence on foreign imports, and to bring about industrial development in central and eastern Anatolia, where geographical conditions for agriculture are less favourable, leaving the Aegean area for intensive crop production, for which, of all regions of Asia Minor, it is obviously the most suited.

Despite high tariff barriers, high interest rates (18% is now charged in some instances), inefficient use of manpower and lack of managerial expertise – all of which mean extremely high internal prices for services, raw materials and small consumer goods – remarkable progress has been made. Industrial production has risen since 1965 at annual rates of between 9% and 12%, with industry now contributing almost one-quarter to G.D.P. At the same time an increasing proportion of production is of capital, rather than consumer goods.

The earlier five-year plans, directed by the state Sumer Bank, gave chief attention to stimulation of the textile industry, with mineral exploitation and chemical industries (producing artificial silk, paper, glass, pottery and fertilizers) as secondary adjuncts. With considerable internal production of natural textile fibres (cotton, wool, silk and mohair) and the new home production of artificial fibres (rayon, cellulose and synthetics), Turkey is well placed for textile manufacturing, which is in fact the largest industrial activity in the country. There are about 3 million spindles and 25 000 cotton looms, 40% of which are privately owned, together with three modern silk mills and a much larger number of smaller and older factories making silk cloth and carpets. The privately owned cotton mills are well placed near cotton-growing areas (at Izmir, Adana, Tarsus, Mersin and Istanbul), whilst the state mills are further inland, on the plateau (at Kayseri, Nazilli, Eregli, Malatya and Bakirkoy). The Kayseri mill is the largest in the Middle East. Bursa, Istanbul and Izmir are the chief woollen-manufacturing towns. Carpet-making has been carried on for centuries as a bazaar trade in many towns, especially those on the steppes of Anatolia. As in Iran, there are traditional patterns and colours associated with particular districts, and recent shifts in taste in Europe and America towards Oriental carpets has had a beneficial effect. Bursa is also a centre of mohair and silk-weaving (both natural and artificial silk), and smaller factories exist at Istanbul and Izmir.

Fertilizer production is developing. Plants have been set up within the last 10 years at Kutahya, Samsun, Elazig, Mersin, Yarimca and Iskanderun and in the Marmara region.

Within the last few years assembly plants for cars and domestic equipment have grown up, using imported parts, with, as the most recent feature, partial replacement by Turkish-produced parts. Aircraft production is now planned.

A noteworthy feature of Turkish economy has been the development of 'agricultural' industries: flour-milling, sugar-refining, packing and canning of fruit and meat, soap-boiling and distilling. Here the distribution of factories is very wide. Many sugar refineries now exist, located close to the three beet-growing areas; fruit-canning is carried on at Istanbul, Bursa, Malatya and Adana. Izmir is the centre of the wine trade. In order to develop the north and east, food-packing factories (meat, fish and cheese) have been established at Kars, Samsun and Trabzon; and the two latter handle an increasing lumber trade that is based on the rich Pontic forests of the coastal ranges. Pulp is used for paper and board production based at Izmir, Dalaman, Caycuma and Giresun. Attar (otto) of roses is distilled at Istanbul and Isparta.

Other industries are chemical production (chiefly associated with the coking plant at Zonguldak) and cement manufacturing, which, in common with conditions elsewhere in the Middle East, has greatly extended, with an annual production of over 5 million tons. Cement is one of Turkey's most significant industrial products. Glass sand is exploited near Istanbul, and Kutahya and Konya have a long-standing ceramic trade. Petro-chemical industries have developed at Izmit (heavy chemicals), Kutahya (nitrates), Samsun, Iskanderun, Mersin and Elazig (phosphates) and at Gemlik where an ammonia plant is to be set up with Libyan participation.

A feature of the last decade had been the growing importance of electric power. Production is doubling every 7 to 10 years, and hydro-generation has played a large part in expansion of supplies. Besides existing schemes at Adana (Seyhan river), Sariya (Sakariya), Hirfanli (Kizil Irmak), Kemer (Büyük Menderes) and Demikopru (Gediz), which together produce over 500000 kW, there is the Keban scheme on the Euphrates. This, completed in 1973, has a dam 204 m high, and impounds an artificial lake to be ultimately 115 km in length. This will eventually make available 1 240000 kW, which will be fed first to the north-west of Turkey, and then, in order to stimulate development in a difficult area that is less advanced, to the east.

A final element in Turkey's economy is the growth of tourism. By 1976 visitors numbered nearly 1½ million and produced an income of about £60 million ($150 million).

**Communications ·**

For long the great size and difficult topography of Asia Minor, together with thinly spread population and limited natural resources, proved very considerable obstacles to the construction of communications. Isolation and remoteness were in turn regarded as important contributory causes to the slowness of economic development. As late as 1950 it was possible to say that despite efforts by the Republic since 1923, Turkey had only 20000 km of all-weather roads, and that many regions, especially in the south and east (including several sizeable towns), were accessible only by mule-tracks. There was 1 km of road to 1025 people in Turkey, as compared with 1:160 in Britain. With the enhanced strategic status as a member of NATO, outside aid, and the improvements undertaken by the Turks themselves, it has recently been possible to develop road and rail links within Turkey itself and with neighbouring countries. A culmination in one sense of the communications programme was the construction of a Bosphorus road bridge, opened 1975. From no more than 17000 km of all-weather roads in 1966, Turkey now has 139000 km, including several express-ways. The road link (completed with CENTO assistance) between Asia Minor and Tehran has become a major artery used by giant commercial vehicles, and extensions to Iraq and Syria are in construction.

### Railways

At the fall of the Empire in 1918 there was only a skeleton railway system consisting of disconnected lines operated by various non-Turkish companies, and suffering greatly from war damage. These lines had been laid without any general overall plan in districts where the prospect of immediate financial return seemed greatest, and in some cases there was an onerous monetary guarantee from the state to the operating company, such as a guarantee of dividends up to 5% or 10% or a downright payment once or annually per kilometre of line laid. Gauges varied, with the Russian broad gauge coming in as far as Erzurum from Russia. The Baghdad line was completed as far as Nisibin by British prisoners of war. In 1925, following nationalization, the state set out to link remoter areas by east–west lines, and to develop hitherto untouched areas. With indifferent roads, the large size of the country and the scattered nature of mineral resources (e.g. coal and iron), railways retain importance, even though they operate at a considerable loss. The latest five-year plans envisage development beyond the 10000 km open in 1976, and the Turkey–Iran rail link, involving a ferry across Lake Van, opened in 1971.

### Shipping

With a coastline over 7000 km long, and difficult relief inland, it is not surprising that communications by sea play an important part in the life of Turkey. Under the Ottomans, sea traffic was mostly in the hands of the Greeks, though Turkish-manned craft were found in the Black Sea; but since 1923 a Turkish merchant marine has been built up, and Turkey has a significant share amounting to about 40% of international exports. Cost of movement of goods by foreign ships is considerable (up to 20% of value of exports): hence Turkey is increasing her own share of shipping.

Attention has recently been given to port improvements: works at Iskanderun and Mersin, including facilities for handling chrome and other

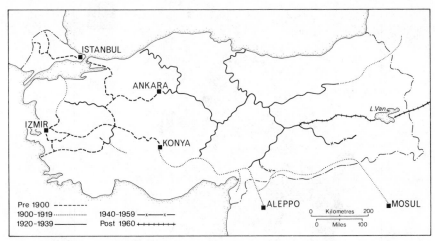

*Fig.* 12.7 Turkey: railways.

ores; improvements at Giresun, Izmir and Samsun, now increasingly active as outlets for the tobacco crop; reconstruction at Haydarpaşa, the Asiatic rail terminal facing Istanbul across the Bosphorus; and the building of a totally new port at Salipazari. Handling over 60% of the total trade of the country, Istanbul is by far the leading port of Turkey (about one-half is foreign trade). Izmir stands next, with about 20%, followed by Samsun, Iskanderun, Trabzon and Mersin.

## Towns

Whereas the overall population of Turkey is increasing at a rate of 2·7% per annum (from 27·8 million in 1960 to 40 million in 1976) urban populations are increasing at more than twice this rate, one reason being that Turkish workers – often rural in origin, who work abroad for a time (nearly 1 million during the peak of 1974, and most in West Germany) – tend to re-settle in towns on their return. Urban populations now number over a third of the total. This means that there are now eighteen towns with a population of over 100000, as compared with six in 1950. Of these cities Istanbul is still by far the largest. The city was founded in 658 B.C. by Greek colonists, who established a settlement on the low plateau formed by the promontory lying between the Sea of Marmara and the drowned valley of the Golden Horn. This site, dropping steeply to the water, was easily defensible by the construction of fortifications on the western (landward) side; and in the centre of the promontory there grew up a succession of fortresses, one of which, the headquarters of the Ottoman rule, came to be known as the Sublime Porte.[1]

[1] Hence the use of the term to denote the Ottoman Caliphs.

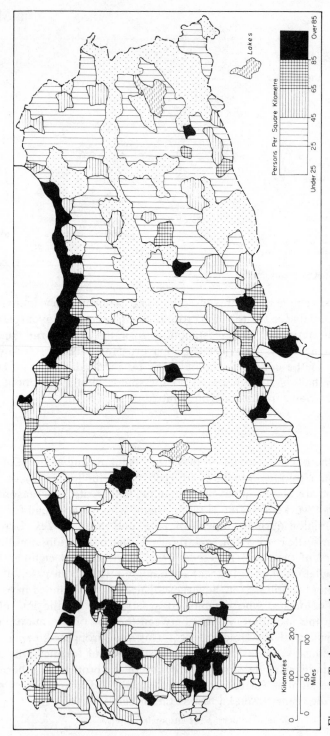

*Fig.* 12.8 Turkey: population (1970 estimates).

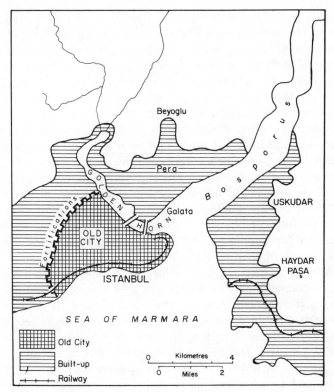

*Fig.* 12.9 Istanbul.

From this ancient nucleus, the city gradually developed; but it was not until the Middle Ages that the opposite (northern) bank of the Golden Horn was occupied and made part of the city. This district, called Galata (new, or foreign), is now the modern business quarter, with the residential district of Pera occupying a ridge well above the city on the north. Uskudar, on the eastern (Asiatic) side of the Bosphorus, was the ferry-point facing Istanbul, and thus the terminal for routes leading eastwards into Asia Minor and the Levant (Uskudar = courier); but in the last two centuries its importance has greatly declined in favour of nearby Haydarpaṣa, which, with a better harbour, has now become the port of entry into Asia Minor, and the terminus of the Anatolian railway system.

The importance of Istanbul derives from a number of factors. Firstly, the Golden Horn is the only good harbour in the entire region of the southern Black Sea, the coastline of which, is, as we have seen, straight, sheer and abrupt, and devoid of shelter during the bad weather that is frequently a feature. Secondly, Istanbul has an important natural resource in the good fishing of the Straits, which is due to the seasonal migration of fish from and into the Black Sea.[1] Thirdly, easy communications by land and sea make it the natural outlet for the relatively fertile Marmara region and its hinterland: though European Turkey is not outstandingly rich, regional differences in land utilization give rise to a variety of products, mainly foodstuffs and animal produce, which are marketed at Istanbul. In addition, however, to this local traffic there were for long two major routes that intersected in the region of the Straits: one by sea from Russia and the Black Sea towards the Mediterranean, the other the land route from south-east Europe to Asia Minor and Iran. Both routes have greatly increased in importance over the past few years: the former with the increase in Russian seafaring, civil and military, the latter because of the growing land trade between Europe and the Middle East, especially Iran and the Gulf.

Central position in relation to Ottoman territories made Istanbul a natural choice for a capital, and it may be noted that, as compared with the bleak uplands of south-east Europe and the arid, 'continental' steppes of Asia Minor, the city has an extremely agreeable climate. Its function as capital attracted many secondary activities – military and naval construction, and administration – so that, like Vienna, Istanbul took on importance as a cultural and economic centre that transcended the limits of a single geographical region. In 1914, Istanbul had over 1 million inhabitants, but after the decision to transfer the capital of Turkey to Ankara, population fell for a time by a quarter. It is now including a substantial and growing outer suburban periphery, well over 4 million. At the present time Istanbul is a market centre for exchange of local produce; a manufacturing centre (textiles, metals, light engineering, glassware, brewing and leather); a fishing and commercial port; and the centre of the expanding tourist trade. Numbers of Greeks and Armenians reside as artisans – the only major Turkish city where they are relatively numerous.

Izmir, until 1950 the second city of Turkey (pop. 1975, 675000), has, like Istanbul, a fine natural harbour, formed by the head of a drowned estuary. A right-angled bend in the lower part of the estuary (due to cross-faulting) provides complete shelter for shipping; but in order to avoid rapid silting up of the port, a feature very common in the Aegean region, the river has been diverted to a new channel away from the town. Izmir is the natural centre for the Aegean coastlands, which are the richest part of Asia Minor; and its position midway between the two largest valleys of the region – those of the Gediz and Büyük Menderes – gives it special advantages from the point of view of communications with the interior. There is a choice of easy routes inland as far as the plateau of western Anatolia.

[1] The name 'Golden' Horn is supposed to refer to the abundance of fish in its waters.

Chief activity is the export of fruit and vegetable products: raisins, figs, olives, tobacco, wheat, barley, opium and vegetable oils are the most important. In addition to these cultivated products of the lowlands, liquorice, valonia acorns, gum tragacanth and nuts are collected from the forested uplands, and Izmir is also the outlet for the pastoral districts of the central plateau. Wool, hides, meat, carpets and woollen cloth are exported, with a return traffic of machinery and cotton goods. There is fishing and boatbuilding – a speciality is sponges, which are exported in some quantity. A fourth activity is the shipping of untreated minerals that are produced in small quantities from the immediate hinterland: chrome, iron, manganese, sulphur, emery and salt. Local manufacturing of soap, spirits and textiles is carried on; and the importance of the city is likely to increase with the greater development of the Aegean coastlands, potentially by far the richest of all the agricultural regions of Turkey. With the current improvements in port facilities, and expansion in demand for Turkish agricultural produce – also its tourist attractions both in its own right and as a centre for the considerable Classical remains of the district – it is well placed for further growth. An oil refinery is in construction.

Ankara was for long the chief regional capital of the northern half of the central plateau, a district formerly known as Galatia. The town had some importance as a Hittite capital, but until 1923 was surpassed in influence by Konya, which, as the centre of the richer southern plateau region, could rightly be termed the metropolis of the entire Anatolian plateau.[1] When, however, the founders of modern Turkey wished to develop Turkish nationalism and break away from the 'pernicious' cosmopolitan atmosphere of Istanbul, Ankara was chosen as the new capital, because of its Hittite associations which have been made much of as the basis of modern nationalist feeling. The city lies at the confluence of a number of streams which are deeply incised into the plateau surface, and the centre portion of the town is placed on a residual ridge surrounded by steep slopes. The surrounding country is open, and relatively easy of access, so that it lies on the ancient routeway from east to west that follows the northern rim of the inner plateau of Anatolia. Ankara is a market for the products of three sub-regions – the forests of the north, and the steppes and cultivated lands of the southern interior – but there is little to parallel the richness of the Izmir region. Chief products are pastoral in origin – wool, mohair, hides and carpets; there is some production of cereals, or temperate fruits (mainly apples), and

---

[1] This is shown by the choice of Konya as the terminus of the Baghdad Railway – Ankara was merely a station connected by branch line to the main trunk route. Another indication of the importance of Konya was the strong religious associations of the city, which became the centre of the Dervish order, and still has some of the finest mosques in Turkey.

of charcoal, a principal domestic fuel of the plateau. Ankara has of course profited greatly from the industrial development undertaken by the Republic, and a wide range of manufacturing of light consumer products takes place, with textile manufacturing (wool, mohair and synthetics), light engineering and repairs, and all the activities associated with an established capital city. Population is now over 1·5 million.

Adana (pop. 1976, 400000) is the natural centre of the Seyhan lowlands, and lies on the ancient highway from Asia Minor through the Cilician Gates to Syria and Mesopotamia. The city is in a sense a second Izmir, for it handles the produce of a rich agricultural region; but Adana, lying 40 km from the coast, must ship her products through the port of Mersin, because the river Seyhan is navigable only by small boats up to Adana. Cotton is the main crop of the district; and other commodities produced are cereals (including some rice and maize), citrus fruits and sugar cane. The Adana plain, one of the most extensive lowlands in Turkey, is, unlike much of Asia Minor, well adapted to the use of modern agricultural machinery; at the present time, considerable development is taking place in this direction, parallel with the development of irrigation and hydro-electric power. With the opening up of south-eastern Turkey both to agriculture and as a source of mineral wealth, Adana has gained considerably in importance. Recent developments also emphasize the expansion of communications and the establishment of NATO bases in the region.

Bursa (pop. 1976, 300000) could be regarded as a replica of Izmir, as the outlet for the Marmara sub-region. It centralizes the trade of the northern Aegean coastlands of Asia Minor, and has its own activities of silk and other textile production. The fig and olive are here less productive – mulberries and nut trees take their place. As well, Bursa has gained generally from its situation on what is now the main axis of Turkish economic activity – the zone between Istanbul and Ankara.

# 13 The Tigris–Euphrates lowlands

For many countries of the Middle East, political boundaries tend to coincide with natural geographical limits. But the major river basin with its twin rivers is divided politically, with little concordance between units of physical geography and political divisions. We shall discuss the geography of this area (as also its western marginal neighbours) on regional environmental basis, rather than as political units.

The origin of the Tigris–Euphrates valley is highly unusual. Although there are opposing theories regarding the origin of the lower valley, equally, if not even more than in the case of Egypt, the land of Mesopotamia is the gift of its rivers. Hence, in beginning an examination of the region, it is first useful to consider the régime of the two streams.

## Régime of the Tigris and Euphrates

Both rivers rise in the Armenian highlands of Asia Minor, and are fed chiefly by melt from snowfall that occurs in winter. In general, both streams can be said to thread an irregular and tortuous way round the east–west running folds of the eastern Anatolian system, following a course towards the south-east. At times, however, quite large folds are directly cut across by deep gorges, suggesting that in some parts, at least, the rivers existed before the mountain ranges were uplifted to their present height, and that drainage is therefore antecedent. Another interesting feature has been the blocking of parts of the Euphrates and Tigris by lava flows, with consequent deviation of the rivers. This is well

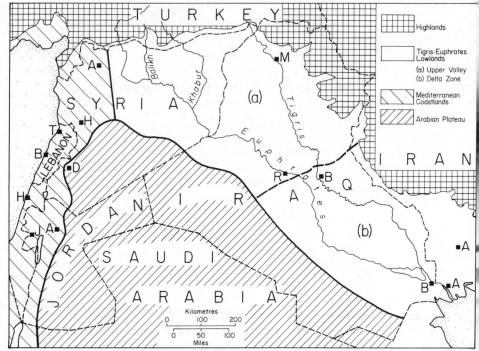

*Fig.* 13.1 Geographical units.

shown south-east of Malatya, where the Euphrates makes a sudden bend south-westwards, because of the presence of lava erupted from the Karacali volcano.

Leaving behind the tangled ridges of Asia Minor, the rivers emerge on to the lower plateau uplands of northern Syria and Kurdistan, and make their way directly south-eastwards to the Persian/Arab Gulf. During its crossing of the north Syrian steppe, the Euphrates receives two important left-bank tributaries, the Balikh and the Khabur, both of which also rise amongst the hills of Asia Minor. No tributaries of any size are received from the Syrian and Arabian deserts (the last right-bank tributary joining the main stream at Carchemish in Turkey), but a number of large empty *wadis* indicate that in earlier times there was substantial right-bank entry of tributaries. The Khabur is the last tributary of any kind to enter the Euphrates, and so for the rest of its course across the hot plains of Iraq there is considerable evaporation, which reduces the volume of water in the river. In this respect, a parallel with the Nile will be noticed.

The Tigris, on the other hand, lies much closer to the Zagros ranges, and along the whole length of its course from Asia Minor to the Persian/Arab Gulf, receives many affluents, some quite large, like the

Great and the Lesser Zab, the Diyala and the Karun; others small, though collectively important in the aggregate volume of water that they supply. The entry of tributaries has important consequences, since the Euphrates, being dependent on rainfall that occurs in a single and relatively restricted catchment area, does not fluctuate rapidly in volume in its middle and lower courses; whereas the Tigris draws its waters from a much wider catchment zone extending from south-east Anatolia to the northern coast of the Persian/Arab Gulf, and local rain in one district can soon affect the height of the river. Sudden floods are, therefore, a feature. Much of the water of the Euphrates comes from slow percolation of melt-water or rainfall through porous rock strata – i.e. temperature conditions in Asia Minor exert considerable control – but a large part, though not all, of the Tigris effluent is due to direct surface run-off from mountain torrents a relatively short distance away to the east. A local rainstorm in the Zagros can thus produce marked changes in river level within a few hours, and a rise of 3–4 m during 24 h is not unusual.

For streams of such large size, the thalweg of the higher reaches of both rivers is distinctly steep. This is the result of oscillation of the land surface during Tertiary and Quaternary times. Most of the fall occurs in the portion between Anatolia and the Baghdad region: the Euphrates drops 244 m between Jerablus and Ramadi (1 in 3000), and hence its current is swift, precluding upstream navigation to all but highly powered boats. The gradient of the Tigris is even sharper, the river falling 300 m between the Turkish frontier and Baghdad (1 in 1750); and though the width of the Tigris is less than that of the Euphrates, the volume of water carried is far greater. The speed of the current in both rivers means also that their erosive action is considerable, hence much sediment is carried at all seasons; and all the year round, the Tigris and Euphrates appear as turbid, rapidly moving streams, in strong contrast to the Nile, which for 7 or 8 months of the year is clear and placid: the Tigris carries as much as 2300 g/m³ of water at flood seasons, as compared with 1700 g for the Nile in flood.

Because of the swift current, sudden fluctuation and great volume of the Tigris, this river is especially subject to devastating floods. An exceptional rise in level may sweep away existing channels, and inundate many hundreds of square kilometres of territory, with the river ultimately carving for itself an entirely new course. Many old channels, still occupied by distributaries, or else used as irrigation canals, are still to be seen: one, for example, at Hilla on the Euphrates, and another east of Baghdad, between Samarra and Ctesiphon.

*Annual régime*

Both rivers are at their lowest in September and October. Decreased evaporation as the result of a fall in temperature during autumn causes a slight but perceptible rise in the Euphrates during November (a feature that does not occur in the Tigris); but the effects of the first onset of winter rainfall, which are clearly to be seen in the Tigris, are almost entirely masked in the Euphrates owing to percolation of rain into the porous subsoil. From December onwards, both rivers begin to rise considerably, because of heavier rainfall over the whole region; yet differences once again become apparent in later spring.

The maximum flood of the Tigris takes place during April, but owing to slower melting, and the effect of percolation, high water in the Euphrates does not occur until May. It is also interesting to compare the volume of the two rivers. At Hit, the Euphrates discharges an average of 250 m³ of water per second in September, and 5000 m³/s in May, with a flood level 3·4 m above low water. At Baghdad the Tigris discharges a minimum of 337 m³ in April, with a rise in level of 5·5 m – this though the Tigris at Baghdad is narrower than the Euphrates at Hit. A further point of importance is that at Baghdad both rivers contain 30–33 parts per 100000 of salt: in the lower courses this figure reaches 90. The Haigh Commission of 1949 estimated that 60% of all irrigated land in Iraq had become salinated to some extent, that 20–30% of irrigated land had been abandoned since 1935 (i.e. 1% of area per annum), and that crop yields had declined by 20% in most areas, and by as much as 50% in some districts.

**Theories of origin of the lower Mesopotamian valley**

According to de Morgan the Tigris and Euphrates at one time (*c.* 10000–5000 B.C.) followed entirely separate courses, and entered the Persian/Arab Gulf by distinct mouths. At this period the shoreline of the Gulf was situated much further to the north-west, and lay only a few kilometres below Baghdad. The two rivers built up separate deltas, which gradually extended towards the south-east, into the waters of the Gulf. Besides the Euphrates and the Tigris, other rivers also emptied into the Persian/Arab Gulf; and two of these, the Karun and the Karkeh, rose in the relatively humid uplands of the Zagros where evaporation was less than on the plain. By reason of their rapid descent from the hills, both these latter streams had enormous erosive power.

Large quantities of silt brought down by the Karun and Karkeh were deposited as deltas along the northern shore of the Persian/Arab Gulf. These latter deltas grew in size more quickly than those of the Tigris and

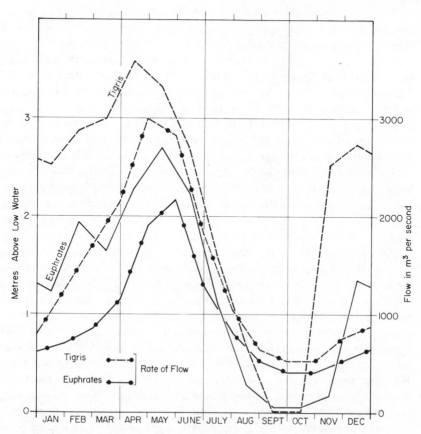

*Fig.* 13.2 The regimes of the Euphrates and Tigris rivers.

Euphrates further to the north-west. Hence a platform of alluvial material was pushed southwards across the head of the Gulf, ultimately forming a barrier beyond which the waters of the Tigris and Euphrates were ponded back in a series of enormous lagoons and swamps. By the commencement of the Christian era, so de Morgan's theory ran, the Karun and Karkeh deltas had joined together and reached the Arabian shore on the southern side of the Gulf, thus partially cutting off the Tigris and Euphrates from the sea. This meant that the latter rivers were slowed down, and their burden of silt, which would normally have been carried away by sea currents, was deposited inland. Vast mud swamps intersected by drainage channels have hence come to be characteristic of the present-day landscape; and this led de Morgan to consider the whole region south of Baghdad as a low platform of alluvium built up by the coalescence of a number of river deltas, with the head of the Persian/Arab

Gulf moving south-eastwards at a rate of 1 km every 30 years approximately. As the coastline advanced, the land behind slowly dried out in places to produce present conditions.

In 1952, however, G. M. Lees and N. L. Falcon put forward another interpretation of the geographical history of the Mesopotamian lowlands. Again in broad outline, these newer views consider that the lowland and upper Persian/Arab Gulf are an area of crustal downwarping, and that the marshlands of lower Iraq represent a delicate balance between the deposition of silt from the Tigris and Euphrates, and subsidence of underlying strata, with oscillation of general sea-level independently of local conditions during the Ice Ages and after as a further complicating factor. Lees and Falcon point out that the rivers flowing from the Zagros and Asia Minor towards the Gulf could be expected to be greatly rejuvenated in Pleistocene and Recent geological times, giving an increased volume of silt over that observable at the present time. Even at the present, measured rates of silt accumulation in the lower valley – 0·559 cm per annum in places – could result in a rate of deposition of the order of 5–6 m per 1000 years. However, between Baghdad and Kut the slope of the Tigris valley is only 6·5 cm per km, and in its lowest part, the Euphrates drops only 0·15 cm per km. Under such conditions, deposition of the order of several metres per 1000 years would make it impossible for the marshes and watercourses to have survived as such for more than a few centuries: deposition would have been too great. The fact that they have so survived points clearly to downwarping. Moreover, the present coastline would appear to have been the boundary between land and sea for a considerable period. Geological deposits of all ages subsequent to the Pliocene are fresh water in character north and west of the present coastline, and marine to the south-east. At Basra, the succession is a complex of alluvial clay and sands with freshwater shells at the base, resting on Miocene bedrock, indicating a subsidence of about 27 m by an original freshwater lake, not a former arm of the sea gradually invaded by silt carried from the north-west. According to the two investigators, the present coastline therefore dates approximately from Pliocene, not Recent or historic times. At the same time Martin draws attention to a series of minor upwarps, the effect of which has been to produce east–west running flexures or ridges. These would appear to have had important effects on the courses of the rivers of Iraq.

Cartographical evidence and navigation charts surveyed fairly exactly at intervals since 1851 indicate that in some restricted parts at the head of the Gulf there has been extensive sedimentation, whilst equally in others there clearly has not. At times, there may have been limited periods of stability when deposition by the two rivers, together with extensive 'trapping' by water surfaces of wind-blown sand from the desert, raised land levels rapidly. Then subsidence occurred, giving rise to local floods, possibly catastrophic over a small area, and re-establishing the line of the coast, with the balance between subsidence and growth by sedimentation extremely finely poised over many millennia. Rather than building forward towards the south-east a normal delta, the Tigris, Euphrates and Karun are discharging into a slowly and irregularly downwarping trough. Further evidence comes from the work of Fairbridge and Purser (chap. 2, p. 25).

Whichever view is taken – and the investigations of Lees and Falcon, though very strongly based, pose difficulties especially for archaeologists – it is also clear that marshland and braided river drainage, which are found only in the last 150 km of the course of the Nile, occupy approximately one-third to one-half of the lowlands of Mesopotamia, covering many thousands of square kilometres. In these extensive shallow marshes most of the water of both rivers seeps away or is evaporated. Below Kut 90% of water in the Tigris is lost, and 63% of the Euphrates volume fails to reach Lake Hammar.

Thus the lowlands of the Euphrates–Tigris can be subdivided into two contrasting regions: (a) the southern, or lower valley, where land forms associated with fluviatile deposition – lagoons, marsh, braided channels and embanked river-courses (levees) with ox-bow lakes – are the chief features; and (b) the upper Mesopotamian region, a somewhat more complex area where features due to erosion predominate. In this latter area are the two increasingly distinctive river basins with smaller tributary valleys separated by a broad interfluve of upland and plateau, within which occur several basins with closed drainage. The boundary between the upper and lower regions of the Euphrates–Tigris lowlands can be conveniently placed at a low ridge or shelf that runs from Ramadi eastwards to a point a little to the south of Baghdad. This, some 80 m above plain level in its highest parts, was regarded by de Morgan, but not of course by Lees and Falcon, as the prehistoric coastline of the Persian/Arab Gulf.

## Geographical sub-regions
### Lower valley

Topographically, this region consists of an alternation of marshland and low mud plain, diversified by sluggish drainage channels. The whole area is extremely flat, with a fall of only 4 cm/km over the last 300 km of the Euphrates, and under 8 cm/km along the Tigris. This means that over a stretch extending for 150 km north-west of Qurna, which lies at the head of the Shatt el Arab, the Euphrates drops less than 3 m in base level, so that annual flooding, which may be of the order of 1·7 to 3 m, regularly inundates immense areas of country (highest flood-level recorded was 9 m – on the Tigris – in 1954). As a result, much of the region is undisturbed swamp, and parts are still entirely uninhabited and unsurveyed. The Shatt el Arab, formed by confluence of the Tigris and Euphrates, is a broad navigable waterway, fringed by a belt of palms for a depth of 1–4 km behind which occur masses of tall reeds sometimes more than 6 m in height. The Euphrates joins the Tigris through an outflow from a large sheet of water, Lake Hammar, which is really an old lagoon now fed by the Euphrates and is no more than 1–2 m deep in many places. Here the fringe of palm trees gives place to reeds and aquatic vegetation that form a canopy over sluggish creeks and sand- or mud-spits. In spring, the season of flood, virtually all the country in the triangle Basra–Amara–Nasiriya is one expanse of continuous marshland.

The inhabitants of these districts follow a mode of life different from that of their countrymen further north. Dwellings are built of bundles of reeds fastened by ropes made of the same plant, and are set either on thick bundles of brushwood as a foundation, or else on the few sand-spits that stand above the water. Rice is a staple, and diet is varied by fish, salted or dried, and by a species of edible rush known as *ageyl*. Water-buffaloes are almost the only animals kept, and these provide curds, butter and cheese, together with dung which is the chief fuel available.

Further north, the zone of marshland decreases in extent, though remaining a uniquitous feature. Numerous old drainage channels occur, and, whilst a good many of these are occupied by swamps or lakes (e.g. Lakes Habbaniya and Aqaquf), others are dry. An important feature is the variation in level between the main streams of the Tigris and Euphrates. From Baghdad as far as Qurna, the bed of the Tigris lies at a slightly higher altitude than that of the Euphrates, allowing the easy construction of free-flow irrigation channels. In the region of Baghdad, the position is reversed, with the Euphrates lying higher than the Tigris. This circumstance has for centuries been utilized with much effect by irrigation engineers.

## Upper valley

Above the latitude of Ramadi, both the Tigris and Euphrates flow in well-defined valleys comparable in certain respects with that of the Nile. In parts, the rivers meander over extensive flood plains; at others, they have cut deeply into soft, horizontally bedded rock measures, and lie in a trench or shallow gorge. Here and there, though less frequently than on the Nile, outcrops of harder rock have resisted erosion, and stretches of rapids or 'narrows' occur. A special feature of the Tigris (and not the Euphrates), is that because of the meandering course of the river, and the presence of natural levees, tributaries enter only with difficulty.

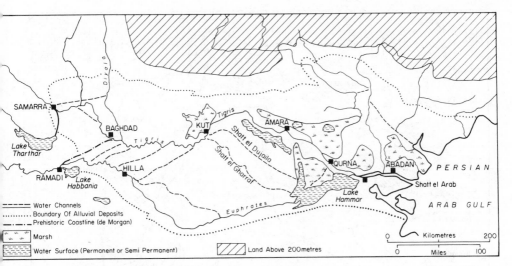

*Fig.* 13.3 The lower valleys of the Euphrates–Tigris.

This is the case on the eastern bank of the Tigris between Baghdad and Mosul, where numerous small streams descend from the Zagros ranges. At their junctions with the Tigris there is sometimes an area of poorly drained marshland.

Relief in parts of the Euphrates and Tigris valleys strongly suggests that the régime of both rivers was at one time markedly different than that occurring now. Much of the river bed even in the plains area is deeply incised, with the river flowing in a notch well below the level of the surrounding plain, and bounded by cliffs sometimes 50–100 m in height. Incised meanders are a common feature on the middle Euphrates, recalling on a larger scale the land forms of the Seine valley below Paris. River rejuvenation at no very distant date would seem to be the causative factor, and this would appear to have taken place as the result of the downwarping of the floor of the Persian/Arab Gulf (already alluded to), combined with the upwarping of parts of Asia Minor. Temporary climatic phases of increased precipitation during Tertiary and early Quaternary times would also have an effect, by producing a temporary increase in river volume.

At the present time, this slotted drainage in upper Mesopotamia has certain disadvantages. Irrigation is difficult in regions where the river is well below the level of the surrounding plain; and miniature gorges and rapids hinder navigation. Thus in some parts the banks of both rivers are entirely isolated from the streams themselves, and wide stretches remain uninhabited.

Between the upper Tigris and Euphrates lies the region known as the

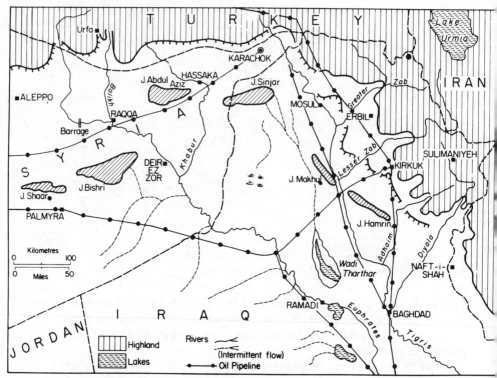

*Fig.* 13.4 The upper valleys of the Euphrates–Tigris.

Jezireh (Arabic = *island*), which is bounded on two sides by the rivers, and on the north by the fold ranges of Asia Minor. For the most part, the Jezireh consists of an undulating plain or low plateau, lying at an altitude of 150–300 m above sea-level, with a number of small closed basins from which there is no drainage outlet. The largest of these basins is a long, narrow trench cut deeply into the plateau and known as the Wadi Tharthar. Streams enter the Wadi from the north, but terminate towards the southern end in a salt marsh. The Wadi may be a tectonic feature, or even an old river valley now dried out; and it is now used as an immense storage basin for floodwaters.

To the north-west of the Wadi Tharthar lies the Jebel Sinjar, a prolongation of the Syrian fold structures. As the highest parts reach 1000 m, there is a heavier rainfall on the upper slopes, and some settled cultivation is therefore possible. The Yazidi, who inhabit the Jebel, practise mixed arable and pastoral farming. Another important feature of the Jezireh is the Khabur valley, the ancient region of Mitanni, where irrigation was formerly developed on an extensive scale, and a relatively dense population maintained. Until recently the prevalence of malaria and heavily charged river water (which is affected by sulphurous springs) prevented exploitation on a large scale, but within the last few years striking changes have occurred, and the region is now one of major development.

The territory on the eastern bank of the Tigris is known as Assyria. Here the land rises in steps from the Tigris towards the north-east, each step being marked by increasingly prominent ridges that are aligned generally from north-west to south-east. The first of these ranges is the Jebel Hamrin (maximum height 500 m), which fronts the Tigris along a part of its course. Numerous tributaries of the Tigris have broken through the ridges, forming gaps or gorges, so that the whole region of Assyria has been dissected, giving on the south-west a fairly broad open plain with occasional higher ridges. This passes towards the north-east into an increasingly broken and mountainous country with scattered lowland basins shut in by hills. Ultimately, the main Zagros ranges are reached on the east, and the Anatolian arcs on the north. Both of these higher upland regions are occupied by Kurds, hence the name Iraqi Kurdistan is often applied to the parts of the mountain massifs and piedmonts that lie within the Iraqi state.

## Climate

The lowland region has two marked seasons – a dry and intensely hot summer, lasting from May to October, and a relatively cold, damp winter from December to March, with spring and autumn as short transition periods between the two.

With the development of summer monsoonal low pressure conditions over the Persian/Arab Gulf and north-west India, air is drawn towards the south-east, giving remarkably regular and constant north-westerly winds over the whole of Iraq. These are known as *shamal*, and blow without interruption during the summer. The air is dry; no cloud forms, and the sun beats down uninterruptedly over the lowland, giving rise to shade temperatures that exceed 35 °C on most days, and not infrequently reach 45 °C. Some relief is obtained during the night, as diurnal variation of temperature is marked; and near the rivers and marshes intense evaporation may lower the day temperatures by a few degrees. Lacking the possibility of moving to nearby hill regions, many Iraqis are driven to constructing underground shelters (*sirdab*) in which to pass the hottest part of the day. A further unpleasant feature is blowing dust, raised by the strong *shamal*, which reaches a climax in late afternoon, and drops at night, but the effect of this wind is also to keep down humidity.

With the wind blowing towards the Persian/Arab Gulf during the summer season, there is little mitigating effect from the presence of the

Climatic data: representative stations

| | J | F | M | A | M | J | J | A | S | O | N | D | | |
|---|---|---|---|---|---|---|---|---|---|---|---|---|---|---|
| **Temperature (°C)** | | | | | | | | | | | | | | |
| Deir ez Zor (Syria) | 7 | 9 | 11 | 19 | 25 | 29 | 33 | 32 | 28 | 22 | 15 | 9 | | |
| Mosul | 5 | 9 | 13 | 17 | 24 | 29 | 35 | 35 | 28 | 22 | 15 | 8 | | |
| Baghdad | 9 | 11 | 16 | 22 | 28 | 32 | 34 | 34 | 31 | 24 | 17 | 11 | | |
| Basra (Shaiba) | 11 | 14 | 18 | 24 | 30 | 33 | 35 | 36 | 32 | 27 | 20 | 13 | | |
| **Rainfall (mm)** | | | | | | | | | | | | | *Total* | *Rainy days* |
| Deir ez Zor | 31 | 25 | 17 | 14 | 3 | 0 | 0 | 0 | 0 | 5 | 37 | 35 | 116 | 29 |
| Mosul | 53 | 76 | 31 | 46 | 13 | 0 | 0 | 0 | 0 | 6 | 45 | 50 | 385 | 60 |
| Baghdad | 30 | 27 | 8 | 11 | 10 | 0 | 0 | 0 | 0 | 3 | 25 | 28 | 144 | 28 |
| Basra | 33 | 30 | 10 | 14 | 3 | 0 | 0 | 0 | 0 | 3 | 27 | 25 | 169 | 21 |

sea – temperatures for Basra, Baghdad and Mosul show considerable uniformity, though continentality is somewhat more apparent in the north, with a wider range of day temperatures in summer. It is also noteworthy that in many places there is little difference between July and August mean temperatures, with the monthly maximum even occurring during August in some localities.

In winter, temperatures generally lower than might be expected can be explained by the presence of snow-covered mountains to the east and north. Differences are apparent between the north or upper basin and the south, the former region experiencing something approaching a continental régime, the latter a milder climate, due to latitude and the influence of the sea. A comparison between Mosul and Basra shows that for the coldest month (January) there is 5 °C difference of temperature.

Another significant fact is that the absolute maximum of temperature recorded at Shaiba in January is 27 °C, and at Mosul 20 °C – i.e. 'hot' spells can occur during winter in many parts of the south, but less so in the north. Diurnal variation is considerable, particularly away from the coast and in summer: at Baghdad there can be as much as 20 °C difference as between day and night, though the average is about 17 °C. Despite low altitudes the whole of the riverine lowlands may experience spells of frost of some severity (absolute minimum temperatures at Deir ez Zor −9 °C, Mosul −11 °C, Baghdad −7 °C, Basra −5 °C). The northern Persian/Arab Gulf is not, relatively speaking, warm in winter; in fact, at sea-level it is at least as cold, if not colder than most parts of the south-east Mediterranean. Coldest weather usually occurs when the Siberian high pressure zone extends beyond the south-west of central Asia, and cold dry air allowing high radiation blankets Iran and adjacent areas, giving especially severe conditions in the hills.

Because of the predominating off-shore wind, the high air humidities characteristic of the Persian/Arab Gulf do not occur on a wide scale in the Euphrates–Tigris region. Nevertheless, as we have seen, evaporation close to rivers and lakes is high, and the air over a short distance can become very humid – on the actual banks of rivers, wet-bulb temperatures of over 27 °C are common, though over the country as a whole humidities are much lower. This fact, which does not always appear in climatological records, is responsible for a difficult 'physiological' climate, in which heat stroke and exhaustion can easily occur; and this goes far to explain the notorious climatic reputation of southern Iraq – a reputation which does not at first sight seem justified until one takes into account the local variation of humidity.

Rainfall occurs only during winter, and is almost entirely due to the arrival of moist maritime air from the Mediterranean, in the form of shallow and somewhat degenerate depressions. The damp air has previously passed over the mountainous country of Anatolia or the Levant, there depositing much of its moisture, so that on arrival in the Tigris–Euphrates basin only a reduced rainfall occurs, with annual totals ranging in the lowlands from 25 to 500 mm. On uplift over the Zagros ranges, however, considerable precipitation exceeding 1000 mm occurs – a figure rather higher than at one time believed – and, in order to explain this apparent anomaly of abundant rainfall from weakened and dried-out depressions, it is necessary to recall that practically all rainfall in Iraq is of the instability type (chapter 3), and is therefore intensified by a mountainous topography. There may also be a further factor: rejuvenation of the depressions by absorption of water vapour from the vast tracts of swamp and lake in lower Mesopotamia, or, more distantly, from the waters of the Persian/Arab Gulf. A strong south-easterly air current, cold and relatively damp, and known as a *sharki*, usually develops in front of an advancing depression, and this can bring moisture northward from the Gulf.

Because of the regularity of land forms, the distribution of rainfall follows a simple pattern. Late January or early February is the wettest period, and normally no rain falls between the end of May and the end of September. Over most of the country annual falls do not exceed 125 mm, but towards the mountains on the east and north there is a rapid increase. The foothills of the Zagros stand out as relatively well watered, and the Assyrian region receives over 375 mm, an amount sufficient to allow cultivation without irrigation. The 375 mm isohyet is of extreme importance in Iraq and northern Syria, since it marks the effective limit between desert and cultivated land.[1] With less than 375 mm annual rainfall agriculture is dependent on irrigation, and settlement is confined to the neighbourhood of rivers. Away from water supplies, the population is nomadic.

## Agriculture

Iraq is traditionally an agricultural country, although today the oil industry accounts for over nine-tenths of its export earnings and provides two-thirds of government revenue. Nevertheless, the agricultural sector remains the main source of employment and offers considerable potential for development as Iraq attempts to diversify the economy in order to reduce the nation's reliance on oil. For many years agriculture received priority in development planning. Large allocations have been devoted to this sector under the various development programmes since 1950, but an important feature of Iraq's development efforts has been a serious shortfall in actual as against planned investment. The performance in agriculture has been particularly poor with expenditure averaging only 38% of allocations between 1951 and 1964, and only 32·4% between 1965 and 1970. More recently, agriculture has received roughly equal treatment with industry in the allocation of development investment. Under the current plan 1976–80 the government is giving precedence to oil and industrial development, but nonetheless the agricultural sector is to receive an estimated ID 3010 million with the aim of achieving self-sufficiency in food supplies. In 1974 foodstuffs, including wheat, rice and sugar, accounted for over one-quarter of all imports.

Iraq is one of the least densely populated countries in the Middle East, but with perhaps the greatest agricultural potential. Unlike Egypt and many Asian countries, it does not suffer from acute pressure of population on agricultural resources, and in recent years, labour shortages at peak seasons, and particularly at harvest time, have emerged as a serious problem. At the time of the agricultural census held in October 1971 the total area of all agricultural holdings in Iraq was 22·9 million dunums[2] which represents 13·20% of the country's total area. Of the total area of holdings, 2·64% was under date palms, and 0·19% was forested. The land allotted to temporary summer and winter crops and land left fallow during both seasons accounted for 84·59% of the total area of holdings. The agricultural population numbered about 4 million (2 million males and 1·94 females) of which 2·1 million were classified as employed.

[1]   250 mm of rainfall is normally regarded as the boundary between arid and moist regions, but in the Middle East, because of high temperatures, the 375 mm isohyet is a better criterion.
[2]   The Iraqi unit of area, the dunum, is equal to 0·25 ha or 0·62 acres.

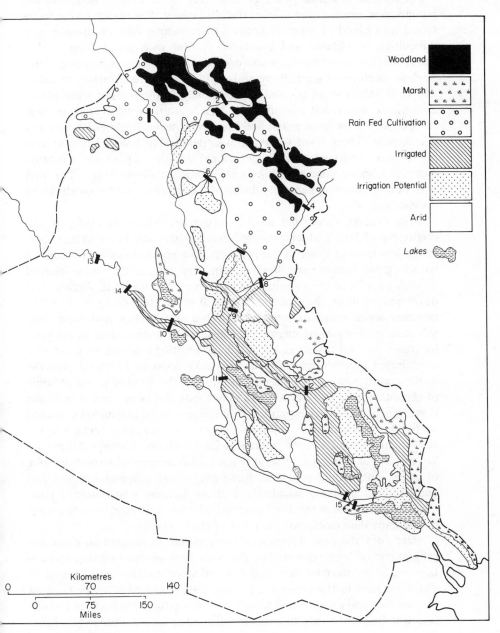

Woodland

Marsh

Rain Fed Cultivation

Irrigated

Irrigation Potential

Arid

Lakes

Kilometres
0          70          140

0          75          150
        Miles

Fig. 13.5 Iraq: land use.

For long agricultural yields in Iraq were lower than in neighbouring regions, and much lower than in the Nile valley. The reasons were to be found in a blend of natural, social and economic factors. Besides the difficulties of climate and the river system with its shifting banks, marshland and rapid floods, insect pests occurred on a considerable scale. Archaic methods of land tenure and exploitation were a further obstacle, and with only a small population potentially fertile regions were often, as we have noted, left uncultivated. As a result the total average income in 1951–53 for an Iraqi *fellah* and his family was calculated at only £14 per annum. Their level of living was deplorably low. They had few possessions; and medical and educational facilities, a pure water supply, electricity and similar amenities were almost totally lacking. Their diet was monotonous and generally deficient, many were undernourished and disease was rife.

Most experts agree that until the 1958 revolution inequality in the ownership of land and land tenure relationships contributed in large part to the low level of living of the peasants. In a political system dominated by the great landowners, land reform was impossible, and it proved difficult to enforce even minimal legislation controlling rents. Agricultural development after the Second World War averted its eyes from the complex social structure and concentrated on irrigation and floodwater schemes carried out by engineers. These great water schemes financed by Iraq's new oil revenues benefited the existing landowning class who contributed little to development and were opposed to social progress in the countryside. In an attempt to improve the level of living of some of the cultivators and yet avoid conflict with the large landowners, the Government after 1945 began to settle farmers on state land to be opened up by the new irrigation schemes. Seven schemes were reclaimed for settlement – Dujaila, Shahrazoor, Hawija, Makhmur, Latafiya, Sinjar and Musayyib – of which the Dujaila scheme was the most important. In spite of many operational problems these settlement schemes brought real improvement in living standards to those farmers who obtained land. Unfortunately, the numbers of peasants who received land were too small to influence the position of the mass of the cultivators.

After 1958 the new Republican Government developed an extensive programme of land reform. The declared aims of the Agrarian Reform Law were to destroy the political influence of the landowners; to distribute land to the peasants; to raise their standard of living in order to stop the rural exodus, and to improve agricultural production. Ownership was limited to 1000 dunums in irrigated areas and double this figure for rain-watered areas. The excess was confiscated to be redistributed in smaller plots (30–60 dunums on irrigated land and 60–120 dunums on non-irrigated land) to new peasant owners. However, although expropriation was rigorously enforced, political rivalry over the implementation of the reform resulted in delays in the redistribution of land. Also because of the problem of organizing co-operatives there was failure to replace functions formerly carried out by the landowner and his agents, especially in the maintenance of irrigation works and in marketing produce. The rural exodus continued and may even have accelerated in some areas as a result of the uncertainty and confusion associated with land reform.

A more comprehensive Agrarian Reform Law was enacted in 1970 further reducing the maximum size of holding. No compensation was paid for land expropriated, while land was redistributed to peasants free of charge. However, expropriation of land has continued to outstrip the government's ability to redistribute it. By the beginning of 1975, 10·2 million dunums had been expropriated since 1958, 4·2 million dunums under the first Agrarian Reform Law and 6 million dunums under the second, but only 5·8 million dunums had actually been redistributed to 157862 beneficiaries.

The government is currently implementing a collectivization programme in the more fertile areas of the country. State farms are being set up, and the new agricultural mechanization programme is mainly concentrated here. In addition, because of the shortage of agricultural labour, Egyptian farmers are being encouraged to settle in Iraq under a joint economic agreement, and the first group of 350 families arrived early in 1976 and were allocated land in the Wahda development project near Baghdad. Unfortunately, while the government fixes prices for agricultural products at a low level to the advantage of the urban population, farming will remain unprofitable and thus Iraqi cultivators continue to migrate to the towns in search of more lucrative employment.

It will be seen that in Iraq a division into two climatic provinces – a wetter (rain-watered) region and an arid (irrigated) region, with the 375 mm isohyet as boundary – has very great significance not only in relation to settlement, but also in relation to the crops grown, because it coincides roughly with another important line of demarcation; that of the northern limit of the date palm. Thus, to the south, barley, rice and dates are staples, all being grown under irrigation; whilst in the north barley, wheat and Mediterranean fruits dominate.

Wheat is the most important crop in terms of the area cultivated and the quantities produced, although occasionally in the past, as in 1965–66, the production of barley has actually exceeded that of wheat. Wheat is a winter crop and is mostly grown in the wetter areas. Hence almost 75% of Iraqi production is from the north and east, chiefly from the *muhafadha* of Nineveh. Other productive areas are along the middle and upper courses of the two rivers, on the Tigris between Baghdad and Amara, and on the Euphrates round Deir ez Zor, Ramadi and Hilla. The

Main cereals – area cultivated, average yield, production 1974/5

|  | Total area cultivated (dunums) | Average yield per dunum (kg) | Production ('oo tons) |
|---|---|---|---|
| Wheat | 5 791 000 | 150·1 | 845 400 |
| Barley | 2 392 900 | 192·6 | 437 000 |
| Rice | 125 610 | 505·8 | 60 540 |

1 dunum = 0·25 ha or 0·62 acres.

introduction of new species from the Punjab and the New World (Mexico especially) has resulted in better yields. Some of these species grow faster, others are resistant to 'rust' or insect pests. Nevertheless yields are still low, and although large areas are devoted to wheat, production no longer satisfies domestic demand.

Barley is also a winter crop, but unlike wheat the area under cultivation has declined by about 50% during the last 10 years. Yields, however, are higher than for wheat. Barley is more tolerant than wheat of aridity and of soil salinity, and its growing period is shorter, a feature which reduces loss by the *sunna* insect pest. Formerly, native varieties of barley predominated, but within the last 20 to 30 years these have increasingly been replaced by better strains introduced from Morocco and California. Main regions of production are the plains of Assyria – Mosul, Erbil and Kirkuk districts, the Middle Tigris valley (*muhafadhas* of Diyala and Wasat) and the middle Euphrates (*muhafadha* of Babylon).

Rice, a summer crop, is grown in the lower valley but is naturally restricted to districts which are regularly inundated, or where irrigation is easy. Although the area under cultivation is small (less than 10% of that of barley and about 4% of that of wheat) a yield of up to three or four times as great can be obtained. Since 1971, however, the area of rice cultivation, yields and production have declined considerably, with a big reduction in 1975 because of a drop in the flow of the Euphrates. As a result large quantities of rice must be imported. The chief regions of rice growing are (1) the marshes of the Amara district (Tigris river), (2) the Shamiya district, between Najaf and Diwaniya, on the Euphrates, and to a lesser extent (3) the lower Euphrates from Nasiriya as far as the head of Lake Hammar. Minor regions of production are the upper part of the Shatt el Gharraf, the district of Samarra, and the lower Khabur valley. Small-scale paddy fields are also a feature of the river banks of Assyria – chiefly around Sulaimanieh and Kirkuk.

Another summer crop is millet, which also demands irrigation in the later stages of growth. As a result, distribution is sharply restricted, even in the wetter zone, to the vicinity of rivers. Chief region of production is obviously the south, where irrigation water is more abundant. Millet is used for animal fodder and as an ingredient for bread, but the area under cultivation has declined by over 50% in the last 10 years, and as yields have not improved, production has fallen steeply.

Maize, also grown in summer, is confined mainly to the middle and upper parts of both river valleys. The area under cultivation is still small but it has been extended in recent years while yields have also risen. Seseme is cultivated on a limited scale.

### Commercial crops

Iraq produces about 80% of the total world supply of dates, i.e. of the proportion of dates that form an article of commerce, because most dates are eaten directly by the growers, or else bartered. The general conditions under which date palms thrive have already been touched upon, and it is sufficient to recall that the palms can flourish in dry, saline, sandy, loamy or even waterlogged soils, although the maximum yield of fruit is obtained when abundant water is available.

The region of the Shatt el Arab is pre-eminently suited to date production, and both banks are lined with date groves extending inland for as much as 2 km. Some 30–35 million palms are cultivated throughout the region, and of these, one-half are found close to the Shatt el Arab, the rest occurring along the river banks as far north as latitude 33° N. A curious feature is the rise of the river under the influence of the incoming tide. Fresh water is ponded back in the Shatt el Arab, and floods the banks to a depth of as much as 1 m to provide natural and regular irrigation of the groves – a phenomenon that from the point of view of the native farmer is wholly estimable.

In order to ensure a good crop, the land is dug over once every 4 years; and because of the frequent presence of creeks and watercourses, this must be done by hand. Artificial pollination is, as we have already seen, highly necessary; and although most groves include 3% of male palms, the district of Fao has developed a special trade in male pollen dust, from which other date-growing regions are supplied.

About 130 varieties of date are known, but three are most widely grown. The *Halawi* palm produces the finest fruit, but gives only a moderate yield (20 kg per tree) (Dowson), whilst the *Sayir* produces slightly less, but is more tolerant of inferior growing conditions and is probably the most widely grown. The *Zahidi* does not give a fruit of high quality, but the yield is over 50 kg per tree, and this compensates for the low price obtained. Fertilization of the female palm takes place in April, and picking begins in August, when large numbers of nomadic tribesmen move into the date-growing areas to work as seasonal harvesters.

Besides forming an extremely important part of local diet, dates are used in the distilling of *arak* – the chief fermented beverage outside the vine-growing areas, and once thought to have value as a prophylactic against disease, chiefly malaria. The crushed stones are fed to cattle, and both leaves and trunk of the palm are used in light constructional work (houses, boats, even bridges) and also in the manufacture of paper. About one-half of the average annual date production of 375000 tons is retained for home consumption, the rest exported.[1]

Cotton is the second commercial crop of the riverine lowlands, but, in strong contrast to the successful development of date-growing, cotton has experienced many vicissitudes. Some cotton has for long been grown to meet the needs of local craft industry, but large-scale production for export began after 1920. Iraq had no modern textile machinery before 1940. There are a number of handicaps, chief of which are insect pests and soil salinity (the latter being especially prevalent on irrigated land). The area under cultivation has remained little changed during the last 10 years, but yields have risen appreciably. There is now a regular home demand from the textile mills installed since 1945, and in some years, also an export surplus, Japan, Hong Kong and central Europe being the chief markets.

## Minor crops

Tobacco is widely grown in the foothills of the north-east, particularly in Kurdistan, but the product is consumed only within the country. Although some improvement has recently taken place following the introduction of new stocks from the Balkans and Turkey, the crop is of moderate quality, and unlikely to compete in outside markets. Vines are also an important feature in the north-eastern foothills, and in some districts of Kurdistan may be said to be a principal crop. Numerous varieties of other fruit and vegetables are also grown, more especially in the wetter zone of the north, though Baghdad is increasingly important for figs and vegetables. As elsewhere in the Middle East, market-gardening associated with growing urban centres is a recent development of increasing significance.

[1] It should be noted that dates are one of the few agricultural products of the Middle East which hold a commanding position in world markets. The situation of the date groves adjacent to tide water allows an unusually low cost of transport, so that competitors in north Africa – especially in Biskra, which has slow and difficult land communications with the Mediterranean – are at a disadvantage. The chief drawbacks to Iraqi dates are: poor packing methods, and variation in quality of the fruits, due to lack of grading and palm-breeding control.

Nitrogen-fixing crops are also increasingly grown – vetches, beans and peas especially. Mulberry-growing for silkworms, once important around Baghdad, has almost disappeared over the last few years with the competition of other fibres. The cultivation of both cane sugar and sugar beet is being encouraged and the area devoted to both crops has more than doubled in the last 10 years, but yields have fallen short of the target set. Cultivation of both crops is at present confined to the governorates of Nineveh and Maisan.

### Irrigation

About a quarter of the agricultural land of Iraq is watered adequately by rainfall. Of the rest much is still irrigated by free flow, seasonally, although lift pumping is also widely practised. Control of river waters for irrigation presents an unusual problem; because of the occurrence of floods in spring, at a time when all crops except rice are partly grown, cultivated areas cannot simply be inundated, as in Egypt, and water must be impounded as far as possible within the banks of the rivers themselves. This is achieved by the construction of large artificial embankments or levees; but at times when the river is dangerously high, breaches are deliberately made in the levees to allow flooding to take place in areas where damage will be least.

Another problem is to drain off stagnant floodwater, which, if left on the land, is very prone to induce soil salinity through accumulation of sodium and magnesium chlorides. About 60–75% of the irrigated lands in Iraq are affected to some degree, while it has been suggested that 20–30% of the country's total cultivated land has been abandoned because of salinity. Of the crops grown in Iraq, cotton and wheat are most susceptible to salinity, dates least susceptible. In ancient times a simple but effective system of canals was created with the dual functions of watering arid areas and draining waterlogged zones, and, to achieve this, skilful use was made of the variation in relative level between the Tigris and the Euphrates. A large number of canals were constructed on both sides of the Tigris from Tikrit southwards, and five major channels also led water from the Euphrates to the Tigris in the region of Baghdad and Babylon. Irrigation reached a peak of development in the early Abbasid period (c. A.D. 850–1000); and from that time onwards there was a prolonged decline. Since about 1880, however, major revival has occurred. Old channels have been cleared and repaired, and a system of new barrages and canals built.

There are two separate problems involved: control of floods in order to prevent destruction on a large scale (much of Baghdad was badly damaged by floods in 1954), and utilization of river water for irrigation

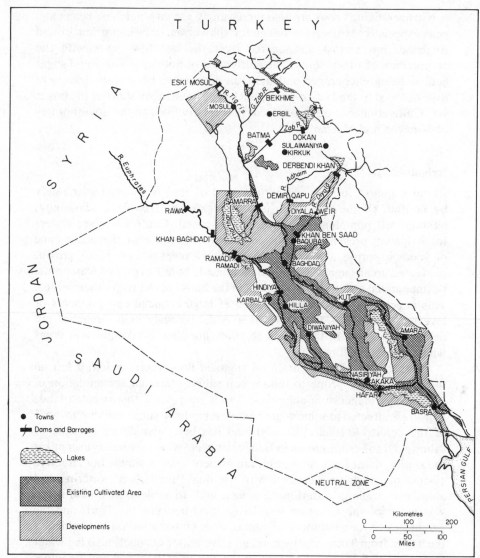

*Fig.* 13.6 Irrigation in Iraq.

and desalination. Flood control on the Euphrates involves two basins,
at Habbaniya and Abu Dibbis. A barrage across the river at Ramadi
(containing a fish-ladder and a navigation lock for river craft) raises the
river level to allow diversion into the Habbaniya depression. Water stored
in this basin can then be led back into the Euphrates in the dry season
by an outlet canal at Dibban. In addition, another channel leads to the
Abu Dibbis depression, which is at present used only to receive excessive

floodwater from Lake Habbaniya in an emergency. So far, water from Lake Habbaniya is not stored at Abu Dibbis for irrigation purposes, since the latter has extensive saline deposits which contaminate the water.

Because of greater volume, the largest flood control scheme of Iraq is located on the Tigris, in the Wadi Tharthar. This is another aretic drainage basin, with its lowest point 3 m below sea-level, and there will hence eventually be produced a lake over 100 km long, comparable in size with the Dead Sea. A barrage has been built at Samarra to deflect in river water through a canal 70 km long, and the fall of level gives considerable potentialities for the generation of hydro-electric power. The Wadi Tharthar scheme was inaugurated in 1956, and some 760 000 dunums are now irrigated from it. As a prevention of flooding, the scheme is also highly successful.

Another regulator dam is located on the Lesser Zab river, at Dokhan gorge some 70 km north-west of Sulaimaniya. This is a high dam (116·5 m), and besides its primary purpose of storing water for irrigation it is an important flood control measure, and a source of hydro-electric power. Extensions to the Dokhan scheme have been carried out at Batma and Vdhaim; and another multi-purpose dam has been constructed at Darband-i-Khan. Smaller new schemes are in operation along the lower Diyala and on the Tigris at Amara.

A number of older barrages and weirs serve to raise the river level for irrigation. The oldest barrage is at Hindiya, on the Euphrates, and was constructed in 1913, with additions in 1922. Its functions are (i) to divert water from the Euphrates into a canal that was one old channel of the Euphrates, and which runs parallel to the modern river through Hilla; and (ii) to raise the general level of the Euphrates and thus allow irrigation in the region of Karbala (on the right bank of the river opposite Hilla), and also upstream on the left bank as far as Ramadi.

Smaller schemes on the Euphrates include (i) the Greater Musayyib project (1956) which has brought under irrigation about 400 000 dunums; (ii) regulators in the lowest part of the Euphrates just before it enters Lake Hammar to expand rice cultivation; and (iii) similar regulators at Shamiyah in order to maintain river level in the dry season.

A barrage at Kut, on the Tigris, was completed in 1943. Some 700 m in length (almost three times the size of the Hindiya dam), allows the cultivation of two extensive areas lying south and south-east of Kut: respectively, the region of the Shatt el Gharraf, and the region of the Shatt el Dujaila, both of which are braided distributaries of the Tigris, but have no outlet at their lower end. Water is not available all the year round in these areas; it can only be supplied during the winter, since the summer flow is required for rice cultivation downstream at Amara.

The Diyala weir feeds six canals which irrigate an extensive area north and north-east of Baghdad. Altogether, about 540000 dunums are watered, as compared with 1·5 million dunums in the Hilla region of the Euphrates, 600000 dunums (Ramadi region) and a potential of 1·2 million dunums round the Shatt el Gharraf and 360000 dunums round the Shatt el Dujaila. In the Kirkuk plain, a canal has been constructed to tap the waters of the Lesser Zab, and 216000 dunums are irrigated.

Within the last 15 years, separate drainage projects have also been developed. These involve the construction of large outfalls, which lower the water table in the subsoil by leading off groundwater either into rivers or natural depressions. Sometimes, gravity flow is possible, but in most cases pumping is required; and because of the prevalence of dust and silt-laden winds, artificial dredging and wind-breaks are also necessary.

Altogether, some 16 million dunums of land are now irrigated throughout the country, and over twelve major dams and irrigation projects are either under way or in preparation. They should eventually give Iraq an additional 4 million dunums of irrigated land. The Kirkuk dam will irrigate 400000 dunums within the next 5 years increasing to 1·5 million dunums by 1987, while the Mosul dam, to be built 65 km north-west of Mosul on the Tigris, is intended to irrigate 1·2 million dunums as well as generate electricity. The Hamrin dam on the Diyala 120 km north of Baghdad will combine flood control, irrigation, and electricity generation and the Falluja dam will irrigate 900000 dunums along the Euphrates near Lake Habbaniya. Preliminary work is also underway for the important Euphrates dam to be built at Haditha. The lower Khalis and Tharthar projects, two important flood control and irrigation schemes, are already under way. A canal has been built to link the Euphrates with Tharthar lake, which is already linked to the Tigris, so that Tigris floodwaters can be diverted to the Euphrates basin. The Lower Khalis project involves the construction of a flood protection embankment on the right bank of the Diyala and an irrigation system covering 625000 dunums of the Diyala basin north-east of Baghdad. Like the Tharthar scheme the Hilla–Diwaniya–Dalmaj irrigation project involves the diversion of Euphrates and Tigris water to wash out salt from 3·5 million dunums of land in the Diwaniya area; and further south, the Sharq al-Gharaf project will provide flow irrigation for an area of 1·15 million dunums. Four other big irrigation schemes, Abu Ghuraib, Nahr Saad, Dujaila and Al Ishaqi, covering some 2 million dunums, are integrated development projects combing livestock breeding and related agro-industries.

Irrigation, drainage and flood control will receive an allocation of ID 600 million under the country's 5-year development plan 1976–80, despite serious water shortages because of a drop in the flow of the Euphrates in 1975 and 1976 – which Iraq maintains was caused by Syria's Tabqa dam. In contrast to the enormous allocations for large-scale projects, services direct to the farmers receive only fragments of the total planned allocations for agricultural development. This emphasis on vast hydraulic engineering schemes merely highlights the longstanding distortions in emphasis over Iraq's development programme. As a result of an inefficient rural bureaucracy, the alienation of the farming community, and many years of neglect, the agricultural sector remains the key problem for Iraq's economic planners and the least responsive to their efforts.

### Stock-rearing

This forms a considerable supplement to agriculture in most of the Tigris–Euphrates lowlands, and predominates in the Jezireh and parts of Kurdistan, so that on balance stock-rearing is more widespread than in many other countries of the Middle East. The reason would seem to be the close proximity of semi-arid or unirrigable land to cultivable stretches; and even in the lower riverine zones one may come across small expanses of higher ground perhaps only a kilometre from a watercourse, yet too elevated for irrigation, and hence fit only for grazing. In Egypt there is a single sharply defined boundary between desert and sown, and in Syria there are broad zones of steppe, but in Mesopotamia the intermingling and close alternation of marsh, alluvial tract and upland ridge provides special inducement to the keeping of animals alongside cultivated areas. However, owing to climate, difficulties in feeding and prevalence of disease, yields are low.

Sheep (numbering 15·5 million) predominate, being most numerous in the Jezireh and on the right (southern) bank of the Euphrates. Other pastoral regions are the southern margins of the Assyrian plains, between the Jebel Hamrin and the first foothills of the Zagros, and the Gharraf region between Kut and Hilla-Daghgara. Generally speaking, the sheep are bred for wool, which, though coarse, is exported in considerable quantities. Some is retained at home for the weaving of carpets and cloaks; most of the remainder goes to eastern Europe, Hong Kong and Communist China.

Goats (2·4 million) tend to be restricted to the north and east, and numbers have declined latterly. Milk is the most important product, forming a large part of the diet of tribesmen; some meat is also eaten, and goat hair is used in the making of tents.

In contrast to goats, which are associated with nomadism, the 2·1 million cattle are kept mainly by settled and semi-settled cultivators living near rivers and marshes, where green fodder is available throughout the year. Cattle are valuable in two ways: as draught animals (for ploughing, for transport and for the operation of irrigation wheels), and as producers of milk. Little meat is eaten. Besides the native Sharabi cattle of the north, there are cross-breeds with Zebu (the Janubi breed) and, more recently, with imported Sindi, Ayrshire and Friesian strains.

There is export of live sheep and cattle to Syria, Lebanon, Jordan and, latterly, Kuwait. Some of this trade is of long standing, with the main route following the steppelands of the Fertile Crescent, and the animals were driven on foot towards the markets of the west by way of Rakka and Aleppo. One handicap was the variable rainfall of the region, which might result in a dearth of pasture along the route, and hence restrict or prevent the movement of animals. Construction of a railway between Iraq, Turkey and Syria altered the position, and Aleppo and Rayak became the principal terminals for the unloading of Iraqi cattle. Now, motor transport is replacing rail movement.

Water-buffalo, numbering about ¼ million, are kept chiefly by the marsh Arabs of the extreme south. Over 80% of the total for the riverine areas are found in the four southern provinces of Amara, Diwaniya, Muntafiq and Basra.

Camels are bred in large numbers in the deserts of the south-west, but in many parts of the alluvial lowlands terrain is too soft and swampy, so that these animals are few outside the steppes. In recent years, with the growth of motor transport across the desert, camels for transport purposes have been much less in demand, and more and more are now bred for sale in the towns as food. In riverine regions the donkey is the chief beast of burden, horses, as is usual in the Middle East, being something of a costly luxury. Mule-breeding is carried on by the Kurds.

In spite of the importance of stock-raising in the economy of the Tigris and Euphrates lowland, production of live animals and livestock products no longer satisfies local demand, and imports, particularly of meat, eggs and dairy products, greatly exceed exports. Consequently, new emphasis is being placed on the livestock sector in the 1976–80 development plan. In addition to the State Company for Animal Production's existing complexes at Suwaira and Fezailiya, four major livestock breeding units are to be created at Abu Ghuraib, Al-Ishaqi, Dujaila and Nahr Saad where large-scale sheep breeding, lamb fattening and dairying will be combined with improved irrigation. Other livestock stations and dairying units are planned, while the State Poultry Company is to set up many new egg and poultry producing units throughout the country over the next 5 years. As part of the Western Desert sedentarization programme twenty villages have been set up near Rutba occupied by former semi-nomadic bedouin who work in the government livestock centres established in the area.

**Industry and minerals**

It was long thought that, petroleum apart, there were few minerals in Iraq. A little coal has been worked at Kifri, south-east of Kirkuk, and salt and gypsum are also traditional products. Intense prospection over the last 10 years has, however, established that there are deposits of chromite, copper, iron, lead and zinc in the northern hill zones adjacent to Turkey. Particularly significant are the discoveries of sulphur and phosphates. The main sulphur deposits are located at Mishraq in the Mosul region and are being developed by a state company. New port facilities for handling liquid sulphur have been built at Umm Qasr and sulphur exports should double in the future. A sodium sulphate and hydrochloric acid plant is to be constructed at Mishraq using sulphur inputs from the existing plant there. Phosphates are found at Akasha close to the Syrian frontier, and a plant producing sulphuric acid, phosphoric and aluminium fluoride, and superphosphate fertilizers is to be constructed at Qaim.

Great impetus to industrial development has come from the greater availability of natural gas now piped to Baghdad from the eastern oilfields, and from increases in the generation of electricity, some of which is based on hydro-electric power schemes in association with new or existing barrages. The northern districts are supplied from new power stations on the Lesser Zab; Basra is now supplied from the Samarra barrage and also from gas piped from the Rumala oilfield: altogether, the consumption of electricity by manufacturing industry has risen from 262 million kW/h in 1960 to over 1000 million kW/h since 1973, representing 45–50% of total electricity consumption.

Since 1964 all major activities were brought under governmental control; major development of 'heavy' industry is in the hands of the national 'General Industrial Organization', whilst a number of small firms in the textile, paper, leather, food and light engineering industries remain in private hands. Textile mills in cotton, rayon and silk occur, mostly in Baghdad, but a large cotton textile plant has been established in Mosul (the original home of muslin), and rayon factories at Hilla and Hindiyah. Sugar refining is carried on at Mosul, Sulemaniya and Kerbela, and cement-making at various centres which now supply total home demand. A fertilizer plant at Basra produces ammonium sulphate as well as urea and sulphuric acid.

Other activities include transformation of agricultural products – date-packing, brewing, canning, cigarette-making and the manufacture of soft drinks. A small electronics industry has started in Baghdad, bitumen is produced at Qaiyarah, south of Mosul, there is an agricultural machinery plant at Musayih and a paper factory at Basra. Furniture, clothing, footwear, and leather are other activities. Out of a total of 30902 industrial establishments recognized in Iraq in 1972, both large-scale and small (which included bazaar crafts), 12098 were located in and around Baghdad. Some of these had only one or two workers per establishment, and the total employed in the country as a whole in 1972 was 187000.

Future plans provide for the major expansion of heavy industry, mainly in the Basra region with oil refineries, petrochemicals, iron and steel, and construction receiving priority. In addition to the two oil refineries recently completed at Basra (1974) and Mosul (1976), two large export refineries are planned for the Basra region together with a third refinery at Kirkuk. The Basra petrochemical complex is to be expanded and a new complex established at Zubair. Two fertilizer plants are also to be built at Basra and Zubair. Construction has begun of an iron and steel mill at Zubair, and an aluminium smelter is to be set up at Basra. New cement plants are to be built at Kufa, Hammam al-Alil and Samawa, and a number of existing plants expanded. Contracts have also been awarded for a number of vehicle assembly plants to be concentrated at Suwairah, and for a number of smaller factories – principally textiles, food processing and a range of other light industries.

## Communications

Unlike Iran, where mountain ranges and deserts have proved severe obstacles to movement, the riverine lowlands stand out as a region of easy access. On either side of the two rivers the undulating plains are not entirely without water and vegetation, and have for many centuries furnished a variety of easy routes from the Indian Ocean to the Mediterranean. Although in the lower valley routes must avoid the lakes and marshland, keeping to the steppes on either side, the rivers themselves are navigable for hundreds of kilometres, even though with some difficulty at certain seasons of the year. Here is a considerable contrast with Iran, where a short stretch of the Karun river below Ahwaz is the only navigable waterway in the country.

In the upper parts of both the Euphrates and Tigris and their larger tributaries, a special form of water transport has for long been a feature. This is by *kelek* – a raft made of brushwood and small pieces of timber, supported by inflated animal skins. The usual number of skins in one raft is 50 to 100, but *keleks* of 250 skins are known, and these can carry loads of 50 tons. These rafts are almost unsinkable, and carry timber, hides and charcoal from the forests of Turkey to the practically treeless lowland region. Because of the numerous rapids and gorges on the headstreams of the rivers, transport by any other craft is impossible.

Owing to the swiftness of the current, upstream navigation is not possible, and on arrival at its downstream terminus the *kelek* is broken up, the brushwood sold, and the timber framework and deflated skins carried by pack animals back to the starting point, where they are used again to construct another *kelek*.

Further downstream where the waters are quieter, numerous types of boats are found, ranging from *mashufs* – small canoes for use in the marshes – to sailing craft large enough to carry 40–70 tons of cargo. Below Baghdad there are river steamers that tow barges between the capital and Basra; but these are small, since the Tigris has no more than 1·3 m of water in winter, and only 1 m in summer. Navigation on the Euphrates is less easy, since the average depth of water in the regions of Hindiya and Lake Hammar is only 0·76 m, and motor launches or small sailing craft replace the steamers of the Tigris.

The waterways until recently carried the greatest volume of traffic; but of late years, partly owing to increased use of the rivers for irrigation, their importance for communication has greatly declined, and they are now supplanted by the railways. The first railway to be laid was a short section between Baghdad and Samarra, built by German engineers as part of the projected Berlin–Baghdad system. This was of standard gauge. During the war of 1914, the British laid a number of lines, of metre and 2 ft 6 in. gauges, using material and stock from India. The disposition of the lines was governed by immediate strategic and economic considerations, so considerable alteration became necessary when the war ended. The 2 ft 6 in. lines were relaid to a metre gauge, giving through lines connecting Baghdad and Basra via Hilla, Samarra, Nasiriya and the Euphrates valley; and another line from Baghdad to Kirkuk and Khanaqin. The former line was routed via the Euphrates, partly because of the denser population and greater productivity of the lower Euphrates, and partly because of the restricted possibility of river navigation on this river as compared with the Tigris; and in the 1960s it was again relaid to standard gauge, thus giving direct connection through Mosul to Tel Kotchek on the Syrian frontier and thence to Aleppo, Ankara and the Bosphorus. This northern portion had been completed by 1940. Another standard gauge line was completed in 1949 from Baghdad to Kirkuk and Erbil.

A number of important new railways are to be built which will more than double Iraq's total rail network by 1980. A new high-speed railway line linking Baghdad with Basra and Umm Qasr on the Gulf will become the backbone of the country's land transport infrastructure. It is expected to allow passenger train speeds of 200 km/h and freight train speeds of 140 km/h. A second line will link Kirkuk and Haditha on the Euphrates via Baiji. Other major railways planned include the Baghdad–Hassaiba line to join up with a new railway in Syria, and a line to be used to transport raw phosphate from the Akashat mines to Qaim where a fertilizer plant is to be constructed. In the future the rail network will be used to transport heavy goods over long distances, and road transport for distances up to 100 km.

### Roads

Up to 15 years ago it was possible to state that there were only about 1500 km of good roads in the whole country. However, the Republic has made considerable changes and pushed forward the construction of all-weather roads to link important centres. There are considerable natural obstacles to road-building. In the plains area, road metal is absent, and the practice was to level quantities of moist alluvium and allow it to dry. This gave a reasonable surface for part of the year, but in the wet season the whole track could degenerate into mud. Seasonal inundation by rivers was a further handicap in many parts. This explains the relative importance until recently of rail and river traffic. Now, with the achievement of flood control since 1956, road-building has gone ahead, and bitumen surfaces are now to be found on most trunk roads, with a number of entirely new motorways. By the end of 1974 there were 4500 km of modern surfaced roads in Iraq, and a further 24 major roads are to be constructed during the current development plan (1976–80).

### Population and towns

At the last census held in 1965 the population of Iraq numbered 8 million. The latest estimate suggests that the population reached 10·8 million in 1974. Distribution is unequal – though less so than in the Nile valley – with most living in the riverine areas, which are moderately populated, and the steppes and deserts are mostly inhabited by nomads. A sharp decline in nomadism has taken place since the end of the nineteenth century, and by 1957 they numbered only 65000, 1·1% of the then population. No official figures for nomads have since been given, but the government is actively pursuing a sedentarization programme in the western desert. Within the north-east, because of higher rainfall, the population is more evenly distributed over the lowland areas, with concentration near rivers much less a feature.

In broad aspect, two fairly extensive regions of relatively dense population can be discerned: (a) the riverine district centred on Baghdad, and bounded roughly by the towns of Ramadi, Diwaniya, Kut and Samarra. Here the extent of cultivable land is large, extending to considerable distances away from the actual river channels. Further south, the alluvial stretches are increasingly interspersed with arid ridges that carry only a sparse population. (b) The wetter zone of the north which

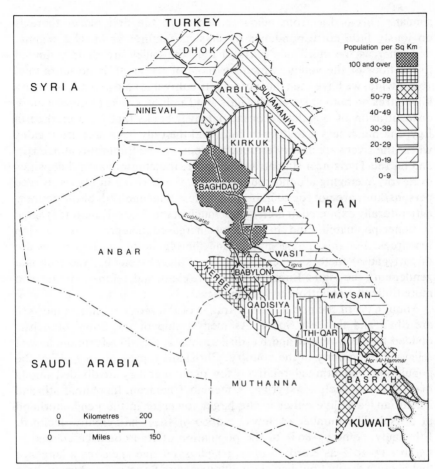

*Fig.* 13.7 Iraq: population density 1976.

may be said to include the Governorates of Erbil, Kirkuk,[1] Sulaimanieh
and Dhok. On the basis of major administrative unit, the Governorates
of al-Muthanna and al-Anbar were the least densely populated with 2 and
3 persons/km² respectively (1974), and Baghdad Governorate (145/km²)
the most densely occupied.

It is customary to regard the Tigris–Euphrates lowlands as closely
similar in physiography to Egypt, and therefore, it has come to be thought
that the population situation in both countries must be again somewhat

---

[1] In February 1976 the new Governorate of Salahuddin was created including the districts
of Tikrit, Sammara, Balad and Touz, with the capital at Tikrit. The former Governorate
of Kirkuk is to be known as Ta'meem (nationalization) and will incorporate the Kirkuk
district and the district of Hawijah. Another new Governorate is based on Najaf and
includes the districts of Najaf, Kufa, Abu Skheir and al-Shabaka.

similar. This is far from being the case. In the first place, there is obviously little correspondence in physical features or in river régime; and whereas the cultivable parts of the Nile valley are sharply limited to the floor of the valley, which for most of its length is no more than 10 km wide, we have seen that potentially cultivable land extends for many kilometres on both sides of the Tigris and Euphrates. The feature of close concentration of population on actual river banks that is so marked in Egypt is much less a feature in Iraq; and the only instances are regions where the rivers are deeply entrenched, e.g. on the Euphrates above Hit, and on the Tigris near Samarra. Moreover, the enormous rural densities in Egypt, averaging around 700 persons/km² and rising in places to 1200 persons/km², are not found in Iraq. With less than one-fifth of the country agriculturally exploited, it is clear that much of the Tigris–Euphrates region is under-populated, and in need of increased manpower to develop resources. For this, physiography and the régime of the two rivers are in part causal factors: whereas, as W. Willcocks put it, 'the Nile is a gentleman', the Tigris–Euphrates are more elemental, temperamental, and more difficult to control for human use.

About 95% of the population of Iraq is of the Moslem faith; some 55% are Shi'a and the rest Sunni. As membership of the Sunni branch is divided between Arabic and Kurdish speakers, the Shi'a form the largest religious community in the country. Christians represent only 3% of the population, and although relatively few in number they are divided among many different sects – Assyrian, Armenian, Chaldean, Jacobite, Latin and Nestorian – and live either in the larger towns or in the neighbourhood of Mosul. The number of Jews, 120000 in 1949, has greatly declined. Ethnically, some 75–80% of the population of Iraq could be classed as 'Arab': 15–20% as Kurds[1] – of larger physique and speaking a language that is quite distinct but has close affinities with Persian. In addition there are 30000 Yazidi who inhabit the Jebel Sinjar and speak a Kurdish dialect, 20000 Mandaeans (Ma'adan) who live in the marshlands of the extreme south, and communities of Turcomans found in a series of villages and towns at the foot of the northern mountains.

A very marked feature of the population situation in Iraq is the rapid migration of rural populations to the towns. The *Iraq Times* stated that by 1956 as much as 75–85% of the rural population in a few localities

---

[1] The majority of the Kurdish population is still found in north-east Iraq, particularly in the Governorates of Dhok, Erbil and Sulaimanieh (the areas in which the Kurds are officially allowed a degree of automony), but also in the Governorates of Kirkuk and Diyala. However, since the defeat of their resistance movement in 1975 refugees forced out of Iran have been among an estimated 50000 Kurds dispersed throughout the Arabic-speaking areas of Iraq. Arab groups are also being moved into the north-east altering the demographic structure of this region.

had moved to the towns; and though this figure is far above the average, it does nevertheless indicate a trend – this despite schemes of agricultural resettlement and re-allocation. As a result, the towns and Baghdad especially, have grown rapidly. J. I. Clarke calculates that between the censuses of 1957 and 1965 the percentage of the population living in towns of over 100000 in size increased from 19·7% to 30%. A recent estimate (1974) suggested that about 59% of the total population is now urban. Most of this migration was and remains towards Baghdad: Baghdad Governorate alone contains about one-third of the country's entire population, while the population of Baghdad itself reached 2·2 million in 1974, 2·4 million including its metropolitan region. One effect of this is that housing, amenity and infrastructure are very hard pressed to maintain comparable growth rates, so shanty and slum building is often the price paid by some for migration to the towns.

It is easy to see why a town should have grown up within the district of Baghdad, but the extra small-scale features that usually fix the site of a town in one particular spot are less in evidence. Local changes in topography due to the shifting of drainage channels have led to the growth of three separate cities at various periods, and so within the Baghdad region there has arisen first Babylon, the ancient capital that lay closer to the Euphrates, some 90 km to the south of modern Baghdad. Babylon was, in turn, succeeded by Ctesiphon, only a few kilometres from Baghdad, and this city remained the nodal centre until superceded by Baghdad in the early Islamic era.

Baghdad itself lies on the Tigris at the head of major navigation of the river and dates only from the eighth century A.D., and a 'golden age' occurred when its Abbasid rulers supplanted the Omeyyads of Damascus and made it the capital of the Moslem world. Baghdad suffered greatly from Mongol invasion, and most of the older buildings have disappeared. The modern city is less distinguished – in fact, a disappointment to visitors who may wish to evoke the 'Arabian Nights'. One factor inhibiting lavish building was, until 1957, liability to frequent flooding. Nevertheless since 1961 most of the squalid shanty towns or *serifas* have disappeared, and their inhabitants have been rehoused by the government in new planned settlements outside the city, principally Al-Rafidain and Al-Thawra, situated to the east of the Army Canal.

Baghdad is the undisputed commercial centre of Iraq, with numerous, but usually small factories, workshops and distributing houses. Industry, still partly carried on in the bazaar, has also expanded into modern factories, and is concerned with textiles, metals, light electrical engineering and assembly, foodstuffs, clothing, building materials and vehicle maintenance. Commerce, once mainly in the hands of Europeans and

Jews, is now more Arabicized, with Armenians and Iraqi Christians as supervisors and clerks. There is a considerable administrative activity, but the once powerful absentee landlord group has declined.

Mosul (pop. est. 1974, 350000), like Baghdad, dates only from the early Islamic era, though on the opposite bank of the river Tigris the ruins of Nineveh go back to the second millennium B.C. As with many other sites in the Middle East, the fallen clay walls of the ancient city form an enormous *tell* or mound. Here, again, is an example of regional factors outweighing local influences in determining the growth of a city. The importance of the city arises from its position in the centre of the upper basin of the Tigris, at the junction of four contrasting geographical regions for which it acts as commercial outlet and exchange focus. These regions are:

(*a*) the plains of northern Assyria, where there is a dense agricultural population;

(*b*) the hills of Kurdistan, occupied by shepherds practising transhumance, and by cultivating groups;

(*c*) the steppes of the Jezireh, where there is a mixed population of true nomads rearing sheep, cattle and draught animals; and sedentary farmers;

(*d*) the uplands of the Jebel Sinjar, where pastoralism and agriculture are carried on by the Yazidi.

As a result, there is extreme heterogeneity of peoples within the city. Arabs are in the majority, with smaller groups of Kurds, Christians and Yazidi, most of whom speak their own languages. An important medieval textile industry declined, but over the last few years has revived, with modern production of cotton and rayon. Processing of agricultural products is another activity, and Mosul is also important for leather working – a reflection of its position on the edge of the steppe. An oil refinery began operation in 1976, and a cement plant is to be constructed. Industry is, however, less important than trade: grain, timber, hides, and manufactured goods are exchanged, and there are long distance communications with Turkey, Iran and Syria. Its dark stone buildings give Mosul a special attraction.

Basra (pop. est. 1974, 423000) is an agglomeration of small sites grouped along the western bank of the Shatt el Arab some 110 km upstream from the Gulf. Basra proper is situated on a small creek 3 km distant from the Shatt el Arab, and the principal port is at Ashar, on the main river. Modern docks have also been constructed at Maqil, 6 km upstream from Ashar, and since 1939 further development has taken place at Tanuma on the eastern bank of the Shatt el Arab, opposite Ashar. Because of the heavy silt deposition and braiding of the channel, dredging is necessary to keep open the channel. Basra still handles the major part of Iraq's foreign trade, but although port facilities are being improved, congestion remains a problem. However, Umm Qasr on the Gulf is rapidly increasing in importance under a major expansion programme, while oil terminals have been constructed at Fao, Khor al-Amaya and in 1975 at Khor al-Khafqa. Basra is the centre of the southern oilfield region, and latterly chemical and petrochemical industries have developed, with many more industrial projects underway or planned in and around the city, some based on natural gas. Surrounded by date groves, Basra is also the centre of the date industry, which, oil excepted, form the chief export item. Grain, wool, hides and liquorice are other items, and much machinery and capital goods as well as foodstuffs are imported.

# 14 The Eastern Mediterranean coastlands

The region lying between the Mediterranean Sea and the interior arid plateaux of Syria, Jordan, Iraq and Arabia, sometimes spoken of – particularly by the French – as the Levant, has a strong geographical individuality. Structurally, it is a zone of transition, where the sediments laid down in the Tethys are folded on to and against the buckled edge of the Arabian platform; climatically, there is a striking 'Mediterranean' rhythm of abundant winter rainfall and absolute summer drought; one can observe a special economy based on intensive 'garden' cultivation, with commerce and craft industries as unusually important adjuncts; and finally, in the sphere of human relations, the concept of a boundary zone occurs once more, since the Levant has in a unique way acted throughout historic time as an intermediary between east and west. Within this general zone, extending from the Turkish Anti-Taurus in the north to the Sinai in the south, is a complex of small, highly individual regions, comparable in their variety and scale to the 'pays' of France, that together make up a general geographical unity based on factors both of physiography and of human relations. Political developments since 1919 have tended to accentuate and exacerbate disunity, but it will be recalled that for centuries before the Versailles settlements the name 'Syria' was held to apply to the whole of the region now described; and the fluidity of political boundaries in this region over the last 50 years could be taken as a further indication of fundamental geographical unity.

**Structural features**

As has been stated, the main feature is the junction of ancient and recent rocks. In the east and south, younger sediments lie thinly, sometimes discontinuously, upon the mass of the Archaean basement, which is exposed in a few places; but towards the north and west, the basement rocks can no longer be traced, and the sedimentary rocks are thicker and more varied. In the northern Lebanon, for example, Jurassic and Cretaceous sediments alone attain a thickness sometimes of 1000 m. Whilst in the south (Israel and Jordan), Archaean strata lie close to the surface, partly providing a core to the hills, especially round the Dead Sea and Aqaba region, in northern Syria the Jurassic is often the oldest series traceable, and is of great depth. From this a number of significant features arise: in the south, rock types are fewer, and, because of the rigidity of the underlying mass, less disturbed, whilst in the north, strata are more varied, and folding is a more conspicuous feature.

A major structural influence is the occurrence of fault lines related to the lateral displacement of major tectonic plates. The most developed of these fault-lines tend to run in a broadly north–south trend, from the Gulf of Aqaba as far as Asia Minor. They are by no means continuous but occur as separate developments: from south to north respectively the Aqaba, Jordan, Beqa and Orontes systems, with breaks or interruptions between, so that there cannot really be said to be an obvious north–south running trough. Parallel faults occur at or west of the coastlines, but on a less developed scale – an important matter in relation to off-shore oil potential. Certain of these faults have helped to define the present coastline, e.g. at Beirut and Haifa.

Besides the major north–south trending fracture-lines, there are also minor faults, many at near right angles to the major series: north of Tripoli and west of Homs, south-east of Haifa-Carmel, and along the lower Jordan valley – the west side especially. As well, episodic folding and uplift have produced elongated domes, which are often sharply terminated by fracture-lines, which have in many but not all instances formed rift-valleys (graben). This gives overall lower relief, the whole arranged in very roughly a rectangular pattern.

The beginnings of the fissuring that led to the elaboration of the Jordan and other rift systems can be traced to the Cretaceous. In Miocene times major fold movements and upwarping of domes took place, with an important torsional movement that produced horizontal displacement; in time, the eastern (Jordan) side of the Jordan valley appears to have been displaced some 40 km northwards in relation to the western side. By late Miocene and early Pliocene times a basin large enough to contain a large water surface had formed, and rift topography was intensified by further earth movements in the late Pliocene and early Quaternary. The floor of the rift sank considerably, due in part to tectonic adjustment along fault-planes, but also in part to the enormous deposition of alluvium on the rift floor. In a few localities, geophysical survey has indicated a thickness of 7000 m of alluvium – an indication of the enormous 'throw' along the major faults.

We can thus recognize a considerable number of separate sub-regions (the 'pays' referred to above), each with its own distinctiveness; and writers on the geography of the region have suggested schemes of division, ranging from a simple outline of coastal plain, mountain ranges and interior lowlands, to a more elaborate classification recognizing some thirty separate sub-regions within Israel alone. In the present instance it would seem preferable to pursue a middle course, and figs 14.1 and 14.2 attempt to delimit the geographical sub-regions in a manner sufficiently detailed to indicate the real complexity and variety of the whole area, and yet to preserve a measure of simplicity. The whole area, despite its apparent simplicity (which is perhaps deceptive), is structurally of very great interest, since there are numerous features which have not so far been fully explained. Here, the plate theory offers very useful explanation, not only as regards the Jordan–Beqa fault-zones, which have in the past been the subject of varied, even opposed theories, but also as regards the 'garland' effects visible in Crete, Cyprus and the Amanus area of Turkey, which are now regarded as phenomena along tectonic plate edges, parts of which are being 'consumed'. Whilst much of the theory of structural origins may be held to be of little direct bearing on the geography of the region, they indicate something of the underlying complexity of conditions, and of the variation in structural forms within a relatively restricted area.

**Geographical sub-regions**

Beginning in the north-west, we may first discuss the Jebel Ansarieh, which consists of a broad, gently folded anticline, with Jurassic limestone as the core, and later series (chiefly limestone and sandstone) on the flanks. The average height of the Ansarieh crest is just over 1200 m, and the highest peak, Nebi Yuness, reaches 1600 m. In the north, where the range is folded against the Amanus, fracturing has taken place, so that the anticlinal structure is somewhat broken up, and fault-valleys alternate with irregular horsts of higher ground. The most important fault structure is the Ghab, a lowland rift 80 km long by 16 km wide, that is now occupied by the middle Orontes river. The valley floor lies 1000 m below the summits of the Jebel Ansarieh, with a steep, almost precipitous western boundary. For long, the floor was swampy, but recently, the Orontes has

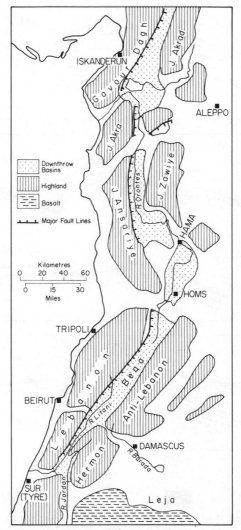

*Fig.* 14.1 The northern Levant.

been regulated and much of the former swamp area is now reclaimed for agriculture.

On the western (Mediterranean) side of the Ansarieh range, oscillation of sea-level has given rise to a number of broad wave-cut terraces covered by marine deposits that tend to be less porous than the limestone substratum. Thus these western slopes of the Ansarieh offer distinct possibilities of cultivation, and are the most densely peopled part of the region. Elsewhere, extreme permeability of the limestone reduces surface

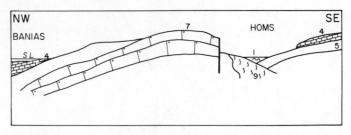

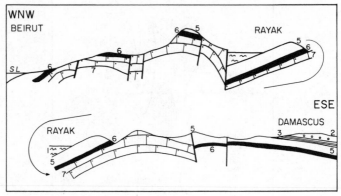

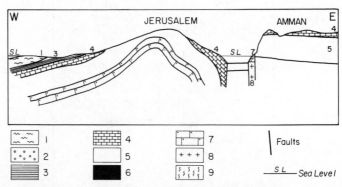

*Fig.* 14.2 Geological sections in the Levant. Strata as follows:
1, Quaternary and later; 2, Miocene–Pliocene; 3, Eocene; 4, Upper Cretaceous (mainly permeable); 5, Upper Cretaceous (mainly impermeable); 6, Middle and Lower Cretaceous (impermeable); 7, Jurassic; 8, Pre-Cambrian; 9, Igneous.

water to a minimum, and although annual rainfall exceeds 700 mm, many parts are karstic, with vegetation restricted to a stunted garrigue. Only in the extreme north (Slenfeh district) are trees at all numerous; and much of the south and east is thinly populated.

East of the Ghab, the land rises gradually to form an irregular plateau, of which the highest parts are the Jebel Zawiyeh between Idlib and Hama, and the heights just east of Hama, where there is a maximum elevation of 500–600 m. Much of this plateau is open, fertile and easily cultivable, giving the impression of a plain rather than an upland; but, because of its altitude, streams are entrenched in narrow, steep-sided valleys, and the raising of irrigation water to the fields can be a matter of difficulty.

Adjacent to the Ansarieh range in the south is the lowland corridor sometimes spoken of as the Tripoli–Homs gap, and sometimes as two separate districts, the Plain of Akkar (Tripoli region) and the Bukeia (Homs region). The gap is occupied by a small river, named ironically, the Nahr el Kebir, which has laid down rich alluvium deposits derived from perhaps the varied sedimentary rocks and numerous basalt intrusions of the district. As a result, parts of the gap are closely settled by a farming population, but the full agricultural potentialities have not as yet been developed. For long, malaria from poor surface drainage was a handicap, but although the disease has now been much reduced, drainage problems remain and other difficulties are the relatively hard winter, remoteness, and recently, political uncertainties.

### The Lebanon range

This is the highest of the mountain massifs of the Levant. The culminating peak, Qornet es Sauda (lying east-south-east of Tripoli), reaches 3083 m, with Mount Sannin (east-north-east of Beirut) 2548 m. The entire range consists of a single major upfold or anticlinal, of Cretaceous and Jurassic series, high and well developed in the north with subsidiary minor folds on its western flank (Tripoli–Jbail area), and more open and plateau-like towards the south, where, below the Litani valley, it passes gradually into the upland of Galilee. Numerous faults occur, along some of which there have been basaltic intrusions. A feature of great importance, peculiar to the Lebanon, is the occurrence of a complex of generally impermeable Lower Cretaceous sandstones, marl and lignite. This series, comparable with the Nubian sandstones of regions further south, has two points of interest: the content of iron oxides imparts a special generally dark reddish colour that, in juxtaposition with the underlying Jurassic limestones, gives a markedly scenic effect; secondly, the whole complex, largely impermeable, lenses out north and south, so it is best developed in the central Lebanon, and absent northwards (Jebel Ansarieh) and southwards (Galilee and Judaea). Above the Lower Cretaceous sands is a Middle Cretaceous complex of more sands, marls and clays, massively capped by porous Upper Cretaceous limestones (mainly Turonian and Senonian) that become marly in their highest parts. These form the highest mountains, where heavy precipitation occurs, with a seasonal snowfall that in the highest parts lies from November to May. Melt and percolation into the porous upper Cretaceous is considerable, so that at the junction with the impermeable Middle and Lower Cretaceous there occur many springs of water, particularly along the western side. Occurrence of these springs at altitudes of 1000–1500 m above sea-level is special to the Lebanon, and as many of them are large – rivers rather than streams – extensive irrigation is possible.

Because of relatively abundant water supplies and a varied, fertile soil derived from different rock outcrops, the middle slopes of the Lebanon range are intensely cultivated, and provide much of the wealth of the Lebanese state. Another interesting feature of human occupation related to the occurrence of these impermeable beds has been the refuge offered to persecuted religious minorities. The soft underlying Jurassic series has weathered into deep ravines, with forbidding cliffs often several hundred metres in height – a considerable obstacle to penetration inland from the coastal plain. At higher levels, where the more resistant Mesozoic strata are reached, erosion has been less active, and there is a piedmont zone that is at once more fertile, and less difficult topographically. Here in past ages refugees were able to settle in comparative safety, and gain a living by agriculture, often in association with nearby Christian monasteries. Now, the western slopes are tourist and summer centres, with extensive building for amenity.

As in the Jebel Ansarieh, the eastern limit of the Lebanon massif is marked by a great fault-line, with a downthrow to the east of 1000–1500 m. This is a single fault rather than a true rift, though superficially at least the presence of the valley of the Beqa, lying between the Lebanon and Anti-Lebanon ranges, suggests that the Jordan rift is continued northwards. This is not the case: the main Jordan faults die down, and are continued on a more reduced scale towards the north-north-west, possibly reaching the Beirut area, where there is a faulted coastline. The Jordan valley is terminated by the Metulla range, which blocks the trough at what is approximately the Israel–Lebanese frontier.

Eastward of the Lebanon anticline is the wide trough of the Beqa, which lies at an altitude of 1000–1300 m. Much of the middle and south of the Beqa has a deep fertile soil, but north of Baalbek, which is at the highest point of the Beqa floor (i.e. on the divide between the Orontes and Litani river systems), soil becomes much thinner and poorer. The site of Baalbek is most impressive. To north and south, the Beqa slopes gradually away, whilst to east and west mountain walls that rise some 1500 to 2000 m higher still, and are covered in snow for a substantial part of the year, provide a remarkable panorama; it is easy to see why Baalbek should have been chosen as the site of one of the largest temples of the Roman Empire.

The Litani river, as the result of episodic uplift and warping, flows southwards on the Beqa floor, and then turns abruptly westwards, cutting

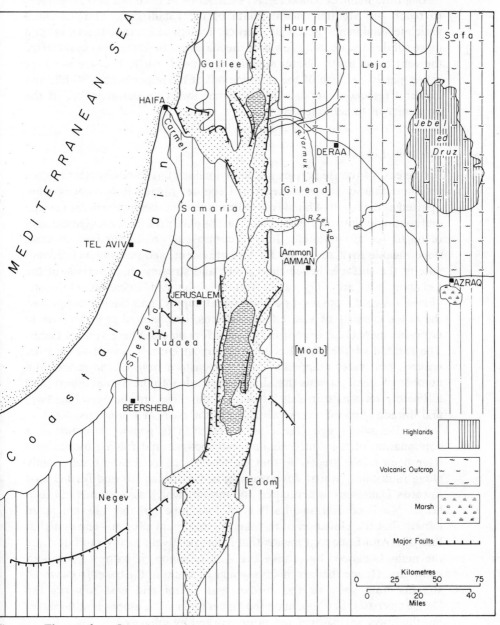

Fig. 14.3 The southern Levant.

through the main Lebanon range, by a series of deep but narrow gorges, to reach the Mediterranean. South of the Litani gorge, the Lebanon anticline diminishes gradually. Relief, though still pronounced, is on a more subdued scale, with fewer of the majestic contrasts that characterize the centre and north. Water supplies are fewer, partly because of lower relief, partly because of the thinning out of the impermeable Middle and Lower Cretaceous series. One becomes aware, geographically, of the proximity of Israel/Palestine.

## The Anti-Lebanon

To the east of the Beqa rises a steeply inclined but somewhat less faulted anticline that comprises the Anti-Lebanon range. Both ranges were uplifted as the result of highly episodic movements beginning in the Eocene and continuing into the Recent phase, with uplift in the Pliocene–Quaternary of up to 100 m amplitude. But, in contrast to conditions further west, impermeable rock series are far less prevalent, and limestones predominate at the surface, hence the springs and streams characteristic of the Lebanon hills are only rarely found in the Anti-Lebanon. Only one village – Aarsal – possesses a good water supply, and the greater part of the range consists of vast karstic uplands, uninhabited or given over to nomadic shepherds, except in the very few places where springs occur. The rainfall of the Anti-Lebanon is almost entirely absorbed into the ground, but water reappears along the eastern base of the range, in a number of small streams that drain eastwards into the Syrian desert, and ultimately terminate in salt basins. Of this kind are the Maraba, Awaj and Barada (Abana) rivers, which form the oasis of Damascus.

The Hermon range (Jebel esh Sheikh) is in general structurally a continuation of the Anti-Lebanon, but tectonic and folding movements have been rather greater so that the whole area has been raised, mainly along fault-lines, whilst downwarping in the Jordan rift and further east towards Damascus accentuated the massif, which now stands out as a horst. Much of Hermon itself is of limestone, so the hills are again karstic, but the elevation of the massif (maximum 2815 m – 600 m higher than the Anti-Lebanon) means that it has relatively heavy rainfall. Like the main Lebanon, but unlike the Anti-Lebanon, it carries a 6 month snow-cap. Hence there is much seepage of water at the base, from which streams flow west to the Jordan and Litani and east towards the Damascus oasis. Settlement on the higher and middle slopes is still sparse, but the lower spring-lines are often marked by villages.

The Anti-Lebanon system may be regarded as comparable with most of the other fold ranges of central Syria, which consist essentially of a simple anticlinal structure, trending from south-west to north-east and dying out towards the Euphrates. Such are the Jebel Kalamun, north of Damascus, the Jebel esh Sharki, the Jebel et Tar and the Jebel Bishri of Palmyra. The upper slopes of these ranges are bare of soil and vegetation, the lower slopes carry grass for a few weeks of the year, and nomadism is the predominant way of life. Permanent settlement is limited to a few oases such as Nebek, Qariatein and Palmyra, where springs occur in association with faults.

## *The Hauran, Jebel Druze and Leja*

South of Damascus and east of Hermon, topography is dominated by extensive lava flows, which began on a large scale in the Pliocene and continued spasmodically until almost Recent geological times, in the form of massive sheets and cones. It has been noted that small-scale intrusions are common in north and west Syria (the largest being in the neighbourhood of Homs, where the marshy course of the Orontes represented the last stage in the drainage of a lake impounded by a basalt sill), but in south-west Syria and northern Jordan much wider areas are entirely buried under igneous material. The whole region as far as central Jordan forms an irregular plateau, lying at an altitude of 300–700 m. In the west, towards the Jordan valley, the landscape is open and rolling, with level stretches and broad valleys interspersed with occasional basaltic ridges or volcanic cones, some of which reach 1000 m in height. The heavier rainfall and sharp winters of this region, particularly in the west, have eroded some of the softer lavas, and given rise to deposits of rich basaltic soil in the depressions. Given a good winter supply, this western basalt zone, known as the Hauran, can be very productive. In Roman times, the area was one of the granaries of the Empire, and once carried a moderately large population; today it is less exploited, and emphasis is more on fruit trees and melons.

Further east, the plateau becomes higher, wilder and more rugged. Vast numbers of boulders scattered over the surface become an increasing obstacle to cultivation, and the highest part of the plateau is reached in the Jebel Druze, an irregular dome of basalt, capped by low volcanic cones, the largest of which, Tel el Jenna, attains 1800 m above sea-level. Again, fertile soil occurs in the lower parts, and the area was colonized after 1600 A.D. by Druze immigrants from the Lebanon, who established cereal and fruit-growing on a relatively important scale – hence the name Jebel Druze, which under the French had political autonomy. Nowadays, vegetable-growing for markets in Damascus and the oilfields has developed.

Further east still, much of the basalt flows take the form of 'pillow lavas' and massive dikes, which appear to cross the landscape as immense cords or ropes. Other areas have been cracked and disturbed by later lava flows, to give an appearance of chaotic vaulting. Lying further into the desert, there has been less rainfall to produce erosion, so that soil is lacking and the landscape is extremely sombre, daunting and difficult, hence the Greek name Trachonitis (dismembered land). Whole areas are totally uninhabited, but numbers of natural caves and the general isolation have attracted outlaws and political dissidents – from which its Arabic name, El Leja (refuge).

### The uplands of Galilee and Judaea

We have noted that there is no real topographical break between the far south of the Lebanon anticline and the extreme north of Galilee, other than the continuing decline of the dome to lower altitudes – though, even here, it is still an imposing and deeply dissected massif.

However, as one goes further south, altitude and intensity of relief decline further; and in addition, instead of the basic structure being that of one major upfold with minor folds on the western limb, the anticlinal becomes broken into a series of small detached blocks, most of which are tilted. The general effect is more that of a broken cuesta than a dome. Limestones form much of the surface, with increasing exposures of chalk, some of which contain small deposits of iron. Thin layers of basalt also occur as sills, and some of these give rise to springs. Altitudes decline from an average of 750 m above sea-level in the north near the frontier with the Lebanon, to under 500 m. This, besides the mere topographical effect, has important influences on rainfall, vegetation and settlement, and the Galilee region is thus further divisible into Upper Galilee, which is a region of broken karst, deep gorges and distinctive peaks, with limited settlement that until recently was often located only on the higher parts; and Lower Galilee, which is more an alternation of ridge or scarp and broader alluvium-filled valley, with occasional detached higher blocks, such as Mount Tabor. Southernmost of the scarps is the Nazareth ridge, which overlooks the lowland of Esdraelon.

The Galilee uplands come to an abrupt but irregular end at a fault-trough which runs north-westward from the Jordan valley to reach the Mediterranean in the region of Haifa–Acre. This is the Esdraelon lowland, bounded on the northern (Galilee) side by an irregular, almost step-like succession; to the south, beginning with the Mount Carmel ridge, the edge is rather more abrupt, but again irregular, with the outlier of Mount Gilboa breaking the continuity and reducing the trough to very narrow dimensions.

Because of the irregular nature of its northern boundary, the plain of Esdraelon varies in width; where it reaches the sea, at Acre, there is a

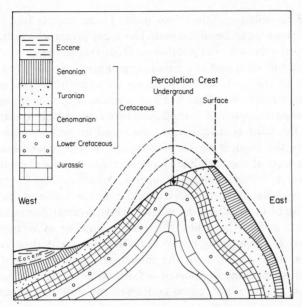

Eocene

Senonian

Turonian

Cenomanian

Lower Cretaceous

Jurassic

Cretaceous

Percolation Crest

Underground

Surface

West

East

Eocene

*Fig.* 14.4 Percolation crests in Judaea, showing eastward diversion of underground percolation.

wide bay some 30 km across, but further inland the plain shrinks to a mere corridor only 2–4 km wide, ultimately widening once again towards the Jordan to an expanse of 8–15 km. The floor of the plain is flat, and formed in the main of a deep black fertile soil weathered from the limestone and basalt of the Galilee plateau. Close in to the sides of the valley, springs emerge, but towards the centre, the water table is low, so cultivation is less easy. In the west, near the coast, the alluvium becomes somewhat more impermeable, and there is a small perennial stream, the Kishon, which once had an extensive area of swamp round it. This, now drained and no longer malarial, as it was to 1943, has developed as an agricultural and especially an industrial region.

South of Esdraelon, the structure of a long narrow dome ultimately becomes re-established, but there is an intermediate zone on a small scale showing the effects of breaching by the formation of the Esdraelon rift, which had the effect of altering and partly shattering the predominantly north–south striking anticlinal. Just as Galilee represents a break in and alternation of the anticlinal that reaches maximum development in the Lebanon, so the hill region immediately south of Esdraelon, known as Samaria, is in a sense a transition to the strongly defined anticlinal structure that characterizes Judaea proper in the region of Jerusalem.

Samaria, then, is a zone of folds interrupted by cross-faulting and differential earth movements producing tectonic basins: what on a larger scale would be called in Asia Minor *ovas*. Three distinct fold structures – small anticlines – can be discerned. The most prominent is the Carmel ridge that runs inland to the south-east from Haifa; the second is much less developed in size, and is a small range known as the Irron hills; the third occurs in the east, where it forms an edge to the Jordan trough. Between these three anticlines are two structural synclines, but one of these, forming the region of Nablus, has proved resistant to erosion, and so parts of the hard synclinal core now stand up actually above all the rest, to form the highest peaks of Samaria, which reach about 900 m, whereas the tops of the anticlines have been breached and eroded away. A much lower syncline – small and narrow – separates the Carmel massif from the Irron hills, and provides a useful corridor between the sea coast and the centre of the Esdraelon lowland. Thus, overall, Samaria has very diverse relief: beside the folds, there are a number of warped blocks; and a number of lower-lying basins are often filled with relatively fertile Terra Rossa soils which, with the moderately abundant rainfall, have throughout historic time supported a farming population of some size. In the period 1948–67 this region contained the bulk of Jordanian Arab farmers.

Further south still the structure of one major anticline or dome becomes dominant, and slightly higher in altitude, reaching above 1000 m in its highest parts, which occur north of Jerusalem, and also south; Jerusalem thus occupies what, in a very general way, one might call the 'saddle'.

Originally, the anticline was higher and more complete, but differential erosion has acted more upon the western (weather) side and less on the eastern (lee) side, so the topographical axis of the dome – the watershed between Mediterranean and Jordan drainage – has been displaced eastwards (fig. 14.4). Differences in rock exposure give rise to striking differences in morphology and land use; there are three distinct parallel zones: the western foothills, or Shefela, the main ridge (sometimes called the Judaean uplands), and the eastern desert, or Wilderness.

The Shefela is a faulted minor downfold, with a number of benches, or broad terraces, and low, rounded hills. Considerable downwash has produced extensive rendzina and alluvial soils, which, on moderate slopes, favour cultivation. Hence this is one of the most highly productive parts of Israel. In contrast, however, to the generally rounded outlines of the Shefela, the main Judaean uplands are much craggier, being composed of limestone that in many places is dolomitic and thus highly resistant. Because of diminished rainfall, erosion is less active, so there is much more the impression of an unbroken high plateau, with fewer diversifying elements and much less cultivation. Expanses of bare rock, occasional small valleys etched in the hillside and seasonally dry, with caverns and deep walls, are characteristic. It is important to note that whilst surface drainage from the topographical crest line is to westward, underground percolation divides at the top of the geological upfold, which, as we have seen above (fig. 14.4), is not the same, and so, in much of the entire substrata of the Judaean uplands, percolation is eastwards; and therefore much of the western plateau top is drier than might be expected, given a seaward aspect.

On the eastern side, chalk and marl replace limestone, often giving rise to greyish-white or yellow hillocks. This is the Wilderness of Judaea, partly the effect of geology, partly due to 'rain-shadow', in that whilst the highest parts of Judaea receive 700–800 mm of rainfall, the amount in the east quickly falls off to 300 mm in the hills, and to only 50–100 mm on the floor of the Jordan rift further east still. The considerable drop in relief to the Jordan means that, despite only small amounts of rain, erosion can be very active, and a number of very narrow, spectacular gorges occur, an element in the defensive site of Jerusalem.

## The Negev

About one-half of the state of Israel in its pre-1967 frontiers is occupied by the Negev, which in one sense is a major transition between the Sinai and the regions just described, but on a broader scale. In the extreme east there is the Jordan trough-line continued as the Wadi Araba to the Gulf of Aqaba, then an imposing hill mass in the centre (with the Beersheba subsidence zone, or basin, on its north-western flank), and finally, a narrow lowland coastal strip bordering the Mediterranean.

Much of the Negev is underlain by the basement complex of north Africa and Arabia. This appears at the surface in the Eilat hills, but is mostly covered elsewhere by relatively thin layers of water-deposited sedimentaries and also aeolian strata. The contrast between the thin mantle of younger rocks at the southern end of the eastern Mediterranean, and the enormous thicknesses near Asia Minor, will be noted. More than half of the Negev is composed of upland; there is a plateau zone in the east made up of fairly horizontal sedimentary layers and a distinctly higher central zone, where the sediments are folded into shallow anticlines and synclines, with relief preserved owing to the relative weakness of erosional factors of rainfall and frost, so that the ridges are anticlinal and the valleys synclinal. It is significant that trends are no longer north–south, but begin to swing round to a north-east–south-west line, and then to east–west, as the Sinai is approached.

The Beersheba basin is noteworthy for its extensive loess deposits which in a few places exceed 30 m in thickness. Aridity means that there is a good deal of blowing dust, and an unfortunate property of these soils, in a régime of alternate rain and drought, is to harden at the surface with the first onset of autumnal rain, so that the surface becomes 'sealed' and later rainfall becomes concentrated as local 'flash-floods' that can then erode deep gullies. Towards the west and north-west, sand replaces loess, as the real Sinai desert is reached. It will be apparent why the Negev is regarded as a 'challenge' by Israelis. Besides being intrinsically a relatively large and unoccupied area, it offers considerable agricultural potential, provided irrigation water can be made available, and the difficult loessic soils properly utilized. In addition, variety in geological structure suggests considerable mineral potential: copper, phosphates and natural gas have been proved, with a possibility of iron. As yet, however, settlements are limited to three towns, Beersheba, Dimona and Arad, and to a number of kibbutzim.

### Coastal plain of the Mediterranean

This is narrow and discontinuous in the north, but increasingly wide and extensive towards the south. In north-west Syria, fronting the Jebel Ansarieh, the plain consists merely of a series of enclaves interrupted at frequent intervals by mountain spurs that reach the sea. Something of the same aspect persists in the Lebanon, where the coastal plain, at its maximum near Beirut, is only 5–7 km wide. At such places as Shekkah and Ras en Nakura, foothills again rise directly out of the sea. Road and railway, where these now exist, must tunnel through the spurs, or cling precariously to ledges cut in the cliff-face; though new roads have recently been made that if necessary cut a wider swathe inland through physical obstacles.

At Haifa a narrow terrace under 100 m wide in its narrowest part separates the slopes of Mount Carmel from the sea, carrying road and rail southwards; but a short distance to the south the plain then widens considerably; about 12–50 km in northern Israel, and as much as 25 km or more in the south.

A marked zonation is visible south of Haifa with three distinctive components: a coastal strip, then the main western plain, and then an inner plain lying along the edge of the Shefela foothills. The coast itself as far as Haifa is sometimes low lying, sometimes with steep cliffs as much as 30–40 m high, but, in contrast to conditions further north, markedly straight. This is because of considerable longshore drift from the south during the Pleistocene down to the present, which has brought extensive quantities of Nile and Sinai silt as far as the Carmel coast. Along the coast is a zone of loose sand dunes with interspersed marshes and swamps that were once more widespread – over the last 50 years they have been drained in some, but not all, localities. Inland, a succession of low ridges delimits the edge of the dune area. These ridges, aligned generally on a north–south axis, are composed of 'Kurkar' – that is, consolidated sands which during the Pleistocene were cemented into fixed and distinctly harder ridges. A second line of Kurkar ridges divides the plain further to the east into what Israeli geographers term the 'western plain' – characterized by light-coloured, sandy, coarse-grained soils that are pre-eminently suited to citrus cultivation – and the 'inner plain', a region of heavier, darker alluvial soils formed largely by downwash from the Judaean hills. The presence of calcretes (*nazzaz*), especially in the western plain, together with the Kurkar ridges which impede river flow towards the coast, means that drainage can be affected, with tendency to swamp formation. This for long made the plains malarial, with human settlement restricted to a few cultivators and robber bands, but in the present century a dramatic change has occurred, with extensive artificial drainage and reclamation. The entire northern section of the coastal plain just south of Carmel is the plain of Sharon, whilst the extreme south, towards the Negev and Sinai, is the ancient Philistia. Here, sand dunes and loess deposits gradually become more dominant as one moves south.

*The Jordan trough*

From the 300 m contour (just north of the Israel–Lebanon frontier), which may be taken as the effective northern limit, a major rift formation extends for some 400 km to the head of the Gulf of Aqaba and then to the Red Sea. This depression is, however, far from uniform either in depth or width. Lowest part of the floor occurs below the northern part of the Dead Sea, which lies 800 m below sea-level at the Mediterranean, but southward of this point level rises and reaches sea-level some 130 km to the south of the Dead Sea. At its maximum width, which is at Jericho, the rift is 32 km wide, but between Jericho and Lake Tiberias, it narrows in one area to under 10 km width. This is because there is one major fault and a series of minor faults that are not parallel to the main fault (fig. 14.3). Almost throughout its length it is bounded by the steep-sided, faulted edges of the Arabian platform to the east, and the massifs of Galilee, Samaria and Judaea to the west. As the Judaean and Jordanian plateaux rise some 1000 m above sea-level, there is a precipitous descent to the Jordan floor, which lies at about 400 m below sea-level at the Dead Sea shore. A number of small streams plunge down the valley sides, and have carved deep notches in the plateau edge, a few of which are used by roads. In many places, however, the descent is too steep, and direct communication, even by track, is impossible.

In the north, a basalt flow across the valley at Rosh Pinna once impounded a small sheet of water, Lake Hule. This was extremely shallow, and it developed thick peat deposits formed from the papyrus swamp that composed most of it. Hule was drained a few years ago and is now entirely farmland.

Southwards, downwarping in the region of Galilee, and possible upwarping immediately to the south, produced a subsidence basin which is now occupied by Lake Tiberias (Sea of Galilee) or Kinneseret, to use its modern Hebrew name. This lake is some 20 km long, by 8 km wide, and covers 166 km². Its shore lies at 213 m below sea-level, and its deepest part is 50 m lower still. Because of the occurrence of a number of mineral springs (some hot) associated with the fault-lines of the region, the waters of Tiberias are saline, containing 250–400 mg of salts per litre, the precise amount depending upon evaporation (which here is considerable) and local rainfall. Some salt springs actually rise on the lake bottom.

Below the junction of the Jordan valley with the side rift that branches north-westwards towards Acre and Haifa, the river Jordan becomes increasingly incised into its bed. Oscillation in level, and the variation in water volume due to arid and pluvial cycles, have given rise to complex terrace formation, which tends to appear as two major sites in the north, and three in the south. On these, deposits of bright-coloured marls and gypsum occur, and have been heavily dissected into fantastic shapes by the ephemeral side torrents that episodically rush down from the plateaux 1300 m above to east and west, and by the Jordan itself, which drops in level by almost 2 m/km. Close to the river, which is now saline, a relatively dense riverine vegetation of willow, tamarisk and reeds is still to be found, whilst the higher terraces consist of 'badlands' that become increasingly saline as the Dead Sea is reached. Here, parts of the shore are salt-encrusted, and there are no settlements other than for commercial purposes: extraction of minerals, or for sun-bathing on a hotel beach, chiefly during winter.

The Dead Sea itself fluctuates markedly in level: it has been observed to have risen by over 14 m during the last century, and then fallen by 5 m between 1900 and 1935, and in 1962–65 it fell by 4 m. These fluctuations cannot wholly be ascribed to climate as controlling inflow and evaporation (see fig. 3.12), so it is thought that there must be some tectonic action affecting the lake bed. The northern basin is larger and, as we have seen, much deeper; the southern basin – separated from the northern one by the Lissan peninsula (= tongue) – is smaller, and only on average 6 m deep.

Immediately south of the Dead Sea is the Hill of Sedom (Sodom). This is a curious formation partly of rock-salt, and capped by sands and marl, thought to be a former evaporation surface of a larger Dead Sea, that became covered by later sediments. The weight of the sediments acting upon the relatively plastic salt forced it up through bedding-planes and fissures to produce a hill some 250 m high that is partially but not wholly made of salt – this is the origin of the Biblical story of Lot's wife. Around Sedom and continuing to the south is a flat lowland flooded at times by the Dead Sea, and covered by highly viscous, saline swamp in some places with a thick vegetation in places that recalls on a small scale the Sudd areas of the Upper Nile, in others, the *kavir* of inner Iran.

From here as far as the Gulf of Aqaba the rift-valley consists of a series of shallow basins. Some of these have springs of fresh water, and appear as oases; parts are covered by coarse sand and gravel, and parts are saline drainage sumps – playas – with marls, gypsum and developed 'badland'. Much of the eastern side of the rift, which is very prominent and precipitous, is composed of pre-Cambrian crystalline rocks and red Nubian sandstone – hence the regional name, Edom (red). Settlement along the entire Aqaba Gulf except at the southern coastal extremities – Eilat and Aqaba – is very sparse indeed.

The fault-lines of the entire Levant are of such recent geological origin (Oligocene and later) that adjustment along them has not completely ceased. From time to time minor displacements occur, giving small-scale earth tremors. These are not on a scale comparable with the earthquakes of the great east–west tectonic zone of northern Asia Minor, though the effects are seen, for example, in the minor earthquake of 1929, which destroyed buildings in Jerusalem, in the shock of 1758 which wrecked the pagan temple at Baalbek, and in the cracking of the floor of the Cave of the Nativity at Bethlehem.[1]

## Climate

The outstanding feature in the climate of the Levant is the rapidity with which conditions alter away from the coast. This is due to the presence of high mountain massifs running parallel to the coastline, which has the effect of restricting maritime influences to a narrow littoral zone. Continental influences hence approach closely to the Mediterranean, and, in addition, because of the height and continuity of the coastal ranges, there is a special 'mountain' régime characterized by distinctly lower temperatures and a higher rainfall.

Besides this well-marked gradation from west to east, climatic differences are also apparent as between north and south. For all seasons of the year, the dominant prevailing wind is from west-south-west, not, as some generalized atlases show, from the north-west. Hence in the north, winds are moister than in the south, since they have a long sea 'fetch'.

---

[1] Also, in certain of the events at the time of the Crucifixion ('And the veil of the temple was rent in twain, and the earth did quake, and the rocks rent, and the graves were opened', Matt. xxvii. 51).

In the south, air is drier, because winds blow from the land mass of north Africa and the Sinai. This is shown by the fact that the extreme north-west of Syria and the Hatay of Turkey have rain all the year round, with a slight but perceptible fall in July and August. In the Lebanon and Israel, on the other hand, there is no summer rainfall, and aridity increases southwards, until beyond Gaza true desert conditions are reached.

## Coastal zone

In this region, winters are mild and summers only moderately hot, and rainfall is relatively abundant. Frost is almost unknown, though slight falls of snow may occur at long intervals – once in 10 or 20 years being the normal for Haifa and Beirut. The coldest period of the year is late January and February, when temperatures average 12–14 °C. There is a fairly pronounced diurnal variation of temperature, with bright sunshine on about half the days of winter, giving a daily maximum temperature of 16–18 °C and a night minimum of 10 °C (January). In March, a rapid change to warmer conditions begins. A feature of spring – and, indeed, winter – is the occurrence of *shlouq* (*khamsin*) conditions, shown by figures of absolute temperature: Beirut has recorded a temperature of 26 °C in January, and Gaza one of 29 °C.

August is everywhere the hottest month – an indication of maritime influence – and although there is considerable uniformity in conditions over the whole zone, there is the rather curious feature that the north is warmer than the south (August monthly means: Iskanderun 28 °C, Beirut 29 °C, Tel Aviv 27 °C, Gaza 26 °C). This is probably due to the sheltering effect of the mountain ranges, which are higher in the north, giving something of the effect of a walled garden.

In summer diurnal variation is smaller than in winter, being everywhere less than 8 °C, and in many parts less than 6 °C. This means that nights are unduly oppressive, though actual temperatures are not particularly high. Summer conditions are prolonged, until October, and temperatures do not usually fall much below 21 °C, until the latter part of November. December too is usually markedly warmer than January or February, and open-air festivities at Christmas are often possible.

Rainfall is for the most part adequate, though great differences are apparent between north and south. The coast of Syria and the Lebanon receives over 750 mm, and Gaza only 355 mm. January is the wettest month, and, except for the extreme north, rainfall has ceased entirely by the middle of June, so that, until the middle of September, aridity is absolute. The fact that much of the coastal zone receives as much rainfall as many parts of Europe, yet in far fewer rainy days (January, the rainiest month, has only 11 to 15 days of actual rain), indicates that

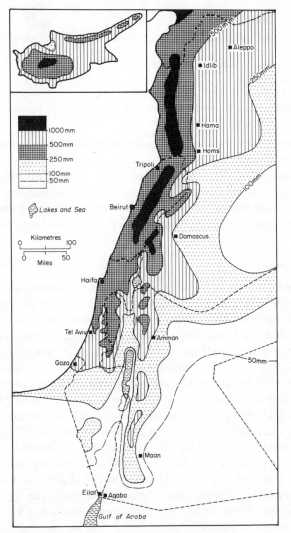

*Fig.* 14.5 The Levant: annual rainfall.

falls are very heavy, but not prolonged. An unpleasant feature is the high humidity prevailing in summer, which, as we have seen, is actually at a maximum in some parts: cf. Iskanderun max. 74% (July), Beirut max. 73% (June), Tel Aviv max. 74% (August), Gaza 77% (January). Dew is as a result extremely heavy, particularly on the coastal lowlands, where, in the words of C. Combier, 'Roofs in the early morning stream with moisture as though there had been a downpour of rain during the night'. Up to 250 nights of the year have appreciable dewfall, and here dew may

Temperatures in August (°C)

|                     | Beirut | Aley |
| ------------------- | ------ | ---- |
| Mean daily maximum  | 30·5   | 29·4 |
| Mean daily minimum  | 22·7   | 17·7 |

account for up to 25% of the total precipitation recorded in certain districts.

High summer humidity, together with only slightly diurnal variation of temperatures, makes the summer season more unpleasant than figures of climate would appear to indicate, and large numbers of town-dwellers, particularly in the Lebanon, migrate into the hills for the summer months.

*Mountain zone*

A remarkable change is found, even in 5–10 km, as one leaves the coastal plain for the mountains. Winters are cold, and snow is of regular occurrence each winter. In the Lebanon range, snow may lie for 2 to 4 months, and the three peaks, Qornet es Sauda, Sannin and Hermon, are white for at least half the year.[1] Jerusalem, at 1000 m, has short falls in most winters. Climatic statistics are fewer for this upland region, but average January temperatures are 6–8 °C lower in the north than on the adjoining coastal plain, and 5–6 °C lower in the south (El Kareya – Lebanon – 5 °C; Nazareth 10 °C, Jerusalem 9 °C). Summer temperatures are again rather lower (by 6 °C in the north, and 5–6 °C in the south), but a special feature is wide diurnal variation in summer, so that the daytime is moderately hot and the night cool. During summer there is thus a most pleasant change at night; and although afternoon temperatures may be very little different from those of the plain, the nights are more restful. This is well shown at Aley, a summer resort only 8 km from Beirut, but 670 m above sea-level.

Considerable diurnal variation of temperature during the summer months is one of the underlying factors in the development of summer stations and holiday resorts in the Lebanon.

As would be expected, rainfall, which is of the instability type, is abundant, even heavy. On the Ansarieh and Lebanon mountains there are annual falls of 1000–1250 mm, though the figure drops to under 700 mm in Galilee, and to 500–600 mm in Samaria and Judaea. The number of rainy days, however, remains low, despite increased precipitation,

---

[1] The name Lebanon is said to be derived from the Aramaic *Leben* (whiteness) in reference to the vista of snow-clad peaks seen from December to June.

averaging 80–85 per annum in Syria and the Lebanon, and 40–60 in Israel: i.e. only 5–10 more than in the corresponding coastal areas, so that rainfall can be termed really intense. This has important effects on the soil cover, which, unless held by a retaining wall, can be soon swept away and lost. Hence terracing on a considerable scale is a feature of all parts of the mountain zone; and in certain districts it is possible to observe hillsides terraced continuously at intervals of 1–2 m over 700–1000 m of altitude. It is the heaviest downpours of great intensity which, though not perhaps very frequent, and short in onset, produce most soil erosion.

*Steppe zone*

Immediately east of the crest of the coastal ranges rainfall diminishes sharply in amount, though the season of onset remains the same. This affords striking indication of the control of rainfall by relief, a relationship that is much closer than is usually the case in cool temperate regions. Aspect and slope are also very significant; though closer to the Mediterranean the western slopes of the Jordan rift are in general markedly drier than the eastern sides of the same rift.

Under such circumstances, the lowland troughs of the Ghab, Beqa and Ghor display a climatic régime markedly different from that of the highlands to the east and west. Although none of the troughs greatly exceeds 15 km in width – being often much less – we can distinguish a separate régime approximating to steppe conditions. De Martonne has given the name 'Syrian' to this type of climate, which is characterized by moderate or somewhat deficient rainfall, with a fairly cold winter and a hot summer. Ksara, on the floor of the Beqa, is one example: coldest month (January) 5 °C, hottest (August) 27 °C; diurnal variation 9 °C in winter, 11 °C in summer; annual rainfall 638 mm.

The great depth of the Jordan rift, and its openness to the direct rays of the sun, give rise to higher temperatures and to a greatly diminished rainfall (Jericho: coldest month (January) 14 °C, hottest (July) 32 °C; diurnal variation 10 °C in winter, 16 °C in summer; annual rainfall 125 mm). Temperatures of over 50 °C have been recorded, and at Sedom annual rainfall is only 50 mm. Evaporation from lakes is high, especially from the Dead Sea, where it attains nearly 15 mm daily – nearly 4000 mm annually. High humidities are thus frequent near water surfaces, and again, dew is important, amounting to 10–20% of the total precipitation in a few areas.

Eastward, there is a heavier rainfall on the uplands of the Anti-Lebanon and the northern highlands of Jordan, but further inland still, a rapid diminution once more occurs, and we arrive again in the steppe régime. Temperatures are more extreme, both in annual and diurnal range (Aleppo:

Climatic data: representative stations in the Levant
*Temperature (°C) and rainfall (mm)*

| | J | F | M | A | M | J | J | A | S | O | N | D | Total |
|---|---|---|---|---|---|---|---|---|---|---|---|---|---|
| **1 Coast** | | | | | | | | | | | | | |
| *(a) Beirut* | | | | | | | | | | | | | |
| Temperature | 10 | 14 | 16 | 19 | 22 | 25 | 28 | 29 | 27 | 24 | 20 | 16 | |
| Rainfall | 195 | 158 | 94 | 56 | 18 | 3 | 0 | 0 | 8 | 51 | 133 | 186 | 906 |
| Rainy days | 15 | 14 | 11 | 6 | 3 | 1 | 0 | 0 | 1 | 4 | 9 | 13 | 77 |
| *(b) Tel Aviv* | | | | | | | | | | | | | |
| Temperature | 12 | 12 | 13 | 18 | 21 | 23 | 24 | 25 | 23 | 21 | 19 | 15 | |
| Rainfall | 124 | 90 | 34 | 2 | 0 | 0 | 0 | 0 | 3 | 18 | 83 | 150 | 519 |
| **2 Mountain** | | | | | | | | | | | | | |
| *(a) Ksara* | | | | | | | | | | | | | |
| *(Lebanon)* | | | | | | | | | | | | | |
| Temperature | 6 | 7 | 10 | 14 | 18 | 22 | 23 | 24 | 22 | 19 | 13 | 11 | |
| Rainfall | 127 | 167 | 49 | 44 | 13 | 0 | 0 | 0 | 0 | 18 | 69 | 104 | 591 |
| Rainy days | 15 | 12 | 10 | 5 | 2 | 0 | 0 | 0 | 0 | 4 | 8 | 12 | 68 |
| *(b) Jerusalem* | | | | | | | | | | | | | |
| Temperature | 9 | 10 | 12 | 15 | 20 | 22 | 23 | 24 | 20 | 15 | 12 | 11 | |
| Rainfall | 153 | 143 | 68 | 23 | 3 | 0 | 0 | 0 | 1 | 9 | 62 | 89 | 551 |
| **3 Jordan rift** | | | | | | | | | | | | | |
| *Tiberias* | | | | | | | | | | | | | |
| Temperature | 13 | 14 | 15 | 18 | 23 | 28 | 29 | 30 | 28 | 24 | 20 | 16 | |
| Rainfall | 110 | 91 | 36 | 19 | 4 | 0 | 0 | 0 | 2 | 14 | 55 | 63 | 404 |
| **4 Steppe** | | | | | | | | | | | | | |
| *Aleppo* | | | | | | | | | | | | | |
| Temperature | 5 | 7 | 10 | 16 | 21 | 26 | 31 | 32 | 25 | 20 | 11 | 9 | |
| Rainfall | 64 | 77 | 34 | 33 | 14 | tr | 0 | 0 | tr | 27 | 44 | 80 | 373 |
| Rainy days | 10 | 10 | 8 | 5 | 2 | 1 | 0 | 0 | 1 | 4 | 5 | 9 | 54 |

coldest month 5·5 °C, warmest month 31 °C; diurnal range 10 °C in winter and 17 °C in summer), and annual rainfall is less, varying from 250 to 450 mm.

In this steppe zone, no more than a narrow strip between the western mountains and inner deserts of Arabia, lie a large number of towns and villages, in which life continues only by the ingenious utilization of a limited water supply. *Qanats* of up to 20 km in length, water channels hacked out of abrupt hillsides, and water lifts of many kinds ranging from small hand machines to petrol-driven *sakias*, are all methods by which man has adapted to his occupation an increasingly difficult environment. It may also be noted that south of a line joining Gaza, Hebron, Beisan and Maan, where the Levant lies within the 'rain-shadow' of north-east Africa and the Sinai peninsula, conditions pass into true desert, and Arabian influences reach the coast of the Mediterranean, interrupting the north–south alignment of the climatic zones of the Levant.

At Aleppo, frost and snow are common in winter, but summer temperatures regularly exceed 38 °C on many days in July and August.

Because, however, of much lower relative humidity in the interior, these higher summer temperatures are much more tolerable than the sultry heat of the littoral, and the traveller finds it difficult to credit that the interior is some 5–8 °C warmer than the coast.

### Agriculture

Because of the varied environment, with rapid topographical and climatic changes, agriculture in the Levant can best be viewed as a mosaic, in which intensively cultivated patches alternate with barren or less productive areas, and where one crop quickly gives place to another, as environmental conditions alter. Over much of the area there is still a pattern of subsistence, with wheat and barley as chief crops, and fruit, vegetables and a little tobacco as adjuncts. Increasingly, however, cash crops have appeared: first, historically perhaps, citrus fruit; but now also cotton, temperate fruits, vegetables for sale, fodder crops and others have greatly increased in importance. The traditional Mediterranean pattern of wheat and barley, vine, olive and fig, with grazing of animals nearby and then on fallow land, still prevails in certain localities, but the growth of towns, with their demand for market-garden produce and fruit, the new markets of the oil-producing areas, and improved transport facilities to Europe, have all contributed to a major change in many areas, with commercial crops providing another impulse. It is therefore less feasible to treat the whole region of the Levant in a general way and developments will accordingly be discussed now on a national basis.

### Syria

Distinction may first be made between the rain-fed areas of cultivation, which in effect mean Syria's share of the 'Fertile Crescent' – i.e. a narrow strip or band of land running north from the Hauran along the eastern foothills of the Anti-Lebanon, then expanding to take in the area between the Mediterranean coast and the edge of the steppe east of Homs, Hama and Idlib, northwards as far as Aleppo, and lastly swinging east along the southern piedmont of the Asia Minor hills into the Jezireh and along the Euphrates valley. Cultivation is by no means entire over all this area, but occurs in patches, with the Hauran, Damascus oasis, Homs-Hama region, the Ghab (Orontes) lowlands and the Aleppo district as the regions of more intensive development.

As well, irrigation is used on an increasing scale; irrigated land now amounts to some 15% of the total cultivated within Syria, and this proportion is rising further as new irrigation schemes come fully into operation. Because of the predominance of rain-fed agriculture, yields

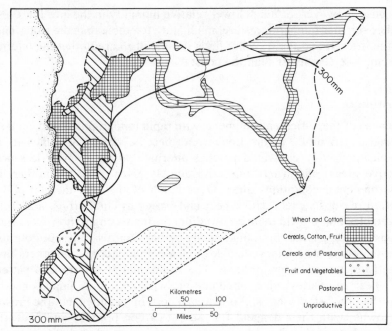

*Fig.* 14.6 Syria: land use.

fluctuate considerably from year to year according to the year's rainfall. but overall the cultivated area has almost tripled in the last 20 years or so.

Chief crop in terms of area is wheat, which is grown over most of the cultivated area, with the north (Aleppo–Homs area) and the Jezireh the most productive regions. In the latter, wheat is grown by dry-farming methods using mechanical equipment on the newly developed territories brought in after 1950. About 1½ million tons are produced on average, but in bad years production falls by one-half or even two-thirds. Barley is the next most important cereal, with a level of production about 35% that of wheat: it tends to be either an alternative to wheat, or produced in the drier, marginal areas, hence production is more affected by weather vagaries. Maize growing has overtaken millet with increased irrigation potential, but oats are now unimportant. Rice growing is another development linked to irrigation, especially in the upper Khabur valley. This means that Syria's position as a producer of cereals has steadily improved, and with average rainfall, there is now an export surplus.

The second crop of Syria is cotton, nearly two-thirds of which is grown under irrigation along the Euphrates and in the Jezireh, with the rest produced in the Aleppo–Hama region. Some cotton has long been grown on a small scale (Damascus = damask), but reductions and variability of

Egyptian cotton exports after 1950 or so were a considerable stimulus, aided by a new strain, 'Coker Carolina Queen', which has a high yield under Syrian conditions. As a result, production has greatly increased, and now fluctuates around 400000 tons annually, being the main export item after petroleum. Another export item is tobacco, produced for export chiefly round Latakia; and following a period of decline, over the last 10–15 years production has revived.

Olives are another important crop, particularly on the hills of the north and west, around Aleppo and Idlib. Vines have a rather wider distribution along the entire western zone of Syria, and nut trees, pistachios especially, are a feature of the Aleppo region. Soft fruits (especially apricots) and figs are widespread, and apply-growing has developed in the cooler western hill zones where water is available. In general, Syria has a very varied production of fruits of many kinds, with vegetables (tomatoes particularly) near the larger towns. Sugar beet has been introduced round Homs and in the Damascus oasis, and sesame is also important. Fodder crops are also grown on an increasing scale, especially in the newer irrigated areas.

Irrigation was until a few decades ago restricted to small-scale works, chiefly local, or rather primitive means such as *norias*. Since 1940, however, considerable numbers of motor pumps have been installed, and great attention has been given by the government to larger-scale irrigation schemes: the five-year plan of 1960–65 allocated 38% of public expenditure to irrigation, and the plan of 1971–75 gave 25% to the Euphrates schemes alone.

Schemes so far achieved, in full or in part, are:

(a) The Ghab drainage and reclamation. This involved the construction of two major barrages to control the Orontes, elimination of a marsh produced by the presence of a large basalt dike, and irrigation so as to allow extensive resettlement in a hitherto unproductive area. Winter crops of wheat, barley and legumes (clover, vetch) and summer crops of cotton, rice, sugar beet and peas are now produced from what had been a totally unused area of rich soil. Begun in 1954, completion occurred in the 1970s.

(b) The Khabur river project, which by a series of barrages and a drainage scheme to remove unwanted salt will eventually bring into cultivation 100000 ha in a region that until a few years ago was little occupied. Much progress has been made, but the scheme is not fully complete.

(c) The Euphrates dam. After a good deal of study (since Turkish and Iraqi agreement was necessary, in that Euphrates water was involved) and difficulties over finance (first West German, then Russian), work began in 1968 on the construction of a major barrage at Tabqa, 200 km east of Aleppo. A dam, 4–6 km long and 60–70 m high, with eight built-in

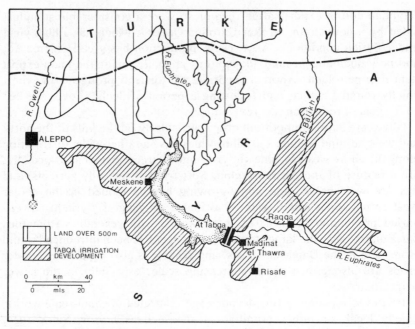

*Fig.* 14.7 The Tabqa barrage scheme.

turbines, began to fill in 1973, forming Lake Assad, which will be over 80 km in length and holding 12 billion m³ of water. From it some 640 000 ha will eventually be irrigated, though the full scheme will not be complete till the later 1990s. Despite earlier studies, Iraq protested strongly during 1975 that the livelihood of 3 million farmers had been put at risk by reduction of the river flow; and a major Turkish barrage at Keban also came into operation in 1974: all pointing to a need for international agreement.

(*d*) Smaller projects: dams south and west of Aleppo, and in the Ghab – here French assistance has been given; and there is an American project along the Yarmuk.

Like many Middle Eastern governments, Syria has undertaken a programme of land reform, designed to reduce the influence of wealthy landlords with large holdings, and stimulate more intensive, enlightened exploitation. Various laws were passed between 1958 and 1967 laying down maximum holdings permitted, and the change-over, though by no means total and complete, is regarded as an important contributing factor in the agricultural expansion of the last few years. Besides resettling landless peasants, the reform has allowed the emergence of an enlightened urban entrepreneur, who, with capital acquired in the towns, has taken over new land as irrigation has developed, and exploited it by mechanical means and with commercial crops as a basis. Despite the 1973 war, or perhaps even because of it, there has been a boom in Syrian agriculture during the 1970s with rising production, expansion of cropped land, and major capital investment.

## Lebanon

Dominating feature in this area is the presence of the Lebanon mountain massif, which far more than anywhere in the Levant gives a range of conditions from near tropical to sub-arctic over very short distances – rarely more than 15–30 km. Further, as we have seen, the structure and height of the massif means that in many areas water is more abundant and better distributed through seepage and springs. A theoretical model based on observed temperature conditions gives a zonation of conditions from humid sub-tropical in sheltered coastal areas through temperate to sub-arctic conditions at heights of over 3000 m, where the mean annual temperature is 0 °C or below (fig. 14.8).

Most, though not all, Lebanese cultivation is located on the western slopes of the Lebanon mountains, where abundant water and varied soil are special advantages. The traditional pattern was of cereal cultivation, mainly wheat with some barley, together with unirrigated olives and smaller quantities of tree fruits (figs, peaches, etc.) and vegetables. This was found in most areas until the Second World War, and is still characteristic of the Akkar region north-east of Tripoli, and of parts of the south towards the Israeli frontier.

Elsewhere, considerable changes have taken place, as the result of enhanced demand for fruit and vegetables from the growing urban centres (Beirut especially), the tourist areas, and from abroad – in the Middle East and in Europe. Consequently, much of the coastal area, the plain and the first slopes has experienced considerable change. Since 1945 citrus fruit groves have developed on a considerable scale both north and south of Beirut. Bananas will also grow, and early practice was to interplant bananas with citrus, since the former bear fruit 4 years earlier than citrus,which needs 6 or 7 years from planting. As the citrus trees become established, the bananas are removed from the open areas, since they do best in the steamier, still and humid valleys. In addition, market-gardening (vegetables, early potatoes, high-priced fruit) has spread, so the lowlands immediately south of Beirut as far north as Batroun are now heavily cultivated wherever soil occurs in sufficient depth. Further to the south, behind Saida and Tyre, vines and olives still remain as major fruit crops on the lower slopes of the hills, with bananas along the Litani bottom land.

Above about 700 m another major change has taken place: the intro-

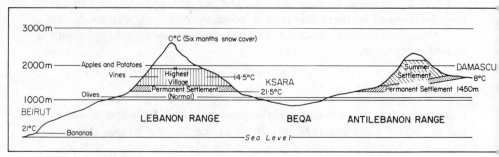

*Fig.* 14.8 Altitude and land use in the Lebanon and Anti-Lebanon.

duction of apple-growing since 1945, when these were first introduced at the instance of the Middle East Supply Centre. The cooler climate is the main factor, and the 'keeping' quality of the fruit makes it especially suitable for oilfield regions – hence considerable markets have developed, and production has increased by a factor of 8–10 over the later 1940s – though now there is overproduction. Small-scale irrigation from tanks or pools fed by springs and provision of refrigerated stores are both essential, so apple-growing is not for the small farmer. Capital is essential, and this has come from city entrepreneurs, who are able to reconstruct the ancient narrow hillside terraces into wider units that will allow mechanization.

Vines are a very important crop and cover over 30% of the total cultivated area of the country. Very much a plant of the lower hills, they are grown all along the western side, and also on the western side of the Beqa: for eating, wine-making and for the making of 'dibs', a sort of syrup or jam.

In the southern Lebanon deep dissection and the absence of water-bearing strata reduce the cultivated area to less than 35% of the total available. Marls and thin limestone soils are a further handicap, hence the traditional pattern of heavy dependence on cereal-growing with some figs is still characteristic. Soil erosion, encouraged by cereal monoculture, is thus a feature, with prevalence of goats as another contributing factor. Some tobacco is grown as a cash crop, but vines, affected by phylloxera some decades ago, have never been replaced. Share-cropping is common, and outward human emigration one result. This southern region thus contrasts strongly with the rapidly changing, dynamic central area, where there is perhaps at times too much readiness to switch to the new, and hotels, casinos and multi-track motorways compete with capital intensive farming for available land. Another somewhat less active area is the Akkar region in the extreme north. Here, climate is one handicap: relatively speaking, the winter is a little harder and longer, and crops are later –

a major disadvantage in market-gardening. As well, there is a good deal of wind. These natural drawbacks, together with relative isolation, the drawing of a political boundary that isolates them to the north and east, and absence of tourists in a not specially attractive region, means that, as in southern Lebanon, change is much less apparent, and we are in the more traditional Middle East.

The Beqa has three distinctive agricultural zones. The extreme north, from Baalbek to the Syrian frontier, is a region of low rainfall of under 200 mm since it lies very much in the rain-shadow of the main Lebanon massifs. As a result, soils are thin and infertile, hence cultivation is greatly restricted, and much of the area is grazing land still used by small groups of pastoral nomads. The centre, round Zahle and Rayak, in contrast has a deep, rich soil and its flatness as contrasted with conditions both north and south makes it very suitable for mechanized agriculture. Water is something of a difficulty away from the western hill slopes, which have spring-lines; but wells and motor pumps are used. However, the supply of underground water is not inexhaustible and there are signs of depletion in some parts. Intensive cereal-growing in rotation with sugar beet, potatoes and fodder crops occurs on the Beqa floor (most of the tractors in the Lebanon are found here), whilst towards the fault-scarps of the Lebanon range, especially around Zahleh, market-gardening, vineyards and orchards are found. The winery at Ksara has functioned for nearly a century, and vines are grown on the lower hill slopes, often on high-level wires to avoid katabatic drainage of cold air from snow-covered Mount Sannin a few kilometres to the west. Salad- and vegetable-growing, together with horticulture, are also important, and there are orchards of peaches, apricots and cherries. Apple-growing has been tried, but is markedly less successful than on the seaward side of the Lebanon – it is remarkable that only a very short distance away the 'steppe' conditions of the interior exert a distinctive influence.

The southern Beqa is rather less developed. Cereals are the chief crop, with longer fallow, and animal-grazing is more important, but development of irrigation from the project is producing more marked development, particularly involving cotton.

Once, there were a number of other commercial crops in the Lebanon. Mulberry-growing (for silkworms) was a major activity in the northern hills east of Tripoli, and again south-east of Beirut (the Jezzine area). Many, though not all, of these trees have disappeared latterly owing to the competition of man-made fibres. Tobacco of varied quality is still produced with some export, and the development of dairying has led to use of fodder crops for stall-fed animals. The Beqa and hill areas also offer excellent conditions for hashish-growing, which in years past was (or is still) a lucrative but illegal occupation for a certain number of farmers. The civil war of 1975–76 has greatly damaged Lebanese agriculture, at least temporarily.

## Jordan

Cultivated areas occur mainly in three regions: (a) the highlands from Amman northwards through Es Salt as far as Ajlun, Irbid and the Syrian frontier, (b) the east Ghor floor, from the river Jordan eastwards in a narrow strip along the foot of the Jordan hills, and (c) the Jordanian portion of the Judaean Highlands, centred on Nablus and Ramallah – this last area now being in Israeli occupation.

The northern highlands of Jordan are a watershed zone, dropping very steeply on the west to the Jordan valley, but more gradually eastwards towards the interior desert plateau. Erosion has been active, with deeply incised valleys on the west leading to the Jordan, but east of this is a tabular or cuesta formation, highly dissected by the headstreams of the Zerqa and Yaarkon (which reach back through the main crests) into a topography of ridge, plateau and vale. Aspect towards the west results in moderate amounts of rainfall (500–800 mm), so rain-fed agriculture is possible in many localities, supplemented by small-scale irrigation from local wells. Cereals, chiefly wheat (and barley in the drier parts), are staples, with olives, figs and vines. Olives were clearly once more widespread, but, like the oak forest that still clothes some of the higher parts, have diminished over the last century. Vines are still frequent. New features are the spread of cash crops in many localities: tomatoes and melons especially, with citrus fruit, artichokes and potatoes, and other fruit and vegetables also. Demand has been stimulated by Jordan's proximity to the Arabian oilfields and the diminished competition from the west bank. Over the last few years, energetic governmental action has taken place to combat soil erosion, which here is a major problem, by terracing, construction of masonry plugs in the beds of valleys to prevent flash-flooding, and agricultural extension work among farmers. As well, forest conservation and grazing control are undertaken by the government, since proximity to the steppelands means that many pastoralists bring up their animals to the hill areas during the summer, and have been accustomed to treating cultivated areas (harvested previously, with luck) as zones of transit and pasture. Here is a social and economic problem of some magnitude.

The Jordan lowland (within Jordanian territory) is highly cultivated in its portion between the Amman–Jericho road in the south, and the Yarmuk in the north. All cultivation is dependent on irrigation from the East Ghor Canal, which runs parallel to the Jordan river on one of the higher terraces. Cereals, fodder crops, tobacco, maize, groundnuts and some fruit and vegetables are grown, and the area has greatly benefited from a special development scheme inaugurated in 1966 and expanded in 1972. This scheme involved a unitary Authority for the East Ghor, that has constructed dams and canals to divert the streams that run westwards from the hills towards the Jordan River. One part of the scheme, the East Ghor Canal project, has added over 100 000 ha to Jordan's irrigated area; a second scheme using the waters of the Zerqa river is in construction; and the current Five Year Plan (1976–81) aims at extending the Ghor irrigation as far south as the Dead Sea. War damage has largely been made good, and with the influx of labour and more recently capital, yields have increased markedly since 1973, though still closely dependent upon weather in a particular year.

The Jordanian portion of the Judean plateau (which pre-1967 produced 80% of the fruit, and 40–50% of the vegetables and cereals of the Jordanian state) is characterized by the same type of cultivation as on the east Jordan plateau. A basic dependence on cereal-growing with vines, figs and olives (Nablus is a major centre for olives) has given way in places to commercial crops such as tomatoes and vegetables; and fodder crops have also come in with the expansion of dairying. The Nablus area is one of the more highly cultivated zones; further south, increasing elevation and chalky, marly soils make cultivation more difficult, except in the hollows and basins eroded in the plateau surface, where soil and water are more abundant.

## Israel

Here, cultivation is carried on in three main zones: the northern coastal plains, the hill regions of the interior, especially the Shefela, and the upper parts of the Jordan valley. Agriculture in Israel differs from that of adjacent countries in several significant ways: first, since the Israelis have colonized gradually from outside, they have been able to plan and direct agriculture in a manner impossible for more traditional existing societies. Second, considerable finance was available, backed by great expertise; for many years, Israel had the largest capital imports per head of any country in the world – consequently, mechanization and rational development sustained by scientific experimentation were keynotes. Third, by emphasizing standards which were European rather than indigenous, labour in agriculture demanded a return well above that acceptable to the average Middle Eastern farmer – Jewish farm labour was therefore expensive and could not be abundant. Last, overseas markets for fruit could rely on the interest of Jewish firms, e.g. in Britain. All this has meant that great effort, human and financial, has gone into what is not intrinsically outstandingly fertile or manageable territory. Specialization

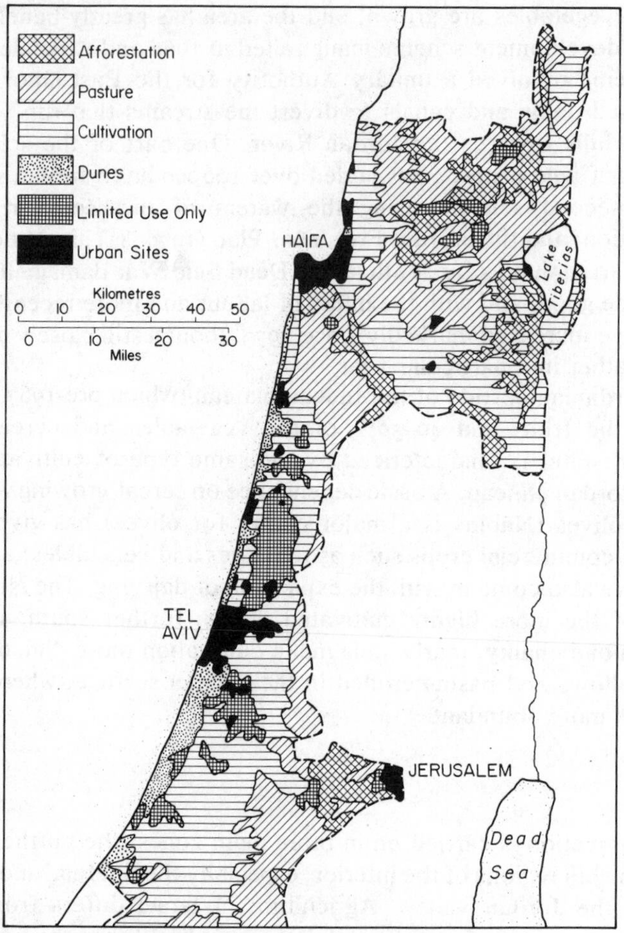

*Fig.* 14.9 Israel: land use.

as between crops, in the light of environmental variation, is very marked
– intensive rational exploitation with a keen eye to markets, and relatively
abundant initial capitalization, are main characteristics. Water, rather than
land, is the chief factor limiting cultivation; and it is noteworthy that,
despite widespread ideas that Israel is a land of agriculture, that only
6% of the total labour force is engaged in agriculture, which contributes
5 to 6% to G.D.P. A basic aim is the attainment of self-sufficiency in
food – due largely to strategic necessities – and some observers believe
that need for self-sufficiency has distorted Israeli agricultural methods
at the expense of full efficiency and total potential.

Cereals (in which Israel is least self-sufficient) are widely grown: wheat
and barley as winter crops, maize and sorghum in summer. Wheat is

especially important on the heavier soils of the Shefela and the Esdraelon lowlands, but is also grown on the lower plateau in Galilee, and on the loess soils of the northern Negev. This winter wheat is largely sold abroad for pastas (macaroni, etc.) and soft wheat for bread-making is imported. Barley is grown on more marginal lands of lower rainfall and poorer soil – especially on the hill margins and in the Negev. Area is actually greater than that of wheat, but yields are lower – most of the crop being used for animal fodder. Maize is also grown chiefly for green animal fodder, and for industrial raw materials (starch and glucose), and when irrigated, yields of 8–10 tons/ha are possible. Clover, alfalfa, lucerne and beans are also grown as fodder.

Principal agricultural export has long been citrus fruits, which have been cultivated on a large scale since the early days of the present century. Oranges (of the Shamuti or Jaffa variety) are the principal item, and they grow best on the lighter, sandier soils of the Sharon area and further south, beyond Tel Aviv. Grapefruit succeeds better on heavier soils, and so is cultivated on the eastern rim of the coastal plain, and in the Esdraelon lowlands. Of the citrus exports about 60% are of Shamuti oranges, 25% grapefruit, 5% Valencia oranges, and the rest lemons and limes.

Vines are at home especially on the lower hill slopes, but also do well on the sandy soils of the west-central coastal plain. Most are eaten fresh, but there is a small wine-making industry centred round Latrun and Rishon le Zion, near Tel Aviv. Other fruits are produced in quantity: peaches, apricots and pomegranates, more particularly in the north, the last named being tolerant of saline soils. Olives are also important, particularly in the Galilee and Samaria regions, while there is a growing export of high-priced, out-of-season items such as avocado pears, guavas, mangoes and strawberries.

Israel grows cotton mainly for her own industries chiefly in the Hule, Esdraelon and Sharon districts, while oil seeds and sugar beet are grown on the heavier soils of the interior lowlands. Groundnuts are an important export crop, and fibre plants are produced, the chief of which, sisal, does well in dry, sandy areas.

Market-gardening is widespread, particularly in view of the high degree of urbanization in Israel. It will also be apparent from the importance given to fodder crops, which increasingly include carobs, that mixed farming plays a role far greater in Israel than in neighbouring areas – probably more, in proportion, than in any other Middle Eastern country. There are about a third of a million cattle in Israel: one for every ten of the human population, which some Israelis regard as excessive, given the geographical limitations of the territory. Export of cut flowers is developing.

*Irrigation in Israel* Of the annual average of rainfall actually falling over
Israeli territory, it is estimated that 65% evaporates either directly or by
transpiration from plants, and 5–10% is direct run-off to the Mediterranean
or Dead Seas. Only about 15–20% of the 6000 million m³ is actually
retained, since a further fraction seeps deeply into the ground and is lost
by deep percolation to the sea. By capturing run-off in small barrages,
and tapping underground percolation, Israeli sources estimate that just
under 2000 million m³ are available – this includes flow from the Jordan
river, some of which is fed by tributaries that rise outside Israel. When
one compares this with the amounts available, say, in Iraq, or even in
the Tabqa Euphrates barrage (40000 million m³), the importance of
irrigation becomes apparent.

Various schemes for overall use of the entire Jordan system and that
of its tributaries have been proposed: there were the Hays/Lowdermilk
scheme of 1930s, and a later scheme by Johnston in 1950–55; but both
were rejected by Arab neighbours who feared that most of the benefit
would ultimately be Israel's. As a result, a smaller-scale water distribution
grid, known as the 'National Carrier', has been constructed. This uses
Lake Tiberias as a reservoir, and from it water is pumped to a height
of 256 m above lake level, on the Galilee side, from where it flows or
is pumped in a series of channels and pipes eventually as far as the coastal
plain, and even the northern Negev. Salinity of the waters of Lake
Tiberias and cost of pumping are adverse factors, now countered by
separating out saline spring waters on the bed of Tiberias and diverting
them down the Jordan; and, of course, the amount of water available
is not large, especially since the Arab governments have diverted
headwaters of streams in the upper Galilee frontier area. As a result, Israel
has been driven to reconstitution of sewage effluent, careful study of crop
needs, use of saline water where this can be done, and desalination of
sea and lake water. There is great need for the most careful conservation
methods, since overpumping of groundwater in the Sharon and Tel Aviv
regions has allowed the rise of sea water into porous substrata – a fall
of 3–6 m in the water table has occurred in several areas since irrigation
schemes began. It is now appreciated that irrigation of crops (especially
tall bushes) by sprinkler methods loses up to 45% of water used; thus
improved methods are coming in which involve plastic pipes near plant
roots, with drip flow controlled by a central computer that is programmed
to operate the flow (*a*) at night when evaporation is less, and (*b*) according
to detailed soil humidities.

Such methods are now used in two recently developed areas: round
Dimona in the Negev, and in the Araba part of the Jordan rift; out-of-season
high grade fruit and vegetables, and cut flowers for European markets
are now produced.

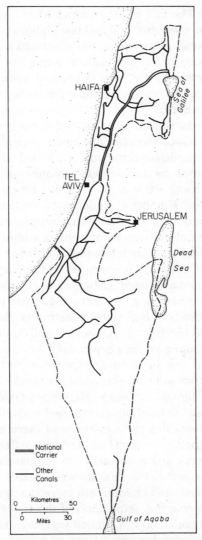

*Fig.* 14.10 Water supply in Israel.

A feature of Israeli agriculture has been the careful arrangement and planning of many rural settlements. Jewish settlement in Palestine/Israel, though spread over many decades, came, as we have noted, in 'waves' rather than as a continuous stream. This probably had the result of invoking strenuous efforts at certain periods to meet sudden demands, and firm policy was therefore arrived at, rather than the general acquiescence in a slowly evolving situation.

Israeli authorities recognize three basic types of village: the moshava, kibbutz and moshav. The first is a type which allows almost all initiative to the individual, who owns his land and installations, and exploits these as he pleases, on a family or larger scale, using hired labour if necessary. This type of settlement is termed 'natural', and has often proved the nucleus of settlements that are now large, and even partially or in a majority commercial and industrial – comparable to the nineteenth-century situation in North America.

The first kibbutz was started in 1909, and these settlements tend to follow the pattern of mixed farming. The land is owned by the state, and all other property is regarded as communal, with food, clothing, recreation and education provided by the kibbutz. Money is not therefore in circulation, and members work at tasks allotted by a local committee elected by all members. Kibbutzim tended to be settlements in 'pioneer' areas, for instance in difficult, arid or defensive situations, and, though there is diversification of activity away from agriculture (e.g. into home manufacturing, fishing, etc), in practice the kibbutz has never grown very large: a population of about 1500 seems to be the maximum, and most have less. Kibbutzim have been criticized as soulless and close to concentration camp methods (e.g. by right-wing Jewish parties) and Arabs regard them as spearheads of imperialist penetration: they have also been praised for the selfless service that can be fostered, and the strong appeal to ideals, especially among young people, both Jewish and non-Jewish.

Moshav settlements are small-holdings worked by the occupant and his family, with a strict limit on size – the tenant cannot acquire more land than he and his family can work. He cannot divide or alienate the land, he accepts mutual defined obligations and responsibilities with the other family units composing the moshav, and there is joint marketing for all produce and supplies. Variants on this basic pattern are the moshav shitufi, in which all work and production are communal, as in a kibbutz, but personal property and family life allowed – meals are at home, not in the central dining hall, and children are more the direct responsibility of parents. It would appear that settlements of this type do not grow much beyond 400 as a total population. A second variant is the moshav ovdim, which is specially designed for immigrants who are inexperienced, and who do not wish to join a kibbutz – instruction and habituation play an important part. The various types of settlement are often recognizable from their ground plan and morphology, with regularity very characteristic of all but moshava villages.

## Minerals

The mineral wealth of the Levant is distinctly more important than was at one time supposed. Within the last few decades oil, natural gas, copper, iron and phosphates have been discovered and exploited in commercial

Chemical content of Dead Sea water (g/l)

| | Surface | 110 m depth | Estimated quantity of dissolved salts (million tons) |
|---|---|---|---|
| KCl | 10·0–11·8 | 15·7 | 2 000 |
| NaCl | 71·0–82·4 | 87·4 | 11 000 |
| MgCl$_2$ | 109·5–142·4 | 169·0 | 22 000 |
| CaCl$_2$ | 31·0–33·0 | 46·7 | 6 000 |
| CaSO$_4$ | 1·3 | 0·6 | 200 |
| MgBr$_2$ | 3·9–4·5 | 7·3 | 980 |

quantities. Lignite was mined on a very small scale in the northern Lebanon, but is now exhausted.

Oil prospection has had varied results. Main discoveries have been in Syria and Israel, with Israel nearly self-sufficient and the former now exporting useful, though not large quantities. Natural gas occurs in the Syrian Jezireh, in the Palmyra area and in the north-east of the Negev (Arad region). Asphalt and bitumen occur in a few parts of the Lebanon, Anti-Lebanon and Ansarieh ranges, and as lumps that form on the bed of the Dead Sea and later rise to the surface. There is little attempt at development of any of these deposits. The Dead Sea is, however, much more important for its mineral salts. Analysis shows that at the surface, each litre of Dead Sea water contains 227–275 g of dissolved salts. At a depth of 110 m, the water is chemically saturated, and the corresponding figure is 327 g.

In 1930 the Palestine Potash Corporation began extraction of mineral salts, using a simple process of solar evaporation, which, as we have seen, is particularly active in the region of the lower Jordan. Pans of Dead Sea water are allowed to evaporate, and after 40 to 50 days, most of the unwanted common salt has crystallized out and can be removed. Evaporation is continued, and a mixture of potassium and magnesium chlorides, known as carnallite, is next obtained. This can be purified by recrystallization (still using solar heat) to give a salt consisting of 20% potassium chloride, 70–80% magnesium chloride, and a small content of sodium chloride. Further fractional crystallization gives a much purer magnesium chloride, and finally, magnesium bromide, from which bromine itself is extracted. The potash salts are used principally as fertilizers, whilst bromine is increasingly valuable in the manufacture of armaments (explosives and lethal gases), and in the blending of high octane fuels, as well as in some of the high-grade chemicals now increasingly produced in Israel. Overall production now approaches 1½ million tons.

Phosphate rock occurs in considerable quantity at Ar Rusayfa, north of Amman. Other deposits are known at Hasa further south, elsewhere east of the Dead Sea, in Syria, and in Oron and Ein Yahat in the Negev. Phosphates are Jordan's chief export commodity, and by 1980, could amount to 7 million tons annually: a fertilizer plant is under construction at Aqaba. The Syrian phosphates located in the Palmyra area and exported mainly via Tartus, occur in association with uranium, exploitation of which is scheduled for 1979. Syria also has an important deposit of iron ore: whilst copper has recently been discovered in the Wadi Araba (Jordan), and is also worked at Timna (Israel) near Aqaba where, however, the ore is 'lean' in quality. Manganese, chromium and other metals are known to occur, but only in quantities insufficient to justify exploitation.

**Industry**

Under Ottoman rule, Syria was the most industrialized region of the Middle East, with a fairly extensive textile industry, in Aleppo, Damascus, Homs, Hama, Beirut and Tripoli, that supplied most of the needs of the whole empire. Palestine was largely agricultural, without any industries of importance, other than a very small textile industry in Nablus. In the twentieth century, however, Syrian trade had begun to decline considerably because of competition from foreign machine-made goods, and this decline was further emphasized after 1918. Since 1960 or so, however, Syrian industry has greatly developed, quadrupling by the mid 1970s, and becoming the principal contributor to G.D.P.

In Israel, the position has been one of almost continuous expansion since the 1930s: it has been Jewish policy to foster industrial development as much as possible, as industrial enterprises can absorb far more workers (and hence immigrants) than agriculture. Hence, even despite a slender basis of raw materials, large injections of capital, a highly skilled population, highly intelligent management and the stimulus of the war of 1939–45 – all these led to much expansion. Since the 1950s development has gone further still, with the concentration of workers into larger industrial units often newly located on the outskirts, or in the suburbs, of the towns. Thus we now have the situation that industries located within the centres of the towns of Israel often employ fewer workers than those at a distance.

The textile industries of Syria and the Lebanon use cotton, silk, rayon and wool as main raw materials, with much (though not all) of the first two produced within the region. Aleppo and Damascus, besides producing cloth for clothing, also specialize in luxury cloths – brocade and *crêpe de chine* – which are bought mainly by tourists, but there is also considerable production of cheaper cloths (poplin, muslin, marocain and coarser cottons), together with some camel-hair cloth worn by richer Badawin. Homs and Hama produce a cotton and silk mixture cloth for everyday use as clothing; but it is significant that most of the home-produced cloth is used in Arab styles, with 'European' clothing worn increasingly by younger people, largely imported. Modern cotton mills at Tripoli produce medium-quality cloth, but the silk industry of the Lebanon has had many vicissitudes, the latest being one of near extinction. Textile production in Syria has greatly increased, partly assisted by local cotton growing, and is a major activity in Aleppo, Damascus, Homs, Latakia and Hama (where a Chinese-built factory has opened).

For a time, textiles in cotton, wool and man-made fibres occupied most of the industrial workers of Israel, but metal-working is now the most important occupation. Originally based chiefly in Haifa and Tel Aviv, textile manufacturing has spread into many of the new towns and development zones, in the Negev and elsewhere, being largely based on home-grown cotton and home-produced artificial fibres.

Metal-working (including the making of small consumer goods and spare parts for vehicles) is most developed in Israel, where over 30% of the entire working population is involved. The Syrian towns also have a certain amount of this activity, and a special feature is the construction of a steel mill at Hama. Type of production thus ranges from craft-style small workshops turning out household utensils and primus-stove parts to larger-scale metallurgical plant in Israel and Syria, with much less in Lebanon, and hardly any in Jordan. Completion of the Euphrates Dam, with its development of hydro-electricity, has led Syria to consider prospects for aluminium smelting (possibly to be located at Latakia), development of nuclear energy (from Palmyra uranium) and further assembly plants for cars and tractors.

Chemical production has greatly expanded in Syria, where there are fertilizer plants of recent construction at Hama and Homs, and in Israel, where, besides heavy chemicals (fertilizers and basic requirements for industry), specialization has begun into higher-quality products – synthetic fibres, rubber and pharmaceuticals. Cement is produced in all four countries of the Levant.

Preparation and treatment of agricultural products, some for food, still remains an important factor, though with the development of modern manufacturing as just described, the relative importance of this type of activity has declined. Because of the abundance of olives, soap-boiling is a traditional feature, being carried on in many towns, Beirut, Nablus, Aleppo and Tel Aviv especially.

Other industries have developed in Israel. Diamond-cutting using imported stones was first introduced into Nathaniya in the Sharon plain during the late 1930s from Antwerp, and now produces gross exports worth

$650 million or more annually, with workers scattered in many localities. Like the watch trade of Switzerland, but even more so, the small quantity of 'raw material' allows dispersion. Other activities are the production of electrical goods and machinery (refrigerators, electric motors, textile machinery) and vehicles, with tyres (based on home-produced products) and plastics also important.

Industrial production in the Lebanon is generally on a small scale, and very small indeed in Jordan. Syria aims at self-sufficiency in a number of commodities as textiles and metals, whilst Israel now exports manufactured goods on a significant scale – one of the very few countries of the Middle East where this is so.

This considerable industrial progress in Israel, by which the number of Jewish industrial workers has risen from 5000 (1925) to about 350000 (1977), has its basis in the following favourable factors:

(1) Availability of cheap sources of power – hydro-electricity, already developed in the middle Jordan, crude oil, natural gas and, exceptionally, the solar heat of the lower Jordan.

(2) Rapid growth of population, both Jewish and (until 1948) Arab, which provided a source of cheap labour, and also an expanding market for finished products.

(3) The marked increase of technical skill, due to Jewish immigration from Europe. Many refugees also brought machinery with them rather than money, especially those coming from Hitlerite Germany, from which the export of currency was forbidden.

(4) The continuing large import of capital ever since the founding of the Jewish National Home in the 1920s, which is still a feature at the present. This has, on a basis of head of population, been consistently the highest for any nation of the world, and is made up of donations of money to the Zionist cause, offers of services free (e.g. on kibbutzim) and loans, mainly from the United States. Funds have hence been available for development projects, private and state-run, that seemed dubious or clearly 'uneconomic' – absorption of all Jewish immigrants and creation of a strong political unit have been overriding considerations.

(5) The stimulus of war, fought by a consistently successful group: in 1946–7, 1956, 1967 and 1973. This, if successfully financed (as it was for reasons given in (4) above), can mean a major expansion for the national economy. It is significant that the largest single industrial enterprise in Israel is the production of missiles and aircraft – passenger and military; whilst the electronics industry has boomed, and begun to export on an important scale.

(6) German reparations, paid by the West German government in compensation since 1953.

Nevertheless, the general financial position of Israel has remained precarious. Between 1963–73 exports amounted to 50–60% of imports: this was hailed as a great advance on the 1948–60 situation; but the 1973 war led to sharp deterioration to below 45%, with considerable foreign borrowing and devaluation of the Israeli pound, which (worth US $4 in 1948) had fallen to 15 cents in 1975. Israel has borrowed some $11 billion since establishment as a state, and now has an outstanding debt of $8 billion. This has in effect made Israel very largely dependent for survival upon the USA, and led Arabs to argue that a similar input of capital applied to Arab regions of similar environmental endowment could have produced equal or better returns.

**Communications and trade**

Location confers on the countries of the Levant important advantages deriving from transit traffic, particularly now that the oil-rich countries of south-west Asia are heavy importers and consumers. The ancient caravan routes have given way to motor tracks and pipelines; and though most of the former passenger traffic that formerly went by sea now moves through the air space of the Middle East often using local airports, there is still a substantial sea traffic, mainly but not wholly involving oil tankers.

*Ports*

Iskanderun (Alexandretta), the natural outlet for the lower Orontes valley, and hence the Aleppo region, was lost to Syria by the cession of the Hatay to Turkey in 1939, and until the 1950s Syria was thus very dependent upon Beirut. Of late years, Syria has made efforts to develop ports on her own coastal façade. Latakia, an ancient site with a moderately good harbour located fairly close to Aleppo, was reconstructed in the 1950s to take larger ships, and rail communication established with the interior after 1952; for long the mass of the Ansarieh mountains had been a hindrance to landward communications. Tartus, further south, is also currently in process of development to handle crude oil exports, and also the phosphate rock now exploited in the interior, but the site is not outstandingly good. Banias, between Tartus and Latakia, is another small oil terminal, which with Tartus handled the Syrian export share of crude oil from the Kirkuk fields of Iraq, and also from the Karachok field of north-east Syria.

Tripoli (*Tri-polis*) is formed by the junction of three small settlements round an original off-shore island. The original Mediterranean terminal of the Kirkuk pipeline, it has a refinery and also handles a small local trade, but as regards general cargo its importance now is only slight. Beirut has a very much better harbour, with a splendidly scenic site, and, despite somewhat difficult landward communications which must cross a col some 1700 m above sea-level to reach the interior, its central position in the Lebanon and moderately wide coastal plain have conferred considerable advantages. Besides its own national traffic, Beirut has developed as the principal entrepôt of the Middle East, with a transit trade to Syria, Jordan, Iraq, Kuwait and Saudi Arabia that in some years amounts to four or five times the value of its own internally generated trade. Beirut is also a very considerable international airport. Some 30 km south of Beirut is Saida, once a Phoenician port but now almost entirely restricted to the export of Saudi Arabian oil. Haifa has a site very similar to that of Beirut, with a harbour formed by a west or north-westward jutting promontory that offers shelter from the prevailing south-westerlies. Haifa, however, unlike Beirut, is not an ancient port site; some assert, questionably, that its harbour was too sheer and deep to allow construction in earlier times, though this is nowadays an undisputed and considerable advantage. Accordingly, the ancient port site was at Acre, on flatter ground. Communications are easy either inland via the Esdraelon lowland, or via the plain of Sharon to Jerusalem and the Negev, but political difficulties have restricted the effective hinterland to Israel only. The port really dates from 1934, and as it is by far the best site in Israel it has steadily taken over the bulk of Israeli shipping activity, which was once shared with Jaffa–Tel Aviv. This last centre has only a small harbour site, formed by a small ridge or hill that extends into the Mediterranean, like a natural pier or mole, giving two small harbours, one to the north, the other to the south.

Eilat and Aqaba are respectively the Israeli and Jordanian outlets at the head of the Gulf of Aqaba, and both are modern developments in response to recent exigencies of political geography. Eilat has an oil pipeline connection to Haifa, which allows the import of crude oil from Iran, either for refining at Haifa or for sale to Europe avoiding the Suez Canal. Aqaba is the only Jordanian port, but is distant and isolated, and the political difficulties of the past few years in the Gulf of Aqaba have restricted its usefulness. Closure of the Suez Canal (1967–75) was a handicap to both Eilat and Aqaba, but both of these have profited from the civil war in the Lebanon coincident with Suez re-opening and have now started to function on a larger scale.

The relative importance of railways has declined: some routes have closed, but others have been improved, notably the Hijaz Railway as far as Maan and now Aqaba. With the enormous growth in road communication, the railway in a region of relatively short hauls and difficult terrain is at a disadvantage – nevertheless, new lines have been developed in Syria between the coast and interior, giving access via Aleppo to Turkey and Iraq.

Tourism/pilgrimage: visitors annually ('ooos)

|         | 1966 | 1975        |
|---------|------|-------------|
| Israel  | 340  | 619         |
| Jordan  | 617  | 708         |
| Lebanon | 601  | 1500 (1974) |
| Syria   | 935  | 950         |

Road and air transport are now extensively developed, beyond the level of most of the rest of the Middle East, making the whole region (political difficulties apart) highly accessible.

*Economy*

The economies of the four Levant states have certain remarkable features: none is wholly self-sufficient in basic cereals/foodstuffs, but must import wheat, edible oils, meat, tea and coffee. There is considerable dependence upon imported machinery and vehicles (including more and more spare parts for assembly), manufactured goods, and in the case of Israel raw materials (diamonds especially) for industry. Syria is now self-sufficient in oil and gas (with an export of the former) but, having returned some oilfields in the Sinai to Egypt, Israel must increasingly import, whilst the Lebanon and Jordan have none of their own. Israel exports cut diamonds (the principal item), fruit and vegetables, textiles, machinery, chemicals and electrical goods; Syria chiefly petroleum and raw cotton; Jordan phosphates and fruit and vegetables; while in normal times the Lebanon has important exports of fruit, but a far greater transit trade. Except in the case of Syria, exports do not balance imports, and the gap is filled by 'invisible' revenue: banking and associated services in the Lebanon; gifts and loans to Zionist political objectives, and remittances sent home by Lebanese and some Syrians living permanently or temporarily in the United States, South America and tropical Africa (where they are often traders and merchants). As well, in normal times, there is the tourist-pilgrim traffic, which brings large numbers of visitors from other countries. Though the individual sums expended may be small, the total amount is great, and much of the commercial activity of Jerusalem is derived from catering for pilgrims, Christian, Jewish and Moslem, in hotels, hospices and monasteries. Moreover, many convents and religious houses are financially supported from abroad, but consume local produce. Pilgrims are also buyers of souvenirs and relics – in olive-wood, mother-of-pearl, and lace-work, the manufacture of which is an important activity in Jerusalem, Tel Aviv, Bethlehem and Nazareth. Further north there are fewer pilgrims, but the scenery and amenities of the Lebanon especially attract summer visitors, mainly Arabs, and there is also a small winter sports activity located in the high Lebanon. In addition, the remarkable archaeological monuments of Amman, Baalbek, Jerash, Palmyra and elsewhere, with the picturesqueness of Damascus and Aleppo and the largely intact Crusader castles of the western hills, amount to a considerable attraction.

### Towns

The towns of this area, though not particularly large in comparison with, say, Cairo, Tehran and Baghdad, nevertheless have played a conspicuous part in the life of the region, and are distinctly more numerous in relation to population. Israel is very highly urbanized, with the great majority of its population in towns; the other three countries have large but not predominant urban populations.

Until recently, the largest urban centre of the Levant was Aleppo (pop. est., 1977, 700000). Many geographical factors have contributed to this supremacy, which is of long standing, for after the decline of Abbasid Baghdad, Aleppo ranked as the second city of the Ottoman Empire. Chief of these factors is the location of the city on the borders of four strikingly dissimilar geographic regions. To the north lies the difficult hill country of Asia Minor, to which relatively easy access is given by the pass of the 'Cilician Gates', and by the upper valleys of the Euphrates, Khabur and Tigris; to the south-west lie the agricultural 'oases' of Hama, Homs and Damascus, with at a greater distance the more intensely exploited Lebanon, backed by the Mediterranean ports of Iskanderun, Latakia, Tripoli and Beirut, for all of which Aleppo acts as distributor and collector of produce. South-eastwards lies the pastoral Syrian desert; and eastwards the steppes of the Fertile Crescent, providing an easier, though longer, route to Iraq and Iran. Hence there is an important market for wool, livestock and hides from the steppes, cereals and fruit from the oases, manufactured articles from the ports and inland towns, and wood, charcoal and metals from Asia Minor.

Besides its commercial relations, Aleppo has, as we have seen, many local industries. Although now overshadowed politically by Damascus, it still retains much trading and industrial activity, and is less affected by Westernization than most other parts of the Levant. As a city it retains many of its ancient monuments, and hence, to Westerners, appears more truly 'Oriental' than many other towns of the Levant. The construction of the Euphrates dam, the opening up of the Jezireh for agriculture, and the oil development at Karachuk, are further favourable factors in the near future.

Damascus (pop. est., 1977, 950000), like Aleppo, owes its rise to trade

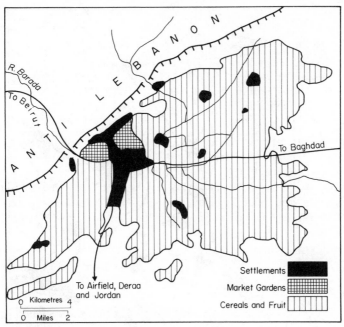

*Fig.* 14.11  The Damascus region.

and industry. Its position as a 'desert port' gave it early importance, and with Aleppo it claims the title of oldest continuously inhabited city in the world. Local advantages are the presence of abundant irrigation water, the availability of local raw materials (cotton, silk, wool, wood, etc.) and an excellent location at the eastern end of a series of gorges and lowland gaps that offer the best east–west route through the Anti-Lebanon range.

Modern Damascus owes most to its agricultural productivity, based on intensive exploitation of the Ghuta (oasis), so, even more than Aleppo, it has become a market for exchange of produce between pastoralists and cultivators. Textile manufacturing continues, and, more than Aleppo, Damascus is in contact with a tourist traffic that provides an outlet for the sale of trinkets, small inlaid furniture in walnut, luxury silks, rugs and carpets. Under the Ottomans, Damascus occupied a marginal position, lying on the edge of the Imperial domain, with Aleppo in a more central and advantageous position. Today, the situation is reversed: Damascus is the metropolis, the centre of political, social and economic planning, with tertiary activities, some manufacturing and a developed communication network, with Aleppo more in isolation, cut off politically from its nearest port-site at Iskanderun.

The rapid rise of Beirut (pop. est., 1977, 650000) has been a feature of recent years. This has been facilitated by the natural advantage of a

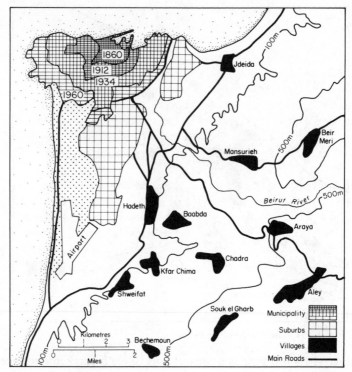

*Fig.* 14.12 Greater Beirut.

fault-defined harbour in the Bay of St George, sheltered, like Haifa, from south-west winds by a westward-jutting promontory. Once the disadvantage of difficult access to the interior had been overcome in the late nineteenth century by the building of a road and railway across the Col du Beidar, Beirut, centrally placed with relatively near access to Syria and Jordan, became the largest port and chief commercial centre of the Levant, handling some Syrian trade and all but a tiny fraction of traffic for Jordan. Textile manufacturing, food-processing, light engineering and production of consumer goods are carried on, with, also, a considerable hotel and tourist traffic. The creation of a 'free zone' in the harbour and the rapid building of a major airport have been substantial advantages.

Most of all, however, Beirut developed as an international commercial centre, by which the profits from oil, gold, diamonds (as international articles of exchange) and other commodities were channelled and sold. Beirut had over eighty merchant banking houses, and gold and foreign exchange reserves of about $300 million (i.e. over $100 per head of national population – cf. Britain, $50). This, for a country devoid of minerals and producing fruit of medium quality as its chief export commodity, is remarkable and is to be explained by the extreme policy of commercial *laissez-faire* practised, with free movement of capital and goods. International firms threatened by nationalization in Cairo and Damascus, the newly rich from oil not wholly certain as to how to handle their complex holdings for the best, traditionally inclined statesmen and merchants not at ease in the 'leftish' atmosphere of the U.A.R., Cyprus and Baghdad, found accommodation in the cosmopolitan culture of Beirut, where a synthesis on *laissez-faire* lines between Christian, Moslem, Jew and pagan lasted from 1945 to 1975. Now (1978) it may have died.

One other element may also be the high level of education. Since Byzantine days, Beirut has had a reputation as a teaching centre, and currently four universities (American, Arab, French, Lebanese National) and the UNESCO headquarters, together with native and foreign schools and colleges, have brought both cultural and economic advantages.

Beirut has grown rapidly from an original Roman nucleus, with a Crusader cathedral (now a mosque) at the centre, on a northward-facing fault scarp facing the Bay of St George. The entire promontory is now occupied, from the extreme west, where Ras Beirut is a fashionable, well-built suburb of high apartment blocks and restaurants, to beyond the Beirut river in the east, which until the 1940s was a malarial swamp largely inhabited by Armenian refugees now a greatly improved zone of light industry and working-class housing. 'Greater Beirut', now estimated to have nearly 900000 inhabitants, extends 5–10 km to the north, south and east.

Tripoli, though lacking a first-class harbour, has the advantages of easy communications inland, and the availability of raw material from the cotton-growing region round Homs. As a result, it functions as a natural outlet for the northern Lebanon, and for long it was the successful rival of Latakia; and the first oil pipelines from Kirkuk were brought to Tripoli by way of the Bukeia–Akkar lowlands, rather than across the Lebanon ridges to Beirut, hence there is a petroleum traffic and oil refining. Tripoli also has some textile manufacturing and, at a distance, cement production, with other smaller activities. Tripoli, unlike Beirut, is predominantly a strongly Moslem town, though its immediate hinterland, the Lebanon hills, is Christian.

Amman, the capital and major city of the Jordanian state, has developed from being little more than a watering point for nomads in the nineteenth century to a present population (1977 est.) of 700000. In Classical times, however, it was the considerable settlement of Philadelphia – a theatre of this epoch still remains in the centre of the city. Amman is the commercial and administrative focus of the country, centralizing rail, air and road links. There are a few medium-scale manufactures, and, as with Jerusalem, water supply has been a difficulty in view of its elevation, so that there is little to parallel the fertile oasis of Damascus or the intense commercial activity (up to 1974) of Beirut. Amman, however, has been a principal beneficiary of the troubles in Beirut, and with an inflow of capital and displaced persons from the Lebanon, there has been a major 'boom' that has transformed the city, and more than doubled its population since 1970.

In Israel, three urban centres stand out. Haifa (pop. est., 1977, 230000) stands at the seaward end of the one major lowland route to the interior. Until 1948 crude petroleum was handled from the Kirkuk pipeline, but when this was closed another pipe was constructed to bring oil from Eilat. Industry of a 'heavy' kind – iron and steel, engineering, vehicle building, chemicals and construction – together with newer 'light' industry has spread across the once-malarial flats as far north as Acre. The town is built on the coastal platform, which is narrow, with industrial plant to the east, and residential areas on the high ridge of Mount Carmel; hence, as at Beirut, there are superb views. Haifa does not, however, occupy a central position within Israel, and its hinterland to the east includes Samaria and Galilee, which are less productive than the coastal plains further south.

Tel Aviv–Jaffa (pop. est., 1977, 375000) is the outlet for the richest part of Israel – the western coastal plain – and is also much more centrally located within the country. Thus it functioned as the provisional capital for a time after 1948.

Tel Aviv began in 1909 as a Jewish suburb of Arab Jaffa. We have already noted the local advantage of a small bluff breaking on an otherwise straight, shallow and sandy coastline that led to the growth of Jaffa as a port in ancient times – it also lies more or less opposite the defiles in the Judaean hills that give access to Jerusalem. Tel Aviv was originally a 'ribbon development' on cheap land – the sand dunes north of Jaffa – and, in days of the British mandate, land was gradually acquired by the Jewish Agency through purchase. Because there could be no compulsion, and Jaffa was a strongly Arab area, development by Zionists took place in a piecemeal, scattered fashion, and the high price asked by Arabs who sold their land meant that often the Jewish immigrants established very small-scale manufacturing premises using restricted quantities of materials, or else they established plant at a distance, on non-agricultural (hence cheaper) land. This led to the development of a rather scattered conurbation, with dispersed small-scale specialist indus-trial plant interrupted by citrus cultivation, and centred loosely on the urban nucleus of Tel Aviv–Jaffa. The Jaffa area was largely abandoned by its Arab inhabitants who fled in 1948, thus allowing restructuring as a single agglomeration. Consequently, Tel Aviv is a centre of service and tertiary activities – commerce, banking, diamond cutting, printing,

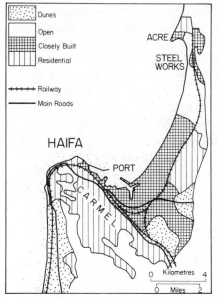

*Fig.* 14.13 Haifa.

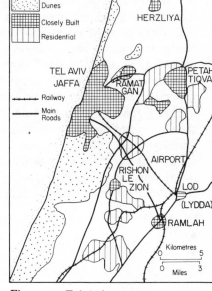

*Fig.* 14.14 Tel Aviv–Jaffa.

publishing and small-scale manufacturing, with larger industrial units of metalworking, production of chemicals, textiles, consumer goods and foodstuffs, on an outer periphery. Beyond to the east lies a ring of satellite manufacturing towns: Ramat Gan, Petah Tiqva, Rishon le Zion, etc., involved in electronics, motor and aircraft production.

Jerusalem (pop., Arab and Jews together, *c.* 360000) has few geographical advantages other than a defensive location at the crossing of routes east–west from the Mediterranean to the Dead Sea and Jordan, and north–south from Samaria to the Sinai along the crest of the Judaean ridge. Relatively difficult of access – the routes mentioned are still steep in places – remote from the major trade routes and lying in an arid, rather unproductive and near-karstic region, its local water supplies have always been difficult, and even now, water, electricity, food and supplies come from outside. There was, however, one advantage – strength as a defensive site, and this probably gave Jerusalem an original importance in early times as a tribal settlement. Since then, religious association and tradition have gradually fostered its growth as a centre of Jewish, Christian and Moslem pilgrimage; and, as in Mecca, the circulation of pilgrims can be said to provide the principal means of livelihood for its inhabitants. Catering, local commerce and now the activities of government are the chief means of livelihood. Under British rule, industry was not encouraged, for political and aesthetic reasons – and anyway, the economic aspect of all this was highly doubtful. With the spread of Israeli control, partial between 1948 and 1967, total after that date, a deliberate policy has been followed to settle the region as thickly as possible with Jewish immigrants and establish Israeli commercial activities. Jerusalem comprises an Old City, still bounded by its sixteenth-century wall and containing most Christian shrines and the Moslem Mosque of Omar, venerated as the third holiest place of Islam, and an outer New City, largely a Jewish creation, planned to accommodate residential blocks in the ridges and higher parts, and the lower basins 'zoned' as parks and amenity areas. Since 1970 the construction of high-rise, high density residential blocks in various places round the periphery of the city has in the opinion of some, including the present writer, adversely affected the urban landscape of Jerusalem.

# 15 Cyprus

The remarkable shape of the island – sometimes compared to that of a lion's skin pegged out to dry – has been determined by two almost parallel and slightly curved fold ranges. The northern arc, known in its western portion as the Kyrenia range and as the Karpass in the extreme north-east, is a simple narrow anticline rising from the sea to a maximum height of about 1000 m some 8 km inland. The southern arc is larger, but has been shattered by great upwellings of magma in the core of the folds, so that the central part of the arc now consists of an enormous boss of plutonic material surrounded by broken fold structures. This boss forms the Troödos range, the highest part of the island, with a maximum height of nearly 2000 m. Between the two arcs lies a lowland plain some 20–25 km wide, known as the Mesaoria. The plain, about 150 m in average altitude, and slightly undulating, is open to the sea on the east and west.

The rock series of Cyprus are all of comparatively recent formation, the oldest being of late Cretaceous age. The Kyrenia mountains are formed of a massive flexure of this Cretaceous limestone, which passes locally into dolomite and marble. The presence of limestone is again a marked feature in Cyprus, since in addition to the Cretaceous series, which is the thickest and best developed of any in the island, there are younger limestones of Miocene and Pliocene, and Pleistocene age. Chalk and chalky marl outcrops are also numerous.

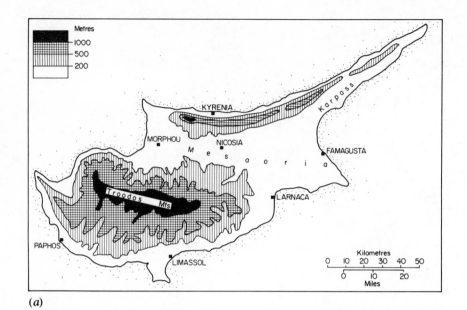

(a)

Pliocene
Miocene
Oligocene and Eocene
Jurassic and Triassic
Igneous
Pillow Lava

(b)

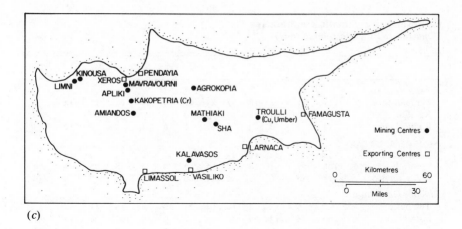

(c)

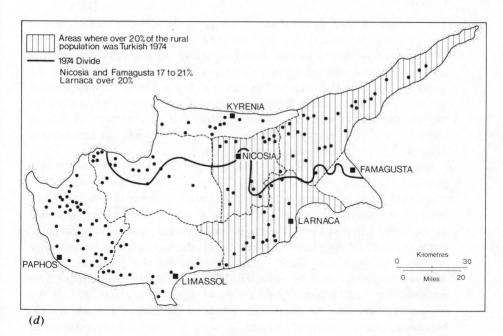

(d)

*Fig.* 15.1 Cyprus: (*a*) topography; (*b*) geology; (*c*) minerals; (*d*) villages and nationality.

Representative climatic conditions
*Temperature (°C) and rainfall (mm)*

|  | J | F | M | A | M | J | J | A | S | O | N | D | Total |
|---|---|---|---|---|---|---|---|---|---|---|---|---|---|
| *Kyrenia (coast)* | | | | | | | | | | | | | |
| Temperature | 12 | 13 | 14 | 18 | 22 | 25 | 28 | 29 | 26 | 23 | 17 | 14 | |
| Rainfall | 115 | 82 | 61 | 22 | 25 | 5 | 0 | 0 | 5 | 34 | 96 | 125 | 575 |
| Rainy days | 11 | 9 | 8 | 3 | 3 | 1 | 0 | 0 | 1 | 3 | 8 | 10 | 57 |
| *Nicosia (Mesaoria)* | | | | | | | | | | | | | |
| Temperature | 10 | 12 | 14 | 19 | 23 | 29 | 32 | 31 | 28 | 23 | 19 | 14 | |
| Rainfall | 109 | 77 | 51 | 18 | 23 | 3 | 0 | 0 | 3 | 28 | 76 | 121 | 509 |
| Rainy days | 11 | 8 | 6 | 2 | 2 | 1 | 0 | 0 | 1 | 3 | 7 | 9 | 50 |
| *Troödos (mountain)* | | | | | | | | | | | | | |
| Temperature | 7 | 9 | 11 | 14 | 16 | 19 | 21 | 20 | 18 | 15 | 11 | 8 | |
| Rainfall | 166 | 128 | 113 | 79 | 60 | 25 | 0 | 0 | 13 | 107 | 176 | 214 | 1081 |
| Rainy days | 13 | 10 | 8 | 5 | 4 | 2 | 0 | 0 | 2 | 8 | 14 | 16 | 82 |

## Climate

The climate of Cyprus conforms strongly to the eastern Mediterranean type. Frost is practically unknown on the coast, but may occur occasionally in lowland areas inland, and frequently on the hills, though the average winter temperature is 4 °C on the higher hills, and 13 °C on the lowlands. Despite the surrounding sea, rainfall is limited to nine months of the year, the summer being completely dry. Control of rainfall by topography is very marked, with annual rainfall varying from as little as 250 mm in a few parts of the plain to over 1000 mm on the highest summits of the Troödos range (fig. 15.1 a).

Reference has previously been made to the frequency with which low pressure systems develop over the island. This gives a degree of changeability in weather greater than for other parts of the Middle East, shown particularly in the greater length of spring and autumn. Because of this, plant life in certain parts is more varied, and a wide range of crops is possible. Another special feature is the high summer temperature of the interior plain. Once again, in view of the presence of the Mediterranean, it could be expected that a modification of summer heat might occur, but in fact, temperatures of 35–40 °C are common on the Mesaoria. This may be due to the effect of the coastal ranges, which, besides excluding maritime influences, may produce a concentration of heat in the basin-like interior. The prevalence of dazzling white calcareous rock series may also be another, very minor, factor. Whatever the cause, however, the effects of summer heating are seen in the dusty and baked appearance of the Mesaoria, which, surprisingly, can recall part of inner Arabia or Asia Minor rather than the verdant slopes and orchards of the Mediterranean coastlands.

**Agriculture**

Whilst the soils of Cyprus are in many instances distinctly more fertile than others of the Middle East (due to formation from eroded igneous material), the two general problems characteristic of Middle Eastern soils persist: low organic content and liability to erosion. Torrential and episodic rainfall occurring in an area of moderately broken relief has eroded much of the soils on higher lands (about one third of the island lies at 300 m or more altitude), giving rise to calcareous coastal and pavement exposures, which are termed *kafkalla* in Cyprus. On the other hand, accumulation of eroded material on margins of the Mesaoria has produced a covering of fertile light loam that is up to 5 or 6 m in thickness.

Chief limiting factor in cultivation is water supply. Few perennial streams exist because of percolation into porous rock measures; and the heavy, intermittent character of precipitation leads to much soil erosion. Hence, though at first sight an average annual rainfall of 500–1000 mm would seem adequate for agriculture, there is, in fact, a considerable water problem. Because of rapid run-off and evaporation, areas of good soil have become saline, and irrigation projects must overcome the difficulties of a porous bedrock and an irregular topography, which, as in Israel, make the construction of barrages difficult. Another adverse circumstance is the system of land and water rights which for long continued as under the Ottomans with the familiar names of *mulk*, *miri* and *waqf*. Only in the last few years has there been a major effort to improve the situation, with the Land Consolidation Bill of 1968. Unrestricted grazing by goats was also a considerable problem (though now distinctly less) and malaria was once extremely widespread. Since 1945, however, the anopheline mosquito has been eradicated from the island.

In 1968 a five-year programme for soil conservation and afforestation was started, with the aim of increasing agricultural output by at least £1·25 million annually. Levelling, terracing, better layout of crops and the removal of old ramifying plants (vines and figs especially) that inhibit deep ploughing, building of small stone walls (to retain soil, demarcate holdings and 'use up' unwanted stone covering good soil) are all involved, the aim being to subsidize the farmer to undertake these wherever possible on a small scale or through local co-operation.

Until recently irrigation was slow to develop. Reasons given were the conservative outlook of the peasants, limited markets for produce, and the deadening effect of traditional subsistence cropping. In addition there are other, environmental factors deriving from structure and topography, since the problems discussed for Israel recur in Cyprus. There is no large river that might be impounded; many of the rocks are porous, so that a large proportion of the rainfall is lost to the surface, and any barrage built must be 'waterproofed' on the floor and sides before it will retain water. Another adverse factor, related to climate and soil alkalinity, is the frequent occurrence of saline deposits which sometimes render irrigation water, even when it has been collected and stored, brackish and unfit for use.

Small-scale irrigation channels have for centuries been used to lead water from the lower mountain ranges to the edges of the Mesaoria. Of recent years, larger schemes have been undertaken, involving the damming of small river valleys near their head and the irrigation of individual areas of over 200 ha in extent. Most of these are on a relatively small scale by no means comparable with the major works on the Nile or Tigris; but the aggregate is most useful: the largest dam so far was completed at Yermasoia in 1968. Now, about 21% of all cultivable land in Cyprus is irrigated – about 10% regularly at most seasons by annual programmes, and the remainder by spate or seasonal irrigation, confined to the winter and spring.

*Crops*

In terms of yield, grapes are the largest single crop of Cyprus, with potatoes second, then citrus fruit. Cereals are important, and rank first in terms of area, with barley occupying more land than wheat. Lower yields from barley, since it is grown in drier and hillier parts, explain this situation. Besides providing fodder and an adulterant for wheaten flour, there is some export of barley for malting and distilling purposes. Production of wheat is, on the other hand, sufficient for only about half total consumption, and quantities are imported. A speciality of Cyprus has been the carob – a moderately large, spreading tree that produces a long, sweet-tasting pod somewhat resembling a large broad bean in appearance. Carobs are eaten as food by poorer people, and also widely used as animal fodder. The taste of the carob makes it acceptable as a sweetmeat in many parts of the world (it was at one time sold in Great Britain under the name of 'locust bean'), and carobs are therefore used in the making of chocolate and confectionery. The pod takes 11 months to form after the flower has appeared, so that it is essential to preserve the ripening pod throughout the winter. Though an unusually 'long-term' crop, even for the Middle East, carobs once had considerable importance. Nowadays, though it is still produced, exports are lower.

Potatoes thrive particularly on the sandy plains of the south-east (Famagusta region) and form an important export item, Britain and East Germany being the chief buyers. Citrus fruit-growing has also developed very considerably in recent years, with considerable exports. Oranges thrive best again on the sandy plains, with grapefruit and lemons on the heavier soils of the piedmonts. Tobacco is of inferior quality, and cultivation is not at present encouraged, though many farmers produce it for their own use.

All the crops mentioned above are for the most part grown on the lowlands and lowest hill slopes below 300 m altitude. Most productive are the lowlands immediately adjacent to the hill ranges, since in these parts rainfall is heavier, streams are more numerous, and the soil richer and deeper. Towards the centre of the Mesaoria lack of water imposes an increasing control, and the inner parts of the plain are often left uncultivated or in long fallow. It is significant that Nicosia, the capital and centre of a rich agricultural region, is located close to the southern slopes of the Kyrenia range, and not, as might be expected from the topography, in the centre of the Mesaoria.

The coastal plain, narrow in many places, is highly cultivated, though exploitation is sharply limited by rapidly rising fold ranges. Terracing exists, but is less a feature as compared with the Lebanon. For the most part the higher parts of the Kyrenia and Troödos ranges are given over to grazing. Because of differences in geological structure, however, there are considerable contrasts between the utilization of the two ranges. The Kyrenia–Karpass folds, being composed of porous limestone, are karstic in many places, and vegetation often consists merely of a thin garrigue, giving scanty grazing for goats and a few sheep. The Troödos, on the other hand, is less rugged, though much higher, and has a heavier rainfall and lower temperatures. As the component rocks are impermeable, there is thus more surface water. Woodland (pine and oak) is a feature in many places, though until recently the area of forest was steadily being reduced by unrestricted grazing and cutting of timber for fuel. Now a scheme of afforestation has begun with control of grazing, and it is hoped to preserve and extend this valuable natural resource.

On the middle slopes of both the Kyrenia and Troödos mountains, vine-growing is important. The most productive areas lie near the south-east of the Troödos boss, where there is a very rich, semi-volcanic soil. Cyprus has for long been the principal wine producer of the Middle East, and wines and spirits rank high in her list of exports. Cyprus wine does not compare in quality with the best products of France and Spain, but there is a moderately extensive market within the Middle East. A special product of the island is 'Commandaria', a heavy sweet wine somewhat resembling port, the manufacture of which is said to have been introduced into the island by the Knights Templar. A 'sherry' type of wine is also produced in considerable quantities, and brandy is distilled at Nicosia and Limassol. Famagusta and Limassol, both close to the major wine region, handle the bulk of Cypriot exports of wine, which now amount to nearly 300000 hl, two-thirds of which goes to Britain, where it enjoys preferential customs duties under 'Imperial Preference'.

Besides their use for wine, grapes are dried and exported as raisins.

The importance of raisins in the export trade of Cyprus is a reminder of the geographical relationship with Asia Minor, where raisins form a chief export. Vegetables, especially tomatoes and carrots, are also produced, as are olives and vetches (for fodder). Cotton is a crop of irrigated lands of the inner Mesaoria, and besides supplying a small home textile industry there is a small export.

## Pastoralism

Of recent years the herding of goats and sheep has been greatly restricted. Now, with more than half the total area of the island under cultivation, herding on a large scale is a feature only of the more arid and mountainous districts. A traditional occupation in Cyprus was mule-breeding, and, as mules are infertile, both horses and asses must also be kept.

## Industries
### Mining

The name Cyprus is said to be derived from *cyprium* (copper), which has been exploited in the island since Bronze Age times. Many veins of copper and other minerals still exist, though most are small and widely scattered. As would be expected, the Troödos area is naturally the most favoured region for the occurrence of minerals, but there are a few deposits associated with the igneous intrusions of the Kyrenia range. Iron and copper pyrites (sometimes mined together) are the most important minerals, but within the last two decades there has been considerable fluctuation in output. Now, iron pyrites easily leads the list of mineral exports in terms of tonnage, though copper is still almost as valuable. The chief centres of mining are Mandios, from which the ore is carried to Limassol and Larnaca for shipment, and Skouriotissa, from which a light railway gives access to Pendayia on the Bay of Morphou (north-west Cyprus). Because of lack of fuel, treatment of the ore is carried out in Britain and the USA.

Copper is mined at Mavravouni (with treatment and concentration at Xeros), and there is also a smaller production from Kalavassos. There is also sporadic working at another centre, Limni, which is an ancient site reopened in 1929 with open-cast workings for treatment of ore formerly rejected as being too low grade. An interesting feature has been recent prospecting by aerial survey for copper and other mineral deposits; this has centred on Mathiaki and Apliki, which are again in the Troödos area. Other centres are Sha, Agrokopia and Kinousa.

Deposits of asbestos occur on the sides of Mount Troödos itself, but these were not at first regarded as valuable, since the fibres are short in length, and could not be used. Modern technique has latterly found a means of handling the short fibres – by using them in packing material, and in the manufacture of 'asbestos board' – so that the Troödos deposits are now exploited, and form the third most valuable mineral export. Amiandos is the chief centre, and an aerial ropeway carries the asbestos to Limassol, the nearest port.

The presence of small igneous dikes has led to metamorphism in surrounding sedimentary rocks, and certain of these metamorphic aureoles contain deposits of coloured earths, two of which, ochre and umber, are exploited on a commercial scale. Both earths are derived from grey Miocene marl, altered by intense heating to a yellowish or brown colour, and are mined in quantity at Mavravouni, north-west of Limassol. Italy and the United States are chief buyers of these pigments. A third coloured earth, known as Terra Verte, consisting of silicates of iron and potassium, is a product of the weathering of basalt. At one time the production of Terra Verte was considerable, but its importance has now declined. Chromium also occurs on the Troödos slopes under conditions that are somewhat similar to those of the Ural mountains of Russia, where platinum and nickel also occur. Moderate production of chromium occurs, but so far the last two minerals have not been discovered in Cyprus.

Another product of metamorphism is marble, characteristic of the Kyrenia range, while Bentonite (Fullers' earth, an aluminal clay) is of some importance. Gypsum of a high purity occurs in the Tertiary series of the Mesaoria, and because of ease of working and proximity to the sea, there is some, but fluctuating export. Unfortunately, however, exhaustion of reserves and the disturbed political situation mean that the importance of mineral production is now declining.

*Industries*

Absence of raw materials precludes the development of extensive industry on a major scale; but a feature of the last few decades has been the emergence of small activities related to processing of agricultural products. Wine-making and brandy-distilling are probably two of the most rapidly growing activities, and there is a small textile and clothing industry based partly on home-produced cotton and wool, together with shoe-making. Olive oil-pressing, cigarette-making, brewing of beer, and meat-packing are other activities, and, as elsewhere in the Middle East, cement-making is a very important item. Although some 90% of Cyprus industrial establishments employ three people or less, industry accounts for 25–30% of the gross national product.

In recent years, with the distinctly cooler summer climate of northern Europe and better air transport, the guaranteed summer sunshine of

Cyprus, its beaches and pine woods of the Troödos (and its situation in the sterling area) had fostered a tourist trade of ¼ million visitors annually, with Kyrenia and Famagusta most popular areas, together with the Troödos uplands.

Fishing, partly for historical reasons, did not greatly develop until recently, but it had begun to expand prior to 1974, in response to the tourist boom; and there is some sponge-fishing. Famagusta, on the east coast, is best placed for traffic with the Levant and Egypt, as well as having easiest communication with the interior, and so up to 1974 it handled over 80% of Cypriot sea cargoes: now that it is in the Turkish zone, it has been overtaken by Limassol, which has the advantage of closeness to the minerals and vineyards of the Troödos – asbestos, potatoes and wine are principal exports. Larnaca also shares in this trade, and has an oil refinery; whilst smaller harbours (Paphos especially) are growing in importance.

Nicosia (pop. est., 1974, 117000) is the natural centre of the island, and acts as a collecting centre for the agricultural produce of the Mesaoria. The town is a focus of routes: one leading northwards through a gap in the hills of Kyrenia and the northern coastlands, another south-westwards to the Troödos, and a third south-eastwards to Famagusta and Larnaca. There are a number of industries: textiles, plastics, fruit-packing, cigarette- and wine-making, brandy-distilling and, in addition, arising from its function as an administrative centre, some activity in printing, building construction and light engineering. One feature indicative of the importance of Nicosia as a route centre is an elaborate system of fortifications, designed by the sixteenth-century Venetian rulers, which still dominates the layout and appearance of the town, and enhances tourist attractions.

### Development

The first Five Year Plan (1961) and its successors attempted to cope with the basic problems arising from a high natural population increase (due mainly to improved public health, especially eradication of malaria) in a highly political minded, literate, and vocal population, within a limited territory that was already by Middle East standards extensively cultivated. Distinct success was registered, with annual growth in G.D.P. of 8%, tripling in value per head between 1960 and 1973.

However, the war of 1974 resulted in the effective partition of the island: the northern 40% becoming Turkish, and the remainder Greek-Cypriot controlled, although Turkish Cypriots numbered only 18% of the total (1974) population of 650000. The United Nations estimated that in 1974 there were 226000 refugees in Cyprus, of whom 184000 were Greek Cypriots. Since 1974 it has been stated that Turkey has encouraged the

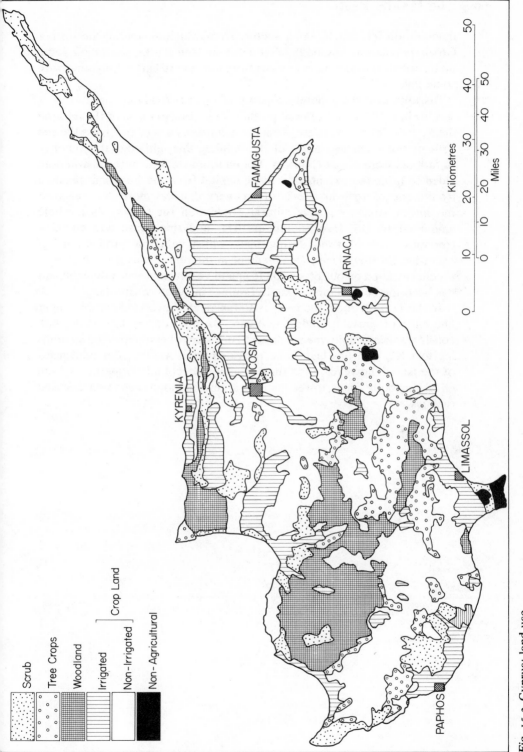

Scrub

Tree Crops

Woodland

Irrigated ⎱ Crop Land

Non-Irrigated ⎰

Non-Agricultural

KYRENIA

NICOSIA

FAMAGUSTA

LARNACA

LIMASSOL

PAPHOS

Kilometres

Miles

*Fig.* 15.2 **Cyprus: land use.**

immigration into the Turkish sector (from which almost all the former Greek population has fled) of 20000 mainland Turks (including some non-Turkish speaking Lazi peoples from north-east Turkey) together with some Pakistanis.

Disruption to the general economy of Cyprus following partition was serious in that 60–70% of total productive capacity (100% of the tobacco fields, 80% of the citrus groves and vegetables, 40% of the livestock and 12% of potatoes) was north of the dividing line, although the majority of farmers were Greek Cypriots. Yet enormous efforts at reconstruction, aided to a limited extent by refugee capital from the Lebanon, resulted by the end of 1976 in a level of recovery that has more than regained the losses after 1974. Agricultural production for Cyprus as a whole amounted to US $220 million in 1972, and this figure was equalled (for only 60% of area) during 1976, whilst industrial production has exceeded the 1972 level. One element in the remarkable growth pattern is concentration on out-of-season fruit and vegetables; and another benefit has been the considerable 'potato famine' in Western Europe.

In the Turkish zone, recovery is so far much slower and partial. Under one-third of previous industries were working during late 1976, with considerable unemployment amongst Turkish workers, so that aid amounting to US $70 m has had to be provided from Ankara. For both parts of the island, however, 1977 showed a tacit acceptance of partition, with efforts in both zones to reconstruct a new economy based on changed realities.

# 16 The Arabian peninsula

From central Syria, where it forms the interfluve between the Euphrates and Tigris rivers to the shores of the Indian Ocean, and from the Red Sea to the Persian/Arab Gulf, there extends the vast platform of Arabia – a block of ancient rocks that appears as a massive detached fragment between the even larger Kraton of Africa, and the fold systems of Iran and Asia Minor. Parallel to the overall structural unity is a climatic uniformity: apart from marginal exceptions in the extreme south-west, annual rainfall nowhere exceeds 250 mm, with at the same time some of the highest temperatures (and extremes of ultra-dry to inordinately humid air) of anywhere in the world. Such physical unity has had an effect on the human geography of the region. From Arabia has arisen the special way of life spoken of as 'Arab'; and though in the main a thoroughly arid plateau environment may appear harsh, yet human activities in neighbouring lands and far beyond have been and are still conditioned by life in the Peninsula, which remains the centre of thought, pilgrimage and aspiration for many millions in Asia and Africa. Arabia thus emerges as the major core, or heartland, of the Middle East.

## Physical units

As noted in chapter 2, Arabia consists morphologically of a tilted block of pre-Cambrian metamorphosed and highly deformed sediments intruded by masses of granites. This block has been subjected to much vertical oscillation throughout later geological time, so that younger sedimentary

461

rocks have accumulated upon it, even in its centre, where one of the most prominent surface features, the Jebel Tuwaiq, is a flexure of Jurassic limestone.

Tilting towards the north and east, and differential erosion acting upon layers of varying resistance, have given rise to a cuesta-like topography, with rather irregular ranges of hills in the form partly of arcs and cusps, partly in straight ranks, often presenting a scarp-face to the west or south, and a dip to the north and east. In quite a number of localities, however, strata are practically horizontal, and the landscape becomes tabular in character: flat massifs diversified by *wadi*-floors of various shape and width, and by blown-sand deposits together with outwash features mostly but not entirely due to rainfall at an earlier geological period.

Two principal and inter-related factors are responsible for the evolution of the present landscape: downwarping of the east, on a major scale; and fracturing on the west. The earlier explanation of the downwarping of the Gulf was that this was due to accumulation of sediments from the four heavily-charged rivers that enter the Gulf: the Euphrates, Tigris, Karun and Kharkeh; a later view is that the Arabian plate has drifted northwards and eastwards due to spreading of the Red Sea floor, and the eastern side of the plate is thus being 'consumed' against the Iranian/Asian plates. Partly due to these differential movements (however explained), which have uptilted the western side of the platform, and partly also because of the torsions involved in continental drift, there has been extensive fracturing particularly in the west and south, where massive step-faulting had formed the downthrow troughs of the Red Sea and Gulf of Aden, together with the smaller continuation, the Jordan–Aqaba rift. Faulting is by no means absent, though on a much reduced scale, on the northern and eastern sides of the block, particularly in the region of the Euphrates valley, where the Wadi Batin west of Kuwait and the Wadi Sirhan have tectonic origins.

In some parts of Arabia the presence of the rigid basement has restricted folding of the overlying sediments to a small extent – as indicated by the very shallow domes and troughs that form the oil-bearing areas of the Gulf coast, and by the fact that copious springs of water exist in certain parts, particularly along the Gulf coast, in and near the island of Bahrain. Flow of water from these springs greatly exceeds the total rainfall of the district, and it is inferred that the source of the water must be the highlands of the Nejd, many hundreds of kilometres to the west – an indication that permeable rock series must extend without great disturbance for considerable distances.

Because of the highly disturbed geological history of the west and south, in contrast to the gentle folding in much of the east, vulcanicity is prominent in the former areas. Throughout the north-west, lava fields

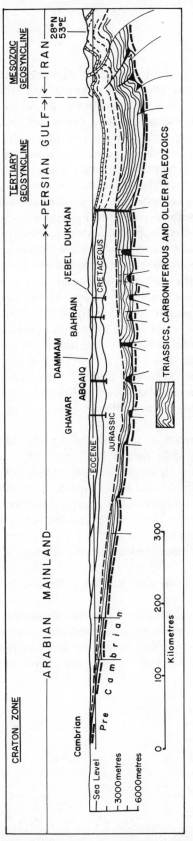

*Fig.* 16.1 Generalized section east–west across Arabia.

(*harras*) of recent formation produce desolate landscapes, whilst in the south lava flows, though less prominent, are still to be found. Here, however, volcanic cones are also numerous and well developed. In some places, as for example near Aden, the basalt sheets are up to 3000 m in thickness, with frequent craters, one of which, breached by the sea, gives Aden its remarkable scenic panorama and useful port site. Further to the east, basaltic eruptions become less prominent, though it should be noted that much of the Musandum peninsula and the Jebel Akhdar of Oman are composed of a core of serpentine rocks.

Although no perennial rivers now exist, the whole Arabian plateau has been heavily dissected by fluvial action, as is shown by the presence of numerous deep *wadis*, many of which are still covered by the thick layers of clay. The best-developed *wadis* are those that follow the dip slope of the plateau in the east and north-east, and hence open towards the Persian/Arab Gulf and Euphrates valley. As we have noted, some of these are basically fault-scarps subsequently enlarged by water action. One of the largest of these latter is the Wadi Batin, which can be traced from the region between Basra and Kuwait, where it is a steep-sided depression 6–7 km wide, as far to the south-west as central Nejd. Another slightly smaller valley, but of similar origin, is the Wadi Sirhan, which runs south-east from the neighbourhood of Amman (Jordan) as far as Al Jauf. Parts of both *wadis* are now filled by deposits of blown sand, and the original outline obscured in places.

A summary approach to study of the Arabian peninsula (which covers an area of nearly 2·5 million km²) can be made on the basis of physiographical units (ignoring political boundaries) defined as follows:

(1) The western highlands with a coastal strip, extending from the Gulf of Aqaba to the hinterland of the straits of Bab el Mandeb in the region of Aden. This includes the districts and territories of the Hijaz, Tihama, Asir, the Yemen and an extension as far as the region of Aden.

(2) The southern coastlands, from the last region as far as the lowland east of Sanqira Bay.

(3) The Oman region, including the Jebel Akhdar as its main physical element.

(4) The eastern coastlands, from the Musandum peninsula as far as Kuwait, mainly, but by no means entirely, the Trucial Coast and El Hasa.

(5) The southern interior, mainly the Rub al Khali.

(6) The northern interior: Nejd, the Nefud and the far northern steppelands.

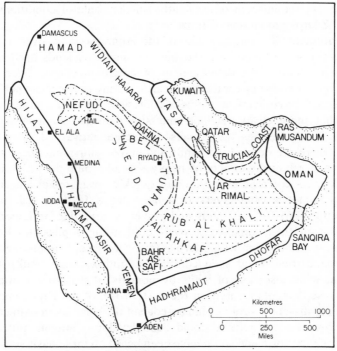

*Fig.* 16.2 The geographical units of Arabia.

### The western highlands and coast

The territory extending from the area east of the Gulf of Aqaba as far as the latitude of Medina (24°N) is spoken of as the Hijaz (Barrier). Beginning in the north as a plateau of 1000–1500 m altitude it becomes higher and more broken and jagged towards the south, with eventually, summits of 2000–3000 m which form the Madian (Midian) mountains. This is a forbidding highland zone formed by uptilting and buckling of the plateau-edge, and composed of pre-Cambrian crystalline rocks (granite, schist, porphyry) with numerous lava flows, mainly of Tertiary and partly Quaternary age. The western side is marked by a series of step-faults that drop rapidly to a very narrow coastal plain. Despite only episodic rainfall at the present time, giving torrents of a few days' duration perhaps once in several years, this western highland rim is heavily eroded into steep, narrow *wadis*, a few of which have cut back beyond the main summit line and further eroded along the geological strike, capturing other streams in the process. Hence in some districts there is a remarkably intricate network of valleys, some deep and short, others rather long and more open, reminiscent on a slightly smaller scale of conditions in the central Zagros mountains of Iran.

In contrast, the eastern flanks of the Hijaz mountains are a zone of distinctly less abrupt relief, and this consequently lends itself more to settlement, and to the development of communications. Even though rainfall is sparse (being for the most part less than 100–130 mm per annum) and, as we have seen, extremely capricious in onset, water can be somewhat more easily retained and stored in the shallower, broader valleys. Here, besides the gravels and scree outwashed from the hill slopes, there are deposits of sands and clayey alluvium. These serve to collect and retain the effects of heavy sporadic rainfall, which in more open districts could be evaporated or quickly dissipated as a flash-flood. Shallow water-bearing layers or lenses are a feature, fed by rapid percolation into surface sands and gravels and resting on impermeable bedrock; on them small-scale oasis cultivation is possible. For long garden-type cultivation with interplanting of cereals, fruit and vegetables has been carried on at such centres as Mudawwara, Tebuk, Ala and Medina, with, also, use of wells by nomads. It was this interior zone of oasis settlements located on the eastern rim of the Hijaz, and not in the deeply dissected broken plateau-edge of the west overlooking the Red Sea, where human activity could best develop. Caravan trade routes linking the far north and south have been based on these oasis settlements over several thousand years: Muhammad himself grew up as a camel driver along these routes, which, involving Mecca and Medina, reached as far as Jerusalem and the Indian Ocean coasts.

On the seaward (western) side of the Madian, run-off is much more rapid, with valleys more deeply incised, and far fewer patches of the clay and sand that allow cultivation. The region remains one of bare, rugged landscapes in jagged black, red or darkly iridescent rocks. A very narrow coastal plain, sandy and almost totally arid in the north, again offers few opportunities for settlement. Here and there the plain is interrupted by narrow deep inlets from the sea (*sharm*) which appear to be the result of drowning of the seaward ends of deep *wadis* produced by downwarping. Much of the coast is rendered difficult of access for shipping by the presence of extensive coral reefs, but some *sharm* (possibly as the result of fresh water draining from the *wadis*, which inhibits coral growth) are clear, and so provide good harbours. Jidda is, however, not favoured in this way.

South of latitude 24° N the mountain fringe decreases considerably in height, with a maximum elevation in many places of only 1000 m. Cross-faulting and foundering of the land on a considerable scale have produced a lowland corridor which gives access to the interior. Here the Tihama ceases to be a mere coastal fringe, and reaches its maximum width.

Because of its central position in Arabia it has come to be a 'gateway' to central Arabia, not merely by reason of its general lower altitude, but also because it lies in the 'waist' of Arabia, which offers the shortest distance between the Persian/Arab Gulf and the Red Sea. Although rainfall is no more abundant than in the Madian, there is a greater concentration of population, due in the first instance to the development of long-distance trade, with the people of the Tihama acting as middlemen, and afterwards, as the result of historical accident, to the growth of pilgrimage to the cities of Mecca and Medina.

Over the greater part of the Hijaz vegetation is limited to a few stunted acacia and wattle bushes, with agriculture (and to a considerable extent even nomadic pastoralism) virtually impossible except on a few *wadi* floors where water is retained near the surface. In such relatively favoured spots there is a little cultivation of dates, millet, wheat, barley and Mediterranean fruits, with stock-rearing on the drier outskirts of the settlement. The towns of the Hijaz were for long mere trading posts, precariously self-sufficient in foodstuffs and dependent for much of their existence on long-distance caravans, by which they could offer services, and hence obtain the means of importing extra food. Since the Muhammadan era the pilgrim traffic has been the chief economic activity of the district, and now that the former overland traffic in incense and coffee is carried by sea, such centres as Mecca, Medina and Jidda would hardly exist at all, certainly not as towns of their present size.

Mecca itself, with a population of about 90 000, is situated on an alluvial-filled *wadi*, and the produce of its oasis can support less than one-fifth of its present inhabitants. Up to 1952 there was a heavy tax on all pilgrims ($110 per head), which was the financial mainstay of the Saudi Arabian state; but with oil royalties the tax has been abolished. Pilgrims now number over 1½ million annually during the Haj season which lasts about 4–6 weeks. The Saudi government now makes great efforts to house pilgrims and provide internal transport (besides imposing health regulations and now attempting to prevent settlement by foreign pilgrims). With the new fervour sweeping through Islamic countries, the moral and social effects of undertaking pilgrimage under some austerity are now increasingly esteemed. Medina was once rather larger than Mecca, as it has a larger oasis and easier communications. Jidda has developed enormously as the principal port of Saudi Arabia, and also as administrative capital of the country (foreign embassies are located here, not at Riyadh), and has a population of 450 000. Besides handling a vast quantity of imports, which can at times severely over-tax the available infrastructures, and some of the pilgrim traffic (including a 'pilgrim city'), there is a growing light industry concerned with consumables, also a steel mill and an oil refinery.

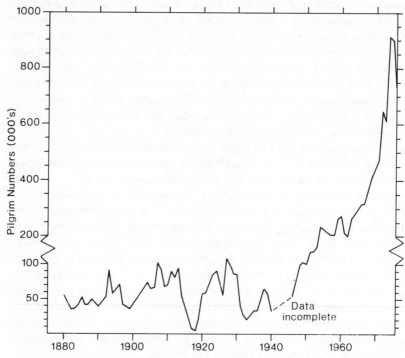

*Fig.* 16.3 Foreign pilgrims to Mecca (data by R. A. Jackson).

Conditions in Saudi Arabia generally are changing with amazing speed, and most of all in the central 'belt' running from Jidda and Yanbo inland through Mecca, Medina, at Taif (a summer resort in the hills), Anaiza, Riyadh, as far as Hofuf and Dhahran Dammam on the Persian/Arab Gulf, linked by a Trans-Arabian highway, and a railway from Riyadh to Dammam.

Although about one-half of the working population is engaged in agriculture or herding (some still nomadic) only 0·2% of the land area is cultivated and agriculture contributes just over 1% to G.D.P. Dates are probably the chief crop, followed by wheat, lucerne, millet and maize, and the production of fruit and vegetables is expanding – the limiting factor being irrigation. Governmental plans aim at improving this, partly by desalination of sea water using natural gas: over 20 plants are planned to be in operation by the late 1970s giving 140 m gallons per day. As well, two schemes using artesian ground water are in progress: the largest at Al Hasa will ultimately bring a further 12 000 ha under cultivation, and the other (the Faisal Settlement scheme) had allowed settlement of 1000 nomadic families. Two barrages use the rainfall of the south-west hills:

the scheme in the Wadi Jizan will allow irrigation of 8500 hectares, and the Al Abha project in southern Asir is of smaller scale.

Industrial development is planned mainly, though not entirely, for the east coast (Gulf) with the oilfields as a base, from which natural gas will be treated in a large plant, partly for export as liquid (making Saudi Arabia the largest world exporter) and partly for internal prime fuel, not only nearby, but by pipeline to the centre and west where Yanbo and Duba will develop as exporters and as smaller industrial centres. Besides the steel mill in Jidda there are new oil refineries planned or in construction at Jubail north of Dammam, and also near Dhahran, and at Yanbo. Plans for iron smelting (at Jubail) and aluminium (in the same area) are under consideration, besides car and tractor assembly. Yanbo on the Red Sea and Jubail (Gulf) are planned to become industrial growth centres at each end of the central 'waist', which will in turn develop further as a more highly populated and active linkage zone.

The great problems for Saudi Arabia are how to make best long-term use of the cash revenues now derived from petroleum, given the small size of the population and lack of infrastructures. There is considerable inflation, with lack of skilled manpower at middle and lower levels; and whilst the country has not had the problem of cash shortage as in Iran, the difficulties remain of developing a viable industry and agriculture over the long term.

*Asir* South of latitude 20° N the Tihama again narrows considerably as the western highland edge again becomes more developed. Massive exposures of ancient schists and granites characteristic of the northern Hijaz once more become prominent, with, however, less of the basaltic lava cover that prevails in the northern Hijaz. The general effect is still unmistakably that of a tilted and dissected tableland, with abrupt westward-facing fault-scarps; but most of Asir lies above 1500 m, with the highest points 3000 m above sea-level.

By reason of their elevation, and also of location in respect of the Inter-tropical Front, which brings them for part of the year under the 'monsoonal' effect of the Indian Ocean, the Asir uplands have a moderate precipitation of the order of 150–300 mm, mainly from summer rains, but also from fog and dew. We here encounter the clear beginnings of a different climatic regime – that of a summer maximum precipitation. Being very much on the margin, the purely climatic effects are not strongly pronounced, though none the less distinctly apparent in their influence on human activity.

One direct result is the occurrence of a number of short but fast-flowing streams for several months of the year, though none of these reach the sea, except during particularly heavy floods.

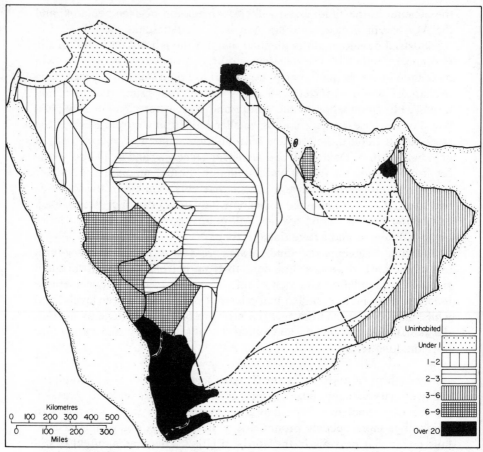

*Fig.* 16.4 The Arabian Peninsula: population densities (1970 estimates) per km².

In their upper courses, the streams are often entrenched in steep valleys, which carry a dense 'jungle' vegetation of evergreen bushes, thorns and moderately sized palms. At some distance away from the valley bottoms, this vegetation changes to thick grassland, with clumps of taller trees. The higher slopes of the valleys have been cleared and terraced for the cultivation of millet, wheat, bananas, dates, coffee, yams and vines. In the west, at the junction of the uplands and a narrow coastal plain, the streams lose themselves in the sand, but here occur fields of millet, and groves of a special kind of palm (the Daum), which produces a hard fruit that is eaten by the Badawin of the region. As Philby has suggested, the entire region of Asir might ecologically be a part of Africa. The savanna-like aspect of the upper valleys, a climatic regime of summer rainfall, strongly African fauna, clusters of beehive-shaped huts made of straw and clay, elaborate basket-work implements and the predominant crops of sorghum, bulrush millet, bananas, mangoes and coffee – all these indicate affinities with the southern Sudan, Ethiopia and east Africa rather than the mainland of Arabia.

Because of its heavier rainfall, Asir offers distinctly better opportunities for agriculture, and it is by far the most cultivated part of the Saudi Arabian state with the largest rural population (fig. 16.4). One unusual feature, now declining with the development of new irrigation (especially the schemes of the Wadi Jizan and al Abha) is shifting cultivation. It is noteworthy that southern Asir has the highest population density of any part of Saudi Arabia – an indication of its relatively high rainfall.

As the land drops towards the Red Sea and the west, the effects of the upper monsoonal damp current are lost, and aridity returns, with a feeble winter maximum of rainfall. On the fringes of the piedmont zone, there are a number of communities of pastoral nomads who rear goats; but close to the coast there is insufficient vegetation even for grazing, and most of the plain is devoid of inhabitants, being little more than sandy scrubland.

*The Yemen* South of Asir lies the state of the Yemen, independent since the withdrawal of the Turks in 1918. The country extends for about 500 km between latitudes 18° and 12°N, with a territory about half the size of Great Britain (one estimate is 120000 km², the United Nations figure is 195000 km²). The first census, taken in 1975, gave a total of 6·5 million inhabitants. Under the rule of its Imams, the country remained largely closed; then there were 7 years of civil war (1962–69) with, later, several years of severe drought, so that information on details of geography is still scanty and uncertain.

As regards topography, structure and climate, the Yemen repeats conditions in Asir, but on a larger scale, and with significant differences. South of the latitude 16°N the granitic upland massifs have a capping of Jurassic and Cretaceous limestones and sandstones, and yet higher above these extensive outflows of basalt have produced a high-level plateau diversified by imposing volcanic vents. The general effect is thus of a high, fairly level platform isolated from surrounding lower areas by abrupt decents: distinctly more of a massive block or butte formation than the general scarp and dip effect in the Hijaz and Asir.

Thus the Yemeni plateau, standing high above the surrounding lower surfaces, and varying in altitude between a general level of 2000–3000 m above sea-level, with a few peaks rising to almost 4000 m (the highest, Beni Sheib, 50 m west of Sana'a), shows most resemblances to the plateau of Ethiopia. Both in fact formed part of a larger single structure later broken down by the fault systems of the Red Sea and Gulf of Aden, and now appear as separate residuals, with basalt covering a sedimentary layer that elsewhere has been largely eroded off.

Heavy dissection (due to altitude and a considerable rainfall) means that the plateau surface is scored by deep watercourses, but there are also extensive level areas, many of which are highly cultivated. On the Red Sea side, the plateau falls steeply to a coastal plain that is a continuation of the Tihama of Asir, but again on a larger pattern; and there is the same feature of streams rising in the uplands but failing to cross the coastal plain to reach the sea. Lava flows are prominent on the plateau, and frequently weather to a rich fertile soil.

Because of the differences in altitude in the Yemen, there is wide variation in climatic conditions. On the plateau, winter temperatures fall below 5 °C, and frost and snow are of regular occurrence on the higher ridges, though actual snowfall is less a feature than in the Hijaz further north. Sheepskins are, however, worn by many Yemenis during the winter. In summer, because of nearness to the Equator, temperatures are high, but by no means as high as in the rest of Arabia, partly because of greater elevation, and partly owing to the fact that there is a well-marked rainy season which gives a cloud cover during the months of July, August and September. This precipitation comes from a well-developed southerly monsoonal current which, like that affecting India at the same season, is moist and unstable. On encountering the barrier of the Yemen hills, rapid cooling takes place, giving the distinctly heavy rain (for Arabia) of the summer months: 500 mm falls over many western parts of the plateau, with 1200 mm probable in a very few of the highest localities. An annual average of 1000 mm is reported from Ibb, 610 mm at Ta'izz, and 300 mm at Sana'a. Being of the instability type, the rain tends to fall as heavy intermittent showers, often at or after dusk; and there are two seasons of onset – a major rainy period from July to September, and a very minor secondary maximum in March, related to the Mediterranean regime characteristic of the rest of the Middle East. Becuse of the importance of dynamical uplift in producing precipitation, the coastal plain adjoining the Red Sea has only a scanty rainfall of 100–150 mm, with a maximum discernible in winter. All this can give rise to seasonal short-lived flooding that in part reaches 3 m in height, with streams flowing for 6 to 9 months out of the year, and, of course, producing heavy erosion.

Some writers see as many as six minor sub-regions within the Yemen. The Tihama is wider here than in Asir, and is in part cultivated where some seasonal water supply exists, or wells can be dug. In other parts, especially close to the coast, there is much loose sand and dunes, with cultivation absent, and vegetation no more than cactus, tamarisk, acacias and a few date groves, with some flushes of succulents and grass that

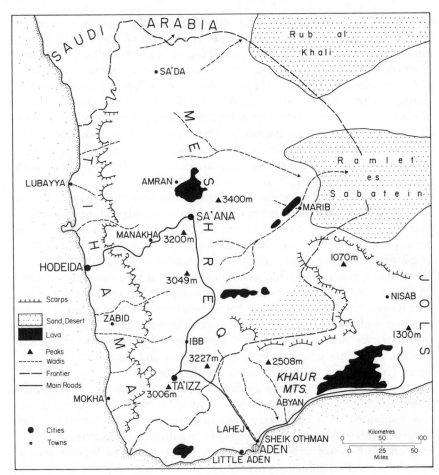

*Fig.* 16.5 The Yemen.

support a small semi-pastoral population. Since 1971 cotton growing has
developed, under the impulse of aid from United Nations, the World Bank
and the Kuwait Development Fund. Already, cotton has displaced coffee
as the Yemen's principal export, and besides cotton, vegetables and
cereals are produced – mainly from the Wadi Mawr and Wadi Zabid,
where modern irrigation has been developed under a Tihama Development
Authority.

The second zone, lying immediately east of the Tihama, comprises the
slopes of the main plateau. In the lowest parts, much of this territory
is deeply weathered into ravines and rocky spurs, with difficult access
that has been an important element in the physical and political isolation
of the Yemeni state. In this lowest foothill zone some water is available,

either from seepage through sand and gravel or from springs that are fed from larger water-tables related to the alternation of porous and impermeable rock layers and the heavier rainfall of the higher altitude. Owing, however, to impeded surface drainage (due to very considerable outwash) and high temperatures, malaria and bilharzia have for long been endemic, another factor reinforcing isolation and difficulty. Further up the flanks of the western plateau-edge, however, the springs of water become more developed, and have an important effect on cultivation. In the lower irrigated levels millet, cotton, sago, castor oil, indigo, mangoes, bananas, tobacco and papayas are grown. Experiments have also been made with sisal.

At altitudes of 750 m or more occur the middle western slopes of the plateau, which form the third zone, or Serat (uplands). Here Mediterranean plants appear: carobs, figs and walnut trees. At 1500 m begins the most productive zone of the Yemen. As well as the availability of irrigation water and natural rainfall, soil quality is a further favourable factor, since besides the widespread occurrence of lava and basaltic soils, there are considerable expanses of wind-deposited loess, especially on the plateau surfaces. Cereals are found wherever soil and water are both available – either on flat ground, or where terraces can be cut – millets, wheat, barley and maize, the first particularly important on the lower plateau. There is a considerable variety of fruit and vegetables: apricots, citrus fruits, vines, pomegranates, onions, tomatoes, carrots and also lucerne. Two plants merit special mention: the coffee shrub, which grows between altitudes of 1200 and 1600 m, and the qat plant. Coffee is not now cultivated on a very large scale, and tends to be restricted to the damper western side of the plateau, in the district of Manakha, which lies behind the once important and now eclipsed port of Mocha, where one kind of coffee gained its name.

The qat (*Catha edulis*) is a shrub somewhat like the tea plant, that grows to a height of 3 m, and its leaves, when chewed or infused, have a strongly narcotic effect like that of alcohol – a sense of well-being is induced, though intoxication is brought on by considerable indulgence. Qat-eating is widely practised by all sections of the population, and extensive areas in the Yemen are given over to its cultivation, with the state deriving much revenue from taxation of qat plantations. The plant itself is restricted, like coffee, to high altitudes, actually 1500–3000 m; and fairly abundant moisture is necessary in the later stages of growth. Whilst it is cultivated all over the Yemen, the main centre of production occurs in the extreme south-west, round Ta'izz; and there is a growing export to neighbouring regions, especially Aden, where, because of lower relief, the plant will not grow. Some observers believe that qat addiction is an important factor in reducing the effective labour potential of many

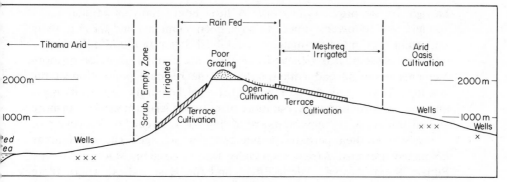

*Fig.* 16.6 Altitude and land use in the Yemen.

Yemenis; others dispute this. However, in 1972 the Yemeni government took steps to prevent further extension of qat growing.

The fourth region could be said to be the highest plateau surface and it lies at 1800–2500 m above sea-level. Here annual rainfall is sufficient to allow rain-fed agriculture, and irrigation is accordingly less important. The valley floors (*qa*) of this plateau surface are actively cultivated, and here occur most of the towns of the Yemen.

Further east still, there begins the dip slope which drops more gently to the interior of Arabia: this is known as the Meshreq. The upper parts are better watered, both from rainfall and from underground seepage, and some cultivation is possible; but in the lower Meshreq, our last sub-region, conditions begin to pass into desert, and there is now very little human settlement. Once, many irrigation works collected floodwater, but none is now usable – the largest, at Marib, broke down in the fifth century A.D. – and pastoral nomadism is the chief way of life. Renewal of the Marib dam (and others) is now under consideration.

In some respects the Yemen platform shows some similarities to the Lebanon: steep eroded slopes rising from a narrow coastal plain to a plateau where abundant springs, adequate direct rainfall and fertile soil patches among a highly eroded and tangled land surface allow a gradation of cultivation from tropical to temperate plants. Climatic conditions show some parallels. Detailed figures are lacking; but at Ta'izz, mean shade temperatures lie between 19 and 27 °C, with mean extremes of 15 and 32 °C. Sana'a, at a higher altitude, shows extremes of −8 and 28 °C.

One other similarity to the Lebanon exists: the marked tendency of Yemenis to migrate elsewhere, sometimes permanently, but more often for a period, so that the Yemen can be regarded as a demographic reservoir from which human streams have spread to various parts of Asia and Africa. Medieval Arab writers refer to the migrations of Yemenis towards the early sixth century A.D. following the destruction of the Marib barrage in the previous century. A little later, many of Muhammad's soldiers and followers appear to have been Yemenis, and these took an important part in the campaigns to establish Islam in the Middle East.

At the present, it is believed that there are about 1½ million or more Yemenis living abroad – one-quarter of the resident population of the country. They go as dockers and short-term labourers to various ports and new construction sites, but more often as longer-term workers in more skilled trades, or as merchants, returning for a 'break' once every 3 or 4 years, and then perhaps permanently in old age. The chief areas colonized are: east Africa, especially Dar es Salaam, Madagascar, the Sudan, Saudi Arabia, Aden, Egypt and the East Indies, where there are over 50000 in Java; and the remittances sent or finally brought into the Yemen are a distinctly significant element in the country's economy.

The people of the Yemen are in the main either Zaidis – that is, followers of a strict form of Shi'a Islam developed in Iran about A.D. 864, which frowns on mysticism and mixed marriages with non-Zaidis and supports 'puritan' views – or else Shaffeites, a sect of Sunnis. These latter tend to look to Al Azhar in Cairo for spiritual guidance, and are orthodox Sunni in other respects – this has an important modern aspect, and partly explains why the republican Yemen formed part of the United Arab Republic. The former rulers, the Imams, were, of course, Zaidis. Both groups claim to amount to about 55% of the population. In addition, there are some 60000 Ismailis mainly in or near Sana'a, and prior to 1950 a fairly considerable community of Oriental Jews, who had been settled in south-west Arabia since the Dispersal. Many Jews were artisans in stone, glass, metal and textiles, others were merchants, and Jewish quarters were a feature not merely of Sana'a (which contained most Jews) but also of many other towns of western and southern Arabia. Since 1951, many, but not all, Jews have emigrated to Israel.

Sana'a, the capital of the Yemen (150000 inhabitants approximately), lies at an altitude of nearly 2500 m, in the centre of a loess-covered basin where there is good access to water. Cereals, fruit and vegetables are cultivated using irrigation from wells and cisterns. Dates do not ripen at this altitude, but there is a wide range of Mediterranean fruit, grapes especially, and sheep, cattle and camels are kept. Other towns are Ta'izz (100000), lying on a lower level plateau at 1500 m and functioning as the main market for the south, Ibb, something of an ecclesiastical centre with sixty mosques, Amran, Manakha, Sa'da, Marib and Zabid, this last hesitantly making the dreadful claim to have the seminary where algebra was first thought of. All are small route centres and markets for their region.

Lacking any considerable foreign trade, ports were little developed in the Yemen: moreover there were no modern facilities, and few had deep

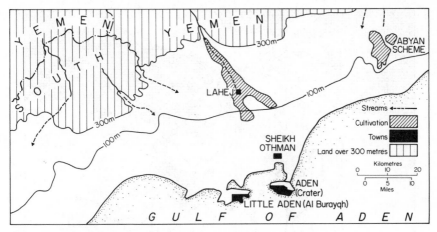

*Fig.* 16.7 Southern Yemen: land use.

water. Competition from Aden, which for long handled between 75 and 80% of all the commerce of southern Arabia, was a further adverse factor. In 1958–61, however, Russian workers constructed a modern harbour at Hodeida, where some increase of trade has taken place, partly also due to civil warfare and the movement of supplies. Improvements have also occurred at Salif, with the aim of developing exports of rock-salt found in the region, and providing alternative facilities (including petroleum imports) to Hodeida, which is showing ominous signs of silting up. Cotton now accounts for 60% of exports, with coffee 20% and hides and skins also 20%. There are only the beginnings of industry in the country: two textile plants (at Sana'a) and small consumer goods plants at Hodeida, Ta'izz and Sana'a.

*Southern Yemen* In simplest terms, one may think of the entire southern coastlands of the Arabian peninsula as a wedge of highland, upstanding in the west, and dropping by irregular stages from this highest western elevation (which is the Yemen plateau proper) to a total lowland devoid of any hills that characterizes the area around Sanquira Bay. This is a drastic oversimplification, but it serves to isolate one problem, that of geographical division. If this eastward tapering 'wedge' is to be regarded as linked to, or an offshoot of, the western highlands which have just been described, how far can it be legitimately described as 'western coastal'? Where may one divide south from west?

There can be no conclusive answer, since a corner of an angle cannot really be defined in terms of 'south' and 'west'. But as a practical and minor categorization, it is possible to discern a number of small-scale changes which differentiate the southern expanse of coast. One of these

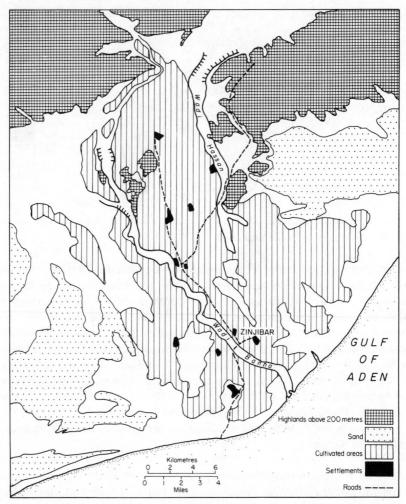

*Fig.* 16.8 The Abyan Irrigation Scheme. The land is cropped in rotation, not simultaneously.

is the Khaur mountain range (fig. 16.5), which continues the structure of the Yemen plateau some distance eastwards, being of the same basic rock types – ancient schists and granites. Here then is a possible termination of our 'western' coastlands if one is needed: justifiable to some extent on terms of physiography, but this is to ignore the political realities that now make the entire territories from Aden eastward the now sovereign country known as 'South Yemen'.

The Khaur mountains lack the capping of less-resistant sedimentary rocks and lava sheets that occur in the Yemen proper – hence the range is of lower altitude, with a lower rainfall, and with fewer patches of good soil. Consequently cultivation is distinctly less developed than in the Yemen and in Asir. The most prolific agricultural region is that of Lahej, just north of Aden, but although very productive in a few such localities, especially as regards the Abyan cotton project further east, cultivation is much more fragmented and scattered, being restricted to the fewer areas of better soil and available water. Round Lahej, cereals (chiefly millet), various fruits, including the citrus, date, banana, coconut and mango, are cultivated, together with vegetables, indigo and coffee. Qat is important at higher levels.

## The southern coastlands

With the Khaur mountains regarded as forming the last element of our 'western coastlands', we may note yet another marked drop in altitude and change in geological succession as we move east. The ancient complex of the Khaur massifs is succeeded eastward by a predominantly limestone upland of younger age, that in many places rises almost sheer from the sea with frequent cliffs and only small enclaves here and there of a coastal plain. The upland is highly dissected by steep, tortuous ravines, and attains 2000 m in many places. In appearance it is often bare and karstic, but in places there are surface deposits of loess. This is the Jols, a highly arid, negative area with few inhabitants, that exists as a pronounced barrier between the coast and the extensive lowland system further north, of the Wadi Hadhramaut.

The Hadhramaut is a major geomorphological feature produced by erosion at earlier pluvial phases within a tectonically disturbed zone. A simple drainage pattern developed during the early Quaternary of northward-flowing streams on the north side of the Jols upland and draining into what is now the desert interior would seem later to have been linked by extensive river capture. The effect of this, possibly in turn brought about by general down-warping of the Arabian basement toward the east, was to produce a highly eroded complex of connected valleys running south-west–north-east, parallel to but 200 km inland from the coast. The whole system then turns sharply towards the Indian Ocean through the Wadi Maseila, probably as a late effect of capture by a north–south running stream, the Wadi Maseila, that was rejuvenated by warping. The complex and varied origins of the Wadi Hadhramaut are indicated by the differences in morphology: some parts of it are shallow, broad and highly dissected laterally, whilst other stretches, including the Wadi Maseila, are extremely deep and narrow. In its upper (south-western) portion, the Wadi Hadhramaut has expanses of level plain, covered partly by shifting sand. Drainage is, so to speak, in a stage of partial activity only. At irregular and often long intervals there is heavy local rainfall, much of which sweeps down parts of the Wadi as a sheet-flood (*seil*) with, eventually, much seepage into the subsoil, and little surface drainage. From these floods and other smaller but rather more regular falls of rain there occur a series of water-tables in the bed of the Wadi Hadhramaut which in places (towards the east especially) give rise to surface flow for most of the year – though the streams do not reach the sea regularly, and there is no perennial flow throughout.

On the higher parts of the Jols uplands, and their continuation east of the Wadi Maseila, there is a slight summer rainfall of monsoon type, but other than the somewhat local exception of the Kara mountains of Dhofar, where aspect in relation to the monsoonal current gives a heavier fall, precipitation amounts decrease eastwards as general altitude declines. At a few places actually along the coast the plateau-edge of the Jols retreats from the sea, giving enclaves of lowlands with reasonably good soil and access to water, where tiny patches of cultivation occur, with the coconut and date palm important. Much more cultivation takes place, however, in and close to the Wadi Hadhramaut, which has by far the largest proportion of inhabitants. Agriculture based on millet, tree fruit (date, citrus, etc.), soft fruit and vegetables is most developed round towns like Shibam and Tarim; but even so, as noted for the Yemen, there is considerable temporary migration of young men, especially to Malaya and Sumatra. As a result, houses tend to reflect East Indian styles, as is also the case in north Yemen and Aden – many-storeyed local 'sky-scrapers', with much intricate carving and ornamentation.

In places on the southern plateaux, usually above 1000 m altitude, where precipitation is slightly heavier, frankincense trees grow semi-wild. Once much more widespread, the trees are still visited seasonally before the onset of summer rains in order to collect the sap from which incense and myrrh are obtained. The wood itself also has considerable commercial value in parts of Arabia, as it is burned in small pieces as the final element in ceremonial household entertaining by the better-off: when the host produces an incense-burner, the guests appreciate that it is time to go.

Collection of the frankincense is partly by migrant Somalis and other Africans. At one time tree numbers and the demand were greater, and there were traditional Incense Routes: the one from southern Arabia striking inland from Bir Ali and crossing the Jols plateau to reach Timna, whence it continued northwards to Jauf, Medina and the Levant. Nowadays the output of frankincense and myrrh is small, most coming from the uplands of Dhofar.

Grass also grows locally on the higher hills, which thus provide grazing for small numbers of semi-nomadic pastoralists who bring their flocks on to the hills after the summer rains, and spend the earlier rainy period

(June–September) in reed or grass huts erected on the valley floors. Here they plant 'catch crops' of millet and vegetables. Pastoralism rather than cultivation is the chief occupation of the eastern parts of the Indian Ocean coastlands – an index of increasing aridity.

As relief declines eastwards and rainfall consequently diminishes, fishing plays an increasing part. Large quantities of shark, tunny and sardines are caught, most of which are dried as food both for humans and for animals (camels particularly). In addition, oil is prepared from the fish for use in woodworking. Mukalla and Shihr are the chief fishing centres, and in these towns rows of fish drying in the sun for food, and rotting in heaps to produce oil, are prominent, pungent and, according to some visitors, unforgettable features.

With a barren hinterland, many activities in southern Arabia centre on the sea; and, in addition to fishing, trading by dhow is important. The Arabs of the south are the Greeks of the Indian Ocean and cargoes are carried between east Africa, Arabia, the Persian/Arab Gulf and India – even, at times, the East Indies. From their sea-trading, the inhabitants of south Yemen and the Hadhramaut derive a livelihood that allows the import of foodstuffs into the country – as it is, local production of food is quite insufficient to maintain the existing population, and part must come from the outside. A cosmopolitan outlook, and wide commercial contacts, strongly contrasting with conditions in the Yemen, are strikingly indicated by the architectural styles in southern Arabia, which as we have seen are much influenced by East Indian models. After a life of trading, perhaps with many years spent away from his country, the southern Arab will return with a small competence that will suffice him for the rest of his life. Pearling, once more important, is also carried on to a limited extent, especially from Socotra Island.

Because of these intrinsic limitations Aden, the chief town and port of this region (pop., est. 1977, 300 000), has relied much more on external relations than upon indigenous trade. Originally in the nineteenth century a coaling station well placed for the India traffic, and with a good harbour formed partly by the drowning of an extinct volcano, it developed oil-bunkering and then, a few years ago, oil-refining, using imported crude. Its position as by far the best harbour between Bombay and Suez gave it importance as a port of call and tourist stop; and for many years its stable political relations, sound location and superior installations also made it the chief import and export centre for the entire south-west of Arabia. Since independence, and above all after the closing of the Suez Canal in 1967, trade declined. Aden of course retains the functions of a local metropolitan city, with import of manufactures and other consumer goods, but lack of a really productive hinterland, growing competition on nationalist grounds of such ports as Hodeida, and the interruption of sea links, have been highly adverse factors, particularly as much as Aden's retail and mercantile activities were carried on by Indians. Nevertheless cotton, coffee and some manufactured goods (small consumer items and textiles) are exported, with, as the major activity, oil bunkering. Re-opening of the Suez Canal has had a beneficial effect.

*Oman* The Dhofari hills continue eastwards from the Hadhramaut structures, and then decline, so that the high coastal plateau edge, with in places a narrow coastal plain, is replaced by continuous desert lowland continuing into the interior. A few fishing and trading settlements take advantage of seepage or springs from the interior hills for oases cultivation – Salalah is by far the largest of these settlements.

Further east still rise the uplands of Oman: structurally distinct, and isolated to sea by cliffs, and to landward by the Rub al Khali: the Empty Quarter. Because of this physical isolation, Oman has had few contacts with the rest of Arabia; and until a very few years ago, when it first became drawn into oil exploitation and hence into the resultant political and commercial upheavals, the country was able to remain very largely apart, looking to the Indian Ocean for its few relations by sea, where these were permitted. Landward communications were almost negligible, and foreigners discouraged.

Oman consists essentially of an extensive upfold of metamorphic and igneous rock upon which rest sedimentaries (chiefly Cretaceous limestones) in discontinuous masses. Much of the centre of the massif, as far north as Dibba in the Musandum peninsula, consists of deposits of almost black serpentine, which has been weathered to produce a stark landscape of jagged crests and highly dendritic valleys. Most authorities regard the Oman folds as an outer flexure of the Zagros system that has been cross-faulted at the junction with the main Zagros, and breached by the sea, but some others, notably Furon, see in the Oman folds traces of earlier (post-Hercynian) folding related to pre-Zagros structures. The undoubted earlier age of the Oman folding movements (Cretaceous, as compared with late Pliocene for the Zagros) is a difficulty in the way of linking it directly to the Zagros uplift. Extensive dislocation, faulting followed by differential uplift in some areas and downthrow in others, has produced a varied topography of marine platforms at various levels, and, in the Musandum peninsula, a sequence of tectonic valleys and small uplifted horsts. Downthrow on a large scale has resulted in a fjord type of coastline, with long, deep inlets shut in by steep-walled cliffs. The largest of these drowned troughs is Elphinstone Inlet at the head of the Musandum peninsula, which is some 15 km long and 500 m deep, and is surrounded by cliffs sometimes over 1000 m in height. This is also to some extent true of the Muscat area, which has a difficult landward approach.

Another serious limitation was for long the extreme humidity of the inlets which, surrounded by cliffs, are hot and humid. Climatic conditions – with wet bulb temperatures that can exceed 35 °C or even 40 °C – have been described as among the worst in the world for sustained human activity; and an earlier attempt to establish a radio station proved abortive. Now, with air-conditioning making a great difference, settlement is easier, but until recently the coasts were sometimes evacuated in summer by the inhabitants, who went to work temporarily as labourers elsewhere.

The interior of Oman is dominated by a tableland of just over 1200 m altitude, rising from a moderately wide coastal plain, with a central ridge, the Jebel Akhdar, that attains 3000 m here and there. Numerous deep and steep-sided *wadis* penetrate inland from the coast into the uplands, some of these being fault-lines and others entirely due to erosion. The effect is to produce a highly dissected plateau surface, with contrasting land forms developed in different rock exposures. Rainfall is generally less in amount than in the Yemen; but certainly greater on the hills (no long-term records exist) than on the coastal plain, some 25–40 km wide, which is known as the Batina. Most rain comes as a result of 'westerly' air streams from the Mediterranean that reach Oman in winter as shallow disturbances via the Persian/Arab Gulf where some rejuvenation occurs, but there is also a sporadic influence from the summer Indian Ocean monsoonal flow, which in some years may intrude westward over Muscat and Oman for a short time. While details are few, it would seem that the lowlands – mainly the Batina – receive 75–150 mm of rainfall per annum, whereas amounts of 250 mm and very exceptionally 400–500 mm are received on the higher ground, partly as sleet and snow. One is here located at an interesting margin of two moisture-bearing currents: one originating from the Mediterranean, the other from the Indian Ocean. Those that pass from the Mediterranean may in some years be feebly developed to follow more of a land track, so that precipitation is then lower than usual. The summer rain brought by the Indian Ocean current may never materialize at all in a given year if the track does not quite impinge on the salient of the Oman peninsula.

The description so far given of the Jebel may suggest the concept of a massive hog's back with gentle upper slopes clothed in green vegetation. This would be erroneous; in reality the area is a region of sharp limestone, schist and serpentine crags and pinnacles, or granitic tors, cut through sometimes by valleys that can be moderately wide with flat currents but are more usually extremely narrow, abrupt and tortuous, with only

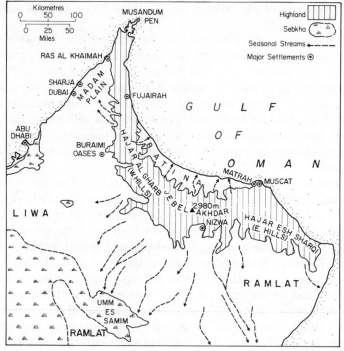

*Fig.* 16.9 Oman.

restricted access to other parts. Many districts present a striking but sombre landscape of dark, heavily dissected rocks with no vestige of soil; others in complete contrast carry pleasant groves of trees, patches of grass and small fields. Another contrast comes from the occasional juxtaposition of light coloured limestone series, and dark serpentine.

Once again, as a consequence of seasonal rainfall over a structure that comprises both permeable and impermeable strata, there is a succession of springs round the hill margins with, also, much outwash of sands and gravels in which rainfall is sometimes retained. The seaward openings of the larger valleys on the north-west as they open on to the Batina offer good opportunities for irrigation, both by direct flow and by the use of *qanats* (here known as *aflaj*). Along the Batina, there is a succession of villages that live by cultivating chiefly the date and coconut palms, also cereals, fruits such as the banana, orange and lemon, lucerne and vegetables, as well as undertaking a good deal of in-shore fishing. The waters here are especially rich in sardines, white-bait and excellent crayfish. Further inland, some valley floors and terraces are irrigated to produce dates, figs, pomegranates, cereals, vegetables, lucerne, and a little coffee, whilst the small seasonal flushes of grass at higher altitudes are used by semi-nomads.

On the inner (south-western) side of the Jebel Akhdar, the effect of the summer monsoon is not felt, and conditions are drier, since the extra land track of the westerlies is significant in an enfeebled air stream. But springs (a few hot) and local deposits of groundwater are to be found; and these allow some cultivation. Chief centre is Nizwa, which, not wholly favoured in the matter of water, has developed oasis-type cultivation alongside its other aspect as a market for pastoralists. Now, like Ibri and Buraimi–El Ain further north-west, it is beginning to feel the beneficent effects of oil exploitation.

The broken nature of the territory, lack of water and soil, and the physical division between the western coast and the Batina, which looks mainly to the east and the sea – until the new roads came the easiest way of driving a car was along the sea beach at low tide – has perpetuated isolation and division. One indication of this is the remarkable political division of the region, with fragmented territorial rights that reflect the movements of one semi-nomadic group, which may cross the path of another, each claiming to own the territory over which it moves (fig. 16.10). Another indication is the fact that down to the mid-1960s, skirmishing, feuding and tribal unrest still occurred in the hill areas; whilst the Buraimi oases had three claimants: Abu Dhabi, Oman and Saudi Arabia. As we have noted, the state of Muscat and Oman had until very recently indeed been able to remain entirely aloof and largely untouched by outside influences, with the gates of its capital city closed nightly at 9 p.m., and the obligation for all its inhabitants to carry oil lamps after dark.

As in the Southern Yemen, the sea provides an important adjunct, sometimes a major part, to the land activities of cultivation and animal-rearing. Until very recently, land communications were difficult, so that most contacts were by sea.

Like that of its south-western neighbour, the population of Oman is of very mixed racial origin; and besides indigenous Arabs, there are some African Negroes and a number of tribesmen from the northern shore of the Gulf of Oman. Structurally an outlier of Iran, Oman displays a curious cultural link with its larger neighbour: in religion the Shi'a faith is dominant; and observers have commented on the fact that some ways of life seem closer to Iranian habits than to normal Arab practice. In fact, both as regards physical and human geography, Muscat town and its neighbour Matra could be thought of as partial outliers of Iran, Pakistan and India.

Muscat, the chief town and port of the region, has some importance through its location at the southern entry to the Gulf of Oman. As a centre of trade, however, it has been retarded by the low productivity of its immediate hinterland, and its formerly difficult landward communications. In one sense, it can be regarded as a mirror-image of Aden on the east side of the Arabian peninsula, since main emphasis is on sea traffic and control of a sea gulf. Now, with petroleum development, and pacification of the interior (including dissidents in the south-west supported from South Yemen) there has been much expansion, with the development of a satellite town and oil port (Matra) a short distance away, since access to Muscat itself is restricted to one very narrow 'corniche' road. Copper and asbestos have been found in the interior, and exploitation of the former is now in progress on a limited scale. There are small exports of fruit, and now beginnings of industry, starting with cement making.

### The eastern coastlands
*The Trucial coast and El Hasa* From the western side of the Musandum peninsula as far as the Shatt el Arab, the coastal region is everywhere below 200 m in altitude and consists for the greater part of an undulating plain, diversified very occasionally by low hills, often anticlinal. Much of the surface is sand- or gravel-covered, and some drifting sand can be traced by its lithology to the regions of origin within various areas of inner Arabia. From this interior reservoir sand is carried by the frequent strong winds towards the east, where it may accumulate in mobile dunes, or as a sheet. Even hillsides may be thinly covered by sand blown from elsewhere. In other areas lie flatter zones of gravel, diversified by shallow *wadi* beds. These *wadis*, like the plains, may have local deposits of silt or alluvium; whilst towards their 'heads' in the interior, there may be extensive coarser outwash deposits from the hills: pebbles, scree and boulders, deposited by the infrequent but considerable flash-floods.

The coastline, being one of oscillation (with the current phase one of gentle and irregular subsidence), is fairly shallow, and fringed by extensive coral reefs. Lagoons and spits are also frequent features, with intricate creeks and salt flats; in some localities it is difficult to distinguish sea from land, with a high tidal amplitude through tortuous channels and winding creeks further adding to the difficulty. *Sabkhas* (salt marsh), some fed by the sea, others by the evaporation of water that seeps to the surface from underground sources, are another prominent feature; and as some parts of these partially dry out seasonally (depending on temperatures, rainfall, winds and tides) to give a muddy, viscous morass covered in places by a temporary salt crust, the *sabkhas* are effective factors in isolating one stretch of coast from another. A large *sabkha* lies at the southern base of the Qatar peninsula; another, 50–60 km wide and over 300 km long, the Matti *sabkha*, stretches along the coast south of Abu Dhabi town.

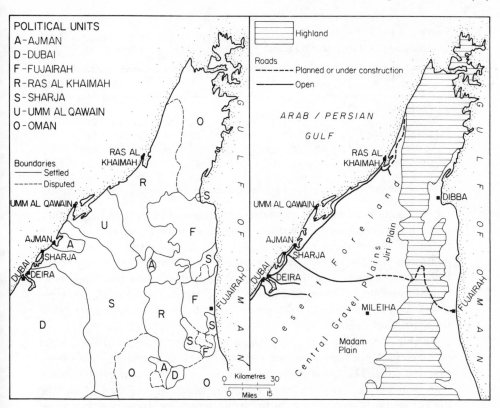

*Fig.* 16.10 The eastern Emirates.

Further to the north-west the region lying between Qatar and Kuwait is termed El Hasa. This is an area underlain by extensive water-tables, some of which appear to be recharged from infrequent local rainfall. Most, however, are not. A great deal of the abundant water often encountered in oil-drilling must originate from further west, and it is thought to be derived from upland regions that receive more rainfall than the El Hasa plain itself: from the Jebel Tuwaiq of central Arabia, and, as has already been mentioned, even the high western edge of the Hijaz mountains. In places, where structure allows, the water rises as natural springs; sometimes it occurs as underground pools in solution hollows; or it may be tapped by wells. On Bahrain Island there is one spring about 10 m across, a natural upwelling of very fresh water that must originate from the mainland, whilst at Hofuf alone there are about forty springs, with freshets of sweet water also occurring in places on the sea bed.

Figures 16.10 and 16.11 gives details of land utilization of a part of the Trucial coast lying south-west of the Musandum area. It will be seen that settlement is closely related either to the coast or to the piedmont,

Climatic data, Dubai (1950–65)
*Temperature (°C) and rainfall (mm)*

|  | J | F | M | A | M | J | J | A | S | O | N | D | Total |
|---|---|---|---|---|---|---|---|---|---|---|---|---|---|
| **Temperature** | | | | | | | | | | | | | |
| Mean max. | 23 | 24 | 28 | 31 | 34 | 37 | 39 | 39 | 37 | 34 | 29 | 26 | |
| Mean min. | 13 | 13 | 17 | 18 | 22 | 24 | 28 | 27 | 26 | 21 | 17 | 14 | |
| Abs. max. | 33 | 37 | 40 | 42 | 44 | 45 | 48 | 47 | 45 | 40 | 36 | 32 | |
| Abs. min. | 4 | 5 | 9 | 12 | 16 | 19 | 22 | 22 | 18 | 16 | 10 | 7 | |
| Rainfall | 29 | 14 | 9 | 17 | 1 | 0 | 2 | 0 | 1 | 0 | 15 | 24 | 112 |

where small-sized villages cluster round irrigated plots with date palms, a few limes, bananas and oranges, tomatoes, onions, melons and a wide range of other vegetables. Although the high central ridges of the peninsula and Oman hills receive rather more precipitation, the coastlands are unaffected by the monsoonal flow of summer that sometimes reaches south-east Oman, and so rainfall is restricted to the winter months. Conditions at Dubai typify the general regime prevailing along the entire southern Gulf coast.

Further west are the large *sabkha* areas that form much of the coastal frontage of Abu Dhabi state, and for long served as a barrier to movement east and west. The Qatar peninsula consists of a shallow limestone dome, with a higher flexure, the Jebel Dukhan, which attains 70 m. Much of the peninsula is inhabited only by semi-nomads or fishermen, but since the exploitation of oil resources there has been considerable expansion of settlement in several areas, and developments of irrigated garden cultivation, especially to the north-west of Doha.

Another small limestone dome forms the island of Bahrain. Differential erosion of Cretaceous and Jurassic strata has produced here a varied landscape crop and lowland basins, whilst in the north the presence of a coral-free inlet and natural artesian water supplies has led to the growth of settlement at and around Manama. For long one of the more agriculturally productive regions of the Gulf, cultivation has latterly declined owing to alternative employment in the oilfield, or in the towns.

Prior to the development of oil resources, life was in general exceedingly hard, since local resources were few: some pasture for nomadic herders, limited oasis cultivation on a very small scale, mostly fishing and pearling, diversified by smuggling, gun-running and a little slaving. Communities were small and scattered, and movement, together with the desire to have better-watered lands on either flank of the limestone crest line, led to extremely diverse political control of a most intricate kind (fig. 16.10). Present population figures for the region (the first census took place only

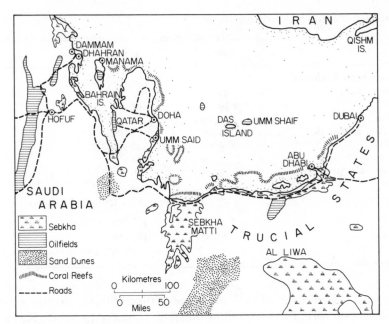

*Fig.* 16.11  Abu Dhabi and Qatar.

in 1968) indicate, even after gains of the last few years, how small in absolute numbers local communities really are.

Whilst there may have been some under-enumeration in the 1968 census, the large increases are the result chiefly of immigration from outside, which is not controlled. As a result, Indians, Pakistanis and Baluchis now form a majority of the population in some regions. Up to the middle of the eighteenth century Iranian influence was probably greatest on both sides of the Gulf. With the decline of Iranian political strength after about 1750, various tribal groups became more prominent: the Qawasim, who occupied the region of Ras al Kaimah, and the Beni Yas, who settled at this period in the areas of Dubai and Abu Dhabi. Bahrain also in the late eighteenth century asserted an independence of Iranian rule. With increased trading activity by sea, the coastal tribes saw a valuable supplement to their meagre way of life in raiding and piracy – consequently the region became known in the west as the Pirate Coast. Modern research has, however, latterly tended to suggest that total emphasis should not be placed on the piratical activities of the Gulf Arab: some part at least of the undoubted warfare and attacks on outsiders was intertribal and political in its aims.

Following British intervention over several decades, the rulers of the seven states were induced, between 1820 and 1843, to agree to a perpetual

Population (censuses of 1968 and 1975)

|  | 1968 | 1975 |
|---|---|---|
| *United Arab Emirates* | | |
| Abu Dhabi | 46 400 | 235 700 |
| Dubai | 59 100 | 206 900 |
| Sharjah | 31 500 | 88 200 |
| Ras al Khaimah | 24 500 | 57 300 |
| Fujaira | 9 800 | 26 500 |
| Ajman | 4 200 | 21 600 |
| Umm al Qawain | 3 700 | 16 900 |
| *Kuwait* | 468 000 | 990 400 (521 300 non-Kuwaiti) |
| *Oman* | — | 750 000 |
| *Qatar* | 63 000 | 180 000 (150 000 foreign immigrants) |

Truce with each other – hence the name 'Trucial States'. British suzerainty and control of foreign relations was later extended to include Kuwait, Bahrain and Qatar. The Union of Arab Emirates came into being in 1971.

Discovery of petroleum on a large scale has recently transformed the economic situation in the Gulf, which had previously depended upon pearling and trading by dhow. Up to a short time ago 250 boats from Manama and 170 from Kuwait took part annually in pearl-fishing, which is a seasonal activity limited to the period May–September. The main market is Bahrain, not only for the pearls, but also shell; however, owing to competition and a shift of fashion pearling has very greatly declined – the latest adverse factor being alternative and far pleasanter occupations produced by the oil boom: pearl-diving is physically exceptionally taxing and dangerous.

Of all the towns in the lower Gulf (Kuwait is here excepted) Dubai has grown the fastest, due to its location on one of the rare deep-water creeks in an otherwise shallow shore. First colonized by Beni Yas tribesmen in 1833, Dubai has in the last 15 years changed from a small dual settlement (Dubai proper on the south bank of the creek and Deira on the north side) to a town of over 200 000, now described as the Beirut of the lower Gulf. Like Beirut, Dubai is a port with very few taxes, based on a good harbour site in an otherwise difficult coast; and though its hinterland produces little, the acumen of its ruler and merchant community (about half of whom are of Iranian, Pakistani or Indian descent) together with a favourable location close to southern Asia have made it a boom town, to which the recent discovery of oil has added a further growth element.

One important element in Dubai's trade is gold, and there was a traditional entrepôt activity in varied commodities. Take-off took place in the 1960s stimulated latterly by the demise of Beirut. At least half Dubai's exports are re-exported (there are no precise figures since full records are not kept), and with petroleum exports since 1964 (though the three Dubai fields are not very large), over 80 banks – about as many as in pre-1975 Beirut, a large deep water harbour and what is one of the three largest ship repair facilities in the world (one dock in construction can take ships of 1 million tons dwt.), Dubai is one of the largest and busiest centres of commerce in the Gulf. An aluminium smelter, light industries and gas and oil plant with a free port zone are other activities, and iron and steel smelting is planned. In 1976 the infrastructure budget for Dubai amounted to over US $150 million, and a development budget of twice that amount was announced. Imports during 1975–6 averaged $1.8 billion – this in a state with a population of less than ¼ million.

Manama, the capital of Bahrain, and once the largest town of the lower Gulf because of its petroleum, pearling, trading and oasis cultivation of dates, has developed less spectacularly than Dubai. Its oil refinery is currently the second largest in the Middle East, but because of limited local reserves (the Bahrain field has been exploited since 1932), three-quarters of its throughput is from Saudi Arabian sources, piped under the sea from the Arabian mainland. Extensive dock services have been constructed (rather smaller than those at Dubai), there are an aluminium smelter, a frozen prawn factory, and extensive warehouse and refrigeration facilities. The government has made great efforts to attract foreign banking concerns by taxation incentives, and besides having a free port zone, there are excellent radio and cable links, with a growing spread of consumer industry.

Doha, the chief town of Qatar, is another example of a tiny port in the formerly unproductive area that has burgeoned following petroleum exploitation. Unlike Dubai and Manama, Doha has no entrepôt traffic, but instead has developed a quick freeze plant for export of prawns, and plans to have heavy industry: iron smelting, aluminium smelting, petrochemicals. The state has made great efforts to produce its own fruit and vegetables, and quantities of these are now exported via Doha to other Gulf States.

Abu Dhabi, a formerly tiny settlement ringed by sea and *sabkha*, has also developed into a major planned city over the last 15 years. As capital of the Arab Emirates, with by far the largest resources in petroleum and natural gas, and with rather more of a hinterland (that takes in Al Ain – part of Buraimi), Abu Dhabi tends to be the leader and patron of the rest of the Emirates. Whilst Dubai is commercially ahead, Abu Dhabi concentrates on maximum oil production: until recently its large reserves of gas were ignored or burnt off, but this is now changing. Petrochemicals, a new refinery, and construction of a deepwater port are planned: one difficulty now is that 80% of the population is non-indigenous. One relatively important interior settlement is Al Ain, where there is a cluster of eight separate settlements, fed by *aflaj* and growing oasis crops, and much transformation is now taking place following oil exploitation. Al Ain is being planned as a town that is expected to number 75000 inhabitants. It is interesting to note that Abu Dhabi city is now building ultra-modern 'tribal housing units'. As tribespeople settle in the town, they prefer to live for the first generation at least in small compact housing units that are allocated in tribal occupation. Later the groups are expected to become more sophisticated, and break up; but for the first decade tribal housing units are to be one basis of planning, in view of the mixed population of tribal Arabs, Iranians, Pakistanis and others.

From Qatar north-westwards the coastlands remain low lying and sandy, with, once more, much *sabkha* development. This is the Hasa region, partly undeveloped and in many places extremely scantily populated but also in part greatly altered owing to oil exploitation. Oqair is the port that handles traffic by truck for the interior of Arabia, but a greater proportion moves via Dhahran, the port which has both road and rail links. Oil development at Dammam and Qatif, and further north at Safaniya, has greatly altered conditions locally; and we have already noted that this coastal complex is in process of developing into a major industrial 'pole' of the Saudi Arabian state.

*Kuwait* Located at the north-western corner of the Gulf, Kuwait is one of the remarkable geographical phenomena of modern times. With an enormously increased urban population, it could be held statistically to be certainly the most urbanized country of the Middle East, and, with Hong Kong, of the world; its national income per head (at about $11 500) is the second highest in the world, after that of the UAE ($43 000 for Abu Dhabi), and its currency is one of, if not the 'hardest' – much better than the US dollar and at least equal to the Swiss franc.

The country itself is a somewhat irregular triangle of land, one side of which is formed by the sea and lower isthmus of the Shatt el Arab, but broken by the extensive Kuwait Bay. A second 'side' to the triangle is the sandy depression of the Wadi Batin, whilst to the south there is little in the way of natural geographical features to sustain a division, and this favoured the erection of the former curious political 'neutral zones' which were designed to facilitate the movements of nomads.

Most of Kuwait is relatively flat with a few slight eminences, such as the Ahmadi ridge of about 120 m height; and the generally higher and firmer nature of the land, as compared with the mud flats of the Shatt el Arab, made it a sort of corridor or even causeway, linking the interior of southern Iraq to the heart of the Gulf. Kuwait had commercial connections with Aleppo in the eighteenth century, and for the same reason Kuwait rather than Basra was designated as the original terminus of the Berlin–Baghdad Railway. A broad bay, unencumbered by coral, gave the original settlement at Kuwait city the advantage of a moderately good trading and fishing site, and so the town grew up as a small market for exchange between nomads of the interior, the pearlers and fishermen of the coast, and the merchants who imported food and implements for sale, exporting in return wool, hides, animals and pearls.

This small-scale trading, pearling and fishing activity was overtaken after 1950 by the dramatic rise of Kuwait to the position of one of the principal world exporters of petroleum. The old walled town has been almost entirely rebuilt – in some cases twice – and besides the oil instal-lations, sited some distance from Kuwait at Ahmadi and Burgan, an industrial complex has grown up within and near Kuwait city itself. Water distillation, power generation and other services are on a most generous scale, whilst food-processing, petrochemicals and smaller consumer goods manufacturing have come into existence. Once flared off, natural gas is now increasingly used for local fuel (e.g. in water distillation) and raw material.

The high level of amenities – free education and hospitals – and the demand for labour of all kinds, have drawn a considerable immigrant population from all over south-west Asia and north Africa, with Pales-tinians one of the most important groups. Foreigners now outnumber Kuwaitis, despite attempts to regulate entry. Stringent laws control ownership of land and commercial activities, which must have predomi-nately Kuwaiti ownership, with one effect that almost all of the outer parts of Kuwait city consist of modern suburbs entirely owned by Kuwaitis, who are abandoning parts of the centre of the city to immigrant non-Kuwaiti tenants. Colonies of 'western' technicians and professionals are to be found outside the main city. With its mixture of the ultra-fashionable and functional buildings lavishly constructed, Kuwait is a remarkable city: one might call it the reality constructed almost instantaneously and in modern idiom by a slave of the oil lamp who knew how to choose shrewdly from American, European and Japanese sources. For the geographer, considerable interest lies in how far, in terms of human geography, Western models can be applied to what is still basically an Oriental social situation; and to what extent economic 'take-off' based on one commodity only can transform what is otherwise almost unproductive desert and coastland into a permanently viable and significant entity for its greatly expanded population of about half a million, most of whom are growing accustomed to rapidly improving standards of life. Kuwait has problems again different from those of

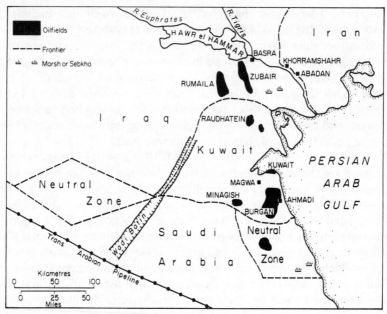

*Fig.* 16.12 Kuwait.

Saudi Arabia and of Iran, in that revenues which in amount approach those accruing in the two latter countries are applied to a very much smaller territory now occupied by an immigrant majority. Basic foodstuffs are subsidized and 70% of Kuwaitis work in what is in effect government-directed employment. Diversification and industrialization have been developed, with a new industrial area at Shuaiba just south of Kuwait City. The state has developed oil tanker ownership, and general shipping in collaboration with other Gulf states. Drinking water is piped from the Shatt el Arab, some 100 million litres of water are distilled daily by plant at Kuwait and Shuaiba, while very useful discoveries of ground water have been made at Raudhatain and Al Shigaia. The demand for electricity increases annually by 20–25%.

### The interior

Interior Arabia is by no means a uniform region, physiographically or in human terms. We are here considering in this chapter Arabia more as a physical concept, not a political one, and so within the totality of the geographical interior of Arabia are included portions of the states of Iraq, Syria and Jordan. In general much (though not all) of the region is a plateau formation: this is especially true of the northern parts, which are surrounded on nearly all sides by valleys and lowlands. To the north-west there is the Aqaba–Jordan trough, then the Qweiq–Orontes lowlands in Syria, and the Euphrates valley to the north and east. Yet as well, the interior comprises a number of obvious hill ridges, and in the south, the plateau surface declines to a low level, generally below 300 m in altitude.

*The Badiet esh Sham* 'Esh Sham' ('the left hand'), in distinction of 'El Yemen' ('the right hand'), imply respectively 'north' and 'south' – i.e. when as a true believer one faces east. Thus this northern area of the interior Arabian plateau (El Badiet) with its capital city Dimashq esh Sham (Damascus) is recognized as a distinctive region, extending from just east of Aleppo and the edge of the middle Euphrates valley as far south as (broadly) the line Aqaba–Kuwait. In the main clearly an upland plateau, the Badiet lies at about 600 m altitude in its southern part, attains nearly 1000 m in the latitude of Damascus, and then declines gradually further north. Here the first effects of geosynclinal folding have greatly involved Mesozoic and Tertiary sediments overlying the basement complex, so that a succession of shallow ridges occur as arcs round the northern border of the basement: the Jebel Kalamun at Damascus, the Jebel Bishri near Palmyra, and the hills south of Aleppo. Except for very small exposure along the Jordan valley fault-plane, the crystalline basement series is completely buried under thick layers of Mesozoic and Tertiary rocks; hence, away from the ridges just mentioned, the north gives an impression of a vast plain interrupted only by shallow *wadis* that trend generally towards the north-east, and are partially filled by alluvial and aeolian deposits. These *wadis* often retain small quantities of water after the scanty winter rains, and are thus the focal points of activity for nomadic Badawin of the region. Two prominent lines of wells have led to the establishment of routeways from east to west across the desert. One line can be traced north-westwards from Jauf along the Wadi Sirhan as far as the Hauran of south-west Syria; the other runs south-west from Karbala as far as Ha'il.

As the result of a rainfall that varies between 50–150 mm per annum (except towards Aleppo where the hills receive slightly more), the northern desert carries a vegetation cover for part of the year: grass in late spring and early summer, and in the autumn after the first onset of rain succulent plants like the *hashish* family, and a number of bushes that provide camel fodder. Hence in the Badiet esh Sham pastoralism finds its fullest development, and the uniformity of the land surface, lacking interior depressions like those of the Sahara, such as Siwa or Kufra (in which cultivation based on irrigation from artesian basins might develop), precludes any way of life other than strict nomadism. Largely self-sufficient, the Badawin cover enormous areas in their annual movements, and the small quantity of agricultural produce that they consume is still in certain measure obtained from cultivators on the desert margins. Though declining in numbers (probably under 90 000) the pastoral nomads are still significant here. Palmyra (Tadmor) one of the few oases of the region, where a warm sulphurous and aphrodisiac spring allows date-growing, was famous in the ancient world as a centre of transit trade. This has to some extent revived in our own time, with cross-desert journeys, and there is a tourist trade based on its magnificent Classical ruins, together with developing phosphate exploitation. Various routes cross the desert to link Damascus and central Iraq. The most ancient tended to be somewhat circuitous, as they relied on wells; but a direct Damascus–Baghdad motor route was first opened by an Australian, Nairn, after 1918, and many companies now operate along it.

Thus until our own time the interior was skirted rather than crossed by routes, leaving much to tribal occupation; but now the Badiet is crossed directly by several sets of pipelines served by surfaced roads. These points of stability in a once uncertain area have much reduced the former isolation of the interior, and travel across the Badiet is now no longer anything other than totally unexceptionable, with many buses leaving daily.

Further south occur expanses of considerable erosion and rock exfoliation which form stony deserts. One of these, the Widian, is located south-west of the Euphrates valley; another, the Hajara, is relatively well provided with sub-surface water, so that despite the difficulties of travel, it has long served as a routeway for nomads and others.

*The Nefud* This is an extensive 'negative' area. Consisting of a major depression or basin some 300 km in east–west extent, and 200 km in its widest part, the Great Nefud is a zone of 'sand sea' enclosed by rocky resistant outcrops, chiefly sandstones. These have been structurally disturbed, so that tilting has given rise to pronounced series of upstanding ridges that have been worn down by water action, and later still, eroded by wind action into grotesquely shaped pinnacles and crags. Between the ridges lie lowland basins that are mostly covered in loose sand, sometimes in the form of dunes up to 100 m in height. Rainfall is extremely rare, occurring only once or twice per annum, or even once in several years; and the enclosed nature of the basins produces a wide range in temperatures. In summer a diurnal range of 20–23 °C is not unusual, with day temperatures reaching 46–49 °C; and in winter, frost is common. A specially unpleasant feature of the Nefud is its violent winds, which spring up and die down with equal rapidity. Owing to the local character of these winds, sand dunes in many parts take on the *barchan* (crescent) form, but because of extreme local variability and strength of the wind, the dunes are aligned in many directions, in a manner quite different from the regular succession that is typical of the eastern Sahara.

In certain of the lowland depressions, water is retained by an impermeable substratum which sometimes lies near the surface. Oasis cultivation of dates, vegetables, barley and soft fruit can be carried on, and the largest of these oases are in the west, where some of the heavier rainfall in the mountains of the Hijaz finds its way eastwards into artesian basins. One well, at Teima, is 20 m deep, and measures 37 m in diameter.

On its eastern side the sand-sea of the Nefud is prolonged southwards as a complex belt of sandy zones broken by high stony ridges that curve towards the south and east, producing overall a corridor or sandy desert and scree that links the major northern desert of the Nefud to the even larger Dahna/Rub al Khali of the south. Nevertheless, despite its frequently loose sandy nature, the frequency of impermeable underlying sandstones means that some rainfall is retained near the surface, and thus a temporary flush of spring grass appears annually in many semi-sandy or even sandy areas. This is used as regular pasture, especially by the Shammar tribes.

*Nejd and the central region of Arabia* This central part of inner Arabia shows a somewhat complex structure, with considerable development of varied sedimentary series. Dislocation of the basement has produced a zone of warping and foundering that, as we earlier noted, runs entirely across Arabia from the region of Jidda to Hofuf and El Hasa. Besides massive exposures of lava, the basement itself appears at the surface, sometimes as an irregular platform, sometimes as a series of mountain massifs that attain heights of over 500 m above the general plateau level.

The sedimentaries consist mainly of Jurassic and later rocks, which, formerly horizontal, have now been tilted in places into extensive scarp and dip country, emphasized and extended by differential erosion. The effect is to produce a series of major ridges and tablelands often aligned north–south, but there is also some flexuring. Most prominent of these ridges is the Jurassic limestone formation of the Jebel Tuwaiq, which rises 300 m above the surrounding plateau.

The drainage pattern originally developed on these scarplands was complicated, though now all valleys are dry, and often, though by no means always, obliterated by sand. There were a number of consequent main streams that flowed eastwards to the Gulf, and in so doing, broke through the north–south aligned scarps, in a way somewhat similar to the Thames as it cut through the ridges of the Clay Vale and the Chilterns. The presence of lowland valleys set at right angles to the main line of drainage also favoured the growth of numerous transverse (strike) streams. Hence at the present time there are considerable differences in topography between the Nejd, which is a diverse region of uplands, small plateaux, scarps, broad valleys and dry river gaps, and the surrounding dune-covered wastes of the Nefud and Rub al Khali.

Rainfall is very small on the lowlands, but heavier showers occur on the higher mountains, and a certain amount of this precipitation ultimately finds its way into the lowlands, or else is retained above the occasional impermeable layers that exist in the uplands. Prevalence of limestone allows the development of underground pools, and in certain districts there are considerable solution hollows of up to 50 m in depth that contain water. This is now tapped on an increasing scale for cultivation, especially near Riyadh.

Oasis agriculture had for long been a feature of the Nejd, but over the last two decades much expansion has taken place as new water supplies with motor pumps are used, new markets develop following internal rises in living standards, and new roads allow transport to market. Dates are still a staple, with cereals, lucerne, vegetables of many kinds (chiefly tomatoes and squashes) and fruit: figs, apricots, oranges and vines. In some localities the water-table has dropped considerably since cultivation began, but in others it has not. The largest of the oases are Riyadh (now the capital of Saudi Arabia with about ½ million inhabitants), Bureida, Ha'il, Jabrin, Anaiza and, on the extreme east, Hofuf.

Nomadic pastoralism still plays a significant part in the economic life of the Nejd, though as elsewhere, its followers are declining. Because of varied terrain, with far fewer of the open stretches characteristic of the Syrian Hamad, nomadism involves distinctly less movement annually, and there are hence many gradations from semi-settled cultivation to full nomadism. The camel is the basis of pastoral life, but each nomad group possesses one or more permanent strongholds together with a few tributary agricultural villages. This somewhat complex social group – chieftains and noble class, warriors and herders, semi- or fully sedentary cultivators, and tributary peasants of the oases – make up a tribal unit. Until 20 or so years ago the king of Saudi Arabia himself moved regularly with his retinue from place to place seasonally.

Within the central triangular zone of better terrain with its varied rock type and alternation of ridge and valley – in a very broad sense a kind of Weald, or Paris Basin – has grown up the Wahhabi state. Though until recently there was little internal or external trade and few natural resources, the Nejd stood out as an island of relative fertility in an expanse of often waterless desert and barren upland ridges. Now the Nejd is the central region of the 'development axis' rapidly taking shape across Saudi Arabia.

*The Rub al Khali* The south and east of interior Arabia are occupied by one of the largest sand deserts in the world: the Empty Quarter, covering over 500000 km$^2$ and measuring over 1200 km by 500 km. The area, to which, perhaps not always accurately, the name Rub al Khali is given, is far from uniform, but consists of an irregular tilted basin that lies at an altitude of about 1000 m in the west to very little above sea-level in the east and south-east, where it adjoins the Trucial coast and inner Oman in the area of Masira (Sanqira Bay). First penetrated and described by Bertram Thomas in 1930 and then by H. J. Philby in 1932, the area had remained largely unknown; but gradually as the oil potential in surrounding regions was realized, and geological exploration pushed further, knowledge became far more complete. It is now clear that the area is much more varied geographically than a single vast sand basin.

In the extreme south-west, adjoining the Yemen, presence of a bounding ring of mountains which produce rain-shadow effects means that aridity is almost, though not quite, complete. Much of this south-west zone is covered by loose sand, often in the form of dunes that may attain up to 200 m in height, or else as flatter 'sand-seas'. This is the Bahr es Safi ('Real Sea') which, with only a very few water holes and springs – that can often be obliterated by drifting sand – has almost no inhabitants. To the south-east, round the western bases of the Oman hills, American geological maps show very extensive *sabkha* and salt marsh of various kinds, with a multitude of saline surface water features. These, in view of the general basin structure of the entire region, can be regarded as forming drainage sumps fed by moisture collected by seepage from the highest ground that frames the region to the west, east and south. Aeolian action, together with hydrostatic pressure from below, produce towards the east a number of hollows like those of the western desert of Egypt (Qattara, etc.) in which water may be found. Closer to the eastern (Omani) hills, considerable seasonal flushes of grass may occur, sufficient to support nomadic pastoralists. This is particularly true of the region inland from Abu Dhabi, towards Al Ain-Buraimi, where, once a coastal dune belt is passed, there is a more level expanse of consolidated sands and silts that give a level plain with, here and there, reddish or ochre-coloured sand deposits, 'enamelled' dark outwash scree and shallow *wadis*. Such relatively smooth surfaces occur in a number of localities: one is the Dhafrah, another the Madam plain inland from Dubai.

In contrast, there are the high dune areas of Al Ahkaf, north of the Bahr es Safi, reinforcing the area of difficulty that separates the Hadhramaut and Southern Yemen from inner Arabia; and the Dahna, a long irregular zone or ribbon of loose sand and dune country that extends in a narrow but continuous arc from the Rub al Khali through central Arabia as far as the Nefud in the north. Though not now a major barrier, the

Dahna serves as a reminder of the arid and difficult nature of much of interior Arabia.

### Economic changes

Exploitation of petroleum on a rapidly increasing scale, together with the price rises (some would say 'explosion') of 1973 and since, have produced economic change on a scale not easily imagined by those outside the producing countries. What had been an industry operated on a relatively modest scale by foreigners, largely self-contained and thus insulated from local life has over the last 15 years, and since 1974 especially, taken on an enormous dimension. The new-rich oil states are endeavouring first to provide infrastructures: roads, ports, tele-communications; then to develop activities that will (a) provide alternative occupation when oil is exhausted, (b) reduce dependence on imported consumer goods and basic equipment, and (c) spread the gains from oil wealth as far as possible through the entire population – otherwise there is strong risk of social instability. Tied in with this last is the provision of social services, hospitals, schools, etc., that in themselves are at first difficult to start (since trained personnel must come from outside) and then need to be closely adapted to the real needs of the country and on the necessary scale.

We may remind ourselves of the volume of oil revenues now accruing to various states in the Arabian peninsula (chapter 9):

Governmental receipts

| | Saudi Arabia | Kuwait | Other Gulf States |
|---|---|---|---|
| | (a) (in US ¢ per barrel of oil exported) | | |
| 1953 | 75 | 61 | 63 |
| 1968 | 88 | 81 | 84 |
| 1971 | 99 | 96 | 101 |
| 1975 | 1 100 | 1 108 | 1 136 |
| | (b) Total Revenue (US $ million) | | |
| 1965 | 655 | 671 | 102 |
| 1971 | 2 160 | 1 395 | 610 |
| 1975 | 27 000 | 7 500 | 9 400 |

In view of the enormous amount of building, production of materials, particularly cement, is a major activity: in Saudi Arabia at Jidda, Riyadh and on the east (Gulf) coast; in Kuwait, and in most of the other Gulf States. Petrochemicals are another very active interest, particularly production of fertilizers (ammonia, urea, nitrogenous) which are increasingly exported to countries of Africa and eastern Europe. Shipping is also a growing interest, which involves dock maintenance and repairs – here Dubai leads but is by no means the only country involved. Another activity is smelting of metals: iron and aluminium; but here, unless very high efficiency can be attained, there is a risk that the various plants now operating or in construction may be too numerous for the limited market, which is already subject to heavy competition, principally by Japan.

Light industry, consumer products and production of food and drink (soft drinks, since alcohol is totally banned in Kuwait and Saudi Arabia) and catering (including hotels of various categories) are now developing actively: facilities for accommodating visitors (who are chiefly technicians and businessmen) are restricted, so that in some countries of Arabia, even entry is now 'rationed' because of hotel bed shortage. Under these circumstances, tourism is not at all developed; but as we have seen, the pilgrim traffic brings well over 1 million persons annually to Saudi Arabia. Most (about 40%) arrive by land, in cars and buses, over 30% by air, and the rest by sea – chief groups originating from (Saudis excluded) in order of importance, Turkey, Iran, Iraq, Indonesia, Pakistan, Egypt, North Africa, the Sudan, Syria, and central Africa, with some even from China. Some even take 10 years travelling on foot. Although there is some cost to the Saudi State, the pilgrims are consumers, and the net effect is to bring in money to the merchants of Mecca, Medina and Jidda.

One final problem in development appears to be the effects of high inflation which in countries of intrinsically limited population and general resource endowment, is only too easily 'imported'. Linked with this is the difficulty of ensuring adequate remuneration to those of the community (e.g. agricultural workers) who are not directly associated by occupation to the oil boom.

# 17 Egypt

## Physical

The extreme north-east of the African continent shows topographical and structural transition from the relatively accidented and disturbed conditions of the Levant to a simpler and more uniform condition of the interior plateaux of Africa. The great tear-faults of the Red Sea system are, however, a reminder of the disturbed geological history. North-east Africa comprises the rifted edge of the main Gondwana Kraton, with crystalline basement rocks underlying most of the area, and occasionally outcropping. Within Egypt, which forms a convenient territorial delimitation, four major sub-regions can be distinguished:

(1) the Sinai peninsula,
(2) the eastern highlands of Egypt,
(3) the Nile valley,
(4) the western desert of Egypt,

and of these, the Nile valley is of overwhelming importance, since it contains over 95% of the total population of the region.

### The Sinai peninsula

This consists for the most part of an irregular tableland or plateau, which is tilted upwards towards the south. The southern half lies between altitudes of 750 m and 1500 m, and occasional peaks rise some 800–1000 m higher, the largest being the Jebel Catherina (2640 m). On the south-

502

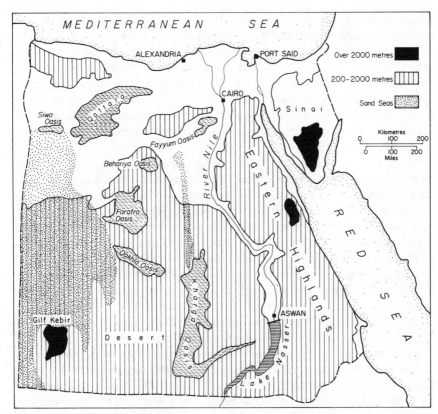

MEDITERRANEAN    SEA

ALEXANDRIA    PORT SAID

Over 2000 metres

200-2000 metres

Sand Seas

CAIRO

S i n a i

Siwa
Oasis

Qattara

Fayyum Oasis

Behariya Oasis

Farafra
Oasis

Dakhla Oasis

Kilometres
0        100        200

0        100        200
Miles

River Nile

Eastern    Highlands

R E D

S E A

Gilf Kebir

D e s e r t

Kharga Oasis

Lake Nasser

ASWAN

*Fig.* 17.1  Egypt: geographical units.

western side of the peninsula, along the Gulf of Suez, the plateau drops
to sea-level by a number of step-faults, the lowest of which forms the
coastal plain of El Qaa, which is 6–12 km wide. In the south-east, along
the Gulf of Aqaba, dislocation is restricted to a much narrower zone,
so that, instead of a series of steps, the highlands approach closely to
the sea, and there is a bold, rocky coastline which is for the most part
devoid of any coastal plain. Towards the Mediterranean Sea, the level
of the plateau decreases, and gradually gives way to a broad coastal plain
below 200 m in altitude, which extends from the Suez region through El
Arish, and passes without break into the lowlands of western Israel. Thus
on the north there is low sandy coastline, diversified by lagoons and
sandspits; and this region has provided a convenient corridor for
movement between the Nile valley and the Levant.

Though now extremely arid, with an annual rainfall of 150 mm in the
north and 50–75 mm only in the south, the entire Sinai region is deeply
dissected by river valleys, eroded at earlier geological periods. In the

north, where gradients are small, the valleys are broad and open, the largest being the Wadi el Arish, which can be traced inland from the Mediterranean to a point south of Nekhl. In the south, the *wadis* are much more deeply incised into the plateau, and often consist of gorges and ravines several hundreds of metres in depth, which break the surface of the plateau into a series of detached massifs. None of these *wadis* contains a perennial stream, but after a rare rainy spell some can fill for a few days, and can overwhelm passing travellers, or even whole villages, as happened in 1969–70.

Many parts in the north are covered by deposits of loose, shifting sand that frequently form dunes. There is difficulty in maintaining settlements and communications, since any projecting object may provoke the formation of a dune several metres in height. Houses, and even railways and roads, can thus become partly buried, and much effort is needed to clear constantly encroaching sand. In a few regions, however, cultivation is possible because rainfall quickly sinks through the sand, and is retained in hollows in the underlying basement rocks. Wells sunk into such hollows allow small-scale irrigation, and there is an oasis cultivation of dates and cereals, the chief of such centres being El Arish, El Auja, Nekhl and Themed. Further south, settlement is either in the plain of El Qaa, or in a few Israeli posts established since 1967. Nomadism still occurs, but on an increasingly limited scale. Following the Israeli withdrawal from western Sinai in 1975 and the reopening of the Suez Canal, petroleum production, mainly at Abu Rudeis and Bel Ayim, and ferro-manganese mining are now being expanded, and the first steps in creating an overall plan for the region are being taken. Sinai is to be linked more closely to the Canal Zone and Nile Delta by the construction of three road tunnels under the Canal, and the cultivated area is being extended by bringing Nile water irrigation to the east bank of the Canal.

## The eastern highlands

This region, a broken upland lying between the Nile valley and the Red Sea, has been formed by dislocation and uptilting of the crystalline basement rocks. In its northern part (i.e. between the latitudes of Cairo and Assiut) there is a covering of later sedimentary series – Nubian sandstone, Jurassic and Cretaceous limestones and sands – but south of latitude 26°N pre-Cambrian series are exposed on a considerable scale. Though somewhat larger in area than the Sinai, the eastern highlands of Egypt are lower in altitude; the general level is between 300 and 750 m, with the highest peak (Jebel Shayeb) reaching 2185 m. Like the Sinai, the highlands are heavily dissected by *wadis* running westwards to the Nile and eastwards to the Red Sea. Many of these *wadis* are narrow, but extremely deep, so that again, as in the Sinai, there is a complicated relief pattern with a series of detached upland masses.

On its western side, the highland region is bounded by the Nile trough; and because of the numerous *wadis* that enter the river from the east, the adjacent edge of the trough is rather less clearly defined than the opposite (western) side, where, owing to the virtual absence of *wadis*, there is a strongly marked, often continuous cliff. On the east, the abrupt change from desert plateau to riverine lowland is slightly less a feature.

Parts of the eastern highlands – more especially the deeper *wadi* floors, which are sheltered from the sun's rays – carry a light vegetation. Water is retained in hollows in the harder rocks, or beneath alluvial deposits in a stream bed; and there are occasional springs at the junction of certain previous sedimentary rocks and the crystalline basement. Water resources are, however, on a very small scale, partly because of a rainfall lower even than that of the Sinai (everywhere below 100 mm/annum), and partly because of the disturbed geological succession, which inhibits the development of large artesian basins. Cultivation is as a result almost impossible, and the few inhabitants live for the most part as nomadic shepherds, or in mineral-working camps. Owing to the difficulty and isolation of the region (there are no trade routes as in the Sinai, and all traffic follows the Nile valley) there is no incentive even to oasis cultivation, and few permanent settlements exist, apart from a few villages on the Red Sea coast and mining colonies.

There are, however, a number of mineral resources. Petroleum is worked in the sedimentary cover of the north-eastern flanks of the uplands at Hurghada, and at Ras Gharib on the Gulf of Suez. New off-shore fields in the Gulf of Suez are also being exploited. Phosphates are produced in significant quantities at Qoseir and Safaga, and manganese also occurs. Iron has been proved in several localities, and the large deposit east of Aswan was the first to be exploited in Egypt.

*The western desert*

This region presents a number of contrasts to the region just described. To the west of the Nile, geographical features are on a vaster scale, and the geological disturbances caused by the formation of the Red Sea rift are absent. As a result, there is an uninterrupted expanse of basement rocks covered by extensive shallow layers of horizontally bedded sediments, giving an expanse of plain or low plateau, with gentle gradients and wide vistas that are relieved only occasionally by light ridges or scarps where one rock series gives place to another. Thus about one-half of the western desert of Egypt lies below 200 m in altitude, and few parts exceed 300 m. The most conspicuous scarps lie in the north-west, along the

Mediterranean coast near the boundary with Libya, with the Gilf Kebir moderately high but not rugged.

There are, however, a number of deep basins, with fairly steep scarped edges, formed by erosion of softer strata either through aeolian action or by solution of soluble rock measures. The largest and deepest of these basins is the depression of Qattara, which covers an area of many thousand km² in the region to the south-west of Alexandria. Here the floor lies some 120 m below sea-level. Other basins are those of Dakhla, Kharga, Behariya, Siwa and the Fayyum (Egypt); Jarabub, Jalo and Kufra (Cyrenaica). Wide stretches of pervious rock overlying impervious basement series have given rise to numerous artesian basins, and it may in fact be stated that most of the western desert consists of one vast artesian basin. Hence on the floors of the depressions, considerable quantities of water are sometimes available. In certain instances (e.g. the Qattara depression) artesian water seeps to the surface naturally, and is evaporated, producing a salt marsh; and in the Fayyum there is a lake, which at one time actually drained to the Nile. For the most part, however, wells must be dug to tap the water, and then cultivation is possible, which much future potentiality. The Qattara depression, with its badlands and marshes, has few inhabitants, but the others have populations ranging from 2000 (Farafra) to over 30000 (Dakhla) and over 1 million (Fayyum). Plans are going ahead to flood the Qattara depression by cutting a canal to the Mediterranean. The chief aim is to produce hydro-electric power from the water flooding into the depression.

Outside the basins, the desert surface consists of an alternation of bare rocky outcrops, stony wastes or loose sand. The latter formation is increasingly prominent in the interior, producing dunes, some of which are fixed and some mobile. In the far south-west, towards the central Sahara, sand covers the entire surface, producing the Sand Sea of Calanshio (southern Cyrenaica). This is a major obstacle to communications, and effectively isolates Egypt from its neighbour Libya. Until the Second World War only one track through was known – but a few others were discovered during the various campaigns. New oil and gas discoveries are beginning to open up this region. Rich deposits of phosphates have also been discovered at Abu Tartur, and in recent years the Behariya oasis, now linked by rail and road to the Helwan iron and steel plant, has become the main source of high quality iron ore. There is a plan to bring agriculture and industry to the region.

*The Nile valley*

The course of the Nile presents many points of interest, with certain anomalies, chief of which is the actual slope of the river bed. In the extreme south, the region of the east African lakes, slope averages 1 in 1200, but further north, from Juba as far as Malakal, there is a fall of only 1 in 139000. This is the Sudd region (*Sudd* = blockage): an alluvial plain extending some 400 km from east to west, and covered by papyrus, reeds and other swamp vegetation. Here is the flattest part of the Nile's course, not, as is normal, near the mouth (cf. the Tigris and Euphrates), but over 3000 km up-stream. Below Malakal the *thalweg* is still extremely flat, falling only 7·9 m in 800 km (i.e. 1 in 101000); but although deep alluvial soils occur, swamps are no longer found. Between Khartoum and Aswan lies the cataract zone – a fairly hilly and almost rainless region through which the river has cut a deep trench. In several localities exposures of ancient granites, schists and gneisses have proved more resistant to erosion than the surrounding Nubian sandstone; hence rapids and cascades are a feature, and river navigation is interrupted. With an average fall of 1 in 6400, the cataract zone of the Nile is remarkable as the only stretch of river outside east Africa and Ethiopia in which active erosion is still proceeding. Here, a Pharaonic monument known to be at river level in 1900 B.C. is now 8 m above the banks, indicating that the river bed is being lowered at the rate of about 10 cm per 50 years – whereas elsewhere in the lower Nile valley deposition of silt is occurring, and the bed of the river is actually rising.

From Aswan northwards, the Nile flows in a well-developed notch cut into the plateau surface, with cliffs forming the boundary of the valley. Two points are of importance here: there are Pliocene marine sediments at high levels along the valley sides, and the valley itself cuts diagonally across a number of Miocene and Pliocene folds and fault-scarps, suggesting an antecedent or possibly superimposed pattern of drainage.

Until it broadens into the delta below Cairo, the river valley is about 10 km wide, and the river itself about 1 km wide. For the most part the Nile flows closer to the eastern valley wall: thus the greater part of the cultivated area lies west of the Nile, though there are many loops and meanders in the river. Below Cairo the delta region begins, with two main distributaries, the Rosetta branch (east) and the Damietta branch (west, and 22 km longer), together with an infinity of smaller streams. Part of the delta is still occupied by lakes and swamps, including four formerly large sheets of water – Lakes Brullos, Idku, Mariut and Menzala – that are now partly in process of drainage and reclamation.

The remarkable pattern of geomorphological units which make up the Nile basin has provoked several theories of origin. One theory postulates that the Nile originally flowed much further west through the oasis belt (Kharga to Qattara); another suggests that the Sudd area was once a large lake basin without river outlet, which was later breached and drained in Pleistocene times through the cutting back southwards of the

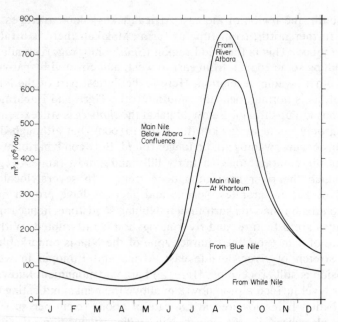

*Fig.* 17.2 Contributions to main Nile floods (after J. Oliver and others).

headstream of a shorter proto-Nile. This 'Lake Sudd' theory involves major changes in east Africa – the existence of river-flow southwards from Lake Victoria to the Indian Ocean, this flow being then diverted northwards about 20000–25000 years ago to swell the pre-existing Lake Sudd. There is further the question of whether the White Nile was 'captured' by strong streams from the Blue Nile, or whether junction came about by a normal shift of course in a very flat terrain. Although varied interpretations exist (the latest major study being that of Butzer and Hansen), it would seem most likely that the present-day Nile developed from linkage of several separate drainage systems in the early Tertiary, by which a stream that originally rose in the eastern highlands and flowed west and then north received headwater accretions from Ethiopia and the Sudan. Later changes have come about through, first, extensive entrenchment of the larger river, then (*a*) later earth movements on a relatively minor scale, (*b*) downwarping and transgression by the Mediterranean Sea, followed by uplift and re-emergence of the land in Pliocene times, (*c*) rejuvenation of the river in humid climatic periods producing down-cutting that was interrupted from time to time by (*d*) arid cycles during which erosion gave place to deposition of silt on the valley floor.

*Régime of the Nile*

The regular annual flooding of the Nile is due to spring and summer rainfall occurring over the highlands of east Africa. The rainfall usually begins as early as April in some areas. Within Egypt the Nile is a combination of three principal streams; the White Nile, the Blue Nile and the Atbara, each of which has different peculiarities. The White Nile is the most regular of the three, providing just over 80% of the total flow (measured at Aswan) during the dry season, but only 10% in the flood period – i.e. its regime corresponds closest to that of a river in temperate latitudes. This is because it passes through a number of lakes, which reduce fluctuation and slow it down, and because of the long course through the Sudd area, which evaporates quantities of water (especially in summer), thus further reducing its flow. Despite all this, however, involving a journey of 28–43 days through the Sudd (Malakal to Aswan), its flood-waters are the first to reach Aswan. Owing to the slow movement, much of the material in suspension has settled out, and its waters remain relatively clear, though with a high proportion of dissolved solids.

The Blue Nile contributes only 17% of the low-water flow; but it rises very rapidly and flows more swiftly, until at high-water season it is contributing 68% of the total water passing Aswan. As its current becomes established, it partially ponds back the slower flowing White Nile. Coming from the extensive lava regions of Abyssinia its waters are highly turbid, owing to erosion of the basaltic *harras*.

The Atbara contributes very little water at low-water season, but rises rapidly after June, bringing 22% of the total high-water flow; and its waters are also highly charged with brown sediment. The Blue Nile and the Atbara are thus more characteristically Middle Eastern rivers, and superimpose an enormous flood upon the more regularly flowing White Nile.

Minimum water level in Egypt was reached during May and early June: and the beginning of the flood period is indicated normally about the third or fourth week of June by the arrival of 'green water' from the White Nile, which contains algae brought down from the Sudd region by the first floods. Later, with the arrival of Blue Nile and Atbara floods, and yet more water from minor tributaries, the main river turns reddish-brown. Persistence into this period of decaying algae (dull red in colour) may on occasion thicken Nile water and give it an offensive odour: hence the 'turning to blood' of the Bible. Maximum flood level is reached in mid-September, and at this period river water formerly took only 6 days to reach the delta from Aswan, as compared to 12 in low-water season. Flow at this latter season averages 500 million cubic metres per second ($m^3$/s) (Aswan) and 8000 $mm^3$/s at flood time, but there is wide fluctuation. In 1913 less than half the normal flow occurred, and in 1878–79, 50%

Flow at Aswan (million m³/day (Hurst))

|  | White Nile | Blue Nile | Atbara |
|---|---|---|---|
| Low water | 37 | 7 | Almost nil |
| High water | 70 | 485 | 157 |

more than usual, with a flow of 13500 million m³/s. Height of flood-water at Aswan can thus vary from 6·4 to 10 m above low water; and if the maximum flood occurs early (i.e. in or near August), even with copious water supplies low water will also take place earlier in April instead of May–June, thus once producing crop famine.[1] It will consequently appear that, despite the general regularity of onset, the actual height, periodicity and hence economic value of Nile floods is distinctly variable (cf. the story of Joseph); and some observers have suggested a cyclical pattern of flood level, related to rainfall cycles and hence to sunspots. More investigation is, however, necessary.

A further matter is the loss of river during its passage northwards. Losses by evaporation between Aswan and Cairo alone are estimated at 15% of the total flow in the cool season, and 27% in summer; and a further 15% at least may seep into bedrock through porous outcrops.

About 110 million tons of sediment were being carried annually into Egypt by river water and, derived from the erosion of volcanic rocks in Abyssinia and east Africa. This silt is extremely rich in mineral substances. Of the total burden of silt, it was estimated that 15% was spread on the land by pumps, 33% subsided to the river bottom and so served to build up the river bed, and the remaining 52% reached Cairo. Here, up to 1968, over 55 million tons of silt were carried by the floodwaters of summer, and the remainder, about 15 million tons, during the rest of the year. Besides suspended solids, considerable quantities of matter are fully dissolved in the river water, and these amounted to 75 million tons at Cairo, all but 14000 tons being carried at the flood season. Principal substances in solution are calcium and magnesium carbonates, and sodium chloride. Thus, the Nile floods were important not merely for the water itself, but also for the fertilizing mud laid down annually. The rate of deposition of Nile mud was as follows:

| Upper Egypt (basin-irrigated lands) | 10 cm per 100 years |
|---|---|
| Lower Egypt (basin-irrigated lands) | 3 cm per 100 years |
| Lower Egypt (perennially irrigated lands) | 0·5 cm per 100 years |

Now some, but not all, of these sediments are retained in Lake Nasser, with effects not yet fully apparent.

[1] The past tense is used now in speaking of the effects of Nile flooding in Egypt, because the Aswan High Dam sluices were closed in 1969, altering all conditions below Aswan.

Frequency of moderate and severe dust storms (J. Oliver)

| | J | F | M | A | M | J | J | A | S | O | N | D | Total |
|---|---|---|---|---|---|---|---|---|---|---|---|---|---|
| 1940 | 1 | 1 | 1 | 3 | 2 | 0 | 0 | 0 | 0 | 0 | 0 | 0 | 8 |
| 1944 | 3 | 4 | 4 | 1 | 3 | 1 | 2 | 2 | 0 | 1 | 0 | 0 | 21 |

When first laid down, Nile mud is soft and sticky, but it soon hardens to a tough, hard earth that can be used for embankments and canals, or, when sun-dried, as bricks. Because of its chemical content, there is, however, a tendency for salinity to develop, particularly under intensive irrigation. This is most noticeable in the northern part of the Delta, where soils approaching a solonchak type are occasionally found. Because of the emphasis on cotton-growing in Egypt – cotton plants being especially sensitive to soil salinity – care is necessary in developing irrigation schemes. This is one reason why parts of the Delta are still unreclaimed swamp.

## Climate

Before discussing irrigation developments in Egypt, a short summary of climatic features may be given. Because of low relief, and a landlocked position, conditions are remarkably uniform over the whole country of Egypt. Summers are hot, with day maxima reaching 38 °C in most places, though nights are distinctly cooler. Over most of the country July is the hottest month, exceptions occurring in the extreme south where, with an approach to inter-tropical conditions, the maximum occurs in June, and in the extreme north, near the Mediterranean, where the maximum is postponed until August. The Mediterranean coast is distinctly cooler in summer because of the tempering effect of the sea; and in Alexandria, which was the summer capital of Egypt, day temperatures are some 5–10 °C below those of Cairo. The prevailing on-shore wind from the north-west is an important factor in reducing summer heat.

Winters are mild, allowing continuous plant growth, and though severe frost is unknown in the Nile valley itself,[1] occasional short-lived cold spells occur, and slight snow showers may spread as far south as Aswan. A factor more harmful to crops than frost is the prevalence of *khamsin* conditions, when hot, dry winds from the desert may scorch the tenuous strip of cultivated land along the river banks. The table above (for Burg el Arab, a few kilometers west of Alexandria) gives an indication of conditions in average, and in bad years.

The whole of Egypt has a rainfall of 200 mm or less. The Mediterranean

[1] Harder frost may, however, occur in the uplands of eastern Egypt, and in the Sinai. The absolute minimum temperature recorded in lower Egypt is −4 °C.

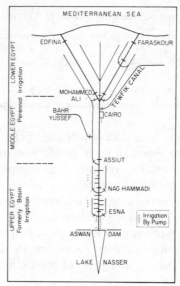

*Fig.* 17.3 Irrigation works on the Nile (mainly from H. E. Hurst).

coast receives 100–200 mm with Alexandria the wettest part of the country; and south of Cairo, the annual average falls to less than 50 mm. This is in some respects a fictitious figure, since a fairly heavy onset of rain may take place only once in 2 or 3 years; and the fact that many inhabitants of Cairo live in houses made of sun-dried mud bricks indicates the scantiness and unreliability of rainfall. Without the Nile, Egypt would be no more than a collection of oases like those of Siwa or Dakhla.

**Irrigation**

There have been two methods of irrigation in Egypt. The first, basin irrigation, was developed in the time of the Pharaohs or earlier, and consisted essentially of dividing off the fields into shallow basins by earth embankments. Floodwater then filled the basins, depositing a layer of fertile silt, and remained for several weeks. This system allowed only one crop per year, since there could be no re-watering; and moreover it could only be employed for 'winter' crops that could grow during the cool months of November–March, since planting had to be in autumn immediately following the summer flood season. Hence wheat, barley and fodder crops were best suited to basin irrigation, and the summer crops (cotton, rice, maize and millet) much less so.

Perennial irrigation involved the construction of large-scale barrages and regulator dams to control and distribute Nile water throughout the entire year. Major element was the original Aswan Dam, 2 km in length, built in 1903 on a site where an igneous dike traverses the valley to form the First Cataract, and heightened in 1912 and again in 1934. In 1970, however, the major project of the High Aswan Dam reached completion and began radically to alter the entire irrigation pattern within the lower Nile Valley. Hitherto, nothing could be done except regulate and re-allocate the flood in one particular season. Although in general the annual flood is regular, attaining 6·3 m in the old days and 4·6 m after irrigation construction, there were, as we have seen, certain significant fluctuations, with occasional failures, and over-floods. The High Dam is designed to store water from year to year, and thus obviate the need to vary the cropped area according to the flood in a given year: up to 1970 the situation was that more can be grown if the flood is high, less if it is low – since everything, in the absence of any significant rainfall, depended upon irrigation. The High Dam, 3·6 km in length and 111 m in height, is located just south of the older Aswan Dam. The new lake created behind the dam, Lake Nasser, stretches as far south as the Sudanese town of Wadi Halfa, and if the projected maximum level is attained it will eventually contain 157000 million m³ of water. In 1969 construction was far enough advanced to close the sluices and in effect terminate annual flooding of the Nile valley north of the Dam, and retain all Nile water, which is released on a controlled annual pattern throughout the year. As a result, the rest of the complicated system of barrages and canals, with a length of 25000 km, have become in effect no more than feeders and distributaries (fig. 17.3).

Before the construction of the High Dam Nile water could irrigate about 6 million feddans.[1] The extra water made available by the High Dam will enable the change-over of some 900000 feddans of basin irrigation located in Upper Egypt to perennial methods, and the irrigation of a further 1·3 million feddans in the rest of Egypt (see fig. 17.5). With this, of course, will occur the possibility of change-over to summer crops (*seifi*).

The advantage which perennial irrigation has brought to Egypt – specialist cultivation of high quality cash crops and doubling or trebling of the food supply, leading to an unparalleled growth in population – are considerable, but these have not been achieved without certain dis-advantages. In the first place, the increase in soil water due to perennial irrigation has led to a marked increase in soil salinity, because of more extensive evaporation from the soil. In some areas, particularly those given over to cotton growing, salinity has become a menace. As might be expected the Delta is the most seriously affected. Salt efflorescence occurs on the lower-lying, poorly drained parts, usually below the 7 m contour. Consequently, drainage of the soil rather than its irrigation has now become one of the most acute problems facing Egypt and is currently being given priority by the Government in its agricultural planning. By

[1]  1 feddan = 1·038 acres = 0·042 hectares.

the end of 1972 about 675000 feddans were provided with tile drains. With financial assistance from the World Bank covered drains are being installed in a further 900000 feddans in the Delta region and 500000 feddans in Upper Egypt. Research has revealed that tile drainage schemes can produce an average increase in yield of 30–35%.

Secondly, with greatly increased frequency of cropping on irrigated land, together with the shift to perennial irrigation, which greatly reduces the deposit of alluvium on the soil, soil fertility has declined in many parts, necessitating the use of artificial fertilizers. First used about 1900, superphosphates and nitrates must be applied on a generous scale, and some of these form an important element in Egyptian imports. In an effort to combat soil exhaustion, the Egyptian government laid down in 1956–60 that basically one-third of every holding should be cultivated in grain, and a further third only in cotton. This, and the new opportunities of irrigation from the High Dam, have led to a shift away from traditional methods of cultivation which tended to be based on a 2-year rotation, in favour of a less exhausting 3-year cycle.

*Two-year cycle*

November–April: wheat/clover
May–July: fallow
August–November: maize
November–February: fallow
March–September: cotton
September–November: fallow/clover

*Three-year cycle*

November–April: wheat/clover
May: fallow
June–November: rice/maize
November–April: wheat/clover
May–July: fallow/maize
July–November: maize/rice
November–March: fallow/clover
March–October: cotton

Certain other unlooked-for effects of the High Dam are already apparent. There has been scouring along some parts of the river bed below the dam, with rapid erosion here and there, instead of the silt deposition hitherto a feature; water-tables have risen in the soil, giving water-logging and salinity; and there are a number of changes in the south-eastern Mediterranean Sea due to diminished volume of Nile flow. Silt is no longer distributed along the Sinai and Negev coasts, and the sardine shoals are less in evidence, since formerly they were attracted by fresher Nile water: this has had a major effect on commercial fishing. There has also been

*Fig.* 17.4 The New Valley scheme; and planned New Towns.

an increase in the incidence of bilharzia. Furthermore, sand and other minerals have been attracted to the transmission lines of the power scheme, producing current 'shorting' of an unusual kind. Some critics have thus termed the High Dam a 'political' device rather than an economic benefit.

Following the discoveries (partly during prospection for oil) of considerable underground water in the western desert, efforts have been made to increase the cultivated area independent of the Nile irrigation system. By far the most spectacular scheme is the New Valley project which aims at reclaiming and cultivating the oasis belt of depressions in the western desert from a chain of artesian wells. The area's potential has probably been exaggerated; the project is frankly problematical in certain ways and is a high-cost matter – as is all land reclamation in Egypt. Out of a total area of about 8 million feddans about 400000 feddans may one day be cultivated. So far only about 50000 feddans have been brought

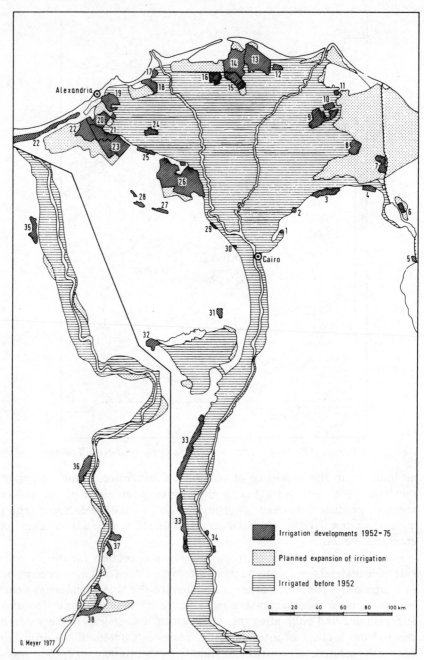

*Fig.* 17.5 Irrigation developments (data by G. Meyer).

under crops, chiefly in the Kharga and Dakhla oases. In addition, a smaller project involving about 16000 feddans has been brought into being in the Wadi Natrun using local groundwater. Ultimately it is hoped to expand this scheme to cover up to 200000 feddans. Other developments occur in the north-west coastal zone. Between 1952–1976 a total of some 912000 feddans have so far been reclaimed in Egypt: a very useful accretion, though only a partial contribution to the need for extra cultivable land.

With the completion of the High Dam scheme, maximum utilization of Nile water entering Egypt has been attained, and further developments can only involve control schemes in the higher reaches of the Nile – within East Africa, Ethiopia and the Sudan. Hence the considerable interest in Egypt in the political future of the Sudan, where a general increase in irrigation facilities could eventually reduce the volume of water available in Egypt, but where also the enormous losses by evaporation in the Sudd area could be reduced. One scheme, at Jebel Awliya in the Sudan, was undertaken solely for the benefit of Egypt, but is of relatively limited importance. Much more might be achieved by raising the level of lakes Albert (Kenya) and Tsana (Ethiopia), which would increase the flow to the main Nile. Moreover, Egypt has contributed to the Owen Falls project affecting Lake Victoria, and in 1975 agreement was reached with

---

Fig. 17.5 (Key)

1. El Gabal El Asfar
2. Enshass
3. El Moulak
4. El Manaief
5. El Suez
6. El Bohairat El Morra
7. El Verdan
8. Baher El Baker
9. El Kasabi and Sand-Sea
10. Abu El Aksar
11. El Serou

*Middle Delta*
12. El Satamony
13. Hafir Shebab El Din
14. West Rira and El Mansour
15. El Zawia
16. Shalma

*Western Delta*
17. El Boseilli
18. Edku
19. Abis

20. El Nahda and El Hagar
21. North Tahrir
22. Mariut and Mariut Extension
23. West Nubaria and Mech. Farm
24. Ferhash
25. El Bustan
26. South Tahrir and El Tahady
27. El Fetah
28. Wadi Natrun

*Middle Egypt*
29. Wardan
30. El Mansouria
31. Kom Oshin
32. Quta
33. Samalut
34. Tell El Amarna and Der Abu Hannes
35. West Tahta

*Upper Egypt*
36. Qena
37. El Rasidia and Wadi Abadi
38. Kom Ombo

Chief crops and orchards (1974)

| | Area ('ooo feddans) | Percentage of total area under crops |
|---|---|---|
| Clover | 2 797 | 25·4 |
| Maize | 1 755 | 16·0 |
| Cotton | 1 453 | 13·2 |
| Wheat | 1 370 | 12·4 |
| Rice | 1 053 | 9·5 |
| Vegetables | 808 | 7·3 |
| Millet | 499 | 4·5 |
| Other crops | 448 | 4·1 |
| Beans | 279 | 2·5 |
| Fruit crops | 273 | 2·5 |
| Sugar cane | 209 | 1·9 |
| Barley | 77 | 0·7 |
| Total | 11 021 | |

Sudan to revive the Jonglei scheme which involves the canalization of the Nile in the Sudd area, with the aim of gaining a further 18 million m³ of water at present lost annually by evaporation.

## Agriculture

The main feature of Egyptian agriculture is the important place held by cotton-growing – far greater than in most other parts of the Middle East. First started in 1821, cotton-growing for export gradually gained in importance, especially after 1900, so that by the 1950s raw cotton accounted for over 70% of Egyptian exports, and occupied 20–25% of the cultivated area. In the early 1950s the governments (Royalist and Republican) attempted to monopolize the long-staple cotton market throughout the world by reducing output, but this policy failed and expansion of cotton growing was then encouraged. In recent years, however, the area allocated to cotton has been again reduced as more land is turned over to food production, and yields per feddan and total production have declined. Egypt is the second largest cotton producer in the Middle East (after Turkey), and the region's top exporter.

As in most other Middle Eastern countries, agriculture is the largest single sector of the national economy. It occupies about half of the total labour force, earns most the country's foreign exchange, and contributes about 30% of the G.N.P. Nevertheless, an official committee of inquiry

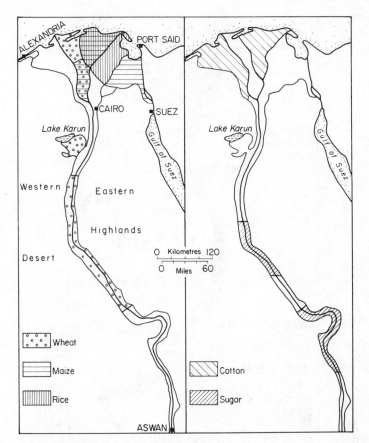

*Fig.* 17.6 Egypt: major crops.

stated that 20–25% of Egyptian cultivators were considerably under-
employed, although a major survey in the mid-60s emphasized that rural
underemployment was essentially seasonal: and there are now considerable imports of agricultural foodstuffs (accounting for about 30% of
Egypt's total import bill).

## Cotton

The reasons for the importance of this plant in Egypt are:

(1) Suitability of soil and climate. Besides the unique fertility of soil,
the long, arid summer, frost-free autumn, and 'controllability' of water
supplies from canals, are specially favourable factors. The effect of all
these is seen in the extraordinarily heavy yields obtained, which are some
of the highest in the world. Moreover, while the old Aswan Dam was

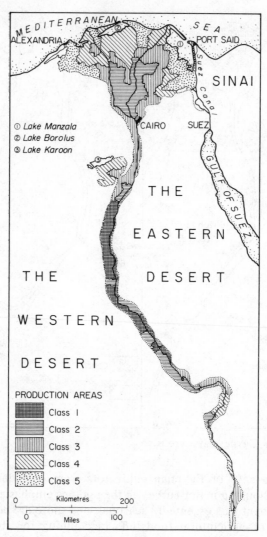

*Fig.* 17.7 Egypt: land capability.

inadequate to prevent seasonal flooding of the Delta areas before the last cotton bolls had matured, this can now be achieved with the new control of water by the High Dam.

(2) Egyptian long-staple cotton is regarded as the best in the world, and Egypt provides the largest quantity of long- and extra-long staple varieties. However, Egypt's position as the first producer has been seriously challenged by the USA, USSR, and India, and occasionally surpassed by Sudan with regard to extra-long staples.

(3) Over a century of experience, backed by careful and assiduous cultivation methods and a vigorous research programme, has led to improvements in cotton-growing over the last 20 years, and the high levels of yield that characterized cotton-growing in its early phases on new land have been regained, following a period of lower yields in the 1940s and 1950s.

Many varieties of cotton plant have in turn been introduced, but quality tended to fall off after a few years, generally because of hybridization (mixing) with other species, as the result of which the specially advantageous qualities of a particular species are lost. In a few instances degeneration has also been due to attack by insect pests. This was the case with the well-known Sakel-larides and early Giza species. Ashmouni varieties, highly cultivated in the 1950s, have similarly declined in importance. In 1974 the main varieties were Giza 67, Menoufi, Giza 68, Giza 66, and Giza 69.

A growing proportion of raw cotton is retained for home manufacture – 53% of the total crop in 1974. Indeed, because of a decline in production in 1974, 20000 bales of US short-staple cotton was imported – for the first time in the history of the Egyptian textile industry – to supply mills and ensure output of utility fabrics. Nevertheless, raw cotton still accounts for about 43% of total exports. In 1974/75 about three-quarters of all cotton exports went to east European countries, the USSR being by far the largest purchaser (38·1%) followed by Czechoslovakia (13·1%). Egypt is the world's fourth major cotton exporter after the USA, USSR and Pakistan, and there are certain manufacturing processes in which Egyptian cotton is exclusively used, e.g. in the making of aeroplane tyres, wind proof clothing and sewing thread. The entire cotton crop is sold in August, and picking is not usually completed till the end of September. Most of the crop is moved to Alexandria for export. Since 1961 when the cotton trade was nationalized and the cotton exchange closed, all cotton exports have been controlled by the state; a public organization for cotton regulates all aspects of cotton growing, marketing and manufacturing.

### Cereals

Cereals occupied 43% of the area under crops in 1974–75. Rice and maize account for 30% and 35%, respectively, of the total cereal supply with wheat now 25%, and millet and barley the remainder. The most important feature of recent years has been the greatly increased importance of rice growing, which has developed with the availability of more irrigation water from the High Dam and reclamation schemes. The area devoted to rice growing has more than trebled since 1952, and the Northern Delta governorates are the main rice-growing region. Rice is well-suited to the Delta because of its ability to produce high yields on the moderate to highly saline soils of that region. After cotton, rice is the most valuable agricultural export, and Egypt has become the world's third largest rice exporter after the United States and Thailand – a further point that distinguishes the country from others in the Middle East. Eastern Europe takes about one-half of rice exports, and the Far East about one-third. Maize and wheat in contrast are grown for internal consumption, and maize and wheat flour mixed form the staple diet. Production of both crops has increased during the last 20 years, especially maize which like rice is a summer crop; maize production almost doubled between 1952 and 1974. Maize and wheat are grown throughout the Nile valley and Delta; wheat mainly in the Northern Delta, and maize principally in the North Delta and Middle Egypt. Millet is important as an alternative summer crop, and flourishes most in Upper Egypt, where temperatures are higher; on the other hand barley, grown in drier, more difficult areas (i.e. on the margin of irrigation), continues to decline in importance.

### Other crops

Sugar cane is also of growing significance: both the area under cultivation and production have doubled since 1952. The plant grows very well and yields are well above the world average, and almost equal to those obtained in the USA. Main area is Upper Egypt where the longer, hotter summer is an advantage, and the cane ripens in a shorter time. Egypt is approaching self-sufficiency in sugar supplies which should be achieved with further expansion of cultivation following the change over from basin irrigation. Berseem, or Egyptian clover, increases the nitrogen content of the soil, and is hence widely grown as a soil regenerator, in rotation with cotton and cereals. The clover is used as animal fodder, both green (in winter) and dried (in summer). Broad beans, which also have the same properties of soil regeneration, are grown to a rather small extent partly for summer fodder, and partly for human consumption. One or other of these crops is grown by most cultivators, and the area under berseem exceeds that of any other crop, amounting to 25% of the total.

Onions and potatoes are grown on a moderate scale, with significant exports of both, especially the former. A wide variety of other vegetables are grown throughout Egypt, and market-gardening (tomatoes, root vegetables, etc.) is of considerable importance near the larger towns. On the other hand, fruit growing is rather less extensive than in other Middle East countries, but the area under cultivation and production have both increased in recent years and a valuable export trade is developing. Because of their export potential, the expansion of fruit and vegetable

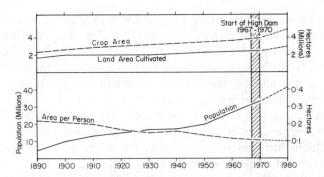

*Fig.* 17.8 Egypt: land use and population growth.

production is now a high priority objective. Foreign investment in agri-business such as building and operating refrigerator plants, preparing and packaging fresh-fruits and vegetables for export, and canning and preserving, is also being encouraged. Dates are grown all along the Nile valley, and especially in the south; oranges are produced in the Delta; and vineyards are found in the extreme north, on the cooler Mediterranean coast.

### Land capability

Official Egyptian sources have recently undertaken a division of the cultivated area of Egypt according to productivity. Five classes are recognized, number one being the most productive in terms of four basic crops: cotton, rice, wheat and sugar – here perhaps it might have been useful to include maize as well. The results are shown in fig. 17.7 which, when seen alongside the details of rural population, shows the interesting point that, whereas in Upper Egypt the better land tends to be occupied by the heavier rural population, this is by no means always the case in the delta, where much of the grade 4 and 5 land carries a higher proportion of agricultural population.

### Land reform

Since the Revolution, Egypt has carried out a series of land reforms designed to eliminate 'large' landowners. In 1952 the very big landowners (owning over 200 feddans) represented less than 0·1 % of the total number of landowners, and possessed about 20% of the cultivated land. At the other end of the spectrum only about 35% of the total cultivated land was owned by the great majority of landowners (94·4%). Under the reform law of 1952 the maximum size of individual holdings was set at 200 feddans with 100 feddans extra allowed for dependent children. In 1961 the maximum limit of individual landownership was reduced to 100 feddans, and in 1966 the limit was further reduced to 50 feddans (100 feddans for family holdings). The expropriated land is being redistributed in plots of 2–5 feddans to small tenants, farmers with less than 5 feddans, and landless labourers. By 1974 some 831 411 feddans (about 12·5% of the cultivated area) had been redistributed. However, the main pattern of landholding remains unaltered, 94·5% of all landowners still own less than 5 feddans but they now control 57·1% of the total cultivated area. All recipients of redistributed land are required to join one of the state-controlled cooperatives which are used as a channel for the distribution of credit and agricultural inputs, and as agencies for the extension of technical services. It is through the cooperative system that crop consolidation and land consolidation are being vigorously promoted. Tenancy regulations have also been improved by the reform laws including the reduction of rents and the legal protection of tenancy. Those who have benefited least from the reforms are the landless labourers who represent about one-third of the total number of rural families; another indication of extreme pressure of population on land in Egypt.

## Livestock rearing

Because of intense population pressure, most attention in Egypt is given to arable farming; but the increasing necessity of maintaining a crop rotation that includes such nitrogen-fixing plants as berseem and alfalfa is leading to a marked development of stock-raising. Within the last 30 years the number of animals kept has risen significantly; but the increase in human food supply has been proportionately much less, as most animals are used for draught purposes on farms, and meat and milk yields are low. As a result Egypt imports quantities of meat and dairy produce.

Sheep, numbering about 2 million, can be seen in most villages, where they are kept either on fallow land or on the edge of the desert. Cattle number over 2 million, but their use for ploughing reduces milk yields, and they supply only one-quarter of the total of milk consumed in Egypt. Water-buffaloes are as numerous as cattle, a fact that is hardly surprising in view of geographical conditions, and these animals supply 70% of the dairy produce of Egypt. Goats have increased in number in recent years and there are now about 1·3 million. Donkeys are still important, but camel-breeding is declining and tends to be confined to the nomadic tribes of the deserts. Official policy is to encourage the Badawin to settle. Most milk produced in Egypt is made into butter, curd or cheese. Poultry production is being expanded, and the quality and size of both birds and eggs improved. Pigeons are kept in many villages, and many owe some of their popularity to the fact that they do not always restrict their eating to the food supplied by their owners.

In the opinion of some experts, there is room for further expansion and improvement of animal husbandry in Egypt. At present, little attention is given to breeding and to improving stocks; but with the extension of crop-growing during the summer, which is the main season of difficulty to animal herders, increased supplies of fodder are now available throughout the year.

### Minerals

Egypt has a fair range of mineral deposits, some of which, like zinc, barytes and magnetite, are on a very small scale; others are more important. Chief resources in order of exploitation value are petroleum, phosphates and iron ore. Mining and quarrying (mainly for hard stone, salt and limestone for cement) contributed 9% of total exports in 1974, and, despite the loss of Sinai after June 1967, efforts have been made with success to replace these losses. Crude oil production expanded rapidly in the 1960s, reaching 14 million tons in 1976, and petroleum has become the chief mineral export. The Gulf of Suez is the main production area and includes the important El-Morgan, Ramadan and July fields. In addition the Sinai fields of Abu Rudeis and Bel Ayim were reclaimed following the interim peace agreement with Israel in 1975. Oil has also been discovered in the Western Desert (Alamein, Yedma, Abu Gharadik and Razzak fields) as well as natural gas (at Abu Qir). Oil and gas have also been found recently in the Nile Delta at Abu Madi. Exploration activity is being expanded following participation agreements between the Ministry of Petroleum and a number of foreign oil companies, and estimates suggest that Egypt could be producing 1 million barrels a day by 1980. Phosphates are mined near Isna and Safaga on the Red Sea (estimated reserves 180 million tons) and at Hamrawein. Rich deposits estimated at 1000 million tons have been discovered at Abu Tartur in the Western Desert, and detailed studies for a rail link to the port of Safaga have been started. Development of the Abu Tartur mine represents the biggest single investment in the industrial sector under the Five Year Plan 1976–1980. Discoveries have recently been made in the Mahamid district in the Nile valley. Plans are in hand to expand production (535 000 tons in 1974) generally in order to gain foreign currency, Australia and the Soviet Union being chief customers. Egypt itself is in need of nitrates rather than phosphatic fertilizers.

Iron ore was first mined in the Aswan area where reserves of up to 1000 million tons of moderately good ore occur close to the surface; production reached up to 500 000 tons/year. In recent years, the main source of iron ore has been the higher-quality deposits from the Behariya oasis, which is now linked by rail and road to the Helwan iron and steel complex. Iron ore production in 1974 was 1·3 million tons. Ferrous sands also occur in fair quantity near Alexandria, and these are in process of exploitation for industrial purposes (chiefly in the manufacture of paint).

Coal deposits, estimated at 80 million tons, have been found near Suez. Manganese deposits are located in the Eastern Desert and in some parts of Sinai. Chrome is being exploited in the Eastern Desert, where deposits of tantalum and molybdenum have also been found. Salt is produced in substantial quantities from the Mex salt lakes (Alexandria) (552 000 tons in 1975), and most of the planned increase in production will be exported. Exploitation by quarrying, simple mining or even collection includes glass sand, dolomite, marble, talc, gypsum, pumice, foundry sand, gold and feldspar. In general, these activities are on a scale larger than in neighbouring countries, but as some of them are undertaken to avoid imports, cost is not always the first consideration.

### Industry

The last 50 years have seen the rise of a number of industries in Egypt. Initial impetus was given by civilian shortages and military needs during 1914–18, when a number of local activities were started, chiefly concerned with textiles, foodstuffs and chemicals. After 1918, certain of these industries proved uneconomic and disappeared; but some survived, and further development took place when Egypt ended Capitulations in 1930, and was henceforward free to erect tariff barriers to protect her home markets against foreign imports.

During the Second World War, an even larger trade 'boom' occurred, with almost all Egyptian manufacturing plant working at full capacity. After 1945 there was some falling off in local production, with a number of uneconomic marginal companies forced to cease production; but in general the level of industrialization remained much greater. A considerable further impetus was given by the Suez War of 1956; and since that time a drive towards self-sufficiency resulted in an intensive industrialization programme. Egypt is now one of the most industrialized countries in the Middle East, and the second largest industrial state in Africa after the Republic of South Africa. In recent years, however, Egyptian industry has been held back by lack of foreign exchange and some excess capacity resulting from shortages of spare parts and raw materials. There are hopes that Egypt's new 'open door policy' and the creation of industrial free zones will attract foreign capital from the Arab oil producers and from the West for further industrial expansion, taking advantage of cheap labour and a favourable location for export to the rich and expanding markets in the oil-producing countries. Already Egyptian industry accounts for 22% of gross domestic production, and provides an increasing exportable surplus; manufactured goods represented about one-third of total exports in 1974. The number of industrial workers has more than doubled since 1952, but is still only about 1 million, whilst industrial production has almost quadrupled.

An important aspect of industrial expansion has been the increase in the availability of electric power. The decision to build the High Aswan Dam was as much related to the development of cheap hydro-electric energy for industry as to improving agriculture: with the cost of land reclamation approaching $2000 per feddan, agricultural return on the capital invested in the High Dam might well be financially very small – great hope is thus placed on the industrial aspect deriving from new, cheap electric power. All twelve turbines in the dam's power station are now working, and the station's generating capacity (10000 million kWh) exceeds the 6102 million kWh provided in the whole country in 1967, mainly from thermal stations with some hydro-electric power from the old Aswan Dam. Transmission lines carry the current from the Dam site to Cairo and the Delta, and plans are underway to develop a national power network. However, the demands of heavy industry, and the programme to extend electric power to all Egyptian villages has emphasized the need for more power generation than the High Dam can supply. Consequently, the possibility of nuclear energy is being explored in agreement with the USA, and the implementation of the Qattara Depression Scheme (to generate energy by flooding the depression with water from the Mediterranean) is being speeded up.

Egypt has a diversified industrial structure and many intersectoral and inter-industry linkages have developed. Textiles and food processing dominate the industrial sector and together account for over half of the total value of industrial output. Cotton textile manufacturing has long been and remains the largest single industrial activity, producing 25% of the total value of industrial output and absorbing just over one-half of the industrial labour force. The main textile centres are located in the Delta at Mahalla el Kubra and Kafr el Dawar. The former town now ranks as one of the more significant cotton textile centres of the world, and a considerable export trade in partly finished and finished cotton textiles has grown up. Production has increased dramatically since 1952, and exports at £104 million in 1974 (47% of all industrial exports) are by far the largest manufactured item. Food-processing ranks closely second to cotton textiles as an industrial activity, and includes sugar-refining, oil-pressing, milling, canning, making of wheat pastes, etc. Together the textile and food processing industries provide almost two-thirds of Egypt's industrial exports.

An iron and steel complex has been established at Helwan just south of Cairo using Aswan hydro-electric power and iron ore from the Behariya oasis. It has a capacity of 900000 tons a year to be raised to over 2 million tons by 1982. The steel is used in the production of consumer durables for the domestic market. An aluminium plant was opened at Nag Hammadi in 1976 using imported Australian and Guinean bauxite; there are also plans to establish an aluminium smelter. Chemicals are produced in increasing quantities, principally superphosphates and nitrate fertilizer. The first stage of the Talkha fertilizer plant was opened in 1976, and the capacity of the chemical industry will increase considerably with the completion of this project; other plants are planned at Abu Qir and Abu Zabaal. The two oil refineries at Suez were damaged during the conflict with Israel in 1967, and after 1969 they were dismantled and moved inland to Musturud near Cairo. The Mex refinery near Alexandria was enlarged, and new refineries were opened at Amiriyah (near Alexandria) in 1972 and at Tanta in 1973. As part of the reconstruction programme for the Canal Zone, the refineries and related industries at Suez are being rebuilt. There is a wide range of electrical production – motors, lamps, meters, pumps, etc.; many consumer items ranging from motor tyres to bicycles and paper are also produced and radio and television apparatus assembled. Another feature is the extensive assembly of motor vehicles mainly for the internal market but with some exports. Fiat cars, for example, known locally as the Nasser, are assembled in Egypt.

Much industry is located in or near Cairo, but there is a scatter over other parts, particularly in the north and west of the Delta. Cement-making and food processing tend to spread over the whole country. If the ambitious reconstruction and development programme for the Suez Canal zone is successfully accomplished the canal will become one of Egypt's major industrial axes.

One interesting activity is the film industry located near Giza (Cairo). Egypt shares or at times leads in the market for Arabic films, which have a circulation throughout most of the Arab lands from Morocco to China, and also in the USA and the Argentine. This activity has grown up as a complement to the film industries of America and Europe, the products of which are not always to Arab taste.[1] In some years, Egypt makes as many films as Britain; and one of its former stars is Omar Sharif. Budgets are small, but the climate is a considerable advantage.

One casualty of the 1967 war was the tourist industry which up to that time drew over ½ million visitors every year, some of them very wealthy.

[1] In particular, 'psychological' dramas, Western racial angles and war films are not greatly liked. Amatory scenes and prolonged kissing are also at times regarded as indelicate by Arab audiences.

The war effectively halved the intake of tourists in less than 2 years, and it was not until 1974 that the number of tourists surpassed the 1966 figure. Almost a million tourists, the majority from other Arab countries rather than the West, visited Egypt in 1976, spending an estimated £E 128 million. An expansion programme is underway to accommodate 1·7 million tourists by 1980. Most of the development is centred in and around Cairo with the north coast as the other big development area.

Until 1952 Egyptian industry was modelled on *laissez-faire* capitalist principles, with dependence on raw cotton exports as the mainstay of the economy and considerable foreign ownership. There then followed a period of increasing state intervention, culminating in extensive nationalization after 1956 of both foreign and internally owned enterprises. For political reasons, too, Egypt developed commercial links with east Europe, and the abortive link with Syria as the UAR strengthened Egyptian determination to pursue radical policies in which state direction and supervision would have the major part. Accordingly, industry, trade and finance are largely, but not totally, nationalized; but agriculture and landholding are not. Hence it could be said that, as agriculture is still by far the largest sector, and contributes most as a single activity to the national output, Egypt does not possess a really socialist economy. In the words of P. O'Brien, what exists is a 'mixture of primitive capitalism public and state enterprise, managerial capitalism, consumers' and producers' cooperatives, and . . . elements of syndicalism'. Following the June war of 1967, attempts were made to expand the privately owned sector, and these efforts gained momentum after 1970 when the Sadat government embarked on a policy of 'economic liberalisation' in order to encourage Arab and foreign investment in the Egyptian economy. Virtually all large-scale manufacturing enterprises remain state-owned and operated, but some 15000 small industrial units in the private sector nevertheless account for 25% of the total value of industrial production, produce a quarter of Egypt's industrial exports, and employ almost half the industrial labour force.

Some Egyptian industries really depend for existence on high tariff protection and war demand: these cannot normally expect to expand beyond the home market. Others (e.g. cotton textiles) clearly do not. There are major shortcomings in the management of many sections of Egyptian industry, and cost per unit of output are high. The cost of assembling a Fiat car in Egypt is still much greater than the cost of making the same model in Italy, even though wages and salaries are much lower in Egypt's motor industry. High costs partly reflect an underutilization of capacity because the domestic market is limited. Also, industries such as the Helwan iron and steel plant have been unable to produce at an output point where they could achieve economies of scale.

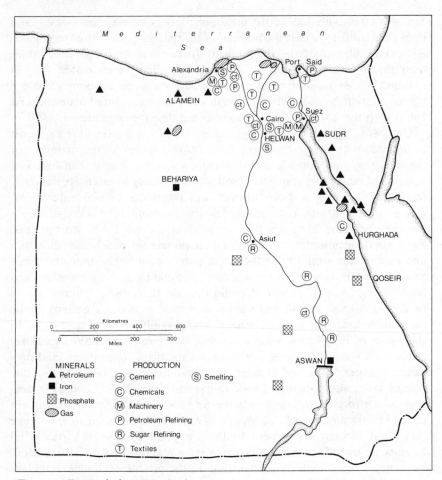

*Fig.* 17.9 Egypt: industry and minerals.

The economy as a whole remains very weak, and in 1975 Egypt joined the ranks of the UNs 'most seriously affected countries' requiring special emergency international assistance. At the root of Egypt's poverty lies its expanding population which is growing at about 2·2% per annum. There were 37 million Egyptians in 1975 compared with only 10 million in 1900; however, while population has increased four-fold, cultivated land has expanded scarcely 50%. Egypt's foreign debts are enormous, and the burden of repayment is a major constraint on economic development. Military debts arising from years of armed confrontation with Israel, are particularly onerous, and scarce resources continue to be diverted to defence spending – about a third of G.N.P. in 1974–77. The need to expand the defence budget, and the government's commitment to providing jobs for the growing number of new graduates and secondary school leavers, mainly in administration and the services, has led to considerable increases in public consumption and a sharp reduction in investment in productive sectors of the economy. The new policy of economic liberalization and foreign investment alone will not solve Egypt's complex economic problems and may lead to serious social injustice and unrest. Many institutional changes are necessary together with an immense injection of capital directed to productive sectors and to the infrastructure. The current Five Year Plan (1976–1980) aims to invest some £E 8000 million. The biggest allocation is to industry (£E 2100 million) followed by transport, communications and the Suez Canal, reconstruction and housing, public services, agriculture and irrigation, oil and electricity.

## Communications and towns
### Railways

The railway network of Egypt is remarkably complete, and on the basis of length of line (4385 km) per inhabited area, Egypt is as well supplied as France. It should, however, be recalled that less than 10% of Egypt is inhabited. Railways were built in the nineteenth century, and added to during 1914–18, so that all parts of the Nile valley are linked by a standard gauge system. Cairo is the hub of the modern rail network. Most lines are double track (unusual in the Middle East) even as far south as Aswan. A major rehabilitation and modernization programme is being implemented with financial and technical assistance from the World Bank. The main lines, which are state-owned, are supplemented by light railways which serve the Fayyum and parts of the delta not touched by main lines. The Port Said railway line, closed since 1967, was reopened in 1976. A new 430 km line has been opened linking the iron ore mines at the Behariya oasis with Helwan, and there are plans for a rail link between the Abu Tartur phosphate mine and the port of Safaga on the Red Sea.

### Roads

About one-third of Egypt's 25000 km of roads are 'surfaced', the rest being usually of earth. Cairo is linked to north and west by new motorways, built in 1960. A four-lane highway connects Cairo and Alexandria. The main artery southwards from Cairo to Aswan is still not good in places, and deviations are necessary, but it is now planned to build a motorway, over 1000 km long, between Cairo and Khartoum, routed via the oases – south of Qattara through the New Valley to Aswan. This would obviate using the valuable Nile land. A long-term plan has

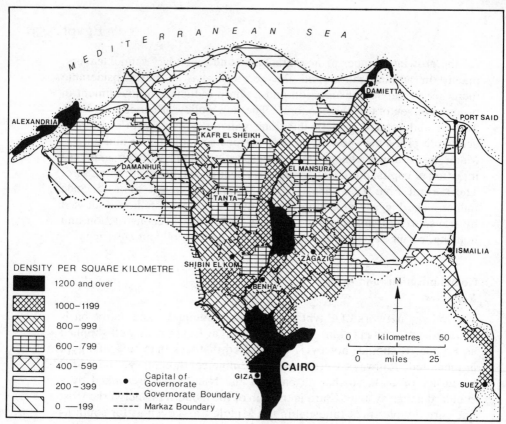

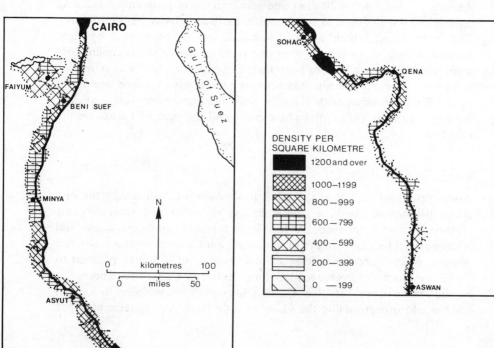

*Fig.* 17.10 Egypt: population density 1976.

been drawn up to surface a total of 4000 km of dust roads between populated centres in the three Suez Canal governorates, and the World Bank have agreed to finance a road linking Port Said to Cairo.

## River transport

From the geography of the country, there would seem to be much scope for this; but water transport is less developed than might be expected, because of the importance given to irrigation, which means a low water level and many works (weirs, bridges, etc.) that impede traffic. Nevertheless, a considerable amount of raw cotton, some of the iron ore from Aswan and quantities of vegetables still move by river, and inland water transport is being expanded to relieve traffic on roads and railways. Navigable waterways total about 3100 km including the Nile between Cairo and Aswan, and the Nubariya, Bahr Youssef and Cairo–Ismailia canals. Now, about half the total freight in Egypt moves by road, with the rest more or less shared equally between railways and waterways.

The Suez Canal, closed in 1967 as a result of the Arab–Israeli war, was reopened in June 1975 and restored to its full pre-1967 capacity by the end of July. The reopening forms part of an ambitious reconstruction and development programme for the entire Canal Zone which includes the creation of free zones and an industrial base along the canal. Traffic has gradually built up, but by the end of the first full year of operation it was still only about half pre-1967 levels. Revenues for the first year after reopening amounted to £130 million – less than half that expected by the Suez Canal Authority. Tanker traffic represents less than one-third of the total tonnage in transit compared with two-thirds in 1966. In contrast dry cargo traffic is up by more than half on pre-closure days. In order to encourage more tanker traffic, the first stage of widening and deepening the Canal is underway and by 1978 ships of 53 ft draught will be able to pass including 150000 dwt tankers fully laden and 270000 dwt in ballast. Plans for the second stage of deepening to 67 ft in order to accommodate fully laden 270000 tonners have been prepared, but their implementation remains problematical. After long delays the Suez–Mediterranean oil pipeline (SUMED) went into operation at the end of 1976. The pipeline transports crude oil brought by tanker to Ain Sokhna, on the Red Sea, 60 km south of Suez, 320 km to Sidi Krer west of Alexandria, and can handle 80 million tons a year. It seems unlikely that both an enlarged canal and the new oil pipeline can be made to pay simultaneously.

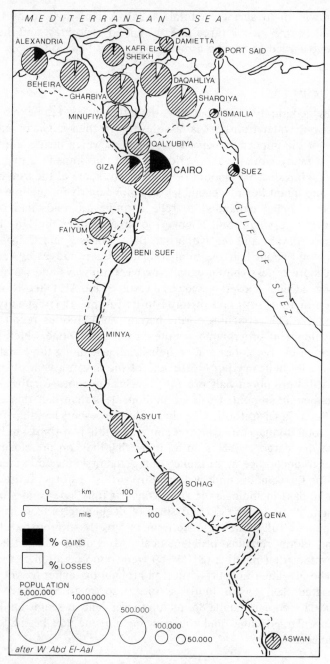

*Fig.* 17.11 Egypt: population change by governorate to 1965 (data by W. Abd el Aal).

*Towns*

About 45% of Egypt's population may be classified as urban. Cairo and Alexandria, as the capital and chief port, the centres of administration and the location of the majority of industry, dominate the urban structure and dwarf all other Egyptian cities. Cairo is located at the head of the Delta, where the Nile waters divide at a spot (as with Paris) where an island provides a convenient crossing place. This nodal site on the border between the two major regions of Upper and Lower Egypt has commended itself to most rulers of Egypt: though Cairo itself dates only from the eleventh century, being founded in 1069 by a former Christian slave, Al Siqilli (the Sicilian), who as a Moslem general conquered Egypt for his master, the Caliph. The town was later much altered by Saladin, the Kurdish opponent of Richard Coeur de Lion. Centrality (between the two major regions of the lower Nile Valley, near the productive Fayyum area, and well placed for east–west communications into Libya and the Sinai) makes Cairo a distribution and market centre for the whole of Egypt. As compared with Alexandria, which does not lie in a particularly productive region and is to some extent isolated by large brackish lakes, Cairo is far better placed for internal exchange; and most of the foodstuffs of the Delta are marketed there. Rail communication with Alexandria, Port Said and Port Tewfik (with a branch at Kantara across the Suez Canal to the Sinai and Gaza) has allowed the import of fuel and raw materials, so that although there is no outstanding richness in natural resources, Cairo has developed a diversity of industries, chiefly concerned with processing of agricultural materials, textiles in cotton and wool (though as we have seen, most of these are at Mehella), iron and steel, engineering, electronics, a wide range of electrical and consumer goods, oil-pressing, printing, cement-making and the other activities of a major capital city.

Like Tehran, Cairo has developed as the real metropolis of its country but, with a population in 1975 of 5·8 million (8·4 million in the Greater Cairo region) it is now by far the largest town in Africa, and the largest in the Mediterranean, overtopping Rome in population. Unlike Tehran, there is an ancient centre, the Citadel, built at the time of Cairo's foundation, and the centre is well built and laid out, with an opera house for which *Aida* was commissioned. War stresses have exerted a deleterious effect on appearance, as has also the disappearance of a former wealthy class of inhabitant, and the rest of the city consists largely of construction in ferro-concrete or mud-brick. Heliopolis, the site of a Pharaonic temple, is now a suburb, as is Giza, the site of the Pyramids, and the conurbation extends practically to the iron and steel centre of Helwan. Cairo is the educational centre of Egypt, with several universities,

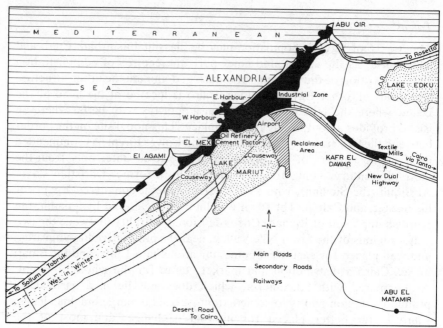

*Fig.* 17.12 Alexandria.

one of which, Al Azhar, is the best known, going back in its origins to the time of Al Siqilli. Very many students come to Cairo from other Arab-speaking countries. Chronic overcrowding and congestion in the capital (over a million people for want of a home live among the tombs built beneath the Mokattam Hills east of Cairo and known as the 'City of the Dead') has prompted the decision to create a number of satellite towns around Cairo, including Sadat city on the Cairo–Alexandria desert road, and a new industrial city, 54 km east of Cairo on the road to Ismailia.

Alexandria (pop. 2·3 million in 1975) is the chief port of Egypt, and handles four-fifths of both exports and imports as well as the bulk of the passenger traffic. There are numerous cotton ginneries, which for the half of the year following the harvest provide occupation for 40 000 people. Rice-husking is another activity, though this is also spread amongst the smaller towns of the northern Delta – Damietta, Mansura and Rosetta. The city lies close to a small promontory of land that runs north to join a small island; in this way there is a kind of natural quay, and a double sea frontage, with an eastern and a western harbour. Much land has recently been reclaimed for agriculture, so the formerly extensive Lake Mariut is now very much smaller. Petrochemical industries, refining and motor assembly plants have developed in the last few years, and there

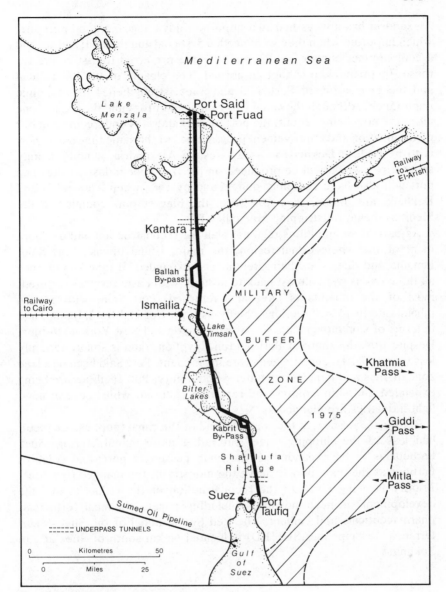

*Fig.* 17.13  The Suez Canal.

is a wide spread of manufacturing activity. In some respects the situation of Alexandria in the extreme north-west of the Delta (so as to avoid the danger of silting by Nile waters) produced a certain isolation from the main economic currents, which, since the construction of the Suez Canal, tended to be stronger in the centre and east of the country. However,

Alexandria has always had two important advantages: a good port site, which imported when they were needed first coal and then oil; and second a cool summer climate, which makes it the preferred tourist centre for those Egyptians who cannot go abroad. The closure of the Suez Canal and the evacuation of Port Said and Suez, strengthened its economic importance. Although the canal was reopened in 1975 and the Canal Zone cities are now being rebuilt, the port of Alexandria is undergoing a major modernization and improvement programme. At the same time a new port is to be built at Dekheila in a bay west of Alexandria, handing mainly sponge iron which will be produced on the free-zone industrial site. The port will also have container quays, and by 1984 when Alexandria and Dekheila are linked, they will form the biggest port complex in the Mediterranean, outstripping Marseilles-Fos.

As part of an ambitious regional plan for reconstruction and development of the whole Canal region, the major Canal towns – Port Said, Ismailia and Suez – are being rebuilt and expanded. By the end of 1976 all three towns were almost back to normal, with basic services restored; most of the inhabitants have also returned. Port Said, with 250000 inhabitants in 1966, functions chiefly as a port of call for shipping, and in terms of ship movements surpassed London and New York up to 1967. Despite this, the share of Port Said in Egyptian trade is small, normally less than 10%. To encourage private investment, Port Said became a free zone in 1975 and imports can enter without duty. Port facilities are being expanded and ship-building and repairing restored, whilst several new, light industries are planned.

Before 1967, Suez, at the southern end of the canal (pop. est. 203000), had less of the shipping trade, but rather more manufacturing. Suez harbour is to be expanded as the main passenger port, and Adabiya harbour as the main port to serve the industry of the planned free zone. Priority is being given to the reconstruction of the refineries and the development of new industries including paper, chemical fertilizers, pharmaceuticals and cement. The Red Sea terminal of the Suez–Mediterranean oil pipeline (SUMED) is located 60 km south of Suez at Ain Sokhna.

# 18 Libya

Both physically and from the human aspect, Libya shows greater geographical affinities to the north-east of Africa rather than to the north-west. In structure, it repeats many, though not all of the basic patterns characteristic of Egypt – a tabular plateau formation influenced by faulting, warping and differential erosion – rather than showing the intense folding characteristic of Morocco and Algeria. Climatically also, there is much resemblance to Egypt with, however, occasional and restricted zones of distinctly heavier rainfall; whilst ethnically it derives in geatest part from Arabia, and forms a stronghold of orthodox Moslem culture. Yet Libya also has an individuality of its own. It is far from being a mere prolongation or continuation of Egypt; and whilst it lacks the clear unity deriving from a single large river valley, a more limited and tenuous social cohesion is conferred by the existence of almost impassable 'sand seas' to the east on the frontiers with Egypt, by the Tibesti uplands in the south, and by irregular and partly sand-covered terrain in the west. Within this loosely containing physical frame have developed distinctive human responses, ranging from the unusual style of dress to the separate sectarian outlook of the Sanussi movement. Recent oil discoveries have assisted the process of consolidation towards a national state and have transformed the country's geographical face, whilst under the leadership of Colonel Muammar Gaddafi Libya has become an unpredictable and turbulent factor in international politics.

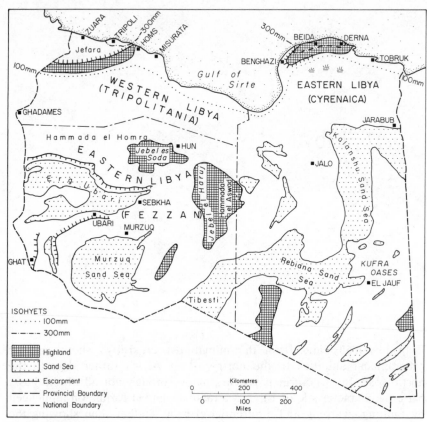

*Fig.* 18.1 Libya: physiography.

## Physical

Unlike Egypt with its river valley, Libya may be regarded as in large measure a part of the unaltered Gondwana plateau. This complex of ancient metamorphosed series outcrops to form much of the Tibesti and associated ranges in the far south, and underlies much of the centre and south of the country. Oscillation of this plateau surface at various geological periods has led to the accumulation of aeolian and marine sediments in layers of varying thickness, and more developed in the north. These are for the most part horizontal or only slightly tilted and deformed, the more ancient outcropping generally in the south, and the more recent in the north. Much fracturing has, however, taken place, with associated vulcanicity (mainly but not wholly of the sheet type), so that extensive *harras* occur, especially in the north-west.

The whole of the pre-Cambrian basement has been generally down-warped towards the geosynclinal of the Mediterranean zone, and dis-

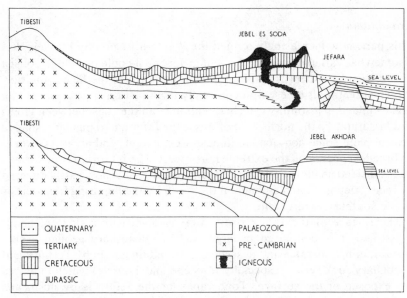

*Fig.* 18.2 Libya: sketch of structural elements.

location becomes more prominent in the coastal areas fronting the Mediterranean. Here, faulting with downthrow to the north is the most important feature; extensive fault-scarps lie actually at the coast in Cyrenaica, whilst in Tripolitania these strike inland from the coast at Homs–Misurata, giving rise to a plateau-edge that is increasingly set back from the sea coast.

In addition, there has been a limited but significant degree of buckling of the sedimentary rock layers, producing shallow anticlines and synclines. As in Arabia, these sedimentary layers above the basement complex extend uninterruptedly over many kilometres, with important results: because of the northward dip, water and petroleum have accumulated at shallow depths chiefly along the northern margins. There are hence broad physical and structural similarities between Libya and the Arabian peninsula. If the former could be regarded as re-orientated through 90°, thus making the Tibesti range run from north to south instead of its true direction east–west, then one might equate the Tibesti with the western uplands of Asir and the Hijaz in Arabia. There is the same narrow upland zone, dropping gradually to a varied plateau surface which shows extensive cuesta formation, and is covered extensively, though by no means entirely, by loose sand. Lava areas occur, diversified by ridges of cones; and there is even a certain limited parallel to the detached and folded outlier of the Jebel Akhdar of Oman in the Jebel Akhdar of Cyrenaica – though in the latter the intensity of folding is much less.

*Tripolitania*

This part, now increasingly termed the Western Region by Libyans, has a somewhat varied physiography, but in general it could be held to consist of an irregular ascent from sea-level in the north to the higher interior. Principal feature is an escarpment, really the limb of a large crescent that strikes inland in a south-westerly direction from the coast between Homs and Misurata. To the north-west of this is the Jefara, a triangularly shaped coastal plain some 300–400 km in east–west extent, and about 150 km at its broadest portion in the extreme north-west. The Jefara is a zone formed by a subsided shallow anticline of sedimentary rocks, now partly covered by recent deposits, and defined on the south by the imposing fault-scarps of the southern escarpment.

The surface of the Jefara rises from sea-level with a slope of about 1:350 and it is composed in large part of Quaternary aeolian sands, gravels, conglomerates and desertic crusts and underlain by Tertiary and Secondary rock series (especially Miocene and Triassic) which in places are exposed at the surface. Topography of the Jefara is by no means uniform: near the coast in some places are extensive dunes; and again inland, especially in the centre and west, loose sand areas occur and build up into ridges and furrows.

The southern escarpment runs inland from the Homs area, and then swings northwards into Tunisia as far as Gabès. The Tripolitanian portion of the arc is by no means regular: in the extreme east near Homs it tends to be fairly sharply defined by straight fault-scarps, but its maximum elevation is not much more than 300 m. In the centre (i.e. between Garian and Jefren), it reaches over 750 m, and its original cliff-like formation has been broken down by many *wadis*, so that there is a more irregular edge, with numerous projecting tongues of upland. Further west, relief is again more subdued, with a general maximum height of about 650 m. Parts of the escarpment are fissured and intersected by lava flows which have locally raised summits by 200–300 m, so that an occasional peak of over 750 m can occur. This is particularly true of the Garian region, where vulcanicity is very prominent. Heavier dissection by several larger northward-running *wadis* has split the entire escarpment into a series of somewhat distinct massifs, each of which has a local name – successively westward from Homs, the Jebels Misurata, Tarhuna, Garian and Nefusa, all of which are, however, usually referred to collectively as 'the Jebel'.

East of Homs as far as Misurata there is a zone of somewhat broken country where the fault-scarps reach the sea; and further east still the land rises very gradually and without major discontinuity from a low-lying coastal plain. This is the Sirtica area, of low relief, land forms being produced by aeolian deposition and the occurrence of marine terraces here and there on a small scale.

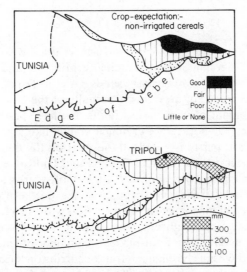

*Fig.* 18.3 The Jefara of Tripolitania.

South of the Jebel area occurs an extensive plateau – *hamad* or stony desert, composed of exfoliated materials upon a partly sandstone and partly karstic surface. In places, also, particularly towards the south-east, there are extensive basaltic exposures, with here and there, lava cones singly or in groups. These latter may form definite ridges that sometimes reach 300 m above the general plateau level, which is 400–500 m above sea-level. Local names indicate the differences in structure and geology: *hamada el homra* (red stony desert), *Jebel es Soda* (black hills), etc.

### The Fezzan

Further south, still, the general level falls and passes into a series of extensive basins and depressions, some irregular in shape, others oval and aligned very generally in an east-north-east:west-south-west direction, and enclosed by rocky ridges, with loose sand in the lower parts. This is the Fezzan, collectively a series of artesian basins where, because of shallow water-tables, oasis cultivation is possible and which form 'islands' in the surrounding sandy and stony desert. Sebha and Murzuq are most important of these basins, which lie in a rough arc from north-east to south-west. Many other water-bearing zones also occur, the most distant being that of Gat, in the extreme south-west corner of Libya near the frontier with Algeria. Perspective is perhaps necessary here: despite the large scale and the intrinsic physical and human interest of the Fezzan, and despite its large territorial area (much greater than that of Tripolitania), it has no more than about 112 000 inhabitants, over two-thirds being oasis cultivators.

*Cyrenaica*

Westward of Egypt the Archaean platform is thickly covered by later sedimentary and aeolian series, principally Miocene and Eocene lime-stones, with overlying Quaternary sands. As in Tripolitania, marked faulting has occurred, but here this is actually at the coast, with a more intricate development of minor cross-faults that have produced bays and inlets. Consequently, northern Cyrenaica stands like a promontory into the Mediterranean, partly isolated on the west by the Gulf of Sirte, and to a smaller degree by the Gulf of Bomba and Gulf of Sollum, with its northern side dropping by a series of steep fault-scarps to the Mediter-ranean. Although by trend and disposition the northern uplands might on the topographical map suggest a connection with Asia Minor or Sicily, folding is in fact largely absent and existing land forms are due to differential movement along fault-planes. A number of small sub-regions may be discerned within Cyrenaica – four occurring on the northern flanks of the massif, and three on the southern edge.

(*a*) *The north* Here the edge of the uplands has been broken by fissuring into several steps, giving a series of fault-scarps or ledges that face north and west. The lowest step, sometimes spoken of as El Sahel, is a narrow and discontinuous coastal plain which is most developed in the Gulf of Sirte and the Gulf of Bomba. It reaches its maximum extent (17 km) near Benghazi, but is sometimes entirely absent further north. Because of this, routes cannot follow the coast, but must be kept inland, particularly towards the north-east. In the neighbourhood of Benghazi and Tocra brackish *sabkha* occurs, fed by seepage from the Mediterranean. Brackish lakes or marshes during winter, the *sabkha* dries out in the summer with some salt effloresecence, hence the plain is less exploited than one might expect, and cultivation is limited to certain parts only.

The second step (El Arqab) appears as a series of ridges in the east, and as a flatter, more developed and open terrace: the plain of Al Marj (Barce) on the south-west. In the east, consequent stream drainage from the interior uplands has heavily dissected the ridges, producing a tangled country of deep *wadis* and isolated hills. Although scattered patches of alluvium may be found on some *wadi* floors, most *wadis* are in general too bare of soil for extensive human occupation, and are covered by *maquis* or scrub.

The third step comprises a moderately high plateau, broad and rolling in the west (inland from Benghazi) but increasingly narrow towards the east, where it rises to just under 700 m above sea-level, and forms in its extreme eastern portion the small dissected ridge of El Hamrin, which is the highest part of Cyrenaica. By reason of its green vegetation cover, the entire plateau is often termed the Jebel Akhdar.

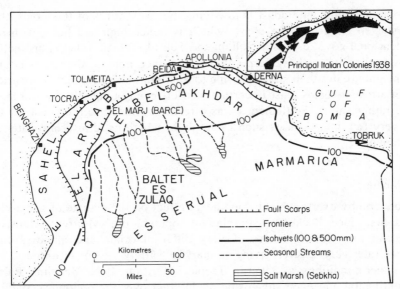

*Fig.* 18.4 Northern Cyrenaica.

(*b*) *The south* To the south of the Jebel Akhdar, the surface slopes
gradually down to the main Saharan plateau. Immediately below the crest
of the Jebel lie a number of deep, southward-running *wadis* that were
developed at an earlier period and are now either occupied by streams
for a few weeks or days only in each year, or else completely dry. This
eroded topography is a remarkable indication of the climate which has
supervened in the Middle East, since no present-day stream could
possibly cut such deep clefts. Further south still, relief is gentler, and
playas – shallow, alluvium-filled basins – separated by low irregular
ridges, with, now and again, a larger hill, are the main features. The
largest playa is the Baltet ez Zulaq, which has several *wadis* and streams
draining into it, and the entire region is termed Es Serual.

Finally, the playa region gives way to true desert – at first formed of
masses of stones with a thin layer of sand. In the extreme south,
however, sand predominates, until in the heart of the eastern Sahara,
we reach the Sand Sea of Calanshio. This consists of many thousands
of square kilometres of mobile sand, with dunes that reach hundreds of
metres in height. Very occasionally, there occurs a lowland basin (e.g.
Kufra) where artesian water is available, and where a very limited degree
of human settlement is therefore possible.

East of the Gulf of Bomba, in the region known as Marmarica, the
variety of topography which is characteristic of central and western
Cyrenaica does not occur. Instead there is a simpler *cuesta* succession
of north-facing scarps rising in a series of shallow steps, or low ridges.

Beyond Sollum, the coast is low-lying; but westwards of this point, the first step occurs at the coast, which is hence high and bold, with an occasional cove, e.g. as at Sollum and Tobruk. Inland, relief is distinctly lower than in north-western Cyrenaicas, since none of the ridges attain a height greater than 500 m. Owing to this, Marmarica is much more arid; but artesian basins exist in certain districts even though their water may be rather saline. Settlement is, as a result, confined to the coast, or to a very few inland oases such as Jarabub, where good artesian water is available.

### Climate

Topography exerts a highly significant effect on the climate of Libya. In the first place, because of its relatively open nature, with few extensive upland ranges, air masses of very different origin and qualities can penetrate very easily, giving a marked variety (even abruptness) in weather conditions, as Saharan, Tropical Maritime, Polar Maritime, Polar Continental and even sub-Arctic air interact over the region. Secondly, position in relation to north-west Africa and the Mediterranean Sea (it should be noted that the coast of Libya is far from straight), together with moderately varied relief, produce certain regional differences. Because of Tunisia and Algeria, the extreme north-west of Tripolitania lies in a definite 'rain-shadow' relative to the moisture-bearing north-westerlies, whilst on the other hand the promontory of northern Cyrenaica, partly surrounded by sea, is much better watered, with its highest points receiving as much as 350–500 mm of rain annually.

Chief feature is, of course, aridity; but along the coast there is a zone of distinctly higher rainfall, brought by depressions that pass along or near the seaboard; and these, as we have noted earlier (chapter 3), can deepen appreciably in the Gulf of Sirte. But these depressions are not always well established, and because of the outward-jutting mass of Tunisia may pass well to the north in a particular season, resulting in drought for the whole of Libya. In addition, extremely hot continental air can flow northwards from the central Sahara, and its normally high temperatures and low humidity are intensified by adiabatic heating on general descent from the high interior to the coast. Variable temperature and rainfall conditions (distinctly more so than in Egypt) are hence a feature of the north in Libya. About twice every 10 years, and sometimes in successive seasons, there is a pronounced failure of the rains. Tripolitania is, on the whole, rather hotter and more arid, and there is greater liability to disastrous sand winds (ghibli). These occur in a severe form on average seven times per annum on the coast, and twelve to fourteen times at some distance inland on the Jefara, whilst moderate

Climatic data: representative stations in Libya
*Temperature (°C) and rainfall (mm)*

|  | J | F | M | A | M | J | J | A | S | O | N | D | Total |
|---|---|---|---|---|---|---|---|---|---|---|---|---|---|
| *Benghazi* | | | | | | | | | | | | | |
| Temperature | 14 | 15 | 17 | 19 | 22 | 24 | 25 | 27 | 26 | 23 | 19 | 14 | |
| Rainfall | 66 | 38 | 18 | 5 | 3 | 0 | 0 | 0 | 3 | 18 | 41 | 61 | 253 |
| *Tripoli* | | | | | | | | | | | | | |
| Temperature | 12 | 13 | 14 | 18 | 20 | 23 | 25 | 26 | 25 | 23 | 18 | 12 | |
| Rainfall | 76 | 43 | 23 | 8 | 5 | 0 | 0 | 0 | 10 | 36 | 66 | 68 | 335 |
| *Azizia* | | | | | | | | | | | | | |
| Temperature | 12 | 13 | 16 | 20 | 23 | 27 | 29 | 30 | 28 | 24 | 18 | 13 | |
| Rainfall | 48 | 33 | 21 | 10 | 4 | 0 | 0 | 0 | 6 | 18 | 30 | 51 | 223 |
| *Garian* | | | | | | | | | | | | | |
| Temperature | 8 | 10 | 13 | 17 | 21 | 24 | 27 | 27 | 24 | 21 | 16 | 10 | |
| Rainfall | 74 | 51 | 41 | 15 | 13 | 0 | 0 | 8 | 10 | 23 | 41 | 54 | 330 |
| *Nalut* | | | | | | | | | | | | | |
| Temperature | 7 | 9 | 13 | 17 | 21 | 26 | 28 | 27 | 25 | 20 | 15 | 10 | |
| Rainfall | 21 | 25 | 23 | 12 | 7 | 0 | 0 | 0 | 5 | 11 | 18 | 19 | 151 |

or slight *ghiblis* occur on 50 to 70 days per annum. As well, the Tripolitanian Jebel has a locally more severe winter: up to 2 m of snow falls in certain years.

Bolder relief in northern Cyrenaica reduces temperatures; in winter sleet is common, and for periods of a few hours the higher hills may carry a snow cover. In summer, too there are distinctly lower temperatures in the Cyrenaican Jebel, whereas at sea-level conditions much resemble those of Alexandria. Inland, temperatures may often reach 38–40 °C, particularly in Tripolitania and the Fezzan. A feature of the northern coastlands, especially in the east, is the formation of dew and early morning fog. The former occurs mainly throughout the summer months, but occasionally in winter – atmospheric humidity is highest in summer near the coast – and this is generally of distinct importance to agriculture, especially on the Jefara of Tripolitania.

## Hydrology

There are no perennial surface streams in Libya, but human settlement is rendered much more possible by the existence of underground water. In the limestone areas of the Cyrenaican Jebel, caverns with underground streams occur, one of these being an underground pool large enough to float a rowing-boat – and there are a few flowing springs and even one

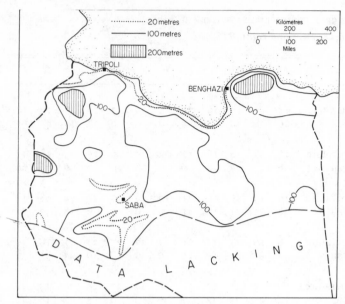

*Fig.* 18.5 Water-tables in Libya (data in part by S. A. Hajjaji and government sources).

waterfall (at Derna). Elsewhere in several parts of the country there are both extensive water-tables at varying depths, and flows of water which either emerge themselves at the surface or can be tapped by wells.

The inland oases of Libya (and also Egypt) have water features of long standing which are of considerable interest. Many of these are large irregular basins, of natural as opposed to man-made formation, with water flows of varying kinds. At Qattara water seeps slowly from the sides and lower parts, producing an extensive salt marsh; at Siwa and Jarabub it rises as a large natural fountain of great force and volume, at Kufra it forms ponds or smaller lakes; and at Aujila and Jalo it must be tapped by shallow wells. Further, the water itself varies considerably in chemical content. It may be fresh and cold, or highly brackish, so that it is unusable for humans or for agriculture, and warm, or even hot, as at Zuara. There may be a considerable gaseous content – of free nitrogen at Siwa, and of carbon dioxide in a few other localities. Recently, however, as the result of oil prospection, considerable quantities of artesian water have been discovered in many areas; round Kufra especially, which is a collection of small oases in the middle of a vast desertic area.

In the Jefara of Tripolitania three separate water-bearing layers are distinguished. The first (phreatic) layer occurs near the coast at 5–15 m depth, but at 30 m or more inland; a second aquifer related to lower Quaternary or possibly Pliocene strata is found at 30–60 m; and finally there is an artesian layer at 250–500 m.

Several theories have been put forward to explain the occurrence of this relatively abundant groundwater in Libya. These range from suggestions that there is a kind of siphoning effect from the Lake Chad basin over the Tibesti; that there is percolation westwards from the Nile; and that there is heavy rainfall over the Tibesti itself (one difficulty here being the absence of any observations of such heavy rainfall); to more solidly based views; (a) that the present water supplies are due to gradual seepage northwards in tilted and porous strata of rainfall in Quaternary and prehistoric times, and (b) that the water is maintained by extremely rapid absorption of present-day rainfall into an exceptionally porous subsoil, i.e. rainfall seeps into the ground before it can evaporate, and thus much of the sporadic but temporarily heavy rainfall is preserved underground. In this connection it may be noted that according to one observer, some 15 million m$^3$ of floodwater on average pass annually down the Wadi Megenin at Tripoli city.

The implications of the last two theories are obviously extremely important. If the first is the real explanation, then most of the groundwater of Libya is a kind of fossil, mineral resource that once used can never be replaced. Space forbids a discussion of the whole problem, which is of extreme interest, and, of course, great relevance; but it is sufficient to repeat that both views are strongly maintained at the present time.[1] Both possibilities could hold, and this is probably the more satisfactory answer, though increasingly, opinion crystallizes that most supplies are 'fossil water', not renewable under present conditions of climate.

## Soils and vegetation

Most of the soils of Libya have been produced by physical rather than chemical weathering, and frequently approach the skeletal, detrital type. Oasis cultivation is often in what many observers would call desert sand; but in the Tripolitanian Jefara a wider range of soil types is found. A few patches of alluvial soils occur on the lower-lying parts, brought from the uplands by temporary streams; and dune sands occur both near the coast and in the interior. Soils of seirozem type also occur both near the coast and in the centre of the Jefara, as fine grey-brown structures, mainly sandy but with a small fraction of clay and loam. Elsewhere solonchak soils and desert crust are widespread.

[1] For example, certain of the natural seepage basins are below present sea-level. They must have been eroded out by aeolian action, or by hydrostatic pressure acting upwards from the aquifer – any erosion by water is largely ruled out. Other problems are (i) the variation of water levels, which in some places is seasonal and at other places not; and (ii) a suggestion now discounted, that the extensive lowland area running east-north-eastwards from the Gulf of Sirte through Aujila, Jarabub and Siwa, and now occupied by numerous salt marshes with marine flora and fauna, was once an arm of the sea. These marine forms are thought not to be indigenous but have been carried by migrant birds.

As a result of distinctly higher rainfall, parts of north-western Cyrenaica have a soil of true Terra Rossa type, but south of the Jebel Akhdar this quickly gives way to seirozems of various kinds, in which extensive crustal deposits occur. Hard pan is especially noticeable in Marmarica, from the region of Sollum as far west as Tobruk, Bir Hakim and even Derna. Then, as the Sahara proper is approached, white solonchak soils are increasingly prominent, until, beyond Es Serual, full desert conditions are reached.

In Tripolitania, natural vegetation consists mainly of scrub or semi-desert types. Extensive date groves and stands of Australian eucalyptus of recent introduction have, however, greatly modified the vegetation in an increasing number of places. Over northern Cyrenaica, the various soil types tend to carry a characteristic vegetation cover. Garrigue is most widespread on the coastal plain, with scattered clumps of cultivated fruit trees (including the date palm) in better-watered conditions. The presence of salt marsh reduces the growth of typical Mediterranean flora, hence tamarisk often takes the place of evergreens. On the second of the plateau-steps (El Arqab) extensive woodland is a feature. This is a low, but fairly dense growth of juniper and lentisk trees, with occasional olives, Mediterranean pines and evergreens; and this vegetation has a surprising extension over northern Cyrenaica. The importance of this 'forest' (or better, shrubbery, since few trees exceed 3 m in height) is considerable, since it provides grazing for animals in poor seasons; and remarkably enough, it seems able to resist even damage by goats. Evans-Pritchard writes, 'There is no evidence that the forest has anywhere been destroyed by goats, or even severely damaged by them'; and it would appear that the goat actually thrives best in wooded areas. Even cattle can be kept there permanently, provided that there are occasional open clearings where grass grows.

The woodland ceases below the crest of the Jebel Akhdar, giving way to more open expanses of garrigue, and scattered grass-covered stretches. South of the crest, steppe vegetation is increasingly a feature, with reeds and lotus in the deeper and damper valleys, and juniper on the uplands. Ultimately again, vegetation becomes extremely sparse, and of true desert type.

**Economic and human**
*Agriculture*

According to the 1971 Agricultural Census the total agricultural area is 9·52 million ha of which 2·37 million ha arable and 7 million ha meadow and pasture. Only 144 000 ha are under permanent crops. Three distinctive patterns can be distinguished, each related to the physical conditions of

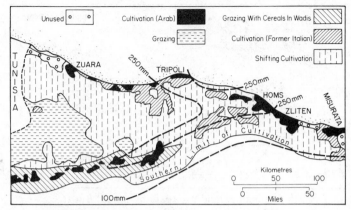

*Fig.* 18.6 Tripolitania: land use.

the locality: (*a*) oasis cultivation within the desert, (*b*) the agriculture of the Jefara and adjacent regions of the Tripolitanian Jebel, and (*c*) the pattern of mixed exploitation characteristic of northern Cyrenaica.

Oasis cultivation is based on two staples, dates and millet. The Fezzan oases consist chiefly of extensive date groves under-cultivated with cereals and vegetables. Altogether, there may be as many as 50 million date palms in Libya; and in the oases, human consumption of dates has been calculated at 500–700 g/head/day with little else to eat at certain seasons. Unfortunately, quality is not high – much below that of Biskra – so there is no trade outside the oasis. Millet (the bulrush type *dukhn*) suits the climatic conditions better than either barley or wheat, though a little of both these last two may also be grown. In addition, a wide range of squashes, peppers, tomatoes and other Mediterranean vegetables are grown together with fruit. A feature of the last few years has been the growth of demand from the oil areas, and from the northern towns.

The Jefara is by far the most productive area of Libya, and is furthest developed, because of Italian activities and more recently as a result of private investment and government subsidies. Barley is the main crop, owing to its tolerance of drier, hotter conditions, with wheat production about 15–20% of this, both being winter crops. A little maize is produced as a summer crop where abundant irrigation water is available, and some farms also grow lucerne for a very small number of stall-fed cattle. Groundnuts have recently been introduced with some success, and another significant crop is broad beans.

Tree crops are widespread: olives, almonds, vines and citrus fruit. Olives are a traditional crop, and probably in terms of weight of crop, more important than barley in some years, though there are very wide fluctuations in yields of both; and of the edible fats and oils consumed

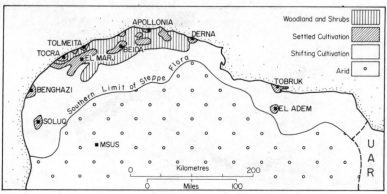

*Fig.* 18.7  North Cyrenaica: land use (data by M. M. Buru).

annually in Libya per head of population, over half comes from olive oil. Chief areas of growth are the eastern Tripolitanian Jebel. In the Jefara and elsewhere the Italians introduced their own stocks alongside Arab varieties, but although they produce more fruit and a better oil, they are less tolerant of poor soil and aridity, hence they have by no means ousted Libyan varieties. There is some export both of oil and the raw fruit. Vines are grown, but much less than in Italian colonial times, since with independence and the Islamic revival which followed the Revolution in 1969, the market for wine has contracted, and there is no export, as quality is not high. Almonds were planted in large numbers during the later phases of Italian rule, and have now reached maturity; there is some export. Citrus cultivation has developed significantly, though once again, quality does not compare with Israeli or Spanish oranges. Vegetables, especially potatoes, tomatoes, onions, aubergines and artichokes, are inceasingly important with the rapidly rising standards of living, and the presence of a relatively large foreign population: oil prospectors, technicians, and constructors, and until 1970 the presence of British and US troops and their families. The irrigated farms of the Jefara produced almost 70% by weight of Libya's agricultural production in 1973 and an even higher proportion in terms of value. However, the further intensi-fication and expansion of irrigated agriculture is limited because of the progressive decline in groundwater levels and difficulties in maintaining supplies of usable irrigation water. Development of the dryland farming area may be a more attractive proposition.

In Cyrenaica (apart from limited areas of irrigated agriculture of the traditional pattern along the coast) there was little cultivation before the Italian invasion. Much of the area remained in pasture with a mainly transhumance economy. The life of many Cyrenaicans could be described as mixed farming, with animal husbandry the major element, and cultivation (except in a few areas) a minor feature. Barley was the chief crop, being sown in the lowlands immediately after the first autumnal rains; but on the plateau lower temperatures often retarded planting until January, with the harvest (which takes place on the coast in May) correspondingly later (often August). By sowing two separate plots, one on the lowlands and another at higher altitudes, it was possible to spread the work of cultivation over a longer period, and to some extent mitigate the effects of capricious rainfall. As barley will grow wild in Cyrenaica it can thrive on a minimum of attention, so that the farmer was able to move off with his animals, and leave his fields unattended till the harvest. Italian colonization in the late 1930s led to the expropriation and development of some of the best watered areas of the Jebel Akhdar. Dry farming techniques were used with emphasis on mechanized grain production with fewer trees and vines than in Tripolitania. However, with the expulsion of the Italians from Cyrenaica in 1942, the traditional economy based on grazing and shifting cultivation gradually revived. A detailed study of the region in the 1960s revealed serious overgrazing and severe soil erosion in many places. Where cultivation did exist, both in the areas where the Italians had established farms (which the Government leased to tribesmen), and in the tribal areas, techniques were primitive and wasteful. Steps are now being taken to modernize farming in these areas which have traditionally been cultivated, to reorganize the ex-Italian farms, to reclaim new areas for agriculture, and to plant trees as part of a soil and water conservation programme. The majority of new farmers will inevitably come from the ranks of the semi-nomads.

Although barley still predominates, wheat has increased in importance, and more wheat is grown in Cyrenaica than in the Jefara and Jebel of Tripolitania. Some millet is found, and maize has recently been introduced, but it is confined to areas where irrigation water is available. The inland basin of El Marj is the best agricultural zone in Cyrenaica, since it has a relatively deep soil layer, and is favoured climatically.

Oil exploitation and its rapid development has resulted in a rapid wave of migration to the towns, leaving deserted farmland in many parts of the country. According to the 1973 population census only 48% of the population gained their livelihood from agriculture whereas nearly 80% of the population lived in the rural and nomadic sectors of the economy before the discovery of oil. Agriculture contributes only 2% of gross domestic product; agricultural exports have declined while the value of imported foodstuffs has risen rapidly. For the 1976–80 plan period the agricultural sector has been allocated 17% of total development funds with the aim of attaining self-sufficiency in foodstuffs, especially wheat and barley, by the 1980s. Industrial crops are being promoted and the vigorous horticultural sector is also being encouraged because of the rising demand from an increasingly affluent Libyan population. New agricultural development and land reclamation schemes are concentrated in the Jefara and Jebel Akhdar, while at Kufra in the Sahara capital intensive, agro-business techniques are being applied to desert reclamation in order to grow irrigated fodder crops for large-scale sheep breeding. Farmers also receive important government subsidies.

### Pastoralism

For centuries the western Jefara, the *wadi* systems south of the Jebel Nefusa and the pastures in and around the Jebel Akhdar have sustained tribes of pastoral nomads. In Cyrenaica, under the traditional nomadic and semi-nomadic systems, many tribes moved south with their animals into the steppe regions during December, after barley sowing; and they returned to the northern plateaux in late spring when pasture in the south was exhausted, but still growing in the cooler, damper slopes of the Jebel. Furthest south reached by most pastoralists was the line Bir Hakim–Agedabia; and by the month of August, most herders had returned to the plateau, though a few sometimes stayed in the region of deep *wadis* and playas where scanty pasture can last all year. The majority of the northern tribes moved only a few kilometres between the coastal terraces and the higher ridges of the Jebel Akhdar. One factor which contributed to this restricted movement was the occurrence over much of the north of a plant, drias (*Thapsia gargantica*), which, when dried for fodder, is poisonous to cattle that have not been previously grazed on it when green earlier in the same year. This meant that animals had to stay in the one region during spring and summer, and could not be moved in from winter pastures in the south. The extreme north of Cyrenaica was given over to goats and cattle, whereas in the south, sheep and camels were the most numerous. Something of a similar pattern of life obtained on the Jebel of Tripolitania and also on adjoining parts of the Jefara.

Today, however, nomadic pastoralism is a disappearing way of life. Over the last few years there has been relatively rapid progressive sedentarization of the nomadic commuity, a process encouraged by government sponsored schemes, while since the oil boom nomads have also been drawn to the towns in growing numbers. The present policy of the Libyan government is to organize livestock rearing and to introduce imported range management practices and techniques with a view to conservation and the optimal use of the country's pastures. One example is the Benghazi plains scheme and the extensive enclosure of areas in the central plains of Surt. In addition to improving local fodder supplies the government has also invested in a number of intensive livestock fattening enterprises and has set up several breeding stations

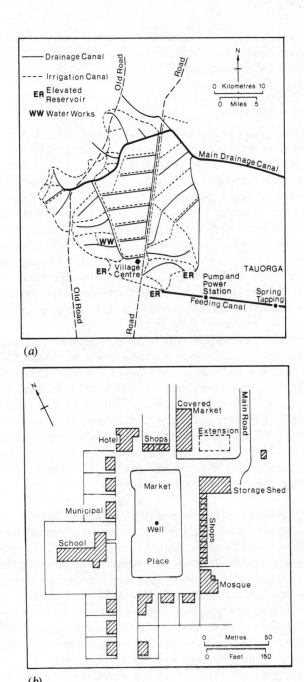

*Fig.* 18.8 Tauorga Irrigation project: (*a*) water canals; (*b*) settlement lay-out.

to maintain the quality of livestock. The aim is eventual self-sufficiency in livestock products. In 1973 there were 3 million sheep, 1 million goats, 120 000 cattle and 120 000 camels in Libya.

### Italian colonization

After the conquests of 1924 (Tripolitania) and 1932 (Cyrenaica), large amounts of land were expropriated (either openly or by legalistic manipulation) in order to allow the settlement of Italian colonists. Two systems prevailed: private concessions, where owners bought fairly large tracts which they would then exploit, partly with local Libyan labour, i.e. somewhat like tropical plantations; and the so-called demographic settlements, maintained financially and directed by the Italian state, with tenant peasant-farmers who could look forward to becoming owners after a period of 20 to 30 years. The kind of crops, grown, and marketing of the produce, were in the hands of governmental agencies. About 75 000 ha were taken over in this way within Cyrenaica, but ultimately entirely abandoned during the Second World War. Libyans have now reoccupied the holdings and continued them in various ways.

In Tripolitania, individual concessions occupied 127 000 ha, and the demographic colonies a further 96 000 ha in all, more than half of all the cultivated land in Tripolitania, and most of it being relatively of the best quality. The concessions, having been established on land carefully chosen for its economic value as a commercial proposition, were best equipped and efficiently handled; and they still furnish the major part of the agricultural produce of Tripolitania. Many Italians left after 1940, but a significant number remained until 1970 when they were expropriated; and among the many problems of the present government are those of ensuring that the former Italian concessions will remain as efficient producers.

Differing answers have been given at various times regarding the importance of the Italians in Libya. For a time, numbers tended to fall as many of the Italian farmers gradually gave up their land, some to return to Italy, others to take up town occupations. In the 1960s the numbers stabilized for a time at 20 000–25 000, with the greater participation of Italians in schemes of technical development. But early in 1970 all Italian-owned land and property, including 37 000 ha of cultivated land, was confiscated and plans made to distribute the expropriated lands to Libyan farmers. It is important that the former concession lands should be maintained as farming land, since they are the best in the country.

The demographic colonies had not begun to show such definite progress. Being on more marginal land, and financed on long-term bases (e.g. 20 to 30 year repayments for stock and capital) with heavy subsidies, they

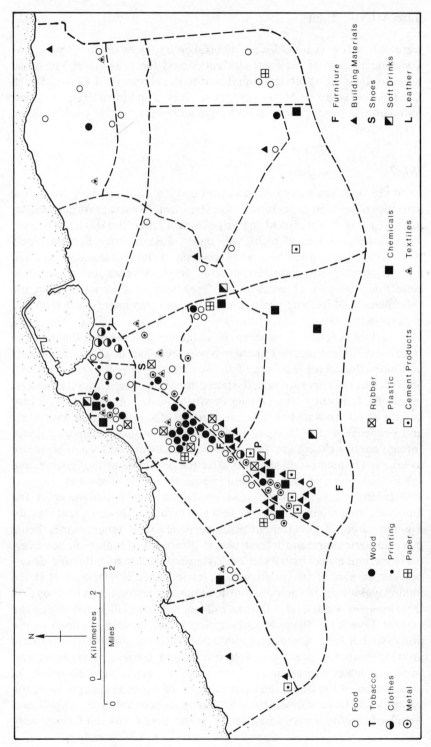

*Fig.* 18.9 Location of industry in Tripoli.

were only a few years old when overtaken by the events of 1939–45. As a significant part of their activity concerned the growing of vines and tobacco, they are much less significant to the economy of Libya, though far from negligible. Moreover, there was a political basis to their foundation; hence they have gradually reverted to full Libyan exploitation.

### Other economic activities

Until the large-scale exploitation of oil in 1960, Libya had relatively few activities other than agriculture and pastoralism. Esparto grass grows wild, particularly on the scarps of the Tripolitanian Jebel; and this has a market abroad in the making of high-grade paper. Just after the Second World War over-collection led to near-exhaustion of the plant, and production is now more strictly controlled at a low level. Another sort of post-war collection was that of scrap metal (especially in Cyrenaica) from the battlefields, and in some years following 1945 scrap metal was a principal export item.

A certain amount of modern manufacturing occurred, dating from Italian days. Most was in Tripolitania with over half of all establishments and more than three-quarters of the workers in Tripoli itself. The main activities were concerned with the transformation of agricultural products, especially foodstuffs; the making of wheat pastes (macaroni, etc.) processing of oil seeds and of tobacco, canning of sardines and tunny, wine- and beer-making for foreigners, soap-boiling. Industry remained under foreign control except in a few cases where Libyans had the opportunity to take over some establishments after the departure of the Italians, and the serious shortage of investment capital restricted expansion.

With the oil boom since 1960 production and employment in the manufacturing sector has grown, although industrial development was not a major target of government planning policy until 1969, priority being given to agriculture and infrastructure. Since the Revolution, however, the government has embarked on a vigorous policy of industrial development as part of its programme of economic diversification. LD 329 million was allocated for industrial development under the revised 1973–75 Development Plan, and LD 1072 million has been allocated under the current Five Year Plan. Manufacturing is still largely confined to the processing of local agricultural products. The most important and rapidly growing branches are food, soft drinks and tobacco, and wood and furniture, which represent 49% and 12%, respectively, of all industrial employment. In spite of the establishment of some new large units, the majority of factories, which are heavily concentrated in Tripoli and Benghazi, are on a very small scale. At the 1971 Industrial Census only

55 industrial units employed more than 50 workers. Nevertheless important developments have been made in petrochemicals. Esso has built a gas liquefaction plant at Marsa Brega, and a refinery (capacity 8000 barrels/day). A 68000 barrels/day LPG plant was established by Occidental in 1972. The National Oil Company (NOC) has a 60000 barrels/day refinery at Zawia, opened in 1975, and output is being doubled to supply 80% of domestic requirements. NOC is also developing a petrochemical complex at Marsa Brega and an export refinery at Tobruk. Exports of liquefied natural gas began in 1971 and naphtha exports in 1974. In addition a major integrated iron and steel complex is to be built at Misurata, with an initial capacity of 500000 tons a year.

Although direct state intervention in the industrial sector has increased since 1969, the majority of manufacturing establishments are still privately owned. Manufacturing industry now employs more than one-sixth of the active population but makes only a small contribution to G.D.P.


**Towns**

The largest city of Libya is the capital, Tripoli, the natural focus of the most populous and productive agricultural region and the country's chief port. The city's population increased from 130000 in 1954 to 552000 in 1973 – or 25% of the total Libyan population. Tripoli has one of the few reasonably good harbours in an otherwise almost harbourless coastline. It was for long a pirate stronghold; and besides controlling the important coastal route east–west was a point of departure for the trans-Saharan caravans. Its walled Old City is still a tightly built maze of covered *suqs*, mosques and dwellings, but today it represents a major planning problem.

Alongside it is the large modern town laid out by the Italians, parts of which have been rebuilt and replanned in recent years. Since the early 1960s the city has expanded rapidly with the addition of modern residential and industrial suburbs characterized by the dull but functional lay-out of the motor-age. The masterplan provides for the continued outward expansion of the city. Since the Revolution, Tripoli has been Libya's sole capital, a function which it shared with Benghazi and then Beida before 1969. It is now the focus of the country's political life, and of administration, the most important business centre, and Libya's major industrial city (with 46% of all industrial establishments employing more than 10 workers, and a highly diversified industrial structure). One of Libya's two universities (Al Fatah University) is also located there.

Benghazi is the second most important urban centre with a population of 282000 in 1973. It lies on a wide coastal plain backed to the north and east by the Jebel Akhdar. Part is salt marsh (*sabkha*), now in process of drainage and development near the city, and part, though not all, is

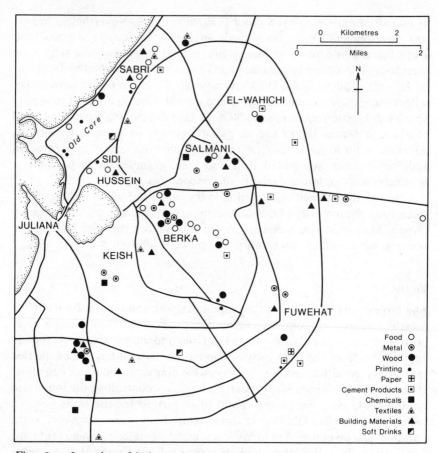

*Fig.* 18.10 Location of industry in Benghazi.

cultivated. Fairly soon to the north the highlands approach the sea, and routes must strike inland, which in any case gives a more direct route eastwards. The original harbour was very small and open to the north-westerlies that prevail in winter, hence there has been no attempt to bring the oil-lines from the south; these have their own terminals at Marsa Brega, Es Sider, Ras Lanuf, Marsa el Hariga and Zuetina constructed during the 1960s. Although for long Benghazi was somewhat overshadowed (as the capital of the less well endowed and remote Cyrenaica) by the more sophisticated and central Tripoli, there was a time when it seemed that Benghazi might rival Tripoli on becoming the administrative headquarters of the oil industry, a growing port, and the natural regional focus for Libya's second most populous region. But the Revolution re-established the dominance of Tripoli. Nevertheless Benghazi remains an important industrial centre (with 14% of all establishments employing more than

10 workers) and the site of Libya's second university (Ghar Younis University).

Between 1954 and 1969 the monarchist government attempted to establish a new federal capital at Beida in the Jebel Akhdar, where construction began of an entirely new town close to a Sanussi teaching zawiya of very small size but far wider repute. The unsuitability of the site, over 1300 km from Tripoli and in a region without major resources, was soon recognized, but nevertheless several government departments, a number of embassies, a university and other services were located there. The division of responsibility between Tripoli, Beida and sometimes Benghazi resulted in frustration and inefficiency so that in 1969 the Revolutionary Council abandoned the project and declared Tripoli the sole capital. Beida has survived as a town of some 30000 people, with some regional administrative functions and a number of university faculties. But it remains a monument to political ineptitude.

The official Libyan definition of 'urban' includes only Tripoli, Benghazi, Beida and Derna, but there are in addition a number of small centres which perform important urban functions and are thriving regional and administrative centres. Misurata has a growing number of industries and is the site of Libya's new iron and steel complex. Its port at Casr Ahmed is being reconstructed to help ease the severe congestion at Tripoli and Benghazi. Homs also has a little manufacturing. Derna has a small but usable harbour which is being reconstructed and expanded; and a new town of El Marj, rebuilt close to the original town (Barce) destroyed by an earthquake in 1963, has a number of new industries in addition to administrative and marketing functions. Tobruk lies on a small creek, and besides acting as an outlet generally for the scanty agricultural and pastoral products of Marmarica, has developed as an outlet for east Cyrenaica oil. In the past proximity to El Adem, a former British airbase 30 km to the south-east, was also a favourable factor. Including these smaller centres, about one-third of the population are urban dwellers.

Many other once-famous centres, Leptis Magna, Sabratha and the Pentapolis (with Benghazi) of Tocra, Tolmeita, Apollonia and Cyrene, are now villages or small towns. Some have extensive classical remains, many of which were refurbished in Italian times, as a matter of Fascist policy. Although the technical methods used have been criticized by some archaeologists, the resulting effect is often very striking indeed. There has been little attempt to develop this considerable tourist attraction.

### Problems of present-day Libya

Libya became independent in 1951 as a federal state. Its division into three semi-autonomous provinces (Tripolitania, Cyrenaica and Fezzan) reflected certain real differences in geographical environment, although their political association antedated even the Italian conquest. Tripolitania has a more developed agricultural base, with increasing emphasis on irrigation from deep wells, which allows the production of cash crops: olive oil, citrus fruits, vegetables and groundnuts, some of which are exported. It holds the larger population, and its wider range of activities has been reflected by the rather more cosmopolitan, 'advanced' city of Tripoli, which for long displayed a more independent 'Mediterranean' outlook.

Cyrenaica with its north highland core, cooler winter, greater dependence on pastoralism and smaller population, and more deeply affected by the religious tradition of Sanussi teaching, gave independent Libya its first (and last) king. Its main products were pastoral: hides, skins, and live animals, which once found traditional markets in Egypt.

Poor and isolated for long, the Fezzan remains harsh and difficult as an area of human settlement. For a time Murzuq and then Sebha were included as, in turn, federal capital in the Benghazi–Tripoli cycle, but this arrangement was abandoned after a very few years as political expediency yielded to geographical realities.

The federal structure of government introduced in 1951 resulted in an over large and costly administration; it merely accentuated debilitating internal political divisions and rivalries; and aggravated the acute economic problems facing the new state. For almost 10 years after political independence in 1951, Libya remained desperately poor, and heavily dependent for its economic survival on foreign financing, grants-in-aid and rents for the use of military bases by Britain and the USA. The country seemed an impossible case for development, and the total recommended budget for 1952–3 was only £2·3 million – representing a bare survival operation. However, with the expansion of petroleum development from the early 1960s, further aided by the closure of the Suez Canal from 1967–1975 (which made Libyan prices even more competitive in the West as compared with oil from Iran and Kuwait), government revenues rose spectacularly from LD 14·2 million in 1962 to LD 663·6 million in 1973. The dramatic price increases at the end of 1973 meant that Libya earned LD 3000 million from oil exports in 1976 even though, through conservation measures, production had fallen to below half the level achieved in 1970. Per capita G.N.P. rose from $40 in the early 1950s to over $4000 in 1976.

Because of the difficulties of dealing with the complexities of oil exploitation and with the management of the funds it generated without a centralized state, in 1963 the federal constitution was abolished, and Libya became a unitary state divided into ten administrative districts or *mohafazas*. In order to strengthen further national unity in a country with a small and scattered population, communications have been greatly improved since the early 1960s with heavy government investment devoted to extending the road network, the construction of new airports, and the installation of telephone and telecommunications systems, and radio and television stations to give national coverage. Wealth is still unequally distributed, but through food subsidies, high wages, popular housing schemes, and a great improvement and extension of social services, especially health and education, most Libyans now enjoy a very much higher standard of living than they did at independence.

But oil wealth has brought its own complex problems. Libya has become a wealthy rentier state, with the economy remaining dependent and underdeveloped. From the early 1960s as the new wealth from oil flowed mainly to the chief urban centres, there followed a rapid wave of migration from the countryside to the coastal towns, resulting in deserted farmland and growing dependence on food imports. Both agriculture and industry stagnated while the services sector grew rapidly. Many of the new jobs created in the administration represented a form of disguised unemployment, and deprived vital sectors of much needed labour.

Since the Revolution more determined efforts have been made to restructure and diversify the economy to prepare for the day when the oil runs out. Investment under the Three Year Development Plan (1972–3) involved LD 2571 million, and total planned expenditure under the current Five Year Plan (1976–1980) is LD 7000 million – compared with only LD 337 million dring the first Five Year Plan (1963–8). Emphasis is being given to the productive sectors, to agricultural development and industrialization. Unfortunately, apart from oil, Libya's resource base is narrow, restricting planning options. At best no more than 2% of the total land area is suitable for cultivation, and groundwater resources are now actually deteriorating in some coastal areas. Industry is constrained by the small internal market provided by a population of only 2·25 million (1973 census). Shortage of Libyan manpower is, however, perhaps the most acute problem affecting the government's development plans. There are a growing number of Libyans who are reluctant to take unskilled jobs or manual work of any kind, particularly in agriculture and construction, preferring employment on easy terms in government service. Consequently the economy has become heavily dependent on imported foreign labour, skilled and unskilled, in almost all key sectors. In 1976 the 337000 foreign workers in the country – the vast majority from Egypt but with a substantial number from Tunisia – represented 40% of the total Libyan workforce. This dependence is likely to increase rather than weaken during the next few years and threatens to become the 'achilles heel' of the Gaddafi Revolution. Uncoordinated planning and spending, wastage and extravagance are aggravating these fundamental difficulties. There is no easy solution to Libya's badly balanced economy.

Under Gaddafi, Libya's growing wealth from oil has been deployed on the international scene, and Libya has begun to play a more forceful role in world affairs. Since 1969 Libya's foreign policy has been dominated by Gaddafi's belief that an Islamic revival is fundamental to the cause of Arab unity and that such a revival requires a world revolution to combat both imperialism and communism. Thus, part of Libya's vast oil revenues has been used to finance the Palestinian *fedayeen* and to interfere in the internal affairs of several Arab states. The Moslem rebels in the Philippines, the Irish Republican Army, and the Eritreans in Ethiopia have also received Libyan financial backing. Although Gaddafi has persuaded several black African states to sever relations with Israel in return for Libyan aid, within the Arab world Libya has become increasingly isolated. Relations with Egypt have steadily declined since Gaddafi's failure to push through the Egyptian–Libyan merger in September 1973, while plans for a union with Tunisia in January 1974 proved a non-starter. By 1977 the situation had deteriorated to actual military clashes along the Egyptian border.

# 19 The Sudan

From a point a little north of the town of Port Sudan, one can draw an isopleth westwards, keeping to the north of Atbara and Khartoum, and reaching the western frontier of the Sudan at approximately 15°N latitude. This line would then delimit a northern zone of indeterminate or slight winter maximum of rainfall from much of the rest of the Sudan, which has a summer rainfall maximum – thus defining in one sense the southern frontier of our 'Middle East'. But there is a zone of aridity even within the region of summer maximum (the 250 mm isohyet occurs south of Khartoum), and this zone of low rainfall (even though now with a summer maximum) reinforces for much of the central Sudan the concept of a hot, arid environment which we take as being 'Middle Eastern'.

Southwards, a strongly differing type of climate becomes established, ultimately passing into a near-equatorial regime of pronounced summer rainfall maxima, with only a short dry season. Associated with these two distinctive climatic environments are markedly different human cultures and ways of life. But because of the overall organization as a single unitary state, in which Islamic and 'Middle Eastern' forms of culture dominate, it is now proposed to treat the Sudan as an integral part of the Middle East. It has been noted earlier in this book that in a few relatively small areas conditions do not easily fit under our basic definition of Middle East: e.g. the narrow coastal lowlands of the eastern Black Sea and western Caspian, and the Yemeni uplands. These are, however, restricted anomalies climatically, and present no major differences as regards their human geography. The Sudan is, however, markedly different in that it is a major area with a sustained transition over considerable territory to conditions that are very far from just locally different.

The largest state in Africa, with an area of nearly 2·5 million km², that extends over approximately 18° of latitude, the Sudan represents basically a lowland transition from the semi-arid and desert zones of north Africa to the savanna regions of the tropical belt. The name Sudan (Arabic = land of black people) underlines this juxtaposition: it refers to the contact of Arabs with Negro populations at latitudes below 15°N.

## Physical

Essentially, the Sudan can be regarded as an immense lowland trough occupied by the Nile system, defined to east and west by irregular masses of higher land, and rising very gradually southwards until, at no more than 100–150 km from its southern frontier, a more abrupt highland rim marks the beginnings of the Ethiopian plateau and the plateau of east Africa. About a half of the entire country lies at or below 500 m above sea level, and only 3% of the country is higher than 1200 m. From the northern frontier, where the Nile valley is only 120 m above sea level (even though over 1000 km inland from the Mediterranean), the land surface rises by a further 200 m over the 700 km to Khartoum – a slope of 1:3500. South again from Khartoum over the 1200 km to Juba, which lies below the East African plateau-edge, the rise in altitude is only 80 m, i.e. a slope of 1:15000. In the west, the narrow but abrupt Jebel Marra of Darfur reaches a maximum of 3300 m, only slightly less than the rim of the African plateau that lies within Sudan territory; whilst along the north-east, close to the Red Sea coast, ranges of hills attain 1500–2000 m, with the culminating peak, the Jebel Asoteriba, of 2200 m. In the centre of the country there is a minor upland complex that rises to a maximum of 1400 m in the Nuba mountains, which is mainly a series of detached inselbergs eroded from a once higher and more continuous mass.

Structurally, the Sudan is very much a segment of the African Basement Complex, which is apparent at or near the surface over most parts of the country. In the south, stability over long geological periods is the main characteristic, but in the north and west extensive phases of downwarping and oscillation have occurred, with the result that, whilst the south has a covering of generally thin and often discontinuous sheets of continental deposits formed of sand and gravels, the north experienced cycles of marine transgression from the Tethys. Consequently near-horizontal layers of sandstones with some shales, mudstones and limestones were laid down during the Jurassic and Cretaceous; these are collectively termed Nubian Series, and once occupied most of the north and west. Fresh-water cherty deposits of Oligocene age also occur, but are now restricted to a very few areas.

Of much more importance are the Tertiary igneous features – sheet flows of basalt on a large scale, together with more local emission features: volcanic ash, tuff and scoriae, extrusive dikes and basalt plugs. Besides forming extensive plateaux on the eastern frontier with Ethiopia these Tertiary features appear as a major intrusive series to form the Jebel Marra, and former plateau basalts are eroded elsewhere into a number of detached summits or flat buttes – inselbergs of varying importance that occasionally dominate the surrounding level plain, and indicate extensive erosion of a formerly more widespread plateau surface.

Because of the flat nature of much of the Sudan, and its generally limited rainfall, two major surface processes can be traced. Over the northern areas the typical effects of arid sub-aerial erosion are dominant, with exfoliation, abrasion and wind transportation of particles, giving rise to sand dunes, sand and gravel plains, and stony rocky surfaces (*hammada*), as elsewhere in the Saharan areas. In much of the south, which as we have noted is especially flat, water-borne sediments of various kinds are accumulating by aggradation. It is pointed out by Andrew and Barbour that because of this very flat zone in the south, little or no eroded material from the Sudan is actually carried by the Nile system beyond the boundaries of the country. For the main Nile, the central Sudan is a vast settling-tank in which sediments accumulate to form the typical minor elements of the present landscape. Most of the river sediment that reaches Egypt is in fact brought down by Ethiopian tributaries: the material in the main Nile is redeposited in the Sudan as silt and clay plains after only a relatively short distance of travel.

Various cycles of erosion and deposition can be traced to earlier geological periods. In the Tertiary, lateritic deposits appear to have been laid down in parts of the south, and later almost entirely eroded away.

*Geographical regions*

With this basis, six major regional units may be defined. These comprise:

(1) The northern Sudan, which is a desertic region that continues east and west of the Nile the general conditions described for the arid areas of Egypt and Libya. This a part of the Sahara, distinguished by some as the Nubian desert, and the narrow trough of the Nile (on average only 2 km wide here) provides a ribbon of cultivation and settlement in an otherwise almost uninhabited territory. The forbidding nature of the Nubian desert for long made an effective southern barrier and frontier to the land of Egypt.

(2) The north-eastern region. This again, continues land forms charac-

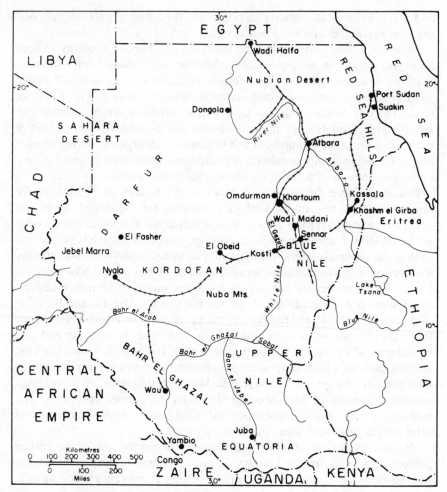

*Fig.* 19.1 The Sudan (including railways).

teristic of Egypt; but in the present instance it is the Red Sea hills that
predominate, giving, as we have earlier noted in chapter 19, an imposing
system of massifs reaching over 2000 m and formed by dislocation,
fracturing and uptilting as the result of movement on the Red Sea fault-lines.
The high edge of the hills drops to a generally narrow coastal plain
fronting the Red Sea, however, the hill mass declines considerably west
of the Atbara river to a low plateau which as an interfluve between the
Atbara and Blue Nile rivers has an undulating surface that is too high
above the rivers to allow irrigation, yet too low also to induce sufficient
rainfall for agriculture. This western plateau is termed the Butana, and
it has only a small population, chiefly of pastoral nomads.

Towards the south of the region a number of outwash areas occur, where streams from the Ethiopian plateau bring down much sediment, but are not sufficiently developed in volume to reach the Nile system, and so do not have mature developed valleys. Largest of these streams is the Gash river.

(3) The central clay plains. A low-lying zone of deposition, with, however, the rivers in generally shallow but defined valley forms, so that they do not flood uncontrollably. Irrigation is thus possible, and this region contains the larger proportion of the Sudan's population.

(4) The western zone. This is a complex area of semi-desert, lowland silt basins, uplands and inselbergs. Most prominent of the relief features is the Jebel Marra, which is sufficiently high to induce rainfall, and thus have a number of non-perennial streams that mainly flow seasonally westwards. Much of the area consists of arid savanna and semi-desert, with, in the centre, a zone of sand dunes – some loose, but most stabilized, among which are small silt basins, the whole area having a hummocky, rounded topography. This is the Qoz region. Some cultivation is possible in the silt and clay basins, but inhabitants are few, with nomadism dominant.

The extreme western sector, Darfur, has episodic drainage and some subsoil percolation from the Jebel Marra. Here we are in the drainage system of the Chad basin, and the cultural history of Darfur reflects central African rather than Semitic affinities.

(5) The southern clay plains. This is, as we have seen, an area of extreme flatness. Some of the chief topographic features are provided by the natural levees which the rivers have deposited, and thick Sudd-type vegetation also produces diversifying elements in the landscape. This sub-region can be held to differ from the central clay plains area in that being so very flat, with natural partially embanked rivers, it is very subject to flooding. Marsh and Sudd form important elements – the whole zone is one of dominance by water features, with agriculture and pastoralism, and hence human occupancy, much restricted. It is significant that the area is not yet crossed by an all-season road, and in 1977 the entire Southern Province had only 10 km of all-weather road.

(6) The uplands of the south. Main feature here is an irregular plateau formation of about 500–700 m altitude covered in ferruginous lateritic type soils – consequently it is sometimes termed the Ironstone Plateau. Outliers of the Ethiopian plateau also occur in the extreme south-east, as in the Boma hills. Climatically related to the equatorial regions, this southern area can in most respects be regarded as an extension geographically of east and central African conditions.

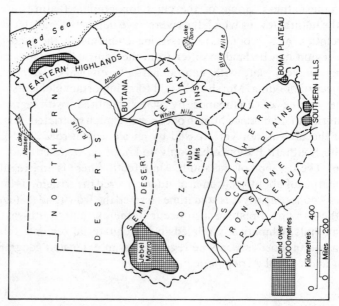

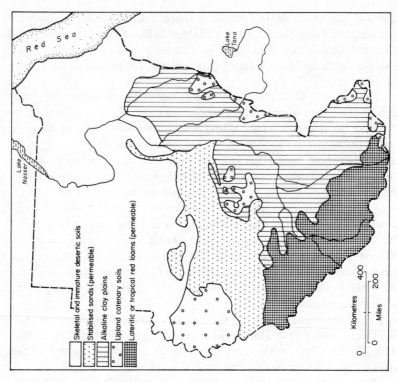

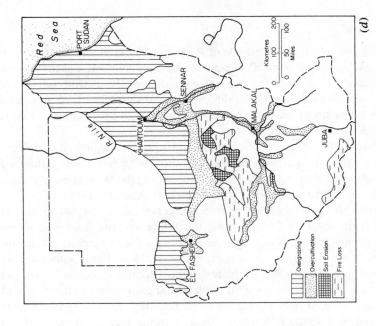

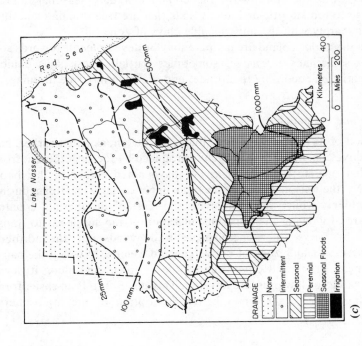

*Fig.* 19.2 The Sudan: (*a*) geographical regions; (*b*) soil types; (*c*) rainfall and drainage patterns; (*d*) degeneration of land.

*Soil complexes*

Over the frequently thick mantle of deposited material that covers much of the lowlands, various soil complexes have developed, and these have been mapped by J. Oliver. Figure 19.2b indicates the distribution of five main groups, as follows: (i) In the extreme north, soils are of a skeletal or immature nature, consisting of loose sand of high permeability, gravels and products of arid type erosion.

(ii) Succeeding these in the centre and west is a region of stabilized sands, without recognizable profile, and thought to have been colonized by low-growing sparse savanna vegetation during the Würm glacial phase, which gave rise to a rainfall distinctly greater than at present.

(iii) The clay plain soils, in an area on average about 200 km wide, that extend from southern Darfur along the White and the Blue Nile rivers as far as the Atbara. These are dark heavy soils of marked alkalinity, that open during the dry season into large cracks. Highly impermeable when not fissured, these clay plains, almost totally level, give a special and pronounced characteristic to the landscape: immense uniformity and monotony, broken only by varied water features near the rivers. Oliver distinguishes a southern variant where extreme lack of slope tends to swamp formation and thus seasonal flooding that induces mottling and gleying on an extensive scale. This is the well-known Sudd region.

(iv) Towards the south-west, higher and markedly seasonal rainfall gives rise to red lateritic and loamy soils that are free draining and thus contrast sharply with the impermeable clays of zone (iii).

(v) In the major upland areas, there may be developments towards soil catenas, sometimes extensive, sometimes partial. These soils exhibit lateral variation according to altitude, and are generally free draining.

**Climate and vegetation**

By reason of its more southerly latitude, the Sudan, as noted earlier, has a distinctive climatic regime, which is produced by factors different from those that operate further north. We have noted earlier in this book (chapter 3) the seasonal occurrence of an upper easterly jet stream during June–October, whilst at lower levels the shift of the thermal equator northwards following the apparent migration of the sun leads to transgression by the southern hemisphere trade winds into the northern hemisphere. A major zone of convergence develops, to which the name Intertropical Front or Convergence Zone is given, and along it, local irregular areas of low pressure develop. Though 'Front' is an easier form of writing, 'zone' is often a better description of the atmospheric condition.

This Intertropical Front migrates seasonally: its northernmost limit, at 18–20° N latitude, is attained in June–July; and it moves south of the Equator (beyond the Sudan) in December–January. Southerly currents at medium and low levels are off the Indian Ocean, and so are very humid, and as they are gradually drawn northwards over the Sudan, rainfall occurs over the southern regions, diminishing northwards as the northern (drier) side of the Intertropical Convergence Zone is reached, with its north-easterly dry winds. The effect of this seasonal swing is to produce four distinctive seasons over most of the Sudan: winter, an early hot season, the rainy season, and a late summer season.

(a) Winter (*Shitaa*). This occurs from about November to March, during which time the Intertropical Front lies well to the south, and northerly, dry air streams are strongly established over most of the Sudan. There is little cloud in this clear air (which is warmed on its passage southwards) and so radiation during daylight hours is unimpeded. Given the lack of marked orography, the main determinant is latitude, with the south much warmer than the north: average temperatures in the coldest month range from 14–16 °C in the north to 25–30 °C in the south. The clear skies also allow much nocturnal heat loss, consequently diurnal variation in temperatures is high – of the order of 10–16 °C. Another important factor in this high level of inward and outward radiation is the absence of thick vegetation cover, especially in the centre and north.

Occasionally, the effects of a Mediterranean depression may extend as far south as the Sudan, and it is the passage of cold fronts associated with south-eastward moving 'lows', when regenerated by contact with the Red Sea, that brings scanty rainfall at this season to the north-east of the country, giving a winter maximum, as at Port Sudan. Further inland, in the Nile valley, there is no rainfall at all of a significant kind – Wadi Halfa has only a few drops of rain in odd years. Relatively cold air may reach the Sudan from southern Europe at this season, giving temporary cool spells.

(b) As the thermal equator begins to move northwards, with the sun overhead, insolation increases markedly over the Sudan, with corresponding rise in air temperatures. In the south, as would be expected, maximum temperatures can occur in March (or in the extreme south at Juba, sometimes in late February); and this maximum is progressively later towards the north: May and June at the centre and north of the country. Absence of cloud and moisture means that heating can be intense, and average daily maxima at the hottest season may reach 38–43 °C. On the other hand, night radiation is also marked, and consequently wide diurnal variation is again a feature, too: 15–19 °C is not uncommon, so nights are distinctly cooler.

Intense local heating of the surface produces convection and marked local instability, with the formation of small local air mass discontinuities. These in the south give considerable rain, but further north the supply of moisture is small, and so there is often considerable wind effect, but little or only moderate rain. Towards the centre and north intense up-and-down draughts associated with local convectional heating, and intermixture of hot with somewhat cooler air produce a phenomenon particularly associated with the Sudan: the *haboob*. This is a violent sand-wind visible as a wall of dust, up to several thousand metres in height, and several kilometres in length. *Haboob* winds develop most strongly in arid areas where vegetation is scanty, and dust can most easily be raised. They also tend to occur at the driest time of the year – i.e. May and June – since there has then been a long period of desiccation of the surface. Quantities of rain may be associated with a *haboob*, but amounts are not usually large.

(c) The wet season (*Kharif*). Gradually, very moist air masses become established over much of the Sudan (other than the north), as the Intertropical Front moves northward in an irregular progression. The whole onset is much less sudden and pronounced as compared with the monsoon of India, to which in terms of mechanism there is considerable similarity. One reason could be the low relief of the Sudan, in contrast to that of the Indian subcontinent, and the descent of air currents from the plateaux of east Africa and Ethiopia may also induce some adiabatic warming that reduces the temperature and humidity contrasts within the air mass.

The general effect of this advection of cooler, much damper air is to give rise to heavy convectional rain during the period April or May to October. Because of the heavy rainfall, mean temperatures drop markedly – causes being (i) increased cloudiness which diminishes radiation received at the surface, (ii) extra absorption of solar radiation by the now abundant water vapour in the atmosphere, and (iii) the cooling effect due to absorption of latent heat as evaporation of free moisture occurs.

(d) The humid season (*Darad*). The period after the maximum rainfall is characterized by the withdrawal of the humid air as the Intertropical Front moves southwards – much more swiftly than its rather fitful northern advance. Cloud decreases and insolation increases again, to give a minor peak of temperature in September–October. Unlike the dry, intensely hot spell of late spring, however, conditions are distinctly more humid because of the prevalence of water from the rains, and mean temperatures can again reach 35–40 °C in much of the centre and north.

Climatic data: representative stations in the Sudan
*Temperature (°C) and rainfall (mm)*

| | J | F | M | A | M | J | J | A | S | O | N | D | Total |
|---|---|---|---|---|---|---|---|---|---|---|---|---|---|
| **1 North** | | | | | | | | | | | | | |
| *Wadi Halfa* | | | | | | | | | | | | | |
| Temperature | 14 | 16 | 20 | 26 | 29 | 31 | 31 | 31 | 29 | 26 | 21 | 16 | |
| Rainfall | | | | | no regular rainfall | | | | | | | | |
| **2 Coast** | | | | | | | | | | | | | |
| *Port Sudan* | | | | | | | | | | | | | |
| Temperature | 23 | 23 | 24 | 26 | 29 | 31 | 33 | 34 | 31 | 29 | 27 | 24 | |
| Rainfall | 11 | 5 | 4 | 0 | 0 | 0 | 5 | 0 | 0 | 8 | 43 | 18 | 94 |
| **3 Centre** | | | | | | | | | | | | | |
| *Khartoum* | | | | | | | | | | | | | |
| Temperature | 21 | 23 | 26 | 30 | 33 | 33 | 31 | 30 | 31 | 31 | 27 | 22 | |
| Rainfall | 0 | 0 | 0 | 0 | 3 | 11 | 41 | 56 | 18 | 6 | 0 | 0 | 135 |
| *Kassala* | | | | | | | | | | | | | |
| Temperature | 23 | 25 | 28 | 31 | 32 | 31 | 28 | 27 | 29 | 30 | 29 | 25 | |
| Rainfall | 0 | 0 | 0 | 0 | 13 | 34 | 105 | 116 | 61 | 12 | 0 | 0 | 341 |
| **4 South** | | | | | | | | | | | | | |
| *Yambio* | | | | | | | | | | | | | |
| Temperature | 24 | 27 | 26 | 26 | 25 | 24 | 23 | 24 | 26 | 27 | 25 | 25 | |
| Rainfall | 12 | 27 | 98 | 140 | 184 | 162 | 179 | 198 | 175 | 151 | 66 | 17 | 1410 |

## Rainfall

Figure 19.2c gives the main features of rainfall distribution, from which the influences of latitude (in relation to the equatorial heavy rainfall zone) and to relief will be apparent. Equatorial conditions of over 2000 mm of annual rainfall are reached in just one small upland region of the south, but by far the greatest part of the Sudan receives under 1000 mm. Variability is also a feature in the increasingly arid north, since we approach the arid 'Middle Eastern' conditions described in earlier chapters. In fact, it is not surprising that rainfall can vary by as much as 50% of average over the north, whilst the figure is under 10% as 'equatorial' patterns of precipitation develop in the extreme south.

Because of extremely high average temperatures, the effectiveness of rainfall is reduced, owing to high evaporation. Thornthwaite's studies of water balance indicate that almost all of the Sudan has a moisture index of less than zero, i.e. net loss of moisture can occur almost anywhere. Only Yambio in the extreme south shows a water surplus. Oliver states that equally, the critical factor in the climate of the Sudan is the length of the dry season, since even during the 'rainy season' there are dry intervals of significance. He estimates that areas of the Sudan with annual rainfall of less than 300 mm – the minimum for rainland agriculture –

cover 47·7% of the total area, areas of 300–1000 mm 37·3%, and over 1000 mm 11·8%, with swamp and open water-surface accounting for a further 5·2%.

Various interpretations of the climate of the Sudan have been made, from that of Köppen onwards. The difficulty is to decide on criteria for aridity, given the variability of rainfall, high temperatures and high evaporation. Barbour distinguishes four major regions: a desertic north, a highly arid area; the south with high temperatures over most of the year low, seasonal and diurnal range, together with a long wet season. The Red Sea coast, with a small but marked winter rainfall, is the third region; whilst the fourth (central) region covers most of the country. This last zone has high temperatures for most of the year, with a 3 to 7 month rainy season, according to latitude. In the south of the central zone, where the rainy season is longer, rainland cultivation is possible; in the north, it is not.

## Vegetation

This is conditioned closely by the effects of climate, and by the soil types, in a remarkable way. A clay soil will hold scanty rainfall, with less available for the plant roots; a sandier soil will be more open in texture and absorb surface run-off to some extent, and make water more easily available to the vegetation. In addition, in an area of episodic rainfall, local geomorphology has a further influence, in determining run-off rates, and hence also the amount of water retained and acquired at the surface. Thus the effective limit of semi-arid vegetation appears in the Sudan as closely approximating to the 400 mm isohyet on clay soils, and to 300 mm on sandy soils – or, as J. Smith put it 'the tree species which requires 3×rainfall on clay soils requires less than 2×rainfall on sands'.

Another important matter is frequent annual destruction of grassland by fires, most of which are started by humans as an aid to cultivation, or to hunting. The repeated effects of these fires, which often spread widely, are considerable.

In the extreme north and north-west, where there is no regular rainfall, vegatation is extremely scanty, or, in some places, non-existent. Low thorn scrub and tough grasses occur here and there, chiefly in the beds of water courses, which may have an occasional flow; and there are some very small species of acacia. A flush of ephemeral grass, as in the Syrian desert, can be a feature following local rainfall.

As incidence of rainfall increases southwards, grasses become more established, with an increased amount of creepers and herb bushes such as hyssop. Where silts or clays provide a non-porous base, as in watercourses, there may be larger bushes or even small, thorny acacia trees. The occurrence of occasional scattered trees among a predominantly grassland zone has raised the question of whether there would be more trees if burning were not so common: ideas differ on this point.

A second major grouping develops in areas with over 300 mm of rainfall (on sands) or 400 mm (on clays). This is described as Low Rainfall Woodland Savanna, and consists of open grassland alternating with expanses of acacia trees, which reach 3–5 m in height and often cluster closely together, with grass growing beneath. One species of acacia, limited to rather drier parts, produces gum arabic, which when collected is a major article of commerce. The reason for alternation of fairly dense tree clusters and open grassland is held to be the practice of burning. Young acacia plants cannot survive this, so they cannot establish themselves in existing areas of grass (which are very liable to be burnt). However, if fires occur at a time of the year that prevents grass from regenerating – e.g. just before the rains – then acacia trees will rapidly establish themselves and form dense clumps of substantial trees without grass and so for a time are impervious to the risk of burning. Southwards again, as rainfall increases further, the acacias are replaced by broad-leaved species that grow more profusely.

A second type of savanna is termed High Rainfall Woodland Savanna. This is the classic 'savanna' type of tall trees and tall grass, including 'elephant grass'. Bulbs and tuberous plants also occur; and one particular tree, the Sudan mahogany, is much in demand commercially. The 'High' type of savanna occurs in regions of 1000–1300 mm rainfall, and passes into full rain-forest in a few places in the far south, with gallery conditions and occasional trees that exceed 30 m in height.

In a few parts of the various uplands, a reduced replica of the rain-forest and some bamboo species occur, with dwarf forms at highest levels. Lastly it remains to mention the well-known Sudd vegetation of the rivers – this covers an area estimated at nearly a quarter of a million square kilometres. Floating vegetation and reeds may occupy almost all of a river channel, leaving only patches of discontinuous stretches of open water, and a particular difficulty is a species of water hyacinth which grows especially rapidly and thickly, obstructing channels within a very short time.

**Occupations**

The physical conditions within the Sudan present a number of important limitations on human activity, amounting in some considerable instances to what is best described as control. The near rainless north is totally dependent on the presence of soil and upon irrigation for agriculture; rainfall cultivation becomes possible only south of 15° N latitude, but it

has proved that the liabilities of shifting sand can be overcome in some
areas by a process of stabilization. Flooding of the plains in the wet season
imposes limitations over large areas of the south; and in the wet season
the presence of tsetse flies inhibits pastoralism in the higher south-west
and a small zone of the south-east whilst the irritation from enormous
clouds of other insects induces considerable human and animal migration
at certain seasons. An absence of large mineral resources is also another
major factor in maintaining dependence upon agriculture and pastoralism,
with consequent necessity of close adjustment to environmental factors.

*Agriculture*

As the rain season becomes longer and more pronounced southwards,
crops of sorghum and bulrush millet are increasingly raised, with, where
water is rather more abundant, groundnuts and sesame. Much depends
not only, obviously on the amount of rain in a given year, but also on
the speed with which the cultivator can get through the routines of
preparing the land and starting his crop. On the northern margins, where
conditions are precarious, only one crop in several years may be possible:
further south, in the far south-west, two crops per annum are sometimes
grown. Cotton is an important adjunct in many areas and vegetables are
also grown with, towards the south, cassava and yams in much wider
variety. Some groups still practise shifting agriculture, and this remains
common in quite a number of areas.

*Irrigation*

Frequently, as local circumstances allow, advantage is taken of the
presence of the rivers and the seasonal flooding of much of the plains
area, to make use of this water either as a supplement to rainfall or as
the principal basis of agriculture. The simplest use of irrigation water is
by planting crops that demand only moderate amounts of moisture, in
the expanses uncovered by receding floods: beans, pulses and some
cereals are grown in this way, with rainfall agriculture alongside in the
non-flooded areas.

Rather more sophisticated devices are small artificial embankments
(*terus*) constructed on interfluves to retain floodwater for a time, as in
the former basin cultivation of Egypt; or the digging of shallow basins
(*hafirs*) which will retain rainwater during much, or even all of the dry
season. *Hafirs* are now often made by bulldozers. The traditional Nile lift
methods (*shaduf* and *sakia*) are still to be found close to rivers, and motor
pumps are increasingly a feature along the main Nile, Blue Nile and White
Nile banks. About 19 m is the usual limiting height for such lift. But in

almost all instances the areas reachable are small, since they are
dependent upon the occurrence of flat terraces, natural and artificial, lying
close to the river bank. Moreover, though the use of *terus* is widespread,
losses from seepage and evaporation can be as much as 50% of the water
stored.

Another method of irrigation, very similar to the *seil* type practised
in Southern Yemen (e.g. the Abyan scheme), is to divert outwash streams
from the high plateaux by regular rotation over deltaic areas where
streams emerge on to flatter plains. This flash irrigation is most developed,
as might be expected, where relief is most marked: the edge of the
Ethiopian–Eritrean highlands and in the valleys of the Baraka and Gash
rivers. Here topography somewhat resembles that of Southern Yemen.

Of late years, considerable development has occurred of large-scale
barrages on major rivers. The fundamental problem involved is the hard
fact that, with irrigation basic to agriculture both in Egypt and also in
the Sudan, the actual flow of water in the Nile system is now insufficient
to supply fully all existing needs, let alone allow development beyond
present levels. H. E. Hurst pointed out that, whilst on average 84000
million m³ of water enter Egypt at Aswan, this figure can fluctuate
between one-half to almost twice as much as the mean quantity. We have
earlier noted that much loss occurs during the passage of Nile waters
through the Sudan: by evaporation, through transpiration by vegetation
(chiefly of the Sudd type) and by percolation into substrata. A second
difficulty is that some river floods occur during the actual rainy season
– an obvious point in one way – so that the extra water is not really needed
at that particular time.

The first joint agreements between Egypt and the Sudan were made
in 1929, and have since been held to be unduly favourable to the former
country. A second agreement in 1959 made greater provision for Sudanese
needs, but also brought in the High Dam proposals, which now involve
the loss of cultivation in the Sudan stretch of the Nile from Wadi Halfa
northward. Altogether, four major barrages have been constructed, three
of which are for storage (Sennar, 1925; Khashm el Girba, 1965; Roseires,
1966), and the other (Jebel Awliya, 1937) as a regulator really mostly for
the benefit of Egypt. In 1975 an agreement was reached with Egypt to
construct the Jonglei Canal to increase the flow of White Nile water
through the southern marshes – a scheme first proposed in 1904. The new
canal will add at least 4000 million m³ of water a year to the Nile at
Malakal and increase Egypt's reserves behind the Aswan Dam. Regulators
near Jonglei will feed a separate canal to irrigate 200000 acres of new
farmland over the next five years. Already, Sudanese use of river water
has doubled since 1959, and by 1982 the full 20 milliard m³ may be used.

By far the most important agricultural region is that known as the

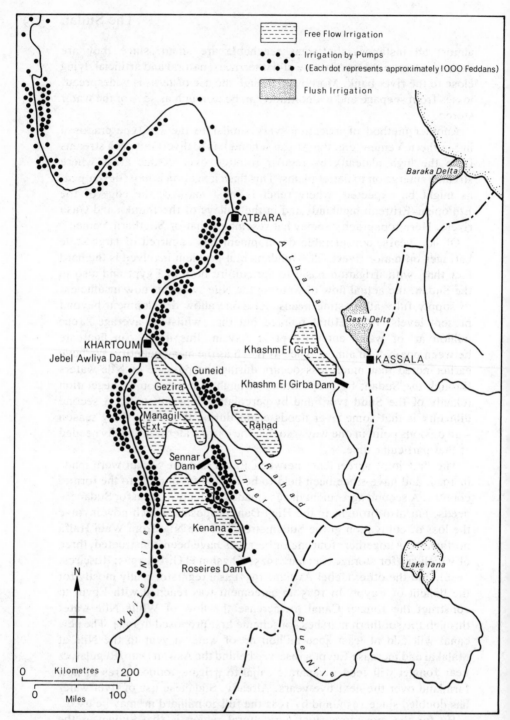

Free Flow Irrigation

Irrigation by Pumps
(Each dot represents approximately 1000 Feddans)

Flush Irrigation

Baraka Delta

ATBARA

Atbara

Gash Delta

KHARTOUM
Jebel Awliya Dam

Khashm El Girba

KASSALA

Guneid
Khashm El Girba Dam

Gezira

Managil
Ext.

Rahad

Rahad

Sennar
Dam

Dinder

Kenana

Lake Tana

Roseires Dam

Blue Nile

White Nile

N

0        Kilometres        200

0          Miles          100

*Fig.* 19.3 Irrigation schemes in the Sudan.

central clay plains. As defined by Barbour and others, this is in effect the region intermediate between the White Nile on the west and the Blue Nile on the east, with a further eastward extension to take in part of the Sudan portion of the Atbara river. The Arabic term for land between rivers is Gezira (cf. Jezireh in Mesopotamia) and this name is applied to the area immediately south-east of Khartoum.

The clay plains are extremely flat, often featureless and made up of a thick layer of clay that cracks deeply when exposed, with an average slope of only 1:7500. Seasonal flooding by the river thus means (in the absence of embankments) that villages may not always lie near the river itself, since the river 'bank' may change seasonally by as much as 1 or 2 km. West of the White Nile the land surface rises slightly, and there is much less possibility of irrigation. To the north, areas of sterile sand enclose the area beyond Khartoum.

Settlement is related to water supply, which can be provided by direct irrigation, by sinking shallow wells in many parts of the Gezira, or by constructing *hafirs*. Most important are the various irrigation schemes that have come into existence following the construction of the three major barrages; and the largest unit is that known as the Gezira Scheme. This began in 1925, partly as a state-directed, partly as a private enterprise; after initial vicissitudes the scheme has come to be outstandingly successful, in that the larger part of the Sudan's foreign exchange and governmental revenue now comes from the scheme. The Gezira scheme covers an area of 1·2 million feddans divided among 46000 tenants. The area was originally divided up into holding of 40 feddans, but many have since been subdivided to accommodate a rising population. As a result about two-thirds of all holdings are now only 20 feddans. The scheme was conceived because of cotton, and its construction and operation are financed almost entirely from the proceeds of the sale of cotton. A strict rotation is imposed which until recently was as follows, cotton, fallow, millet, fallow or beans, fallow, cotton, fallow, fallow. Within the last 10 years, however, new crop rotations have been introduced to include groundnuts, wheat and rice, making the Gezira the major producing area of all three crops as well as cotton. In 1974 the Government announced a programme of further crop diversification in the Gezira by reducing the area under cotton by a third and increasing the area devoted to wheat and groundnuts.

The farming system is far less intensive than that followed in Egypt, and only about two-thirds of the irrigable area is cropped in any one year. The technique of growing cotton is to plant in August, apply about fifteen waterings each at intervals of about 16 days, pick the crop during January–April, and then remove all plants from the fields by May, in order to prevent the spread of plant disease. Only two types of cotton are grown

The Gezira–Managil scheme – cropping pattern 1975–76

| Crop | Area cultivated (feddans) |
|---|---|
| Cotton | 395 637 |
| Groundnuts | 423 604 |
| Wheat | 561 047 |
| Rice | 12 288 |
| Vegetables | 23 618 |
| Dura | 341 357 |
| Lubia | 1 467 |
| Total | 1 759 018 |
| Gross area | 2 100 000 |
| % Cropping | 85% |

(medium and long-staple): Sakel and a local derived species. This again contrasts with Egyptian practice in that the Sudanese growers prefer to improve and breed a reliable unvarying plant, rather than shift to new varieties at frequent intervals.

Financial arrangements are that the Government receives 36% of net profits of the cotton in return for irrigation costs; the tenant, who supplies labour and a share of extra costs such as insecticides and transport of cotton, receives 49% of which 2% goes to the Tenants Reserve Fund; the directing Gezira Board takes 10% and the remainder is divided between the Social Development and the Local Government Councils within the irrigated area. The tenant also takes all the other crops in their entirety. Naturally, the relative shares allocated to each group come under criticism from time to time.

One of the major problems to emerge since the scheme began is the lack of improvement in the yield of cotton crops in spite of the introduction of modern pesticides and fertilizers, while significant year to year variations in yields also occur. Although areas with naturally saline soils were excluded from the scheme, the possibility of secondary salinization has caused much concern since the earliest days of irrigation, and the lack of yield response to fertilizers and other modern technologies has led to discussion of the possibility of a decline in soil fertility.

But the concept is successful, and has been extended, first into the Abd el Majid area lower down the Blue Nile, then (1960) into the Managil region immediately to the south and west. The Managil extension was divided into holdings of 15 feddans, and as from the 1975/6 season the tenants were permitted to grow 5 feddans of cotton, 3¾ feddans of groundnuts, 1¼ feddans of dura, and 5 feddans of wheat. The Gezira scheme and its extensions now covers an area of about 2 million feddans.

A somewhat similar scheme has been developed at Khashm el Girba on the Atbara, to absorb farmers affected by the flooding of the Wadi Halfa region by the High Aswan Dam (this has been paid for by the Egyptian Government). The Rahad Scheme currently being implemented will eventually irrigate 820000 feddans south-east of the Gezira with water pumped from the Blue Nile using power from the Roseires Dam. The first phase covering 300000 feddans, on which 13000 families will be settled, is due for completion by 1978. There are developments also in the Kenana district, partly from water from the Roseires Dam, and partly from pumping directly from wells, or from the river, though at the time of writing there are major difficulties over finance.

Motor pumps are now established along the clay plain portions of the White Nile and Blue Nile in considerable numbers. The largest single group serves the Guneid sugar project close to the Blue Nile; and construction of the Jebel Awliya regulator made possible much more river pumping than had been previously possible. Because of flowing in a very flat valley, the effective irrigated area could vary by as much as 2 km from high to low water. Now, the Awliya scheme means that water is held along the White Nile for a period of 6 months at a fairly constant level, whereas previously the bank line fluctuated, inhibiting the construction of pump intakes, and even the more primitive *sakias* and *shadufs*.

Another important crop area is the delta of the river Gash, just north-west of Kassala. Here the turbid floodwaters have built up a delta fan of outstandingly fertile alluvium, along the edges of which two braided distributaries flow, the eastern one on a natural levee, like the Tigris is near Baghdad, from which an area some 110 km by 40 km is irrigated by free flow. The Gash Board now controls a tenancy scheme, by which 1 year of cropping (80% cotton, 20% millet) is followed by 2 years of fallow.

Despite the greater abundance of water in the southern areas, agriculture is far less developed than in the central Sudan. Some cultivation does, however, occur; sorghum, millet, maize, sesame, groundnuts, beans, vegetables, cotton, depending in part on current prices. Most of the south is, however, pastoral country rather than given over to cultivation, and the inhabitants devote greater interest to their animals.

In the western parts of the Sudan, agriculture is largely confined, as we have seen, to various localities in Darfur; and here, small temporary dams are often built to retain water supplies.

Although the cultivable area in Sudan is estimated to be about 200 million feddans, only 14·2 million feddans were utilized in 1974/75 of which nearly 2·5 million feddans were irrigated. Irrigated lands therefore accounted for only 17% of the total area under crops in that year, but for 52% of total production.

Area under cultivation ('ooo feddans)

| | 1965/66–1969/70 | 1972/73 | 1973/74 | 1974/75 |
|---|---|---|---|---|
| Rainfed | 6729 | 10498 | 11064 | 11563 |
| Irrigated | 1685 | 1994 | 2210 | 2480 |
| Flooded | 123 | 149 | 144 | 181 |
| *Total* | 8537 | 12641 | 13418 | 14224 |

Source: *Economic Survey 1974*, National Planning Commission, Khartoum, July 1975.

Cereals occupy much of the cultivated area in any one year, particularly the rainfed lands which accounted for three-quarters of the total production in 1974–75. Sorghum (*dura*) is by far the most important cereal crop of the Sudan, and millet (*dukhn*) second. 1·8 million tons of *sorghum* were produced in 1974/75 and 470000 tons of *dukhn*. To meet a growing demand among the urban population wheat production has increased rapidly during the last 10 years to a record level of 362000 tons in 1974/75. Although rice production is still small compared with sorghum, millet and wheat, 15000 tons were produced in 1974/75 compared with only 5000 tons in the previous year.

Some 1168000 feddans were devoted to cotton, Sudan's major export crop, in 1974/75 producing 670000 tons. However, the Government plans to reduce the area under cultivation to lessen Sudan's heavy reliance on cotton exports. In contrast the area devoted to groundnuts and sugar cane has continued to expand. In 1974/75 nearly 2 million feddans were devoted to groundnuts with production reaching a record level of 991000 tons. The rapid increase in sugar cane production is in line with Government policy which aims to produce locally the country's needs as well as to have a surplus for export. Some 40000 feddans were devoted to sugar cane in 1974/75 (28000 in 1969/70) from which 1·4 millions tons of sugar cane were produced.

Sudanese agriculture is subject to a number of hazards, and crop production, particularly in rainfed lands, can fluctuate dramatically from year to year. A drop in total amount of rainfall, as in 1968–9, together with seasonal maldistribution, can be disastrous for most crops, while pests, notably grasshoppers and locusts, can devastate large areas. Nevertheless Sudan's agricultural potential remains considerable, and Sudanese agronomists with financial backing from the Arab Fund for Economic and Social Development have formulated a 25-year plan (1976–2000) which aims to make Sudan a major producer of foodstuffs for the whole Arab world. Under the first phase of this ambitious plan

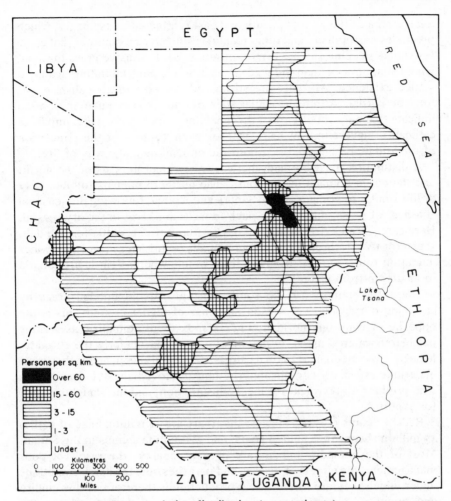

*Fig.* 19.4 The Sudan: population distribution (1970 estimate).

(1976–86) implementation of over 100 large interrelated schemes are envisaged including both agricultural and livestock projects. The plan aims to raise agricultural production by more than 6% a year, to improve production methods and to diversify farming.

## Nomadism

We have seen how substantial environmental controls operate within the Sudan. There is the arid zone covering much of the north and centre; the greater part of the southern clay plains are flooded for a good portion of each year, leaving only limited areas of higher ground as quasi-refuges;

a large area of the extreme south and east is affected by tsetse fly, which precludes pastoralism; and other localities still have mosquitoes that carry fever and sleeping sickness (trypanosomiasis). Extensive grass-burning, whether natural or man-induced, is also an element militating against a settled existence. All these are strong inducements to nomadism either total or partial. Although official sources (the 1973 population census) indicate that only about 11% of the inhabitants are full nomadic, unofficial estimates suggest that at least 20% or even 30–40% of the population of the Sudan are engaged in a nomadic or semi-nomadic way of life.

A distinction must be made between the camel nomads of the north, and the cattle nomads of the south. The northern nomads follow a way of life similar to nomads of the Sahara and Arabia, following the seasonal 'flushes' of grass, and moving back to wells and *terus* in the dry season. Here camels can exist for several days without water; cattle for one day, sheep for two or three. Thus camel nomads (with sheep) can cover wider migration routes, up to 50–80 km from water, whereas cattle are limited to 12–20 km from water.

The cattle nomads of the south must also avoid flooded areas by gathering during the wet season on zones of higher ground; this is the opposite of what one normally understands about nomadism as seeking out better-watered areas. Other tribal groups, particularly the Baggara, located in the median areas own camels, cattle and sheep; hence they must undertake especially complicated rhythms of movement. It is these tribes who produce all the meat for local consumption, and the slaughter stock for export.

Recent figures (1974/5) suggest that there are 14 million head of cattle, 13 million sheep, 10½ million goats, and 2½ million camels in the Sudan. Most of the nomadic animals are of poor quality, the result of poor management, the effects of disease and parasites, and the harsh conditions under which they are raised. Meat production is therefore of low quality and quantity. Nevertheless, the contribution of the nomads to the Sudanese economy, in the production of meat, milk, wool and hides, is significant though not outstanding.

Some nomads have already settled and become cultivators, and spontaneous settlement around newly established water yards is an ongoing process in many parts of the country. For example, in the savanna lands nearly 30% of both the Messeriya Humr and the Rizeigat, and 80% of the Ma'alia, traditionally nomadic tribes, are now settled. Other nomadic tribes, e.g. the Baggara of the western savanna, have been modifying their traditional migration patterns for some time. Instead of being completely nomadic some now tend to settle, at least temporarily, in cultivation areas where they grow crops, while their herds are sent south by other members of the family. However, the Government's declared

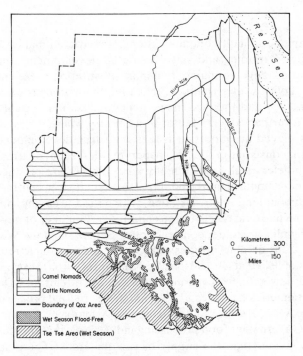

*Fig.* 19.5 Nomadism in the Sudan (J. Oliver).

policy is in support of full settlement, and its 'anti-thirst campaign' with its proliferation of bore-holes and water yards is one expression of this policy which is unlikely to be reversed. Unfortunately in all too many cases the result of these new centres is overgrazing coupled with uncontrolled cultivation leading to accelerated erosion. The application of stricter control measures are needed to both grazing and cultivation around existing water yards. Some Government measures are also devoted to improvements in the animal husbandry and range management practices employed at present by the nomads, and the provision of facilities for integrating animal and crop husbandry so as to raise it above subsistence level.

Among a number of new livestock projects planned with financial backing from the Arab oil producers, a Saudi Arabian and a US company are to develop a million feddans for commercial cattle farms near the Blue Nile aimed at increasing Sudan's meat exports. However, this project and others like it are essentially agri-business projects and involve few Sudanese pastoralists.

*Industry*

Lack of capital, difficult communications, a restricted market and a low level of human training and skills restricted development, and the first large industries, devoted mainly to import substitution, were only created after 1960. Political uncertainties, including the nationalization of many factories in 1970 and then extensive denationalization measures in 1973 have been a further adverse factor in a country where the private sector has always played an important role in industrial development. A small range of light consumer products – paper, textiles, soap, pharmaceuticals, ceramics and electrical goods (chiefly air coolers) – are produced mainly in Khartoum – Omdurman, the country's main industrial centre. There are many cotton ginning factories, and two cotton weaving mills began operation in Khartoum North in 1964 and 1966. A number of new spinning and weaving mills are under construction of Sennar, Gadow, Wad Medani and Butri. Considerable progress has been made in sugar refining with factories established at Guneid in 1961, Khashm el Girba (1963) and Sennar (1975), and new refineries planned at Assalaya, Melut and Dongola. A number of tanneries have been built, and there are food processing plants at Kareima, Wau, Kassala and Babanousa. A major problem associated with these Government food processing industries is that their production capacity is greater than the supply of raw materials. There are cement works at Atbara and Kosti, and two new plants are under construction at Mesa Arakiyai and Dirbab in the Red Sea Province which will eventually export much of their output. An oil refinery has been built at Port Sudan and a second refinery is planned there to be jointly owned by Sudan and Saudi Arabia. A number of industrial projects in the Sudan are being financed by the Arab oil producers, particularly Kuwait, Saudi Arabia and the UAE. Many of the new industrial developments are located outside the Khartoum area, and industrialization is seen as one aspect of Sudan's regional development programme. So far, however, manufacturing activities of all kinds contribute less than 10% of the gross domestic production.

*Minerals*

There is a surprisingly wide range of minerals known to exist in the Sudan, but amounts are generally very small, and prospection is far from complete. Over thirty minerals of commercial interest have been proved. Iron ore is known to exist in four localities: at Fodikwan in the Red Sea hills about 250 km north of Port Sudan, at Dar Messeriya in southern Kordofan, and at Sufaya and Ankura between Kassala and Port Sudan. Most of these ores have an iron content of at least 60%, but only the highest grade, that at Fodikwan (71%), is exploited, by a Yugoslav firm, and the scale of operations is small.

Manganese is fairly widely distributed in the Red Sea hills, but there is only a very small level of exploitation – at Halaiv. Chromite of very high grade is known to occur in the Inganessana hills of the centre, and also towards the south-west, but again production is not large. Gypsum is produced in several localities; there is sporadic production of gold; and copper may exist in commercial quantities in Darfur. Plans are underway to exploit the asbestos deposits in the Inganessana hills and in the area of Qala el Nahl. But particularly hopeful is the recent discovery of oil in commercial quantities and natural gas off Sudan's Red Sea coast. Mineral exploitation is being actively pursued in collaboration with West Germany and Saudi Arabia. In 1978 it was announced that important oil resources had been discovered in the southern plains, near Muglad and Bentiv (Kordofan and Upper Nile Provinces respectively).

*Trade*

Since the establishment of the Gezira scheme, cotton has dominated Sudan's exports. Between 1960 and 1973 about half of total exports from the Sudan were accounted for by sales of raw cotton, although in 1974 cotton's share fell to 38% as a result of a sharp decline in world demand. Gum arabic, groundnuts, sesame and animal products make up most of the rest. Machinery and vehicles, textile, foodstuffs (wheat, sugar, tea and coffee) and petroleum are the chief imports. Italy, France, China and West Germany are the chief buyers of Sudanese produce, and Britain, China, India, West Germany and the USA the chief suppliers. Overall, the EEC is now Sudan's chief trading partner, and an aid and co-operation agreement was concluded between the Community and Sudan in 1975.

**Peoples**

K. M. Barbour points out that, though the name Sudan is Arabic, the majority of the inhabitants belong by racial origins to non-Arabic groups. The Arabs of the Sudan (like the Normans or Moghuls in other regions) are a dominant immigrant group within an indigenous cultural and racial pattern that is of a quite different character. Following the overthrow in the fourteenth century A.D. of a once Christian kingdom based on Dongola, Arab immigrants of very varied geographical origins have gradually settled in the north and centre of the Sudan as far south as 10° N latitude, so that Islamic culture and the Arabic language are now firmly established in these areas and in the major towns and cities.

Several non-Arabic languages, however, such as Beju, Nubian and Tigre still survive (see fig. 5.3.). About two-thirds of all Sudanese are Arabic-speakers and acknowledge Islam.

The south would also seem to have been occupied by immigrants, but of negroid origin: Nilotes, Hamites and Sudanic tribes, of whom the Azande are probably the best known. Many of these southern groups other than the Nilotes who may be indigenous, appear also to have come in relatively recent time either from the east (Ethiopia–Eritrea) or from the south-west. The Nilotes include the Nuer, Luo, Shilluk and Dinka peoples: now, with the Azande, they provide classical and revered names in the literature of anthropology. These diverse peoples speak a variety of languages, though Arabic is often employed as a *lingua franca* and English has special recognition in the southern provinces.

In the country containing many different ethnic groups, languages and ways of life, unity has been maintained only with difficulty. The 'Southern Policy' introduced under the British administration separated the three southern provinces – Equatoria, Bahr El Ghazal and Upper Nile – from the rest of the country, and accentuated contrasts between North and South. The south was closed to northerners, and Southerners were discouraged from visiting or seeking employment in the North. Efforts were made to eradicate all traces of Islamic and Arabic cultures in the South, and instead assistance was given to the work of the various Christian missionary societies operating in the Southern region. After independence in 1956 the southern provinces presented a serious challenge to the unity of the Sudan and until 1972 the region was in revolt against the central Government. During these years an estimated 300000 Southerners fled into neighbouring African countries, while a further 800000 were homeless in the South. The Addis Ababa Agreement of 1972 between the central Government and the southern Sudanese rebels gave the South regional autonomy within a federal system of government, and demands for secession and creation of a separate and independent state in the South were dropped. With international assistance a massive programme was launched to resettle the refugees living in Zaire, Uganda, Ethiopia and Central African Empire, and to aid the homeless within the southern region. Most of the work of resettlement had been completed by 1974.

Sudan is also a sparsely populated country. The preliminary results of the 1973 census give a total population of 15 million compared with 10¼ million at the previous census held in 1955–56 and thus an average density of 5·9 inhabitants/km². There are, however, vast uninhabited areas. The highest densities are found between the Blue Nile and the White Nile to the south of Khartoum where destinies of over 60 inhabitants/km² are recorded. Away from the Nile, areas of high density occur in parts of the highlands of Darfur and in the Nuba mountains, but over most of the central parts of the country densities are low – between 3–15 inhabitants/km², sometimes falling to below 3 inhabitants/km² in the north and south. The reasons for these variations, and for the generally low densities, are varied but include the depopulation of certain areas in the past as a result of the slave trade and revolts, the occurrence of numerous endemic diseases and the shortage of water in many areas for agriculture and for drinking. This situation has been further complicated by recent migrations, for in addition to the considerable population movements in the southern provinces, some 50000 refugees from neighbouring African states, mainly Zaire and Ethiopia, have been permanently settled in the Sudan since 1960, and there are still 40000 recent refugees from Eritrea living in camps in the Sudan.

### Communications

A large area, small-scale, low level of commercial activity, seasonal flooding, and lack of road building material in some areas go far towards explaining the dearth of road communications and consequent emphasis on the railways, river steamer and air. There is no real north–south road, let alone a system, and the Nile is used to communicate with whole areas even in the dry season.

Most of the roads or rather tracks are constructed merely of 'graded' clay and are usually passable only in the dry season. There are few all-weather roads, and they are found mainly in the vicinity of the larger towns, and in the centre of the country. No major road connection exists with the south. The absence of an adequate road network is regarded as an important element in the economic retardation of the country, and as a result first priority has been given to transport and communications under the revised five year plan 1970/1–1974/5. The major project under construction is the Port Sudan–Khartoum highway via Gedarif, Kassala and Wad Medani, over 1000 km in length to be completed by 1980. This road, being built with Italian, Chinese, British and Yugoslav assistance, will also link Egypt and Sudan through the road link proposed between Port Sudan and Bernis on the Red Sea in Egypt. Also underway are feasibility studies to build roads between Sennar and Roseires, Jebel Awliya and Kosti, and Debibat and Obied.

The railway system, Government-owned, on a 3 ft 6 in. gauge (107 cm) links Port Sudan via Atbara to Khartoum (fig. 19.1). From Atbara another line leads to Wadi Halfa on the Egyptian frontier, and south of Khartoum the line continues through the Gezira area to Sennar, then west to Kosti and El Obeid. Further extensions run beyond El Obeid west to the Darfur area at Nyala, and south to Wau; with another link from Sennar through

Gedaref to Kassala – this taps the Khashm el Girba irrigated area. The volume of freight and passenger traffic handled by Sudan Railways, however, has not grown significantly over the last 10 years – 2·8 million passengers and 2·5 millions tons of freight were handled in 1973–74. Considerable efforts are currently being made to upgrade the existing network and to increase traffic handling capacity. In addition a new railway link between Wadi Halfa and the High Dam station south of Aswan in Egypt is to be completed by 1980. As well, there are river services covering 3000 km as far as Dongola in the north, from Kosti to Juba in the south, on the Blue Nile, and via the Sobat as far as Ethiopia. Efforts are being made by the River Transport Corporation to modernize and replace the obsolete fleet of barges, tugs and river buses. Air services have, on the other hand, developed considerably both on a local and national scale: the country is well adapted for these.

**Towns**

In very strong contrast to some other Middle Eastern states, where urbanization is considerable and 35–40% or even more of the population live in towns, the urban population of the Sudan numbers no more than about 13–14% of the whole. Khartoum has a large share of this, and in the extreme southern provinces, no more than about 2% of the inhabitants live in what could be properly described as 'towns': an index of the generally low level of commercial activity.

Khartoum has come to dominate the Sudan only really in the last century and a half. Before 1800 it was very small indeed, but its growth arises from a central position in what is now by far the richest zone of the country – the central clay plains – and centre of routes by rail, road, river and air. The town is really tripartite. Khartoum proper grew up at the confluence of the White Nile and the Blue Nile with Khartoum North a short distance away. Across the river from Khartoum is Omdurman, traditionally more of an 'Islamic' centre and a focus of nationalist interest, this deriving to some extent from the presence of the Mahdi and his political supporters. Whilst Omdurman, longer established as a large town, became increasingly residential, Khartoum became the centre of British rule, and drew in, because of its better communications, a number of industrial and commercial activities. It is significant that Khartoum province is the only part of the Sudan where workers in secondary and tertiary sectors of occupation outnumber primary producers.

Of recent years, industrial growth has continued – though much less in absolute terms than in many other Middle Eastern capitals. New industrial complexes have developed, producing foodstuffs and light consumer goods: paper, textiles, and light electrical goods (refrigerators and air coolers especially), with plant mainly in small industrial complexes in Khartoum North and Khartoum itself. Some 70% of all industrial employment in Sudan is found in the 'Three Towns'. Latest statistics (1973) give Khartoum 321 666 inhabitants, Khartoum North 161 278 and Omdurman 305 308, a total for the complex of 788 252.

The next largest town is Port Sudan, which has grown from tiny beginnings since about 1900. Previously Suakin was the main sea outlet from the Sudan, but a restricted harbour site and difficult seaward approach through coral reefs led to the decision to create a new port some 65 km further north. Port Sudan is on a well-developed sharm (see p. 466). Situated on a very humid, but arid and unproductive coastal plain, with very few local resources other than fish, means that the town is wholly reliant on its outside links. Food is imported either by sea or from regions much further south in the Sudan. Now, Port Sudan handles almost all the exports of cotton, groundnuts and livestock, and takes in most of the imports of manufactured goods and petroleum. With almost a monopoly of outside trade, the town has grown from negligible size to a population of 123 000 (1973). Although the harbour site is good, consisting of a creek and an unencumbered approach, water supply has been a recurring difficulty, first to meet the needs of the inhabitants, then of the ships that called (there were for long only two Red Sea ports where fresh water could be obtained regularly and in quantity – Port Sudan and Suez, now also Jidda), and then to allow functioning of the oil refinery. The port is also severely congested, and as a result the World Bank is financing a major development and improvement programme. Port Sudan will soon be linked to Khartoum by an all-weather road, and in addition an oil-products pipeline has been built to the capital capable of pumping 600 000 tons/year from the Port Sudan oil refinery, and putting an end to the inefficient and wasteful use of rail tankers.

**Planning and development**

Enormous size, few roads and high cost of public and social services for a scattered population are especial difficulties, and it is significant that in 1974 average per capita income was only US $130 – one of the lowest of all the countries in the Middle East. In addition, overgrazing in pastoral areas, and excessive cutting of trees for fuel have been factors in considerable soil erosion and ecological deterioration. A ten-year development plan, the country's first experience in planning, was inaugurated in 1961, with the aims of expanding agricultural production by providing irrigation facilities (e.g. the Roseires and Khashm El Girba dams) and of stimulating industrial activity along the lines of import substitution.

However, after the first 4 years the plan was abandoned, and although a new five-year plan was drafted it was also abandoned in 1965. Its physical targets nevertheless continued to provide guidelines for development planning. A new Five Year Plan (1970/1–1974/5) was produced in 1970 and later substantially revised to give first priority to improving transport and communications.

The present plan, due to end in 1977, allocated (in broad terms) 25% of funds to industry, 20% to agriculture, and 20% to transport and communications: aims were to expand industrial production and reduce dependence on imported goods and foodstuffs, thus providing employment for the rapidly growing population. The eastern bloc (including Yugoslavia and China) have provided specific plant and services, whilst the west has provided finance, technical aid and foodstuffs. International sources, as we have seen, have also made grants and loans for infrastructures such as dams and communications; and for social relief, particularly in the south. In 1976 it was announced that a Ten Year Plan would be undertaken by the Arab Fund for Economic and Social Development, which would involve $6000 m., and aim to produce foodstuffs (cereals, meat and sugar) on a large scale both for the Sudan and for Arab countries. Annual growth rates of 6% in 1976 would rise to 8% by 1985. Saudi Arabia has also made loans, including financing of a major new refinery at Port Sudan, which will use Saudi oil.

Servicing loans to the government (by no means all of which are without interest) now takes 8% of budget revenue, and thus the 1976 AFESD proposals come at a somewhat critical time. Given success in organisation which would include technological and managerial inputs, tranquil political conditions and sustained, enlightened participation by the sponsors of the Ten Year Plan, there could be a major development of considerable proportions that would make a really significant contribution to the problems of the Middle East as a whole.

# Glossary of geographical terms

*Unless otherwise shown as Greek, Persian or Turkish, all words used are of Arabic origin.*

Ab – water
Abu – father of (tribal)
Ada (T) – island
Ain – spring
Ak (T) – white
Akhbar – greater
Akhdar – green
Ala (T) – grey
Asir – isolated
Aswad (also Soda) – black
Aya (Ayos) (G) – saint
Bab – gate, strait
Bahr – sea, lake
Balkan (T) – wooded hill
Bandar (P) – harbour
Beit – house
Beqa – fertile plain
Bir – well
Birkeh, Birket – pool, tank
Büyük (T) – great
Col (T) – desert
Dagh (T) – mountains
Dar – dwelling

Darya (P) – sea
Deir – monastery
Derbend (P) – defile
El (al, em, en er, esh, et) – the
Gezira, Jezireh – island
Ghab – wooded
Ghor – hollow
Göl (T) – lake
Hamad – stony plateau
Harra – lava field
Hasa – gravel
Hijaz – boundary
Hor – lake
Hosn, Husn – fortress
Ibn – son of
Irmak (T) – river
Jaus – basin
Jebel – hill
Kara (T) – black
Kasr, Qasr – castle, barracks
Kebir – great
Kefr – village
Khan – night stopping place

595

Khor – channel, creek
Kizil (T) – red
Köy (T) – village
Kum (T) – sand
Maaden (T) – mine
Maidan (P) – open expanse, small plain
Mar – saint
Masjid – mosque, temple
Mawsil – confluence
Merj, Marj – plain
Meskin – poor
Mina – harbour
Nahr – river
Nakle – palm tree

Ova (T) – plain, basin
Qalat (P) – defensive point
Qanat (P) – canal
Ramle(h) – sand or dune
Rud (P) – river
Sabkha, Sebkha – salt marsh
Sahel – plain
Seil – stream, flood
Sidi – tomb of holy man
Su (T) – river
Suq – market
Sur (P) – fortress
Tel, Tell (plural Tulul) – small hill
Tuz (T) – sediment

# Bibliography

**General**

ADAMS, M. (ed.) (1971). *The Middle East: a handbook*, Anthony Blond, London.

AMIN, G. A. (1974), *The modernization of poverty – a study in the political economy of growth in nine Arab countries 1945–1970*, E. J. Brill, Leiden.

ANTOUN, R. and HARIK, I. (1972), *Rural politics and social change in the Middle East*, Indiana University Press, Bloomington.

ARABIAN AMERICAN OIL CO. (1968), *Aramco handbook – oil and the Middle East*, Dhahran, Saudi Arabia.

BAER, G. (1964), *Population and society in the Arab East*, Routledge & Kegan Paul, London.

BARTHEL, G. (1972), *Industrialization in the Arab countries of the Middle East: problems and trends*, Akademie Verlag, Berlin.

BEAUMONT, P., BLAKE, G. H. and WAGSTAFF, J. M. (1976), *The Middle East: a geographical study*, Wiley, London.

BERQUE, J. (1964), *The Arabs: their history and culture*, Faber, London.

BEYDOUN, Z. R. and DUNNINGTON, H. V. (1975), *Petroleum geology and resources of the Middle East*, Scientific Press, Beaconsfield.

BIROT, P. and DRESCH, J. (1953, 1955), *La Méditerranée et le Moyen Orient*, Vols 1 and 2, Presses Universitaires de France, Paris.

BLANCHARD, R. and GRENARD, F. (1929), *Asie occidentale et Haute Asie* (Géog. Universelle, vol. VIII), Armand Colin, Paris.

BONNÉ, A. (1960), *State and economics in the Middle East*, 2nd edn rev., Routledge & Kegan Paul, London.

BRICE, W. C. (1967), *South-West Asia*, University of London Press, London.

BROWN, L. C. (ed.) (1973), *From madina to metropolis: heritage and change in the Near Eastern city*, Darwin Press, Princeton, New Jersey.

BRUNING, K. (1954), *Asien* (Harms Handbuch der Erdkunde III), Frankfurt.

597

BULLARD, R. (ed.) (1961), *The Middle East*, R.I.I.A., 3rd edn, Oxford University Press, Oxford.

BUTZER, K. (1958), *Quaternary stratigraphy and climate in the Near East*, Bonn.

CLARKE, J. I. and FISHER, W. B. (1972), *Populations of the Middle East and North Africa: a geographical approach*, University of London Press, London.

CLAWSON, M., LANDSBERG, H. H. and ALEXANDER, L. T. (1971), *The agricultural potential of the Middle East*, Elsevier, New York, London, Amsterdam.

COOK, M. A. (ed.) (1970), *Studies in the economic history of the Middle East*, Oxford University Press, London.

COON, C. S. (1951), *Caravan. The story of the Middle East*, Holt, New York.

COOPER, C. A. and ALEXANDER, S. S. (eds) (1972), *Economic development and population growth in the Middle East*, Elsevier, New York, London, Amsterdam.

COSTELLO, V. (1977), *Urbanization in the Middle East*, Cambridge University Press, Cambridge.

CRESSEY, G. B. (1960–3), *Crossroads (Land and life in S.W. Asia)*, Lippincott, Chicago.

DEMIR, S. (1976), *The Kuwait Fund and the political economy of Arab regional development*, Praeger, New York.

DENHAM, H. M. (1964), *The Eastern Mediterranean: a sea guide*, Murray, London.

DICKS, B. (1975), *The Ismailis* (Series: How they live and work), David & Charles, Newton Abbot.

DUBERTRET, L. *et al.* (1957), *Lexique stratigraphique internationale*, Vol. III, Asie, Centre National de la Recherche Scientifique, Paris.

ENCYCLOPAEDIA OF ISLAM (1954– ), Brill, Leiden.

EUROPA PUBLICATIONS (1978), *The Middle East and North Africa, 1977–78*, 23rd edn (annually), London.

FALLON, N. (1975), *Middle East oil money and its future expenditure*, Graham & Trotman, London.

FAO/UNESCO/WMO (1962), *A study of agroclimatology in semi-arid and arid zones of the Near East*, Geneva.

FIELD, M. (1975), *A hundred million dollars a day*, Sidgwick & Jackson, London.

GENERAL UNION OF ARAB CHAMBERS OF COMMERCE (1972), *Arab economic report*, Beirut (annually).

GILBERT, M. (1974), *The Arab–Israel conflict; its history in maps*, Weidenfeld & Nicolson, London.

GILSENAN, M. (1973), *Saint and sufi in modern Egypt: an essay in the sociology of religion*, Clarendon Press, Oxford.

GOTTMAN, J. (1959), *Etudes sur l'état d'Israel et le Moyen-Orient*, Colin, Paris.

HANCE, W. A. (1964), *The geography of modern Africa*, Columbia University Press, New York.

HARRISON CHURCH, R. J. (1967), *Africa and the Islands*, Longman, London.

HERSHLAG, Z. Y. (1964), *Introduction to the economic history of the Middle East*, E. J. Brill, Leiden

HERSHLAG, Z. Y. (1975), *Economic structure of the Middle East*, E. J. Brill, Leiden.

HILLS, E. S. (1966), *Arid lands: a geographical appraisal*, Methuen, London.

HOGARTH, D. G. (1905), *The Nearer East*, Heinemann, London.

HOLT, P. M., LAMBTON, A. K. S. and LEWIS, B. (eds) (1970), *The Cambridge history of Islam*, Vols 1 and 2, Cambridge University Press, London.

HOPWOOD, D. and GRIMWOOD-JONES, D. (eds) (1972), *Middle East and Islam. A bibliographical introduction*, Bibliotheca Asiatica 9, Zug.

HOURANI, A. H. (1947), *Minorities in the Arab world*, Oxford University Press, Oxford.

HOURANI, A. and STERN, S. (1969), *The Islamic city*, Cassirer, London.

ISSAWI, C. (1966), *The economic history of the Middle East 1800–1914*, University of Chicago Press, Chicago.

JACOBY, N. H. (1974), *Multinational oil – a study in industrial dynamics*, Macmillan, New York.

JOHNSON, D. J. (1969), *The nature of nomadism – a comparative study of pastoral migrations in S.W. Asia and N. Africa*, Department of Geography Research Paper 118, University of Chicago, Chicago.

KAEUBLER, R. (1966), *Das Wasser in dem ariden Gebieten der Alten Welt*, Leipzig.

KIRK, G. E. (1964), *A short history of the Middle East*, Methuen, London.

LANDEN, R. G. (1970), *The emergence of the modern Middle East: selected readings*, Van Nostrand–Reinholt, New York.

LAPIDUS, I. M. (ed.) (1969), *Middle Eastern cities*, University of California Press, Berkeley.

LAQUEUR, W. (1969), *The struggle for the Middle East. The Soviet Union and the Middle East*, Routledge & Kegan Paul, London.

LONGRIGG, S. H. (1968), *Oil in the Middle East*, Oxford University Press, London.

LONGRIGG, S. H. and JANKOWSKI, J. (1970), *The Middle East: a social geography*, Duckworth, London.

LUTFIYYA, A. M. and CHURCHILL, C. W. (eds) (1970), *Readings in Arab Middle Eastern society and culture*, Mouton, Paris and The Hague.

MANSFIELD, P. (ed.) (1973), *The Middle East: a political and economic survey*, Oxford University Press, London.

MUSREY, A. G. (1969), *An Arab Common Market*, Praeger, New York.

NELSON, C. (ed.) (1973), *Desert and the sown: nomads in the wider society*, University of California, Institute of International Studies, Berkeley.

NUTTING, A. (1967), *No end of a lesson, the story of Suez*, Constable, London.

PATWARDHAN, V. N. and DARBY, W. J. (1972), *The state of nutrition in the Arab Middle East*, Vanderbilt University Press, Nashville.

PFEIFFER, C. and VOS, H. F. (1967), *The Wycliffe historical geography of Bible Lands*, Moody Press, Chicago.

PLANHOL, X. DE (1959), *The World of Islam*, Cornell University Press, Ithaca.

PLANHOL, X. DE (1968), *Les fondements géographiques de l'histoire de l'Islam*, Flammarion, Paris.

RIFAI, T. (1974), *The pricing of crude oil*, Praeger, New York.

ROUHANI, F. (1971), *A history of O.P.E.C.* Praeger, New York.

SAYEGH, K. S. (1969), *Oil and Arab regional development*, Praeger, New York.

SHERBINY, N. A. and TESSLER, M. A. (1976), *Arab oil*, Praeger Special Study, New York.

STEPHENS, R. (1976), *The Arabs' new frontier: a history of the Kuwait Fund*, revised edn, Temple Smith, London.

SWEET, L. E. (1970), *Peoples and cultures of the Middle East – anthropological reader*, Vols 1 and 2, Natural History Press, New York.

THOMPSON, B. W. (1965), *The climate of Africa*, Oxford University Press, London.

UNITED NATIONS (1962), *Problems of the Arid Zone*, Paris.

UNITED NATIONS (1968), *Studies on selected development problems in various countries in the Middle East*, Beirut (annually).

VAN NIEUWENHIJSE, C. A. O. (1965), *Social stratification and the Middle East*, E. J. Brill, Leiden.

VITA-FINZI, C. (1969), *The Mediterranean valleys: geological change in historical times*, Cambridge University Press, London.

WALTON, K. (1969), *Arid zone*, Hutchinson, New York.

WARRINER, D. (1962), *Land reform and development in the Middle East*, Oxford University Press, London.

WARRINER, D. (1969), *Land reform in principle and practice*, Clarendon Press, Oxford.

WEULERSSE, J. (1946), *Paysans de Syrie et du Proche-Orient*, Gallimard, Paris.

WRIGHT, H. E. (1968), *Climatic change in the Eastern Mediterranean Region*, Minnesota.

## Atlases

*Atlas of Israel: cartography, physical geography, history, demography, economics, education* (1970), Department of Surveys, Ministry of Labour, Jerusalem, and Elsevier, Amsterdam.

*Atlas of Jerusalem* (prepared by Department of Geography, Hebrew University Israel) (1973), De Gruyter, Berlin.

BECKINGHAM, C. F. (1960), *Atlas of the Arab World and the Middle East*, Macmillan, London.

BEEK, M. A. (1962), *Atlas of Mesopotamia: a survey of the history and civilization of Mesopotamia from the Stone Age to the Fall of Babylon*, Nelson, London.

BRAWER, M. and KARMON, Y. (1964), *Atlas of the Middle East*, Yavneh, Tel Aviv (in Hebrew).

HAZARD, H. W. (1954), *Atlas of Islamic history*, 3rd rev. edn, Princeton University Press, Princeton.

*Oxford regional economic atlas: The Middle East and North Africa* (1960), Oxford University Press, Oxford.

ROOLVINK, R. et al. (1957), *Historical atlas of the Muslim peoples*, Djambatan, Amsterdam.

TANOĞLU, A., ERINÇ, S. and TUMERTEKIN, E. (1961), *Türkiye Atlasi/Atlas of Turkey*, Milli Eğitim Basimevi, Istanbul.

## Regional

ADMIRALTY, NAVAL INTELLIGENCE, London
> Turkey (2 vols), 1942–43
> Palestine and Transjordan, 1943
> Iraq and the Persian Gulf, 1944
> Persia, 1945
> Western Arabia, 1946

AMERICAN UNIVERSITY, FOREIGN AREA STUDIES DIVISION, AREA HANDBOOKS, Washington, D.C.
> Iran, 1971
> Iraq, 1971

Israel, 1970
Cyprus, 1971
Jordan, 1969
Lebanon, 1969
Libya, 1969
Saudi Arabia, 1971
Syria, 1971
Peripheral states of the Arabian Peninsula, 1971
Sudan, 1964
Turkey, 1970
Egypt, 1970

## Iran

AVERY, P. (1965), *Modern Iran*, Ernest Benn, London.

BARTH, F. (1961), *Nomads of South Persia: the Basseri tribe of the Khamseh confederacy*, University Press, Oslo.

BEAUMONT, P. (1973), *River regimes in Iran*, Occasional Publications (New Series) No. 1, Department of Geography, University of Durham, Durham.

BEMONT, F. (1969), *Les villes de l'Iran: des cités d'autrefois à l'urbanism contemporain*, Fabre, Paris.

BHARIER, J. (1971), *Economic development in Iran 1900–1970*, Oxford University Press, London.

BILL, J. A. (1972), *The politics of Iran: groups, classes and modernization*, Merrill, Columbus, Ohio.

CLARKE, J. I. (1963), *The Iranian city of Shiraz*, Research Paper Series No. 7, Department of Geography, University of Durham.

CLARKE, J. I. and CLARK, B. D. (1969), *Kermanshah, an Iranian provincial city*, Research Paper Series No. 10, Department of Geography, University of Durham.

COSTELLO, V. F. (1976), *Kashan: a city and region of Iran*, Bowker, London.

ELWELL-SUTTON, L. P. (1976), *Persian oil – a study in power politics*, Hyperion Press, Westport, Conn.

ENGLISH, P. W. (1966), *City and village in Iran*, University of Wisconsin Press, Madison.

FESHARAKI, F. (1976), *Development of the Iranian oil industry; international and domestic aspects*, Praeger, New York.

FISHER, W. B. (ed.) (1968), *The Cambridge History of Iran*, Vol. 1 (*Land and People*), Cambridge University Press, London.

LAMBTON, A. K. S. (1953), *Landlord and peasant in Persia*, Oxford University Press, London.

LAMBTON, A. K. S. (1969), *The Persian Land Reform 1962–1966*, Clarendon Press, Oxford.

PLANHOL, X. DE (1964), *Recherches sur la Géographie humaine de l'Iran septentrional*, Centre de Recherches et Documentation Cartographiques et Géographiques, Paris.

OBERLANDER, T. W. (1965), *The Zagros streams*, Syracuse University Press, Syracuse.

WILBER, D. N. (1963), *Contemporary Iran*, Thames & Hudson, London.

## Turkey

ABADAN-UNAT, N. (1976), *Turkish workers in Europe 1960–1975: a socio-economic reapparisal*, E. J. Brill, Leiden.

ASFOUR, E. (ed.) (1975), *Turkey: prospects and problems of an expanding economy*, John Hopkins University Press, New York.

BENEDICT, P. (1974), *Ula, an Anatolian town*, E. J. Brill, Leiden.

CAMPBELL, A. S. (ed.) (1971), *Geology and history of Turkey*, Petroleum Exploration Society of Libya, Tripoli.

COHEN, E. J. (1970), *Turkish economic, social and political change: development of a more prosperous and open society*, Praeger, New York, Washington and London.

DAVIS, P. H. (1965– ), *Flora of Turkey and the East Aegean Islands*, Vol. 1, Edinburgh University Press, Edinburgh.

DEWDNEY, J. C. (1971), *Turkey*, Chatto & Windus, London.

DRAKAKIS-SMITH, D. W. and FISHER, W. B. (1975), *Housing problems in Ankara*, Occasional Publications, New Series, no. 7, Department of Geography, University of Durham.

HALE, W. M. (ed.) (1976), *Aspects of modern Turkey*, Bowker, London.

HERSHLAG, Z. Y. (1968), *Turkey: the challenge of growth*, E. J. Brill, Leiden.

HINDERINK, J. and KIRAY, M. B. (1970), *Social stratification as an obstacle to development. A study of four Turkish villages*, Praeger, New York, Washington and London.

HIRSCH, E. (1970), *Poverty and plenty on the Turkish farm: an economic study of Turkish agriculture in the 1950's*, Middle East Institute, Columbia University, New York.

MANSUR, F. (1972), *Bodrum – a town in the Aegean*, E. J. Brill, Leiden.

NEWMAN, B. (1968), *Turkey and the Turks*, Herbert Jenkins, London.

PAINE, S. (1974), *Exporting workers: the Turkish case*, Cambridge University Press, Cambridge.


## Iraq

ADAMS, R. MCC (1965), *Land behind Baghdad*, University of Chicago Press, Chicago.

BOIS, T. (1966), *The Kurds*, Khayats, Beirut.

FERNEA, E. W. (1968), *Guests of the sheik, an ethnography of an Iraqi village*, Hale, London.

FERNEA, R. A. (1970), *Shaykh and Effendi: changing patterns of authority among the El Shabana of southern Iraq*, Harvard University Press, Cambridge, Mass.

JALAL, F. (1972), *The role of government in the industrialization of Iraq, 1950–1965*, Cass, London.

LANGLEY, K. M. (1962), *The industrialization of Iraq*, Harvard Middle East Monographs, Cambridge Mass.

LONGRIGG, S. H. and STOAKES, F. C. (1958), *Iraq*, Praeger, New York.

RECHINGER, K. H. (1964), *Flora of lowland Iraq*, Hafner, New York.

TREAKLE, H. C. (1965), *The agricultural economy of Iraq*, Washington Foreign Regional Analysis Division, Economic Research Service, U.S.D.A., Washington D.C.

*The Levant*

BEN GURION, D. (1974), *The Jews in their land*, Rev. edn., Doubleday, Garden City.

BERLER, A. (1971), *New towns in Israel*, Israel University Press, Jerusalem.

BLAKE, G. S. and GOLDSCHMIDT, M. J. (1947), *Geology and water resources of Palestine*, Government Printer, Jerusalem.

CHURCHILL, C. (1954), *The city of Beirut – a socio-economic study*, Dar al-Kitab, Beirut.

COHEN, A. (1965), *Arab border villages in Israel; a study of continuity and change in social organization*, Manchester University Press, Manchester.

COPELAND, R. W. (1965), *The land and people of Jordan*, T. Lippincott, New York.

COURBAGE, Y. (1973–4), *La situation démographique au Liban*, Vols 1 and 2, Université Libanaise, Beirut.

DETTMAN, N. (1969), *Damaskus – eine orientalishe Stadt zwischen Tradition und Moderne*, Frankische Geographische Gesellschaft, Erlangen.

EVENARI, M., SHANAN, L. and TADMOR, N. (1971), *The Negev: the challenge of a desert*, Harvard University Press, Cambridge, Mass.

FULLER, A. H. (1961), *Buarij: portrait of a Lebanese Muslim village*, Harvard University Press, Cambridge, Mass.

GUBSER, P. (1973), *Politics and change in Al-Karak, Jordan; a study of a small Arab town and its district*, Oxford University Press, London.

GUINÉ, A. (1975), *Syrie*, Delroisse, Boulogne.

GULICK, J. (1975), *Social structure and cultural change in a Lebanese village*, Viking Fund Publications in Anthropology, No. 21, New York.

GULICK, J. (1967), *Tripoli: a modern Arab city*, Oxford University Press, London.

HALPERIN, H. (1957), *Changing patterns of Israel agriculture*, Routledge & Kegan Paul, London.

HAMIDE, A. R. (1961), *La ville d'Alep: étude de géographie humaine*, Damascus.

HEPBURN, A. H. (1966), *Lebanon*, Doubleday, New York.

HITTI, P. K. (1967), *Lebanon in history*, 3rd edn, Macmillan, London.

HOPKINS, I. W. J. (1970), *Jerusalem: a study in urban geography*, Baker Book House, Grand Rapids.

KARMON, Y. (1971), *Israel – a regional geography*, John Wiley, Chichester.

KHALAF, S. and KONGSTAD, P. (1973), *Hamra of Beirut. A case of rapid urbanization*, E. J. Brill, Leiden.

KHURI, F. I. (1975), *From village to suburb: order and change in greater Beirut*, University of Chicago Press, Chicago.

KLAYMAN, M. I. (1970), *The moshav in Israel*, Praeger, New York.

KUTCHER, A. (1973), *The new Jerusalem – planning and politics*, Thames & Hudson, London.

LEON, D. (1969), *The kibbutz*, Pergamon, Oxford.

LUTFIYYA, A. M. (1967), *Baytin – a Jordanian village*, Mouton, The Hague.

ORGELS, B. (1962), *Contribution à l'étude des problèmes agricoles de la Syrie*, Centre pour l'étude des problèmes du monde musulman contemporain, Brussels.

ORNI, E. and EFRAT, E. (1976), *The geography of Israel*, 4th edn, Israel Programme for Scientific Translations, Jerusalem.

OWEN, R., et al. (1976), *Essays on the crisis in Lebanon*, Occasional Paper No. 1, Ithaca Press, London.

PETRAN, T. (1972), *Syria*, Nations of the Modern World, Ernest Benn, London.

POLK, W. R. (1963), *The opening of South Lebanon 1788–1840; a study of the impact of the West on the Middle East*, Harvard University Press, Cambridge, Mass.

SAFA, E. (1960), *L'émigration libanaise*, Université Saint-Joseph, Beirut.

SALEM, E. A. (1973), *Modernization without revolution: Lebanon's experience*, Indiana University Press, Bloomington.

SALIBA, S. N. (1968), *The Jordan river dispute*, Martinus Nijhoff, The Hague.

SHAIK, K. A. (1965), *Planning for a Middle Eastern economy: model for Syria*, Chapman & Hall, London.

SPARROW, J. G. (1961), *Modern Jordan*, Allen & Unwin, London.

SULEIMAN, M. W. (1967), *Political parties in Lebanon. The challenge of a fragmented political culture*, Cornell University Press, Ithaca.

SWEET, L. E. (1960), *Tell Toqaan: a Syrian village*, University of Michigan Press, Ann Arbor.

VAUMAS, E. DE (1954), *Le Liban (montagne libanaise, Bekaa, Anti-Liban-Herman. Haute Gaililee libanaise) Etude de géographie physique*, Firmin-Dibot, Paris.

WOFAST, R. (1967), *Geologie von Syria und der Libanon*, Gebrüder Borntraegerm, Berlin.

## Cyprus

BITSIOS, D. S. (1975), *Cyprus; the vulnerable republic*, Institute for Balkan Studies, Thessaloniki.

CHRISTODOULOU, D. (1959), *The evolution of the rural land use pattern in Cyprus*, World Land Use Survey, Bude.

EHRLICH, T. (1974), *Cyprus 1958–1967*, Oxford University Press, London.

HENDERSON, C. (1968), *Cyprus: the country and its people*, Queen Anne Press, London.

LOIZOS, P. (1975), *The Greek gift – politics in a Cypriot village*, St Martin's Press, New York.

MEYER, A. J. and VASSILIO, S. (1962), *The economy of Cyprus*, Harvard University Press, Cambridge, Mass.

## Arabia

ABIR, M. (1974), *Oil, power and politics: conflict in Arabia, the Red Sea and the Gulf*, Cass, London.

ALI, S. R. (1976), *Saudi Arabia and oil diplomacy*, Praeger Special Study, New York.

AL-RUMAIHI, M. (1977), *Bahrain: social and political change*, Bowker, London.

ATTAR, M. S. EL (1964), *Le sous-développement économique et social du Yémen, perspectives de la révolution Yéménite*, Editions Tiers Monde, Algiers.

EL-MALLAKH, E. (1968), *Economic development and regional cooperation: Kuwait*, University of Chicago Press, Chicago.

FENELON, K. G. (1973), *The United Arab Emirates: an economic and social survey*, Longman, London.

FFRENCH, G. E. and HILL, A. G. (1971), *Kuwait, urban and medical ecology: a geomedical study*, Springer Verlag, Berlin.

HAWLEY, D. F. (1970), *The Trucial States*, Allen & Unwin, London.
HAWLEY, D. F. (1976), *Oman and its renaissance*, Barrie & Jenkins.
HICKINBOTHAM, SIR T. (1958), *Aden*, Constable, London.
HOPWOOD, D. (ed.) (1972), *The Arabian peninsula*, Allen & Unwin, London.
INGRAMS, H. (1966), *Arabia and the Isles*, Murray, London.
KELLY, J. B. (1964), *Eastern Arabian frontiers*, Faber, London.
KNAUERHASE, R. (1975), *Saudi Arabian economy*, Praeger, New York.
LEIDLMAIR, A. (1961), *Hadramaut*, Bonner Geog. Abhandlungen No. 30, Geographisches Institut, Universität Bonn, Bonn.
MAKTARI, A. M. A. (1971), *Water rights and irrigation practices in Lahej*, Cambridge University Press, Cambridge.
MILES, S. B. (1966), *The country and tribes of the Persian Gulf*, London.
NIZAN, P. (1967), *Aden Arabie*, Maspero, Paris.
PESCE, A. (1974), *Jiddah: portrait of an Arabian city*, Falcon Press.
PURSER, B. H. (1973), *The Persian Gulf*, Springer, Berlin.
RUGH, W. A. (1969), *Riyadh, history and guide; a brief historical survey of the development of Riyadh from a small desert town into the capital of Saudi Arabia*, Al-Mutawa Press, Dammam.
SKEET, I. (1974), *Muscat and Oman – the end of an era*, Faber, London.
WENNER, M. (1967), *Modern Yemen: 1918–1966*, John Hopkins Press, Baltimore.

## Egypt

ABDEL-FADIL, M. (1975), *Development, income distribution and social change in rural Egypt (1952–1970)*, Cambridge University Press, Cambridge.
ABU-LUGHOD, J. (1971), *Cairo: 1001 years of the city victorious*, Princeton University Press, Princeton.
AMMAR, H. (1954), *Growing up in an Egyptian village*, Routledge & Kegan Paul, London.
AYROUT, H. H. (1963), *The Egyptian peasant*, Beacon Press, Boston.
BARBOUR, K. M. (1972), *The growth, location and structure of industry in Egypt*, Praeger, New York.
BUTZER, K. W. and HANSEN, C. L. (1968), *Desert and river in Nubia*, University of Wisconsin Press, Wisconsin.
DUFF, R. E. B. (1969), *One hundred years of the Suez Canal*, Clifton Books, Britain.
ELISOFON, E. (1964), *The Nile*, Thames & Hudson, London.
HARIK, I. F. (1974), *The political mobilization of peasants. A study of an Egyptian community*, Indiana University Press, Bloomington.
HURST, H. E. (1952), *The Nile: a general account of the river and the utilization of its waters*, London.
HURST, H. E., BLACK, R. P. and SIMAIKA, YU. M. (1965), *Long-term storage, an experimental study*, Constable, London.
LITTLE, T. (1965), *High Dam at Aswan*, Methuen, London.
LITTLE, T. (1967), *Modern Egypt*, Benn, London.
MABRO, R. (1974), *The Egyptian economy 1952–1972*, Clarendon Press, Oxford.
MABRO, R. and RADWAN, S. (1973), *The industrialization of Egypt: 1939–1973 policy and performance*, Clarendon Press, Oxford.
O'BRIEN, P. (1966), *The Revolution in Egypt's economic system*, Oxford University Press, London.

OWEN, R. J. (1969), *Cotton and the Egyptian economy: 1820–1914*, Clarendon Press, Oxford.

RADWAN, S. (1974), *Capital formation in Egyptian industry and agriculture 1882–1967*, Ithaca Press, London.

WILBER, D. N. (ed.) (1969), *The United Arab Republic, its people, its society, its culture*, Human Relations Area Files, New York.


## Libya

ALLAN, J. A. *et al.* (eds) (1972), *Libya: agriculture and economic development*, Frank Cass, London.

BLAKE, G. H. (1968), *Misurata: a market town in Tripolitania*, Department of Geography, University of Durham.

DOYEL, W. W. and MAGUIRE, F. J. (1964), *Ground water resources of the Benghazi area*, US Government Printing Office, Washington D.C.

ELDBLOM, L. (1968), *Structure foncière, organisation et structure sociale: Une étude comparative sur la vie socio-économique dans les trois oasis Libyennes de Ghat, Marzouk et particulièrement Ghadames*, Lund.

EVANS-PRITCHARD, E. E. (1949), *The Sanusi of Cyrenaica*, Oxford University Press, London.

FIRST, R. (1974), *Libya – the elusive revolution*, Penguin, Harmondsworth.

HAJJAJI, S. A. (1967), *The new Libya*, Ministry of Information and Culture, Tripoli.

JOHNSON, D. L. (1973), *Jabal al Akhdar, Cyrenaica*, University of Chicago, Chicago.

KANTER, H. (1967), *Libyen–Libya; a geomedical monograph*, Springer Verlag, Berlin.

PELT, A. (1970), *Libyan independence and the United Nations: a case of planned decolonization*, Yale University Press, New Haven.

WARD, P. (1969), *Tripoli: portrait of a city*, The Oleander Press, Stroughton.


## Sudan

BARBOUR, K. M. (1961), *The Republic of the Sudan: a regional geography*, University of London Press, London.

BARNETT, T. (1976), *The Gezira scheme. An illusion of development*, Cass, London.

BESHAI, A. A. (1976), *Export performance and economic development in the Sudan 1900–1967*, Ithaca Press, London.

CUNNISON, I. (1966), *Baggara Arabs – power and the lineage in a Sudanese nomad tribe*, Clarendon Press, Oxford.

CUNNISON, I. and JAMES, W. (eds) (1972), *Essays in Sudan ethnography*, Hurst, London.

DENG, F. M. (1971), *Tradition and modernization: a challenge for law among the Dinka of the Sudan*, Yale University Press, New Haven.

GAITSKELL, A. (1959), *Gezira: a story of development*, Faber, London.

HENDERSON, K. D. D. (1965), *Sudan Republic*, Benn, London.

HILL, R. (1965), *Sudan transport: a history*, Oxford University Press, London.

LEBON, J. H. G. (1965), *Land use in the Sudan*, World Land Use Survey, Bude.

ODUHO, J. and DENG, W. (1963), *The problem of the Southern Sudan*, Oxford University Press, London.

WAI, D. M. (ed.) (1973), *The Southern Sudan: the problem of national integration*, Cass, London.

WHITEMAN, A. J. (1971), *The geology of the Sudan Republic*, Oxford University Press, London.

ZIEGLER, P. (1973), *Omdurman*, Collins, London.

# Index

608